NARRATIVE
OF A
JOURNEY TO LHASA IN 1881-82

NARRATIVE
OF A
JOURNEY TO LHASA IN 1881-82

SARAT CHANDRA DAS

GYAN

Published by

Gyan Publishing House
5, Ansari Road
Daryaganj, New Delhi-110002
Phone: 011-47034999, 9811692060
E-mail: books@gyanbooks.com

Distribution Network
gyanbooks.com
India, USA, Canada, UK, Australia

ISBN: 978-93-7097-635-1 (HB)

First Published, 1885

2nd Impression 2025

Printed at: Gyan Press, Delhi.

NARRATIVE OF A JOURNEY TO LHASA IN 1881-82

Author: SARAT CHANDRA DAS

NARRATIVE

OF

A JOURNEY TO LHASA

IN

1881-82.

BY

SARAT CHANDRA DAS.

1885.

PREFACE.

I HAVE embodied the accounts of my travels and residence in Tibet, and the experiences derived therefrom, in two little volumes of about equal size. The first of these, containing the Narrative of a Journey to Lhasa in 1881-82, and a supplementary paper on the Government of Tibet, is now published.

The second volume, which will shortly follow, contains the Narrative of my journey round Lake Palti, the explorations of Lama Ugyen Gya-tsho, and a series of papers written by me on the history, antiquity, customs, manners, &c., of the people of High Asia.

The work of revising the proof-sheets was very kindly undertaken by Mr. H. M. Percival, one of the distinguished members of Her Majesty's Bengal Educational Service. But he has done much more than that. Indeed, my grateful thanks are due to him for making the following pages readable.

SARAT CHANDRA DAS.

The 25*th March* 1885.

NARRATIVE OF A JOURNEY TO LHASA, 1881-82.

PART I.

NARRATIVE OF A JOURNEY TO SHIGA-TSE AND TASHI-LHUNPO.

I.—JOURNEY FROM DARJEELING TO THE KANGLA-CHHEN PASS.

7th November 1881.—On the night of my departure from Darjeeling, the moon was shining brightly, though dark clouds presaged a slight fall of rain. Our eyes often turned with anxiety towards the mountain-tops on the eastern outskirts of Nepal, to watch if snow was falling on them. The fear of death in the snows, and the hope of overcoming the obstacles of nature, alternated within me as I left my solitary residence at Darjeeling, soon about to bid a long farewell to my native land, with no great confidence that I should ever see it again. A few minutes' walk brought me to the door of my chief, Mr. Croft, who from first to last has assisted me in all my adventures by every means in his power, and in whose forethought and advice I placed implicit faith. He conducted me to his drawing-room, in order that I might get some hints on the collection of plants from a learned doctor then residing with him. While we were thus engaged in pleasant conversation, Mr. Macaulay, who had shown much interest in my work, was announced, and seeing me, asked how far I was going that night. The clock had struck eight, and knowing it was full moon, I replied that I intended to ride as far as Gôk, where I should halt a few hours. After a few minutes' private conversation in the moonlight with my honoured chief, I took my leave. Deeply interested as he has ever been in my success, the remembrance of my leave-taking from so kind and warmly-esteemed a master will never be effaced from my memory.

I rode on silently, and, to my great relief, unnoticed by any person, and meeting no one except one or two Bhootias who were proceeding towards Darjeeling. I heard the songs of the work-women at Takvar and the music of their pipe and drum. A chill breeze blew, but as I gradually descended towards the valley I felt warmer and more comfortable. On approaching the side of the stream, I saw many blazing fires, by which hill travellers were sleeping. While riding through the plantain groves of the little Rungeet, I heard the familiar voices of some Bhootias, and, much frightened lest I should be recognised, quickened pace that they might take me for a belated hillman. My attendant had a short talk with Kansob, the head Lama of Ging Gonpa, who, accompanied by two Bhootia servants, both known faces, was returning from a place in Sikkim where he had lately been invited to perform some religious observances. On being asked who I was, he told Kansob with an air of indifference that somebody looking like a Nepali was riding ahead, and that he had come down that distance in order to meet his cousin Ugyen Gyatsho, who was going to Sikkim. I congratulated myself on having passed unrecognised, for otherwise the story of my proceeding to Tibet would have spread all over the market of Darjeeling next day. Coming to the river, which was rather broad at this time of the year, I met Lama Ugyen Gyatsho, who was waiting to help me in crossing. Three or four bamboos were loosely laid upon the main stream, which I crossed with some difficulty, glad enough that I had not slipped and wet my clothes. After a short rest on the long grass near the opposite bank, where in the wretched traveller's shed called a *Dongkhang* a few Limboos were cooking, I rode up the ascent, which was steep, along a path overgrown with weeds, and dangerous for a night-ride. With the help of one attendant, an intelligent Bhootia, I managed to journey on till at half-past one, after many a tumble, I arrived at Gôk, now a deserted village. In place of the shops and the pretty Hindu-Buddhist shrine which formerly stood there I found only a cowshed, where a Nepali was snoring fast asleep. I had visited this place on two previous occasions, when I had found it a prosperous village with about a dozen shops, and handsome ponies for relays. Gôk was formerly a very remarkable place, resorted to by *madesia* (up-country grain-sellers) for buying indian-corn and cardamom in large quantities for sale at the Darjeeling bazar.

At a short distance from the cowsheds, on one side of the way, we spread our rugs to sleep in the long grass. Various kinds of insects crept over my clothes and shirt, and made me uncomfortable. The prickly points of brambles and other weeds, and the long grass, penetrated through the thin rug on which I lay. All these, and particularly the uneven nature of the ground, kept off sleep for a long while. My pony rolled about on the weeds close to my head, and disturbed my rest several times. At 3 A.M. slight showers of rain fell, which wetted our clothes and blankets as we lay on the bare ground, and broke our sleep. Dismissing the pony, which would be no longer of any use, as our way lay through jungles and pathless defiles, we started on our journey at 4 A.M. The path, hardly a foot broad, was almost choked with weeds and long grass. As bears and snakes were said to abound in this place, I did not think it safe to go ahead unarmed. Lighting my lantern, I followed Phurchung, with my fowling-piece tied crosswise on top of his load. In this way, suffering from many a small mishap and frequent slips, we descended to the valley of the Rummam at daybreak.

8th November.—The Rummam, one of the principal feeders of the Great Rungeet, rises from the Singlee mountains, and forms the boundary between British territory and Independent Sikkim on the north-west, all the territories to the right of it belonging to the British Government. It is a furious torrent, bridged only by a temporary contrivance of bamboo framework. In the middle of the stream there is a huge boulder on which bamboos are placed and kept down by the pressure of large stones. The Lepchas and Limboos catch fish in the pools, where water lies during the cold season. Large fish are sometimes found, which the Lepchas sell in the Darjeeling bazar. *Sál* forests abound here. On the hill slopes there were cardamom and cotton patches with pods burst open. On the larger cultivations guards were stationed in bamboo watch-houses to scare away monkeys and bears with the sound of bamboo clappers. On our approach a number of small monkeys fled away swiftly. I was told that a large species of monkey is found here, which are a terror to the agriculturists and solitary female travellers. To kill them the Lepchas generally place cooked edible roots and occasionally rice mixed with dogbane and other poisonous roots. On nearing the bridge we met some twenty orange-sellers proceeding to Darjeeling. Our coolies talked with them, while I passed to the other bank, crossing the bridge unnoticed. I did not like that men should spread a rumour about me and my journey to Tibet, as it might produce unpleasant consequences on my reaching the frontier outposts and coming across the officials. Before proceeding many yards, one of my attendants met the wife of Sonam Sring, formerly interpreter at the Darjeeling court. Both she and Sonam had come up here to supervise their cultivation. I was very uneasy lest Sonam should recognise me, but to my great relief I learnt that he was as afraid of being known by one of my position as I was with regard to him. However, I took precautions not to be seen by him by taking a different path. I was here much fatigued after my journey on an empty stomach, and some of my coolies who had gone ahead of me prepared some rice and cooked a pheasant for breakfast. I was very thirsty and unable to walk, and lay down exhausted on the bare ground; however, my servants soon brought me water. At 12-30 A.M., after changing my Indian dress for a Tibetan one, we resumed our journey up-hill, leaving the Mitogang road to our right. The ridge that we ascended is the property of our friend Kabi Athing. There is a small stream dividing it from Mitogang village, situated on the hill top. Here antelopes and wild goats abound, offering a rich field to the hunter. But the people are very poor, having hardly half a dozen matchlocks in the whole village. The Nepalese settlers are numerous here, and among them I noticed some Brahmans and Chhetris, who chiefly live by selling milk and butter. We passed by several paddy-fields prepared out of the flat slopes, in the form of terrace-steps, so as to hold water, and cultivated by ploughs drawn by buffaloes. The Bhootias as a rule never use ploughs for cultivation, but raise an inconsiderable harvest with the hoe and clubs made of oak. Although they know the advantages of the plough and the terrace-steps on slopes, which give a better yield than their rude mode of cultivation, they do not resort to them, but adhere to their ancestral system. This year's indian-corn crops were very rich, and the paddy was growing fit for the sickle. There were many hillmen engaged in splitting bamboos and in making wicker-work to enclose their cultivations. After ascending several hill-sides by steep foot-tracks, we came to the top of a ridge, the entrance of which is marked by a *mendang* and a *chhorten.* There was a rill close by, from which our men fetched water, and Limboo houses to our right and left in the valleys, whence dogs barked angrily on our arrival in the neighbourhood. Here I saw my coolies halting; they had pitched my little tent and spread my carpet, and were waiting for my arrival. I was extremely exhausted, and thanked them for not pushing me further that day. I refreshed myself with some biscuits and oranges and a good bottle of *marwa* beer, and in recognition of the kindness of my servants (four persons altogether) I ordered them to buy for their own use some country *arack* (*rakshi*) distilled from indian-corn. Phurchung, as soon as he heard this, ran down the hill to a quarter mile's distance to a Limboo village, where he bought two bottles at four annas each. Some Limboos brought us some vegetables, which I purchased for our evening meal. This ridge commanded a picturesque view of the neighbouring places. The place is called *Mani-dara* by the Paharias and *Chhorten Gang* by the Bhootias, both names having the same meaning, *i.e.* the ridge of the sacred *stupa*. The flat valley of Dhuramdeen, dotted with numerous houses, was visible through a hazy atmosphere. There were several Limboo huts, near which dwarf pigs were running about grunting. To our right and left, as the evening was closing upon us, we saw smoke rising up, which reminded me of the way in which the Bhootias reclaim their fallow land. They keep the soil fallow generally for three years; after three years' continuous cultivation, the weeds are allowed to grow, and then cut and burnt for the preparation of the soil. Here, at Chhorten Gang, we halted for the night.

9th November.—The previous day's tiresome journey had given me pains all over my body. We started after breakfast. The way was easy, and the numerous rills on either side overgrown with luxuriant weeds. We passed by Limboo houses here and there, with sheep-folds and pigsties in front of them. They seemed also to possess a few goats and cows. Their fowls are not so remarkably big as those of the Bhootias. I gave the coolies a four-anna piece to buy some *arack* for their refreshment. This detained them for half an hour in one of the Limboo houses at the village of Singling. As I journeyed on, we talked of some of the Limboo customs, the most remarkable of which is that of beating drums on every trivial occasion. Every Limboo family, be it poor or rich, as a rule possesses three or four drums shaped like tambourines, which they beat on going out of, or returning to, their villages. The wife or children beat them in honour of husband or father when he goes out, and the latter when *they* go out. As we ascended we came across a large hole about three feet deep, in which about a week ago a venomous snake had been captured. At 3 P.M. we crossed the saddle of this range of hills, and entered on a richer soil, as appeared from the growth of the vegetation and the abundance of trees. Here we saw long canes growing luxuriantly. There was quite a forest of plantain trees, indicating the warm nature of the soil. It began to rain at 4 P.M., and our clothes being wet, though I knew that our day's march had been short, we halted in a Gurung village, called Saryong. Our tent was pitched on a flat slope, sheltered from the north-west wind by a hillock. It was spacious enough to accommodate two or three persons, but at present it contained only myself and my clothes. It was constructed after the Tibetan fashion, resting on a ridge piece, supported by two posts, and standing like a house with two gables. A fire was lighted in front of it and kept up the whole night. The coolies slept round it. I was disturbed by leeches, which crept over my breast and legs. These pests not only drink their fill, but leave a wound from which blood oozes out in streams for several minutes after they drop off. Phurchung now wanted to fire off my gun, and after many entreaties on his part, I allowed him to try one shot. He said that it would warn off evil-doers. The number of our servants and the neatness of our tent disposed the natives of this place to think that I was some high functionary, and the Lama a deputy of the Sikkim Raja. Some Bhootias of Sikkim, who had spent the night under a large, branching tree about a quarter of a mile up the hill, passed by our tent before we had got out of bed. As some of them, according to my servant, knew me, I did not care to appear before them in my Tibetan dress, or give them an opportunity of making any inquiries respecting me. As they passed by our tent, I heard them speak, but did not see them.

10th November.—The sky was cloudy and the atmosphere filled with a fog, scarcely allowing us to find our way through the thickets of the mountain slopes. For a short distance the way was dry and easy, after which our troubles began. We met some men, employed by the survey party, proceeding to Darjeeling for a fresh supply of provisions. We crossed two hill streams, which looked more like cascades, and made their way downwards through bushes of ferns, rattans, and other mountain weeds. The trees that stood on the bank of the streams and studded the mountain slopes were chiefly tall pines and giant ferns. At 11 A.M. we made our way through the dense forests of the Hee range, the sky being scarcely seen through the lofty oaks, pines, and magnolias that over-arched our way. At midday we seemed to be journeying in the dark, the drizzling mist alternating with a feeble sunlight. The way was muddy and slippery owing to the previous night's rain. After one hour's hard ascent we arrived at the Rishi *chhorten,* which has a *mendang* attached to it, all covered with thick moss. The Hee La commences here, and the presence of the *chhortens* announced that the neighbourhood was inhabited; and their position indicated that the way lay along the top of the range rather than on its sides. This place commands an excellent view of the south-western part of Sikkim, including Tonglu and Singlee, and the hills of Darjeeling now enveloped in ascending masses of fog. I stood here for about ten minutes, leaning on a slab of the *mendang,* to hear the gun-fire of Darjeeling, to correct my time, and also to know how far in a direct line we were from Darjeeling. The gun-fire was distinctly heard, from which I knew that I was not many miles from Darjeeling. We met some Bhootias and Lepchas, whom I carefully avoided. In the thickets on either side were the marks of the passage of wild pigs, and their foot-marks in the mud. There were, according to our coolies, wild bears at some distance, peeping from their lairs in the hollows of old trunks hoary with moss. The forest was filled with monkeys that fed on acorns. At about 1 P.M. we crossed the top of the range, about 6,000 feet above the sea. At 3 P.M., after crossing many rills which poured their contents into the Rishi streamlet, we passed by the sheds of a cowherd. The cows and bullocks of this place seemed to be very fine, large in size, and parti-coloured, and most of them having snow-white patches on their forehead. Our coolies observed the fatness of the bullocks, and their mouths watered at the thought of the beef. The muddy state of the way increased as we proceeded along the track of the cows. Though very tired, no rest was possible, as I could see the leeches making for me with the utmost haste, spanning their length with swift but measured paces. At 4 P.M. we commenced our descent from the *la* (top of the ridge), which is marked by a *laptse*—here a bush of dwarf bamboos, with some scraps of red cloth tied to it, near which Phurchung uttered his *Lhâsol,* or invocation to the mountain deities. At 5 P.M. we halted for the night in a small opening in the jungles at the foot of a gigantic oak, a few miles above the village of Lingcham. The cries of antelope at a short distance made Phurchung run off with my fowling-piece full of hopes of venison, but he returned late, and unsuccessful. The giant-nettle creeper here attains its largest growth; some more than 100 feet long. The tree-nettle also abounds in this forest. Our servants searched for the common nettle, the tender leaves of which make excellent soup. Heavy rain fell during the night, wetting our bedding and clothes.

11*th November*.—We resumed our journey at about 10 A.M after breakfast, having dried our rugs by exposing them to the draught. The sky was overcast with clouds, and there was rain and sunshine at the same time, which phenomenon the Bhootias call *Metog-chharpa*, or "flowery shower." This kind of rain presages further rain in reserve—a circumstance undesirable to us. The descent was very abrupt to the edge of the river Kalay, also called Kalliat. The village of Hee, by which we passed, contains several Bhootia, Lepcha, and Limboo houses. The Limboos seemed to be prosperous. They cultivate paddy, and use a plough drawn by buffaloes. The paddy-fields here differ from the barley and *murwa* cultivation by their terrace steps for holding water, which is essential to the growth of paddy. A few hundred yards above the river Kalay, we saw cardamom patches carefully fenced. The passage was overgrown with long grass. After missing it several times, we at last found the right way. I and Phurchung went in advance, leaving the rest behind. At 3 P.M. we crossed the Kalay river, which was rapid even at this season of the year. It rises in the Singlee La, and after making a circuitous journey for about 20 miles, empties itself in the great Rungeet near the foot of Tashiding hill. We passed by cultivation and villages up and down this river for many miles. The villages are situated on ridges, which look like lateral ribs of ranges running on either side of the Kalay from west to east, generally sending forth southerly spurs. There were other Limboo villages on spurs towards the west, resembling that of Hee, but we failed to find out their names. The valley of the Kalay on both sides is overhung by lofty trees growing on steep banks, access to which seemed impossible from the river-side. The river is bridged by two long, stout bamboos placed on a huge boulder in the middle, and kept in position by the weight of stone slabs. There were also bamboo balustrades. In the shallow parts of the stream piles are driven to hold a network of bamboo for capturing fish. The Kalay torrent is well known for its delicious fish, probably owing to the water, which comes from the Singlee La and the snowless slopes of other neighbouring ranges. The fish of the Teesta is not much valued, whence I also inferred that the glacial waters are not favourable to either the quantity or the quality of fish in these mountains. We passed by several Limboo houses and saw cultivations of the *Na-dag Shig*, a tree the leaves of which are used to poison fish that swarm in the stagnant nooks of the river. My journey through the Limboo districts of Sikkim led me to inquire into the history of this primitive race, who, though they dress like Nepalis, differ greatly from them in physiognomy and mode of living. I obtained very accurate and interesting information regarding the Limboo people from a very well-informed and learned Limboo priest, greatly revered by all the Limboos of Sikkim and Eastern Nepal. There are five classes of priests among the Limboo people to perform their religious and secular ceremonies. They are called *Phedangba*, *Bijuba*, *Dami*, *Baidang*, and *Srijanga*. The Phedangba enjoy the privilege of conducting the religious ceremonies and of dealing in omens and fortune-telling. The Bijuba are trained to the Shamanic or mystic worship, of which fantastic dances are the chief characteristic. The third order practice witchcraft exclusively, and are said to be able to eject evil spirits through the mouth. The fourth class, called Baidang, are the physicians who cure diseases. The name Baidang is undoubtedly derived from the Sanskrit "Baidya." The fifth, which is the most important of the five, have the exclusive privilege of interpreting the religious books and of studying religious observances and rites. Our informant, though a Srijanga, combined in himself the qualifications of the other four orders. Hence his reputation among the Limboos, who consider him endowed with divine attributes. At half-past three we resumed our up-hill journey through long grass and thickets of reeds, which are traversed by the wild pig, their foot-tracks being distinctly visible. The porcupine abounds here, and is said to be very mischievous to pulse and radish fields. The people here chiefly live on a kind of wild yam, which both the pig and porcupine feed upon. On ascending about 3,000 feet from the Kalay valley, we enjoyed distant views of Pema-yangtse, Yanthang, Hee, Sakyong, and other villages on the high but flat ridges on either side of the Kalay and the Rathong rivers. The village of Lingcham, with its orange groves and numerous *murwa* cultivations, was just on our right. At 5 P.M. we halted on a spacious flat above the house of a Limboo, the only resident in this continuous wilderness. When I passed by his house he and his wife hastily shut the door as if to conceal themselves from our view, being evidently afraid lest we should enter his house and deprive him of his indian-corn. I gave him a two-anna piece, which he received with delight, and gave me a bamboo bottleful of fermented maize, which I gave to my coolies to suck up after the fashion of *murwa* beer. The place where our tent was pitched was, a few days ago, occupied by some officers of the Raja who had come to collect revenue. Some temporary huts close by were surrounded with heaps of *bangma* or *murwa* refuse. Around us was a large indian-corn cultivation lately harvested, the stalks remaining to serve as food for cattle. Our coolies rooted up some of these and ate them as sugarcane. I was told that some stalks taste as sweet as sugarcane, while others are insipid, the difference being caused by the quality of the soil on which they grow. There were wild onions (*la-gog*) growing in the crevices of rocks, which our coolies brought to spice our curries with. *La gog*, though smelling like the common garlic, is not half so strong, and adds a peculiar flavour to the meat. It is said to cause coughing. At the end of our day's toil, after refreshing myself with buttered tea and a dish of rice, I slept soundly.

12*th November*.—The morning opened with a clear sky. After breakfast at nine on a cup of rice moistened with buttered tea, we started. The steep slope through which we passed, with difficulty finding the track, was here and there dotted with indian-corn cultivation. After an hour's hard walk we came to two Limboo houses, where a few goats, some dwarf pigs, and a few fowls were feeding about. The place appeared as wretched as it was wild. Leaving these unsightly cottages, we ascended further up, when we saw two Limboo women busy in reaping *murwa*, one of whom had collected a basketful of wild apricots. At 2 P.M. we arrived at the top of the ridge, on the furthest extremity of which, to our right, was situated the Sangñag Chhoiling (Changachelling) monastery. Near our way stood a very old *chhorten* thickly covered with moss. The descent from this place was very abrupt, through thickets of tree-nettle and other wild plants. A drizzle now commenced and increased the slipperiness of our way. Passing through dense forests of old oaks and tall pines clothed with thick moss, at 4 P.M. we halted on a small flat at the entrance of the village of Tale, which contains about twenty Limboo houses. There were several mares, buffaloes, pigs, and a large number of cows feeding near us, which led us to think that the villagers were well off with their cultivation. The year before last, when the panic of Phodang Lama's disturbance spread, Yangthang Tsomo, wife of the Yangthang chief, came to this village with her jewels and other valuables to escape being plundered. Some Limboos came to ask if we had any salt to sell, as they would like to barter for it some excellent *chhang* (beer made from indian-corn). We said that we had no more than we required for ourselves. On account of the October fall of snow, the Yangpung salt-dealers had not up to this time made their appearance, so that salt was scarce in these villages. Phurchung and his brother went towards the neighbouring dairy for milk and butter, while the other servants went to gather firewood and to fetch provisions from the village. After the tent was pitched I spread my rug on the ground and joined its edges to those of the tent cloth by stone weights, to prevent leeches creeping inside. After refreshing myself with a cup of buttered tea we sat down to gossip about the place and its inhabitants, some of whom had come to our tent. The country between the Arun and Tambur is called Limbuan by the Nepali natives, and the aboriginal people who have resided there from time immemorial are designated by the name of *Limboo*, though they call themselves by the name of *Yakthanga*. In the same manner the tribes inhabiting Kiranta, or the regions between Dudkosi and the Arun, are called *Kirat*, which name is as old as that of the great Hindu deity Mahádeva. The Kirat of the north, now called Khambu, and the Limboo of the south are allied tribes, intermarrying among themselves. They were known to the ancients by the name Kirata, on account of their living by hunting and carrying on trade with the natives of the plains in musk, yak-tails, shell-lac, cardamom, &c., from the earliest Hindu periods. Hence Arrian heard of the *Kirhædi* of Nepal and Bhot. The Kiranta includes Rongshar, Shar Khombu, Madhya Kiranta, Limbuan, and Panthar. Ronshar is a country of defiles through which the Dudkosi flows. It lies between the great mountain range running from north to south, of which the culminating point is Lapchhyikang (called Mount Everest in English maps), and that lofty range which commences east of Ñanam (or Nilam) to terminate at the junction of the Sun and Dudkosi rivers. The Tibetan extension of Lapchhyikang westward along 28° north latitude, which forms the southern snowy wall of great Tibet, south of the Tengri district of Tibet, is its northern boundary. Shar Khambu, of which the loftiest peak is Chomo Kankar of the Lapchi range, lies to the west of Arun and south of the Pheruk district of Tibet. Madhya Kiranta lies between the Arun and Tambur rivers, the most remarkable places in it being Tsanpur, Walung, and Shingsa. Limbuan includes the eastern defiles, forming the valleys of the Tambur and Kangpachan rivers. Panthar, or Pathar in Hindi—probably the region of rocks—includes the eastern and western flanks of the lofty range which runs north to south full one degree between 28° and 27° north latitude, having for its culminating points Jesang La on the north, the Kangchan Jongna group in the middle, and Samdubphug of the Darjeeling frontier to the south.

The Tibetans and the Bhootias of Nepal and Sikkim call the Limboos by the name of *Tsang*, which is probably given to them on account of their having emigrated from the Tsang province of Tibet. Both tradition and written Limboo works relate that the Limboo people partly emigrated thither (to Limbuan) from Tsang in Tibet and Kashi in the Madhya Desh, and partly sprang from underneath a huge rock in the village of Phedab situated to the north-east of Tsanpur. So that the Limboo people were divided into three great tribes, according to their original homes, *Tsang, Kashi,* and *Phedab*, which in later times split into numerous clans. The first branch from Tsang spread themselves over Tambur-khola, Phalung, Miwa-khola, Mayiwa, and Yangrub, being designated by the Tibetans as Tsang Monpa, or the Limboos inhabiting the defiles. Those who came from Kashi occupied Chaibisa, Kai-khola, and Tshothar. Those that sprang from underneath the great rock of Phedab were also called *Bhaiphuta*, and were widely distributed in the valleys of Wallung, Tambur, Mewa, Mayi, Tshothar, Pathar, and Chaibisa. The name of the place in the middle of which stands the huge slab of rock, measuring a hundred fathoms on either side, was Phedub Panggi-loma, which evidently is a corruption of the name *Phedub Pangi-lungpa*, or the land of pasture in Phedub. The self-same rock cave, according to the statement of the Limboos, still exists, and the pious among them make pilgrimages to it. According to a prophecy mentioned in their holy books, the Limboo pilgrims are forbidden to speak in their mother tongue in the neighbourhood of this their only sanctuary. On approaching the sacred cave the devotees carefully avoid speaking Limboo, trying to explain themselves either by signs or in some other dialect with which they are familiar. What the cause of this restriction may have been, my informant was unable to explain.

The Bhaiphuta Limboo were the most powerful and numerous. Their Chief, Bhaiphuta Han Raja, ruled over Eastern Nepal. All the Limboo tribes, as well as the Kiratas, paid him tribute and military assistance in a manner resembling the feudal system of Europe. The family of Han Raja ruled for many years; after its decline the third tribe became powerful, and its Chief massacred all the members of the Han royal family and enslaved those who were their adherents. In this act of bloodshed the Tsang Limboos helped the *madesia* Limboos, for those of the Han army and nobles who had fled towards Tambur were captured by the former. Two nobles escaped, whose descendants are now called Tongpup (a Limboo word) and includes all the Bhaiphuta Limboos under it. The tribe which claims to be of Tibetan origin is called Srisobhaphapu. The Kashi Limboos are called Tumbonphehule. After the fall of Bhaiphuta Han's dynasty there was anarchy all over Eastern Nepal, there being no supreme ruler to keep all the clans of Limboos and Kiratas in peace and unity. In this way they continued for several years, when at length there sprang from among the Srisobha tribe a powerful man called Marang, who succeeded in reconciling the different tribes to each other. He was elected king by the common consent of the people to rule over all the aboriginal tribes of Eastern Nepal, for then the southern part, including the great valley of the Sun Kosi, was ruled by a Newar Chief (from that circumstance called Newarland, or in Tibetan Palyul). After a prosperous reign of many years, Marang Raja died, and among his successors in the chieftainship founded by him, Mokani Raja became distinguished. After Mokani's death the Limboo tribes again fell into anarchy, there being none able to persuade all the tribes to live peacefully together, which state of things lasted for more than a century. At last, probably in the ninth century, appeared the famous Srijanga, the deified hero of the Limboos. The cis-Himalyan Bhootias identify him with an incarnation of Padma Sambhava. Srijanga taught the Limboos the art of writing by inventing a kind of character. Tradition says that Marang Raja was the first man who introduced writing among them, which, however, owing to the long prevailing anarchy, fell into disuse till revived by Srijanga.

13th November.—After breakfast at 9 A.M. we set out. Our way lay through the courts and along the houses of the Limboo villagers, passing which one after another we reached the Ringbee river, a stream as rapid as the Kalay. There was a strong bamboo bridge over it, but we crossed the river where it was narrowest, over a deep channel bridged by some bamboos laid side by side. Here we met some half a dozen Limboo villagers coming from the other side of the river. To the north-west of Tale village, on a parallel ridge projecting northward from the same range of hills, was the village of Nambura. Passing by the left bank of the Ringbee, sometimes approaching and at others receding from the roaring stream in a wearisome zigzag, we again crossed the river about five miles up, a little below the village of Nambura, by means of a long log laid upon a huge boulder, on which there was a small bamboo bridge in good order. As we ascended, our way lay along the side of a cliff, dangerous and fearfully slippery. With great difficulty we walked on, placing our feet in the fissures of rocks, and holding fast by creepers and grass, which were the only means of support. If my feet had slipped, I should have been lost. Thus following the course of the Ringbee, we ascended towards the village of Ringbee, and on looking back we saw many villages, such as Tale, Nambura, &c., perched high up on the sides of mountains several thousand feet above us. Though situated on separate ridges wide apart from one another, yet distance made them seem as if lying on one side of the same mountain range.

Passing under a huge rock, below which the stream had cut gullies, we crossed it by means of bamboo and wooden ladders. Looking up once, I saw some stuffed pheasants and a Tibetan shirt of red cloth hidden in a fissure of the rock, evidently by some bird *shikaris.* Birds of different hues, especially several sorts of pheasants, abound in these forests, frequented by *shikaris* who earn a livelihood by selling stuffed birds at Darjeeling. After journeying about a mile and following the river up, we arrived at the village of Ringbee, situated on a beautiful flat backed by a craggy hill; to the north and east the Ringbee roared at a considerable depth below. The wild plantain, the gigantic rattan, and numerous pines and oaks filled the forest on the other side of the torrent. There were about a dozen houses, the residents being all Limboos who grow rice, indian-corn, *murwa* and other millets. As soon as Phurchung had laid his load on the ground, he flew towards the house of a Limboo acquaintance of his to buy for me some bottles of beer, and presently returned with three bottles, of which he knew one would be given him. Our tent was pitched towards the river-side of the flat. The rugs being spread, I stretched myself at ease, forgetting the fatigues of the journey. There were a few ravens and kites perched on the trees near our tent. I was alone, the servants having dispersed, some to collect firewood, some to pick out edible wild plants, and others to buy vegetables for our evening's meal, and nothing broke the silence save the sound of the rushing torrent below. Our provisions falling short, to recoup our stock I intended to spend the following day in search of provisions. For this purpose I ordered Phurchung to go to the village of Nambura early next morning. I slept soundly, my mind being occupied more with the future than the past.

14th November.—The morning was clear, the fogs of the valley having ascended to the upper regions. The sun shone brightly and made me regret having delayed the day's journey. I was glad that there was no rain, for rain in the valleys means snowfall on the mountain-tops. The view on all sides was superb; the eye, though familiar with the mountain scenery of these singular defiles, seemed to draw fresh entertainment from their wild grandeur. We waited and waited for hours, but Phurchung not appearing by noon, we dismissed all thoughts of journeying that day. In the afternoon Phurchung returned from Nambura, loaded with bags of rice, maize, *murwa*, eggs, vegetables, &c., and leading a ewe before him, which had cost him Rs. 4 as he said. He was very drunk; but conscious of his position, he begged to be excused, and after numerous *salams* and lollings of the tongue after the Tibetan fashion, he vanished from our sight. His friends of Nambura, most of whom were from Nepal, had reached him here, fearing he might fall into the rapids while crossing the precipices and crags on the river-side. As I wore a Tibetan hat, and was dressed in a *Gelong's* raiment, they failed to recognise me. The Limboo villagers came to ask if we had salt, as they were suffering from the want of it, like their neighbours of Tale. They had collected many large bundles of the dyeing creeper called *tsuo*, which grows here in abundance, and which they exchange for salt. We took the boiling point and read 203° in the hypsometer at 3-15 P.M. Phurchung regretted that one of his best acquaintances, a Limboo of the village, was not present during our stay, as he could have lent us much help. He had gone to attend some marriage in a distant village. The marriage customs of the Limboo people are very curious and interesting.

Some families among the Limboo people, at the time of marriage, consult astrologers; others do not. When marriage is contemplated, the parties very commonly, without the knowledge of their parents, meet together in some place of common resort, or in some market, should there exist any, in order to sing witty songs, in which test alone the male is required to excel his fair rival. If the candidate is beaten in this contest by the maiden whose hand he covets, he at once runs away from the scene, being ashamed of his defeat; but if, on the other hand, he wins, he seizes her hands and leads her triumphantly to his home without further ceremony, a female companion generally accompanying her. If the candidate had previously won the maiden's attachment by any means whatever (the best place to meet being some fountain or rill where the maiden goes to fetch water), and thereby had opportunities of discovering her efficiency in the art of singing, he pays a bribe of a couple of rupees, or its equivalent in kind, to the maiden's companion to declare him the winner in the singing competition. Generally, marriage is contracted by courtship among the parties, when the above described means are not resorted to, before their parents are informed of their intentions. This takes place when the candidate obtains free access to the house of the maiden's father, which is easily effected by presenting the nearest relation living in the house with a pig's carcass. This kind of present is called *phudang* in the Limboo language. When the marriage ceremony takes place, the bridegroom, if rich enough, kills a buffalo, or else a pig, which is presented to the bride's parents with a silver coin fixed on its forehead. But generally among the lower people the parents of the bride seldom know anything about the marriage till the return of the girl from her victor's house. At the time of marriage the friends and relations of the parties assemble, each bringing a present of a basket-ful of rice and a bottle of *murwa* or *arack*. Then the parties meet in a spacious courtyard attended by their friends and neighbours. The bridegroom beats a drum, to the music of which the bride dances, outsiders also taking part in the dance. This over, a priest, called Phedangba, conducts certain religious ceremonies, beginning with the *mantra*:—"According to the commands handed down from ancient time, and the doings of the patriarchs, we bind our son and daughter to-day in marriage." When the Phedangba repeats the *mantra*, the bridegroom places his palm on that of the bride, they at the same time holding a cock and a hen respectively, which is then made over to the Phedangba. At the end of the service the throats of the fowls are cut and the streaming blood is received on a plantain leaf, from which omens are drawn. In another leaf some vermilion paint is placed. The bridegroom, then, dipping his middle-finger in the paint, passes it by the forehead of the officiating priest to touch the tip of the bride's nose. The bridegroom then says "henceforth from this day, maiden, thou art my wife," and shouting repeatedly "maiden, thou art my wife," puts a vermilion mark on her brow. The slain fowl is thrown away, so that whoever picks it up gets it. The following morning the priest invokes some friendly spirit, who thus advises the married couple: "You two should henceforth live as husband and wife as long as you live on this earth," to which the parties suitably reply, "we will do as you command." Unless this period of a life-time is mentioned, the marriage is not considered auspicious, and to make it auspicious certain other ceremonies are prescribed, which open up new sources of gain to the priest. Those who bring presents of *murwa* bottles are admitted as guests to the marriage, when first of all *murwa* and roasted meat (generally pork) are served, after which a dish of rice is presented to every one of the party. At the termination of the marriage ceremony the bride, released from her captor's hands, for the first time returns to her parents. Two or three days after her return comes the *parmi* (intermediator, or umpire) to settle differences with the bride's parents, who now for the first time are supposed to learn the matter about her and the bridegroom. He brings as a rule three things—one bottle of *arack*, the entire carcass of a pig, and a silver coin—as presents to the bride's parents. Just as he goes to make the presents to the bride's parents, they are bound to fly into a passion and threaten to beat him, whereupon he entreats them not to beat him, and tries to pacify them by producing another rupee from his pocket. The bride's parents then interrogate him in an angry tone, saying, "Why did you steal away our daughter," and so on. When their anger subsides, he pays the price of the bride, which, according to his means and resources, varies from Rs. 120 to Rs. 10. When the money is not forthcoming, its equivalent in kind is given. But in all cases a pig must accompany the price. When the bride's parents are satisfied, the demand of presents for the *soffas* (*subahs*) and village aldermen is made. Usually a sum of Rs. 12, or its equivalent in kind, is paid, which the *subahs* and other officials of the village appropriate to themselves. The payment is called *turayimlag* in the Limboo language, meaning satisfaction for appeasing the anger of the bride's parents for stealing their daughter. This amount, though due to the bride's parents, is now-a-days appropriated by the village officials. Like the Tibetans, the Limboos present white cotton scarves to all who are interested in the marriage. At the time of delivering the bride to the *parmi*, the parents must say "Oh, our daughter is lost! She is not to be found; somebody must go and find her." So when a couple more of silver coins are produced as remuneration, but not before, one of the relations discovers the lost bride, who generally conceals herself in the store-room of her parents' house, and delivers her up to the *parmi*. Now-a-days this searcher does not generally make his appearance on marriage occasions, but the bride discovers herself when the money is paid.

15th November.—The villagers told us that we had better not start at all, as the passes were still untraceable and closed by snow: instead of waiting on the mountain-top, it would be far more convenient to stay at Ringbee, where provisions were easily procurable. We weighed carefully the arguments for and against halting for a week at least at Ringbee. If I waited there, various reports would be spread to prejudice the frontier guards of Tibet against us, and we should have very little means of ascertaining the exact time when the snow would get hard enough to enable us to set out on our journey, as the passes were three or four days' march from that village. Besides, any delay seemed to tire our patience, as I experienced from a single day's halt at Ringbee. Our coolies gave the villagers to understand that we *shikaris* had very little to do with the passes, except for going to Kangpachan, where more abundant game could be found: if we failed entering Ñamga-tshal, we should most probably return by Jongri to Darjeeling. The fowling-piece which Phurchung carried, and the load of cartridges which he showed to all he met, chiefly to show what a great personage he was, enabled him successfully to pass us off for *shikaris*. I was not interrogated by any villager or traveller about myself and my occupation, for my rich Gelong's dress revealed me to outsiders as one to whom respect and reverence were due. I walked with becoming dignity when any travellers passed by me, always maintaining an unconcerned appearance, and seemingly absorbed in high and divine thoughts. The villagers were perplexed at seeing us determined to ascend to the Yampung La, which still remained free from snow. We passed behind the village, where there were some tall cypresses and a solitary juniper tree. This last they erroneously called *chandan* or sandal-wood. At a short distance from the village we passed the road leading to Dechan Phug, or the cavern of bliss, a huge rock the hollow of which is the haunt of numerous demons and evil spirits.

Here and there on the way we met Limboos making bamboo mats and collecting osiers to thatch their houses. The way was comparatively easy, as we had to travel only along the ups and downs of the river valley. The lateral rills were well bridged, the steep banks carefully crossed by small stone dykes, steps being cut in the rocks where necessary. The hillmen seemed to take more care of the roads than their Bhootia countrymen. At one place Phurchung's feet slipped, and he was about to be plunged into the river below, when the huge load, as he rolled down on his back, held him fast, having stuck in the nettle bushes. Such was the mercy of the Dispenser of our destinies that the guide, in whom lay all our hopes of a successful journey, was snatched from the jaws of death by the very means which would otherwise have hastened him to a watery grave. We travelled slowly, and at 1 P.M. arrived at Paongthang, where there is a wretched shed (*dongkhang*) for travellers. Its roof was good, and rested on piles of loose stones laid irregularly one above another; numerous ants and centipedes were creeping everywhere in the interstices of the stones. We could hardly walk erect inside, but every time we got up from our rug, our heads struck against the roof. There was a slight drizzle outside, so we were obliged to cook our food inside the miserable shed. The smoke and dust raised by the bellows nearly suffocated us. In this wretched way did we accommodate ourselves at Paongthang. Although we had a tent which could have made us comfortable, the obstinacy of the servants compelled me to yield to them. To them the *dongkhang* was a comfortable shed, and so they wished that I too should make myself comfortable in it. On the opposite bank of the river were a few yakmen tending their flocks. The yaks, called *yak-chhung* here, were of diminutive stature. The calves of the yaks, very pretty-looking creatures, more lovely than the calves of the cow, frolicked here and there near their dams. Phurchung told me that he had a cousin among the herdsmen whom he wished to see. I let him go, with instructions to bring me curds, milk, and butter. After an hour's absence, during which time he must have emptied some three *murwa* bottles, he returned, bringing with him a quantity of milk, cheese, and some very good fish. The last was most welcome, as I had not tasted fish since leaving home for Tibet. He told them that I was a *pandit* Lama who understood *dharma* and was going on a visit to the Kangpachan monastery. He also gave out that I was a profound scholar in the Shastras of the Buddhists as well as of the Brahmans. I dismissed the yak-men with a reward of a few two-anna and four-anna pieces in silver, which greatly satisfied them. After refreshing ourselves with some *murwa*, we listened to an interesting repartee between Jordan and Tonssang, two of our companions. Although they carried our loads, they were men of much respectability in their own country, and were induced to do menial work only to oblige me, as

I did not care to trust outsiders with the secrets of my movements. The harangue which Jordan made when he was offered the *murwa* bottle enlivened our evening circle. Some yak-men were also present, who now and then added fuel to the glowing fire. All listened with eagerness and delight. I amused myself with observing the wit of the orator; and really wondered that even among the uncivilised dwellers of the hills wine could inspire eloquence. He did not speak mere nonsense. Among the volleys of his eloquence were quotations from a book of "traditional sayings," called Rinchhen Thenwa.*

"A dir tshogs thams-chad s uan g san-par shu ;
"A Dab chhags byahi gyal po khyun yin,
"Chig-gi chhags-pa kun-gyi chhags.
"Chan-gssan-gyi ; gyal-po Senge yin ;
"Chig-gi m chhons-var kun-gyi m chhoñs,
"Tam-gyi gyal-po chhawmi yin.
"Chig-gi sad de kum-gyi nan.
"A Dab-chhags mauste khyun chhen rgyl-po dokan.
"Metag mau ste Udum-várá dkon.
"A Dam-seu man set seuge karpo kon.
"Chhas byed ma ste, byan chhub Sems d pah d kon.
"Chhan sna man ste, Arog dud rtsi kon.

"All here assembled, pray attend.
"The eagle is the king of birds; when he rises all rise;
"The lion is the king of beasts; when he leaps all leap;
"He that drinks† is the prince of speech; when he speaks, all hear."

Here Jordan's analogy broke down, for he should have said—"when he speaks all should speak;" but as his were quotations, he could not introduce any alteration. Ugyen told me the lines were contained in the little work called "The precious rosary."

Our orator, however, went on :—

"Though birds are many, king-eagles are few;
"Though flowers are many, the *udumwara* (fabulous lotus) is rare;
"Though marsh lions are many, the white lions are few;
"Though devotees are many, saints are but few;
"Though wines are many, nectar is rare."

It is not possible to follow any further the flight of our companion's oratory. I have added the last line in order to finish his unending recitations. At night Jordan and his brother Tonssang sang a few Sikkim and Bhutan songs.

16*th November*.—In the morning at sunrise, the yak-men with their wives and children came to pay their respects to me, bringing presents consisting of yak-milk, butter, and fish. I received these with thanks, and dismissed them with a suitable return in silver pieces, after a hearty exchange of compliments. We finished our breakfast at eight, and dismissing Jordan and Tonssang to carry letters and my Indian clothes to Darjeeling, we resumed our journey. After a mile's journey up-hill along the leaping course of the Ringbee, we ascended the hill called Lungmo La, which was thickly covered with a species of dwarf bamboo and mossy oaks of immense size. At 2 P.M. we came to the junction of the two head-waters of the Ringbee called Chhoonjom, where there is a well-made bridge with very strong approaches made of boulder piles. The river here presented a very picturesque appearance in consequence of its bed being covered with thick green moss, for the bed being level here favoured the growth of the hairy moss. At 3 P.M. we halted at a place called Keta, in the midst of dark forests, the abode of wild bears, pigs, and Sikkim leopards. We spread our rug on an incline where with difficulty I could stretch my legs. There was a tree near it on which we hung our clothes and the remaining pieces of mutton and fish. We lighted a large fire to keep off wild animals. As we had no tent now, we sheltered ourselves from the inclemencies of the sky by a contrivance made with our bed-clothes. After dinner, which consisted of under-boiled rice and indian-corn, moistened with buttered tea, we slept soundly. At night we were disturbed by owls which wanted to rob us of our meat, and by mice which stole a little of our butter.

17*th November*.—After breakfast at 9 A.M., we resumed our journey through the dense forests, the bramble weeds on either side of the way catching our clothes and scratching our heads and faces all over as we passed. Our hearts quaked with the fear of encountering a man-eater, which was reported to have killed two Nepalese wood-cutters in the Singlee La. The year before last a tiger came up to Jongri, where he killed half a dozen yaks. We feared lest this year the same tiger might come to make havoc on the Yampung yaks. In ascending, we crossed several fences erected to divide the pasturage and property of the residents, as also to bring certain fallow ground under cultivation. In crossing one of the fences, we got a pheasant, which had been caught by the neck in a hair-trap laid for its capture. The way was exceedingly steep and stony, here and there clayey owing to the snow melting on porous soil. The cold made us shiver. At noon we reached the zone of rhododendrons. At midday, passing through the graceful pine forests, from which at our approach there flew out

* Rinchhen Aphren-wa, or the precious rosary.
† Chhan-mit, the man under the influence of wine. Wine is universally believed to be the mother of oratory.

pheasants and other birds of beautiful plumage, we entered a ridge covered with patches of snow. This passed, after an easy walk we commenced ascending another steep spur crested with jagged rocks, along the steep side of which we threaded our way up in a zig-zag course. This was the place, we were told, where the Lepcha troops of Sikkim had offered a bold resistance to the Goorkha invaders. From the wood on the west of the rocky precipice they shot arrows, and when these were exhausted, they rolled down detached rocks to crush the enemy. The embouchure overlooking the path below is very fearful, and the account that the Lepchas killed many Nepalese soldiers at this place seemed to me probable. On account of this reverse the Goorkhas are said to have abandoned this route. After half an hour's walk we got over the precipice, when the danger of the ascent seemed to diminish, as the way ran over easier gradients and continual slopes. The sky was bright. A brilliant sun shone out to help us in our ascent to the colder region. We were here shown some beehives, which by no means resembled those of the plains; they looked like so many white fungi projecting from the rock in front of us. My guide wanted to climb the precipice in order to fetch me some honey, but as this would occasion a day's delay, I did not allow him.

On all sides the rhododendron bushes were fast withering, for they lose their leaves before the pines; yet we could smell the fragrance from the pods of the different species. Their novelty pleased us, for our eyes were tired of the continual sight of the lower forests. As we proceeded higher up, the leaflessness of all kinds of vegetation became conspicuous. At 2 P.M. we arrived at the Dok of Yampung, which is situated on the lee side of the range. Long *mendangs* mark the approach to the village, and the flying flags show the vicinity of yak-sheds and houses. The slopes were filled with pasture on all sides; the patches of unmelted snow here and there, and the blocks of ice glistening in the sun, gave a fine appearance to the village. On approaching nearer, that beauty vanished, as the forlorn and deserted nature of the village became manifest. There was not a living being in the village, not a yak, not a dog, only some hungry ravens perched on the flag-poles and the roofs of the sheds. The village contained about a dozen houses, all built in a very rude style. The walls were made of loose stone slabs piled one above another, with some degree of evenness outside. The roof was constructed of long pine-planks kept in their places by stones. The larger houses were locked up, and the doors of those that had no locks were sealed by strings. In front of the house we occupied, there were four flag-poles with inscribed flags. It was unfinished towards the west, and a breeze rushed in through the opening upon our fire-place. There were large heaps of firewood, a quantity of which we burnt to warm ourselves. I spread my rug on a broad plank and seated myself cross-legged. Phurchung helped me to keep off the cold by wrapping my blankets around me, as the wind was freezing my limbs. The coolies collected blocks of ice and began melting them on the glowing fire. The warm water thus obtained served to melt fresh quantities of snow to get sufficient water for tea and *chhang*. One of the servants of the Dokpas, whom we met at Paongthang, had accompanied us carrying a part of Phurchung's load. He shewed us a basketful of *chhang* hidden in a nook of the wall, and sold it to us for a rupee and a half. I distributed some bottles among my coolies. The salt trade of East Nepal extends to this place in the summer months, and in November after the October snow has hardened. Heaps of red-dye creepers were kept in every house, and our house contained more than a dozen huge bundles intended to be exchanged for salt. The Limboos and Lepchas of Western Sikkim annually come here to buy salt, wool, tea, and Tibetan earthenware in exchange for *murwa*, maize, rice, dye-creepers, and other petty commodities of the Darjeeling bazar. Phurchung, with my permission, baked the pheasant and made a hearty meal of it.

After my evening meal, which consisted of rice moistened with tea, shortly before sunset I went to a little eminence for a view of the setting sun; but the heat of the day had filled the valleys with ascending vapour which gradually enveloped us, so I returned to the house unsuccessful, to gossip with my companions on the quality of the *chhang*, maize, meal, and buttered tea, for in other subjects they seemed to take little interest. For some few minutes they talked of the snow which now obstructed the passes, but when I perceived they despaired of crossing the snow, I diverted their attention to other topics. I went to bed early, and scribbled a little with my pencil in the diary. The following morning the Lama took hypsometrical observations, and found water boil at 189° F. Before we started, we saw two Limboos who had descended from the top of Yampûng La, and were going to snare pheasants near Jongri.

18th November.—At 9 in the morning, after breakfast, we set out on our journey, resolved to face the snows. I implored the Great Dispenser of our destinies for mercy as I looked at the snow-clad tops of the peaks which bounded the horizon. The Yampung La, though not lofty, yet presented much difficulty in the ascent. The vegetation on its slopes did not appear so luxuriant as that of Jongri, which is nearly of equal height. After the first mile the road seemed to become steeper. Reaching the top of Yampung La, I took a short rest, and surveyed the regions to the south and west. The great range of mountains led away to the south in a series of precipitous crests, almost bare of vegetation, and conspicuous in their ghastly nakedness. On the summit of the peak I stood buffeted by the west wind. The fog presented the appearance of a boundless sea, the bristling crags representing ships. To the north the range continued to skirt the snows of the famous Kangchan, the dreaded Khumba Karna of the hillmen. The eye on all sides, except to the east, was met by snow; and as I ascended to the south-western flank of the Du La (Demon Mount), I cast an anxious look backwards to the deep gorge through which the

Ringbee leaps with ceaseless roar. The glacial lake which receives the snow streams of Yampung La is called Tamachhu on account of its crescent shape. The Nepalese call it Lampokri. It is about half a mile round when full.

Here our troubles commenced. The Du La was filled with snow, and as we travelled upwards it seemed to recede. After walking for a short distance, I asked my guide to point out with his finger which was the Du La. He pointed to a peak which lay before us, but when we reached that point the Du La rose higher up, and so we ascended peak after peak, not knowing where our troubles would end. The difficulty of breathing increased more from the exertion of the ascent than from any other cause. Ugyen complained of headache and breathlessness, and said he was sick with *la-dug* (mountain sickness). To add to our troubles a strong gale blew, and threw me to the ground several times. At last, when I could no longer resist it in a standing position, I sat on the ground, and did not rise till the wind fell. One of our coolies (the one from Yampung) here fell down helpless, his toes being frost-bitten. All the coolies surrounded him, and consulted what was to be done, whether halting in that dreary and unsheltered place to make him a pair of boots out of our blankets to protect his feet, or to carry him on their backs. On my arriving at the spot and learning what the matter was, I gave the man my shoes and Cabul socks for his use, I myself putting on a new pair of Tibet boots which I had purchased for the journey. The coolie with his new equipments walked through the snow, limping with inconvenient pride and satisfaction, for this was the first time in his life that he had put on a pair of English shoes. The direct way to Gumothang was blocked by snow, which had not yet become passable, and our guide consequently prepared to lead us by a roundabout passage on the northern and western flanks of the Du La. The detour, though troublesome, gave me a chance of seeing once more the eastern gorges of Jongri and the defiles adjoining it. Here the snow was condensed, and in some places turned into ice, on which walking was very dangerous. Our coolies slipped several times, some rolling down with their loads to many yards distance. I walked carefully, using my hands when my feet slipped, and when both failed I lay prostrate, trusting to my weight against the furious gale. The gorge here is terrific, and so deep that it tires the eye to follow its windings. The snow flows down in a kind of solid stream to form the head-water of the Yong Dso Chhu, which runs past the foot of the Jongri snows. In the descent through the western flank of the Du La my coolies seemed to be experts, and I could scarcely follow them. As to me it appeared more dangerous than the ascent, I walked with the greatest care to avoid being thrown down by the wind, and consequently fell behind, sometimes failing to see how far my men had advanced, and sometimes calling to them to walk slower, to enable me to catch them up; but I cried in vain, for my voice, owing to the tenuity of the air, could not reach them. At last I proceeded by following their foot-marks, which were still unobliterated by the flying storm of snow-dust. Fortunately there was no fresh snowfall. In travelling through the western flank of the Du La, after the snowy parts were passed over, we again came in sight of the deep defiles, filled with forests of pine alternating with pasture lands, and overhung on either side by rugged precipices. I thought our way would lead us thither, and flattered myself with the prospect of soon seeing our day's labour terminated. But alas! Our guide informed us that the gap was the head stream of the Rathong, and if we followed it we should be taken to the west of Jongri. He assured us that he would soon conduct us to the very place from which the stream issued. We again commenced to ascend another spur, beyond which lay Gumothang, our next stage for halting. We plodded on extremely exhausted. The wind seemed to diminish its fury as we caught sight of Gumothang, a deep gorge about two thousand feet below. From here it appeared like an extraordinarily well-shaped receptacle into which huge glaciers from all sides moved down like streams. We followed the course of one of the glaciers. Our coolies had already gone down, and Ugyen was more than three hundred yards in advance of me. The sun had disappeared, and it was five by my watch when I began to descend to the gorge of Gumothang. The rhododendron bushes and dwarf juniper shrubs, relieved of the heavy weight of snow, were gradually recovering their erect position, and the melting of the ice increased as we went further and further down. In this march it is not easy to number how many tumbles I had, or how many times I slipped down on the crystal plates of ice, owing to the heavy dress that wrapped me, and the Tibetan boots I had on. I suffered very few bruises, although I got severe pains in my arms and legs. At six I descended to the Gumothang gorge, and found it flooded with torrents caused by the melting of ice towards the north-east. Phurchung helped me in crossing the torrent, which was three to four feet deep and about 40 feet broad. On the back of the precipice (a ridge of the Du La) which overhangs Gumothang is the lake called Lachmi Pokri, or the Lake of Fortune, which is believed to contain mines of gold and precious stones. It is a mile in circumference, its colour deep black, and its bottom is said to be the abode of fabulous water-elephants.

Gumothang is a narrow gorge, but a beautiful wooded spot, the receptacle of glacial deposits. It was now intersected by a glacial torrent, which we had just crossed. This clear, cool, murmuring stream presents alternately a series of rapids and shallows as it flows out of the gloomy chasm. For a moment, seeing the cedars, the various kinds of pines and firs, the tall rhododendrons, and the grassy pasture in the middle, I forgot that I had entered the domain of snow. We entered a wretched shed, probably erected by the Limboo huntsmen and herdsmen of Yampung, the roof of which leaked in several places; but as the rain was not heavy, I could save myself and clothes from getting thoroughly wet. My rug was spread on a charcoal heap, the remains of some traveller's fire-place. At seven in the evening Phurchung cooked some rice and fish curry for me, but they were only half-cooked. I was much exhausted, and my knees and feet pained me much. There was no *murwa* beer, and so I had to go to bed after a cup of tea. Gumothang is not far from Yampung, but during the snowfall a mile's journey here is more tedious than a day's march in places free from snow. The height of this place is nearly equal to that of Samdubphug.

19*th November.*—The morning was bitter cold. After breakfast, which consisted of rice moistened with tea, and after dismissing our Yampung coolie, who was required to go back to Paongthang, we resumed our journey. The coolie whose feet were snow-bitten walked with gloomy thoughts of dying in the snow, as the skies were not to be trusted. We crossed a small stream with water knee-deep flowing towards the east to feed the Rathong, and commenced the ascent of Bogto La. Firs and juniper of various species overhung our way, which lay along the sides of a dry, glacial channel, having a stream of water in the middle and filled on either side with debris. Our guide pointed out to us the different species of juniper, the leaves of which serve as incense in Buddhist temples. There were numerous pheasants feeding on the rhododendron berries. There are two tracks from here to the only traveller's shed on the slope of Bogto, one following the course of the glacial stream that comes down from the Tshonag lake, and the other that which we now followed. The former is much frequented by the herdsmen of Yampung and by traders in salt from Yangma. The other, though shorter, is not much in favour with the herdsmen, as there grow on both sides of it a plant (called *dug-shing*) which is a deadly poison if eaten by yaks and sheep. There were herds of wild sheep grazing on the slopes of Bogto, which we could have killed, but were dissuaded from the attempt by Phurchung. Though the way was exceedingly steep, I succeeded marvellously in rapidly ascending it, with but few pauses to take breath. I succeeded because I had now become practised in mountaineering, and my heart expanded to the work with greater zeal. At noon we arrived at the shed, which, being constructed of stones piled on all sides, resembled a cell under a cairn. I did not enter it, the weather being pleasant, and there being sunshine outside. There was no water to enable us to make our tea, so I sent off my coolies in advance of me. Within this shed, shut up by snow, some time ago died two young women from Mali Gonpa in Sikkim. One of them was the beautiful daughter of Mali Lama, who, accompanied by a maid-servant, arrived at this unlucky place on her way to Tibet. Shortly after their arrival heavy snow fell and communication was stopped with Yampung and Nepal. There was no water to be had close by, and the unfortunate travellers subsisted for a few days on the scanty residue of the provisions they had brought with them and water melted from snow. When that was exhausted, they died of starvation. A few days after some salt-dealers coming to the place saw the bodies lying within the shed yet fresh, one possessing some traces of beauty, though pale and cold in death. The relics of the unfortunate women were still visible (their bones and teeth lying strewn about the neighbourhood), and filled my mind with gloomy reflections of what might await us in our further progress. Ugyen boiled water in the hypsometer over a candle flame and read it at 188° in my presence.

On the left flank of Bogto, an immense treeless slope, runs the passage to Jongri, with which an interesting story is connected. Previous to the invasion of Sikkim by the Goorkhas under General Undur Sing, there lived a Dokpa (herdsman), named Ssangpo, who possessed a number of yaks. One day a she-yak went astray, and being left behind by the other yaks did not return to the herd. The herdsman searched for her everywhere, but in vain. At last he went to the margin of a little lake at the foot of mount Kabur, the highest point of which immediately overhangs the Jongri ridge. Suddenly he saw his lost yak accompanied by a snow-white bull yak which had miraculously sprung out from the glacial lake. The herdsman, from the colour and size of the white yak, guessed him to be the god of yaks, about whom he had heard different stories from the old folks of his village. On his return home he told the story to no one. In due course of time the she-yak brought forth a snow-white he-calf of extraordinary beauty and possessing red marks resembling an impression in sealing wax of Kanchan Jonga. On account of this peculiarity, the calf was considered as something sacred, and of divine origin. The neighbouring herdsmen, hearing the story of the extraordinary size and appearance of this yak, brought their cows to consort with him. Thereby, within a short time, a numerous progeny of yaks was produced, the male portion of which resembled their father. These were allowed to graze in every pasture land without restriction. The white bull is said to have wandered as far as the Tashiding Monastery in Sikkim. Once Ssangpo, missing him for several days in the neighbourhood of Jongri, came to Tashiding, where he found him in a standing position, his horns stuck in the trunk of a huge oak. The herdsman fondled him, calling his favourite by his name, Karchan, when the yak slowly drew out his horns from the tree, and a tiger's body dropped down putrid and full of maggots. This tiger had attacked the yak, who had crushed him against the oak, and stood in the same position with unabated rage, thinking his ferocious enemy was still alive. It was full one week that the tiger had been pinned to the oak by his horns, yet his rage did not abate till fondled by his master. The herdsman, when returning homewards, found a gigantic landslip on the ridge of Jongri bordering Rathong, which was looked upon as a portent of some great calamity to his sovereign. It is even now a proverbial saying in Sikkim that whenever huge landslips occur at Jongri (or the castle hill) some danger must befall its chief. About this time the Goorkha troops under Undur Sing invaded Sikkim and drove the Raja from his seat at Rabdan-tse to take shelter in the stronghold of Tholung. The herdsman fled with his herds to the Guchak-la (or key-mountain) pass. But on the way he died, and his flock led by Karchan, the great white yak reached Tholung without any other mishap.

We threaded our way up the south-western slope of Bogto La through a mass of dwarf rhododendron and diminutive creeping juniper, which, as we ascended, became smaller and smaller, till they finally disappeared. There were occasionally here and there in the clefts of the rocks a few spongy lichens and moss-like vegetation. Snow was moving down towards the stream that slowly issues from the frozen lake of Chhonag. As the shrubs gave place to grass and débris our difficulties increased. The wretchedness of our food, which was ill-suited to sustain life in these great ascents, was the chief cause of my feeling unwell and exhausted. We had used partly animal and partly vegetable food while journeying in the lower valleys and the Sikkim defiles, but here there being no meat in stock we had to load our stomachs with rice and tea only, which, on account of their bulk, added to our troubles and inconvenience in walking. All my strength was exhausted. I walked on with a frame emaciated by hunger and exertion, dejected and oppressed by the heat and the rarified air, suffering from a violent headache and a tormenting desire to vomit in my efforts to draw a full breath. There was extreme lassitude, and I walked upward with little control over my body for about half a mile, when I fell prostrate on a piece of sloping ground, exhausted and almost breathless. My coolies were all in a worse condition than myself, as they had to carry loads on their backs, while I had nothing except my heavy Tibetan robe. Ugyen had his own weight to carry, which was heavy work. Phurchung laid down his load near me, and searched for a spot for me where I could lie at full length. Failing in this, he prepared an artificial flat by placing his loaded basket lengthwise below my feet to prevent me from rolling down the abyss. The wind now turned to a chill gale, and the clouds moved swiftly in the skies. One of our coolies prepared some tea, which seemed to increase my desire to vomit; but pressed by Phurchung, I drank two cups and wrapped myself up in my whole stock of blankets and clothes. Our guide carefully tucked me in so that no chill breeze could penetrate my blankets. I could scarcely stretch out my arms to take hold of anything. Though my stomach was empty, yet there was no desire for food, and giddiness compelled me to keep my head still. The eyes alone had the power of moving. I wanted to fall asleep as soon as possible, but sleep would not come to me. The extreme height appeared to be the real cause of my sleeplessness. A little before dusk the weather brightened, the wind ceased to blow with fury, and the rays of the setting sun threw the snowy summits before us into a glorious blaze. As the sun withdrew his rays I drew my head into the inmost recesses of my blankets, thinking rather of death than of the morrow's toil. Phurchung now, slowly putting his hands within my blanket, gave me a boiled egg to eat, but when I put it in my mouth, I found it was frozen, the white and the yolk breaking like pieces of sugar crystal. He also gave me some dried fruit out of my bag. At midnight I felt thirsty, and broke off a piece of ice from the side of the rock which served me for a pillow. In this wretched plight, half asleep from fatigue and half awake, I spent my night on the snowy slopes of Bogto, while my companions were snoring in deep slumber. In the morning we found the uppermost blanket was frozen stiff, the pores being filled with crystals of ice, and the whole piece of cloth resembling a hide. The pains that I got in my back and sides recalled to my mind the dismal night I had passed in the snows of Chathang La a couple of years before.

20th November.—The skies were overcast with dark clouds, a gentle wind blew, and the sun shone occasionally from underneath some thin clouds. This threatening attitude of the skies was ominous to our guide, who reluctantly resumed his load and set out for the ascent after chanting some of his *mantras.* After a breakfast of half-boiled rice and tea I left this dreadful place called the Ñoga slope. A few hundred yards of ascent brought us to the neighbourhood of Chho-nag-tsho, which is a glacial lake now entirely frozen. There was no water; but massive crystal ice, resembling glass blocks, was seen in the distance as we scrambled up. It was of a dark blue colour, and of an oval shape, about 400 yards long and 200 yards broad in the middle. The reason why our guide prevented us from shooting *argali* (*ovis ammon*) became evident from the following story:—Not many years ago, when some-trade in rock-salt was carried on through these passes, a family of the Yallung valley became well known for cattle wealth. Once the father of this family with his son arrived here for a night's halt on his way to Yampung, his wife and daughter having gone in advance towards Bogto La. In the evening a Gurung acquaintance of his presented him with the head of a goat. The son lighted a fire with some dry juniper twigs and flint, and the father baked the goat's head and made a hearty meal of it. The baking of the goat's head gave umbrage to the *Shibdag*, the mountain deity, who, assuming the shape of a huge black bull, sprang out from the middle of the lake, bellowing loudly. To this the boy replied by mimicking the lowing of a cow, *law, law.* But *law, law,* in the vulgar colloquial of the Tibetan herdsman, also means "yes, yes." The bull again bellowed, and the boy again provoked him with the same reply. At midnight, when the father and son were fast asleep, the same bull came and crushed the boy to death to avenge the insult, and disappeared. The father, seeing his son dead, fled for life towards Bogto, where he met his wife and daughter. After relating the sad story, he too died vomiting blood from his lungs. Whether the poor herdsman suffered this fate for baking the goat's head, or for his son's insulting the mountain deity, our guide could not explain; but I saw easily what it was that killed them, and mustered all my courage to avoid succumbing to a similar fate. I had no fear of becoming a victim to the fright of spectral visions and the dread of the devil; but to over-exert myself in climbing, so as to bring on congestion of the lungs, to which most probably the poor herdsmen owed his death, was what I dreaded, so I slackened my pace to the surprise of our friend. The ascent was sometimes easy but oftener precipitous, crossing ridge after ridge, paved as it were with massive plates of ice, distributed in fantastic forms, in different stages of conversion from snow into ice. These forms were mostly regulated by the superficial contour of the ground. The scenery was of the wildest grandeur, and the solitude most appalling, no sound of water, nor even the fall of an occasional avalanche, being heard. There was no sound produced by the stamping of our feet on the snow, which in some places yielded under their pressure. Where the snow was condensed into semi-fluid ice, we had to dig our heels with some exertion and caution, though our coolies occasionally slided or skated along the slanting surface. There was a profound silence all about us, none speaking, every one intent on the journey. After a mile's ascent we arrived at the margin of a glacial lake, now frozen to ice as hard as stone. The strata of ice in their different stages of congealation presented a magnificent spectacle, and their dark blue appearance was a relief to the snow-sick eye. Our guide hastened to lay down his load, and ran to prevent us from going round the margin. He forthwith collected some scraps of snow and splintered ice, which he sprinkled along the frozen surface of the lake to show the path and keep us from the dangerous slips which so commonly happen on smooth, glassy surfaces. This lake, only about 200 yards broad at this season, and twice as much lengthwise, is considered an object of sanctity in the sacred books of the Sikkimese. It is called Chho Domdongma, or the "lake of peacock's spots," and the eyes of the enchanted devotees may realise something like spots made by the bubbling water under the icy sheets of the lake. The glorious peak of Chhum-bab La rose right in our front, and broken, forked ridges ran sharply out from each side of its snowy summit. As we forced our way onwards up the steep ice slope of Chhum-bab La, the clouds rapidly enveloped the sun, and within half an hour's time nearly the whole vault of the sky was hidden from our view. Here courage failed our hitherto intrepid guide. "Why proceed further up, Sir," said he; "death awaits us in this desolate place; one hour more and we shall be gone." "What do you mean by this, Phurchung?" said I; "what makes you see death?" "Sir, look at the sky, those very clouds will shortly fall on us as heavy snow from which no earthly means will enable us to escape. If you do not get buried in the snow on this side of the La, you will surely not get out from it on the other side. There is but one hour's ascent to take us on the neck of that towering La." He trembled and looked pale and depressed. No doubt a fall of snow was threatening, and he had read many ominous things from the frowning aspect of the sky. He cried, and said "Oh, Sir, we *pon-yog* (master and servants) will perish here if you do not return to Bogto. The skies are portentous, and I entreat you to turn back towards the Bogto La." He repeated his entreaties with childish tears, but in vain. I told him and the coolies that I was determined not to turn back a single step, and that all his entreaties were to no purpose. In one hour's time we could scarcely reach Bogto, and if the snow fell in the meantime, we could hardly escape; besides such a course would not shorten our troubles, as we should have the risk of re-traversing the distance we had now travelled over. There might be a chance of a second snowfall, when we should again have to turn back. I told him the season of heavy snowfalls was over, and the portentous cloud would soon disappear. And turning back to Ugyen, I observed: "To go back is inauspicious, and one unlucky thing might draw a train of unfortunate events. We have been thus far fortunate; why should we then embrace an inauspicious course?" He admitted the force of my arguments on religious grounds, and so our guide being silenced, began to crawl upwards, though with dejected spirits. I took the lead, and with the fresh energy that accompanied this resolution, toiled on crawling along a blue, glacial indentation underneath which some half-melted ice was seen to run down. We now constantly looked towards the skies as the source of all our fears. After an hour's hard ascent we reached the summit of the pass, quite exhausted. Here was the Lap-tse, where a few scraps of red cloth, tied on small, dwarfish bamboos, fluttered in the wind. Three or four baskets full of *tsuo* (dyeing creepers) were half buried in snow, probably left by their carriers during a snowfall. Some of our men tried to find out if there were the remains of any who might have been buried under the snow. They drove their sticks into many places of suspicious appearance, but no traces were found. We took a short rest, and enjoyed the grand and impressive scenery. The skies now cleared up, the azure heavens again smiled on us, and the welcome re-appearance of a brilliant sun dispelled our fears. The distant views of Sundubphug in imposing blue to the left, the towering pinnacles of Kanglajang-ma to our right, the rounded spire of the lofty Lap-chyi in the Sharkhambu district of Nepal peeping from the midst of occasional fogs, and above all the vast expanse of the Nepal valley, which bounded our vision on all sides, rose blended together in the distant haze. The valley of Chhum-bab La is called Chhu-loknyo ('the spoon of water') because it receives the water of the surrounding mountain in a spoon-like receptacle. Ugyen took the boiling point, which stood at 184·4° at midday. Our ascent to the La was not the end of our troubles, for they, in truth, here commenced. I had hardly time to congratulate ourselves on our success, when our guide, now smiling, put his arms into the *namlo*, or the tie-rope of his load, and uttering the usual prayer (*Lhasol*), resumed his journey. The descent was fraught with immense dangers, as the snows were trackless, so that to guess which way the safe path lay was very difficult. Our guide surveyed the entire slope with his stick and not finding any track, at last selected a way which, though circuitous, seemed to his experienced eyes practicable. He walked first, the rest of our party following his footsteps. Properly speaking, there were no footsteps, as each step took us two or three feet deep in the snow. The sun now shone brilliantly, and increased the glare of the snow so much that I had to protect my eyes with a pair of coloured glasses.

After walking about an hour, we saw that we made very little progress; and with the idea of getting a path through shallow snow, we followed the foot-marks left by a Tibetan long-tailed leopard (*sah*). I wondered the animal should have suceeded in walking over the snow in so remarkable a way, for its foot-marks were all uniform, and in no place were the animal's heels sunk unevenly. This my men attributed to the supernatural powers of the animal, which they said was indeed the goblin of leopards. An hour's struggle in the snow, with numberless tugs and tumbles, exhausted my strength, and I found myself incapable of proceeding further. Our guide opened some of the packages and repacked, putting all the brittle substances in one, and the clothes and provisions, &c., into another. The latter he plunged down with a great push. For a short time I followed the groove made by the rushing load; but when its progress was arrested by some heavy block, my difficulty recommenced. Ascertaining the direction we should follow, I adopted the dangerous course of passing directly down the steep, snowy slope (*thur*). I held the corners of my blanket robe with both hands on the outer side of the knees to prevent any injury to my hinder parts, and accommodating myself as if I were in a sledge, I slid down smoothly on the half-hardened, smooth, but yielding snow. On the slippery slopes it was hard to check the plunge, but whenever I found myself in the vicinity of a crevasse with green-blue gaping chasm, I diverted my course by working my elbows as if I was swimming in a lake. This course answered well, and I advanced far ahead of my companions; but remembering the treacherous crevasse I had seen on a former occasion, I apprehended much danger in proceeding further, as my men could not then come to my assistance if any mishap occurred to me. The ice chasms were numerous; yet rest being necessary I halted close to a huge boulder, in one side of which there was a yawning gap, the ice and half-melted glacial snow moving downward.

Our men arrived by a different path, which was about twenty yards above the place where I stood with my feet and legs freezing, for one does not experience the greatest effect of cold when walking; it only overpowers him when he halts. But as my feet and legs were well protected by Tibetan boots and Kashmir socks, I escaped the consequences of frost-bite, which too often paralyses the limbs of inexperienced travellers. I now felt that we were safe, and devoutly thanked Heaven, for had there been the least snowfall, our fate would have been sealed. At about 3-30 P.M. we descended a long way into the chasm of Chhu-lonkyok, where patches of snow alternated with a grassy surface. In the snow there were lean stalks of a kind of alpine shrub called *upala*, with large, pink leaves at the top, resembling those of the water-lily, flapping in the rushing wind that now rose again. Landed as it were on *terra firma*, I put off my shoes and trousers, wherein crystals of snow had penetrated and were freezing my feet and legs. The coolies now walked with greater swiftness, leaving me at a considerable distance. At times looking back, they signalled to me to quicken my pace. I clambered onwards unmindful of the rugged stones and the icy rills that lay across the way. The gradual re-appearance of the grass, rhododendrons, and juniper bushes freshened my spirits as I walked on, frequently halting to take breath. In this way did I traverse the dreadful slopes of Chhum-bab La, and at the approach of sunset quickened my pace to arrive at the night's shelter. What that might turn out to be nobody yet knew except the guide. As I descended to the grassy pit of Chhu-lonkyok the sun dipped below the horizon, his beams shining for a few moments on the peak of Chhum-bab La, and then disappearing. Shortly afterwards I lost sight of my men and walked at random for more than half an hour, no track or passage being discernible, before I found Ugyen waiting for me. Here was a small hillock and saddle-shaped spur full of pasture of luxuriant growth. There were no shrubs or juniper bushes with which we could light a fire to cook our food. From this spur we descended to a depth of about 500 feet in a ravine filled with bushes of rhododendron, juniper and several species of prickly, sweet-scented shrubs, resembling the thistle of lower elevations. It was past six and gloom had overtaken the earth, when I descried a distant boulder, underneath which our men had lighted a smoky fire. On either side of our pathway there were juniper bushes which had encroached on it by the weight of the superincumbent snow, now melted down. From these and from others at a distance, which I did not see on account of the darkness, came a delightful and most welcome fragrance; and cheered at the end of the day's trouble, and with hopes of a night's comfortable rest, I arrived at the boulder. In front of it there ran a stream about four feet wide. This is said to be the head stream of the famous Kabilee of Nepal which receives the waters of the Chhum-bab and Semarum mountains. My companions had spread my rug on a heap of juniper twigs, which were laid upon the splintered stones to keep off damp. The rug being thin was supplemented by a blanket, but yet these failed to remove the unevenness of the place. Tea was prepared, and I emptied my cup very frequently. I always carried my China cup, which I used to put in a copper cup-shaped case during the march. It was an indispensable article, as we often suffered from thirst in our up and down hill journeys. It took a couple of hours to cook rice, as the fuel, consisting of moist and undried juniper, did not burn well, and smoked very much to our great annoyance. We felt no appetite for any food, but the extreme exhaustion of the body threw me as it were into a state of collapse of the vital powers—the eyes wandered, and there was no strength to move the limbs. After an hour's rest I recovered strength and rose from my sleepy prostration; such is the life-infusing climate of these lofty altitudes and their exhilerating tendency to allay pain and fatigue. Phurchung lighted my lantern and held a cupful of rice moistened with tea before me. I ate my meal sitting within the folds of my blanket. There was a slight fall of sleet, but no snow nor much wind. I slept a good though interrupted sleep owing to pains.

21*st November*.—In the morning there was a brisk movement among the coolies, packing up their loads and talking to awake me. I was not asleep, and heard quietly what was going on outside from within the folds of my blankets. When I looked out, my eyes were dazed with the glare of daylight. The skies were cloudless and of the deepest blue, against which on all sides the snowy summits of numerous peaks pierced the vault of heaven in indescribably grand array. The sun light, though not yet visible in the valley, had already gilded the snow-clad tops of the giant peaks. Removing the upper blanket, which had become encrusted with slight snow during the night, our guide requested me to get up soon; "the weather is tempting, and we must cross the *La* as quickly as possible." I asked him to give me some tea. He said all the utensils and cups, &c., were packed up and despatched, and the coolies having gone some distance could not conveniently be called back. What disappointment I felt, and how exhausted I was, my good servant failed to understand, but judged from my previous day's feats that my little thin frame possessed extraordinary powers, and knew not that my strength was unequal to the task before me, and that I walked only because I could not help walking. I reproved him for his inconsiderateness in thinking me as strong as himself. He begged pardon, explaining that he thought the weather being good in the morning would most probably turn bad in the evening, and that to be able to cross the second snowy pass early in the day would be far more safe. Dressed very lightly, in order to be able to ascend quicker, I set out on my journey, following his footsteps. The ascent was at first not difficult or rugged, and so I walked with some cheerfulness, often asking to be shown the exact position of the pass we should have to cross that day. There were a few birds resembling sparrows, which twittered as they flew, issuing from the clefts of rocks hanging over our head. We crossed saddle after saddle of mountain ridges, and so had numerous ups and downs; but of that we thought little, for to ascend or descend five or six hundred feet was *now* nothing to us; it was the sight of abrupt ravines and gorges five to six thousand feet deep that made us uncomfortable and full of dismay. Walking in this manner for a few miles, I again felt exhausted. Our guide observing this, said the pass was not very far off. "There it lies: we shall soon reach it." Encouraged by his words, I walked on again, but arriving at the foot of what he called the *La*, I found that it had gone further up! After a mile's journey further up, I found it to be no *La* at all, but a passage resembling a gateway lying between two rocky cliffs. Here commenced the region of scanty vegetation that invariably lies at the foot of the limits of the lower snowy zone. Here our coolies had halted, and having collected some juniper twigs on their way up, had lighted a fire, which, when I arrived, smoked very much. They prepared me a cup of tea, with which I moistened my mouth, dry and bitter with thirst. I ate some indian-corn, as our biscuits were consumed all but one tin. The fuel having burnt out before any snow could be melted, the coolies failed to quench their thirst; however, they licked up the water dropping from the melting ice in the clefts of rocks; some picked up snow-flakes and ate them, though with difficulty. At about nine we resumed our journey, passed various formations of snow and ice in their several stages of congelation and melting. The ice was all that we dreaded, for no feet could rest on them without slipping down. The hard snow was welcome to us, being pleasant to walk over. The heels scarcely sank more than a few inches in snow. The icy regions lying at the lower limits of the snow were slippery in the extreme, and most dangerous in consequence of the steepness of the slope. After a couple of hours' hard and tedious ascent over different stages of melting snow, we reached the pass, which was protected from the south and west by a very rugged cliff resembling the outspread wings of an eagle both in colour and shape, and inspiring me with a strange feeling of dread. Sitting near the Lap-tse, I enjoyed one of the grandest scenes I had ever beheld. Though very tired and unwell, I was much impressed by the grandeur and sublimity of nature. No poet could adequately realise nature's exploits in this part of the world. No pencil could delineate these romantic scenes. I thought for a moment that the sages of old were wrong in their ideas of heaven. When one looks up from below, he naturally conceives paradise to be somewhere on high, but on reaching such lofty altitudes, where breathing is a natural and unsurmountable difficulty, I could not but smile at the ignorance of those sages in their ideas of heaven. They must have been deluded with the grandeur of the void that encompasses the universe, to risk the situation of their paradise in such a desolate region. From my position here on the top of hoary Semarum, I saw paradise below, while above me were nothing but eternal snows where death alone can dwell. The hanging glaciers, the towering pinnacles, the rushing snow drifts, the thundering avalanches, the yawning crevasses, the splintering of rocks from frost, and above all the cold,—all were but various appendages of the Lord of Death. He chose to make his abode here, to rule the skies as well as the world below with his thunder and rain. Verily might one say that the sages of yore in their ideas of the celestial regions were not happy; for when, after encountering immense hardships and endless privations, one arrives at the loftiest regions, he is utterly surprised that paradise should have been sought there.

Legend has it that many years ago, at this very pass, a certain cunning and designing Limboo of Tambur Khola had secretly concealed under the rocky ground a red earthen jar filled with charcoal, with the dishonest object of establishing his heir's right over the whole easternmost part of Nepal, called Yangoro, which also includes Singlee-la. Before dying, he left a written will bequeathing all this land to his heirs. A few years after a quarrel took place between the Limboos of Tambur Khola and of Yangoro, which lasted for nearly twelve years, during which time the Gurungs were the chief sufferers, as their cattle were robbed by the Limboos of either party who disputed the possession of the land, both parties claiming rent for pasture lands. The great dispute was at last settled by the Chaubisi Raja, who ruled at Bhatgaong, in favour of the Yangoro Limboos. The trick played by the cunning ancestor of the Tambur-Khola Limboo was found out, the Raja agreeing that the earthen pot which the Tambur man dug out from the Semarum La must have been concealed with no other view than that of falsely claiming the Yangoro lands. The Yangoro Limboos therefore hold this place as very auspicious.

The forked cliff of Semarum proudly piercing the blue space stood frowning on us with its numerous brown ribs of rock, now bare of snow. To our north-west, at a great distance, I saw numerous snowy ranges, said to be the Shar Khambu mountains, whose tops were wrapped in clouds. I got out my field-glass from my bag and feasted my eyes on the splendid scenery of the grandest and loftiest of the world's mountains,—Choma Kankar (the lord of snows), which overhangs Lap-chyi, the famous mountain of great Buddhist sanctity. The highest of the three peaks that were visible, Choma Kankar, reposing in calm majesty in the shape of a rounded dome, rose high above all, and the two others that stood side by side, like his ministers, resembled blunted cones. They were resplendent with the rays of the sun, the shadows being cast to the north-west. To the north-west of these were the Sharkhambu mountains, which, gradually enveloped with ascending fogs, soon vanished from our sight. To the west, beyond an immensely wide and stupendous chasm in the valley of the Tambur, were the valleys of Leylep, Yallung, Dhunkota, and Tambur, all of which were faintly visible when pointed out by our guide's finger, for there was a haze, so that a dark-blue colour overspread all the scenery. After half an hour the wind blew from the west, making it inconvenient to take the height by the hypsometer, as the flame was several times blown out. However, by surrounding the instrument with a screen, we obtained the boiling point, which stood at 184·5°. We took bearings of the passes of Shingsa, Takpola, and Wallung, and other important snowy peaks. These finished, we resumed our journey. After walking about 50 yards, we found ourselves entangled in a maze of glaciers and trackless snowy surfaces. The glacial furrows were the natural tracks which an unwary traveller would follow; but those furrows were in some places very deep and treacherous on account of the crevasses formed on the side of huge boulders; so that when one follows a furrow he descends into an abyss surrounded by walls of ice without any accessible passage out. Our guide brought all his past experience of mountains to bear at this critical place, and yet failed to come to a satisfactory solution. We all consulted together, and each advised the others to follow some particular glacial furrow. At last I thought it best to give preference to our guide's suggestion to follow the track which he, disencumbered of his load, would make for us. He started the other coolies, dividing his own load among them. After wading for about twenty yards, he found himself half buried and scarcely able to get out. He had sunk to the waist, and snow filled his sleeves and the great pocket at his breast. I turned back at his signal, without trying to go to the right or left of our track, and retraced my footsteps. After ten minutes' struggle Phurchung succeeded in getting out of his difficult position. Although my other coolies tried to persuade me to follow this or that track, yet none came forward to take the lead. Observing Phurchung's discomfiture I made a different though dangerous resolution as to our *modus operandi*. I begged them to let me go ahead, and to follow me when they saw I had obtained a firm footing on the snow. First of all our guide drifted his huge load and watched which way it went. This having plunged down where the track might lead it, I girded up my clothes, and holding the edges of the lower part of my robe slipped along. Instantly I was carried down and hurled to a depth of more than a hundred feet below. There I brought myself up by fixing my elbows into the snow like a brake, at the same time lifting my hinder part a little. Ugyen followed me in the furrow I had made, and would have dashed on me with his whole weight, had I not taken the precaution of turning myself to one side of the track. I then embarked on a second slide down a still steeper snow-slope, and was at once shot forth to a greater distance than before. In the third slide we met with slippery ice rather than snow crystals, and consequently got pains in the back, caused by friction on the harder substance. When there intervened a flatter surface, a slide became inconvenient, and we commenced wading with great difficulty. We made very little progress, as it took much time to draw up our legs from the foothold two or three feet deep in snow. Here my men tried the expedient of dragging their loads after them by strings tied to the edges of the baskets, as they found it impossible to wade in the snow with such heavy loads as they carried. I saw the foot-marks of some wild animals, such as the wild rabbit and the snow leopard, and also of a kind of bird called *chamdang*, probably the snow pheasant. I really wondered that wild animals should have been able to preserve the equilibrium of their bodies so well as to stamp the snow uniformly all over, for the animal or the bird had no doubt to rest its weight on its foot-marks. Why these should have remained uniform, while ours were deep and irregular, I could not understand. For a considerable distance on the flat, icy slope I followed the foot-marks of a snow leopard, and at last I found I was being led the wrong way. Phurchung and Ugyen had ascended a ridge on my left, while I laboured down the deep gorge. Although, abandoning my first track, I soon overtook them, yet I found they were equally mistaken in their route. Our intrepid guide now mustered all his knowledge of travelling in snow and glacial regions. When we saw it was past three in the afternoon, and that we had to make a long journey still to reach the next stage—Namga-tshal—our countenances were overcast with dismay and anxiety. Our progress was very slow. There being no water for our men to quench their thirst, they chewed half-melted lumps of snow. At last our guide made a detour round another ridge which lay to our right. After half an hour's ascent we found ourselves on the top of a huge, snowless rock, about 40 to 50 feet high. The coolies descended down this with wonderful agility. I took a short rest, sitting down on a slab. There were loose stones and debris brought down by the melting snows, which we were warned by our guide not to throw down carelessly, as they would crush the coolies in their descent. I descended the steep side of this block of rock, being helped by one of the coolies, who held fast my right arm and the girdle of my robe. Our bundles of clothes and other articles were plunged down as before, to be brought up short at the bottom of the snowy gorge, and I again prepared for a series of slides. This time the slopes were steeper than ever, but their end was visible, for which reason we were bolder than before, as there was no crevasse to devour us at the bottom. Although in one slide I rushed down unable to check my motion by my elbows, yet fortunately a projecting boulder covered with snow arrested me in my headlong progress. The third slide, which took me to the pit where our troubles in the snow were to end, I really enjoyed as if it were an amusement, and we all laughed at each other's achievements. Arrived at length at the very bottom of the gorge, I stood on a turf by the side of some rhododendron bushes, and shook my garments to clear myself of the snow which had penetrated inside my trousers and inner shirt. Here my watch dropped down and the keys with it; one of my coolies picked them up shortly after. At 4 P.M. we all reached the region of stones and vegetation, and our hearts were filled with the joy of a successful termination. Cheerfulness brightened every one's face, and especially mine. After a short rest we again resumed our journey along the gentle rill which leaps down from here with a pleasant murmur. It is called the second head-water of the Kabilee, although the part of it which we followed empties itself into the Namga stream. Half an hour's quick journey along the fragrant, turfy margin of this glacial stream brought us to the Namga river, our old acquaintance, which rises from the Kangla Nangmo Pass near Jongri. We recognised the old track which we had traversed in 1879, and had a distant view of the Kangla Pass. The snows on either side of the Namga river shewed us that the Kangla Pass was equally inaccessible at this season of the year. Snow had fallen several miles below it in October. The autumn fall of snow is called *shingsa pahmo*, and affects the lower altitudes of luxuriant vegetation. Our way was now easy, and overgrown with dwarf rhododendron and bushy juniper, besides other new varieties of shrubs, the sweet scent of which I enjoyed as I passed. A kind of prickly shrub with red fruit was abundant, and often its thorny twigs caught in our garments. There were several kinds of mosses and lichens growing on the sides of the river and on the slopes of the mountains on either side. The Namga stream was also frozen, large ice floes being in motion where the stream was narrow; but the greater part was covered with snow, underneath which the water forced its way down-stream. Towards our front, but a great way off, the pine-clad flanks of Juona, through which the Yallung rapids threaded their silvery way, were set on a blaze of fire by the sun now quietly setting in the west. I wished much to get into the sunshine, but our way seemed endless; and as we advanced, the sun's rays ascended higher and higher along the mountain flanks. Our way now lay between two snow-covered ranges, the lower flanks of which were densely covered with rhododendrons and pines, chiefly the *dungshing* or cedar. To follow the meandering Namga was a tedious affair. We plodded on till at 6 P.M. we reached the extensive flat of the Namga river, called Namga-Tshal (the grove of joy). It was overgrown with rough pasture now withering, and also with thickets of various alpine trees and shrubs. Passing through several pasture lands, and crossing the Namga river by a wooden bridge about 40 feet long, constructed after the East Nepal fashion, we arrived at the halting stage under the wide-spread branches of a high cedar. There were marks of other travellers having spent the night at its foot, such as the fire-place, the collection of fuel, and the bamboo water-vessels. We cleared the spot of all the rubbish and spread our rugs on the ground. To protect me from wind and snow my coolies erected an enclosure of rhododendron twigs round my bed and covered it with a sheet of cloth. Phurchung, who had been for several days entreating me to be allowed the use of my fowling-piece, now quietly took it and asked if he could use it. I gave him leave, and said that he must bring me a pheasant. It was dark when he entered the thicket to shoot any solitary *chamgdang* (pheasant) that might fall in his way, but after firing two cartridges he returned without any game. Our coolies busied themselves with collecting fuel, lighting a fire, and fetching water. After taking a few cups of tea and a dish of rice, I stretched my length on the rug, and was soon asleep.

22nd November.—The morning was bright and clear. My fatigues were to some extent allayed by the genial climate of this grove, and with a mind released from the fear of snow, I lingered under my blankets. There was a gentle breeze, and the whole grove appeared enlivened by the cries of pheasants and different species of the bird called *abla*.

Lha-tsun, the great Buddhist patriarch of Sikkim, I was told, when first coming to visit these Himalayan regions, spent a few days here, struck with the fine scenery and the spaciousness of the valley. He performed the inaugural rites of the work of converting the Lhopas. The fatigues of his long and perilous journey from the northern solitudes of Tibet down to this place had broken down his health, but the few days that he spent here greatly restored him, not only by the delightful scenery of the place, but more especially by the comforts that he obtained here, both religious and physical. After the termination of his toils he called it *Namga Tshal* (the grove of joy). He left directions for the guidance of Buddhists of his school to consider this place as very sacred, and to perform their annual inaugural religious ceremonies at the cavern where he had spent a few days. We had the self-same cavern in view from our halting place, and were told that the Sikkim and East Nepal Buddhists even now resort to this place occasionally on pilgrimage.

I got up from bed at 7 A.M., and finishing the accounts of the previous day in my scribbling diary, sat to breakfast, which consisted of tea, rice, and some red pulse brought from Darjeeling. Dressed as usual, I started for the day's march. Phurchung muttered his sacred *mantras*, invoking the saint Pema-jung-ne and his two wives to help us on our journey. We now walked with cheerfulness, the pleasant recollections of the scenes of our former journey becoming more and more vivid as the boulders and precipices re-appeared to our view. Thickets of *deodars* and other pines, black through age, were perched over the steep slopes, from the deep recesses of which crowed the mountain pheasant. There were one or two Limboos carrying down loads of dye-creepers. After crossing two streams, the margins of which were somewhat swampy, we ascended a short way up-hill through the thickets of rhododendron, where numerous green pheasants were picking the berries. Ugyen Gya-tsho could not resist the temptation of shooting some: he shot at several, but missed them. I was asked to walk noiselessly so as not to stir them. At last one unfortunate pheasant was hit, but it flew to some distance, and Phurchung's brother chased and captured it. I arrived on the bank of the Yallung river, which unceasingly washes down the glacial debris of the giant Juona, which stood to our right unspeakably grand and in stupendous glory, its head shooting to the skies. There was a wooden bridge of cedar-logs and silver-fir planks on the river, which we easily crossed. The grove through which we then passed for a while made me forget that I was travelling in the mountains. There was a sluggish stream filled with leaves of trees and twigs, and its course overgrown with creepers. Phurchung and his brother now arrived, brimful of exultation at having killed one pheasant after several fruitless shots. They shewed me the poor bird, which was just breathing its last. It was of the colour of the green parrot, with spurs on its legs and a deep, thick red line round its eyes. The legs and toes resembled those of the domestic cock, which in size it much surpassed. Shortly afterwards Phurchung and Ugyen left us, telling me to proceed slowly and that they would presently overtake me. So with only one coolie I clambered up the slopes of the lofty Choonjorma. The way was very steep; besides we had taken the wrong way. Having had a somewhat heavy meal, I found much difficulty in ascending rapidly, and took rest, sitting in a reclining posture on the trunk of a large tree which with its rope-like hanging twigs swept to and fro in the wind. My coolie gave me some berries to eat which he had plucked from the thorny shrubs growing by the side of the road. A few minutes after we were joined by Phurchung and Ugyen, who had failed to shoot any more birds. After a short march the difficulty of ascent increased. I now resolved not to take rest by sitting, for when I did so, I felt a languor in my knees, which disinclined me to get up and resume the journey. I had got pretty well habituated to mountaineering, in consequence of which I hardly suffered from quick and frequent breathing, and my heart now beat less and my lungs were less exhausted by the up-hill journey. The coolies, who had to ascend with heavy loads on their backs, gasped like ponies. When, after climbing two or three hundred feet up-hill, they stood supporting their loads on a short stick which they carried in their hands, I too rested standing. After ascending about 1,000 feet along the middle flank of Choonjorma, we reached the top of a huge rock, on which I sat for a while to get a view of the spacious grove of Namga-tshal, situated between the Yallung and the Namga rivers, and extending as far as their junction. The two streams wound along their silvery way amidst the dark groves of tall silver-firs, bleached juniper trees, and several kinds of rhododendrons. Deep, gloomy chasms yawned below to our left and right, and the great grove of Namga-tshal seemed hemmed in on three sides by craggy cliffs of great height. Their wild appearance, here and there broken by torrents carrying down landslips of large dimensions, and presenting a chalky appearance from a distance, was very impressive and awful. The more we climbed up, the less we perceived the noise of the torrents, and the roaring of the Yallung river now sank into a faint murmur. The abrupt height of Choonjorma, its isolation from other mountains on three sides—south, east, and west,—and its rounded rocky appearance, compelled us to ascend it with feelings of the awful and the sublime. Up to this height we had not met with any snow, and our hearts palpitated with the fear of again meeting with snow on the summit of Choonjorma. We still heard the cry of the pheasants and other mountain birds which love to make their nests in the hollows and crevices of the gigantic rocks of these stupendous precipices. After a hard climb of half an hour we arrived at the top of a flat rock, the lower sides of which were overgrown with a kind of thorny creeper with bunches of berries, some red and ripe. I asked the coolies to take rest for a while at this place, and myself opening Phurchung's load, took out the field-glasses to enjoy the superb scenery of the surrounding mountains. Looking to the south-east, the eye failed to follow the endless labyrinth of the mountain valleys, through which threaded numerous torrents. There were no mists nor any thick, hazy atmosphere to limit our view. On our right stood Cho-kangchan Juonga, receding somewhat towards the north-east, with its dome-like conical head reaching the sky, but overtopped by the great Kangchan and others to the further north and east. The grandest and the largest moraine on this side of the snowy range presented itself to our view. The huge white boulders, called in Tibetan *Kang-se*, which were thickly scattered over the place, the different glacial furrows which intersected this moraine laterally, and the rock-slips caused by the combined action of avalanches and glacial currents, were the most remarkable features on the western slope of Cho-Kangchan. For a while I mistook the whitish-brown boulders for snow in the shade, but on close inspection with the binocular I became convinced of their being nothing but rocks, though at such extraordinary heights. That there should be rock-covered moraines free from snow at about eight or nine thousand feet above the place where we stood, while comparatively lower altitudes were entirely covered with snow, was a curious phenomenon. There were patches of verdure visible just below the snow limits. A few hundred (probably a thousand) feet below the green spots were woody slopes. Phurchung here told me that the yaks of Yallung village in August and September advance so far up as to graze in the green patches we saw, just at the foot of Juona. In the woody solitudes lower below, on the waist of this romantic snowy mountain, was seen the monastery of Dechhen Rolpa, with six monks, famous for its consecration to Cho-Kangchan. The head Lama of Dechhen Rolpa, who is a friend of our guide, is named Jigma-Gya-mtsho, or "the fearless ocean." He is now aged fifty, and by the grace of Cho-Kangchan will, it is believed, live an unusually long life. His predecessor, named Jigma-Pao, is said to have by dint of his saintly character visited Na-Pemathang, the most sacred and secret sanctuary consecrated to Kang-chan-Juonga. At Pemathang, according to our guide's narration, Jigma-Pao met seven Lepcha couples, who cultivate the excellent soil and raise luxuriant crops of rice, indian-corn and *murwa*, and live in plenty throughout the year. I was about to believe in the story of our friend, but when he proceeded to say that these seven couples beget no children and never die, I took the story for what it was worth. Pemathang is the paradise of the Lepchas, from among whom up to this time only seven happy families have succeeded in entering it. To these dwellers of paradise Pema Jung-ne, the Dinghsenē of the Lepchas, makes himself visible on the 10th of every lunar month. Jigma having succeeded in penetrating into this mystic abode of the pious Lepcha patriarchs, is given the name of Pao, 'or the dauntless hero,' by the Buddhists of this part of Nepal. Last year a native of Yallung penetrated into Na-Pemathang, situated between the Cho-Kangchan and Juonga. He was enveloped in mists, and although he saw forests and pastures, he failed to see any trace of human abode or cattle, and encountered immense difficulties from snow-falls.

The village of Yallung, which is situated about three miles to the west of the monastery of Dechhen Rolpa, was not clearly visible from the place where we stood. It contains twelve families, who spend their summer in tending yaks at Yallung and their winter at Yanku-thang in the valley of the Kabilee. These twelve families, consisting of about thirty-five souls, are now under Lapa, the headman of Yallung, a friend of our guide. The view into the Yallung gorge, overhung by the grand mountain, was unspeakably grand, and held me chained to the spot until I found my companions had resumed their journey, and my guide stretched his hand for the binocular to put it into his big package. Reluctantly I followed him after a parting look at the scenery. After an hour's ascent we left the zone of tall trees and arrived at the rocky waist of the mountain, when I guessed that the two small lakes called Tsho Chhung Donka were not far from us. Shortly after, we reached the eastern lake. I at once went to the edge, and put my hand into the water for a draught, when I found it solid and hard as stone! The lakes were all frozen deep, and under the glossy layers were visible a few bubbles issuing forth from the sandy bed. Ugyen threw some stones to see if water could be struck out. I feared lest the stones might rebound towards us from the frozen surface, but they slid smoothly to the furthest margin. We resumed our journey, and after a walk of a few minutes arrived at the margin of the other lake. Phurchung prevented Ugyen from throwing stones on it, saying that the goddess of the lake would take offence at his doing so. The two lakes are said to be presided over by two mountain deities—husband and wife. These deities take offence at any attempt of travellers to boil the water of the lake for any purpose. [Once three Nepalese arrived here, one of whom lighted a fire to make tea, the second fetched water, and the third, who was an old man, fell asleep through fatigue. When the water began to boil there was heard the sound of thunder from the cloudless sky. As the roaring continued, the three travellers fled towards Yallung, leaving their loads of mutton and wool behind.] These passed, we ascended to the top of Tsho Chhung Donka and enjoyed a view of the western mountain ranges. Here I thought the trouble of ascending would cease, but it was not so. Our guide said that the way by the western flank of this *La* was covered with snow and ice, and consequently impassable. We therefore had to ascend the Nango Lap-tse, the shortest but the steepest route, being upwards of 13,000 feet above the level of the sea. Up to this place, which receives the rays of the sun from the east, there was only a sprinkling of snow. Passing the Lap-tse after the usual votive offering of a few scraps of rags inscribed with the *mantras Lha sol-lo, Lha kyal-lo* (God be praised, God be praised), we descended to a small dip filled with snow. This part of the pass midway between the Lap-tse and Mirkanla, where the road from Nepal past Khan-Dophug joins it, is called the Choonjorma (collection of cascades). The snow was deep, although settled down. From the foot-tracks left on the snow, and the droppings of yaks and sheep yet fresh, it was evident that three or four days ago some herdsmen had passed by this way. We followed this foot-track, and journeyed on very carefully. In several places we sank to our knees in snow, but there being no crevasses we walked on with spirit. I only feared lest from the steepness of the slopes on the west I might slide down to the foot of the *La*. In some places I was helped by one of our coolies, who had lagged behind on account of the weight of his load. The lake near Khan-dophug was spacious, and the green, turquoise-like colour of its water was seen from a distance. This passed, we arrived at the spur of Mirkan-La, which was partially free from snow. Our road lay on its western flank, which we found easy. From Mirkan-La we passed on into another saddle of bristling crags, called Tha-Miran Kukyab. The chief of these crags is believed to be the self-grown image of the horrid deity *Tamdin* or *Haya-griba*. The rock resembled the head of a horse looking towards the Kang-chan. Below this, at a mile distance, is Pangbo La, where we observed grass. Leaving the dip of Pangbo, we ascended upwards of a mile and a half to reach Sseenon-La, whose flanks were coverd with juniper and rhododendron bushes. Our way now lay towards the Kang-pachan valley, where the descent was gradual. A mile's journey brought us to an extensive moraine called Dolung-phug. The boulders here were large and numerous, and of a brown-red colour. The spur of the moraine was covered with snow, which gave us much difficulty in traversing it; but the track laid out by herds of yaks and sheep a few days ago was of great help to us. The sun now entered the clouds of the western horizon (the approach of evening being rather early), and painted the stupendous, sublime peak of the imperial Kang-chan-juonga with a dazzling expanse of gold and amber. I stopped for a while to enjoy the view, the most majestic that ever was presented to my eyes, though my companion hurried on to reach the night's stage. The different glacial furrows studded with pale amber-coloured boulders were also distinctly seen on Kangchan beginning gradually to be covered with fog, but the summits remained unsullied by clouds. I heard Ugyen calling from a distance to me to quicken my pace, and I hastened on. At this place a few years ago two Khamba from Darjeeling were overtaken and killed by the natives of Kang-pachan for kidnapping a girl from their village. A good descent of nearly two miles brought us down to Mudan-phug. The snow was deep, and darkness coming on, we plodded on our way very much embarrassed. In the meantime our good guide, after depositing his load at Mudan-phug, came back to carry me. He tied me to his broad back with my comforter, and walked off with long strides. I did not ask him to carry me, but he saw my difficulties and of his own accord came to my help. How invaluable were his services to me in this most trying journey, when my strength had failed me, it is not easy to describe. At about 7 P.M. we arrived at Mudan-phug, on a table-land with a stream of clear, sparkling water flowing by. Near a small bridge I dismounted from my friend's back and walked down to the side of a boulder, where a fire was lighted by our coolies. My rug was spread before I arrived, and a candle in a broken lantern flickered in the wind. The inside of the *Phugpa* (the hollow of a rock) was damp, leaky, and uneven: some ashes and charcoal, the residue of the fire of travellers who had preceded us, were spread beneath my rug, which hardly removed the unevenness of the ground. With great difficulty did I accommodate myself in the rock-hollow to pass the night. Phurchung and his brother were now in excellent sprits, and cheerfulness brightened their faces, as they were nearing their homes. Phurchung told us that he noticed smoke at a distance of about a mile, which was probably Menda-phug, and where the natives of Kang-pachan generally halt on their way to the Rong-Yanku-thang and other places. Tea and rice were prepared as usual, with which we satisfied our hunger, and conversed as to how we could best manage to pass unrecognised at Kang-pachan, where the natives were all our old acquaintances. Phurchung told us that he could easily manage to throw dust in the eyes of his friends by telling them we were *shikaries* from Darjeeling, and this he would prove by shewing them our fowling-pieces. He also told us that if he met his friend Phuntsho, he would not care much for the Kang-pachan people, as he had confidence in Phuntsho's ability and courage. Ugyen told us that that plan would hardly answer our purpose, as the natives of Kang-pachan were not all fools. I told Phurchung to speak the truth to everybody, and to enlist their friendship by small rewards. Phurchung answered *la-la-so*, 'yes, sir.' I then covered myself with the blankets and went off to sleep.

23rd November.—Before getting up from bed I heard the voices of some men, who, after greeting Phurchang, opened a conversation with him. They enquired who we were, and what had brought us there, and some among them, without asking him any questions like strangers, at once enquired why Babu *la* was going to Tibet at such an unusual time. From inside my blankets I could hear, though not distinctly, all that they said, and Phurchung seemed not to answer their questions, but inquired why they were so late in their winter emigration to the lower valleys, and where his friend Phuntsho and brother Dao Namgya were. No sooner had he asked these questions than they arrived, and his joy knew no bounds, and he laughed long and loud. I did not care to get up as long as these new-comers remained; but when I was assured that they were all friends, and liked to see me, I got up. They also enquired if Ugyen was with me. Phurchung then asked his brother and Phuntsho to wait a few minutes, and came to inform me of his friends' arrival. I gave him some bright two-anna and four-anna pieces to distribute among them as *chhang-rin* (wine-money), to stop their mouths, that they might not spread the news about our journey to Tibet. When I appeared before them, they all bowed before me with the usual loll of their tongues as a sign of respect. They feared it would be impossible for us to cross the snowy Kangla-chhen, which, probably, was already blocked by the October fall of snow. Some among them advised us to enter Tibet by the Wallung Pass, which was easy and snowless. After a few minutes' conversation, after receiving the presents of silver-pieces, they bid us farewell. Their women lingered behind, as much as to say that they had received no *bukshish*. I ordered them a two-anna piece each, on receiving which they scampered off to overtake their friends. They told me that they would halt at Namga-Tshal for the night. After a cup of tea, leaving the coolies behind, I and Ugyen started in advance. Our way now lay along an extensive ancient moraine, the *débris* of which, consisting of huge reddish boulders, were covered with creeping tamarisks and dwarf junipers. We felt the presence of vegetation by the fragrant smell of the different species of shrubs, of which the latest blossoms were now withering. After a mile's continual descent we arrived at Mendaphug, which is a hollow between two gigantic boulders standing one inclined towards the other. There was some firewood left by the men whom we had met in the morning, and some bamboo vessels for water. The sunlight being powerful, and the shadow of the mountain too cold, an artificial shade was prepared for me by spreading two bed-sheets on a ledge of the boulder, on the lee side of which we had taken shelter. Our men arrived within a few minutes of our reaching this place, and at once busied themselves in fetching water, gathering firewood, and preparing our breakfast. Phurchung now assumed a dignified tone in conversation, having arrived at his own village, where he is counted among the respectables. Finishing a wretched breakfast, consisting of rice and buttered tea, at about 12 A.M. we resumed our journey. From Menda Phug to Mendala the way along the mountain side for about a mile is comparatively easy, so that one could ride leisurely in perfect safety. We were again in the midst of vegetation, which was gradually growing luxuriant as we descended. The Kang-pachan valley was now coming in view. The sight of the thick alpine forest in the deep glens refreshed our eyes, so long tired with looking on barren rocks and extensive moraines. The cries of pheasants, deer, and antelope could be heard in the distance. From Mendala to Tamala the way, nearly two miles, is fair but narrow. Here we saw some shepherds with their flocks and yaks. The pleasant recollection of the different rhododendron bushes and the juniper and cypress trees of our first journey in this great valley now vividly came to our mind, and I cheeringly pointed them out to my companions. It was here that Ugyen had asked me very seriously about the religious persuasion I really belonged to. The dip here commences to continue down to the valley of Yamatari torrent, and the top of it is consecrated to a mountain nymph called Mamo. In a rhododendron hedge I saw several white and red strips of cloth, tied as offerings to the fearful Mamo, so greatly dreaded by the people. Dao Namgya, our guide's step-brother, here asked me to furnish him with a strip of white rag to offer to the Mamo. I had no such rags on my person, and to search out our packages would incur loss of time. After some hesitation I offered to tear out a bit from my own red waist-band. He smiled and said that the Mamo preferred red rags to white. From this place I was shown the whole labyrinth of the Kang-pachan river. On the spacious bank is situated the ruins of the former Magar forts of Pholi, Gebla-Jong and Rigur Sampajong, Paniphadingjong, Taplajong and Lagyejong, the last of which is in the neighbourhood of Lelyep. These ruins show that once the Magars held sway over this part of the country, and that their power was considerable. The Magar tribe either mixed with the Kiratas of these regions, or were driven to the west by fresh colonies of Limboo, Khambu, and Tibetans from Tibet.

Finding me very exhausted, Dao Namgya begged me to mount his back that he might carry me to his village, telling me that he had carried loads heavier than myself with ease on steep slopes of craggy precipices. After some hesitation I yielded to his request, and no sooner did he find me on his back than he walked down with a quicker pace, and soon overtook Ugyen and others who had preceded us. Phurchung now, sticking the fowling-piece in his girdle, and giving his load to his cousin Phuntsho, marched ahead of us to make arrangements for our accommodation at the village. When I found the way easy, being on the north-western flank of Tama La, I got off Dao Namgya's back and walked down to a flat, grassy valley with tall rhododendron and fern bushes of different kinds. This place is considered singularly auspicious to Phurchung, being connected with associations of his infancy. It was here that he, while an infant, was blest by Dr. Hooker about thirty-five years ago, who, while exploring this part of Nepal, happened to be passing by the place where his parents tended their hairy flocks. His father, who was suffering seriously from eye-disease, caused by the glare of snow, hearing of the fame of the great doctor, went to him, led by his wife. The latter brought him some presents, in return for which she begged for some medicines for her husband's eyes. Dr. Hooker not only favoured her with excellent medicines to apply to her husband's eyes, but also gave her a pretty-looking coin to hang about the neck of her child, the self-same Phurchung, then only twelve months old. This proud possession adorned Phurchung's neck for about four years, after which it was taken from him by his brother. Phurchung exultingly remarked that he was particularly fortunate, for although other mothers and children subsequently went to beg for similar gifts, Dr. Hooker did not give them anything. His parents, as well as the villagers, predicted that Phurchung would some day become a great man.

On my return from Tibet, while reading Dr. Hooker's 'Himalayan Journal' I came across the passage,* which curiously enough describes the exact story of Phurchung and his mother's interview with Dr. Hooker.

* "Ascending, we reached an open, grassy valley, and overtook the Tibetans who had preceded us, and who had halted here to feed their sheep. A good-looking girl of the party came to ask for medicine for her husband's eyes, which had suffered from snow-blindness; she brought present of snuff, and carried a little child, stark-naked *yet warm in December*; prescribed for the man, and gave the mother a bright farthing."

At about 2 P.M. we arrived at Yamatari, a torrent which is formed by the glacial meetings of Chokangchan and Kanchan Jonga, and which forms the deep chasm between those two lofty snowy mountains. The Yamatari gorge possesses very imposing and magnificent scenery. The blue glaciers of its opposite flanks topped the craggy precipices which overhung the forest of silver firs and larches covered with pendant mosses waving like feathers at every blast. There were huge *deodars* and other tall trees on two sides of our way, in the hollow of which the black bear finds shelter. Two such hollows were pointed out to us, in which two bears were captured by the villagers last year. There is a little bridge on the Yamatari torrent, just at the entrance of Kang-pa-chan (Gyunsar) village, which we crossed, and got a view of the village flat, perched on which were the wooden huts of the villagers. Some of the houses were now deserted; a few ugly old women, most of whom had goitre, sat basking in the sun, spinning at the thresholds. Phurchung, who had arrived before us, and was rather drunk, came with two of the villagers to receive us with much demonstration of respect. *Chhang* was ready in wooden bottles, and his mother poured boiling water into them as soon as we were seated on the cushions that were spread for us. Some incense, consisting of a few dried juniper leaves, was burnt, and two incense-sticks smoked before us. After we had emptied half of our *murwa* bottles each, the housewife prepared fresh bottles, but we politely declined the offer, with the expression, La-me, La-me—'no madam, no madam.' Then two brass plates full of red, boiled potatoes were presented to us, and I tasted one or two. This course being over, rice and boiled mutton was served in large quantities, the former wrapped in the broad leaves of a kind of hill plant. The fire was blazing in a corner of the room, fed by fragrant fuel of flesh-coloured rhododendron and other alpine firs. After sunset we all sat round the fireplace, each with a bottle of *murwa* before him. On account of the fatigue of the journey sleep soon overtook us, and so I went to bed earlier than usual.

24th November.—I got up at 10 A.M., but could see no sun, though there were no clouds in the sky. I thought my watch was going wrong, and consulted Ugyen's, which, however, pointed to the same time. The valley of Kang-pa-chan being very deep and overhung by very steep snow mountains, which hem it on all sides, is not touched by the sun till 10 A.M. Evening, on the other hand, makes its appearance there earlier than in other places situated in the deep gorges of the Himalayas. After finishing breakfast, which consisted of tea, potatoes, and indian-corn, I went for a walk in the village, which consists of several terraces sloping down towards the south-west. The houses were surrounded by stone dykes, raised to keep off cattle from destroying the barley. The village, being situated in an alluvial moraine, abounds in boulders. Its position is most advantageous, as several insignificant streams, with clear sparkling water, coming from the right and left, flow into the Kangchan river intersecting the village. The steep flanks of the mountains covered with snow half converted into ice, like some running molten metal, frown over the village on both sides. Their lower slopes were clad with thick forests of tall silver firs, deodars, and larches, with pendant mosses on their branches, and a variety of juniper trees. The village was wooded with various species of rhododendrons. Flocks of wild pigeons flew from one plot of land to another. Dao Namgya fired a few cartridges at them, and shot two pigeons, which were immediately taken to his mother, to be prepared for our dinner. Some sprightly yak calves frisked and played in the dyke enclosures near our host's house. Although the river flowed within a hundred yards, yet its sound was muffled by the flatness of its bed. Higher up and lower down its roar was ceaseless, though faintly heard from our friend's house. On my return to the house I found two men, who saluted me by lowering their hats and lolling out their tongues. They then prayed me to accept an invitation to drink *chhang* at their houses. First I declined their offer, but on second thoughts, considering that to refuse them would be making them unfriendly to us, which was not desirable at such a time, I accepted. Accordingly, at 2 P.M., accompanied by Ugyen and conducted by one of them, I visited Jorgya's house.

This was a new house constructed on a plank platform about six feet from the ground, laid on walls of loose stone. Beneath it a few yak-calves were confined, and two or three *Di* (she-yaks) were being milked. Jorgya, the host, received us very kindly at the threshold, and seated me on a thick mattress-like seat covered with a piece of Khamba carpet. A newly-made bamboo bottle filled with *chhang* was placed before us, its edge touched with a little butter. Tea was first brought, and the housewife stood with the steaming kettle in her hand before us, expecting that I would produce my maple-knot cup from my breast coat to receive the frothing drink. The cup was not forthcoming, and our host, perceiving his mistake, at once ran to another room to fetch a China cup for my use. It is customary in Tibet for men of equal rank with the host, or lower, to carry their own cups to drink tea or liquor. But as my position was known to be higher than what any of the villagers could boast of, Jorgya was taken to task by his friends. In haste the cup was brought, and tea served. Then a brass plate full of potatoes was placed before us on a little table. Our host regretted that he could not treat me with yak, of which he had a large supply in his house. I thanked him for his kindness. Parched indian-corn, milk, and butter were given to the party in abundance, of which we took our fill. Our host then advised us not to attempt going to Wallung, as we would be sure to meet much difficulty. He whispered in my ear that I should quietly go to Yangma, and enter Tibet by the Kangla-chhen Pass, which, according to him, was not wholly inaccessible at this part of the year. After some uninteresting talk, which according to the prevailing custom was the repetition of the same thing over and over, we took leave of our host, and went over to Pemassang's, who is an uncle of Phurchung.

This man's house, not so large as that of Jorgya, was glazed; and his little chapel was tastefully covered and painted. His son and wife respectfully received us at the top of the ladder, and conducted us to the interior of the house, where the fireplace was blazing with fragrant juniper twigs. Pemassang had thick, knotted, flowing curls on his head, which he never combs nor dresses. He wears two gold pendant earrings, made in the shape of magnolia flowers. With these he sometimes sits in meditation for the purpose of stopping hail-storms, &c., by the efficacy of his charms. He was grave and serious in his looks and talk. He too advised us to cross the Kangla-chhen in preference to the Walung Pass, for the same reasons as those given by Jorgya. After a few minutes' stay, and a sip through the *murwa* pipe, we bid him good-bye, and hastened to pay a visit to the Tashi-chhoiding monastery. Accompanied by Ugyen and Sonam (Phurchung's youngest step-brother), we crossed the bridge to get to the other bank of the river. Arrived at the monastery we found it almost empty, only here and there one or two old women turning and twirling the prayer wheels. The *mendangs* were newly painted and roofed with deodar planks loosely placed and kept in position by boulder weights. After crossing two ladder stairs, we entered Kangchan Lama's house. The old Lama received us very kindly, and said it was owing to his prayers that he was able again to see us; while his *ani* (female friend and helpmate, but more a mistress) received us with great concern, for the old gentleman was suffering from *pa-kan* (acidity), and entreated me to let him have some medicines. I gave him a dose of castor-oil and soda. After a sip or two from the *murwa* bottle we took leave of the old Lama and returned to our lodgings. At 4 P.M. the sun disappeared from the valley, but his rays still gilded the snowy summit of the eastern mountain groups. Phurchung, Phuntsho, and Dao were now busily engaged in pounding indian-corn and barley for the coolies' provisions during their journey through the Kangla-chhen. Some rice was obtained for me, but no mutton could be had, as the sheep of the villagers were taken to the warmer valleys of the Tambur and Kangpachan rivers. We sent a man with a letter to Om-dse Pema at Kangpachan with the customary present of a rupee and a scarf, requesting him to sell us some butter and a couple of sheep. In the evening his wife invited us to drink *chhang* at her house, but we politely declined the invitation, whereupon she sent a *murwa* bottle to our house, and we returned her an eight-anna silver piece.

In the evening, before dark, Ugyen, when trying to open our canvas bag to take out silver pieces, found the key broken. He was astonished to find that somebody had attempted to open, or had opened, the bag to steal money. His face flushed with fear of loss, and more particularly because if it was so, we were actually surrounded by a set of rogues. Ugyen was about to count the contents of the bag to ascertain how much was taken out, but I prevented him from doing so, fearing that the counting of money before so many strangers would cost us our lives. "What good," said I, "will there be to count the money? What is lost cannot be recovered. We would only place a fresh temptation before the thief's eyes; and, on the other hand, might suspect those who are innocent among our faithful friends. If you think the money is lost, I will quietly suffer the loss, for we should have been careful not to leave the money and our property unprotected." So the money was not counted. Ugyen suspected Phurchung, but not I. This event ruffled our cheerfulness, and we went to bed with much uneasiness of mind. Altogether six persons slept in the same room with me. My bedding was spread on a black bear skin. Beside me slept Ugyen and Phurchung. My sleep was a disturbed one, I often waking with the impression that the remaining silver was being stolen by some villain.

25th November.—I awoke rather early, anxious to leave the place as soon as possible, and began to count the minutes and hours as they passed. Phurchung had not yet slept off the effects of his previous night's drinking, and snored fearfully. At 10 A.M. Dao Namgya brought me presents consisting of potatoes, *murwa*, millet, rice, butter, and a goat. We received the presents with great delight, as the goat would be most useful as provision on our way through the snows. I paid him five rupees as a return present (which he accepted most gladly) and asked him to buy us another goat. The widows and other poor people of the village waited upon us with presents consisting of eggs, potatoes, and *murwa* bottles. This they did, not out of any great respect or veneration for me, but evidently with an eye to return presents, which they expected would cover the highest value of their presents. Fortunately there were few people in the village, otherwise they would have drained me of my cash. At 12 P.M. I ordered Phurchung, gradually recovering from the effects of wine and *murwa*, to make for me some pairs of *kyar*, or wooden snow shoes, used in the snowy tracts of this part of Nepal. Phuntsho, one of our newly-engaged coolies, told me that he had lately crossed the Kangla Pass with the help of a pair of *kyar*, and reached Jongri, where he had met Captain Harman, who praised much the usefulness of this rude-looking snow-shoe. New ones could not be made on so short a notice, so we had to borrow some pairs of *kyar* from the villagers. In the evening our coolies busied themselves in slaughtering two kids brought for us. The blood was held in a bowl, and then poured into the washed and cleansed intestines of the kids. Ugyen, who was an expert in preparing Bhootea dainties, mixed barley-flour with the blood, with which he stuffed some of the larger intestines. These they boiled in water and packed up in a small wicker-work basket for use on the way. The skin of the stomach of the kids also served as dainties to the coolies.

The legend which I heard of the Kangpachan people and of the Magar, the ruins of whose forts and town we saw in the Kangpachan valley, is very interesting. People say that the account is correct and true. The upper valley of the Kangpachan river, through the grace and the blessing of the royal Kangchan-Jonga, was peopled by men of Tibetan extraction called the *Sherpa*, whose original home was in the mountains of Shar Khambu, or Eastern Kirata. Though inhabiting a place almost surrounded by snowy barriers, they enjoyed immunity from the ravages of ferocious animals and murrain. The lower valley, a few miles below Kang-pachan village, on account of the comparatively sluggish course of the river, contained many spacious banks fit to be the habitation of the hillmen. The Magar tribe of Nepal occupied these tracts. Their chief, who had become very powerful, extended his sway over the people of Kangpachan, and exacted a heavy tax from them. His deputies always oppressed the people to squeeze out money from them, so that at last they were driven through desperation to take revenge on their enemies. Once, when the Magar chief had gone to visit the village of Kangpachan, the people who had matured a conspiracy against him, killed him and his followers, and concealed the dead bodies under ground. The party not having returned to their homes, their relations went all around to search for them. When they failed to get any clue to the cause of the wholesale missing, the queen herself went to Kangpachan to ascertain the cause of her husband's disappearance, but after searching enquiries, failed to clear up her husband's mysterious disappearance. One day, while walking close to the river side, all on a sudden a boulder undermined by a current of the stream slid down, and from underneath some flies flew out buzzing. The queen observed this, and suspecting that something underground must have attracted the flies, instantly dug out the ground, when, lo! she discovered the corpses of her murdered husband and his retainers. To the surprise of all she quickly returned home with the exhumed corpse, where she planned the best means of wreaking vengeance on the Kang-pachan murderers. She ordered grand funeral observances for the honour and benefit of the departed soul: great preparations were made for the funeral obsequies, and large bowls filled with wine were brought to entertain the villagers and her followers. The funeral was appointed to take place about six miles up the river, near the Rapachan torrent, midway between the two great villages of the Kangpachan valley—Gyunsar and Yarsa—so that all the villagers might assemble there. In the wine-bowls poisonous drugs were secretly mixed. After the queen's followers had finished drinking, the poisoned wine was given plentifully to the Kangpachan villagers, who, not suspecting anything, drank freely. At the end of the ceremony all the Kangpachan people were dead drunk and stupified, and slept a long sleep from which they never awoke. In this way nearly one thousand men and women died. The infants in arms were taken away by the queen's followers. Only such people escaped who were absent from this dreadful scene. The place where this foul deed was committed is now called Tong-Shong-phug, or 'the place which witnessed a thousand murders.' The few who survived this massacre carried the news of this horrible affair to Tibet, and invited a large army to wage war on the Magar. The Tibetan army invaded the several Jongs belonging to the queen, when she shut herself up in one of the castles. She had made no preparations to fight the enemy, but her soldiers defended the place for three months. The Tibetans continued the siege, intending to compel the Magar to surrender by starving them and depriving them of water, the supply of which they stopped from outside. At last the queen, aware of this intention, threw all the water she had in store towards the Tibetan camp. The Tibetans thinking that she had abundance of water-supply inside the castle, raised the siege and went to a distance to watch the movements of the Magar. She immediately collected her men and tried to pursue the enemy, when a skirmish took place, in which she fell nobly fighting. The Tibetan expelled all the Magar from the country (Kangpachan and Tambur valley), and left their properties to the Kangpachan people. Such is the past history of the people of this deep mountain gorge, the like of which I never heard in my journey until I had reached the heart of the Himalayas. The natives, it is evident, were able to harbour the blackest motives in their mind with profound dissimulation. But I rejoiced to have obtained in this region, the wildest and the most gloomy in the Himalayas, the services of the steadiest and most faithful man that I ever came across in the Himalayas. Although Ugyen distrusted him, and he abhorred Ugyen, yet I placed implicit confidence in Phurchung's sincerity and ability, while his devotion and fidelity towards me was boundless.

26th November.—In the early morning we commenced making preparations for starting. The coolies altogether were four in number, of whom three were newly recruited from Kangpachan. They now busied themselves in collecting their outfits, such as blankets, *kyar*, covering for the head, provision, bags, and baskets to carry loads. Our guide now inspected the distribution of the loads among the coolies, himself carrying the fowling-piece as a mark of honour and importance. But the red broadcloth sheath, its most attractive ornament, had been stolen last night. Phurchung had become furious when he had heard of it, and wanted to delay a day or two to detect the thief and recover the lost article. I did not agree to it, but cautioned the coolies lest some articles from their baskets should unaccountably disappear. They nodded with a *La Laso*—'yes, sir, be it so'; and one after another lifted up their respective loads on their backs, which they had been careful to cover with thick folds of their blankets. When the coolies were started, Phurchung's load being carried by his youngest brother, Sonam Dorje, I, Ugyen, and Phurchung remained behind. Two ponies, which were engaged for us at a hire of eight annas each to take us half way up the Nango La, were saddled and brought to the gate. After a hearty breakfast we resumed our journey at 9 A.M. The *ama*, or old matrons of the village, now assembled to make us the *chhang-kyel*, or the presentation of wine. It is the custom of the Tibetans invariably to present wine at parting to friends setting out on a distant journey. In our case, it seemed, a little kindness and great hopes of getting return presents led them to make this demonstration, for many persons joined the party who were previously not known to us. With bowls of wine in their right hand and platesful of parched barley and flour in their left, they waited at the eastern approach of the *ssampa* (bridge). I walked up to it through rows of pretty-looking, red-coloured brambles which grew side by side with rhododendron shrubs. Each of the *ama* approached to pour a little wine from her wine-jug into a China cup and put a pinch of barley flour in it, and begged us to take a sip as an auspicious observance. "May we present similar *chhang-kyel* on your safe return" was their prayer to the gods and Buddhas. We thanked them for their kindness, and walked off after placing a couple of rupees in one of their plates, Phurchung telling them to divide the same among themselves. Much pleased with the present, they all went off except Phurchung's step-mother, who shed tears, saying she feared her son would hardly think of returning to Kangpachan within a year. The *kangssam*, or wooden bridge constructed of planks, is about four feet broad and 20 feet long between the abutting approaches on which they are supported. The planks are loose, but firmly held in position by stone weights, no rivetting or screwing being known in this wild country. After crossing the bridge we mounted our ponies and rode on slowly, observing with interest the splashing and bounding waves of the river and the several prayer-wheels turned by streamlets, which come from the back of the monastery to flow into the Kangchan river. A few minutes' ride brought us to the Kani Chhorten, which is only one mile from the monastery, where we found two of our coolies waiting for Phurchung. The latter, who carried a bamboo jug full of wine for the use of the coolies, unable to resist the temptation, here opened the cloth and he and the two coolies emptied the whole bottle here. I told them that they would be without any wine on the *La* (mountain summit). The way being stony and steep, I asked Phurchung to follow me, so as to help me in difficult ascents. The work of conducting the pony seemed very unpleasant to him, and he begged me to go alone, as the ponies were very sure-footed on the rocky ways. Our way lay amidst thick woods up to Daba-ñonpu, a distance of about three miles from Kani Chhorten, whence the natives formerly used to get their supply of blue clay to make images with. They consider the clay of this place to be particularly pure, since brought down from the summit of a holy mountain by a hill stream. This place belonged to our guide, whose yaks grazed in the pasture lands. It is the base of a moraine, and is overgrown with long grass and alpine forests. The ascent of the moraine was very tedious for the ponies, as the loose boulders slid down very often under the pressure of their hoofs. Close to this place is a lake bed, almost dry at this time. Ascending the rocky way for a mile from this place, we came to a place called Kamai Phugpa, where the trees diminished in size and the ground was a mass of boulders. Here we crossed a glacial channel, now dry, much resembling an artificial canal. After a few minutes' ride we arrived at another part of the moraine, called Kha-ma-kang-tung, where there is a large table-land. The trees now disappeared, and were succeeded by the region of shrubs and dwarf plants. At the distance of a mile from here we passed another place, called Nango Pungsa, which is the limit of the yaks' pasturing land on this side of the Nango La. Half a mile from this place we passed the steep flank of a black mountain overtopped by the Nango La, where a flock of spotted birds (*Pragpa*) were picking their food from the stones just freed from snow. This place, called Luma Goma, is generally selected as a halting-place by hill travellers. The collection of débris in immense heaps bespoke the desolate nature of this region. Here and there were a few huge boulders, which being near the stream were covered with lichens. The skies were clear, and the sun shone very brightly. Ugyen here wished me to alight from my pony in order to enable him to shoot some of the *Pragpa*. He fired twice into one of the flocks. Two only were hit on their legs, and flew towards the top of the mountains, where they evidently dropped down dead. The *shikar* being unsuccessful, we resumed our journey, dismissing our ponies and Sonam Dorje, to whom I gave a rupee as reward, and some biscuits and parched indian-corn. As he was alone, I feared he might be attacked by wild bears, which are said to rove even thus far. He parted from us very much affected: his eyes moist with tears. It was now 1 o'clock, with a light gale blowing. Leaving this desolate region, we commenced ascending the snowy Nango La, a lofty mountain, at the base of which, 14,000 feet high, we passed sometimes over solidified snow, at others on soft snow, knee-deep. The bluish shade of the snow and the molten crystallised ice were very pleasant sights, but the effect of the snow was quite different on the feet, which, though inside of felt boots, were getting benumbed with our slow plodding in the snow. The way seemed endless. Tired and exhausted I desired one of the coolies, Phuntsho, to take me on his back. He laid down his load on the snow, and leaning on a boulder, took me on his back, and reached me to a distance of nearly a quarter of a mile, and then, leaving me on a snowless patch, returned to fetch his own load. Ugyen and others followed our tracks, and we arrived at the source of the Lungkyong Chhu, the course of which we now followed. Two miles to the west of the Nango-Lap-tse is a place called Sayong-kong, a flat table-land, which we found entirely covered with snow. From this place there is a direct route to Yangma. Below Sayong-kong, a mile distant, is Sayong-hok, descending whence about two miles we arrived at the valley of the Lungkyong Chhu river. Vegetation reappeared at Sayong-hok, and gradually increased in size and in number as we descended, until the plants gave place to trees on the sides of the Lungkyong Chhu. We crossed here and there some unmelted snows and, following the downward course of the torrent, arrived at a comparatively flat terrace, where underneath a huge boulder we halted for the night. Phurchung, who had come ahead of us, had collected some long, dry grass growing in the clefts of rocks, and spread them to conceal the damp appearance of the boulder cleft where he had spread our rugs. At 6 P.M. we arrived there and each remarking the other's weary appearance, rested to discuss the fatigues of the journey. A large fire was lighted and tea prepared. There was slight sleet at night. Red pulse badly cooked with rice and a little kid served for my food. Our companions made a hearty repast of the blood-stuffed intestines of the kid. I slept soundly, though my sides ached in the stony, uneven bed, and the pains over the whole body increased as I got up from bed to resume our journey next morning.

27th November.—The morning was not misty, though the sun was not bright on account of distant fogs, which prevented his rays from shining on the forests we were now entering. Without a cup of tea or a handful of parched indian-corn, we resumed our journey. The way glided easily along the eastern bank of the Lungkyong Chhu, at times approaching the margin of the murmuring stream, and at others receding from it. The track showed some traces of the frequent passing of men and cattle. Our guide, looking at the fresh footmarks, told us that some men had passed this way the previous day. In fact this is the only passage for communication between Kangpachan and Yangma and Wallung. The mountains on the left were almost screened from our eyes by fogs; their winding ledges with massive rocks here and there being sometimes visible through the occasional rents in the fleecy envelope. As we descended further and further, the Lungkyong Chhu increased in volume and noise. At nine we entered a woody spur to avoid the detour along its side, when we found ourselves in a thick forest. The trees were tall and grew thickly together. and I could see no signs of felling. The rhododendron and juniper gave place to the fir, feathery larch, ash and deodar. The descent from the spur may be said to be abrupt, although the track sometimes had turnings, where we took a few moments' rest, standing. Ugyen here complained of increasing pains in his stomach. I attributed it to his eating voraciously the boiled intestines of the kid slain at Kangpachan. The entire forest was filled with numerous kinds of pheasants and different other wild fowl. The coolies and the guide told me that there were abundance of musk-deer and wild sheep in these alpine forests. At about 11 A.M. we arrived at the *tasa-ssampa* (wooden bridge) on the Yangma river. It was about 36 feet in span, and constructed after the usual manner in this part of the country, the main part resting on the overlapping plank approaches. The Lungkyong Chhu joins the Yangma at a distance of nearly two miles below, westward of this bridge. We had not met any traveller thus far. Then, ascending along the Yangma river, we passed through many flats, the woods of which have been thinned by the natives, and arrived at Thingugma. Travellers generally halt here on their way to Yangma from Wallung. There were no sheds, but here and there were fireplaces and collections of fuel. I felt very hungry and tired. Our coolies laid their loads at the foot of a tall poplar close by. Phurchung fetched me a cup of water, with which I quenched my thirst; soon a large fire was lighted and the kettle steamed, while I sat on my rug, spread in the shade, waiting for the tea. Some rice was next boiled, and I sat to breakfast with rice moistened with tea and mixed with some kid curry of the previous night. At half past one in the afternoon we resumed our journey, and before we had proceeded a hundred yards we met a party of Yangma natives. They had about a dozen yaks laden with blankets, yak-hides, barley, salt, a few sheep, and a white hound with them. Phurchung recognized them, and, exchanging compliments, asked them if the Kangla-chhen Pass was accessible at this time: some of them told us that we could easily cross it, but others expressed their doubts about it: for, according to them, three feet of snow had fallen a few days ago. Some travellers had lately arrived, whose footsteps were by this time obliterated by a snow-storm. We also inquired if there were yaks to be had for hire at Yangma. "There are no yaks," they said, "but you might get *Di* (milch-yak) if they let them for hire." At this season there being plenty of grass in the lower valleys, the herdsmen bring their flocks to graze in warmer zones. These men were going to a village called Chaini, on the Tambur river, to sell blankets, &c., and exchange salt for rice and indian-corn. Walking a mile, the way being easy, we arrived at a place called Maya Phug, a cavern consecrated to sylvan goddesses called *Mamo*. Some scraps of paper and rags being attached by our coolies to the votive mound in honour of the deities, we clambered up a hill, on the top of which were flat slopes overgrown with different species of juniper, which gives the place its name of Shugpa-thang. The foot of this hill is about a mile and a half from Maya Phug. Ugyen here fell very ill with severe pains, on account of obstruction of the bowels. I gave him a dose of sulphate of soda with a few drops of tincture of ginger. Pitying Ugyen's position, I ordered Phurchung to carry him on his back, but he showed much reluctance, saying that he had got pains in his waist, and that if he carried so heavy a man as Ugyen on his back, the pains would certainly increase; yet out of respect to my words he said he would carry him. On the top of the *La* there are several old *mandang* and cairns

*

overgrown with fragrant shrubs. Phurchung here placing his live load on a stone slab, addressed his usual invocation to the mountain deities. While Phurchung was busy thus with his *mantras* and Ugyen with his cries of *achi-che-apa-ouh* (an expression of pain), I feasted my eyes on one of the grandest views I ever beheld. How refreshing was the prospect of travelling in a cool, extensive, grassy plain intersected by sluggish but transparent rills, and dotted all over with chalets and huge massive boulders. At my back the entire mountain of Shugpa-thang was filled with massive, reddish granitic rocks looking like ruins of the gigantic ramparts of some ancient town. The black, rugged appearance of the ridge was more conspicuous on account of the scantiness of the rhododendron and juniper bushes. But I looked more before than behind, and was deeply impressed with the grand and superb scenery of the vast plain before me, with the surrounding lofty mountains, one rising above another in sublime succession, their tops clad in snow, while intervening gullies glistened with accumulated ice and snow. Ridge after ridge raised their gigantic bodies as if from a reclining position. This vast plain is probably an ancient moraine nearly two miles by half a mile. The chalets of the Yangma valley, which were scattered about, were made of loose stone walls roofed with rudely-formed planks. The Yangma river, meandering, flowed sluggishly through the middle of the plain, which was now a vast sheet of yellow, owing to the drying of the grass at the approach of winter. The stupendous mountains with their rocky flanks, snowy summits, and dark woody base, under a vast canopy of blue sky, stood like an enchanted land before my eyes. On my right towards the south-east, was the lofty Nango La, partly enveloped with fogs and partly displaying his craggy flanks and snow white crests in all the naked majesty of his race. Beyond the north of Nango La there is said to be another vast plain, known by the name Sumdongma, though four or five times as large as the one before us. Much occupied with these wonderful sights, more and more impressed with the supremely wondrous intelligence of Him who is the author of these stupendous works, I started, alone, ahead of my companions in a pensive mood. After walking a few hundred yards, I looked back, and saw Dao Namgya plodding on towards me with his heavy load, Phurchung and Ugyen being still on the Shugpa-thang. There is a bridge in the middle of Dsari-thang (or the plain filled with heaps of gravel, boulders, &c.), which I crossed easily. The river here at this time of the year, having divided into several channels, looked rather sluggish when compared with its course both higher up and below. From here our way lay towards the north. Walking half a mile, we arrived at the foot of a steep ridge, where a serpentine stream, very shallow now, joins the Yangma river. I crossed this stream at three different places, managing not to wet my shoes. There was a slight wind blowing, and evening approached before I could get up to the top of Dola (or bleak, rocky mountains). This spur is a dip about 200 feet above Dsari-thang, and entirely barren where we crossed it. Walking about two or three hundred yards downwards, I found myself again on the bank of the rushing Yangma river, its banks filled with alpine forests. There is a wooden bridge, or *kangssam*, over the river, about 30 to 40 feet long. Some logs were being carried away by the stream, and some villagers were crossing the bridge, before I reached its eastern approach. The sun was now set, and I loitered for a few minutes after crossing the bridge at the foot of the great terrace on the top of which the monastery of Yangma is situated. About twenty minutes after, Phurchung, Ugyen, and the coolies arrived. We ascended up the terrace, which is spacious and filled with bushes of arborescent plants and other dwarf fragrant shrubs. The sky was enveloped with a darkish hue, and we lost all views except that of the rushing and resounding Yangma. Phurchung and Ugyen with the coolies went ahead towards the monastery, and I remained alone seated on a grassy spot. Having arranged for our accommodation in the cell of one of the monks of the monastery, Phurchung soon returned with a smiling face to conduct me to the lodging. I ascended to the terraces, of inconsiderable breadth, and then reached the Manding Gonpa. Our lodging lay a few yards to the south of it, on a higher plain. As it was dark and windy, having once entered the wretched cell which was destined to be our night's shelter, I never came out of it during the night. Ugyen lay prostrate, wrapping himself with all the blankets I could spare, shivering and groaning and crying "*achi-che-apa-ouh.*" I felt his pulse, and found that he had a slight fever. Two nuns were engaged in helping Dao Namgya in cooking our food, one of them fetching water and firewood, and the other blowing the bellows. Phurchung obtained a few eggs and some milk from the Lama of the monastery, and he and the coolies were invited to dinner by the Lamas, who were now engaged in their annual reading of the Kahgyur scriptures. Phurchung, in return, at the end of the dinner, presented the congregation with a good quantity of *chhang*, purchased at a cost of one rupee. The head Lama, we were told, is the father of Phurchung's friend, and hence a warm reception was accorded to him by the assembled monks. At this time there were fifteen monks and seven *ani* (nuns) in the monastery. The readers returned to their respective cells at 7-30 P.M. to assemble again at 5 A.M. the next day. I lighted my lantern, and, spreading my blankets as if to go to bed, sat for a while reclining on a small table which was to serve for my pillow at night. Dao Namgya, being new to the work entrusted to him, did not prove a good cook. The rice was partially boiled, yet with the help of the eggs and milk I succeeded in swallowing a quantity of it. Ugyen did not take any food.

I extinguished the light, fearing the candles were fast consuming, but did not sleep till late in the night, my mind being uneasy for the illness of Ugyen, and through fear of detention in such a wretched place.

28th November.—In the morning I got up rather early from bed. It was freezing cold, but as we were in a strange land, the people of which could stop us from crossing the frontier, I became anxious to escape soon from their hands. I waited only for Phurchung and his comrades, who had not returned to the house during the previous night. They were drunk, and my anxiety increased lest in this state they should recklessly disclose the secret of our journey. I waited and waited for their return till my eyes were tired looking at the way. At seven Dao Namgya prepared some tea, and we breakfasted on some barley paste made of the same. Ugyen also got up from his bed, and said, "Sir, we are here in an enemy's country, and do not know what may happen to us. If we be turned out by the Nepalese from this place, it would be somewhat better than our being taken to the Nepalese court; look, how foolish our men are" Some time after, all on a sudden, Phurchung and Phuntsho appeared, *salaaming* to me several times with much lolling of the tongue. They asked me to wait for a day here that we might start all together on the following morning. I was indeed in a difficult position, for if I lost temper and used rough language towards my companions, unpleasant consequences would follow. I told them that they were at liberty to do what they liked, but as for me, I was determined to leave the place that day at any risk. I also told them that they were behaving very unworthily, and that I was very much surprised at their conduct. Ugyen Gyatsho, who had lately learnt smoking the *hukka* as a luxury, had brought with him a fine cocoanut-shell *hukka* for his use. Phuntsho, in order to show that he had a *hukka* to smoke, took it with him to the meeting of the village elders. He assured me that he could obtain the headman's permission to let us proceed without much difficulty, and that he could also try to avoid the payment of customs duty, called *chua* in this part of Nepal. I told him I was prepared to pay *chua,* whatever its amount may be. Saying "*ausi, ausi,*" "never mind, sir," they proceeded towards the monastery. The elders one after another arrived, the richest man being known by his *tamuksi* hat, the long single earring, and a *purug* (deep red serge robe). He had arrived from Yangma village riding on a *jo,* which, with the saddle on its back, was tied at the gate of the monastery. I anxiously waited to know the result of the conference, and in great anxiety prayed to the Supreme Dispenser of our destinies that nothing might happen unfavourable to ourselves and our journey. Dao Namgya had faithfully served us, taking charge all the while of the cooking. After washing I went out to enjoy the view of the surrounding scenery, but more to divert the mind to other thoughts, and to examine the extent of the monastic establishment and the residence of the monks. To the right and left of the monastery-temple there were a dozen houses on another narrow, gravelly terrace at the foot of the steep, precipitous, black mountain overhanging the temple. In front, a little towards the right-hand side, rushed down the Yangma river. To my right, standing as I was, facing the north, were the eastern lofty peaks, and immediately on the river was the huge *Dola*, the grandest and longest moraine I ever saw. It was a gigantic bank of huge boulders and reddish rocks. There was not a plant or shrub to be seen here, while all over Dsari-thang we had seen the ground covered with arborescent shrubs. I was told that both at Yangma and Manding Gonpa, fire-wood being scarce, people go there to collect fire wood. What grand operation on the part of nature must have produced these gigantic formations and denudations that were continually going on and changing the course of the glacial streams and torrents!

The convent or monastery of Manding Gonpa is situated at the mouth of a gorge on a large terrace about 40 to 50 feet above the river. There are several terraces one above another, the largest of which has the convent on its western extremity. These terraces were all overgrown with shrubs and grass, and two or three streamlets flowed across them. The monastery is a tolerably large house, built of stone after the fashion of the Sikkim *Donpa*. The huts or cells of the monks in its immediate neighbourhood are all irregular and ugly, the doors, windows, and cornice being all very rude and wretchedly executed. They are all painted with a kind of red clay obtained from mountains. Every house is enclosed by a loose stone enclosure resembling a dyke. These are intended for the shelter of sheep and yak. The *Lhakhang*, or the temple, is the only remarkable building in the village inviting attention. The walls were massive and the sides neatly executed, the doorway new, and the folds painted. This monastery is called Nub-Manding Gonpa, *i.e.*, the western Manding monastery. On the back of this place, in the gorge, is a rock cavern called Ssimphung, where Lama Lha-tsun lived an ascetic life for three years to discover medicines of wonderful efficacy. He is said to have obtained three medicinal pills, one of which came flying miraculously and fell at the spot where Manding Gonpa how stands (*Man* in Tibetan means menicine, and *ding* flying). The second pill fell at the place a little above the monastery, where the Yangma people now burn their dead. The third pill fell at the place where the great Chhorten was erected. Manding Gonpa is held very sacred, being one of the earliest monasteries of cis-Himalaya founded by the great red-hat Lama Lha-tsun. I sent some presents to the monastery, and a rupee to the head Lama, and eight annas as *chhang-rin* to the monks. I did not visit the monastery, and consequently could not ascertain what church furniture, books, &c., it contained. Kangpachan monastery, I was told, is considered second, and Wallung as the first in wealth and in strength. Manding contains a rich set of 125 volumes of the Kahgyur collections. To the south-east side of the monastery some monks were sitting reading. After enjoying the scenery and the external appearance of the monastery, I returned to my lodging and found breakfast ready. Dao Namgya told me that one of our coolies, named Urgyen, had heard that every thing was proceeding in our favour at the conference. Phurchung was asked to inform them whence I was, and what I intended to go to Tibet for. He told them that I, his master, was a *nakorpa*, or pilgrim, who talked Tibetan and dressed as a Tibetan. The head Lama of the monastery observed that he was not aware of any order from the Government of Nepal which authorized him to stop pilgrims on their way to Tibet: in the present case the pilgrim (meaning me) talked Tibetan with greater fluency and accuracy than many of the Nepal people and to stop him purely from *tog-pa*, or suspicion, or as one not of Tibetan nationality, would be unjust and objectionable: as for himself, he would nither stop me nor ask me to proceed to Tibet, the former being an impious action, but would deal with me as a pilgrim only. The Gopa, or the village headman, said he would not stop me, but would compel Phurchung to sign an agreement holding himself responsible for my being no other than a traveller. An agreement was accordingly written, and Phurchung affixed his seal to it. He also paid a customs duty of eight annas per head for us all. After the meeting dissolved, Phurchung came out exulting at his success. I was glad that the result was known so soon, as any delay would cause much embarrassment to us, all the coolies being drunk, and talking things which they would never have done in their sober moments. Fortunately for us, Ugyen Gyatsho felt better and was anxious to be off soon. Although Phurchung begged me to remain here during the night, and to start early next morning, yet I determined to leave the place forthwith. Phurchung informed me that the Gopa and the Lama were coming to bid me farewell, and whispered that I should receive them respectfully and be careful, after exchange of compliments, to say *sangpoi jachhag* (may we meet again next year). The big folks now arrived, and the Gopa, conspicuous by his earrings, boots, and the serge robe, slightly nodded his head and lowered his *tamuski shamo*, or hat. I received him with great courtesy, and enquired after his health. He asked me why I had selected such a bad time to go to Tibet. I told him that I did so in obedience to the command of our holy and learned *Tsa-wai*, Chief Lama, and not by my own wish. His object in coming was to see if I spoke Tibetan and knew the Buddhist religion. My fluency in Tibetan, and the citing of one or two proverbial sayings in course of conversation, made him think highly of my proficiency in the sacred texts and histories, as well as of my character and holiness. "*Laso, laso*" ("yes, yes,"), he said, and apologised for not having brought anything as a present for me. I replied that our acquaintance had now commenced, and there would be time in future to cultivate it, and expressed a hope that we might meet next year. So saying, I presented him a scarf, which he received with delight, saying "*sangpoi jachhog*." The Lamas of other villages, who were spectators, expressed many wishes for our welfare. But some one among the crowd said that I was certainly not a Tibetan, another swore that I was an Indian, and a third said that they should not feel much anxiety on my account. "That Hindu," added a fourth, "will surely die in the snows, and his servants will soon return here with the news of his death." I could not distinctly hear all this at the time, but learnt it afterwards from Dao Namgya. The sun was now past the meridian, when the coolies reluctantly one after another took up their loads. Phurchung, who carried my fowling-piece and a long knife, was delayed by several young women come to make him presents of wine—a ceremony which is carefully observed by female friends. It is called *chhang-kyel*. Phurchung spent about five rupees in responding to the attentions shown to him by his fair friends. I was in excellent spirits, having escaped the anticipated obstruction from the Yangma people, on whose mercy and good will we entirely depended. As they allowed me to go, I thought within myself that a large portion of our troubles were at an end. We passed a few *Mandang* and *Chhorten*, situated at the entrance of the convent, and arrived on the steep but high bank of the Yangma river. The valley is narrow here. This crossed, we arrived at another terrace on the bank of the Yangma river, which was filled with snow, the juniper shrubs in some places bending under the weight of snow. We then reached another small flat, called Kya Shongma, or white plain, which formerly was the scene of a deadly quarrel between the Yangma and Chhusharpa villages. There was formerly a village on the east of the river Yangma, called Chhu Shar, containing about a dozen families. Once a dispute arose about the grazing lands round about Kya Shongma. After many interchanges of hot words they agreed to refer the question to the gods. There was a rock above Kya Shongma, which contained the image of Dsam-bala, or the god of wealth, which the people revered for its supposed miraculous powers. It was agreed that this sacred rock should be rolled down. To whichever side it would turn its *back* on stopping, that party would lose all claim to the disputed pasture land. The sacred rock was pushed down. It rolled and rolled till its progress was stopped by some other boulders. Unfortunately for the Chhusharpa villagers, its back chanced to be towards their viliage. Fearful omens were seen by the villagers of the ruin of their village, and just when the quarrel was about to be settled by divine intercession, a huge landslip took place, entirely burying the village of Chhushar, and not one out of its twelve families survived the dreadful catastrophe, only those escaping who were absent from their homes. A little above Kya Shongma is a pretty lake now filled with ice. The water, though frozen, appeared like water, the difference being that it was solid instead of liquid. As we were hastening towards our night's stage, which we thought would be a few miles beyond Yangma, I had no time to enjoy the scenery. This lake was for a long time the haunt of mischievous spirits, by whom several persons were mysteriously killed every year. In order to suppress them, two handsome *chaits* were erected by Lha-tsun. The mountains to our west were black and craggy, through the gaps of which snow gleamed out. These were standing in fantastic order, looking as if grinning and frowning at us.

The mountains on our east were snow-covered: the upper parts of their flanks marked with gigantic landslips. In one of the lateral valleys a few years ago many wild sheep were found frozen to death on account of a heavy snowfall. The lake is a little less than a mile long, and is called the *Missa*, or man-eating lake. The Yangma river appears in some places as a lake, owing to its confinement by the snows, although one would on closer examination find that it stealthily forced its way several feet below the surface of the snows. Gravel deposits were in some places visible. All these clearly showed how moraines are generally formed by glacial action. The *chhortens* and *mandangs* were very handsome things in these wild places, the height of the former being very impressive. They are called *Thongwa kundol, i.e.*, 'the very sight of which brings to all emancipation from misery.' A couple of years ago these were repaired by the head Lama of Wallung. Before we had proceeded a few hundred yards from this spot, we saw six wild sheep (*noa*) coming down one after another to drink from the stream. They saw us, and yet did not care to run away, as if they were perfectly domesticated. They were very fat, tall, and with broad horns, and each as big as the biggest domestic sheep, if not larger. Dao Namgya and Phuntsho were very anxious to shoot them, as one of them carried my gun loaded with ball. The sheep were within range, and we could easily have shot at least one. I asked Dao Namgya why the Yangma people do not kill them. He replied that the mountain gods take offence when people molest these *nao,* for they are the favourities of the *Shibdag* and *Ri-lha* (lords of the land and the mountain gods). Ugyen told me that as we had given ourselves out to be simply pilgrims, any attempt on our part to shoot the *nao* would be inconsistent with our assumed character, and suspicion would be created in the minds of the Yangma villagers. Though much tempted to shoot them, yet these considerations checked me. The *nao,* after drinking, quietly, retraced their steps up-hill, when Phuntsho and Dao shouted at them, which made them start off with great swiftness. Dao Namgya then showed me some boulders on the steep edge of the river, which are worshipped as the *rangjung*, or self-sprung images of Pemaguru and his two female disciples. It was about half-past 3 P.M. when we got sight of the village of Yangma. There were several spacious terraces one above another in succession towards our left and right, reaching the higher summits of the west. These were strewn with boulders and overgrown with a kind of dwarf sedge, now turning yellow in the wintry frost. A stream comes down from the east to flow into the Yangma river, which rushed past our left. This was also a vast moraine studded with numerous lakes, and marked by huge collections of débris and gravel all over. We then arrived at the bridge across the river, which, though rapid, was not very broad here. The valley here undulated, and walking became pleasant to us. The terrace on which Yangma village is situated is broad and irregularly sloping, situated on the southern flank of the lofty mountain receding to the north. The houses of the village from a distance could not be distinguished from the huge boulders except by the smoke from their fireplaces. Approaching near, we saw the houses, which resembled more the Tibetan houses than those of Kangpachan, or Himalayan style, which latter were beautifully constructed of numerous planks.

There were not more than a hundred houses in the village. The cultivated lands were distinguished from the pasture lands by stone dyke enclosures. The smaller enclosures were for the sheep and yaks of the villagers, and within I saw young yak calves and lambs frisking about. The dams were grazing outside the dykes. There were unmelted patches of snow here and there in heaps in the court-yards and on the roofs of the huts. We passed through the village and reached the top of the north-western part of the village. Our way lay by a lane between two huts, through the middle of which a drain ran. The houses contained stone enclosures, and were two storeys high. In the lower storey we saw yak-calves feeding on barley straw. Phuntsho and Ugyen were accosted by many of the villagers, chiefly women. They inquired if there was *chhang* beer and rice for sale. Hearing there was, they unloaded themselves and walked inside one of the houses, while I and Ugyen Gyatsho ascended a little up the village where, on a small flat, we sat down. After half an hour they returned drinking *chhang*, having spent a couple of rupees on rice and parched indian-corn. The Yangma people get these articles of food from Yang-kuthang and other villages in the warmer valleys. The entrance to some of the houses was filled with snow still unmelted. Some houses had snow-heaps even a few feet within their doors. Ugyen Gyatsho drew my attention to these, and observed how wretched this village was, and how hard and sluggish the life of people must be. The part of the village where we sat was nearly 14,000 feet high. Buck-wheat, barley, sweet turnip, radish, and potatoes grow here. The people do not take care to clear the fields of stones, and we saw boulders scattered all over the enclosures where these vegetables grew. The country appeared very barren.

The village of Yangma in ancient time was not inhabited. Once on a time a *dokpa* (cowherd) of Tashi-rabka lost one of his yaks, which, grazing on towards the

Kangla Chhen Pass, entered the Yangma valley. The *dokpa* missing his yak, went towards Dorjethag rock, whence he crossed the pass and arrived at the Yangma valley, where to his great delight he found his hairy property lying on a rock with a full stomach. In the morning he again missed it, and proceeding further down in the interior met it at a place which is now called Shophug, grazing on a rich pasture land. Here, being charmed with the luxuriance of the pasture as compared with his bleak and barren country, he sowed a few grains of barley which he had obtained from a certain Tantrik priest as a blessing. On his return to Tashi-rabka he gave a good account of this place to his fellow *dokpas*, but nobody would believe him, nor would any one undertake to visit his discovery on account of its position beyond the snows. The *dopka*, however, with his wife, went to Yangma valley to tend his flock. To their surprise they found the barley well grown On his return home he showed the barley ears to his friends, who were now induced to emigrate to the new land to grow corn. Thus was the village of Yangma first inhabited. It is indeed a purely Tibetan settlement, as the houses testify. The name Yangma was given to the place for the spaciousness of the valley, its numerous moraines, lake-beds, and flats. The extensive terrace beds of the river Yangma, the high, steep mountains with dark flanks and white tops which stood awfully overlooking the valley on all sides, and the snowy, giant peaks of Chabuk La which run their array of heads towards the furthest east, whence a streamlet comes to supply water to the indolent Yangma people, all vanishing in the shade, combined to make me think that I was in the midst of an enchanted land, and to forget the filthy village with its tiny flag-poles and banners, *chhortens*, *mendangs*, and wretched huts perched over the flat along with the boulders. I deplored that such a marvellous land should have fallen in the hands of a people so wretched, filthy, and indolent as the Yangmas: lands they have enough, but they will not cultivate them, choosing rather to live wretchedly as pigs. But though the men here were so idle in their habits, the women showed much stir and briskness. Some of the latter were engaged in threshing corn, some in collecting fuel, and others in the different branches of household life, while the stupid and savage-looking men were sitting by the side of their hearths, wrapped in blankets swarming with vermin, whose bites alone make them move their limbs. The character of these lethargic people reminded me of the famous theory of the Sankhya philosophy, that *Prakriti*, which is identified with *Sakti*, is more powerful than *Purush*. The men looked with indifference towards us, and it is from the women of the village that we received any help: they told us that the pass would be impracticable.

It was nearly 5 P.M. when we resumed our journey, in spite of the reluctance of the coolies to proceed further. They said that there was no place for our night's shelter within a distance of about eight miles, and that we would do well to halt for the night at the village. I inquired if by halting at Yangma we could arrange for some *jo* or yaks to carry our things. The coolies forthwith went to some of the rich villagers to ask them to lend us their beasts. I instructed them to offer high rates; but they returned unsuccessful, having been laughed at for making such proposals. The yaks and *jo*, they said, could never walk in deep snows, and it was clear to them that we would be compelled to retrace our steps towards Yangma on account of the inaccessibility of the *La*. Hearing this, I at once got up from the ground and resumed the journey in right earnest. I told Ugyen Gyatsho that the object of the coolies in halting at Yangma was simply to get drunk during the night like Phurchung, who, by the bye, had not yet returned. Before, however, proceeding a few hundreds of steps, we heard Phurchung calling to Dao Namgya at the pitch of his voice. We stopped for a while by the side of a *chhorten* situated on a flat, to know what was the matter with him. He arrived, and with a great deal of lolling of the tongue asked my pardon for his helpless state. I did not say much, but quietly walked along. He returned to Yangma, and we ascended up another terrace. On our way we met several *di* (she-yaks), which are all milked at this season. The she-yaks bring forth one calf annually, and scarcely cease to give milk, except a month before calving. We met dwarf rhododendron bushes and creeping juniper scarcely measuring more than six inches in height. The sunset was glorious. No trace of fog was visible in the atmosphere, save the fantastic array of variegated clouds in the western sky. The snow-clad peaks here and there made their appearance and added to the sublimity and impressiveness of the scenery. At 6 P.M. we halted at Kiphug, a cliff overlooking the frozen Yangma. There was no place free from snow even here on which we could spread our rugs. After much search we found a boulder perched slantingly on another huge boulder half buried in the ground. In the cleft between these two we elected to spend the night. Some creeping juniper twigs were spread underneath to remove the unevenness of the spot, and a square slab of stone placed before me to serve for a dinner-table. Dao and his colleagues at once collected some fuel, consisting of dried yak-dung and some dried stalks of arborescent plants, probably species of rhododendron growing in the snowless crevices of rocks. The fire was lighted with a flint-stone and tinder, and kept up by a continual supply of dried moss scraped off the top of the boulder. Tea was prepared and distributed, after which rice was boiled. The day's journey had not been long, consequently I was not fatigued. While my companions were engaged in blowing the fire, I walked up a little distance to enjoy the scenery, which it would hardly fall to my lot again to witness. It was dark, and though the distant views were half shrouded in a bluish dark haze, yet I feasted my eyes on one of the grandest spectacles of nature—the radiant effect of the sunset, the appearance of the moon after it, and the summits of an irregular row of snow-clad mountains peeping from an envelope of purple clouds. Feeling a little cold, I returned to my cleft and sat down, wrapping myself in blankets. The cooking was not done well. I, however, managed to swallow some of the imperfectly boiled rice, with a couple of boiled eggs. Some of the latter were reserved for next morning. There was complete stillness, the river having to make its passage through a depth of several feet of solid ice. A keen, chill breeze, accompanied with slight sleet, blew during the night, but I did not much feel its effects, being secure within my boulder cleft.

29th November.—Leaving Kiphug a little after sunrise, we proceeded on our journey. The way lay on the side of the Yangma, which was scarcely distinguishable, snow and ice in different forms covering its entire bed. In some places snow in a crystallised form overspread the slopes in little motionless waves. On these we walked lightly, our Tibet boots being now very convenient. Passing this stage of snow, we came across a vast plain of sheeted ice, exceedingly dangerous to cross; so our coolies dug out some earth to scatter on the ice to make it less slippery. We now descended to the river bed. It was easy to walk on snow, and whenever we came across an extensive sheet of ice, we longed for a snowy surface to walk on. There was no life stirring; no birds or clouds in the sky; no noise on the frozen river, save the sound of our boots on the crystallised snow. The entire lake-bed, for the river was a lake here, was strewn with huge boulders, the biggest as large as hillocks. The river meandered, sometimes contracting in a deep gorge, at others opening into lake-like beds. The mountains on either side seemed to touch the skies. The eastern flanks of the lateral spurs were less covered with snow, and whenever we happened to cross them we wished a continuance of their slopes further. Crossing spur after spur and lateral frozen feeders of the Yangma, we arrived at another lake-bed of the river, where a long ledge of a lateral spur overhung the river. It was 11 A.M. when we got sight of water in a shallow part of the river, caused by the melting of the snow by the sun. Our coolies had picked up some tufts of sedge grass on the way, and throwing them on the ground, they unloaded themselves. I now found much relief in halting, as rest was most necessary, having travelled for nearly three miles on an empty stomach. This place is called Tsher-chan, or the place of summer pasture of the yak herds (*Tsher* in Tibet and in cis-Himalaya means common pasture land). Luxuriant pastures grow here in the months of July, August, and September, when numerous *dokpas* pitch their *dok-kur* (tents) at this place. Phurchung now suddenly made his appearance and cleared a plot of snow, and spread my rug thereon. A fire was lighted and tea prepared. Being very hungry, I unshelled a boiled egg, but it was frozen, and cracked beneath the teeth. The yolk was hard, resembling amber, and the white hard as conch-shell. Tea was prepared, though with much difficulty, the fuel having burnt out before the water could boil to the desired extent. I soaked the remainder of my last night's meal in a cup of tea to serve me for breakfast. The coolies managed to moisten their parched indian-corn and barley flour with the share of tea given them by Phurchung.

Breakfast finished, we all prepared for the greatest hardships that we had yet encountered. Our way now lay along the frozen Yangma. We were at the foot of Pophug, bearing north north-west. A snowy mountain stood before us bearing direct north. I took it for Kangla-chhen, not liking to ask our guide if my supposition was correct, lest he should say that it was not Kangla-chhen. After much struggle within myself, I asked Phurchung at what time he could take us to the pass, to which he replied "Oh sir, the *La* cannot be seen from this place. You may possibly get a glimpse of it to-morrow morning." Much disappointed, I plodded my weary way, and at 1 P.M., crossing the frozen bed of Yangma twice, we arrived at Pophug, a distance of nearly three miles, which was entirely snow-covered, only some patches on the steep eastern flanks here and there being laid bare by the melting of the snow by the direct rays of the sun. Passing Pophug, we arrived at the higher flanks of the steep mountains, which were to a great extent free from snow on account of the sun, and were covered with scanty blades of grass. This place, called Luma Goma (*Luma*, fountain, and *Goma*, the head) is the source of the river Yangma. We encountered a herd of *nao*, about thirty, that were coming down probably to drink water. The moment our coolies saw them they stood stock-still, and we whispered to one another to ask what was the matter. Dao pointed out to me the *nao* that were approaching towards us, but had not seen us, there intervening a steep ridge between us and them. At last the *nao* arrived on the top of the ridge before us, and looked towards us. Phuntsho asked me if we would shoot them. I told them that if they could carry the booty along with them, they were at liberty to chase and shoot them. Cartridges were put into the breech-loader, and Phurchung, who carried the gun, was asked to take aim. "Oh sir, the mountain god, the *Shibdag*, will take offence if we fire a gun here. These mountains are never disturbed by the sound of a gun, and, look there, the wild sheep have smelt gunpowder, and are running off towards the summits of the mountain." "We have not yet fired our gun, how could they scent the powder," said I. "Oh sir," replied Phuntsho, "the *nao* are very powerful smellers. They have perceived that we have cartridges and powder in our cans." "If that was your fear," added I, "why have you carried the gun so far?" But Phuntsho had never used a gun in his life, and would perhaps have dropped it while firing. In the meantime the *nao* had ascended far beyond our reach, and were followed by another flock containing about twenty-five. Dao counted them as they passed. These animals always follow one another, and scarcely disperse unless closely chased. As the idea of shooting was given up, the coolies now sent up a shrieking yell to frighten the fleeting flock. The distance between this plain and Tsa-tsham, which the guide pointed out to us, was nearly a mile. After an easy ascent of half an hour we arrived at Tsa-tsham, the limit of vegetation.

Leaving the limit of vegetation we arrived at the region of active moraines, where denudation by snow is carried on actively and unceasingly, giving rise to ridges formed by the alternate accumulation and dispersion of débris through glacial action helped by the sun. Leaving Tsa-tsham we arrived at a grand ridge of accumulated boulders, about a quarter of a mile in breadth and nearly three miles long in a line. This from a distance appeared like an embankment about three to four hundred feet above the surrounding bed of snow. The south-eastern flank of this extensive ridge was laid bare by the melting of the snow, but the north-western flank remained fully clad in snow, the sun being too weak to exert any influence when past the meridian. The frequent blowing of the wind from the west seemed also one of the causes why snow did not melt on the west. On our right and left there was a vast expanse of snow. This great and long glacial spur is called Chyang Chhub Gyalam ('the high road of saints'). There was no path, not even a foot-track; but our guide, whose knowledge of these snowy regions was remarkably good, never missed the right way. In places where snow lay unmelted he carried me on his back, dividing his load with his brother Dao and Phuntsho. It would have been impossible for me to have passed this "highway of saints" had it not been for his kindness in taking me on his back, without my asking. Fortunately there was no gale nor snowfall. A serene sky gleamed over-head, and water-vapour was rising like smoke from the melting snow. Here and there distant avalanches were heard, but nothing else stirred the atmosphere except our solitary footsteps on the snows of Chyang Chhub Gyalam. The lofty peaks, some isolated and others in continuous ridges, bounded our views to the north-west and north. Their array and distance, their sublimity and dazzling whiteness, were imposing, but their glare exhausted us as much as the height of Chyang Chhub Gyalam and the journey along it. Added to this, the great tenuity of the air and the exertion of the lungs in continuous up-hill work, the uninterrupted journey on snow and immense accumulation of boulders, paralysed our strength. I was also oppressed with thirst, which, as I journeyed on, became unbearable, when we descried a pool of crystal water. I joyfully approached the precious discovery by deviating a little to the east of my route, Phurchung following, but, to our great disappointment, there was no water: the lake was entirely frozen, the thick crystalline surface was about a foot deep, if not more, and in some places bubbles were seen rising. Tempted by this, we tried with all our might with stones to break the hard surface, but no indentation could be effected, the stones generally sliding off after falling. After several unsuccessful attempts I turned back and resumed our journey in a worse condition than before. The entire ridge of Chyang Chhub Gyalam stretches from south to north. At its termination we came to a yawning gulf of snow filled with dreadful crevasses. Having crossed it with much fear and uneasiness, we ascended another spur bearing eastward, and more exposed to the power of the sun, and consequently less covered with snow. It was a huge accumulation of black rocks irregularly heaped. For a short time we lost sight of the white glare, our eyes being engaged with the black, dismal appearance of this place, which is appropriately called Dsama Nagmo, or the black rock. Before we had half passed this dreary scene the Dsama Nagmo was shrouded in darkness. We began to despair of being able to reach our destination, Phugpa-karmo (the white cavern). Travellers from Tibet or Wallung who happen to journey by this pass generally take shelter here, for on account of its whiteness the rock is conspicuous in this region of black rocks in the summer months. Still we plodded on our way with a hope of reaching Phugpa-karmo. The darkness caused by the fogs helped to increase our difficulties. Our feet were benumbed, and frequently sank into the crevices and clefts of loosely accumulated black rocks. Our suffering from cold, the temperature being several degrees below the freezing point, was unendurable. At last at 7-30 P.M., finding it would be impossible to reach Phugpa-karmo, or fearing that it might have been left behind, we halted on a heap of black, loose stones. Phurchung and Phuntsho scraped out some snow which lay in the clefts, and spread my rug between two large pieces of stone. The space was hardly a foot and a half broad and about two feet long. I could neither stretch myself nor turn on my sides. Phurchung packed me, as it were, in my blankets. I sat down with knees drawn up, hugging myself, and remained in one and the same posture.

How exhausted we were with the fatigues of the day's journey, how overcome by the oppressive tenuity of the air, the killing severity of the cold, and how completely prostrated by hunger and thirst, it is not easy to describe. The very remembrance of the sufferings of that dreadful night makes me shudder, but I quickly recover under the inexpressible delight I feel at the consciousness of a great success. This was the most trying night I ever passed in my life. There was a slight gale attended with sleet. The latter pressed the folds of my blankets down with its weight, which helped us to get more warmth than the woollens would otherwise yield. We sorely needed rest; sleep accommodated itself inconveniently, as it were, to our eyes, as we accommodated ourselves to the miserable cleft of the rocks of Dsama Nagmo. Ugyen slept by me, his head touching mine, and Phurchung slept at my feet. The rest of the party slept on the bare stones, their heads sheltered by the baskets which contained our indispensables, and which were kept erect by their *togma*, or support sticks. Thus oppressed by hunger and thirst, without taking even a morsel of dry food, and placed as if in the grim jaws of death on the bleak and dreary regions of snow, where death alone dwells, we spent this very dismal night.

30th November.—The KANGLA CHHEN PASS. Although I awoke from sleep earlier than on the preceding days owing to the uncomfortableness of the cleft which accommodated me yet fearing the severity of the cold, I did not get up from my miserable bed before 7 A.M

There was much glare of the sun, which rose earlier on the summit of the ridge where we were than lower down. The coolies having reloaded themselves, we resumed over journey, and our guide commenced the recital of his *pema jung-ne sam-ba dub-ba* and other *mantras* in his gravest tone. I always followed Phurchung, Ugyen generally following me, very seldom heading the party. The morning was gloriously radiant, and the great Kangla Chhen towering peerlessly glittered in our front, bathed in a flush of golden light. I could not fully enjoy the grand scenery owing to the fatigues of the previous day, which, instead of being slept off, were aggravated by the wretchedness of the cleft of Dsamo Nagmo. The sight of such majestic, sublime, and stupendous scenes very seldom falls to the destiny of men who can enjoy them, and perhaps they are least accessible to those who travel luxuriously. Fortunately for us no fresh snow had fallen in these regions lately, otherwise we could hardly have crossed the lofty pass. When Phurchung got a view of the eastern flanks of Kangla Chhen he was transported with joy, exclaiming *La-la khang bab ma-song* (no fresh snow has fallen on the mountain). After journeying about a furlong, we came to Phugpa-karmo. This was no cavern at all, as the word *Phugpa* would seem to imply, but a large crevice between two huge blocks leaning against each other amidst a collection of massive rocks. From Phugpa-karmo we descended to a gully full of snow, several feet broad. This crossed, we ascended to the eastern flank of Kangla Chhen. The distance from Phugpa-karmo to the foot of Kangla Chhen we estimated at half a mile of easy slope. The ascent was most tiresome owing to the many broken, rocky ridges, some stopped on their way down from the higher summits. Our entire attention was engrossed by the glaciers, which concealed under their semi-fluid surface many a treacherous crevasse. The bluish and emerald-like depressions we carefully avoided. Our guide now leaving his load in charge of his brother, took the lead with a long stick in his hand, driving it into the ground in front and then slowly advancing his feet for a foothold. I followed his footsteps with confidence, myself in the middle of the train; but when my strength failed me, I fell back, and advanced by cautiously placing my feet in the holes dug by them. Where the footholds were too deep, I dug new ones with my heel, but always keeping the other foot in an old foothold. Occasionally I slid down short distances in making attempts to cut new footholds, when I leaned backwards, and held on to the snow with one of my elbows and knees. From Phugpa-karmo the *La* (top of the Kangla Chhen) bore almost due east nearly two miles off. Just at the waist of the great mountain there is a sandy flat with a huge rock perched in the middle. This place bears the encouraging name of *Thar-pa-gang*, or 'the place of salvation,' because travellers when they arrive here are confident of reaching the summit of the mountain. Our troubles, we imagined, would shortly end: the highest summit attained, there would be less chance of greater and steeper ascents. We took out some parched indian-corn from the bags and put them in our breast-pockets. Owing to great thirst and stickiness of the saliva I could eat hardly a morsel of food; but my companions really made a feast. I steadily followed the track of our guide, and did not consent to his taking me on his back, thinking if I succeeded in ascending to the highest summit of Kangla Chhen without any help, I could look to the achievement with greater pride. Ugyen, who wished to be carried on somebody's back, now pretended to be very ill, and with many groans begged me to enable him to follow me. "I cannot ascend, Sir," said he; "I am very unwell; *ah-yeo, ah-yeo do-mi-chhu*, what pain! I cannot proceed." Fearing that any delay here would be injurious to us, as we were in the very heart of the snow, I begged Phurchung to take him on his back; but he grumbled: "Look here, Sir," said he, pointing to his waist, "I have got a pain here. How can I carry him?" I pressed him again, telling him he should listen to my request, as I could not leave my companion at such a stage of the journey. After some more grumbling and whispering Phurchung took off his *pagri*, and putting it round Ugyen's body, lifted him on his back. How many times Phurchung had to take rest in a standing position with the corpulent load on his back! After every ten or twelve paces of steep ascent he halted with a low groan and a yawning mouth to take breath. The more I approached the Lap-tse the more vigorous and hopeful I became, and my companions were really surprised to see the revival of spirits in my hitherto drooping heart. Frequently, when traversing a zig-zag on the steep snow and ice, I threw a glance upon the amazing scenes we were leaving below. What a grand gathering of snow-clad, towering pinnacles, arrayed in all their savage grandeur; hanging glaciers round us glowing in their turquoise-blue tint, avalanches disturbing the serenity of these desolate regions, yawning crevasses, and snowy spurs and ledges of rocky cliffs: all seemed to make up a dream even in those wakeful hours of active journey. After an hour's hard and rapid ascent we reached the Lap-tse, or the summit of the pass. It was 3 P.M., and the sun shone brilliantly to aggravate our sufferings by increasing the intolerable glare. The sky was cloudless and of the deepest blue, against which the snow-clad world of mountains all round stood out in splendid contrast. From the exalted position we had now gained our eye surveyed the valleys immediately round us, and, far beyond them, what looked like a boundless ocean of snow, the distant ridges and spurs looking like the billows of the sea. The snowy mountains of Pherug in Tibet stood towering up far, far to the north-west. The mountains of Sharkhambu, probably the great Lap-chye-kang, stood gloriously to the west, piercing the deep blue vault of the sky, but the Kanchan Jonga was not visible from here. I was really transported to enter an entirely new region never visited by any European or Indian. These splendid scenes of wonderland, the grandest and the most sublime that my eyes ever beheld, which then baffled my utmost powers of admiration as they now do my pen to describe, inspired feelings of deep gratitude to Heaven, by whose mercy my life had been spared thus far. What reverential awe I felt in beholding the majesty of God in nature, and His mercy in myself! We had come thus far in search of Death as it were and to be his guest in these abodes of his dreaded legions, but we missed him and his messengers altogether. A few minutes after Phurchung arrived, breathing hard, and placed his cumbrous load (Ugyen Gyatsho) before me. I smiled at him, but could not draw out a smile from my friend's face. I asked him to take out the thermometer. He did it immediately, and lighted a candle. The thermometer gave a reading of 182° at 3-45 P.M. The summit of Kangla Chhen is a great plateau, about two miles long from east to west and about 1½ mile broad from north-west to south-east. From the place where we stood, which was the extreme prominence to the east, the plateau descended towards the west in an inclined plane. To the north-west this table land is skirted by a snow-clad mountain of considerable height. While we were engaged in boiling water and taking bearings, our coolies rested and refreshed themselves, each with a mouthful of parched indian-corn. Phuntsho and Ugyen took out the *kyar*, or snow-shoes. There were altogether three pairs of *kyar*. Phuntsho and Ugyen each wearing a pair, at once fled away as fast as they could with their loads, fearing that others might come to dispossess them of their precious snow-shoes. The third pair was given to me for use. But Dao, whose toes were severely, frost-bitten required a pair, so I gave him mine, and had to walk in the deep snow with my Tibet boots to protect my feet. I was very much displeased with Phurchung for his carelessness in not providing us with a sufficient supply of *kyar*. I had asked him to order at least half-a-dozen *kyar* to be made at Kangpachan. I followed Phuntsho, always placing my feet in his foothold. Sometimes I sank up to my knees, at others to my thighs, in the deep snow. The table-land was somewhat undulating, being, in fact, a gigantic glacier across which we had now ascended the southern flank of the Dorjethag range and slowly plodded our way towards Dorjethag Phugpa. Our track was entirely new, as the old track had been lately effaced by a snow-storm, in consequence of which the journey was most tedious and difficult. While descending from a saddle point towards a deep gorge I fell into a crevasse, and would have been lost had not Ugyen and Phurchung come to my rescue. The blue tinted crevasse, though deep, was hard enough on the upper surface to support my hands; besides there was a boulder supporting a portion of the surface snow, which was very fortunate for me. We then commenced our descent along the glacier, and after many tumbles and slips arrived at a slope of the Dorjethag precipice. From this place we cast a look towards the deep abyss, where a number of huge rocks, half covered with snow and half bare, could just be seen lying irregularly about. We sent Phurchung and Phuntsho to see if any spot of ground free from snow could be found out in the neighbourhood, that we might spread our rugs thereon to spend the night. It was now 6 P.M., and though darkness was fast enveloping the skies, yet the whiteness of the snow to some extent seemed to keep it off. After dusk there was moonlight, and we scraped out snow from a tolerably flat slope, where our rugs were now spread.

On all sides there was nothing visible but an ocean of snow. Innumerable snowy peaks touched with their white heads the pale leaden skies where stars were visible. The rattling roar of distant avalanches was frequently heard, but having succeeded in crossing the greatest and the loftiest of snowy passes, I was too much transported with joy to be frightened with their thunder. Though my body was weather-beaten and very much pulled down by most trying privations, yet my mind grew stouter and more hopeful through success, and I expressed my gratitude with uplifted eyes towards the clear, starry heaven. Loss of strength and extreme exhaustion made me lie down before my faithful friend and guide had time to spread my rug, but he instantly warned me not to do so. He then quickly opened his package and got out my blankets. He was going to make my bed thicker, and more comfortable and warm, when I stopped him; for, as Ugyen had not brought woollens for his use, I had to share with him my own blankets. I felt extremely cold, my extremities freezing inside the socks, and I thought for a moment that I would succumb to the increasing effects of cold. Phurchung saw that such thoughts would tell seriously on me, but my companion, shewing perfect unconcern for me, kept up his cries of pain and exhaustion, and sat shivering on my rug. My condition bore no comparison with his, as he was fat and corpulent, and consequently possessed of a larger quantity of animal heat. Yet, when I saw him shivering, I forgot his silly behaviour, and invited him, as usual, to wrap himself with half of my woollens, which Phurchung unceremoniously threw towards him. There was no even surface where we could stretch ourselves at full length. The rock being abrupt on either side, Phurchung feared lest I should slide down towards the glacial abyss if I rolled during sleep. He therefore fixed his packing baskets lengthwise on the abrupt side, and propped them with a few pieces of ice. On my left Ugyen made himself comfortable, sleeping on my rug and covering himself with his *rari* blanket, besides half my woollens. Phurchung's brother stretched himself at my feet, and he himself sat reclining near my head to sleep in that posture. There was a slight snowfall, and I could hardly bring my hand outside my wrappers, so Phurchung put a handful of biscuits close to my mouth. There was no water to drink, and after eating three or four biscuits I felt my tongue dry, and hardly able to swallow. The saliva too was very sticky for want of food during the day. I gave Ugyen a few, although he was then keeping his teeth busy with grinding some parched maize. We had no tents to shelter us from the rigour of the freezing wind, and if we had one, we could not have pitched it in this unprotected, unsheltered region. In this most deplorable condition, harassed by hunger and thirst, and more so by snow and the chill wind, short of clothes where clothes were most needed, we laid ourselves down to rest, entirely resigning ourselves to the care of Him who had brought us safe over the lofty pass. I slept uneasily and dreamt of my lamented father, whose presence once, in a dark night while I was ten years old, had banished from my mind the terrors of an attack from a half burnt skeleton ghost. The same spirit was present here to infuse strength into my mind, for I never imagined till my sleep broke that my affectionate parent was not in the land of the living.

II.—JOURNEY FROM THE KANGLA CHHEN PASS TO TASHI-LHUNPO.

1st *December*.—I awoke before it was dawn, but remained quietly inside my blankets to delay rising as much as possible. To my disappointment, Phurchung, after muttering some sacred *mantras* in which *pema jung-ne sambo dubba* were several times repeated, unceremoniously took off my outermost covering, which he shook for a minute or two to disencumber it of its load of snow. I now felt the bitterness of the cold, and at once found that the weight of the superincumbent snow which had fallen on the blanket had kept me warm, the freezing of the moisture in it having made it a tough-like hide, through which chill winds, not to speak of snow, could not penetrate. Ugyen and the coolies next got up and busied themselves in their task of packing up. The track was hardly visible; below our path lay the great glaciers, extending for miles, which feed the Tashi-rabka river with a sluggish supply. The retiring snowy slopes of the lofty mountains to the other side of this glacier were furrowed by different glacial streams clearly visible in their varied shades of blue and green. On the glacial pools, which were distinguished by their exceptionally bluish appearance, there were huge rounded bodies, evidently boulders concealed under ice, producing an unevenness on the surface, but yet reflecting the overhanging snowy summits. There was no sign of life in this desolate region. We carefully followed the footsteps of our guide, who always took care to spread dust on the slippery parts of the ice-covered way. In this way we crossed several spurs and ledges of the Dorjethag range before we saw any trace of vegetation. We found no trace of water to quench our pressing and increasing thirst. At every appearance of water we rushed forward with eagerness, but as continually met with repulses, the water being frozen. As we descended we gradually came to crags and rocks free from snow, from which vapours were issuing. It was a great relief to find the paths free from snow after we had been so long struggling in the icy and snowy slopes of steep precipices. At the end of six miles' continual march we came to an easy path along the ridge of an ancient isolated moraine, on two sides of which the glaciers flowed to a great distance. Sometimes we treaded our way on the right bank of this moraine and sometimes on the left, the yak-dung helping us in keeping to the track over heaps of debris and collections of immense boulders. In some places there were sand accumulations in which we saw foot-marks of stray yaks. As we descended towards the great plateau of Tibet the mountains lost their whiteness, and black and ochre-coloured crags in forked array presented a scenery quite peculiar to Tibet. The slopes of the great moraine alongside of which we passed were overhung by giant rocks and dotted with enormous blocks of stone which had descended to add to the wildness of the scenery, and to show to what convulsive changes these mountains were subjected in times past under the devastating operations of glaciers.

The sun shone with increasing brightness as we proceeded towards the plateau which extended before us, dissected by numerous blue mountain ranges where occasionally one or two snow-capped peaks broke the monotony of the scenery. The snowy mountains of Pherug were the most prominent objects within view, and the far-famed Chomo-kangkar now slowly vanished from our sight. We now began to feel more keenly the effects of our last two days' fasting There was strong headache accompanied by feverishness and great lassitude. We were anxiously walking on more for a halt than to make any progress in our journey. At last our ears were refreshed with the welcome but faint murmur of a stream which was feebly pushing its way through the snow-covered ice-beds; and our eyes were directed eagerly to find out where this stream flowed clear of the ice. With the advance of the sun the frozen stream begun to melt, and the fountains, released from their fetters, trickled down. There were some prickly shrubs and some dwarf species of rhododendron with a few flowers not yet withered. Further down the fountains increased, and in their wet nooks and corners fragrant shrubs nestled regardless of the approach of winter. Small twittering birds flew to our left and right, and seemed evidently to subsist on rhododendron berries. At noon we came to a sparking rill, close to which there was abundance of dwarf juniper, the leafless twigs of which were well suited for fuel. Here we halted. My rug was spread under the shade of a steep, huge rock, and I sat reclining on a boulder. One of our coolies at once ran to the rill to fetch a kettleful of water with which to quench our thirst. The baggage being opened, some yak-dung was collected, which, with the twigs of shrubs growing near, was fired with the help of our goat-skin bellows. This reminded me of the method of cooking on the banks of the Chhorten Nima river nearly three years ago. The sun now declined towards the west, and his rays falling directly on my face, I ordered one of our coolies to spread a cloth against the sun. Within one hour our simple breakfast was ready: rice half-boiled and a few cups of buttered tea. From this place we saw at a distance several herdsmen tending their hairy charge, and in one place some smoke rising. Breakfast over, I shaved myself sitting in a secluded nook, two of our coolies watching for the approach of any new-comers from either way. Shaving of the beard is unknown in Tibet, and so to be seen shaving would be a very embarrassing thing to me. I would not have cared to shave my head in public, as all monks in Tibet shave their heads, but shaving the beard would at once betray my foreign nationality. I tied my neck-tie round my head and chin after the fashion of the Tibetans, and resumed our journey at 1-30 P.M. The rill now assumed the appearance of a gurgling stream, and acquiring strength in its downward progress, rushed sweeping onward in its course many ice blocks and much snow. The yak pasture appeared on wide, refreshing, greenish banks, where several yaks were grazing. Dao Namgya told us how a yak, belonging to a rich resident of Yangma, had last year come here, and how it was pursued by the herdsman thus far. The yak was killed by wolves, but the man fortunately escaped. The visit of wolves is not unfrequent here, and I was pointed out the place whence packs of wolves found their way into this solitary valley. The biggest bull-yak of the herd, called *shalu*, a most savage animal, had been exiled here for his vicious conduct. He is seldom molested by wolves, who fear his pointed horns. With great apprehension of danger from him, I passed this pasture land, though closely guarded by Phurchung. Here, near the narrowest part of the river, the banks are dyked to obstruct the *shalu's* way towards the adjoining pasture-land where the she-yaks, called *di* in Tibet, were grazing in large numbers. At 3 P.M. we passed Dsongo, where there are the ruins of a stone house erected on a huge boulder. My companions said that this place was formerly the halting-stage of the Sikkim Raja's labourers who had been employed in conveying his provisions from Tibet to Sikkim or from Sikkim to Tibet when the Yangma and Wallung districts belonged to him. From the name Dsongo I could know that the place is the furthest entrance to the district of Tashi-rabka (*Dsong*, a district; and *go*, an entrance). Heaps of loose stones, small and large, with thin pointed boulders in the middle were piled on the side of our way. Our servants, as they passed, added a stone each to these votive cairns, which we always kept to our right. These were said to be the offerings made to the presiding mountain deities of these parts of Tibet. At 4 P.M. two herdsmen passing, made enquiries as to whence we were and where we were going. On Phurchung's replying that we were going on pilgrimage, they passed on with a *La laso*. The yaks that they were tending here all belonged to one Gambo Tashi, a chief of the *dokpas* of Tashi-rabka. As we left Dsongo we came to pass by the tents of the herdsmen, where there were two swarthy-looking women and a fierce Tibet mastiff. Phurchung left his load on the road-side, and begging me to look after it, entered their tents and sat down to chat. They offered him some thin curds, called *thara* in Tibetan, drinking a good draught of which he turned to me, and said that there was no milk to be had. The way now lay along a broad, grassy bank, intersected by the channels and off-sets of the main stream in several places. The journey was pleasant, the scenery refreshing, and the breeze most delightful. I wished much to throw off my head-tie, but Phurchung did not allow me to do so. Ugyen was overpowerd with fear and thoughtfulness how we would escape from the hands of the *Tongssung-pa* (thanadar) at Tashi-rabka, now fast coming into view. Phurching was also much overcome by fear, but Phuntsho frequently addressed me with '*ausi-ausi metog*' (do not fear, never mind) to keep up my spirits. On two sides of the stream, the course of which we had been following after its rise from the glaciers of the north-western flanks of the great Kangla Chhen, rose in forked peaks lofty, bleak mountains with sharp and craggy edges looking like ribs. Extreme barrenness marked the general aspect of the hills in our front, much contrasting with the fertile slopes of the southern but loftier peaks. The arid and dry character of the climate was at once perceptible, these mountain-tops being devoid of snow, while lower elevations at our back were white with it. These lateral mountain ranges appeared to me as northerly projections of the central trans-Himalayan range. Two almost parallel ranges, enclosing a river which debouches from the northern slopes of the great Himalaya, extended northward till they terminated in the lofty southernmost plateau of Tibet, through the middle of which flows a river from east to west. On advancing four miles north of Dsongo, I obtained a glimpse of the great plateau, which seemed to be an immense country filled with blue, waving, interminable mountain ranges. We left numerous gigantic piles of boulders, one after another, which, with some grassy patches, formed an immense moraine.

At about 6 P.M. we arrived at the vicinity of Tashi-rabka. In one place there were a great many huge rocks collected together. We ascended over these, and then, led by our guide, entered a gigantic crack in the rock, about 8 feet by 25 feet, close to which some curious long grass resembling sword-blades in shape and size, were growing. Some travellers on a previous day had burnt some of this grass as fuel for cooking. Here we halted for a few hours; tea was boiled, and some barley which we had brought from Yangma was moistened to satisfy our hunger. There was a glorious hue produced by the sunset, and the western snowy peaks were bathed in a gradually vanishing tint of purple. After two-and-half hours' rest we resumed our journey. The skies were somewhat covered with masses of white cloud running fast before the wind. The moon shone brilliantly at intervals, and helped us on our way to Tashi-rabka. First we came across the flat, rocky bank of the river, which here turned towards the west, and then, descending to the east of this bank, we met a long wall in ruins, about three to four feet thick. This wall, raised by the Tibetans during the Nepalese war, is said to have resisted the attacks of the Nepalese for several days. It being night, I could not ascertain the height, but it was evidently five to six feet above my head at the place where I stood for a few minutes leaning against it. I could see at this time about 200 feet of the length of the wall, whose winding up and down hill reminded me of pictures of the Great Wall of China, with the exception of the towers. Here Phurchung shewed me the route to Wallung, and told us how the Tibetans, under the generalship of Shape Shata, in one day erected about five miles' length of this wall to defend their position against the Goorkha army. The general is said to have allotted a fathom length (*Dom*) to each soldier under him to be erected in 24 hours' time. The wall was built of hard turf and stone, and the dryness of the climate has enabled it to remain standing to this day; but the portion which stood on the bridge had been carried away by the river. On the bridge eight towers were erected, each containing a sentry for the defence of the army. The ruins of the wall, I was told, still extend to a little more than five miles in length, terminating at the steepest parts of the two ranges of mountains on both sides of the river Tashi-rabka. We entered Tashi-rabka by a passage, probably made by a portion of the wall having fallen down. Overhead, where we stood, hung a wing of the wall overgrown with grass. Ugyen and Phurchung were now motionless, afraid lest the guards stationed here should detect us as foreigners The former been to tremble, not knowing whether to turn back towards the Kangla Chhen Pass or to proceed onward towards the *chhorten*, where resides the *Tongssung-pa*. Phurchung's position was no better than Ugyen's. I mustered all my courage, and found Phuntsho alone equal to the task. He said, "if the guards are found awake at this part of the night, we will sing some of our national Wallung songs and will make them pass us for Walungpa." I was now in excellent spirits, and said to my companion, "well. God has brought us safe thus far across the most inaccessible snowy mountains; He will surely help us in overcoming the present difficulty. Proceed forward, Ugyen," and, turning to Phurchung, I added—"why does your courage fail you here?" I asked Phuntsho not to sing or make a noise, so as not to disturb the sleeping guards. Once I thought of avoiding the guards by walking round the hill behind Tashi-rabka, but on second thoughts I abandoned the idea.

Before coming to the *chhorten*, a voice from a yak-hair tent cried, "whence are you and where do you go?" To this Phuntsho replied, "we are Walungpa. and are going to Shigatse;" and in turn asked whence he was, and what brought him there. Before his reply could be heard, we had proceeded on our way and passed by the *chhorten*—the dreaded spot where our destinies were to turn. The terrible mastiffs which were tied in front of the Tongssungpa's house did not bark, and there was no one awake to notice our movements. We passed in perfect silence along the lines of *chhorten*, keeping the two largest ones to our right. At a distance of about 30 yards from the *chhorten* is situated the bridge on the Tashi-rabka river. It was about 30 feet long and made of stone slabs and rough logs. I feared there might be some noise produced by our walking on the bridge, but nothing happened to awake the guards. It was a miraculous escape indeed that we made that night. Not a dog barked and not a guard awoke. We passed in silence up to a distance of 300 paces from the bridge, where I first broke the silence with thanks to merciful God who had enabled us to overcome the most dreaded of all difficulties, and which had chilled the spirits of our stoutest friend, which the snows of the Kangla Chhen had not daunted. The Tashi-rabka river was frozen, but the current in the middle of it was powerful, as it carried down blocks of ice of large size with some velocity. We then kept the stream to our right and, helped by moonlight, proceeded on our way. Being entirely a stranger to the country, and journeying in the moonlight, I could not observe the aspect of the country we passed through. There was a range of mountains to our left, the frozen river, faintly murmuring, flowed to my left, to the south of which a line of lofty mountains seemed to journey along with us. After nearly five miles' walk we arrived in the neighbourhood of a snowy range. There is said to exist a glacial lake close to it, which we did not see, and possibly could not see. In one place two Tibetans were heard speaking, when Phurchung, now bold as a lion, at once proceeded to enquire who they were. I did not wait for him, but proceeded on my way. After a few minutes talk with the travellers, Phurchung returned and told us that they were *gyagar-khamba*, or poor traders, who were going to Wallung to sell a young wild sheep, *nao*, they had lately captured. This place, called Lang-lung-pang-thang, is an extensive pasture-land extending from west to east. Proceeding along the river for three miles eastward, we arrived at Ri-oo, to the north of which, at some distance, is situated a glacial lake, and the snowy mountains reared their dome-like heads. There is a large Ningma monastery at Ri-oo. Here we met with a man proceeding to the village of Sar. Phuntsho talked with him for a few minutes about the trade at Sar and the current price of barley-flour and firewood there at this part of the year. This man told us that he had been to the house of one of his friends, a herdsman of Ri-oo, and was now proceeding to his house at Sar, which he must reach before the third watch of night. He was alone, and we wondered how one man in this dreary solitude could travel so fearlessly as he did. Before arriving at the bridge two fierce-looking mastiffs came howling towards us from a distance of several hundred yards in the direction of the uplands. Purchung and Ugyen threw stones towards them, and made one of them run away limping. Near the bridge the Sar man parted from us, his way being to the left side of the river along the mountain edge. The river here was evidently shallow, as a large area was covered with ice, the water flowing in two channels under the superincumbent ice. The wooden bridge on the first channel was about 20 feet long, and shook as we crossed it. The second bridge, which was about 10 feet long, was not so strong as the first one, and my leg was about to slide into a hole in it, when, with Phurchung's help, I extricated myself from the dangerous position. Our way now lay along on a sandy and gravelly plateau extending between two lofty ranges of mountains. After walking two miles we came lose to an encampment of grain-dealers, who, with about two dozens yaks, were proceeding to Tashi-rabka to buy rice from the Nepal traders of Wallung. They were all asleep. Some of the yaks were still grazing and others were lying down as if to sleep off the fatigues of the day. Here a third range of mountains intervenes, the snowy ranges which bound Tibet on the south now lying to our right. Along the northern flank of this third range, which was to our left, a road leading to Shiga-tse is said to exist. After nearly eight miles' hard walking we arrived at a sand-covered hillock called Shara, where we halted for the night. It was nearly 12 P.M., and the moon had just disappeared when Purchung conducted us to a sheep-fold to spend the night. A loose stone dyke-like wall surrounded the sheep-fold. Phurchung at once, without consulting us, threw our traps in it and began to spread our rugs thereon. There was a slight gale and intense cold. Close to our sheep-fold was another, where two hunters were staying. They had a matchlock and a *shyhakhi* (hound) with them. Phurchung went to bring fire from them, but they did not get up from their bed to oblige him, simply telling him there was no fire there. I felt very thirsty on account of the hard journey and the consequent fatigues. Our guide, who also felt thirsty, went a little distance forward to fetch water, but returned disappointed, as the streamlet which flowed past Shara was entirely frozen. As soon as the blankets were spread, I laid myself down to rest, and now that we had passed the greatest danger, I slept soundly. We were come down to the Tibetan plateau, where the air seemed to be favourable to breathing. The atmospheric oppression in the head was gone; only my knees were somewhat painful.

2nd December.—Early at sunrise we resumed our journey. An extensive, barren tableland extending towards the east lay before us. After an hour's journey we got sight of the village of Guma Shara, which stood at the foot of another range of mountains extending from north-east to south-east. I enquired from our guide if any yaks or ponies could be obtained or hired if we went to Guma Shara. He replied in the negative, but shortly after he said that 18 rich families of herdsmen resided there. Although yaks could be obtained there, our guide seemed unwilling to walk to Guma, as it would entail on us an out-of-the-way journey of four miles. Then turning a little to the north, and leaving Guma Shara behind us, we proceeded towards Langbula. The mountains on our left were bleak and barren; their summits rocky and of the most fantastic forms and array. Enlivened by the bracing breeze of the morning and the genial rays of the sun, I felt myself in good spirits. There was not a single soul to be seen in this vast table land, and only a few little birds like swallows twittered on the hill-sides close to our way. A few kites were flying in the sky a little to the north of Guma Shara. The plateau we were travelling in gradually rose towards Langbula, and we felt keenly that we were ascending a steep incline. After about two miles walk we arrived at a sheep-fold without a roof. There was a strong, chill gale blowing from the north. The stone wall of the fold protected us for a time from the inclemency of the weather. We resumed our journey after a short rest, when the fury of the gale had abated a little. Here Phurchung begged me not to require him to carry Ugyen Gyatsho on to Langbula. I told him that I would be the last man to subject him to unnecessary troubles, but if Ugyen was really ill, we could not by any means leave him behind. Ugyen *was* somewhat ill on account of the previous night's hard journey, and made but little progress in journeying. We had not taken any food this morning, and were travelling on empty stomachs. In fact there was no water with the exception of snow and ice here and there. We then quickened our pace to cross Langbula, beyond which we were told there was water. After proceeding half a mile further, we saw several yaks grazing on the slopes of Langbula. Of course it was a welcome sight, as it indicated that water was near. Walking slowly, on the gradually rising slopes of Langbula, we arrived at its foot. The way to the summit was by a zig-zag cut in the rocks, which appeared to me very steep. Long slabs of stone lay here and there, sometimes across, sometimes in the bends of the road. The track was evidently much frequented by caravans, as could be known from the dung of yaks and ponies. Langbula is a rocky mountain about 700 feet over the plateau, with some furze-like shrubs growing at its foot The mystic syllable "*Om mani padme hum*" was seen engraved on every available even surface on the rocks. After ascending to some height, I became exhausted, when Phuntsho carried me on his back up to the top of the pass. Ugyen, who had mounted Phurchung's back, was at the foot of the La while we were on its top. Phuntsho wanting to wait for them on the top near the Lap-tse, that all of us together might offer our *lhasol* (invocation) to the mountain deities, I complied with his wish. From the Lap-tse I enjoyed a magnificent view of the surrounding country. At our back were the snowy south Himalayas with their white, glistening peaks arrayed in wild, fantastic array. Due north, perched on a lofty peak, was the distant Lhakha of Sakya. Almost due west were the snow-clad peaks of the lofty Pherug mountains. The north-eastern slope, on which we treaded our way to take us to the northern foot, was flat, with deposits of sand in waves. Phurchung, carrying Ugyen on his back, arrived at the Lap-tse half an hour after us, and said he had got pains in his waist carrying Ugyen's weight. He then uttered his *lhasol*, saying "*so so-lhakyal-lo*" (pray, pray to the mountain gods). This mountain is believed to be the abode of numerous demi-gods.

Proceeding about a furlong from the northern foot of the La, where the table-land begins, I and Phuntsho reached the fountain where the Geh river springs. There was not sufficient depth of water to dip a cup in. We saw traces of grass in the neighbourhood. Some stones were kept piled one above another near this fountain, which shewed that the herdsmen while tending the yak during the rains stayed here for a day or two. Although I could have proceeded further on, yet I took a short rest here, sitting on a slab of stone and chatting with Phuntsho. After ten minutes Phurchung and the rest arrived, when we resumed our journey. Before proceeding a hundred paces we heard the whistles of some herdsmen coming towards us. I was quite perplexed, as this was the first time we would come across the Tibetans, ever since we left Yangma. Our party divided into two groups. The larger, consisting of Phurchung, Phuntsho, Ugyen, and others went ahead of the second party, consisting of Ugyen Gyatsho and Dao Namgya and myself. Three herdsmen and two *gelongs* (monks) with a dozen yaks and half a dozen donkeys, seeing us from a distance, stopped for a few minutes. Perhaps they took us for robbers, but afterwards, when Phurchung approached them, one of them at once recognized and greeted him. While they were thus engaged in talking, we walked past them. One of them asked who we were. Phurchung replied we were certain *Lamas* proceeding on pilgrimage to Shiga-tse, and he was accompanying us as our servant. I and Phuntsho proceeded along the way without waiting for our other companions. I would certainly have been interrogated by the herdsmen, and my being a foreigner exposed by my appearance and talk. These men, called *dadubpa*, or rice-collectors, were proceeding to Tashi-rabka to buy rice from Wallung grain-dealers. Our way now lay along the bank of the Geh stream, which, as we proceeded northwards, increased in size. In some places a slight verdure was visible, and yaks were feeding on the scanty blades.

Proceeding onward, we met other parties of swarthy Tibetans, in which the women were conspicuous by their *patug*, or head dress. Their dirt-covered complexion, filthy dress, and gleaming white of the eyes and teeth, were quite disgusting. Some of them accosted Phurchung and enquired if he was coming from Wallung. At 1 P.M. we arrived at the foot of Thag-la, where the pathway lay along the steep bank of the Geh-chhu. About 50 feet above the margin of the rivulet, beneath a steep, rocky cliff, there was a large cave, which the natives call Thagphug, or rock cavern. On two sides of this rock cavern two loose stone walls about three to four feet high were erected by some travellers. There was a slight breeze, which drove the smoke from the fire-place towards me. Seeing that the breeze would not change its direction, I removed my seat to the furthest end of the cavern, a distance of nearly 40 feet. Here I sat at ease, leaning upon one of the baskets which contained some of our blankets. There were several dwarfish weeds growing on the bank, from which an agreeable smell was blown towards us by the breeze. After breakfasting, at 3 P.M. we resumed our journey. The way lay sometimes along the flat basin of the rivulet and at others along its steep bank. After walking two miles we crossed the rivulet by a bridge consisting of two beam-like slabs of stone laid across the narrowest part of it. We had again to cross it in another place where there was no bridge at all. But the upper part of the stream was so frozen that we found no difficulty in crossing. The valley now gradually opened towards the north-east, and at 5 P.M. we found ourselves in an extensive plateau several miles broad ; I could not ascertain its length. The river now suddenly turned towards the west, probably to fall into the great Arun. To our left there was an extensive mountain range, by the south-eastern edge of which the Arun flowed. Phurchung here pointed out to us the place where there is a large under-ground convent, the *tsuglag-khang*, or the chief temple of that convent being cut out of a massive rock. There were altogether twenty souls living in it. The church furniture and the images of the deities contained in it are said to be of very ancient date. Ever since its foundation, which took place several hundred years ago, it has never been visited by any kind of religious or political vicissitudes. I had never heard before of the existence of an under-ground convent in such an unknown part of the country. We now turned our face towards the north-east and plodded our way in a wide, bleak, and barren country, entirely destitute of vegetation. At the place where we left Geh-chhu are two *chhortens* and several *mendang* with inscribed stones, but nothing more was seen with the exception of a few bits of inscribed rags. At about 7 P.M., we arrived at a sandy plain near the bank of a rivulet. Walking nearly a hundred yards on the sand-bank, we descended towards the margin of the rivulet, which is about 12 feet broad. Going down, we came to a barley field where the soil had been lately ploughed and ready for sowing. The ground was rocky and several boulders lay scattered on the ploughed lands. The river was frozen, with only a current in the middle. Phurchung, after laying his load on the bank, tried to cross it, but his legs sank into the ice-cold water. He tried to cross it at three different points, at all of which he failed to find a fordable place. He then proceeded nearly half a mile up the river to find out the bridge, but returned without success. We then walked about 100 yards down the stream, where, finding a part where there was less ice, we crossed

*

over. Phuntsho carried me on his back while Ugyen mounted Phurchung's back. We then proceeded in an easterly direction. Towards the south the glorious snow-clad Himalayas stood in stupendous array one behind another in endless succession. The Tibgyu-chhu which we had just crossed is said to come from the snows of Chabug La, at the foot of which is situated the Chalug monastery. Phurchung told us that his master, Kusho Tonga Rin-pochhe, the high priest of Wallung, Yangma, and Kangpachan, was then residing at Chabug, and that Dao Namgya was required to meet him on his return journey there. Proceeding several miles eastward, we passed the village of Wena, consisting of about six families. The mastiffs of the village howled at us, but Phurchung kept them off. We had now come to the side of the north-eastern range of hills, which lies laterally between Tibgyu-chhu and the basin of the eastern feeders of the Arun. Nearly at a mile's distance from Wena is the village of Chanee, where, according to our guide's statement, lived about ten families of *misser* (serfs). The Chanee people are said to be somewhat rich in cattle as well as in grain. They cultivate the fertile margin of the Tibgyu-chhu. In this village there still lives the *metshang* family named *Chhyugpo mepang*, or the rich men who never replied "no." When travellers passing by this place asked the *Chhyugpo* if there was such and such things to be had at theirs, they never replied in the negative. One day, in the month of August, a traveller who had heard this story regarding the family, in order to examine the truth of their reputation, asked the housewife to favour him with a piece of ice which he very much required. The housewife immediately gave him a piece of ice out of a butter cask; on another occasion a traveller begged for a chilly in February, which the housewife immediately produced. For these reasons people here regard the family as one favoured of heaven. Our object in travelling during the night was to enter the territories of the Tashi Lama before daybreak, for we did not consider it safe to travel in the Lhasan territories without a pass or *lamyig*. Our *lamyig* was from Tashi-lhunpo, and it would only be obeyed within the Tashi Lama's territories. Ugyen now complained that he was completely exhausted, his strength gone, and he could proceed no farther. The country was overgrown with a kind of furze, the thorns of which penetrated inside our felt boots. Selecting an even, furzeless place, we spread our rugs on the bare ground near the village of Polé. The sky was serene and the moon was bright as ever.

3rd December.—We got up from bed before sunrise, and resuming our journey, crossed several frozen streamlets. At a distance of nearly one mile from the place where we slept last night we came across a rivulet about 15 feet broad, the waters of which were rushing on in a strong current towards the north-east, carrying down ice blocks. We selected a shallow part of it, across which Phurchung waded, carrying me on his back. From this stream, in which I saw some small fish, channels were cut to irrigate the neighbouring barley-fields. We crossed them, sometimes leaping over them. At 7 A.M. we arrived at the *dok* of Polé, situated in the middle of the plateau, which extended from west to east for nearly 10 miles, and was bounded by the Arun on the north. Here and there were several sheep-folds or enclosed places surrounded by walls made of large sun-dried bricks. In the corner of these folds there were turret-like houses which sheltered the shepherds from the severity of the weather. The walls of the folds were six to seven feet high and two to three feet thick. There was enough of cowdung, which our coolies collected for fuel. Near one of these folds, on a clean place, my rugs were spread, and I seated myself. A thick piece of turf was then placed before me to serve as *chok-tsi*, or dinner table. Our companion soon made aquaintance with one of the shepherds who was milking his cow when we arrived there. He fetched us water, and obligingly said his services were at our disposal. Soon tea was prepared and poured in my China cup. Shortly afterwards two women, a boy eight years old and an elderly-looking man, arrived from the village of Polé. They surrounded us, some admiring my China cup, others praising my carpet, and all dazzled with the richness of my flannel *boku*. In fact our little possessions were all of the coarsest kind, but the people of this place, who had never gone out of the village, looked on them as wonders. Phuntsho now begged me to let him have the revolver which I carried in my breast-pocket. He made a grand exhibition of it by cocking it and aiming it at the women. Our men got some dried curds and butter of ewe's milk from the shepherds, with which they prepared some barley broth. My breakfast consisted of tea and boiled rice, and when I was sitting to it, there arrived two herdsmen with several cows and oxen. I asked if Phuntsho could arrange with these herdsmen to provide us with two *jo* or oxen for our conveyance. He at once went to them and asked if they would let their oxen on hire up to the village of Thebong, which was about six or seven miles off from here. They agreed to give us two oxen provided we paid two *tankas* as hire. As we were very much exhausted, this news was most welcome to me. I distributed a few English biscuits among the people standing about us. We resumed our journey at 9 A.M. mounted on the oxen saddled with pack-saddles, and with collar ropes instead of bridles, while a servant named Talogpa, whose face and clothes were covered with dust, whistled behind me to keep the beast in motion. The entire plateau was covered with a kind of thorny shrub amidst which a slender, long grass grew, which the cows and *jo* were picking. From these furze-like bushes rabbits and *wa* (Tibet fox) ran away, startled by our approach. Midway between Polé and Thebong, on the mountain side, lies the village of Mûg with about 40 families or *mitshang*. Within a mile's distance from the village of Thebong we met three flocks of

8th December.—We left Eago a little before dawn, walking for nearly half a mile in the faint moonlight. At 10 A.M. we entered the village of Thamar, where our grooms exchanged two sheep-skins for some forage. The fertile valley of the Rhe-chhu here is thickly dotted with hamlets. Numerous flocks of pigeons and swallows were picking worms and grain in the harvested fields. Ugyen told me that the pigeons are a great nuisance to the people, as they cannot kill them, bird-life being considered very sacred. Rhe-chhu was not much frozen, and we crossed it on our ponies. The country about Rhe is thickly populated. We purchased three basketsful of barley straw at a cost of one *tanka*. This year's produce, we were told, was below the average, and consequently a general scarcity in grass and food-grain was anticipated. We passed by the foot of the hill on which Rhe-gyuipai Gonpa is situated. At 2 P.M. we called at Labrang-Dokpa, but finding the doors shut, proceeded towards Nambula. In ascending the gravelly slope of Nambula, owing to the slackness of the girth, my saddle slid down, and I had a fall, but our Tang-lung grooms immediately came to my assistance. At 5 P.M. we crossed the Nambula, and seeing the village of Nambu situated immediately in front of it, we made towards it to spend the night. The *Nabo*, an acquaintance of Phurchung, was absent, but his wife, a woman of about forty, received us very kindly.

III.—ARRIVAL AT TASHI-LHUNPO, AND RESIDENCE THERE.

9th December.—We got up from bed at about 3-30 in the morning, and dressing ourselves in our best woollens by candle-light, and bidding good-bye to our hospitable *Namo*, set out for Tashi-lhunpo. There was moonlight sufficient to shew the way, and though a very chill wind blew, freezing our ears and nose, we walked on with much spirit. Parties of travellers conducting laden donkeys and yaks were proceeding towards the Nambu-dungla. Their peculiar wild whistle encouraging the laden animals was very familiar to me, and I admired the activity of the people. My health was much pulled down under the immense fatigues of the journey, but I was in high spirits. When I felt tired walking, I rode, and when my feet began to freeze, I again dismounted to walk. My companion was ill, and fretted fearfully, but our obliging grooms begged him respectfully to use the pony. His appearance was now most repulsive, and his language towards the grooms very abusive, yet the good Tang-lung men bore it with much patience. I often smiled at them, and shewed appreciation of their kindness by returning thanks for every slight mark of attention on their part for my comfort. We crossed beds of the several frozen streamlets with much caution. In some places the hoofs of the ponies were much cut. The custom of shoeing is not much understood in this part of the world, but the hoofs of mules and ponies, though left unshod, seem to be eminently adapted to the rocky soil, and are seldom injured in the stony paths amidst the gravelly table-lands of Tibet. This is owing chiefly to the Tibetan practice of ambling instead of galloping their horses.

Two ridges of mountains ran from west to north-east amidst the narrow defiles, in the middle of which lay our pathway, and after a few miles they end, and give place to two others of low altitudes which run parallel, enclosing a table-land in the middle dotted over with several hamlets and groves. We were met by several parties of traders and caravans of donkeys and yaks proceeding to Rhe. Lobssang, a native of Tang-lung, who had served me on my first journey from Tang-lung, recognized me at once, and saluted me by lowering his yellow felt turban (*bogto*), and with the honorific expression *chhyag pheb* (welcome); he talked with the Lama for a few minutes about the Ampa's row at Shiga-tse and the arrival of the two Shape. We asked him the current price in the town of barley-flour, meat, and forage. I was glad that Ugyen did not shew his fretfulness towards this good man. We then met a second caravan of donkeys from the north-east with tinkling of iron bells attached to their necks. We also passed some Gyagar Khamba (men who carry on a petty trade in Indian commodities from Darjeeling and Calcutta), who were proceeding to Darjeeling with a few laden sheep and dogs. The leafless trees of the *linka* (groves), and the occasional *chhortens* and piles of inscribed stones irregularly distributed at the foot of bluff spurs, were the only objects which we observed on the way. In one place some large, black cranes with white necks were feeding. Phurchung quietly took out my revolver from my saddle-bag, and approaching the half-frozen pool, fired a shot. At this all the cranes flew away, flapping their wings above our heads, not one being hit. I asked if he had a mind to eat the flesh of the *tungtung* (crane), and he replied that beggars *do* eat the same. There was a bright sun, whose rays were diffused on the mountain-tops, but the shades of steep cliffs over our winding pathway did not allow us to journey in the sunshine. At 9 A.M. we passed the village of Chhuta, and at 10 A.M. came to the village of Jong Luguri. The people here were engaged in selling forage, barley, and eggs. The laden yaks were tethered close to the court walls of the villagers. I passed them riding, and was received by the *Namo* Lobdon-puti and her husband, our acquaintances of 1879. Our hostess, after exchange of complements, spread a thick rug and placed two little dining-tables, and conducted me to a seat close to the window opening to the courtyard, where I sat reclining. Lobdon, knowing that we were fatigued, brought me a cup of good tea and a bowl of malt beer. I preferred taking the former with some parched barley and four boiled eggs. I quite appreciated the kindness of our hosts, and thanked them heartily. My other companions, too, were shewn suitable attention. The refreshments finished, we reloaded our ponies, and paying the *jaltse* or bill, and bestowing a reward on the host, we rode on towards Tashi-lhunpo. Two men stopped two fierce mastiffs which were barking furiously at us.

In the afternoon, at 4-30 P.M., we arrived at Tashi-lhunpo. Approching the western private entrance, in front of which there are two *chhortens*, one very large, with a gilt spire, and the other, though small, yet neatly constructed, and keeping the former to my left and the latter to the right, I arrived at the gate, where, dismounting from my pony, I reverentially entered the grand monastery. I mustered all my knowledge of Buddhist ceremonies and monkish etiquette, that I might not be criticised by the passing monks as one unacquainted with the duties of the wearers of the sacred costume. I walked slowly and with gravity, but secretly observing everything around me. There were a few yaks under the charge of three or four wildly dressed herdsmen, waiting lazily probably for the return of some of their number from within the monastery. Some monks, riding on mules, passed us from north to south. A few parties with heavy grain packages on their backs were entering the monastery along with us. The rays of the sun, now slanting on the gilded spires of houses and tombs in the monastery, presented a very magnificent view to the eye. Though the news of the minister's absence had somewhat damped my spirits, yet the pleasing thought of having been able to visit Tashi-lhunpo a second time cheered me up. The lane, about six feet broad, lined on either sides with lofty buildings, was well known to me, as well as the several houses that stood on its sides. The house of Dachan Tanga, in the court-yard of which a fierce mastiff was tied, and which howled at me from inside the closed doors, was most conspicuous in the row of buildings. At a distance of about 20 yards from it I met an old acquaintance, Machan, the head cook of the minister, who with his hands stretched, greeted me with the expression *Pandib La, Chhyag-phebnang*, "Pandit, Sir, welcome." I nodded pleasantly to him, and replied *La-yo*, "Sir, I am come." Then followed mutual exchange of compliments, after which he said that his holiness was absent from Tashi-lhunpo, having gone to Dong-tse, his native town. Conversing thus for a few minutes on the way, I was soon conducted to the gate of Thargod Chyi-khang, which the minister had selected for my residence till his return from Dong-tse, and Machan La, opening the huge padlock with a key about five inches long, flung the great door open. The building is a three-storied one; the ground floor, adjoining to which there were two stables, being used for godowns. The rooms on the first floor were spacious and neat, but very cold on account of the height of the roof and the want of sufficient sunlight. The third storey, though it looked snug, was exposed to the cold winds, which did not make it appear to me very comfortable. The doors of the several rooms were opened, and I was conducted to several of them to choose my accommodation.

Shortly after Phurchung and our Tang-lung grooms arrived, who unloaded the ponies and tied them to the stable, giving a handful of grass to each. The loneliness of the house, its nearness to the minister's residence, and above all its being situated in the vicinity of the western gate, gave it peculiar advantages, which seemed to me very essential for my comfort. When I was inspecting and deliberating on the comparative advantages of the several rooms, Machan left us without any ceremony, and there came in Nerpa La, the store-keeper of the minister, with a huge bundle of Tibet keys hanging down from his waistband. He too greeted us, but with an air of dignity which was evidently due to his position in the service of the minister. He recommended the rooms on the first floor for our residence, on the ground that they would be warm in the winter, when much air is not desirable. In fact these rooms were the best in the house, and on expressing our desire to occupy them, the Nerpa ordered the house furniture, consisting of about 200 books and a heap of printing blocks, boards, and tables, &c., to be removed to the adjoining *lha-khang* (chapel). When the rooms had been swept out and dusted, several thickly stuffed cushions were spread by the Nerpa's attendants, on which our carpets and rugs were spread. The Nerpa now begged me to be seated, and small tables being laid, and china cups placed upon them, tea was brought from the minister's kitchen and served us by the Machan. A few twisted biscuits and some pieces of mutton were given me with some barley flour. From a second pot tea, which was evidently inferior, was poured into the cups of our companions. They had only a kind of coarse barley flour to be eaten after moistening with tea. The Nerpa then informed us that the minister, anticipating our arrival, had left him instructions to accommodate us in the present house and to look to our wants. He also told us that if we did not feel comfortable here, we might write to him for granting us better accommodation, and he would forward our letter to Dong-tse. We were really delighted at the forethought of our only patron and friend, who had been so anxious for our safe arrival and accommodation. At the end of the conversation, when we were left alone, both Nerpa and Machan having retired, I consulted Ugyen about making presents to the servants of the minister and to our former acquaintances, because by doing so we would be better introduced to them than by mere exchange of compliments. Money being very scarce in Tibet, is valued above all other things, so that for the renewal of our former acquaintances we could do nothing better than make presents of silver coin and scarves. In the evening, after sunset, we returned visits to the Nerpa and his comrades, and presented them with coin, consisting of rupees, eight-anna and four-anna bits, according to their rank in the service of the minister. With difficulty could we persuade them to accept the presents, for they feared that the minister might take offence at their receiving money from me. I pressed them several times, and told them that I would be really sorry if they declined my presents, which were only meant to commemorate our second happy meeting: at last we induced them to put the silver in their pockets, which they did with great reluctance. The Nerpa said that the minister's commands to serve us were very clear; to be useful to us in any way was his and his comrades' duty. On account of the fatigues of the journey, which had told severely on my weak, weather-beaten constitution, I really became an object of anxiety to Phurchung and Ugyen; yet, having reached the much wished for destination, I felt that my troubles were at an end.

Phurchung now hastened to spread my blankets on the stuffed seats which were sent by the Nerpa for our use. I stretched myself on the bed. He tucked in the edges of the bedding to be sure that no chill might penetrate inside. Some tea was brought for me by Machan, but owing to extreme exhaustion I was disinclined to bring out my head from inside the heavy load of blankets that wrapped me; in fact I had no appetite or thirst, and so in a low voice I asked Phurchung to let me alone. I slept soundly till 7 A.M.

10th December.—In the morning Ugyen and Phurchung, who got up at daybreak, were busy making domestic arrangements and buying fuel, firewood, &c. After getting up from bed I called Phurchung, who helped me to put on my stockings and outer robe and girth. The Tang-lung men arrived, and begged for rewards. I thanked them for their obedience and readiness to help me when I required their help, and gave to each of them six coins of Tibetan currency, which pleased them greatly, as it was more than they expected. As they were not immediately starting for Tang-lung, I asked them to give me a call any time in the week, or before they left Shiga-tse. I also gave them each a few twisted Tibet biscuits to carry home for their children. After the night's sound sleep I found myself somewhat refreshed in the morning. I felt it a surprising novelty that I had now no journey to resume, so accustomed had I become to that as my first work in the morning. After washing I sat reclining on a cushion spread in the balcony of our house, facing the east, and with a good frontage lighted by the morning rays of the sun. Ugyen sat by me to make lists of purchases. Tea was served by Phurchung. We were now altogether three—myself, Ugyen, and Phurchung. The last being single-handed, the necessity of another servant was much felt, and we settled to engage a Tibetan to help Phurchung in fetching water and in blowing the hearth. The market-time of the Shiga-tse *thom* being between 11 A.M. and 1 P.M., we had no breakfast till noon, for our provisions were exhausted, and until fresh provisions were brought from the market we had to fast. Ugyen and Phurchung both went to the *thom* at 11 A.M. As soon as my companions reached the *thom*, they were surrounded by two parties of Rogyaba beggars, clamouring for alms. Finding Ugyen to be a man from Sikkim, with alternate threats and solicitations they succeeded in squeezing out some silver pieces from him. When one party was satisfied other parties made their appearance, to all of whom Ugyen distributed some silver pieces. He then witnessed an altercation between a woman selling salt and some *khamba* traders. One of the latter having bought five seers of salt from the former, paid a debased *tanka*, which the woman declined to accept, and asked him to pay in better coin or to return the salt. At this the *khamba* became furious, scattered the salt on the ground, and calling six or seven of his friends, was about to assault the poor woman. There were no policemen near to come to her help. After witnessing this short affray, in which the poor woman lost her salt and the savage *khambas* walked off without paying, Ugyen returned with his purchases, which consisted of butter, salt, mutton, barley-flour, *phing*, and a few Chinese cakes for me. In the afternoon, mutton curry and rice were cooked by Phurchung, on which I made a hearty repast. Ugyen then expressed his surprise and terror at the lawlessness of the people in the *thom*, their violence towards the helpless, and the want of police supervision. I smiled at his fears, and desired him to take a hearty breakfast. In the afternoon I sent a man to enquire if my old acquaintance Lob-ssang Tanzing was still at Tashi-lhunpo. My immediate neighbour was also one of my old acquaintances. In the evening, I called at the Phuntsho Khangsar and had some talk with the Nerpa, who told us that Kusho Tungchhen, the Minister's Secretary, would return to Tashi-lhunpo on the following afternoon. After a cup of tea I returned to my residence. Having very few out-door engagements, and not liking to go out of my residence either for a walk or for making *chhoikor*, I walked round the monastery like the other monks. I began to feel the acuteness of the cold, which now slowly increased in severity. Besides, the lattice shutters of my room not being papered, chill breezes rushed through them at night, which made my room freezing cold. However, being as it were, through Phurchung's kindness, hermetically packed in my bed with several blankets, I managed to sleep well.

11th December.—My slumber was deep and long, extending through the whole of the night, and when I was roused by Phurchung at 7 A.M., the sun was shining bright. Tea and some biscuits were put on my little dining-table with a cupful of *thugpa*, a broth-like preparation of barley-flour, radish, marrow, and minced mutton, with a little salt and dried milk. The butter being rancid, our tea was anything but good, so I preferred the *thugpa*. After breakfast Ugyen and Phurchung prepared themselves to start for the *thom*, and asked me if I had any particular purchase to order. I named books and manuscripts. My companions started for the *thom* at about 11 A.M., which was a little early for the market-time. On the way Ugyen met Chhoi-tashi, a Mongolian monk, whom during his stay at Darjeeling I had helped with food and money. The faithful Mongol had not forgotten my kindness. As soon as he saw Ugyen, clasping his arms round him, he led him to his residence inside the monastery. He was transported on hearing of my arrival, and begged Ugyen to furnish him with my address. Ugyen took the opportunity of enquiring of him the whereabouts of Lob-ssang Tanzing and others of my Mongolian friends.

Lob-ssang, he informed Uggen, having failed to pass the final examination for admission into the monastery, in which 120 pages of selected sacred texts are required to be repeated from memory without an omission or mistake, had been denied subsistence allowance, and his name struck off from the roll of the monks. In consequence of this failure he had been compelled to leave Tashi-lhunpo about four months ago for his native country, with an intention of visiting Lhasa on his way thither. Lately Chhoi-tashi had received a letter from him from Lhasa, announcing his intention to start for Mongolia. After drinking a few cups of tea, Ugyen managed to take leave of this friend, and went to the *thom*, where he was met by an old acquaintance of his, a Chinese head-constable, the head of the Shiga-tse police, who too showed much kindness to him. After his *ani* (mistress) had offered *chhang* and *gya-thug*, the Chinaman opened the talk with an account of the late row in which the junior Ampa was involved, how he was sent as messenger to Lhasa with letters to the senior Ampa, with what incredible swiftness he had ridden, how he had represented the story of the late disturbance to the Lhasan public, &c. As the senior Ampa, accompanied by Shape Rampa and Lhalu, had arrived to settle the disturbance, the head-constable thought his mission as special messenger was eminently successful. The Ampa and the Shape were now engaged in taking evidence from the parties involved in the row. On arriving at the *thom*, Ugyen heard of the compulsory currency of debased coin. The topic was in the mouth of all, that the Shape in consultation with the Ampa had decided to enforce the currency of all coin that had any trace of silver in them. It was also rumoured that the distinction made in Shiga-tse market regarding coin, as good and bad, was considered to be productive of much commercial inconvenience. For this reason they thought that by public notice the ruinous distinction should be forthwith removed. Formerly such a distinction existed at Lhasa, but lately it was removed by Government to the great convenience and satisfaction of the people. The same law, therefore, the Shape maintained, should apply to Shiga-tse. Secret orders were issued to arrest the few respectable monied men who might be found objecting to the general currency of coin in the market, and it was thought that matters could not be set right before a few instances had been so handled and punished. Being informed of this secret affair, Ugyen took precautions to avoid falling into any trouble by changing our Indian currency for Tibet *tanka* within the monastery. In the *thom* were also several parties of beggar-prisoners, each loaded with chains weighing 20lbs. or upwards. Some had their hands manacled, others their arms put into the pillory; not a few had their eyes put out, probably for having killed their teachers. As the Government never cares to feed these prisoners, they were let loose in the *thom* to beg their sustenance in the market. They were more troublesome than the Rogyabas, and poured forth curses and abuse on all who hesitated to give them alms, always persisting in their obstinate solicitations with loud and boisterous harangues. Our friend returned at 2 P.M. to a bad dinner which was prepared by Phurchung. He never was a good hand at cooking, and often forgot that we were no longer journeying, but being at ease in our residence we would be more particular about our dishes. Sometimes, disgusted with his slovenly habits, I used to go to the cookroom; but the suffocating smoke raised by the continual blowing of the goat-skin bellows would drive me out, so that Phurchung always remained master of the kitchen. After forcing down a wretched meal I sat to converse with Ugyen on the topics of the day, after which Ugyen shaved my head clean, myself shaving my beard. At 4 P.M. the water-carrier of Phuntsho-khangsar came to call Phurchung to accompany him to the well for fetching water, and told us that Kusho Tung-chhen, the Minister's Secretary, was arrived, and wanted to see me. I dressed myself in the Lama costume, and accompanied by Ugyen, carrying a few coins and some presentation scarves, proceeded towards Phuntsho-khangsar. Tung-chhen was seated in the *ni-hok*[1] on a Chinese cushion, and deeply engaged in drafting some letters, among which was one meant to be sent to Dong-tse. On being conducted to his presence, I presented him with a scarf and a couple of rupees. Ugyen followed me in paying him compliments, but produced only one rupee as a present. We received in return scarves of a superior quality, and were requested, after the Tibetan fashion, to seat ourselves by his side with a genuine air of cordiality and kind attention, which pleased me much. A raised, stuffed seat, covered with a China carpet, was spread for me, and a small table of a height suitable to my supposed rank placed in front to hold tea-cups. Plates of dried and boiled mutton, together with barley flour in wooden bowls, were placed on them. The attendant fetched handsome china cups from the Minister's shelves, and rubbed them with towels in my presence to shew that they were not dirty. I was requested to drink tea with "*Pandit, La sol-cha-she*" (Pandit, please to take tea), at which I raised the cup to my lips and drank *one-third* of the contents. Replacing it on the little table, I commenced replying to his queries with much gravity and cheerfulness. Neither Ugyen's table nor his seat was so high as mine, to show the difference of rank between us, and of the attention we each deserved. After an exchange of compliments and congratulations on Tung-chhen's part, we returned to our residence. Phurchung had lighted an oil-burner, the light of which flickered much, and kept muttering some of his favourite hymns of *Padma Jung-ne*. When I got to my bed-room he took off my

---

(1) Ni-hok is an open quadrangle on the roof of a house, enclosed on all sides by walls, and provided with two door-like openings in two of the walls.

boots and the big robe from my person, and packed me, as usual, in the folds of my heavy woollens.

12th *December*.—Tung-chhen sent a man to inform us that he would be sending a messenger to Dong-tse in the evening, and if we wished to send any letter to the Minister we had better prepare them before noon for despatch. We at once applied ourselves in drafting our letters, which was no easy business. The form of the paper, the margin to be left at the top and bottom, and the selection of complimentary words at the heading, had to be carefully looked to. We tried to make the Minister understand our position clearly, how sorry and disappointed we were in not having had the honour and delight of meeting him at Tashi-lhunpo, and how thankful we felt to him for his great kindness in arranging for our comforts and accommodation. We begged him, if possible, to return to the capital for the good of all living beings, as also of ourselves particularly, who depended solely on his mercy for the security of our lives. We also informed him of the arrival of the lithographic press so close to the Tibetan frontier as Lachan, where it was detained by the headman of Peepon village under instructions from the Jongpon of Khamba. Ugyen also addressed a letter to the Minister separately. The cover being well sealed and properly packed, I went to deliver them to Tung-chhen, who received me also this time with much kindness. He read me the contents of the letter he was addressing to the Minister, and in my presence dropped a few lines recommending his master to vouchsafe his sacred protection and mercy to us who had come thus far after encountering incredible hardships and risks. His language was eloquent, and we could perceive the difference between our poor attempt and his masterly style. Thanking him very much for his sincere kindness, and after emptying the cup of tea that was offered to me, I returned to my residence. Here I met Lupa Gyantsan, one of our former acquaintances, who was waiting for my return. I presented him with a rupee and some twisted biscuits. He had brought us some provisions and other necessaries, and assured us that as an old acquaintance he was bound to make our purchases, and to see that we were not cheated in the market. He seemed very obliging, and undertook to buy for us fuel and barley flour from the *thom*, and also to send us a good servant. After numerous expressions of *La la so* and *thug-je-chhe* (yes, Sir, great mercy), he left us. We then examined our account book to see what amount had been expended since we left Darjeeling. In the evening one of my respectable old acquaintances, Kusho Dechhang, hearing of my arrival at Tashi-lhunpo, sent for me to see him. Accordingly after sunset, dressed in good apparel, with a scarf and a couple of rupees in my hand, I visited him. He was delighted to see me, and rising up from his cushion he addressed me with a "*Chyag-pheb nanb chig,*" (accept my welcome.) I was then seated on a carpet-covered cushion next to his seat. At a short distance from my seat a rug was pointed out to Ugyen, on which he seated himself quietly. After an exchange of compliments and wishing of healths, I was requested to drink tea by the *solpon* (steward). Kusho Dechhang himself at the same time pressed me to taste the preparation of tea. After some delay and three or four pressing requests I lifted up the cup to my lips and emptied it of one-third of its contents. It is customary in Tibet not to drink more than one-third of a cup's contents at the first instance. To drink a smaller quantity would be a reflection on the cook or the host. As soon as I had placed the cup on the little table, the *solpon* poured a fresh supply from his silver *chhambim* (teapot). Kusho Dechhang then asked me about the present condition of Aryavarta and its government under the *Feng* (Europeans), the harvest and the general prosperity of the Indian people. Then came enquiries regarding the troubles I had encountered on the way, and how I succeeded in entering Tibet without being stopped at the frontier outposts. The conversation then turned to the Ampa's row and the probable punishment to be inflicted on the prisoners. These he conveyed to us in a very low voice, and wished us to maintain a profound secrecy about them. He asked me what things I had brought from India, and especially if I had brought any medicines which would be of benefit to himself, as he was suffering a little from cold and cough. I promised to give him medicines some other day, and rose to take my leave of him, thanking him very much for his kind remembrance of me. Again I was pressed to sit, and again promising to see him very frequently I took leave of him, and pouring the remainder of the contents of our cup into the *shalu* (slop-basin) as a sign of departure, I walked out.

13th *December*.—To-day at 12 A.M. a great number of men, about 15,000, assembled in the *thom* and its neighbourhood. All the alleys of Shiga-tse, the court-yard of Kesar Lhakhang, and the adjoining gardens were filled with men, all eagerly waiting to see the *tema* or *tamasha* of the arrival of the Kashmir Envoy with his guards and escort in military uniform. The confusion in the *thom* was great, every one trying to guess in some way or other the nationality of the approaching military party—the Envoy of the Maharaja of Kashmir with about 50 *sowars*, all in uniform, besides a hundred followers of various nationalities, all mounted on ponies, among whom could be distinguished a few Siks, Mahomedans with their flowing beards and white turbans, Ladakis in their clumsy lamb-skin dress, Murmis from Nepal, Dukpas from Chang, a few Nepalese and some Tibetans from Kirong. They were entering Shiga-tse from the west past the monastery of Tashi-lhunpo to encamp in the *maidan* near the *thom*. The vast number of spectators were struck with the appearance of the envoy and his escort, the richness of their uniforms, and above all the variety in their nationality and colour. When they approached the *thom*, men ran to the right and left to catch a good sight of them. The Kashmir Government, we were told, sends an envoy to Lhasa every three years with presents under the name of tribute to the grand Lama. In order to arrange for the safe transit of the envoy's party, the

Tibetan Government, on receiving due notice from the Kashmir Government, sends agents to the different towns and villages on the grand road to furnish the envoy's party with about 500 *Ta-oo*, relay of ponies or mules, and coolies for their transit from the boundary of Ladak to Lhasa. Although so great a number of relay of ponies and men is hardly necessary for the envoy, who only makes presents of precious things of small size, yet the party, taking advantage of the Government sanction, utilizes the ponies and coolies for the carriage of personal property or merchandise to or from Lhasa. There were several merchants dressed in a princely style, attended by servants in liveries of silk and laced cloth. Some of the ponies belonging to them were also richly adorned with ornaments of silver and gold brocade. The people in the *thom* remarked that all this splendour and ostentation was at the expense of the Government of Lhasa and to the ruin of the poor people of Tibet. The origin of this tribute from Kashmir to Lhasa is as follows:—After the conquest of Ladak, Balti, and Skardo, Zorwar Sing, the famous Sikh general of Maharaja Golab Sing, turned his arms against Rudok and Gar in the year 1840-41. These two provinces, which produce the richest wool, and contain the richest and most sacred monasteries of Tibet, were considered by the great Buddhist ruler of Tibet as his most valuable possession, and the Sikh general, by attempting their conquest, excited the wrath of the Lhasa Government, who, applying to their suzerain, the Emperor of China, brought more than ten thousand soldiers to the field. Zorwar Sing with five thousand men invaded Rudok and Gar, when the *Gorpan* (the Governor) fled to the interior of Chang Thang, leaving the fort and the country to fall into the invaders' hands without a struggle. A portion of the Sikh army were scattered over the country in detachments, and the general established his garrison in the vicinity of the sacred lake Mapham (Mansaravara). He sent one of his commanders to Purang near the Nepal frontier to watch the arrival of the Lhasan forces, and employed his gallant deputies to pillage and spread desecration into the holiest of Buddhist sanctuaries at Mapham and Kailas. The combined forces of Lhasa and China, amounting to upwards of 10,000 men, advanced towards Rudok and Gar under the leadership of a *Shape*. Zorwar Sing, whose contempt for the Tibetan soldiery was great, and who underrated the strength of the approaching force, sent first of all small detachments of his armies against the enemy; but these were all cut to pieces. At last he himself at the head of his gallant and veteran army advanced to encounter the Lhasan forces. The two armies fought for two days and nights without any decisive result; on the third day the Sikh general fell in battle, and victory was declared for the sacred Lamas. The defeat was complete, and the number of the slain immense on both sides. The victorious troops now threatened the conquest of Ladak, when the Maharaja sued for peace between his and the Lhasan Governments, and a treaty was concluded between the Agent of Maharaja Golab Sing and the Government of the Dalai Lama, of which one of the conditions was the payment of a tribute triennially.

At about one o'clock there arrived at the *thom* from the different leading thoroughfares of Shiga-tse, north, south, east, and west, several warders preceded by heralds, who announced to the public the punishment inflicted by the Ampa on the poor wretches who followed them. These unhappy prisoners were flogged as they were ignominiously paraded round the *thom*, and dragged mercilessly along, for they could hardly move, each having a large, wooden collar-board, 3 feet by 3½ feet, and 3½ inches thick, attached to his neck. The board is in two parts, each of which contains two half apertures. The half boards are screwed together so as to form a huge collar-frame, leaving the head and one of the hands visible above. A chain is attached to the board, by the other end of which the warder drags the prisoner. On the board are inscriptions in Tibetan and Chinese, giving an account of the nature of the crime and of the penalty inflicted on the prisoner. The poor wretches were ready to sink under the weight of the board, but this they were not allowed to do; whenever one attempted to sit down, the whip of his cruel warder served to keep him up. The men who were thus parading their broad collars were the ringleaders in the assault upon the junior Ampa. Not that they were ringleaders literally, but being the *tsho-pon*, or the circle headmen under Government, they were seized and punished for the conduct of the mob, which consisted mostly of men belonging to their circles. The two Chinese residents at Lhasa annually by turns inspect the Nepal-Tibet frontier in order to ascertain the discipline of the garrison at Tengi, and the state of the fortifications and military resources of the several frontier forts. As the task of inspection of the forts and army is most tedious and fatiguing owing to the desert-like condition of the greatest part of the Tibetan plateau in the vicinity of the Himalayas, the Ampas cast lots to ascertain who is to undertake the inspection tour. In the latter part of October it fell to the junior Ampa to go to Tengri and Shiga-tse. He started accordingly, accompanied by a *tsipon* (civil officer), named Kong-Chyang-lochan. The latter, an experienced officer, arranged, as usual, for the transit and conveyance of the Ampa and his retainers by sending *ngondo* (messengers) beforehand to the different stages and stations on the road. The Ampa selected the Changlam or the northern road *viâ* Toilung Tshorphu. Now, according to the prevailing custom, the Ampa's daily allowance is four *dochhe*, or 500 rupees, which is to come from the Tibetan treasury. But the Government of Lhasa, instead of paying the money from the Government treasury, raises it from the people at the time of the Ampa's tour, so that the duty of raising the Ampa's daily tour allowance naturally devolved on the Tsi-pon Kong Chyang-lochan. The junior Ampa on his arrival at Shiga-tse demanded six *dochhes*, or Rs. 750, instead of four as was the custom. The civil officer notified the demand of the Ampa to the *misser* between Shiga-tse and Tengri: on their refusal or inability to comply, extortion was resorted to; the headmen of the villages were flogged, and their ponies and properties sold to recover the daily allowance of the Ampa. On his return to Shiga-tse, the Ampa halted for several days, and required the people to pay charges at the rate of Rs. 750 per diem. This the Shiga-tse people were unable to bear. They complained that it was with much difficulty that they had paid up his allowance twice according to his arbitrary demands, which were in defiance of established custom; and that to compel them to pay his halting allowance at the rate of Rs. 750 per diem would drive them out of their homes. The Ampa was inexorable, and the soldiery busied themselves daily in torturing the poor subjects in various ways. The civil officer, tired of the Ampa's unprecedented tyranny, was anxious to resign his commission if he could. When, in spite of the various means of oppression day after day, money was not forthcoming, the Ampa began to treat him with harshness and insult. In the meantime the people combined in a body to resist the exaction, and with the connivance of the Jongpons, openly refused payment of the Ampa's unjust demands. The Ampa grew furious, and ordered his Chinese officers and soldiers to arrest the Jongpons, and to handcuff the civil officer for failing to realize the full amount of the allowance he had arbitrarily fixed. The soldiers returned unsuccessful, the Jongpons having absented themselves from the Jong, and were stoned on the way by the people. The Ampa then threatened to flog the Tsipon. On the second day, still finding that the money was not forthcoming, he suspected him of complicity with the people, and ordered him to be tied to a pillar of his house: about fifteen or sixteen cuts were inflicted on the hinder part of the Tsipon, when volleys of stones were flung towards the Ampa's residence, who was severely hurt before he could save himself by running into the interior of his house. The Dahpon of Shiga-tse, with the soldiers under his command, came to the Ampa's rescue, and saved him by timely intervention. The Ampa then sent some *sowars* with a special message to Lhasa to intimate the state of affairs at Shiga-tse. The senior Ampa, accompanied by two *Shapes*, viz. Sa Wang Rampa and Lhalu, forthwith started for Shiga-tse, and arrived there shortly before our arrival at Tashi-lhunpo. A commission was formed to investigate the matter, with the senior Ampa as president, and Shapes Rampa and Lhalu of Lhasa, Kyab Vying Chhenpo, the temporal minister of the Tashi Lama, and Chhumig Phogpon, the paymaster of the forces, as members. After hearing the preliminaries, charges were framed and evidence from witnesses on both sides was taken. The Commissioners delivered their judgment on the 12th December (yesterday). The Tibetans were found guilty of several grave offences, for which the following sentences were passed:—

I (1) That the two Jongpons of Shiga-tse be degraded to the fourth rank; to wear crystal buttons on their official hat; and to be debarred from wearing *mome* buttons, which is the privilege of officers of the 3rd class.

(2) That they be removed from their Jongponships, and be allowed to hold the minor office of Jong-ner under new Jongpons.

(3) That two hundred bamboo cuts be inflicted on the hinder parts and palms of each of the Jongpons after the Chinese fashion.

II. That the six Tshogpons, or village headmen, receive four hundred bamboo cuts on their hinder parts, and be sent to the distant jails of Rhe and Khamba Jong for a period of two months.

III. That the eight Ganbu, or aldermen, receive fifty cuts each, and wear the wooden collar for six months.

It being also proved that the junior Ampa did claim more allowance than usual, the Commissioners recommended that henceforth the Tibetan subjects be allowed immunity from paying allowances to the Ampas, and the rules regarding the transit arrangements of Ampa's party remain intact as before. For this, sanction would be asked from the Court of Pekin, which the senior Ampa undertook to obtain. In fact, there existed no order from the Imperial Court requiring the people to pay the Ampa's travelling and halting allowance; but by established custom and usage the subjects were bound to arrange for the conveyance of the Ampa's party when he left his head-quarter, Lhasa, to make a tour in the interior of the country. But at the instance of some shrewd and cunning Ampas the system of exacting travelling allowance from the people was insidiously introduced and got the sanction of time. The two *Shapes* of Lhasa, it is said, offered a bribe of 15 *dochhes*, amounting to Rs. 1,875, on behalf of the Government for a favourable report regarding the Tibetans, to free them from further payment of travelling allowances to the Ampa.

Such being the state of affairs in Tibet in respect of the Ampa, the Emperor's authority over the country seemed to be as great as ever, and rebellion against the authority of his representative a most unpardonable crime, which would meet with the severest punishment. The people, who waited only for an opportunity for a general rising against the authority of the Ampa, were cooled down by the beneficial policy of Sawang Rampa, which freed them from further payment of what was called the baneful Chinese tax (*Gya-thal*). The people seemed, however, to some extent indifferent to the proposal, which, they thought, was devised only to appease them. The sincerity of the Ampa's promises was also questioned by many. In the evening I saw Kusho Tung-chhen, with whom I conversed on different subjects, the principal among which was the justice shewn in the above question. He felt much curiosity to know what view I took of the matter. I observed that the sentences were rather savage and cruel, and that the Jongpons should not have been punished with 200 cuts each, their degradation being enough punishment for men of their exalted position; while the wooden collars and 400 cuts on the hinder parts of the headmen and the elders were simply inhuman. Kusho Tung-chhen added that other brutal punishments had been inflicted on the prisoners, the palms of the hands of the Jongpons having been stripped of flesh and skin. Among the six aldermen two were very rich, who begged the Ampa to let them go free on paying a heavy fine of Rs. 2,000 each, but the *mandarin* was inexorable. When half the number of stripes were gone through, they cried in the most pitiful manner, "oh, don't kill us; oh, don't kill us; have mercy and let us off: we will give all that we possess," but the inhuman executioners redoubled their fury on the prostrate prisoners. After emptying a few cups of savoury buttered tea I returned to my residence.

14th December.—In the morning Tung-chhen sent to me one of his acquaintances named Norpu Tondub La, a Donnger of Dong-tse, with a request that I should let him have some medicines, as he was suffering from acidity and indigestion. I had only a small box containing a dozen and a half medicines, which I kept for my own use. I therefore gave him to understand that the medicines were not intended for any except myself and the minister, whereupon he returned to Tung-chhen, and informed him of his discomfiture. Tung-chhen again sent a man to inform me that he would feel greatly obliged if I could remove his friend's illness. As any further refusal would offend Tung-chhen, I walked up to his house carrying the box myself. I opened the lid, and displayed the several bottles with their sparkling contents, Tung-chhen, his friends, and the menials all looking on with much amazement, while Norpu Tondub, at the very sight of the bottles, seemed to become certain of his recovery, and said he would pay as much money as I might ask. I replied that even then I could not let him have any medicine, as when those few bottles would be emptied no amount of money would enable me to get a fresh supply of medicines from India, since the passes were closed by the Government of Tibet. At this Tung-chhen looked anxious, but I opened the cork of one of the bottles, and called for a China cup: three or four persons ran to the kitchen, and brought me half a dozen cups, large and small. I weighed the medicine in my brass balance. The drams and scruples, which glittered like gold coins, perplexed them much, as they thought me to be a miracle-worker who used gold coin for weights. They were convinced that the weights were real gold, until I disabused them of their mistake. I now told them that the two separate medicines when mixed would "boil" (*i.e.* effervesce). The very announcement of this seized the spectators with a kind of dumb surprise, and made the patient tremble with fear; he looked towards Tung-chhen's face and towards heaven with anxiety, evidently repenting for having pressed me for medicine, and seemed anxious to escape from my hands. Tung-chhen too looked aghast; but the medicines were mixed, and to his mind they were too valuable to be thrown away; so having examined if the two mixtures were hot, and satisfied himself that they were not, he encouraged the patient, saying that I was a very great *amchi*, physician, and that he had no cause to apprehend danger from my hands. I told the patient on my part that he could depend on my words that I was not going to administer a poison to him. I then asked him to prepare himself to take the draught as soon as it frothed up. All waited with eager expectation to see the phenomenon, when lo! the mixture frothed up with a hissing noise, which made our patient shrink back! I then asked him to dip his finger in the frothing mixture, which he did, and found it to be cold; so uttering the mystic sentence "*om mani padme hum,*" he drank it, and pronounced it to be pleasant and refreshing. He then immediately put his hand in his great pocket next to the breast, and producing a scarf with a few coin approached me with profound veneration to present them to me. Laying the scarf on the ground before me, he addressed me thus "Great Amchi, accept this little token of my gratitude to you; although it is not worthy of your acceptance, yet considering that you are a pious man to whom money is no consideration, I venture to hope you will accept it." I declined the money with thanks, but at the request of Tung-chhen accepted the scarf. With looks of open-mouthed astonishment and feelings of endless admiration for the marvellous properties of the medicine and for the marvellous Amchi who cared not to accept money, the little circle of spectators now returned to their own houses and work.

In the *thom* there was a prevailing terror for the Chinese; every one talked of the severe punishment inflicted on the Jongpons and their colleagues. The Tibetans were struck with panic, seeing that the Ampa was bent on finding opportunities and pretences to inflict punishment on the people. They apprehended fresh dangers at the hands of the insolent Chinamen swaggering about the streets of Shiga-tse. In the *thom*, people who had come from a distance to sell their goods were packing them up unsold to return home. No provision could be had, no purchases could be made, and the great crowd in the *thom* seemed all to have come to make purchases while there were no goods nor sellers to be found. Ugyen met some grain-dealers whom he knew, and entreated them to sell him some rice; none of them would confess that he had any grain to sell. At last he met an old woman who formerly used to sell us rice. He accosted her, and asked if she would supply him. "Talk not about rice," she said whispering in his ears, "before the Chinamen, for as soon as I expose my rice for sale the Chinamen and their friends will surround me to take it away, after throwing some bad coin on my cloth: please come after an hour or two when these villains will have gone away, and you will get what you want." So he loitered about to while away the time, when he met a silversmith, an old acquaintance of his, who greeted him with much delight, and conducted him to his shop. Tea was soon prepared for him. and conversation went on after due exchange of the usual health compliments The silversmith was preparing some cups for the rollers of some wall pictures belonging to the Grand Lama. Very glad he was, he said, to meet an old friend after the lapse of a couple of years, and inquired if he had brought any *chhong* (merchandise). After a short stay at the silversmith's, Ugyen returned to the *thom* to make the necessary purchases. Just as he was measuring a rupee worth of rice, there appeared at one end of the *thom* the paymaster and captain of the militia with a few soldiers, whereupon the rice woman packed up and hastily disappeared. When this dignitary was out of sight, for he never meant to make any purchases at the *thom*, the frightened woman returned, and completed her sale. On one side of the *thom* there is a large *ssakhang*, or hotel, where Phurchung and Ugyen repaired to appease their hunger. When they were busy with their chop-sticks, there appeared the proprietor of the hotel, who is a nobleman of Tashi-lhunpo and chief of the Tondub Khang Sar family, and who now holds the post of Chhyanjov to the Tashi Lama. He asked whence Ugyen and his friend were come, and what *chhong* they had brought, and where they put up. Ugyen replied that he was a monk of Pema Yangtse monastery in Sikkim, and had come to Tashi-lhunpo on pilgrimage, and was staying at Phuntsho Khangsar. The lady, under whose immediate supervision the hotel was, was no less a person than the wife of this dignitary. Her manners were gentle and dignified, she talked to them in a very sweet and polite manner. Her head-dress was covered with innumerable strings of pearls which could not be estimated at less than Rs. 3,000 in value. Besides there were corals, rubies, and turquoises, and other precious stones of great value. Although she is one of the richest and noblest ladies of Tsang, besides being connected with the family from which the Tashi Lama has sprung, yet she did not feel it beneath her dignity to keep the daily accounts of the hotel or supervise and watch for hours the work of hotel servants.

15th December.—To-day, the 25th of the 10th lunar Tibetan month, is one of the holiest days of the Gelugpa Buddhist Church, being the day of Tsonkhapa's departure from mundane existence. The holiday is called *Gah-dan namchhoi*. In every chapel and in every temple new *torma* or painted water-like offerings of barley paste were prepared, the old *torma* being thrown away as useless. Late in the afternoon, the Mongolian monk who had been my guest at Darjeeling, and whom I had helped with money and clothes during his stay there, arrived to pay his respects to me. He presented me with a long scarf, expressed his gratitude and thanks in a touching manner, and apologised for his delay in seeing me. He then placed before me the carcass of a large sheep which he had brought from the *thom* as a present for me. This honest man had only a few day ago been released from jail where, during an incarceration of two months, he had been subjected to frequent whippings on mere suspicion of being implicated in a case of forgery. His tutor had been sentenced to three years' rigorous punishment, and removed to the jail attached to Khambajong. In the evening, after sunset, the monks of Tashi-lhunpo busied themselves in illuminating their chapels. Hundreds of lamp-burners fed with butter were tastefully placed in rows on the roof of every building in Tashi-lhunpo. The Tashi Lama's Government supplied butter to every house and to the cell of every resident monk to enable them to add to the illumination of the city. Tung-chhen sent butter to our house that we might light some of our lamps. I went on the roof of Phuntsho Khangsar to have a good sight of the illumination. The fantastic roofs of the four *ghyophigs* (tombs) of the Tashi Lamas were illuminated in the best style. The mitre-shaped Ganjeras, Gyal-tshan (spires), and the upturned corners of the temple-eaves had a beautiful effect, and resembled so many fully illuminated *tajiahs* in a *mohurum* procession in India. The grand monastery of Tashi-lhunpo being situated at the foot of the slope of a hill, presented a magnificent appearance. For an hour the illumination remained undisturbed, but after 7·30 P.M. the wind turned into a gale, and blew howling, extinguishing most of the lamps and sending me to my house shivering with cold.

To-day being a holiday for the monks of the reformed school, was taken advantage of by one of the newly incarnate Lamas of Tashi-lhunpo, who had just arrived from the province of Tu-kham in Eastern Kham, to get himself admitted into the Tu-kham-tshan order of monks. He had invited the Panchhen from Kun-khyab-ling, and to celebrate the occasion presented alms to 3,800 monks at the rate of one *tanka* each. Besides, he made large presents to the Grand Lama, his court, and the College of Incarnate Lamas. At about 8 A.M. his holiness the Panchhen arrived, being received with due honours by the monastery and the state officials. The road for a distance of 300 yards was lined with red broad-cloth and banners. Some old Lamas stood in a profoundly reverential attitude on both sides of the roads with divers sacred paraphernalia to receive the *chhyagwang*, while the Chinese trumpet, the melodious *gyaling*, and the resounding *tongchhen* (a huge Tibet trumpet) sang his praise. In the grand hall of worship, *Tsho khang*, he was seated on the altar as the president of the inaugural service. The incarnate boy, now admitted as novice-monk of Tashi-lhunpo, had gone through the usual course of moral discipline and study like ordinary monks. Within one year from the date of his admission, every monk is required to pass an examination in selections from the sacred books, of which 125 leaves are to be repeated from memory without a single mistake. Candidates coming from outside Tibet are generally allowed three years to prepare for their final admission, which gives them the privileges of a resident monk with an allowance for food. Any temporary monk failing to pass the final examination forfeits altogether his seat and allowance in the monastery. Once admitted in this way, the monk may rise by dint of industry and study to the several grades of Lama-hood. At about 10 A.M., morning, the service was over and the monks were seen going cheerfully to their respective cells, each carrying large plate-like cakes, treacle-sticks, and strings of beads. Phurchung and Ugyen, whom I had sent to the *thom* for books, returned at 2 P.M. with a large load of books. After dinner I sat on my rug to turn over the pages of different printed volumes, to see which would serve my purpose. In the afternoon the book-seller's son, a smart fellow, arrived to fetch the volumes I did not require. I talked to him about different books, regarding many of which he gave me accurate information. We engaged a new cook to work in the place of Phurchung, whom we now proposed to send to Khambajong to arrange for the conveyance of our lithographic press from Lachan to Khamba. Just before sunset I went to Tung-chhen's. He was right glad to see me, as there was a man arrived to beg some medicine from me, and to invite me to see a patient at Shiga-tse. When I asked who the patient was, Tung-chhen, after a smile, added that he was one of the two rich Tshagpons who were the other day punished by the Ampa with 400 stripes. The man was a devoted admirer and well-wisher of our friend the minister. He was in a precarious state of health from the brutal wounds inflicted on his hinder parts by the cruel Chinese executioner. Hearing of me as a great *amchi*, the dying man had asked if I could vouchsafe to him any hope of life. I was indeed sorry that my stock of medicines and medical appliances was so small, and therefore declined to go to Shiga-tse or to supply him with any medicines, although I was pressed to give some kind of drug. Tung-chhen now urged the necessity of not returning the man empty-handed, because then the patient would think that even the minister had forsaken him in his last moment. Being much pressed, I gave the bearer a small bit of alum to make a lotion of and to apply to the wound.

16th December.—Getting up from bed at 7 A.M., I spread two wool-stuffed mattresses on the third floor of our house, opened the shutters, and, basking in the sun, and sipping tea placed on my little table, began to turn the pages of one of the newly purchased books. The residents of the neighbouring houses peeped from their windows as if to observe my habits and manners. Henceforth I commenced to conduct myself like a good *gelong* (monk). Reading attentively, writing, and making notes was my chief business during the hours of the day. It was not my habit to chant *mantras* or hymns, or count beads. In the former I never became proficient and in the latter I could only separate one bead from another on the string in recurring numbers of one hundred and eight without any knowledge of the prayers meant to accompany that mechanical operation. The new cook was a sloven, although I promised him a reward for cleanliness. He never washed his face nor cleaned his teeth, and his mouth and clothes smelt offensively when he happened to talk to me. With much difficulty I succeeded in making Phurchung wash his clothes and person. Our usual breakfast consisted of one or two pieces of Tibet bread, a few cups of tea, and one or two cups of *jamthug*, or thin paste made of boiled barley flour, with mutton and dried milk. At 12 A.M. there was a large gathering of men between Tashi-lhunpo and Shiga-tse Jong (fort), and men and women dressed in holiday apparel were going to the scene. The monks from Tashi-lhunpo also assembled—some standing at a distance from the lay people and others mixing with them. There were several Chinese among the crowd. This was the occasion of the annual rope-dancing. A long rope was stretched from the top of the Jong to the foot of the lower castle bridge, a distance of 300 feet or upwards. The *thom* was deserted,—the sellers alone left in it to look after their goods. At about 2 P.M., from the midst of the expectant crowd there came out an athlete with a white scarf tied round his neck, who stood at the upper end of the rope near the *Jong*. With his face upwards, he invoked the gods; looking downwards he invoked the snakes of the nether world, raising his voice to its highest pitch, and at times shrieking in a terrific manner: then scattering flour on all sides he sang some repartee to which somebody from among the crowd at the foot of the *Jong* sang a suitably funny reply. The athlete thrice exchanged repartees before arriving at the lower end of the rope, when he finished off with a shriek.

In the evening I met Tung-chhen and talked to him about the conveyance of our packages from Lachan. If he had friends at Tondub Khangsar, the head of the family there having charge over Khambajong, there would be very little difficulty in procuring us a pass for the safe transit of our things to Tashi-lhunpo. Tung-chhen promised to do the needful on the following morning. Two of his friends were then sitting by him, one of whom was engaged in mincing a piece of boiled mutton. When I asked them what they meant to do with the mutton, they told me that Tung-chhen having a toothache caused by worms in the roots of his teeth, could only eat pounded or minced mutton. Tung-chhen shewed the cavities, which, according to him, were dug by *rhing-pa* or 'thread-shaped worms': he had killed several of these worms, he added, by inserting red-hot pins into the cavities. Tung-chhen read out of several books, and asked me if I understood him. Finding my pronunciation bad, he allowed me to follow him in reading one of the manuscripts for half an hour. He then wished me to call every day at his house, and to take lessons in reading from him. After thanking him for his kindness I returned to my residence.

17th December.—At about 10 A.M. a messenger arrived with a letter from the minister, in which both I and Ugyen were kindly asked to proceed to Dong-tse to enjoy the scenery of the place. The Minister was unable to return to Tashi-lhunpo agreeably to our solicitation on account of the pressing request of the Chhyan-dso Kusho, his friend, to stay a few days more at Dong-tse. He would like to have us in his company at Dong-tse, where he was alone. There were other circumstances which prevented his leaving Dong-tse at an early date. He also mentioned that he had already instructed his Chhyan-dso to arrange for the despatch of a letter to Khambajong, directing the authorities there not to stop the lithographic press, &c., on their way to Tibet from Lachan. We were delighted to see that the Minister was impatient for the things, and had already issued orders to supply us with ponies and mules for our journey to Dong-tse, a distance of about 40 miles, and to look to our comforts on the way thither. I was impatient to start Phurchung for our things, but delay was caused by the officialism of Tondub Khang Sar. As the cold was daily increasing in intensity, I keenly felt the necessity of warmer suits of clothes. A pair of trousers and *kua-tsi*, or China coat, lined with lamb-skin were considered indispensable. My friends, both old and new, advised me to keep myself warm at any cost, and recommended lamb-skin suits. I accordingly sent Lupa Gyantsan and Ugyen to the *thom*, where they bought about 60 pieces of fine lamb-skins at a cost of Rs. 7-8. These appeared to have been obtained from very young lambs, which evidently had died from natural causes just after birth. The cost of a single piece of skin was not more than three to four annas; but as the lambs when alive would fetch double that price or more, it is not likely they had been killed for their skins. It is of course not unusual for the *dokpa* (shepherds) to kill ewes for the soft skins of their unborn lambs when these fetch a high price. The demand from China for this kind of lamb-skins is gradually now-a-days becoming inconsiderable, and the practice of killing ewes is becoming rare.

Our house, like all houses in Tibet, had no chimney, and as the ceiling was of very fine China satin, dung-fuel was objectionable. I therefore ordered coal to be burnt in earthen *jalang* or stoves. About a *maund* weight was bought at one rupee four annas. The earthen stove that was bought for the purpose was nicely made and very fine-looking. At about 12 A.M. a grand procession arrived from Dechan Phodang, preceded by flag-bearers and several cavaliers, to see which I immediately went to the roof of the minister's building, which commands an excellent view of the southern and western quarters. Arrived there, I was told by Tung-chhen that it was a holiday for the Chinese, being the anniversary of the present Emperor's accession to the throne, when all Chinamen and subjects of the Celestial Empire are required to offer him homage and to pray to heaven for his long life and prosperity. Within the monastery there exists an image of the Emperor of China, probably of Chhing-lung, to pay reverence to which the procession, headed by the Lhasa Shape, the senior Ampa, and Shape Bora of Tsang, were just marching on. The numerous Tibetan officials, dressed in their best gala apparel made of *kinkab* satin painted with the dragon of the Tartar period, and China satin of various colours and patterns, and riding on their richly equipped ponies, were marching solemnly and slowly towards the western gate of the monastery. The Chinese were conspicuous by their pig-tails and petticoats, and though very well dressed, were all black and of a villainous appearance, greatly contrasting with the respectable-looking Tibetan gentry, which forced me to think that they all were recruited from low class people of Western China. I was told by Tung-chhen that these Chinamen were also notorious for their dissipation and immorality in Tibet. I saw men carrying long boards of timber, about two feet square, containing the inscriptions of the Ampa's titles and diplomas and his appointment to supreme authority over the whole of Tibet. Those written in Chinese were carried by Chinamen, and those written in the language of Tibet by the Tibetans. The Shapes also rode, escorted by their body-guards on horseback. Of the three guards who escorted a Shape, two kept themselves on two sides and one marched in front; two grooms ran behind his charger holding its tail, and his advance was heralded by two men who warned the passers-by to be careful and to keep out of the way. This portion of the guard was employed the whole way to keep off the crowd with their whips, of which they made a liberal use. The house-tops of the monastery were crowded, and the walls, staircases, and the *labding* (a walled accommodation for travellers) were thronged with spectators. The party consisted of about 300 dignitaries and gentlemen of the provinces of U and Tsang, besides the followers and retinues of the Ampas. The Ampas' sedan chair was carried by eight Chinese soldiers, and the sedan bars and the net-like string framework were supported and held by about fifty Tibetan soldiers.

After paying homage at the sacred chapels and the tombs of the departed saints, the party came out of the monastery by the eastern gateway, and, headed by Shape Bora of Tsang, marched towards Kun-khyab across the *thom*. The flags, carried in tasteful array, were all of China silk, containing inscriptions in Chinese and Tibetan, those on the points of the lances of the guards being of brocade. They now marched in regular order, always keeping their rank and position. First marched the ordinary officers of the State, then followed the party of the Phogpon or paymaster, then the Chinese officials, followed by the Ampa carried in the state sedan chair. Throughout the march the Tibetans appeared to occupy a subordinate position, and the Chinese displayed their superiority in all possible ways. The crowd in the *thom*, though it apprehended a whipping any moment from the hands of the Chinese who ran on all sides, were not here beaten by the Ampa's guards. The junior Ampa was delighted at the sight of the prisoners under heavy chains, and groaning under the weight of the block collars on both sides of the road, as he followed the senior Ampa on horseback. His sedan chair was carried by the number of soldier-bearers usually allotted to such service. His retinue and followers resembled those of the senior Ampa, except that the latter had no prisoners to proclaim to the world his exploits with their loud wailings. After the junior Ampa marched the Shapes, followed by their respective retinues, their arrival being loudly proclaimed by the two heralds warning the passers-by to keep at a respectful distance. The guards were all armed with Chinese matchlocks and long spears. Then followed the captains and lieutenants of the army with their escorts numbering one hundred, and their red and white flag-bearers. Behind these marched the yellow and black turbaned officers of Labrang and the Jong. The Ampas, we were told, were received by his holiness the Panchhen with due honours, and they paid him the reverence due to his exalted position and holy character. In the evening I saw Tung-chhen, who gave me a very valuable manuscript, giving a general description of the world, which I carried with me to my house to read.

18th December.—Tung-chhen sent one of his store-keepers, named Tshering Tashi, to Tondub-khangsar to arrange for the *lamyig*, that we might send Phurchung to Khambajong and Lachan to bring our heavy luggage. Had not Tung-chhen favoured us with several blankets, rugs, and mattresses, we would surely have suffered much from cold which increased in intensity as the winter advanced. The water that my servants used to throw on the roof and the court was generally congealed after a few minutes' exposure either by day or night, and in the lanes the urine of the ponies and the drain-water used to get congealed. So fast did the urine stick to the ground that the scavengers could hardly scrape it up. Once Phurchung brought some eggs which we kept in one of the outer niches of our house. These were frozen as hard as stone when taken out to boil next morning The tailor came in the morning, and commenced his work at 7 A.M. We kept ready for him a kettle of tea on an earthen stove. A cup, a few pieces of boiled mutton, and a wooden bowl filled with barley flour always remained before him for his refreshment. He busily plied his needle, and every one or two hours moistened his mouth with draughts of tea. Thrice in the day he took his meals. His breakfast consisted of mutton, barley flour, and tea. At noon we gave him a dish of rice and mutton curry, on which he made a hearty repast. At 6 P.M., after taking a few balls of barley paste, he put on his yellow *bakto* (Tibetan turban), and making a low salute walked off briskly towards Tashi Gyan-tsa. I was really pleased with his steady working habits, which had already earned him the proud title of Uje-Chhenpo, 'the head craftsman,' and a rate of wages at one *tanka* a day, exclusive of food.

19th December.—In the morning I sent Ugyen to press Tung-chhen to send for the *lamyig* as early as possible. Tshering Tashi was again sent on that mission. The delay to obtain it was occasioned by Tung chhen's not paying any gratification to the clerks and to the authorities in whose immediate charge Khambajong was, and who expected some consideration from us. They made unnecessary delays, and kept our messenger frequently running to and fro between Tashi-lhunpo and Tondub Khangsar. Disgusted with this conduct, Tung-chhen requested one of his respectable acquaintances to exercise his influence to obtain us the *lamyig*, so our messenger, accompanied by this friend of his, was sent back for the *lamyig*. I sent Ugyen and Phurchung to the *thom* to make some purchases for our journey to Dong-tse. They went at the usual hour, and found a great increase in the number of Chinese present, who were fully one half of the Tibetans assembled there. This was probably owing to the gathering of the Chinese to make purchases for their journey to Lhasa. The senior Ampa started to-day for Lhasa *viâ* Gyan-tse and Nangar-tse-jong. His numerous retinue and guards were furnished with ponies both for riding and for loads. Almost all the ponies belonging to the residents of Shiga-tse were employed for the conveyance of the Ampa and his party. The junior Ampa and the Shapes of Lhasa could not be started for want of sufficient conveyances, so that, after reaching the senior Ampa to Gyan-tse, the local authorities in charge of the *Ta-oo*, or *dâk* business, had to arrange for the transit of the parties of the junior Ampa and the Shapes. At this time the Chinese proved themselves very intolerable and haughty. They strolled in parties in the *thom*, and carried away the best of everything by paying, if they paid at all, a nominal price for the goods. Unable to bear this, the sellers had packed up their things and gone away, so that no rice, mutton, oil, or butter could be had in the *thom*. Travellers from other parts of Tibet found much difficulty in riding to the *thom*, for there the *Ta-oo* officers were in constant search of ponies to employ for the Ampa's service. Whenever they got a pony they seized it at once and sent it laden to Gyan-tse. Ugyen and Phurchung returned without making purchases. They bought some mutton and rice from within the monastery, so that we now learnt that good things could be had there at a comparatively cheap price.

20th December.—Before I got up from bed, our tailor, ever punctual to his time, had arrived. I felt rather ashamed of having slept so late in the morning, because it is unusual for religious persons, specially monks, to keep in bed after dawn, and feared he might entertain doubts about my sacred character. The chanting of sacred *mantras* in the morning, after the manner of the Tibetan monks, did not form a particular part of my day's business, and in fact, as I had not the skill to utter the mystic hymns in the peculiar intonation of the monks, I always refrained from attempting to show my inefficiency in the sacred recital. After taking a few cups of tea I went to Kusho Tung-chhen, and negotiating for an hour for the issuing of the *lamyig*, returned to my solitary room to engage myself in the reading and writing of the task of the day. Lately I had got a fresh supply of books and hymns, the composition of the second Dalai Lama, from the Lhasan booksellers. To-day there arrived five men from Gyan-tse, whose arrival was at once detected by the Rogyabas, for these pests of beggars always remain on the look out for new-comers, whom they at once surround with clamorous solicitations for alms. Few men can escape from their hands without paying them something. These Gyan-tse men, as soon as they arrived, were at once surrounded by some hungry Rogyabas, while others set off to inform the rest of the fraternity of the new arrivals. Their business resembled that of the vultures, whose name they bear, (*ro* in Tibetan means a corpse and *gyo* a vulture; hence *Rogyabas*, 'the vultures of corpses,') except that strictly speaking they are the vultures of the living. The new-comers from Gyan-tse brought the news about the fresh orders of the Lhasan Government to stop strictly the egress or ingress of traders at the frontier passes. The two Jongpons of Phagri were very busy with the work of stopping travellers and traders on their way from and to Tibet. Not one man is said to have till then succeeded in going to Darjeeling. Some Bhutanese traders on their way towards Lhasa were stopped by the Jongpon of Phagri. But a second party, consisting of a large number of Bhutanese, proceeded towards Lhasa, setting the authority of the Jongpons at defiance. The Bhutan Government does not like such interference on the part of the Tibetans in trade matters. According to them, it was against custom and practice to stop communication with the border people who have been trading with Tibet from ancient times. The Bhutanese would not listen to any representation on the part of the Jongpons, and resorted to force to make their way to Lhasa. Failing once or twice to stop them, the Jongpon of Phagri sent armed men to stop the Bhutanese, whom no ordinary resistence or show of power could intimidate. Some weak parties were stopped and turned back, after which it was said the Jongpons succeeded in enforcing their orders on travellers of all races. There was now a busy concourse of men between Dechan Phodang and Shiga-tse. The senior Ampas resided in the former and the junior Ampa in the latter. The constant running of ponies, monks, and officials on horseback to and fro occupied a portion of my attention, as everything could be seen from the window of my study-room.

21st December.—To-day is one of the holiest days of the month, being the new moon, or *namgang*, 'full night.' Offerings and oblations were made at the different tombs and chapels by the monks. The conch-shells were blown at their utmost pitch to call the monks to join in the service. Everything on all sides seemed religious and monastic. From the break of day to one hour after sunset a large number of men and women made the *chhaik* (circumambulation of the monastery). Some carried strings of beads in their hands, others the *mani* prayer wheel, keeping them in constant motion to the ever-recurring recital of the mystic syllables, "Om mani padme hum," and thus walked round and round the monastery several times in the day. Early in the morning the Nepali Buddhists circumambulated the grand monastery, beating their cymbals and chanting Sanskrit *mantras* loudly. After 10 A.M. a pious scene to the east of the monastery engrossed our attention. Between the *mandang* of the *thom* and the eastern gateway of the monastery the entire place was thronged with beggars. The streets and lanes were all filled with ragged men and women. In the middle of this anxious crowd was the well known Lhagpa Tshering now busily engaged in distributing alms to the beggars who were real objects of pity. Among them there were many from Amdo and Kham, whose eyes had been pulled out of the sockets for high crimes, such as the murdering of Lamas and spiritual guides; some were quite crippled or walked with the help of crutches; some in heavy chains, drawn on wheel-barrows; some maimed, some dumb and deaf, some still bearing traces of torture, some with knees and joints pinned down; so that the entire crowd consisted of a sickening mass of misery and pain. To these poor people the pious Lhagpa distributed alms at the rate of one anna each. He has been distributing alms in this way at every new moon without interruption for the last ten years. The circumstance which led this worthy man to undertake giving alms to the indigent is very remarkable and instructive. Formerly Lhagpa was a silversmith by profession, who by patient work and industry amassed considerable wealth and started business as a jeweller and banker. For several years he had been carrying on this business with profit. His shop, which was rich with goods from Western China, besides pearls, corals, turquoises, and jade, was resorted to by all the great men of the country. He had become celebrated for his liberal donations to the monastery of Tashi-lhunpo, and the annual expenses he made to feed the monks of that great congregation. About ten years ago, there lived a very learned and pious Lama by the name of Chyab Tan Lama in the district of Shang. The purity of his life, the sanctity of his morals, and his vast learning made him adored by all classes of men in Tsang. The jeweller Lhagpa, believing that he would derive a hundred times more profit from his trade if he made offerings to this holy personage, once went to Shang, and begged to be permitted to present him Rs. 1,250, besides numerous other things of value. When he approached him with the presents, the sage replied, "O merchant, not a fraction of these valuable things and money is the results of your honest earning; take them back to your house, and do what you choose with them; I require them not, for they are undoubtedly the property of a sinner who has deceived many a good and honest person. You had been in your former birth a great sinner, and in your future existence you are sure to be born as a crocodile." So saying the Lama returned him the presents and dismissed the astonished merchant from his presence. Struck with horror at the idea of being born a crocodile in his next existence, and also with the Lama's absolute contempt for wealth, Lhagpa on the following morning, with his palms joined reverentially, approached the sage, and begged to be allowed to know how he could avoid this dreadful fate. "Oh sage! I entreat thee to enlighten me by thy divine knowledge how I may hope to obtain a higher life than that of a crocodile. Tell me what acts of piety, what acts of charity, will make me a man in my next existence, and afford me immunity from a sea-monster's life. I shall devotedly follow thy advice. Vouchsafe thy mercy to me." To this prayer that day the sage made no reply. Next day Lhagpa again approached him in a humbled and abject state of mind. "*Thug-jechhe* (great mercy), oh Lama!" said he, "shew me the means of my deliverance from a sea-monster's existence." The Lama then consulting his transparent mirror of divine knowledge added, "Know that henceforth if you give alms to the poor and helpless of whatever rank, creed, or country they may be, on every new moon annually without interruption till your death, you will surely get immense wealth as well as immunity from the horrible state of being a crocodile in your next life. There are no other means to save you." He again declined what was offered him as presents that day. From that date Lhagpa commenced the practice of almsgiving to the poor and helpless on every new moon. The sacred Lama died a few years ago. Lhagpa himself gave out this anecdote of his interview with him, and it is known to almost everybody in Tsang.

Lhagpa's example has produced a wholesome influence on the merchants of Kham, who now shew some hesitation in cheating. A Buddhist trader generally, when he cheats others, thinks that the amount thus gained was due to him in a former existence. This is a dangerous principle.

Close to the cemetery of Shiga-tse, called *Kega-tshal*, is the graveyard of the Chinese. There were about three hundred tombs of varying size and very rude construction, indicating the poverty and low rank of those whose remains they mark. They seemed, owing to the uniformity of their make, to have been designed after some prescribed model different from the Indian *chaits*, probably constructed in obedience to some recognized funeral rules of China. They all were in the form of half-oval flat domes, generally three feet by six feet. There were no inscriptions on them, although it is customary in China to put inscriptions containing the names, titles, dates of birth and death of the deceased on a slab of stone cut in the shape of a tortoiseshell. At a short distance from the graveyard is the parade ground, about half a mile square, called *jah-hu-tang*, or in Chinese *ta-thag*, whence was often heard a distant booming sound. To it is attached a walled enclosure, in the centre of which is a large house used by the Ampa for target shooting with arrows and bullets. On four sides are some high towers, generally used by the drum-beaters and trumpet-blowers. Here to-day all the headmen (*ganbu*) of the towns and villages of Tsang were assembled in order to muster the porters and pack ponies. At present about three hundred ponies were ready for service. One of the *ganbus* being asked the reason of the gathering, said that the Ampa had issued orders to collect all the ponies that could be found in Tsang, no matter whether they belonged to subjects, merchants, or pilgrims. The assembled headmen here conferred on the best mode of starting the Ampa's followers, and how many servants should go after them to take charge of the ponies at the relay stations, and at last decided that one man for every pony would be sufficient. They all reviled the Ampa in their own language, and cursed him for his late cruel treatment of the Tibetan officials. In the afternoon I sent for a copyist, and Gya-tsho brought Khamba Tungyig, one of the best writers in the monastery. He belongs to the province of Kham, has large projecting eyeballs and an intelligent countenance, is about 45 years old, and talks in his native dialect of Kham. He addressed me '*kugo*,' instead of '*kusho*,' whence I guessed that "*sh*" is either not easily pronounced by the Kham people, or that *kugo* was the equivalent of *kusho* in Kham. (It is remarkable that a similar difference or peculiarity in pronunciation holds also in India, where "*sh*" is generally pronounced as "*kh*" in Behar, the North-West Provinces, and Western India; for instead of pronouncing *rishi* they will pronounce it *rikhi*, and so on). Khamba Tungyig said he could furnish me with rare books. He agreed to copy the book "*Dsamling gya-she*" and the General Account of the World, which Tung-chhen had kindly lent me to read. In the evening Tung-chhen sent all his ponies and mules to be confined in the stables attached to our house, that they might not be seen by the Ampa's spies. Other parties also shut up their ponies in their houses for the same purpose.

22nd December—To-day, at 9 A.M., the junior Ampa with a retenue of 300 men on horseback left Shiga-tse for Lhasa. The owners of the relay ponies also followed them on foot, keeping pace with the ponies. Those among the latter who lagged behind were whipped by the men on horseback, to the terror of the poor people, some of whom ran after their properties weeping; others falling back to some distance disappeared, abandoning their property rather than undergo this ill-treatment. By the order of the Commissioner the six Tshogpons who were awarded 400 cuts each were deported to the Jongs of Rhe and Khamba. Out of these one died on the way to Rhejong, and one was struggling between life and death. The deceased was much attached to our freind the Minister, as we could know from Tung-chhen's conversation. It was for this man that I had been asked to prescribe.

In the evening the Tang-lung man arrived. I made flattering remarks about their kindness towards me, and also made them understand my position at Tashi-lhunpo as having many influential friends and acquaintances. This I did that their fear of serving a foreigner from India might to some extent be diminished. I presented them with large, twisted biscuits besides rice, which gratified them very much. My accommodation and style of living, which to their eyes was grand, inspired them with much respect for me, and they seemed to repent not having recognized me ere long as a learned man from India. They now more frequently lolled their tongues with many a *Lala-so*, *thug je-chhe*, &c. I settled with them about the conveyance of my things from Lachan, they agreeing to my proposals provided I furnished them with a *lamyig* from the Jongpon of Khamba.

23rd December.—To-day Shape Lhalu with one hundred followers, all on horseback, left for Lhasa. The ponies and their owners, mercilessly treated and forced to serve without food, were, I heard, reduced to skeletons. This kind of enforced service is patiently borne by the people according to the custom of the country. The followers were required to take with them their own provisions as well as provender for their beasts. Having received but short notice, they were ill-prepared for the journey, but were, however, compelled to follow the Ampa and the Shape without provisions to a great distance from their homes.

The *thom* to-day received a large supply of pottery brought from the villages of Tanag and Lholing situated on the Tsang-po, a few miles north-west of Shiga-tse. In these places excellent clay for pottery is obtained, and the people carry on a profitable trade in earthenware with the surrounding districts. The Tanag pottery, which is considered very good and durable, has an extensive sale in Tibet as well as in the cis-Himalayan countries where untinned copper vessels are generally used as utensils; while the Sikkim and Darjeeling people use them universally in preference to cheap potteries manufactured by the Nepalese inhabiting the lower Himalayas. Different sorts of potteries were brought for sale, some so glazed and varnished that they could be favourably compared with China and European earthenware seen in the shops of Calcutta. There were a few very huge and heavy vessels meant for keeping wine or water, the largest of which could hardly be lifted by two porters. These were prepared at Lholing and brought to Shiga-tse *viâ* Tanag in hide boats (*ko-du*). The Tanag potteries are also conveyed up to the banks of the Tsang-po on donkeys, where they are transferred to hide boats. Here the boatmen take charge of them and deliver them at the Pathama ferry about four miles to the north-east of Shiga-tse. At this place there are about 200 families who raise good crops by cultivation. The alluvial soil on this side of the Tsang-po is considered very fertile. The people here also derive their subsistence from fishing and ferrying. The Pathama dealers bring their potteries to the Shiga-tse *thom* on donkeys, which plod on their way slowly ringing the large bells attached to their necks.

There were in the *thom* many *Dokpas* of the Chang province, very wildly dressed. The females wore apparel so heavy and fantastic that a new-comer might well be taken aback at the first view. From a distance these savages looked as if, with their costume, they wished to imitate the peacock's outspread plumes. There were so many pendants of glass beads, corals, ambers, and turquoises suspended from their head-dress, that one could hardly see their face.

To-day the tailor gave us our winter suits, consisting of a *kwa-tse* (China coat) and *pishu* (trousers). The lining of lamb-skin in all the new suits was pretty neatly executed. I was also furnished with a new *wahpa*, or fox-skin hat, made after the Lhasa fashion. Provided with these, I was well equipped for my journey to Dong-tse. In the evening Tshering Tashi brought us the *lamyig* from Tondub Khangsar, which was to remove objections on the part of any Khambajong authorities against our things being conveyed to Tashi-lhunpo. Although it is customary to issue the *lamyig* in open covers, yet the official of Tondub Khangsar enclosed it within a letter to the Jongpons of Khamba, and we were thus precluded from knowing its contents. We guessed that something evasive or unsatisfactory must have been communicated, probably orders to examine narrowly the packages. Tung-chhen did not entertain doubts about the sincerity of Tondub Khangsar, although we did.

24th December.—In the morning, after washing, I went upstairs to sit in the sun. Machhen brought tea, and placed the *chambim* (tea-pot) on the *jalang* (earthen stove) before me: shivering with cold I brought out my right hand, which was almost frozen, so that I could hardy hold the cup. The warmth of the cup somewhat restored the use of my fingers. I had emptied three or four cups when the manuscript copyist Tungyig Phurching arrived carrying a roll of blank papers, and lowering his hat saluted me, which I returned with "*Chhyag pheb nag chig*" (may it please you to come), extending my right hand towards him. The Khamba Tungyig arriving next, I half raised myself from my seat as a mark of respect for him, and seated him on my left-hand side on the same rug. After an exchange of compliments he opened his bundle of papers and shewed me an almanac which he was engaged in copying for the Minister. He begged to be excused for his inability to copy my manuscripts at present, and recommended Tungyig Phurching for the work. I counted the leaves of the *Dsam-lin-gyashe*, a treatise on the geography of the world according to the Tibetan system, and he agreed to copy the manuscripts at the rate of six leaves for a *tanka*, exclusive of the ink and paper, which I was required to supply. I poured some tea in a fresh cup, and pressed Khamba Tungyig to take it. Phurching brought out his wooden cup from his breast-pocket, which he filled several times before leaving me. My English inkpot seemed to be an object of great curiosity and admiration to him. He meekly asked if I could let him have one like it. As I could not part with it, I satisfied him with a few pen-holders and nibs. At the time of parting, Khamba Tungyig poured the remaining contents of the tea cup into the *shalug* (slop-basin), and took his leave wishing me, as is customary, a prosperous journey to Dong-tse. To-day news arrived of the death of Kusho Shanku, one of the victims of the Ampa's wrath. He was the richest of the six Tshopons who had been transported to the prisons at Rhe and Khamba. I saw several monks and laymen carrying from the monastery three huge caldrons of copper, about five feet in diameter, to the town of Shiga-tse. On asking what they were being taken for, we were told that they were being carried for boiling tea and *thugpa* (a preparation of barley flour, minced meat, and radish) for the entertainment of upwards of a thousand beggars in honour of the deceased. The caldrons belonged to the monastery, and were taken on loan for the occasion. During market time Ugyen went to his Palpo friend in Shiga-tse, and was welcomed very warmly. He was seated on a thick rug and served with tea. On being asked what kind of trade they were now-a-days carrying on in Tibet, the Palpo said, "Oh, Sir, trade is very dull now; our concerns are fast falling off. In former times the Nepalese (Palpo) traders used to make cent per cent profit, but now-a-days the introduction of Calcutta goods by shorter routes has seriously affected our trade. We suffer from a twofold disadvantage, viz. the expense of the carriage of our merchandise by a circuitous route *viâ* Katamundu, and the length of time in performing the tedious detour." The chat lasted for about an hour, during which the Palpo pressed Ugyen several times to take tea. He returned to the house after loading his stomach with several cups of egg soup and Chinese gruel at the neighbouring inn. About half an hour after his return one of Tung-chhen's men arrived to inform us of the arrangements made for our journey to Dong-tse. We were required to be ready to start with him for that place on the following morning, and were asked to see, if convenient, Tung-chhen in the afternoon, which we did at 3 P.M., when he handed over to me the pass to enable Phurchung to go to the Sikkim frontiers to bring our packages from Lachan. We were not required to carry many things with us, as our stay at Dong-tse would be very short. He therefore dissuaded Ugyen from hiring donkeys to carry our baggage, telling us that the Minister was expected to return to Tashi-lhunpo very soon. We then left him, pouring the residue of the tea into the *shalug*, and returned to our house. In the evening we busied ourselves in writing our letters for home, to be sent through Phurchung.

IV.—JOURNEY FROM TASHI-LHUNPO TO DONG-TSE, AND RESIDENCE THERE.

25th December.—We got up from bed early in the morning, finished our letters, and equipped Phurchung for his journey to the Sikkim frontier. After tea I sent Ugyen to the *thom* to purchase provisions for our own journey. A large quantity of *phing*, a piece of mutton, besides some vegetables, were bought. Having lately acquired a liking for *gya-thug* (Chinese egg gruel), I sent Phurchung to the *thom* to get some of it rolled for us. Two strong ponies, saddled, in charge of a groom, waited for us at the western *gyal-go* or gateway. Our traps and bags being made over to the charge of Tung-chhen's men, at 3 P.M. we left Tashi-lhunpo accompanied by Tung-chhen, and rode at a gentle trot towards the village of Tashi Gyan-tsa. Tung-chhen was dressed in his church raiment, and a silk-lined *chosha*, or clerical hat, covered his head. Arriving at Tashi Gyan-tsa, which is only three-quarters of a mile from Tashi-lhunpo, he put on a fox-skin hat lined with brown satin outside. There was a strong chill gale blowing from the south-west, which necessitated the use of our fox-skin hats and lamb-skin suits. Tung-chhen conversed with me about India and its sacred places. The view of Tashi-lhunpo from Tashi Gyan-tsa was very magnificent and picturesque. The four gilded tombs of the four preceding Tashi Lamas situated in the middle of the grand monastery glittered from afar, and the rays of the sun threw them into one blaze of fire. The approach to Tashi Gyan-tsa is made by a lane excavated as it were through a gentle slope. The village is situated on an eminence about 20 feet higher than the surrounding places. The lanes are irregular and filthy. The houses of the village were surrounded by walls enclosing generally a court in front, and painted with stripes of red, black, and blue clay. The *mandang*, situated on the left of the main road, was neatly constructed. The entire village is inhabited by the clerks, copyists, painters, and artizans of Tashi-lhunpo, most of whom get their allowance from Labrang. The houses were not mean in appearance. The *chhorten* which we passed on our left was new, and the images in relief were evidently recently painted. The *jo* was plentiful in the village. A few yaks with pack-saddles on their backs were being led off from the village by two tall, savage-looking men, dressed in goat-skin *bokhu*. The village elders (*gyanbu*) and old men and women were sitting at their porticoes, and glanced towards us as we passed. Though the village is three-quarters of a mile to the south of Tashi-lhunpo, yet it appeared to us that the latter was not more than 100 yards off from it. This was probably owing to the clearness of the atmosphere. At a distance of about 300 yards to the south of this village there is a *chhorten*, which appeared from a distance like an obtuse, conical mound of earth. A caravan of donkeys and yaks had halted here, probably for refreshment. We passed by the left of it without caring to know whose they were. The irrigation canals were all frozen, and even the moisture on the ground was so frozen that the encrusted soil was crushed like brittle glass under the hoofs of our ponies. We passed by Perongshavea, a group of hamlets, in the middle of which there was a little garden and a plantation of willows. Beyond this village we passed another village called Dekirabdan. At a distance of two miles from Tashi Gyan-tsa is the large village of Khara Tedong, the Chief of which is a Dahpon, the Commander Tedong, who was lately dismissed from his office at Gartoi near Rudok. The village seemed prosperous judging from the outward appearance of the houses. At a distance of nearly two miles from this we crossed the stream Numchhu, now almost dried up, which came down from the mountain lying to the north-west of Narthang along the plateau-like valley of Chhyugpu Shung. On our way to Numchhu we passed the villages of Sunapara and Sarsha, leaving Doring and Semaron on our right-hand side. To its east is the large village of Gyatsho Shar containing about a dozen hamlets in two or three groups. At 5 P.M. we arrived at the village of Chyang Chhu, which belongs to our friend the Minister, and is 400 yards from the Numchhu. There is a little garden to the east of the hamlet, where the Minister takes his autumn baths. In the southern corner of this garden stands a snug little house called *Lobding*, where the Minister spends a few days during the autumn holidays. As we were entering the village, Kusho Tung-chhen told us that this place was his *kyisa*, or birthplace, and he would conduct us to his own residence. At the gate were chained two big mastiffs with lower jaws hanging down. Two servants forthwith came out to help us in alighting from our ponies, and two stout men stopped the fierce mastiffs from jumping at us. A number of females and boys also assembled at the gate to see the new-comers. The headman of the village, Deba Shikha, received us, addressing me with "*Amchi La Chhyag-phendnang*" (Doctor, Sir, may it please you to come). He had at once recognized me, although I failed to do so till the following morning. We were conducted to the central room of the upper story by this gentleman, where two stuffed seats (*bu-dan*) were spread for us. The room, though spacious, was dark, dusty, and full of soot. There was a heap of yak-hair bags, resembling Indian *gunnies*, in one corner of the room. Our servant, Lhagpa-sring, after spreading my khamba rug on the stuffed seats, busied himself in fetching our bags and traps from the outer court. Deba Shikha presently arrived, and begged us to refresh ourselves with tea and *chhang*. Lhagpa, looking with peculiar eagerness towards the maid-servant who was pouring *chhang* in Ugyen's cup, winked at her to fill his cup from her bowl, but to his disappointment she turned to another direction. Another maid-servant came with a still larger bowl to pour wine in the cups of the menials. The housewife (Deba Shikha's wife) came out last, with a handsome, pretty jug in her hand, to pour wine in my cup, but I politely declined to accept the gift, and thanked her for her kindness. After a few minutes dinner was served in slightly-tinned copper dishes resembling salad bowls. The first course consisted of dried mutton and barley flour. My companions moistened barley flour with tea to make into paste balls for greater ease in swallowing. The second course consisted of minced mutton and *gyathug*. Deba waited upon us to shew us the attention due to a guest from a distant country. After dinner, at 6 P.M., Tung-chhen, who had taken his meal in a separate room, came to make the usual compliments to us, and asked if we were comfortable. He then conducted me to his mother's room, where the *jala* (earthen stove) was blazing. The fireside was glowing, and the ruddy faces of Damdul, the Deba's boy, and of his mother, who sat opposite to us near the fireside, enlivened the scene. Tung-chhen's mother, Angla, a venerable old lady who had seen upwards of eighty summers, and whose hair was all white, welcomed me with—"*Kusho Amchila chhyag pheb-nang*" (Doctor, may it please you to come). I humbly replied with a nod "*La yo*" (Madam, so it is). Then after a slight exchange of compliments I emptied a few cups of warm tea, warmly pressed by the housewife and the old lady, who every time I put down the cup on the table after a sip said "*La nang, la nang*" (Take sir, take sir). Kusho Tung-chhen, the Deba, and his wife now joined our fireside company, and shortly after the maid-servant, Dao Dolma, waited upon us, *chambim* (teapot) in hand. The old lady now made several inquiries respecting the sacred cities of Vajra Shana (Buddha Gaya), Varanasi, and Kapilavastu, and the condition of Buddhism in modern India. She sighed regretfully several times when I told her that the sacred places of the Buddhist were entirely in ruins in modern India. I then gave her a short history of ancient India and Tibet, which delighted the whole party, and Kusho Tung-chhen expressed himself highly pleased with my narration. Before taking leave of our kind host to go to bed, I presented Tung-chhen with a couple of rupees, and Angla with one rupee. They very reluctantly accepted the presents, saying that as it was their duty to please me, they would not deny me the pleasure of making kind presents to them. I was really delighted with the sincere and polite treatment accorded to me by the first respectable family I came across this time on my arrival in Tsang. After an exchange of thanks (*La-thug-je-chhe*), I took leave of the party at 9 P.M., and was conducted by Lhagpa to the bed spread for me in one corner of the room where we had taken our dinner. The Deba again came to see us, and finding my woollens rather light, fetched me two thick blankets with which my servant wrapped me up.

26th December.—The Deba has several milch *jomo* and cows yielding plenty of milk. A *jomo* yields four times the quantity of milk which a cow or a female yak gives. The *di* yak cow which pastures on mountain-tops, ordinarily yielding only two seers of milk a day, is not much valued for milk, although yak milk is considered both delicious and wholesome. The Tibetans always fix a high price on *jomo* on account of the quality and quantity of her milk. She is most useful, too, in husbandry. Our host has a dozen *jomo*, and the maid-servants belonging to the family were now engaged in milking and churning butter. They had got up from their beds probably at 4 P.M., and were busily employed in their respective duties for the day. After washing, I walked up and down in the courts and on the roof of the house for half an hour. The roof was uneven and badly beaten. In one corner of the central court of the Shika a big hound was tied with an iron chain. I saw some very old ewes and rams, judging from the length and the twist of horns which are supposed to indicate their age. These, I was told, were never slaughtered, being kept for breeding purposes. After tea I took a walk round the house, and was shewn the *lobding* (garden house) of the Minister from a distance. The village of Chyang Chhu belongs entirely to the Minister. Though from a distance it appears like one large house, it really contains a large cluster of houses with a court in front of each. It is vulgarly called Tog-tshang, or the *ant-hole*, on account of its being inhabited by a large number of serfs. Our breakfast consisted of boiled mutton, minced radish, and *pagthug*, or balls of barley flour cooked in broth made of dried mutton. At 10 A.M. we left Chyang Chhu Shika, mounting our ponies near the *mandang* which marks the entrance to the village. There are two hamlets adjoining the one we had just left; our way lay between them. To the south-west of Gyatsho Shar opens the table-land of Chhyugpu Shung, dotted with numerous hamlets all over its fertile area, with Lhena Jong as its chief town. At a distance of nearly two miles from Chyang Chhu is situated the village of Norgya Nang-pa with a group of hamlets surrounding it. A mile and a half to the east of Norgya, where the valley approaches the edge of the southern mountains, is the village of Kena, including within its boundaries about half a dozen hamlets. The houses of Kena are well built, and there were signs of prosperity in the large size of the houses and the tasteful appearance of the door-frames and the windows. The walls of most of the houses were painted with long blue and red stripes on the outer walls, these being the favourite colors with the people in Tibet. From Kena the mountains of Pankor-shor-nub, notorious as a stronghold of highwaymen, were clearly seen. Far to the east, on the other side of the Nyangchhu river, the village of Sangaling was also seen, though very faintly. At Kena an irrigation canal comes down from Nyangchhu, on which there is a culvert about 15 feet long, which we crossed. From this place our way lay across a barren plateau more than two miles broad, in the uplands of which were seen several villages, the most important of which contains the Shalu monastery. Near the mouth of the Shalu rivulet, a little above its junction with Nyangchhu, is the hamlet of Chhuta Chyangma with three or four dilapidated clay houses. This place was overgrown with thistle bushes and other prickly shrubs, and we were told the Grand Lama's camels were pastured here in winter. We met some Tibetans who were proceeding towards Tashi-lhunpo with donkeys. The Nyangchhu was divided here into several channels, and some cranes were picking a scanty subsistence from underneath the icy crusts of the stream. Going south-eastward for nearly two miles and a half from this place, we arrived at a fertile tract of land containing the villages of Panam-gang, Jorgya, Pishi, Penagang Do, and Natog, which, we were told, belonged to Hamdang Kham-tshen of Tashi-lhunpo. At Jorgya there is an irrigation canal cut from the Nyangchhu, and on its bank is a beautiful garden lined all round with poplars and willows and other shapely trees. The walks in the garden were tastefully laid out, and the central castle-like house, a neat two-storied building, was the most remarkable thing we had noticed since leaving Tashi-lhunpo. Jorgya is in the possession of the Jongpon of Phagri, who had stopped Sir Richard Temple near Chhumbi. In the middle of the principal lane of Jorgya there is a deep well about four or five feet in circumference on the top. A number of swarthy-looking women were engaged in lifting water from it with buckets made of the membrane of the stomach of sheep. From Panam-gang, Jorgya is nearly one mile. There is no regular road in this country. We alternately rode and walked owing to the frozen condition of the irrigation canal and the little rivulets which feed the Nyangchhu. Riding about five furlongs to the south-east, we arrived at Pishi Mani Lhakhang, situated in a grove of poplars and willows. The village of Pishi is famous in Tibet for the manufacture of the superior serge and broad-cloth called *unam*. It belongs to Deba Pishi, and contains a spacious orchard and several hamlets. The castle of Fishi appeared from a distance to be larger than the one we had seen at Jorgya. The Mani Lhakhang is a *chhorten*-like temple, with rows of drum-like prayer wheels constructed at the entrance. At a distance of about five furlongs to the east of Pishi Mani Lhakhang we passed by the village of Panam Doi, whence, after a ride of two miles, we arrived at the village of Taoogang. Here, observing a flock of lambs without a single ewe or ram among them, I asked Tung-chhen if it was not true that all the old sheep had been killed to supply the winter stock of meat. Tung-chhen, with a nod of his head, replied 'yes.' I added that the Tibetans, it seemed to me, raised a crop of live-stock annually. Riding a distance of above two miles eastward from Taoogang, we arrived at the village of Pa-tshal, whence we saw the castle of Pa-tshal gleaming from amidst a thick grove of poplar, about two furlongs to our north-east. The Mani Lhakhang by which we passed is now deserted, two old women who occupied a hut to the south of it being probably the only residents of the place. The willow stumps indicated some age, and their leafless condition would lead one to think they were dried up. We here met some men, leading yaks and laden donkeys, proceeding towards Shiga-tse. Two furlongs to the east of Mani Lhakhang we passed Tongtaipa, a hamlet where resided only three families of the Tongtai clan. Next we passed through another large village with 50 or 60 houses. The lane we passed along was six feet broad, lined with stone houses on two sides. The *mandang* which marks the entrance of this village is neatly constructed, and the deities in its niches had been recently painted. From this place the monastery of Belung is seen. Then proceeding about two and a half miles south-westward we arrived at the village of Penjang, containing a cluster of respectable looking houses with a small willow grove at its east corner. At half a mile to the south-west of Penjang we passed the village of Tagong, whence we obtained a view of the great monastery of Kahdong Gonpa, situated in the *Phug*, or uplands, on the right bank of Nyangchhu. We were now in the district of Panam, and the fort of Panam, situated on a hillock, was clearly seen. This tract of land is said to be very fertile, to which the number of clustering hamlets bore witness. The river Nyangchhu flows nearly a mile off. Northward from Tagong is a group of hamlets called Ssam-dopa, being in the neighbourhood of Panam *Ssampa* (bridge). The chief hamlet is called Chasang Norpo Khangsar, with fine buildings in the middle. From Tagong, proceeding southward for nearly a mile, we arrived at 3-30 P.M. at the village of Tashigang, which is situated on a barren, gravelly tract of land. There was not a blade of grass or a stump of a tree to be seen, and the village at once suggested to me the extreme poverty of its residents. We were to spend the night here. The lady of the house was a Tibetan of upwards of 60 years of age. There was a court in front of the house where we dismounted from our ponies. The servant of the house bustled out and led us to the top floor, where rugs were spread for us. The matron, Angputi, received us at the entrance of her house with much cordiality. Her *patug*, or head-dress, was studded with flawed turquoises and faded corals. She had worn it for nearly 20 years, and purposes to leave it as a legacy to her second son. In the ground-floor of her house she keeps her cows, *jomo*, and donkeys. A flight of stone steps led to the upper floor, where we followed her. The central room, which is supported by a couple of poplar pillars, was selected for our accommodation. It was open towards the south, and the wind rushed in from that quarter. Two thick, coarse rugs were spread for our reception, and two little tables laid in front. Shortly after we were seated, her daughter, a nun who had lately arrived on leave from her convent, brought us a kettle of tea and two wooden bowls of barley flour. Tung-chhen was accommodated in the room which the Minister uses on his way to and fro *viâ* Tashigang. It is furnished with several volumes of *Yum* scriptures, a small chapel, two dozens bells, oblation cups, some nice-looking tables, a sofa-like altar, a number of pictures, several curtains, and a silk canopy. The cushions, made of the finest fleece of Panam, were the most remarkable furniture of the house. Our servant, Lhakgpa, got out our China cups, and placed them before us. Ugyen sat on my left. I was offered *chhang* by the nun, who, on my refusal to take the same, with a smile withdrew to the kitchen. In Tibet a married woman is called *chhangma,* or 'wine companion,' a part of whose principal business is presenting wine to her friends and guests. It was to avoid this position that women generally enter a convent life. After taking a bowl of *chhang,* Lhakpa prepared tea for me, when I refreshed myself with several cups of the same. Angputi now brought us some boiled pieces of mutton, together with a portion of dried sheep carcass, some barley flour, and tea. This kind of present is generally made to guests under the name of *solchi,* or 'the first show' of attention from the host. After tea, our servant served us with rice and *gyathug*: the latter we had obtained from Shiga-tse bazar, but from pressure in the luggage box, the tape-like preparation of eggs and corn-flour stuck together and could not be boiled well. We prepared mutton curry with *phing* brought from the Shiga-tse bazar. I was a little fretful towards my servant for cooking our food badly that evening. Owing to the exposed nature of the house, it was intensely cold during the night.

27th December.—We resumed our journey at 9 A.M. after breakfast. On taking leave I presented Angputi with two *tankas*, and offering her our best thanks, we rode off towards Dong-tse. In the uplands above Tashigang we noticed four hamlets, the residents of which outwardly appeared to be better off than those of Tashigang. In these there were trees to be seen. Passing the Tashigang valley, we arrived at the north edge of the mountains bordering the Nyang valley on the left; here an irrigation canal is cut from the Nyangchhu, which fertilizes this part of the district. At a distance of two and a half miles towards the south-west, where the Nyangchhu washes the foot of the mountain, is a precipice called Ritong, where about 20 years ago two generals of Lhasa were assassinated by the usurper Gah-dan Gyahu. From Ritong a grand view of the fort of Panamjong, Gontai, Takar, Palri monastery, and other monasteries was obtained. At a distance of a few hundred yards from Ritong, the Nyangchhu again recedes towards the north-west, and its banks are here overgrown with furze, a kind of bramble, and other thorny plants, which are said to be very much liked by camels. Riding nearly two miles westward we came to a large village called Tsog-chi. This place was formerly the residence of several noted generals of Tibet. At present it is in the possession of one of the head Dung-khors (civil officers) of Lhasa. The castle appears very splendid and magnificent from a distance. Three furlongs off Tsog-chi is the village of Dukpanagpa, formerly a town of the Shamans called Nagpa, but now it is fallen in ruins, and contains about half a dozen families. At a distance of a mile and a half from this village we arrived at Norpa Khyung-dsin (Eagle's gem), formerly an important seat of the Karmapa Lamas. The ruins of the monastery on the hill top are seen from a distance, and the village, containing about 100 houses, is scattered along the foot and slopes of the eastern ledge of a range of hills. The irrigation canal, which brings a supply of water from the upland, was now frozen, and the village children, about a dozen in number, were engaged in sliding on the glassy surface of a broad frozen pool, so that we had to dismount from our ponies in order to cross it. In the neighbourhood of Norpa Khyung-dsin are the villages of Nembotong and Pangang. After a ride of two miles across a broad plateau extending east and west from Norpa Khyung-dsin, we arrived at the village of Thaimen, containing three huts, and surrounded by heaps of sand on all sides. A sluggish stream flowed from the upland, and the wind had formed the sandy surface into little waves. There was a large, old solitary poplar in front of the village. In the uplands, which are said to be very fertile, there are the villages of Phola and Wangdan. The former is the birthplace of King Miwang, and the latter is noted in Tibet for its carpet manufacture. At the head of the open valley, which opens between Norpa Khyung-dsin and Thaimen, is the foot of the Gingu La mountain, across which a track runs to Rhetoi or Upper Rhe near Eago. From Thaimen Gingu La bears almost due south. From Thaimen was also seen far off in the upland the fort of Darchhung-jong, at a bearing of 220° from Thaimen. Then following the river Nyang-chhu for a distance of two furlongs, our way turned southward, whence, riding a mile westward, we arrived at the village of Sharchhyog Añing, also called Isa.

Though the hamlets in this village are scattered, yet the abundance of poplar and willow groves makes it very respectable-looking when seen from a distance. Here we met one Daosring, a monk of Dong-tse monastery, who was sent by the Minister to fetch some religious books from Kahdong monastery near Panamjong. Daosring had a bundle of incense sticks on his back hanging down like a quiver. His tall and slender frame meagrely covered with torn raiment, his curious boots and head-dress, all evoked occasional smiles from us as he walked swiftly, keeping pace with our ponies. In the uphill side from Sharchhyog Añing we crossed many irrigating channels the waters of which were frozen, and passed by several hamlets the names of which I did not care to know. In the village of Teling, a mile and a half to the west of Sharchhyog Añing, we met several beggars clamouring for alms. Tungchhen told me that they were bad men, and would have waylaid us had we been alone. Proceeding three furlongs up, we arrived at the village of Dao-Targay, which contains six or seven families. Further up, at a distance of six furlongs, we passed the hamlet of Pangri with only three families. Proceeding three furlongs to the west of this place, we came to the village of Pishi, whence the way to Nesar is along a good road. Before reaching Nesar we encountered a rabid mastiff. Some travellers who had preceded us had disturbed it by throwing stones. When Ugyen saw it making towards us, he cut at it with his whip, when it turned towards our companions who were walking on foot. They threw stones at it and drove it off, but in running away it bit several donkeys that were grazing in the field. I begged Tung-chhen to be permitted to shoot it with my revolver. He smilingly stopped me, saying "no use." A few minutes after the dog again made its appearance across our way, and being again driven off, it rushed into a village and bit an old man. Nesar contains about 20 families, with a neatly-built temple in the middle and small towers on the hill overhanging it, dedicated to the *Mamos* or sylvan goddesses. The images of Chanrassig and Padma Sambhava were also painted on the walls of the Mani Lhakhang and the turrets on the hillside. The *mandang* at the entrance of the village is also filled with sculptured images. In the shadow of the *chhorten* a monk-traveller was taking rest when we passed by the village. We warned other travellers to be on their guard against the rabid dog, and slowly rode along the gravelly way. At a distance of nearly a mile and a half to the west of Nesar, we passed by the village of Tangtai Pao, with four families in it. Here we met four Khampas, each armed with a long sword-like knife, but carrying no other articles with them. Their mode of walking and appearance shewed that they were highwaymen. Their dress and features shewed them to be natives of Gyarong in Mar-kham in the eastern part of Tibet. At a distance of a little more than a mile, gleamed out the village of Riso with a beautiful grove of poplars and willows attached to it. Here our way turned to the rocky foot of the mountain, and the road henceforward was well beaten and frequented by large numbers of men. From here the hill on which the monastery of Dong-tse is situated is seen. Then riding south-westward for a mile and passing by two *chhorten*-like gateways, now in ruins, we arrived at the village of Khângma near Dekiling, the property of Deba Dong-tse, whence the town of Dong-tse is only one mile off. At half-past 5 P.M. we arrived at Dong-tse. The monastery is situated on the top of Dong-tse hill, which is about 300 feet higher than the flat of the town. This was of a rocky formation all over, with the exception of the eastern flank, where there is a sandy patch now laid out as a small garden. Climbing about 50 feet we came in front of a *chhorten*, keeping which to our right we ascended another flight of steps which took us to the front of a large niche containing painted images and frescoes of Chanrassig and Amitabha. This passed, a long flight of stone steps brought us to the gateway of the monastery: formerly it was walled all round, but now the walls were out of repairs and fallen down in many places. The grand congregation hall is a lofty structure; the walls high and well made. A little above the gateway, on a flight of neatly laid stone steps near the entrance of the grand temple, I was received by Shabdung, the Minister's page, who greeted me with a *chhyagphe nangchig*. I was conducted to the eastern room of the Minister's residence (which I was told was selected for our accommodation), where tea was immediately served. Before we had taken a couple of cups of tea each, a message arrived calling us to the Minister's presence, who was anxiously waiting to see us. With two scarves and a couple of rupees in our hands we proceeded to the drawing-room, and entering approached his holiness with profound salutations, when he touched our heads with his palms and gave back our scarves by tying them round our necks. His holiness graciously inquired after our health, and asked if we had not suffered great privations and hardships on the way. We gave a brief account of our troubles in the snows and also of the miraculous escape we had effected at Tashi-rabka. By the grace of the three holies, added I, we had overcome all difficulties, and now our delight was boundless in being able to present ourselves at his holiness' feet at last. The Minister expressed his regret at our sufferings, but was exceedingly glad that we had safely returned to his presence after an absence of three years: it was time for going to his prayers, but being very anxious to see us, he had sent for us at this unusual hour. He then ordered that proper attention might be paid to us in matters of food and accommodation. Large dishes of biscuits, bread, fruit and meat were placed before us, and tea was poured from his holiness' own *chambim* into our cups as a token of high respect. The Minister, before dismissing us from his presence, asked Kusho Tungchhen if proper arrangements had been made for the delivery of our packages from Lachen. The queries being answered, we were ordered to occupy the adjoining room to the south.

28th December.—Early in the morning Kusho Tung-chhen knocked at the door of our room, which, being opened, the cook Deba Machan made his appearance. Tung-chhen inquired after our health, and requested us to give orders for tea, breakfast, &c., to Deba Machan. After we had finished taking tea, Kah-chan Gopa called us to the Minister's presence, who very graciously inquired after our health and requested us to drink tea. We gave him a detailed account of the difficulties and privations we had encountered during the journey. After listening with attention, he observed: "Pandibla, I fail to understand the reason of your selecting such a dangerous route as Kanglachhen and Tashi-rabka. You had a passport with a road bill attached to it, to return to Tsang if you liked, and that should have helped you in your journey to this country. Did not the Khamba-jong people act according to the orders contained in the *lam-yig* last time?" We replied by saying we feared that difficulties might have been raised by the Sikkim Durbar at the instance of the Phodang Lama, who had lately created disturbances in Sikkim. The Minister expressed himself much interested in our successful journey across the lofty pass of Kanglachhen and our miraculous escape from Tashi-rabka. He again said that there was no necessity of our undertaking such a difficult and perilous journey across the jurisdiction of Tinki-jong while we had the Grand Lama's *lam-yig* to travel across the Lachen Pass, which was very easy and free from snow. After a short conversation he retired to his contemplation room. In the evening, accompanied by Kusho Tungchhen, we took a walk round the group of *chhortens* and *mandangs* situated to the south of the monastery buildings.

29th December.—After about nine in the morning we had an interview with the Minister in the *Nihog* under a spacious canopy pitched on the roof of the *Tsuglakhang*. His holiness told us that since our departure from Tibet he had composed two large volumes on the history of the philosophical schools of Tibet, which were now being stereotyped at the Namring monastery. He shewed us the manuscripts of the second volume, and read a part of it

30th December.—After breakfast, which consisted of preserved vegetables and gruel made of radish, barley, and dried minced mutton, Ugyen Gyatsho and I went downstairs to make *chhoi-jal* (obeisance to the deities). A bundle of incense sticks, two *tankas* worth of clarified butter, and about a dozen scarves, were all that we carried with us to present as offerings to the gods. After descending a strong but steep ladder of about a dozen steps, we reached the lobby of the *du-khang* (the congregation hall) of the Tsug-la-khang. The portico, which fronted the east, consisting of a row of timber posts, with capitals most fantastically carved and painted, was very picturesque to look at. The walls were painted in fresco. The four Dik-Rajas (the fabulous kings of the four quarters), dressed in all sorts of cumbrous, gaudy, and barbaric apparel, stood in most wrathful and hideous attitudes in the four corners of the portico. The images of the sixteen *Sathaviras* (sages), called the *Naten-Chudug*, all in relief, were gorgeously painted. I had seen many Buddhist and Brahmanic dieties in India, the remembrance of which forced me to think that the early Tibetan sculptors were very inferior to the Indians. The alto-relievo images were very badly and irregularly executed. There was no uniformity or symmetry in the projections from the ground on which the images were sculptured. The images, however, were thickly varnished, and the wall from a distance presented a very smooth and glossy appearance. The most remarkable thing in the building was the floor made of pebbles, nicely set and smoothly beaten to make a glossy surface. The "hall of congregation" is about twenty-five feet long north to south, and about twenty feet broad east to west. The deities were arranged to the south-west and north next to the wall, each seated on a beautifully carved wooden and metal dais. The principal images occupied chapel-like niches. Most of the images were of very ancient date, with numerous ornamental figures impressed on them, indicating much ingenuity on the part of the artists who had constructed them. On account of their being very old, the images at first sight appeared to be of brass, but on closer inspection I found they were of gilt copper, or what is called *ser-ssang* (gold copper). The images of the *Ñonthopa*, or the attendant disciples of Buddha, such as Sharipu Moungal kyi pu, were in standing postures On either side of Buddha half adozen *Ñonthopas* (sravakas) were standing in a very reverentially attentive attitude. The image of *Chyamba* (Maitreya Buddha) was in a standing posture holding a miniature *chhorten* tomb in his hand. Kusho Tung-chhen asked me if the images were beautiful, and informed us that the image of the Chovo (Lord) Buddha was constructed by a miraculous Indian Buddhist in imitation of the great image of Shákya Thuba at Lhasa. The founder of the monastery, Je Lha-tsun, once prayed that the gods might send him a skilful artist for helping him in the construction of images for his monastic shrine, and accordingly an Indian Buddhist visited Dong-tse, constructed the images, and returned to India Tung-chhen then smilingly asked if I was not an incarnation of that Indian Buddhist. I felt proud to hear of my countryman being so highly admired and venerated. Among the deities the following were most conspicuously placed—Jam-yang, Chhyag-na-dorje, Chan-rassig, Chyamba, Paldan Yishe, Shákya Simha, Paldan Atisha. At the entrance of the outer passage of the *du-khang* stood the image of Manlha (the god of medicine). Ugyen Gyatsho prostrated himself before every one of the images, and received benediction from them by touching with his head their feet or person. I also shewed a proper veneration for those sacred images by touching with my head their right hands as if receiving their *chhyag-wang* (benediction). My companions uttered *mantra* and made prayers to them, while I felt reverential gratitude to the Supreme Ruler alone whose merciful providence had brought me safe thus far.

The roof of the *du-khang* was supported by two rows of wooden pillars, on the artistically constructed capitals of which shields and quivers full of arrows were hung. These, I was told, were the armour of the Dharmapalas with which they protected Buddhism against the evil designs of demons and heretics. From the ceiling were hung rich China brocades embroidered in gold and silver and containing magnificently worked dragons Among the pictures the most interesting was that of the first Dalai Lama, Lossang Gya-tsho. In it he was portrayed as receiving the kingdom of Tibet from the Tartar conqueror Kushi Khan. The celebrated Desi Sangye seated on his left was evidently thanking the magnanimous and liberal conqueror for the munificent gift on behalf of his thrice holy liege. I was also shewn the dais which is reserved for the special use of the Minister. The chair on which the head Lama of the monastery sits during service was three feet high and placed opposite the Minister's seat at the top of the second row of seats. There was accommodation for about eighty monks in this hall of worship to read the sacred books or offer prayers to the all-merciful Buddhas. I was told that a religious service is daily held at this hall, when the majority of the monks attend. These monks get a pittance of 60lbs. of barley per head every month from the *Labrang-gsi* (church endowment property), which they grind into flour at their own cells and carry with them to the congregation hall in little bags. They get tea thrice during every service held in the congregation hall from the *Labrang-dso* (church store).

On my return from the *chhoi-jal* I was called to the Minister's presence, who was seated on a raised seat covered with satin, under the genial shade of a spacious canopy fixed on the roof of the third floor of Dong-tse Tsug-la khang (the chief temple). I was accommodated with a stuffed seat a foot high on his immediate left, and Gopa placed a cup of warm tea on a little table before me. After tea, twisted sugar-biscuits, prepared very cleanly, and several pieces of boiled mutton brought on a square wooden tray, were placed before me. Gopa then begged me to taste the barley-flour, meat and biscuits, but I only replied to his kindness with *La thug-je-chhe* (sir, great mercy). The Minister then, before raising his tea-cup to his lips, graciously asked me, *Pandibla solcha nang* (Pandit, take tea). I at once replied by drinking one-fourth of my cup as etiquette required, and every time he drank I also took a sip. He made several inquiries respecting the lithographic press and the various articles which I had sent him as presents and which were now at Tashi-lhunpo. After dinner, he shewed me the work he was writing on history, rhetoric, astrology and science. The last was most interesting, as it contained two chapters on chemistry and photography. The latter he had composed from the notes I had supplied him from Tassinder's Manual of Photography in 1879, and I was delighted to see the diagrams he had drawn to represent the different photographical apparatus I had left with him last time. He read a portion of his chapter on photography, and asked me if it was correct. He had rendered many chemical names into Tibetan, such as *nul-chhu* (silver-water) for nitrate of silver solution, *shal-thu* (face-wash) for "developer;" but as for collodion, iodizer, &c., he had found no names in the Tibetan vocabulary. He now wished me to help him in the accurate translation of these names. He then read to me an account of the theories of the Tirthikas (Brahmans) of ancient India, how they held obstinate controversies with the orthodox Buddhists, and how, finally, the followers of the Tathagata triumphed over their heretic rivals. I felt much interest in these accounts, and prolonged his narrations by asking pertinent questions at intervals and by expressing delight at the success of the Buddhists and wonder at the logic of the Tirthikas. While we were thus engaged in pleasant conversation, Shabdung, the page, came and informed the Minister that Dah-pon Phala and Kung Chyang-chan were about to arrive at Dong-tse. The former being the chief of Dong-tse, the monks of this monastery were bound to show him due respect. Accordingly, when the party was seen approaching the town by the road at the foot of the Chhoide hill, two monks in full dress sounded a pair of long copper hautboys. The Minister and I stood on the top of the fourth storey of Dong-tse Chhoide, whence we could see the foot of the hill very clearly. The party, consisting of a dozen gentlemen, all on horseback, was proceeding towards Dong-tse *phodang* (castle) at a gentle amble. The Dah-pon and his friend rode on two spirited mules gaudily dressed with brocades and tinsels, and were preceded by five *sowars*, and followed by an equal number, all carrying lances with banners at their points. When the party arrived at the foot of the hill of Dong-tse Chhoide, two other monks sounded a pair of *gyaling* (a clarionet-like instrument possessing a very pleasant and sonorous sound, while the hautboys were very disagreeable and hoarse. When they reached the *linga* (grove) situated in front of the castle, Chhyan-dso Kusho received them with his band, which consisted of a *gong* and a pair of tambourines. The Minister in course of conversation told me that of the four Dah-pons or commanders of forces in Tsang, two are ordinarily stationed at Shiga-tse, one at Gyan-tse and one at Tengri. It was past four in the afternoon when the party entered Dong-tse *Phodang*, and when the Minister also returned to his study. Coming to my room, Ugyen and I looked from our window towards Gyan-tse Jong, which glimmered in the eastern horizon. Ugyen told me it was eight miles from here, and could be reached in two hours. "If it is so near," said I, "I should like to take a trip to it."

31*st December*.—Rising early in the morning, I talked to Ugyen Gyatsho to arrange for a trip to Gyan-tse. He very properly observed that as we were just come to this country, it would not be wise on our part to shew ourselves in the *thom* (market) of Gyan-tse, which is frequented by Bhutia traders from Darjeeling and Phagri. At nine we were called to the Minister's presence, and, as usual, were presented with tea and biscuits.

After reading a few sentences in English from the Royal Reader No. I with him, I begged him to be permitted to make a request: it was if I could go to see the Pal-khor Chhoide of Gyan-tse. "If you like to visit Gyan-tse," said the Minister, "I will arrange for it; but you should bear in mind that the Gyan-tsepa (men of Gyan-tse) are not good men. They speak much, and are in the habit of spinning a great deal out of little. I will request Tung-chhen to take you up there." "Thank your holiness," said I humbly, joining the palms of my hands according to the custom of the country. Ugyen Gyatsho then respectfully asked if he could start that day for Gyan-tse to buy some blankets for me, as I had several times complained to him about the insufficiency of my woollens. "Yes, you can at once start for Gyan-tse; as for Pandib, I should like to send him with Tung-chhen," said his holiness. Ugyen Gyatsho left Dong-tse at 12 A.M., riding on one of Tung-chhen's ponies. On the road he met some of the muleteers of Deba-Dong-tse Phala who were proceeding to Lhasa with a supply of provisions (barley, butter and meat) for consumption at Bangye-shag, Phala's residence. Ugyen Gyatsho inquired from them the state of the road to Lhasa and the best time to make a journey to U. They told him that winter is the best time to go to Lhasa, when there are no rains and no inconvenience in fording streamlets and crossing the Tsang-po, and when, besides, provender is cheap, and meat and barley and wine are easily obtainable everywhere. Ugyen Gyatsho first went to the town in search of an old acquaintance of his, but he being reported to have died, he took quarters in the house of a layman to the south of Gyan-tse Jong.

1*st January* 1882.—To-day, after breakfast, I went to the Minister's presence and read with him one page of the English Primer. For about half an hour he practised writing the Roman characters on a wooden slate *(chyang-shing)* about two feet long and ten inches broad. A string was tied to it, at the further extremity of which hung a small cotton bag containing chalk-dust. After cleaning the slate with water, Gopa dried it in the sun. The Minister now gently rubbed the chalk bag on the slate, when a thin film of fine dust covered it. Then, with a steel pencil, about a foot long, he scratched letters upon it. Looking at this writing apparatus, I observed "Kusho Rinpo-chhe La" (your precious honour), "this is a rude and dirty contrivance. It soils the hand. In India we have very fine and neat slates, which easily fold like books and can be written upon with chalk pencils and the writing easily rubbed off." He smiled at me, and said "My *chyang-shing* is a nice one. Even the great ministers of China use these rude ones. Yes, they are not clean. If you could procure me one or two of your Indian slates from Calcutta, I should thank you very much." In the afternoon we conversed on religious matters, such as the difference of the Ningma and Sarma schools (old and new philosophical schools of Tibet).

At Gyan-tse, Ugyen Gyatsho visited the *thom* (market) at 10 A.M. According to his accounts both Gyan-tse and its *thom* are inferior to Shiga-tse in respect of wealth and commodities brought in there for sale. There were sellers of Calcutta goods and also of Chinese goods of very inferior quality. He saw about fifteen to twenty Nepalese shops and half a dozen pastry shops kept by a few Chinamen. The *thom* is the property of the Pal-khor Chhoide, the great monastery of Gyan-tse, and contributes largely to its maintenance. The monastic authorities also collect rents from the shops in the vicinity of the *thom* which do not belong to the Government or the *gerpas* (landholders). Barley sold at Gyan-tse was reported to be inferior to what was sold at Shiga-tse. *Chhang* (fermented malt liquor) was cheaper, but inferior in strength and quality. Ugyen Gyatsho saw there a larger supply of mutton and butter than in the Shiga-tse *thom*. This was owing to the nearness of *dok* lands (mountain pasture lands), where there are numerous yak herds and shepherds. On the whole, according to our friend's estimate, Gyan-tse is a poorer place than Shiga-tse. Its *thom* lasts only three hours, commencing at 10 A.M. and dissolving at 1 P.M. At Gyan-tse, for the first time, he saw women selling meat and dried carcasses of sheep and yak. At Shiga-tse women never take part with men in selling meat, &c. Some of these butcher-women had amassed much wealth by this profession, and wore rich head-dresses (*patug*) thickly studded with pearls, amber and turquoises.

On return to his lodging Ugyen made the acquaintance of a *dingpon* named Nima Tshering, also a lodger in the same house. He entertained him with *chhang*, and when he became very jolly over it, asked him, in course of conversation, about the military arrangements of Gyan-tse. The *dingpon* related that there were 500 Tibetan soldiers ordinarily stationed at Gyan-tse. This force was divided into two battalions under two *rupons*. Under each *rupon* there were two *gya-pons* (or captains) who commanded companies of 125 soldiers each. Under each *gya-pon* were four *dingpons* (or lieutenants), who headed twenty-five soldiers each. The *dah-pon* (commander) of these five hundred regular troops at Gyan-tse was Te-ding-pa, who had been lately recalled to Lhasa to explain his conduct in connection with a complaint preferred against him by the residents of Toi-gar near Rudok. Besides these regulars, there were others called *yul-mag* (or country soldiers). There is also a militia of fifty Chinese soldiers under a Chinese officer called *da-loye*. The troops both at Gyan-tse and Shiga-tse are under the inspection of the Paymaster (*phog-pon*) of Shiga-tse. Nima Tshering told Ugyen that the Tibetan soldiers are very poorly paid by the Government. The Emperor of China contributes only at the rate of five rupees per head per year, and the Government of Tibet pays them at the rate of 40lbs of barley per head a month, but no pay whatever, on the ground that they are furnished by the landholders at the rate of one soldier for every *kang* of land which yields a revenue of 55 *srangs*. The *dingpons* and *gya-pons* receive pay at the rate of 13 *srangs* and 25 *srangs* annually from the imperial treasury, but receive no larger grain allowance than the ordinary soldier from the Tibetan Government. As the Chinese soldiers have to serve in Tibet, a place far away from China, the Emperor has permitted them a family allowance of 6 *srangs* a month and 60lbs. of rice per head as subsistence allowance in Tibet, in addition to their monthly pay of 6 *srangs*, so that the Chinese soldiers are better off than the Tibetan soldiers. In the evening, Chhyan-dso Kusho informed the Minister that both the *dah-pon* and his friend the *tsi-pon* would call at his place to-morrow morning.

2nd January.—In the morning preparations were made to give a grand reception to the august guests. All the furniture of the rooms occupied by us and Gopa were replaced by choice furniture from the Minister's store-room. Silk ceilings and curtains were hung to give a gorgeous appearance to the waiting-room and lobby. Beautiful silk cushions were spread in the Minister's drawing-room, the ceiling of which glittered with orange-coloured China brocades. The artistically-worked dragon made its appearance everywhere—in the ceiling, the curtains, and even on the floor carpets. Handsome dining-tables, each measuring three feet by eighteen inches, and two feet high, were placed before every raised and cushioned seat. The Minister's seat, as usual, was placed in front of a gilt chapel three feet high; on the right hand side were placed the cushioned seats of the two guests, each about two feet high; to the left were placed two more cushions each about eighteen inches high, on which the sons of these gentlemen were to sit. Pretty china cups and painted and gilt bowls (wooden and metal) were placed on the little tables. All the fancy goods and curiosities here in the possession of the Minister were displayed in conspicuous places. At the corner of his table was placed the beautiful stereoscope we had presented him, with about 200 slides. In the middle of his table were placed the calendar-watch and some toys which I had lately presented to him. Different kinds of dainties, Tibetan and Chinese, were prepared by Deba Machan (the head cook), under the directions of Kusho Tung-chhen. To the arrangement of the seats and decorating of the room the Minister himself attended. He kindly permitted me to attend on him while he was busy with his furniture. When there was no one present I took the opportunity of asking him to introduce me to the *dah-pon*. He promised to do so in course of conversation with him during dinner. Thanking him for his kind promise, I went to the roof of the monastery to see the procession of monks appointed to give the guests a state reception. There were two roads leading to the monastery from the castle of Dong-tse, one in front of it and the other at the back. The monks kept themselves ready on both the roads to receive him with the band and flags. The former consisted of a pair of *gya-lings*, a very grave and sonorous wind instrument, a pair of *dung-chhen* or brass hautboys, a pair of drums resembling tambourines, a pair of bells and a gong. About a dozen flags were carried to do honour to the august scion of the Deba Dong-tse, who had founded the monastery and endowed it with a rich grant of land.

At 1 P.M. the *dah-pon* and his friend the *tsi-pon*, accompanied by their sons, were conducted to the Dong-tse Chhoide by Chhyan-dso Kusho. They were dressed very simply, although the spectators expected to see them in their richest apparel, as they walked up to the monastery hill, which is about 150 feet higher than the top of Dong-tse castle. The *dah-pon* appeared to me to be about 30 or 32, and the *tsi-pon* was a little older of the two. Their clothes consisted of a silk outer robe, a Chinese jacket, a yellow hat of the softest wool, velvet boots and silk trousers. From their right ears long earrings hung down. Arrived before the Minister, they thrice prostrated themselves before his holiness, each time touching their foreheads with their joined palms. I was surprised to see such powerful and wealthy chiefs perform the *kootoo* before the Minister. So great is the triumph of the church over the laity that even the great ministers of state submissively fall down to pay homage at the feet of incarnate Lamas! (His holiness is said to have been the spiritual guide of the Gya*l*-pos of Lhasa from a time even prior to the days of the famous Mivang. Mivang used to fall down to perform the *kootoo* before the predecessor of his present holiness. Even the celebrated Shata, the late illustrious Regent of Lhasa, whom the Abbé Huc saw, is said to have fallen down at the feet of the Minister when he was only six years old.) The Minister touched their heads with the palms of his hands, and blessed them. They presented him with two pieces of red English broadcloth and a handful of silver coins each. The dinner was served in perfect gravity: nobody talked, but as soon as grace was pronounced by the Minister all were busy with their chopsticks and spoons, and course succeeding course in the midst of profound silence. After dinner, tea was served, when at last the guests broke silence and conversation began. The watches and the stereoscopic views were the most important of the curiosities which interested the guests. On their inquiring how the Minister could become possessed of these, he replied that Pandibla, one of his devoted and zealous pupils from Aryavarta, had presented him with them, and that he was now in his study-room. They did not ask him to call the Pandibla to their presence, nor did the Minister talk further of him. He, however, allowed them to take home these two curiosities as a loan. At about 3 P.M. they took their leave with profound salutations, and walked off to the Dong-tse castle. In the evening there was a review of the *yul-mag* or country soldiers, when exercises in musketry, running, archery, &c., took place in the presence of these two dignitaries. During their stay at Dong-tse they preferred the garden-house situated in front of the castle, where there were tall poplars planted tastefully in rows along the stately walks. The place of exercise was situated in the pleasure grove or *linga* of the commander.

At Gyan-tse, Ugyen Gyatsho made the best of his time to-day. He surveyed the town and its great monastery, Palkhor Chhoide. A stone wall nearly two and a half miles long goes round the town. He estimated its length, by means of his beads, to be

4,500 paces. At each pace he dropped a bead and uttered once the mystic phrase "Om mani padme hum, while the good people of Gyan-tse, who accompanied him in his *Linkor* (or "monastery circumambulation") little suspected the nature of the work he was really doing. Arrived at the foot of Gojogs, a *mandang* situated to the north of the Jong, he took an observation of Tse-chan monastery, one of the most ancient religious establishments of Tibet. It bore to the south-west at a distance of nearly three miles. To the north of Gyan-tse was seen Ritoi Gonpa, a recluse monastery with five or six long houses containing a large number of cells. To the south-south-east of Gyan-tse Jong is the road to Phagri in the direction of Na-nin monastery and Niru-chhu, one of the principal feeders of the Nyang-chhu, which drains the northern glacier of the Chumo Lhari mountain. To the north-east of Gyan-tse is seen the course of the Nyang-chhu for a great distance. Judging from its position, Ugyen Gyatsho guessed that Nyang-chhu must have come down the snowy Noi-jin Kang-ssang mountains which extended their snow-clad heads towards the north and north-east. In the northern uplands of Gyan-tse, at a distance of nearly three miles, is situated the monastery of Chhoilung Gonpa. The monastery of Dong-tse was seen at a bearing of 304 from the *mandang*. Descending the hill of Gyan-tse Jong, Ugyen Gyatsho came down to the plain, where he saw the Chinese cemetery situated a little above the trunk road to Lhasa, but at a distance of three miles from this town. He counted there three hundred tombs, some of which were very old and dilapidated, but a few quite new.

The lofty Jong of Gyan-tse, a very strong castle, was built by the famous Chhoigyal Rabtan, who ruled over the province of Nyang, of which Gyan-tse was the capital in the 14th century. The hill with the Jong on its top is nearly five hundred feet above the town. Chhoigyal Rabtan had constructed a long stone house running from the Jong to the foot of the hill, through which he meant, in times of siege, to keep up a supply of water. There are three deep wells dug at the foot of the hill on its three sides, which Ugyen visited. Six water-carriers were engaged in drawing water from the wells, with ropes about 150 feet long. They use pulleys to work the ropes, and hide buckets to lift the water.

3rd January.—After tea, I was asked to read English with the Minister. He transliterated the English words and read them, but did not take the trouble of spelling them. I explained to him the importance of knowing the method of constructing words and syllables, as otherwise Ganot's Manual, which it was his chief aim to understand, would ever remain a sealed book to him. He observed that as he had little leisure from his ordinary duties, he could hardly devote much time to the study of English, with which his acquaintance would therefore be unavoidably superficial : it was his desire to ask permission from the Grand Lama to be absolved for a time from the heavy religious duties of the church : if he succeeded in that, he would apply himself assiduously to learn English. Breakfast was now brought by Deba Machan in trays, and consisted of a kind of pot-herb called *pa-tshal,* cured in the cold draught, and potatoes and radish preserved by being kept in sand under ground. In the course of the talk at table, I asked him if he would allow Tung-chhen to accompany me to Gyan-tse on the following morning. "Yes, we shall make arrangements about that," said his holiness. In the evening Gopa secretly told me that he was very anxious to visit Gyan-tse Pa*l*khor Chhoide, and would feel very much obliged if I spoke to the Minister to send him with me instead of Tung-chhen. I agreed to the proposal on his telling me that he was known to the head Lama of Pa*l*khor Chhoide. After sunset the Minister called Tung-chhen, and desired him to start early in the morning to shew me Pa*l*khor Chhoide ; but as I was going to open Gopa's request, Gopa, I knew not why, prevented me from doing so by a side-glance. Order was now issued to the grooms to make ready two ponies early in the morning.

At Gyan-tse, Ugyen saw the landlord of the Lithophug sub-division of Gyan-tse, who in course of conversation told him that the very house where he was putting up was the scene of a great calamity to the ex-Dewan of Sikkim. About eighteen years ago the ex-Dewan came to Gyan-tse on some state business, and stayed there for about a month. One night about fifty sinister-looking Khampo traders suddenly entered his house and laid violent hands on him. They robbed him of all his property, stript him of all his clothes with the exception of his night-drawers, beat him with clubs to the effusion of blood, tore his earring off his right ear, and a large turquoise off his left, severely thrashed his servants and compelled them to run away for life, and then, in the dead silence of night, they subjected him to all sorts of indignities to avenge themselves for his maltreatment of them at Chhumbi. Some of the robbers ran away from Gyan-tse carrying away his property, mules and ponies, but on the following morning, when the matter was brought to the notice of the Jong-pon, the chief of the robbers, who had stayed behind, proved that about a year ago the ex-Dewan had put them to much difficulties during their stay at Chhumbi on their way to Darjeeling, exacting from them the last pice they had in their purse, besides depriving them unjustly of all their property to the value of upwards of Rs. 500. It was estimated that the ex-Dewan's loss exceeded Rs. 1,000 in cash, besides jewellery, clothes, &c. At 1-35 in the afternoon Ugyen took a boiling-point observation, and found water boiled at 188°. To-day a well-informed Ningma Lama, the manager of Pa*l*ri Kusho's estate near Panam-jong, put up in the same house with Ugyen, who made his acquaintance and became very intimate with him. They discussed the Ningma religion, and were delighted with each other's conversation. The Lama was just returning from Lhasa, where he had stayed for two months after his return from pilgrimage to the Tsari country. His master, the Pa*l*ri-Kusho (an incarnate Lama), was now studying sacred literature at Lhasa. He promised to let Ugyen see the books in the Pa*l*ri library, and to lend them to him on the security of the Minister or his Chhyan-dso. This Lama told Ugyen that the town of Gyan-tse was formerly the capital of the province of Nyang, when it was a dependency of the Sakya heirarchs and ruled by Chhoigya*l* Rabtan. There were two printed volumes about that celebrated king who founded the Pa*l*khor Chhoide with its eighteen *ta-tshang*, or schools, for the study of the eighteen schools or philosophical sects of Tibet. The histories of Gyan-tse and king Rabtan were now kept as a *terchhoi*, or sealed book, by the Government of Lhasa. Ugyen also learnt from him that a complete account of the life and writings of Lama Lha-tsun-chhenpo, who introduced Buddhism in Sikkim, were to be found in the recluses' monastery of Lhari-ssim-phug situated in a solitary mountain to the east of Panam-jong. He was told that at this time the weather at Gyan-tse was very bad, there being high winds every day, which raised dust-storms and covered the persons of travellers with thick coatings of dust. During this time of the year people spend their time idly, having very little occupation besides that of weaving and spinning.

4th January.—At 6 in the morning Lhag-pa-rida, the groom, came and informed Tung-chhen that the ponies were saddled and ready for our journey. I hastily shaved myself and drank a cup of tea. The Minister wished us to carry a few scarves to present to the deities of Pa*l*khor Chhoide, and Gopa gave me a few *tankas* to buy for him some fur felt. I saluted the Minister and received his benediction, and mounting our ponies we rode off towards Gyan-tse. Our way lay across barley fields watered by the Nyang-chhu. This valley is one of the richest in Tibet, and extends from Shiga-tse to about fifteen miles beyond Gyan-tse, including a distance of 60 to 70 miles with an average breadth of 10 miles, every inch of which is cultivated. In course of conversation Tung-chhen told me that this valley was famous for the extreme fertility of its soil, for which, and especially for its being favourable to the growth of different kinds of millet and pulses, the whole province is called Nyang, or "the land of delicacies," and the river which fertilizes the soil is called Nyang-chhu, or "the river of delicious water." Our way lay along the banks of the river, but sometimes it receded far from it. Flocks of wild geese and ducks were swimming in the water, and here and there long-billed cranes stalked about in search of food. From the bushes of furze and other thorny plants with which the river banks were overgrown, rabbits leaped out and made off towards the mountain recesses. Beautiful small birds, probably allied to the family of kingfishers, were also fishing in the river. Tung-chhen told me that this bird, though very pretty outwardly, is a very defiled animal, emitting an offensive smell from its body. Passing a few villages, we arrived at a place where a stream coming from the south joins the Nyang-chhu. The waters of this stream, a few hundred yards above its junction with the Nyang-chhu, worked two flour-mills. Between Shiga-tse and this place we noticed at least twelve mills worked by water. With the exception of the two mills above Pishi Mani-lhakhang, which were worked by irrigation canals cut from the Nyang-chhu, the rest were worked by smaller streams which flowed down from the upland mountains to the Nyang-chhu. Though these streams were insignificant in volume, yet, being on a higher level, their tiny affluents carefully applied to the mills proved good moving agents. The mills that we observed were very large, with mill-stones four times the size of ordinary grind-stones. In the Himalayas the affluents of rapids are utilized to move prayer-wheels only, but here the streams are used only for turning flour-mills. The people of the village of Gyab-shi seemed to be very industrious. The women were engaged in the work of the loom and the spindle, and the men in tending sheep and collecting fuel from the fields. When we came within two miles of Gyan-tse, the most prominent object which attracted our attention was the Tse-chan monastery. Tung-chhen told me that this monastery was nearly eight hundred years old, and that it was there that Tsongkhapa, the great reformer, spent several years in the study of *tshan-nid* (metaphysics). Tse-chan monastery presented a picturesque view from a distance. The entire north-eastern slope of a hill was filled with closely-built white-washed houses, looking from a distance like a gigantic castle hanging on a great height. The mountain in the south-west also presented an imposing aspect, novel and singular to my sight. I was shown the Tinkarla pass, by which herdsmen travel to the foot of the Lachung pass of Sikkim, it being a shorter and more direct route to Sikkim from Gyan-tse. A few minutes' ride brought us to the wooden bridge on the Nyang-chhu. It was a very light temporary construction about 20 feet long and 6 feet broad, and stood on the frozen surface of the river. Crossing the bridge we were met by some herdsmen proceeding to Gyan-tse with laden yaks and donkeys. Leaving them behind, we entered the town of Gyan-tse by the side of a long *mandang*, on both sides of which, at a distance of about 10 or 12 feet, there were several houses. Some old women were going round the *mandang*. Entering a narrow lane, probably a short cut, we came to the gate of Gandan Lhakhang, situated on the left side of the main street confronting the grand *chhorten* and the Pa*l*khor Chhoide. The *kuner*, or priest of Gandan Lhakhang, was an acquaintance of Tung-chhen, and at once greeted him and offered him a cushion to sit upon. Tung-chhen smilingly sat down, desiring me to sit by his side on a second cushion. The *kuner* immediately ordered his servant to bring tea. My cup was with the groom, but Tung-chhen offered me his, which he had brought in his saddle-bag. Lhagpa-rida bought a few bundles of hay from a neighbouring shop, and giving them to the ponies, hastened to prepare tea for us. Tung-chhen had brought a small bag of barley-flour and a few pieces of boiled mutton, some dried milk vermicelli, Chinese pastry, and twisted biscuits. While going to buy curds from the *thom*, our groom met Ugyen and told him that we had just arrived and were putting up at Gandan Lhakhang. Ugyen arrived just when we were sitting to breakfast. Our host provided him also with a seat, and we divided the meal among ourselves. Several pilgrims, uttering some sacred hymns, entered the chapel of the Gandan Lhakhang, and added some spoonsful of butter to the oil-burner to feed the sacred fire. Some of them stared at me and Ugyen, observing to one another that we were strangers from the other side of the Himalayas. They at once took Ugyen for a Sikkimese. As for me, they entertained some doubts whether I was from Ladak or from Besahir. Tung-chhen smiled, and said that he met many Ladakis at Gyan-tse. At the request of Kusho Tung-chhen, the *kuner* of Gandan Lhakhang accompanied us to perform *chhoi-jal* at the different shrines of Gyan-tse. Ugyen Gyatsho presented him with a scarf and a *tanka* as remuneration for his kind services. The grand *chhorten* is a splendid edifice built in curious artistic taste. The architecture is indeed unique in its nature. Hitherto I had been under the impression that the *chhortens* were nothing more than tombs, intended solely to contain the remains of departed saints; but now the sight of this grand *chhorten* changed my ideas respecting them. It was a lofty temple nine storeys high. Ugyen, I, the *kuner*, Lhagpa-rida, and Lhagpa-sring, our servant, entered the enclosure, and waited for a few minutes at the entrance of the shrine, where several other pilgrims and travellers were also waiting to see the *chhorten*. Our guide, the *kuner*, went up to the service hall where the priests were assembled to perform religious ceremonies. Hundreds of oil-burners were lighted, and incense-sticks were smoking profusely so as almost to darken the hall. We at once ascended to the topmost storey of the *chhorten*, but the other pilgrims, most of whom appeared to be from Ladak and Chyang-thang, did not follow our example, but performed *chhoi-jal* from the bottom upwards. Though this is generally the practice with pilgrims, yet sometimes they fail to reach the topmost storey, getting quite tired after having walked round and round the lower ones. The *chhorten* was about 100 to 120 feet high, the top covered by a gilt dome. The copper-plates being very thick, have stood for centuries the wear and tear of the weather. From the topmost part, called the *pumpa* (cupola), immediately under the gilt dome, I enjoyed a magnificent view of the town and the monasteries of Gyan-tse. The surrounding hills and the distant mountains, their bleak appearance broken here and there by some solitary white monasteries, presented to the eyes a singularly wild aspect. In going round the *chhorten* to see the different chapels, we were required to go from left to right according to Buddhist usage. There were numberless niches filled with images of Buddhas and Bodhisattvas. During the time of Chhoigya*l* Rabtan there were eighteen Buddhist sects in Tibet, all of which had received encouragement from him. He founded eighteen establishments for the study of their respective religious theories and philosophies, all of which he endowed with grants of land. Under his benign rule Gyan-tse was raised to eminence and Buddhism received a fresh impulse, and the study of literature was encouraged.

In the first floor we were shown his statue and those of his ministers surrounding him. The *kuner* of the *chhorten* touched our head with the sword of that illustrious monarch, and said that by its *jin-lab* (blessing) we could triumph over our enemies and enjoy longevity and prosperity in this world. Here we were specially pointed out the two images of Dorje Chhang, the supreme Buddha of the Gelugpa church, one of which was very old and small, and the other large, glittering and handsome. Once on a time the grand Lama of Tashi-lhunpo visited this *chhorten* and touched the breast of the old image to feel if it was warm and living according to popular belief. But he soon repented for having dared on so great a sacrilege: he confessed his sin, and as a testimony of his penitence he constructed the gold image of Dorje Chhang, which he placed by the side of the old one. The base of this sacred edifice was fifty paces square, as we found by counting our paces as we went round it. Then returning to the Gandan Lhakhang, we refreshed ourselves with copious draughts of tea. In the meantime parties of pilgrims came to the chapel of Gandan Lhakhang, and uttering sacred hymns, presented incense-sticks, scarves and butter to the deities. The abbot of the Pa*l*khor Chhoide, with half-a-dozen disciples, came to make reverence to the great image of Buddha in this shrine. in the portico of which we were sitting. On the two sides, right and left of the chief image, were the images of Tsonkhapa and Maitreya. To-day being the full-moon—a sacred day with the Buddhists—the doors of all the sacred shrines were thrown open. The *kuner* told us that I was peculiarly fortunate in having come to Gyan-tse at such an auspicious time, the doors of the great *chhorten* being only opened to the public at the full and the new moon. After an hour's rest, accompanied by Kusho Tung-chhen and Ugyen, I paid a visit to the great monastery of Pa*l*khor Chhoide. The Tsug-la Khang, or the grand temple of learning, is a splendid and lofty edifice, the inside of the hall being lighted by 1,000 lamps. On three sides—the north, east and west—there were lofty niches, inside of which were placed three huge images of Buddha—Jam-yang Chanrassig and Maitreya—and of numerous Buddhas and Bodhisattvas. The first was constructed of *ser-ssang* (copper) overlaid thickly with gold-leaf. Five hundred monks were engaged in the divine service, and about two hundred monks were engaged intently in reading the sacred scriptures. No one lifted his eyes to look at us, so exemplarily strict was the discipline observed at this place. We were conducted to the great library, the very sight of which inspired feelings of awe and reverence in our minds. The books were very old, broad-leaved, and some two to four feet long. I was shown the sacred scriptures, all written in gold. The library is not accessible to the public, but the *kuner*, an acquaintance of Kusho Tung-chhen's, did all in his power to oblige us. With what assiduity and perseverance the

Buddhists perform the sacred duties of their religion, what interest they take in the collection of sacred books and images, and with what zealous care they preserve them, can be only gathered by visits to such places. I was shown the sculptures executed by Indian Buddhists, and also some stone images like those I had seen at Buddha Gaya. The gilt images of the Sravakas, such as Saripu, Moungalputra, Ananda, Kashyapa, and other Arhats, artistically wrought by Indian hands, some in a standing and a few in a sitting posture, were objects of the utmost interest to me, and awoke a deep desire in my mind for the thorough study of Buddhism and of the history of mediæval India. On the four sides of the image of Shakya Buddha the monks sat in four rows of twenty each. In front of them were hundreds of lamps fed with butter. On the back of the seats of the monks were kept drums, each placed on a post, which the monks at intervals beat, and sounded cymbals and blew brass hautboys (*dung-chhen*) and the sonorous *gya-ling* (clarionet), uttering sacred hymns to the accompaniment of the music in a peculiarly profound tone. When exhausted by continual recitation of *mantras*, they refresh themselves with tea. Wine is not brought within the precincts of these Gelugpa monasteries, and in fact all drinkers of wine are expelled from the order of monkhood of the Gelugpa church. After feasting my eyes on all these novel and grand sights, I came to the lobby of the monastery, where there was a grand collection of stuffed animals such as the snow leopard, wild sheep, goat, the yak called *dong*, stag, wild mastiff, &c. Among these I also saw a stuffed Bengal tiger. Kusho Tung-chhen and I made several rounds outside the great *chhorten*, counting the beads as we walked. This religious trip being finished, we returned to the Gandan Lhakhang, when the *kuner* conducted us to the second and third floor, where several recluses were reading the sacred books. I was told that when the Tashi Lama visited the Pa*l*khor Chhoide he put up at this house, and I was shown the raised seat occupied by him during his visit here. The successful students among the monks of Tashi-lhunpo are sent here to complete their study of the first course of sacred texts before they are allowed the degree of *Tom-ram-pa*, or bachelor of sacred literature. The Pa*l*khor Chhoide alone enjoys the privilege of conferring this degree. Here we dismissed the *kuners* who had taken the trouble of accompanying us to the several sanctuaries. Two monks, just arrived, attempted to talk a little Sanskrit with me. One of them asked me to read the signboard on which the names of Tsong-khapa and the monastery were written in Sanskrit, viz. Sumati Kirti and Tushita Vihara. They seemed to understand these names, and said that I was correct. I also read in their presence the inscriptions in the "ume*d*," or "headless" characters of Tibet, *i.e.* characters without the *Mátrá*. In the portico as well as below the eaves of the house several sorts of flower-plants in blossom were kept. At about 3 P.M. we left Gyan-tse, Ugyen returning to his lodgings at Lithophug. The skies were somewhat cloudy and a strong gale now blew, and we made haste to reach Dong-tse before dusk. I warmly thanked Tungchhen for the trouble he had taken to show us the celebrated and most interesting sanctuaries of Gyan-tse, and added that, not to speak about the Minister, whose kindness for us was incomparable, he (Tung-chhen) was one for whom I had the highest regard. He smiled at this, and observed that he was glad that we were able to appreciate his holiness' *thug-je* (mercy) towards us and all living beings. Conversing in this way we arrived at the foot of the Chhoide hill, where Shabdung, the Minister's page, came to receive us. I was at once conducted to his holiness' presence, and supplied with tea to refresh myself. "How did you enjoy your trip to-day? Were you not tired? Could you see all the sanctuaries?" were the Minister's gracious inquiries. "Yes, by your holiness' grace I have been very fortunate and successful in my visit to Pa*l*khor Chhoide. To-day being the holiest day of the month, the doors of the great *chhorten* and the grand monastery were thrown open. Religious services on a grand scale were being conducted in the Pa*l*khor Chhoide when we visited it. The whole hall was illuminated by a thousand lamps, with the help of which we could see many things very clearly that at other times could not be seen at all." "I rejoice at it," added the Minister, "and I must say that *lhat lam tan song* (the gods have shown you the way), for it did not strike us that to-day was a holiday. If you had gone tomorrow or yesterday, you would have seen very little."

5th January.—This morning the *dah-pon* and the *tse-pon* left Dong-tse at about 7 A.M. On account of the previous day's fatigue I got up from bed a little too late to see the procession at their departure. After breakfast I went to the Minister's presence and gave him an account of my trip to Gyan-tse and the impressions it had left on me. He told me there were half a dozen *chhortens* in Tibet like the one we had seen at Gyan-tse. He admired the power and devotion to religion of Chhoigya*l* Rabtan, who in fact had raised Gyan-tse to importance, erected the Gyan-tse fort, and founded the great religious establishment of Pa*l*khor Chhoide, with its college for the eighteen Buddhist schools of Tibet. There were about six hundred monks in the Pa*l*khor Chhoide and about six hundred more in the neighbouring monasteries. In former times three thousand monks are said to have been on the register of the college. I then explained to the Minister a few diagrams from Ganot's chapter on photography. At Gyan-tse, Ugyen Gyatsho, on the previous day (after his return to Lithophug, a distance of half a mile from Pa*l*khor Chhoide,) had been warmly received by the Chhandso Kusho of Pa*l*ri monastery, with whom he entered into a long conversation. He learnt from him that much information about the antiquity of Gyan-tse could be gathered from a work called "Nyang-chhoi-jung Nimai-ho*d*sser." Ugyen Gyatsho returned to Dong-tse at 2 P.M., when he was called to the presence of the Minister, and asked to give an account of his experiences of Gyan-tse. I was present, and observed with interest how inquisitive and curious the Minister was. Ugyen Gyatsho expressed himself much pleased with his visit. He said that he had obtained lodgings at Lithophug in a gentleman's house, where both the *Habo* and *Namo* showed him much hospitality, and at parting repeatedly entreated him not to forget to call at theirs if he happened again to go to Gyan-tse. Ugyen Gyatsho presented the Minister with a dozen oranges, which he had bought at Gyan-tse *thom* at one anna each. I told his holiness that the oranges were from Sikkim (Demo-jong), and that our friend's house was surrounded by orange trees. "Oh, indeed," said his holiness, "then his home must be a happy land. In Tibet no oranges grow; at Lhasa there are orange trees producing small oranges, but they do not ripen." I accounted for this by saying that even in Sikkim oranges borne by trees on a height over 6,000 feet above sea-level were very sour and small, the cold climate being unfavourable to their growth. Ugyen Gyatsho also related how an accident had befallen him through the bridge of the Nyang-chhu having been damaged and the river channel obstructed by a large block of ice. It was with much difficulty that the ponies were landed in safety on this side of the bridge: he himself had fallen down in the icy water, a portion of the ice having cracked by the sliding of the bridge beams In the evening my companion narrated to me the stories he had heard from the Chhyan-dso of Palri monastery, one of which I relate here:—Once on a time when Dugpa-kunleg, the famous but eccentric saint of the red hat school, was staying at Khang-toi Shikha in Lhasa, he saw from the upper floor the wife of the host stealing a piece of amber from the bag of a beggar-guest then residing in her house, and putting a small apple in its place. Dugpa-kunleg told her it was both sinful and criminal to do what she had done, and related to her an old tale by way of instruction. In ancient India there lived two friends, one living in the uplands who was a dishonest man, and the other residing in the lowlands, a sincere and honest man. One day these two friends, while walking in a mountain valley, found a bowl of gold, at which the lowlander said to his comrade, "Well, now that by fortune's favour we have got a treasure, let us first make adorations to the different local gods, and then divide the remainder among ourselves." At this proposal the upland man said, "Friend, the day is much advanced. We can conveniently do the same tomorrow; let us go home to-day with the bowl." The lowlander agreeing to this, the upland man returned to his home carrying the bowl with him. Next morning the former called at the house of his friend in the uplands, and found him in a corner of his house crying and shedding tears. His friend tried to console him, saying "Friend, do not cry; tell me what is the matter with you." At which the other said "Ah friend! my heart is filled with grief and shame. How can I tell you! Friend, the bowl of gold, when I arrived here last evening, miraculously changed its contents, for this morning I found it filled with sawdust. The gods alone know who stole the treasure. This event, I am grieved to say, will put an end to our friendship, inasmuch as it will create in your mind a suspicion against me." So saying, he began weeping afresh. His friend, perceiving the design of his false friend, with wonderful evenness of temper said "Friend, you need not cry. The treasure is not the most important thing for the loss of which we should be depressed. If we two live long as friends, we should consider ourselves very happy. Chance brought the treasure, and chance has taken it away: crying will not bring it back." The false friend, thinking that he had gained his end without creating suspicion in his friend's mind, soon dried his tears. His friend, before taking leave to return home, said "Friend, I have not mentioned to you one thing." "What is that," asked the false friend. Said the other, "In my orchard very excellent mangoes and other delicious fruits are ripe. I have no children who can eat them: let your two sons accompany me to my house that I may entertain them with the choicest fruits in my garden." The false friend gladly agreed to the proposal, and his two sons accompanied the honest man. He on his return to his house bought two monkeys, to whom he gave the names borne by the two sons of his friend, and trained within a short time to come when called by their names. One day the false friend came to the lowlands to take back his two sons, and knocked at the door of his friend's house, when his friend came out crying in a loud and pitiful voice. "What is the matter with you," inquired his friend. "Friend, my heart bleeds to tell you the misfortune that has befallen us! Your two darlings are changed into monkeys!" The father replied: "Friend, it is a curious story; how can I believe it?" "If you doubt it, you may call your sons, and they will immediately present themselves." The father called his elder son by his name, when the elder monkey instantly came leaping, sat in his lap, and began to fondle and chatter as if the upland man was an old friend. Surprised at this, the father called his second son by name, when the second monkey came frisking and leaping, and sat in the lap of the guest. After a while the lowland man asked his friend "How can it be possible, friend? Tell me how the bowl of gold could turn into sawdust?" The upland man, fearing his sons were transformed into monkeys by the incantations of his friend whom he had deceived, replied "Friend, I deceived you when I told you that the gold was turned into sawdust. I have got it with me. We will divide it between ourselves equally." He then asked "Is it true, injured friend, that my sons are transformed into monkeys." "Oh no, how can men turn into monkeys? Your sons are in excellent health in one of my distant orchards." So the two friends returned to their homes with their respective treasures—the one with his children, the other with his gold. Years elapsed before the two friends were summoned to the court of the lord of death in order to have their good and bad acts weighed. Their moral merits and prayers were also weighed and found tolerably in their favour. A game of chess was played by the gods and the demon, in which, by means of artful casting of dice, the merits and demerits of the gods and men are ascertained. In the mirror of *karma*, or mundane actions, the two friends saw and blushed for the evil actions performed by them—the gold turned into sawdust and two human beings converted into two monkeys. The lord of death ordained that the upland man should be incarcerated for five hundred years in hell, and that the other should be born as a monkey for five hundred births. Greater punishment was to be inflicted on the latter because he had the audacity to steal human beings and say that they were turned into monkeys! But because he had wished to make offerings to the gods when the gold was found, the gods pleaded for him.—Having finished his tale, the sage Dugpa-kunleg exhorted the hostess to leave off her stealing habits and threatened her with similar punishments if she persisted. Then the woman put back the amber in the beggar's bag, and the sage returned to Lhobrag.

Ugyen Gyatsho also related to me the account he had heard of the Terton Lama of Sikkim. Last year a mendicant, native of Gyan-tse, visiting Sikkim gave out there that he was one of those discoverers of sacred books mentioned in the Ning-ma history of Sikkim, and showed a very old Tibetan manuscript volume on the propitiatory ritual of "Guru Thag-mar," a fearful deity of the Ning-ma pantheon. The Sikkim Rajah gave him a very warm reception, and in consultation with the chief Lamas of his *durbar*, arranged to make block-prints of that book. Lately this imposter had returned to Gyan-tse carrying with him many valuable brass and copper articles, silk robes and cash.

6th January.—Both Ugyen Gyatsho and I were called to the Minister's presence to breakfast with him. He told us that the Grand Lama had expressed himself very anxious to buy a calendar-watch in which the dates and the days of the week are indicated. Kashmiri and Nepalese merchants brought for sale different kinds of watches, cheap and dear, but he had never met with one of the above description. I begged him to give me the calendar-watch which we had lately presented to him, that I might make a present of it to the Tashi Lama at the time of paying my reverence to him, promising to procure him (the Minister) another of superior quality. "Pandib, this watch is very handsome: do you wish me to part with it?" said his holiness looking towards me. I humbly replied that as our things from the Lachen Pass had not yet arrived, I did not know with what suitable present I should approach the Grand Lama when I went to receive *chhyag-wang* (benediction) from his holiness' hand: that it was for this reason that I made the proposal, but would act according to his advice. The Minister replied that Phurchung would shortly be due here, when we would be able to select presents for the Grand Lama.

I then explained to him the rules of division in arithmetic, and made him do some exercises on the *chyang-shing*. He observed that the English method of arriving at results by the process of multiplication and division was simple though tedious: the only advantage it had over the Tibetan process was that, the workings being left on the paper instead of being rubbed out according to the Tibetan practice, helped the memory in finding out mistakes. He also said that he knew some merchants from Nepal and Kashmir who with wonderful facility and readiness worked long and tedious sums in arithmetic, which it would take the Tibetan experts days to work correctly. He evinced much interest in the working of "simple rule-of-three," by which he was able to calculate the number of grains in a given bushel of barley. The signs of plus and minus amused him not a little. I told him that the Nepalese traders who worked long sums with great facility must have practised themselves in mental arithmetic, and if his holiness took the trouble of exercising himself in mental arithmetic, the next time he met those merchants he would wonder less at their quickness in calculation.

The Minister's mother, accompanied by a maid-servant, came to-day to pay reverence to her saintly son. When I was first told that she was the mother of the Minister, I felt much difficulty in believing the statement, for while we were seated she reverentially approached his holiness, made three profound salutations by touching the ground with her forehead, and received his benediction. She then presented him with a few balls of yak butter and a scarf, and cried much on hearing that his holiness would be off to Tashi-lhunpo after three days. In the evening the Minister informed us of his having accepted an invitation at Kye-pa Khangsar, Chhyan-dso Kusho's house. He desired us to return to Tashi-lhunpo on the following morning, as, after staying three days at Chhyan-dso Kusho's, he also would return thither. Rice, barley-flour, butter and meat were supplied to us as provisions for our journey. Jerung-la, the second son of Chhyan-dso Kusho, who came to see him after dusk with a message from his father, entreated him to take us with him to Kye-pa Khangsar, as his father particularly wanted to see Pandibla (myself) in order to consult me about his son Chola Kusho's eyes. The Minister directed Jerung-la to personally invite us, and he accordingly called on us and begged us to accompany the Minister to Kye-pa Khangsar.

7th January.—Early in the morning we received a message from the Minister to postpone our starting for Tashi-lhunpo and to see him at once. He told us that Chhyan-dso Kusho very much wished to see me, and he would feel greatly obliged if I would accompany him to his house. I accepted this opportunity of cultivating his acquaintance, and dressed myself to join the procession of the Minister's visit to Kye-pa Khangsar. The monks of the Chhoide were in their church apparel, and bustled about as if busy with some important religious service. The parents of the Minister, accompanied by their youngest son, came to pay reverence to their saintly son. The father, a quiet and respectable-looking elderly man, saluted me by lowering his yellow felt turban, and inquired after my health. After exchanging compliments, Ugyen Gyatsho and I presented him and his wife with ten *tankas*, which they accepted with much hesitation. They were then ushered into the Minister's presence, who, as soon as they rose from the ground to receive his benediction, touched the crowns of their heads with the palms of his hands. I was indeed struck with this singular spectacle, and wondered that the parents should fall at the feet of their son!

At 2 o'clock in the afternoon the Minister, dressed in a Buddhist cardinal's costume and accompanied by Kusho Tungchhen, ourselves, and his domestics, left his residence and entered the Du-khang, or grand worship hall. Tungchhen carried a bundle of incense-sticks and a few scarves in his hands. The head Lama of the monastery threw some grains of barley towards the Buddhist deities and uttered some sacred *mantras*. The Minister conducted a short solemn service standing, and approaching the great image of Buddha, lowered his own mitre-shaped hat and offered a present of a scarf. The head Lama of the monastery, taking the remainder of the scarves, flung them one by one towards the faces of the other deities, while monks who accompanied him threw flowers towards the sacred images. Then walking slowly round the chapel from right to left, we circumambulated the monastery and descended to the foot of the hill by the eastern exit, where the son of Chhyan-dso Kusho, dressed in a Mongolian noble's costume, was waiting for the Minister's arrival. Two spirited ponies, richly equipped, waited in charge of grooms in livery. A stool covered with a velvet cushion was placed between the two ponies. Arrived at the foot of the hill, his holiness was helped by a servant to stand on the stool, whence he mounted the pony brought from Chhyan-dso Kusho's stable. As the distance from this place up to the gateway of Kye-pa Khangsar's was inconsiderable, Kusho Tungchhen, Kahchan Gopa, Ugyen Gyatsho, and I walked on. The band, consisting of drums, hautboys, bell, gong and a pair of *gya-ling*, discoursed grave music as the procession moved towards the *sho* (lay town) of Dong-tse. Passing through a broad road lined by tall poplars and other aged trees, we arrived at the gate of Kye-pa Khangsar, where Chhyan-dso Kusho was standing to receive the Minister. He was dressed in a rich scarlet satin robe girded by a silk scarf, a yellow woollen turban, and a pair of velvet Tartar boots. His tall stature, graceful looks, broad forehead, and uncommonly well-proportioned nose, gave him a commanding appearance. He greeted the Minister with a profound salutation and the presentation of a scarf, and in return received his sacred *chhyag-wang*. A stool covered with a velvet cushion was ready for his holiness to dismount. Ugyen Gyatsho preceded me and was *salaamed* by Chhyan-dso Kusho. Kusho Tungchhen, perceiving that Ugyen Gyatsho did not pay his *chhyam-bu* (presenting of the hat) to Chhyan-dso Kusho, turned back and whispered to him to salute the nobleman, who it appeared had mistaken Ugyen Gyatsho for me. All of us then ascending a flight of steps entered Kye-pa Khangsar. The Minister was conducted by Chhyan-dso Kusho to his drawing-room, while Tungchhen and we were led by his third son, Phuntsho Yu-gyal, to the chapel, which is the central room on the first floor. The house appeared to me very neatly built, with walls of durable rubble masonry and beautifully carved beams, evidently of aged poplar. There was a skylight in the centre of the roof, which strongly lighted up our room. Long stuffed seats, overlaid with Khamba rugs, were spread, on which we were respectfully asked to sit. Tungchhen was given the first place, I the second and Ugyen the third. Platesful of Chinese cakes, buckwheat cakes and twisted sugar biscuits, and wooden bowls full of barley flour, were placed on small tables in front of our seats, and tea was served by Chhyan-dso Kusho's page, Pinu. About half an hour after, Ugyen Gyatsho and myself were conducted before Chhyan-dso by Kusho Tungchhen. Saluting him according to the Tibetan custom by lowering my hat, I presented him with a scarf and a couple of rupees. Ugyen did the same, and he received us both very graciously. We then presented scarves to his wife, Ama-tungla, and his daughter-in-law, Pa-tsha Rinpo-chhe, and returned to our respective seats. After dinner, which consisted of Chinese gruel, *pag-thug* (Tibetan gruel), boiled mutton and buttered rice, we were conducted to a dormitory on the south side of the chapel. There were three bedsteads, one for each of us. At about 9 P.M., after taking a cup of warm tea and some gruel, we went to bed. Tungchhen's servant spread his knapsack, while our servant Lhagpa helped us in wrapping ourselves with our woollens.

8th January.—Early in the morning, after tea, we asked Chhyan-dso Kusho's leave to start for Tashi-lhunpo. He expressed much reluctance to let us go, and said that he would feel much pleasure in entertaining us in his house for a day or two more. We begged him to allow us to act according to the Minister's wish, as his holiness was our master and protector. He immediately went to the Minister to ask if he objected to our staying at his house for a day or two more. Kahchan Gopa communicating to me the Minister's consent, we postponed our setting out for Tashi-lhunpo. Breakfast was brought by a *shetama* (maid-servant) and Pa-tsha Rinpo-chhe, the daughter-in-law of Chhyan-dso Kusho. The latter is by courtesy called Pa-tsha Rinpo-chhe, or "the precious lotus," being the only wife of Chhyan-dso Kusho's two sons. She also bears the title of *Chyam-kusho*, though she is seldom addressed by it. She is a young lady of about twenty, of modest manners and intelligent looks. She told me that the dishes were cleanly prepared and I could take them without repugnance. The servants and other guests having all gone out during our breakfast, Pa-tsha Rinpo-chhe lingered in the room evidently to converse with us. Ugyen Gyatsho opened the conversation by asking her if he could take the liberty to enquire from what family of Tibet she was sprung. She meekly replied by asking if Ugyen had ever heard the name of Kusho Mankipa of Tanag. "Yes," replied he, "do you speak of Manki Kusho, who is the maternal uncle of our Chief the Rajah of Sikkim?" She nodded assent, and with a sigh added, "My father died last year. I could not see him. Are you a subject of my cousin Den Jong Gya-po (Chief of Sikkim)? Oh, how I long to see my aunt." Turning to Ugyen Gyatsho, I said, "Is Kusho Mankipa dead, that gentleman who came to see us at Tashi-lhunpo during our last visit?" Pa-tsha Rinpo-chhe, looking towards me, said "Did you know my father?" "Yes, Pa-tsha Rinpo-chhe. Kusho Mankipa was an acquaintance of mine. He was very kind to me." She thereupon shed tears, and frequently wiping her eyes said, "It is now full three years that I have come here, during which time I have never once been allowed to see my paternal home. Oh, I am miserable! I have to work continually at the loom, supervise the work-women and do the duties of the kitchen and the table. My mother-in-law is relentless. She thinks that my frame is made of iron. Though this family is rich, yet they work as if they are no better than ploughmen." She then begged Ugyen to communicate to Lha-yum Kusho (the Sikkim Rajah's mother) the tale of her misery, and to persuade her, if possible, to take her to Chhumbi for a couple of months. She was exceedingly delighted with having met in us her father's acquaintance and her cousin's subject. I told her that she possessed excellent personal accomplishments, was the wife of one of the richest families in Tsang, and would within a short time become the mother of children: how could she then say that she was miserable? "Sir," she asked, "do you know palmistry," and placing her right hand on my dining-table, begged me to tell her fortune by examining the *lagri* (lines of the hand). I was much embarrassed, but at last told her that I knew very little of palmistry. Just then a servant came to call us to Chhyan-dso Kusho's presence. He received us very kindly, and politely motioned us to two cushioned seats on his right hand side. His wife, Ama-tungla, was seated on his left. Ugyen Gyatsho was given a seat at some distance from us, and interpreted for me. Chhyan-dso Kusho began with: "In the sacred books we find mention of Indian Panditas who laboured for the diffusion of the enlightened religion (Buddhism). If you be a Pandita, as I hear from the Minister that you are, we must be fortunate to have you in our midst. I also learn that you know medicines, in which I shall hereafter avail myself of your kind services." Then looking to his wife, he said, "If Nima Dorje (his eldest son) were here, we could have asked the Pandita to examine his eyes. What a pity he is not here, to-day!" He then begged me to see his elder brother, Kusho Jambala, and then called his son, Phunsho Yugya*l*, and desired me, to my great embarrassment, to foretell his fortune by examining the *lagri* on his palms. Being considered an Indian Pandit, it was rather hard for me to say that I did not know an essential science like palmistry: so after grave reflection I told him that although I had read a few pages of a work on palmistry, yet I never attached much importance to its mystic explanations of men's fortune. The science was very little known, and in my opinion it deserved to be less known: nothing was more unpleasant than a prediction of one's misery. Human destiny was full of misery, and it was for deliverance from its recurrence that Buddha had expounded the doctrine of Nirvana. Chhyan-dso Kusho listened to this speech with much attention, and seemed to think highly of me. He said that if he knew how long he and his son would naturally live, he could devise means for the prevention of accidents in consultation with the Minister, for in the sacred books mention is made of religious remedies by which calamities brought on us by *de* (devils) might be averted. He pressed me to examine his palms first, and stretched it towards me. How could I refuse to see it, or how could I predict falsely! so I told him that there are certain figures and lines in the palms of the hand from which the experts in palmistry draw indications of a long or a short life. In Chhyan-dso Kusho's palms the line indicated a long life, and as to fortune it was well known that he was favoured of the gods. Ama-tungla then showed me her hands, on which I said: "Ama la (mother), you are very fortunate. Being the mother of three sons, all of whom are grown up and accomplished, and also the wife of such a great man, what more do you want from the gods?" She smiled at this, and said she had been suffering from a cough since last Saturday: could I give her some medicine that would bring her relief from the obstinate coughing? I asked for some black pepper and sugarcandy, with which I prepared a powder for her. At noon we were called to dine with the Minister and Chhyan-dso Kusho. I sat by Tungchhen with Ugyen Gyatsho to my left. The dishes were prepared after the Chinese fashion, and brought dressed in Chinese trays, and placed on little tables. A servant brought about two dozens of wooden and ivory chopsticks and a few clean spoons, from which I picked out two chopsticks and a spoon. There were no forks. The first course consisted of *gya-thug*, a tape-like preparation of wheat flour and eggs cooked with minced mutton, and a cup of soup. With the chopsticks, which were to be held like tweezers, I pinched out one tape of *gya-thug* and tried to put it into my mouth, but in the midway of its passage it dropped down. Forthwith, not to be laughed at, I attempted a second pinch, and was successful. I relished it well, and would have considered it almost a dainty if there was less of onions. The Minister did not take *gya-thug* on account of his having taken the vow of abstinence from eggs; but a kind of mock *gya-thug* was presented to him. The second course consisted of rice and half a dozen preparations of mutton curry, viz. mutton with preserved vegetables, white and black mushrooms, Chinese green-grass, pea-vermicelli, potatoes and fresh shoots of peas; the third course of buttered rice and sugar; the fourth and last, of boiled mutton, barley-flour and tea. When the dinner was finished I asked Tungchhen how many courses would be served in sumptuous dinners, and was told that thirteen *leu* (literally chapters) are generally served to noble laymen, such as *Dah-pons* and *Shapes*. About an hour after dinner we were conducted by Jerung-la, the second son of Chhyan-dso Kusho, who had betaken himself to monkhood, to the castle of Deba Dong-tse. It is one of the oldest and loftiest buildings of Tsang. The great reformer Tsong-khapa is said to have visited it in order to hold controversies with Lama Lha-tsun Rinpo-chhe, the saint whose fifth incarnation our patron the Minister is. The building, about 600 years old, is built of stone of the best quality. It faces the south, and has balconies (*rab-sal*) in front of every one of the five storeys, provided with shutters. The building, built partly after Indian and partly after Tibetan style, encloses a courtyard about 100 feet broad and 200 feet long. Round this court, on the south, east and west, the three wings of the building rise three storeys to a height of 40 feet. Instead of railings, every one of these storeys is provided with a row of prayer-wheels on pivots, ready to be twirled. These prayer-wheels were each two feet high and two feet in circumference, and resembled little drums, and there were about three hundred of them in front of the nine balconies of the three wings. To the north of the court stood the lofty main building, about 60 to 70 feet high. Although we visited it purposely to see the chapel, yet the keeper (*kuner*) of the house being absent, we had to ascend to the highest floor by a steep ladder, where we were shown the *gonkhang*, or the shrine of the guardian deities. It contained terrible figures, among which I noticed three deities called *Mamos*, resembling the maimed deities of the Hindus—Jagarnath, Balavadra, and Subhadra. There were several chapels, in each of which there was a resident priest called *am-chhoi*. In the balconies of the wings two or three old women were weaving blankets. At the entrance of the house a huge mastiff was chained, which furiously attempted to rush upon us.

To the south of the castle, at a distance of about a hundred yards, is the garden or *linga* attached to it. In the middle of this *linga* is a garden-house very tastefully constructed after the Tibetan style, its cornice and other external decorations being remarkably pretty. Tall poplars, some of which were 80 to 100 feet high, and four other kinds of trees, all leafless now, were planted in rows along the four avenues of the *linga*. In front of it, but at a distance of about 100 yards from the garden-house, was the target for exercise in musketry and archery. A greyhound roamed at large within the *linga*, but did not molest us. On our return we passed by the village, where, under tall poplars, some potters were heaping earthenwares for sale. We met four yellow-turbanned men who, we were told, were the rent-collector's orderlies. In the evening the Minister requested me to examine the eyes of Kusho Jambala, the elder brother of Chhyan-dso Kusho, who had been suffering from ophthalmia. Chhyan-dso Kusho observed with sorrow that eye-disease had been a general complaint in his family, his son and brother both being afflicted with it.

9th January.—After tea we asked Chhyan-dso Kusho's leave to return to Tashi-lhunpo; but he told us that it would be convenient for us to accompany the Minister on the following morning. Tea was supplied to us, and as is usual in the houses of great men of Tibet, a servant continually waited upon us to replenish our cups. During breakfast Pa-tsha Rinpo-chhe made her appearance. She again related the story of her hard work and merciless treatment at the hands of her stern mother-in-law. I asked if her husband did not much like her. "Oh, Sir," she said, "we both are one soul and body. But he generally remains at Shiga-tse, where he serves as the Dah-pon's *nerpa* (store-keeper). Once while young, my husband's right eye was injured by an accident. It has now a *dib* (shade) over it. Could you, Panditla, cure his eye?" "I must see it before I can say I can cure it," replied I. She then told us that she had heard a very happy piece of news: her cousin, the Rajah of Sikkim, would come to Tibet to marry. If his mother came with him, she could surely prevail upon her to take her to Chhumbi for a couple of months. She hoped we would not return to our homes before that, and if we remained at Shiga-tse, she would let us accompany her to Chhumbi. She also remarked that her mother-in-law should not have given her the fond but high-sounding name of Pa-tsha Rinpo-chhe (the precious lotus-stem), for Rinpo-chhe is properly applied to incarnate Lamas and Chiefs. I replied "Well, do not you know that handsome and accomplished ladies can also be designated by that precious name of Rinpo-chhe?" She smiled, and withdrew. We were then called to the Minister's presence, where we met Chhyan-dso Kusho and Tungchhen. After a short conversation we got up from our seats to wash our hands. A large copper washing-bowl, called *katora*, was placed before the Minister, who washed his hands, rubbing them with a kind of wood-dust called *sugpa*, which served the purpose of soap. The *sugpa* is a kind of plant which grows in Tibet. Dinner was then brought and served precisely as on the previous day. At 2 P.M. Chhyan-dso Kusho made presents to the Minister consisting of blankets, Tibet serge, three pieces of red, scarlet and yellow English broadcloth, Gyan-tse rugs of superior quality, Khamba rugs, embroidered China satin, spotted woollen chintz, about two bushels of barley-flour, a large quantity of buck-wheat cakes, twisted sugar biscuit and some thick Tibetan bread, besides one hundred rupees in Tibetan currency. He then made profound salutations to his holiness and received his *chhyag-wang* (benediction). He next in a speech begged his holiness to pray to the gods to make him prosperous and happy. Chhyan-dso Kusho then made presents to Kusho Tungchhen, which were half of what was presented to the Minister. Kahchan Gopa received half of what was presented to Tungchhen; next I was presented with a pair of Gyan-tse rugs and two pieces of spotted blankets together with a scarf; and lastly Ugyen Gyatsho obtained two small rugs of inferior quality and two pieces of coarse blankets. Then alms were distributed among the monks of Dong-tse and the menials of the Minister. When the work of presentation was over, Chhyan-dso Kusho returned to the Minister's presence, where we also were. In course of conversation, he hinted the advisability of my presenting an elephant to the Tashi Lama, and inquired from me the cost of one. I replied that I did not much care for the cost of an elephant: what I feared was that it would be very difficult to bring an elephant to Tashi-lhunpo. He said that lately two elephants were taken to Lhasa to be presented to the Dalai Lama from the Sikkim Rajah, and gave a graphic description of the animals, and said that one of them had died on the way. I answered that if the Government of Lhasa provided me with a passport to enable me to come to Tibet freely, I could easily present an elephant to the Tashi Lama, and told him that the elephants presented to the Grand Lama of Lhasa were presented to the Sikkim Rajah by the Government of Bengal. I then explained to him the relation existing between the English and Sikkim Rajah. He asked me, if the English were good men, why had they fought with Sikkim and snatched away from him the best part of his territory. I thereupon gave a short account of the history of Sikkim and Nepal, how Nepal had conquered Sikkim and expelled the Chief from his territories, how the British Government came to his rescue and reconquered for him his territories from the hand of the Goorkha government, and what return for all these good services the Rajah of Sikkim had made to his benefactor the British Government. I related how the *Dewan* of Sikkim had insulted inoffensive travellers like Drs. Hooker and Campbell, and kidnapped refugees from the protection of the British authorities; and how readily, when the Rajah repented of his actions, the British Government pardoned him and granted him a pension of Rs. 12,000 a year. He then said that if we could procure him a pair of elephants, he would pay the cost-price. I replied that I myself could present him with a pair of elephants if he could take charge of them on the British Sikkim frontier. He then turned the conversation on the superiority of Indian metal images over those made in Tibet, and said, looking towards the Minister, that the bell-metal images of Magadha, called *jaikhim*, are very rare things in Tibet. "If Panditla had brought some of them, or those called *sharli* (bell-metal images of Bengal) and *nubli* (those of Uddayana or the lower Indus Valley), your holiness would have been really delighted. Indian articles of gold and of other precious metals are superior to the glass and other fragile things which they have presented to your holiness." Then turning towards me, he said, "Pandibla, we Tibetans do not care for fancy toys. We like useful things. The next time you bring presents for his holiness, please do not bring glassware and other useless toys." The Minister smiled at this. Chhyan-dso Kusho then said that his holiness had showed him the things we had presented him a couple of years ago. I then gave him a short account of the early history of Tibet as I had read it in Tibetan books, and concluded by observing that the Tibetan Government of the present time was very weak compared with the former Governments under native Tibetan kings. In the evening it was settled that the Minister would start for Tashi-lhunpo next morning, and that Kusho Jambala should accompany me to Tashi-lhunpo to avail himself of my medical treatment.

10th January.—We got up early in the morning, and equipped ourselves to start for Tashi-lhunpo. There was a brisk movement among Chhyan-dso Kusho's servants, who prepared tea and Tibetan gruel for us all. Tungchhen La advised me to start ahead of the Minister's party who, he said, riding swiftly, would overtake us very soon, and kindly allowed me to select the quietest pony from the Minister's stable. We paid our respects to Chhyan-dso Kusho, and, accompanied by his brother, left Dong-tse. When we were passing by the village of Dong-tse, a few beggars followed us supplicating alms. We satisfied them by throwing a two-anna piece for them all. Before we had proceeded four miles from Dong-tse, we saw the Minister accompanied by four attendants, all mounted on ponies, rapidly approaching. They overtook us near Dekiling, where I was taking a short rest, and without waiting rode on swiftly. I intended to ride slowly with the pack-ponies and Kusho Jambala, who, being an old man, was unable to ride fast; but Ugyen Gyatsho urged me to keep up with them and, whipping his pony, ambled off. I followed him. The Minister's party having ridden about a mile, had dismounted to cross a broad, frozen irrigation canal, and we overtook them at the sixth mile from Dong-tse. Then proceeding together for about three miles, we found ourselves on an extensive table-land through the middle of which a streamlet, now dry, cut its way to flow into the Nyang-chhu. A little above the junction we all halted for about an hour. The Minister dismounting, ordered his page Shab-dung to fetch him a basketful of earth from a particular place which he pointed out. The earth being brought, he sat cross-legged on a rug and uttered some *mantras,* after which some barley-flour was strewed and water sprinkled. On my asking the reason of this evidently religious service, Tungchhen La told me that here the Minister having a fall last time from his pony, it was supposed that some unfriendly evil spirit (most probably a *Naga*) was maliciously bent upon hurting him. The service was to threaten the evil spirit to leave the place at once. At the conclusion of the service the Minister gave me some dried dates and other Cabul fruits, while Kusho Tungchhen distributed treacle, biscuits and parched barley to Shab-dung and Ugyen Gyatsho. Then proceeding eastward, we passed in front of Norpu Khyung-dsin (the jewel eagle's peak), on which are the ruins of an ancient Karma-pa monastery. When we arrived at Rissur, where the Nyang-chhu washes the rocky ledge of a bluff, the Minister showed me the narrow passage on the side of a rock where, about twenty years ago, two powerful dignitaries were assassinated, being thrust into the Nyang-chhu by the agents of the notorious Gah-dan Gya-oo, who wanted to usurp the supreme authority at Lhasa. Gah-dan Gya-oo was the treasurer of Gah-dan monastery, which is under the control of an abbot. He gradually rose to distinction, and became the right-hand man of the Regent, when he was well-known under the name of Dayan Khanpo, but at last conceived the idea of usurping the sovereign power of the Dalai Lama and of confining the Dalai and the Tashi Lamas in two monasteries where they would be compelled to perform exclusively religious duties. He accordingly organized a secret conspiracy, and treacherously put several noblemen and powerful officials of Tibet to death to pave his way to the supreme power. His secret designs were also directed against the four Shapes, all of whom he planned to capture and throw, hermetically packed in hide bags, into the Kyi-chhu. Shape Thimen and his colleagues were first imprisoned in the jail of Du-chhung Jong situated to the north-west of Dong-tse, but Dayan Khanpo, suspecting that Thimen's case might be espoused by many powerful Chiefs of Tibet, secretly sent a letter inviting him to Lhasa to fill some high office under the Government. When the unsuspecting Shape was passing by the Rissur early in the morning, he was thrown headlong into the water by some ruffians employed by Dayan Khanpo. At last when the atrocities practised by him became unendurable, the chiefs and nobles of Lhasa unanimously declared him to be an evil spirit who deserved to be despatched by the sword, and sent a large body of soldiers to arrest him, but he managed to run away from Lhasa towards Rigyal, when, seeing that he could not escape his pursuers, he induced one of his servants to strangle him to death with a scarf. At about 4 P.M. we reached Tashi-gang, where Ang-putti received us with much reverence and cordiality. After refreshments the Minister took his seat on the roof of Ang-putti's second storey to enjoy the view of the surrounding hills and the famous Lhundub-tse Jong of Panam. Here he called me and Ugyen Gyatsho up, and asked us to teach him the English system of land surveying. Ugyen gave him the prismatic compass which he had with him, and also the pocket compass by which vertical angles could be taken. We explained to him the use of the instruments, and expressed regret that we had no tape or chain with us with which we could take the measurements, carefully concealing from him the fact that approximate measurements could be taken by pacing. Had we mentioned that, he would surely have suspected us of being surveyors, and withdrawn his patronage from us. The Minister still expressed much eagerness to learn surveying, and we, in reply, reminded him that he had kept with him the tape and mathematical instruments which we had brought when we last came to Tibet, and then returned to us. "What a pity *akha-kha* that I did not keep it here. Is there no means now to get them here?" He then told me that he was in earnest to obtain a sextant, an illustrated work on English astronomy, some mathematical instruments, together with a chest of medicines, and asked if we could not make arrangements to send somebody to bring them from India. I replied that unless I myself went down to Calcutta, nobody else could select things which he would consider useful and good, and in my absence Ugyen Gyatsho would be the proper person to give effect to his wishes. Of course, if we sent orders to our friends in India for any articles, they would send them, but they certainly could not divine what things not mentioned in such a list would be acceptable to the Minister. He then asked why Ugyen Gyatsho could not go to India to buy those articles, on which the latter said he could and would certainly go if his holiness wished him to do so, but there was one thing in the way which made him hesitate to leave Tibet. "Tell me, Ugyen, what that is," said the Minister. "Your holiness, how can I leave my friend Pandibla alone here? Besides, the desire of visiting Lhasa was one of the principal objects of Pandibla's coming to Tibet this time, and before that end has been attained how could I return to India leaving him here without a companion? The Minister replied "That is not a matter of difficulty. I can undertake to look after him. There is every probability of the Grand Lama's going to Lhasa to ordain the Dalai Lama into the order of monkhood in the 4th month (June), when we may arrange for Pandibla's going to Lhasa. Both Shape Rampa and Phala are my friends; they will help him. However, we will think of it afterwards when we return to Tashi-lhunpo." He then said that there were four persons in Tsang who took an interest in science and study in general. We begged to know their names. He said the four were Shape Porapa, Kusho Tung-yig Chhenpo, the Donner Kah-chan Dao, and himself. "There are many other learned men at Tashi-lhunpo and in different other monasteries of Tsang, but they mostly interest themselves in the works of sacred literature only. They do not care to know the sciences and improvements of other great countries, such as Philling and India." I then asked if his holiness could not arrange to establish a meeting of these four great personages to improve the educational status of the monastery and to introduce the study of elementary science. He replied, "Although we are the most influential men in Tsang, yet it is not within our power to induce men to study and work after our own way and wishes." "How that can be possible I cannot understand." said I. The Minister then told me that he intended to visit tomorrow the convent of Kyi-phug situated about three miles off in the uplands of Tashi-gang. The lady superior and her *tsun-mos* (nuns) had repeatedly solicited him to pay a visit to their convent, but for want of leisure he had not been able to do so even once in the course of the last six years. He therefore advised us to proceed slowly towards Tashi-lhunpo after tea tomorrow, in company with Kusho Jambala, whom he desired to put up in his house.

11*th January*.—The Minister and his party left for Kyi-phug convent at 7 A.M. Tungchhen La gave us a letter to Gyatsho Shar. We breakfasted at Tashi-gang, and set out for Tashi-lhunpo at 10 A.M. Kusho Jambala being an old man was unable to keep up with us, who rode fast at a graceful amble which he admired, but himself would not urge his pony. His yellow satin mitre-shaped cap, his spectacles, his manner of sitting his pony, and his tall thin singular appearance, recalled to my mind the appearance of the Knight of La Mancha as he followed the muleteers who were in charge of the Minister's baggage. With his leave we proceeded ahead of the party, and arrived at the margin of the Nyang-chhu at the eastern corner of the table-land of Shalu. The river here was divided into three channels, the shallowest being in the middle, while the deeper one was undermining the fields. Ugyen Gyatsho opened his saddle-bag and gave me a piece of boiled mutton to eat. A crust of ice about a foot deep was formed on the surface of the Nyang-chhu. The place where we refreshed ourselves was overgrown with a kind of thorny shrub resembling the silver fir. Proceeding thence in a westerly direction we saw a woman in the middle of the table-land engaged in sweeping the field. On asking her what she meant by it, she replied that she was clearing away the frozen crust of moisture that her cattle might the more easily pick up the grass. At this time, we were told, many sheep died for want of grass, for crusts of ice formed on the surface of the dry pasture grass injure the health of the sheep. At 4 P.M. we arrived at Chyam-chhu in Gyatsho Shar, where we were kindly received by Deba Shikha, the head of the farm, to whom we handed Kusho Tungchhen's letter. He read it and ordered tea for us. After refreshment, when we were about to cook our own food, the Deba's wife brought us Chinese gruel, barley-flour and boiled mutton, on which we made a hearty repast. Deba Shikha and his wife made grand preparations for the Minister's reception. Two ponies were equipped with saddles and saddle-bags, the latter filled with cakes, buckwheat bread and fine barley-flour. Two bowls of curds, well packed, were giving to the messengers to carry the Pishi Mani-lhakhang, where the Minister generally refreshed himself when journeying between Dong-tse and Gyatsho Shar. These men never started before dusk, so we took a short walk in the Lobding, and saw the garden-house where the Minister's quarters were arranged. At night, after a couple of cups of Tibetan gruel (*jam thug*), Kusho Jambala was accommodated in a snug little room opposite Deba Shikha's sleeping-room, while we occupied our former place on the first floor of Deba Shikha's house.

V.—RETURN FROM DONG-TSE TO TASHI-LHUNPO AND RESIDENCE THERE.

12*th January*.—After breakfast we took a walk round the *linga* (grove) belonging to the Minister, situated in front of his *cham-chhu* or bathing villa. It was surrounded by a wall of partly sun-dried bricks, stones and turf, seven feet high. In the south-eastern corner of the grove stands the two-storied snug little house where the Minister in October spends a few days of his autumn recess. This house had a balcony to the south, a bath-room and dormitory in the upper floor. It had three spacious windows on the west, south and east, provided with shutters easily removeable. In the sleeping-room, well furnished according to Tibetan fashion, two yellow church cloaks were kept erect on the cushion, just as gown patterns are kept in millinery shops in Calcutta, so that at first sight one would believe that somebody was in the room dressed in the cloaks. There were no out-offices near the house. We were told that during the Minister's stay here, cooking and bathing are performed under yak-hair tents pitched in the western avenues of the grove. At nine in the morning we left Gyatsho Shar, and riding slowly, arrived at Tashi-lhunpo at noon. We first called at Phuntsho Khangsar, where we were warmly received by Nerpala and other domestics of the Minister. As usual tea was served and flour and boiled mutton presented to us for refreshment, which we did not touch, but after a few minutes stay to inquire after each other's health, returned to our lodgings at Thorgod Chyikhang, where we met Phurchung, who had arrived yesterday from Khamba jong. After saluting us, he said that as Rinzing Namgya*l* was in charge of our baggage, the Jongpon of Khamba-jong did not allow him (Phurchung) to proceed beyond the Tibetan boundary, for last year Rinzing having accompanied Captain Harman up to Thangu, the Tibetan boundary, he was believed all over this frontier to be a Government employé connected with the Survey Department. The Jongpon, who knew Phurchung, told him that unless he came armed with a passport from the Tashi Lama's Government, or from the Commander of Shiga-tse, he could not let him cross the frontier; adding that there were definite orders from the Lhasa Government not to let anybody cross the boundary, even if he came with recommendations from the high officials of Labrang, who are unconnected with the charge of the frontiers. Besides, Rinzing Namgyal had brought to Lachen many articles of a suspicious character, such as English guns, chairs, &c., belonging to Captain Harman or some European gentlemen, and had given out that he would enter Tibet. Phurchung also told us that some natives of Lachen had secretly informed the Jongpons about Rinzing's connection with the Government and his object in entering Tibet. Rinzing had accordingly gone back to Darjeeling, leaving our baggage at Lachen Peepon's house. In the afternoon tea, barley-flour, &c., were sent to us from Phuntsho Khangsar. In the evening we cooked our own food and conversed with Phurchung about the treatment he had received at Khamba-jong and the report spread about us by the Tang-lung natives.

13*th January*.—The cash which we had brought from Darjeeling having been almost spent, we now felt the necessity of selling the pearls and gold we had with us. When going to Dong-tse we had left a few *tolahs* of pearls with our old acquaintance Lupa Gyantsan of Shiga-tse. I sent Ugyen Gyatsho to Shiga-tse *thom* to purchase provisions, and also to inquire if the pearls had been sold. He found Lupa Gyantsan engaged in casting bell-metal oblation cups, but as soon as the latter saw our companion he left his work to receive him, and his wife immediately spread a little table and poured tea for Ugyen's refreshment. Lupa Gyantsan told him that he had shewn the pearls to a merchant of Lhasa, who had not offered more than our cost-price for them. Lupa observed that the market for pearls had of late considerably fallen, and that we could not expect much profit out of them within a month or two, but promised to show our pearls to other parties and let us know the result. Lupa also asked if we had not brought any gold with us. Ugyen Gyatsho replied that he had no gold to sell, but would inquire from me if I had any for sale. On my arrival at Tashi-lhunpo I had warned Ugyen Gyatsho not to tell anybody that we had gold with us, as then we would tempt robbery. Lupa Gyantsan also told him that great preparations were being made by the Grand Lama for his visit to Lhasa in May, when he would ordain the Dalai Lama into the order of monkhood. On that occasion the Tashi, according to the custom of the sacred order, would have to make return presents and money rewards to the different officials and chiefs of Tibet, for which robes, boots, &c., were now being largely ordered. Ugyen Gyatsho also met other acquaintances of his, who inquired if he had enjoyed his trip to Dong-tse. He returned in the evening, when I arranged to remove my study-room to the second floor where the sunbeams used to fall earlier, the first floor being very cold, being seldom visited by the sun. The shutters and doors of the second floor were not in good order, so Ugyen and Phurchung stuck some paper on the shutters to make the room habitable. The Nerpa came to see us in the evening and inquire after our wants.

14*th January*.—After breakfast Ugyen Gyatsho went to the *thom*, where he found Lupa Gyantsan waiting for him. Lupa whispered in his ear that some traders from Chhumbi and Rinchhengang were just arrived, most of whom were known to Ugyen. He (Lupa) knew that some among them were bad men, and, as he understood from their conversation, not well-disposed towards us. He was waiting here to prevent Ugyen Gyatsho from incautiously coming across them unprepared. Following Lupa's advice, Ugyen went to the furthest corner of the *thom*, where pastry was being sold, whence he entered the lane leading to the police-station, where he had an acquaintance in the Chinese *havildar* of Shiga-tse. Then ascertaining who were the men come from Phagri, Chhumbi and Rinchhengang, Ugyen met them and made many inquiries respecting the state of the passes. They told him that it was only through the Government of Lhasa having declared the Phagri Pass open that they had been able to come. As regards the Sikkim Rajah's coming here, they could not give him any definite information, but there was much talk of the Rajah's marrying the daughter of a great man of Lhasa. After making purchases in the *thom*, Ugyen Gyatsho went to Lupa Gyantsan's house, where he arranged to buy a pony for me, for which the owner asked Rs. 75. Through Lupa he induced the owner to send it to Tashi-lhunpo for our inspection. Accordingly, at about 2 P.M., the pony was brought to our house when, after a short trial, I offered to pay Rs. 50 for it; but not agreeing to that price, the owner went back to Shiga-tse with his pony. At four o'clock the Minister, who had arrived at noon, sent for us. Being conducted to his presence, we saluted him as usual, and on his graciously inquiring after our health and the fatigues of the journey, we told him that we were allright by his mercy. He told us that the lithographic apparatus sent to him some months ago had not been opened by him for fear of small-pox. "May I ask what your holiness thought of the press," said I. "I thought that the packed cases contained some miraculous remedies, which when applied could neutralize the effects of small-pox coming out from the tubes enclosed among the lithographic articles," replied his holiness. "You wrote in your letter that you had sent different powerful chemicals along with the press, and, as you had promised to send some vaccine matter, I thought you had sent it with the chemicals. One night I smelt some gaseous emanations coming out from the boxes, which I thought contained the germs of small-pox, so I did not sleep that night, my mind being troubled with the dread of small-pox attacking us." We laughed heartily as his holiness went on relating these ludicrous fancies of his. I told him that the vaccine matter enclosed in hermetically closed glass tubes was not yet come, having been by mistake put into the packages now lying at Lachen Pass. At last he was convinced of his delusions and laughed at his groundless fears. He asked me if Phurchung was come and had brought our baggage from Lachen, whereupon I related to him the circumstances connected with Phurchung's failure.

15th January.—After breakfast we were called to the Minister's presence. After a short conversation we went to his library where the packages were. In his presence the boxes were opened and the portable lithographic press set up. The Minister seemed to take much pleasure in the fixing and setting up of the apparatus. He himself unfastened the screws with the screw-drivers, fixed the rollers, wheels and cylinders, and gave orders to carpenters to make a pair of tables to fix the press upon. The pony-seller brought the pony for our inspection a second time. I begged the Minister to ask Kusho Tungchhen to examine the pony and to let me know its proper price. Permission being granted, Tungchhen took the pony outside the monastery and made a monk try it for a short distance. He said that the pony was worth 20 *srangs* or Rs. 50, but even if we paid 22 *srangs* it would not be dear.

16th January.—The lithographic press and other apparatus had become rusty through lying long unused. We tried to clean them with cocoanut-oil which we had carried for using in the magic-lantern, but with little effect. We then tried Tibet rape-oil with emery powder, and found it answer well. After breakfast, which we took with the Minister in the west drawing-room of Phuntsho Ḳhangsar, he told us that he was very anxious to get the articles left at Lachen. Phurchung, he said, was not intelligent enough to persuade the Jongpons not to obstruct him, and even if he were provided with a proper passport, as required by the Jongpons of Khamba, he would hardly succeed in satisfying their shrewd inquiries. He therefore thought that unless Ugyen Gyatsho undertook to go to Lachen, the things would hardly come to Tashi-lhunpo. He had heard that Ugyen had relations at Lachen—a circumstance which would go a great way to help him in his mission. Ugyen in reply said he had no relations at Lachen, but that one of his sister's daughters was married to the headman (Peepon) of Lachen. The Minister observed that he did not wish to send Ugyen to Lachen merely, but that as he had other articles, such as calendar-watches, books on science and arts, and particularly on astronomy and geodesy, to order from Calcutta, none but Ugyen could be entrusted to buy them, whom he would therefore like to go on to Darjeeling for the purpose. Ugyen Gyatsho in reply represented that it being the middle of winter, the journey between Tashi-lhunpo and Darjeeling would be fraught with immense dangers. The Kangra Lamo pass must surely now be blocked with snow, and the cold must be extremely severe between Khamba-jong and the Kangra Lamo pass. He feared he might die in the snows or fall ill on the way. However, as he was bound to give effect to his holiness' wishes, he must consent to go down to India in spite of the difficulties he was sure he would encounter on the journey. He would do anything in his power to please his holiness, provided he was furnished with a *lam-yig* (passport) the draft of which would be made by himself. The Minister undertook to provide him with a *lam-yig* containing very favourable conditions, and to propitiate the gods in order that they may protect Ugyen Gyatsho from dangers from man or beast or disease till the 1st of the third Tibetan month (end of April 1882). Ugyen Gyatsho then thrice prostrating himself before the Minister, reverentially addressed him, "Your holiness, may it please you graciously to excuse me, as, being a man of the petty state of Sikkim, I am ignorant of the honourific language used in China and Tibet, and consequently am unable to address your holiness in suitable language befitting your exalted and sacred position; yet your holiness, out of your great mercy and generosity, will be pleased to hear my prayer. Allow me to pray that in my absence your holiness will take charge of Pandibla, who, as your holiness knows, has no friend or acquaintance in this distant land, except your holiness. I pray also that your holiness will promise to look after his health, and will not allow any injury to be done to him by our enemies or by the Government authorities on the ground that he is a foreigner." After a pause the Minister said, "Do not you fear that Pandibla will die before your return: he may suffer from illness, but die he will not." Ugyen Gyatsho then begged the Minister to favour us with a letter in which the following conditions were to be inserted :—

1st.—That the Minister take charge of Pandibla (myself), that he may not be molested by the Government, that his person and properties may not be subjected to any kind of injury from outsiders, and that his comforts be looked after here.

2nd.—That when Ugyen Gyatsho returned in the spring, he and I might be sent on pilgrimage to Central Tibet without opposition from any quarter.

3rd.—That we must not be thrown or allowed to be thrown into any difficulties of a political nature during our residence in Tibet on the ground of our being foreigners.

Besides these, which were to be written in the form of an agreement, he would keep the rest of his holiness' promises and assurances in his heart as objects of hope and cheerful confidence, like the lotus flower in the allegorical story of the sun and moon. Thus did Ugyen Gyatsho supplicate the Minister and charm me at the amount of foresight he displayed. It was a very wise provision he was making for his own responsibility towards our Government; for if owing to any cause whatever I happened to die in Tibet during his absence, he could produce this letter to show his anxiety on my account. The Minister, in reply, said that it was unnecessary for Ugyen to be anxious for my safe residence in Tibet. He would keep me in his own house as a member of his own family, and defray all my expenses. As regards the second question, it was his intention to send us to Lhasa with the Tashi Lama's party in May next, as there was every probability of his visiting Lhasa in the beginning of the summer; but if neither the Grand Lama nor himself went to Lhasa, he would make separate arrangements for our pilgrimage. As for the third point, he was aware of his own responsibility when he invited us to come up to Tashi-lhunpo, and he readily agreed to give Ugyen Gyatsho a letter assuring him that he would not allow us to be molested by anybody during our residence in Tibet. We offered his holiness our cordial thanks for his very kind assurance, and Ugyen promised to start for India within a week's time. In the evening he told me that the promised letter would be of great use to us, as, if difficulties arose, it would be easy to extricate ourselves by producing it. I told him that I knew Tibet and the Tibetans well: nobody could give us trouble: if anybody or the Government suspected us, we would simply be sent back to the Sikkim frontier under a suitable escort. Under such circumstances it would be unnecessary for us to produce the Minister's letter, which may entangle him with us. I knew full well what influence the Minister had both at Lhasa and Tashi-lhunpo. In the latter he was the right-hand man of the Grand Lama, and at Lhasa the two senior Shapes who ruled over the country were his devoted admirers and worshippers. Our business was simply to mind our own work—the study of the language and literature of Tibet.

17th January.—In the morning, at about 7 A.M., the Minister went to Shiga-tse to bless and grant absolution to the departed soul of Kusho Shang-po, who had lately died from the effects of a cruel and severe flogging in connection with the Ampa's row. At his departure he instructed the Lama to clean and set up the lithographic press. Accordingly, after breakfast, Ugyen Gyatsho, Phurchung, and myself engaged ourselves in the press business. Phurchung and Ugyen polished the apparatus while I set up the machinery and instructed the carpenter to make tables in my presence, as the one he had prepared would not answer. We took our tiffin in the library room, where the press-work was to be conducted.

18th January.—After breakfast, we went to the Minister's presence, who told Ugyen Gyatsho that Kusho Badurla, the head of the conveyance department, wished to see the pearls we had brought with us. We gave him the pearls, with a request that we might be paid in silver through him. He therefore sent Ugyen with a letter to Kusho Badurla to settle the price of the pearls. Ugyen did not find Badurla at home, but conversed with his wife, whom he at once recognized, having seen her at Tumlong and Chhumbi, she being none other than the elder sister of the present Rajah of Sikkim. She gave him a very kind reception, and talked with him for nearly one hour. He was treated with tea and *gya-thug* (Chinese gruel), and was asked to call again.

19th January.—To-day being the day of the new moon, nearly a thousand beggars lined the two sides of the road leading from Tashi-lhunpo to Shiga-tse. Lhagpa Tshering, the well-known almsgiver, was distributing alms to the poor. At noon Ugyen visited the *thom*, where he witnessed a quarrel between a Tibetan woman and a Khamba over a *tanka* worth of barley-flour, in the course of which the woman challenged the latter to take an oath very common in Tibet, namely, that if he told an untruth, he might never see the Grand Lama's face. Ugyan Gyatsho, who was present all the time, separated the parties. The people of Kham are a fierce race who infest the solitudes of Tibet, and generally carry on depredations in the isolated villages north of Lhasa. They are a dangerous class.

20th January.—Early in the morning we received an invitation to dine with our acquaintance Lupa Gyantsan of Shiga-tse. We were told that to-day was the new-year's day of the working people, being observed by all the people of Tibet with the exception of the clergy. To my mind the question arose how could *two* new-years' days come to be observed by the Tibetans. The solution was not at present possible. After many excuses we agreed to dine at Lupa's house in the afternoon. After breakfast we went to the presence of the Minister, who asked if we had come to work with the press. On Ugyen Gyatsho's answering yes, he thanked us copiously, and leaving his other business came to the library-room. He carefully washed the lithographic stone himself, which Ugyen Gyatsho dried by keeping it near an earthenware stove blazing with charcoal fire. Everything being ready, I asked the Minister to print a very auspicious hymn at first, that the first fruit of our labour might be a sacred composition. The Minister at once ran to his study room and fetched a very old manuscript, containing a stanza or *stotra* composed by the present Grand Lama in honour and praise of the Minister. I opened the transfer-paper roll from the tin case, and asked him to dictate to Ugyen Gyatsho. He wished himself to write on the transfer-paper with the transfer-ink, although Ugyen hesitated to entrust him with that task, which requires good practice. I told the Minister that I had no objection to his undertaking to write the first copy. If it turned out bad, we could easily wash off the impressions from the stone and print fresh copies. He was quite delighted with my offer, and with the greatest caution and attention wrote upon the transfer-paper, which, being placed on the stone, he eagerly took hold of the handle, fearing lest Ugyen or I might forestall him. He turned the wheels, Ugyen having put the ink with the roller (*tobchhen* in Tibetan). I counted the turnings—once, twice, and thrice,—when an excellent impression was obtained. "So it is a charming print ! the press is a miracle !" said the Minister, quite transported with joy. He sent Shabdung, his page, to call Kusho Tungchhen and three of his Lama friends to witness the miraculous affair. The *do-par* (stone-press) was now given the name of *tul-par* (or the press of miracles). The Minister in the presence of his friends printed twenty more copies in the course of an hour and a half. Ugyen Gyatsho secretly told me that he would take one of these twenty copies to Calcutta to show the first print of the press to Mr. Croft, our kind master, who had specially indented for the press from England to present it to the Minister. It being tiffin-time, Kah-chan Gopa brought tea and biscuit with a few sticks of boiled mutton. While I was engaged in reading the directions about working the press, which the Minister wanted to translate, the latter lifted the tea-cup to my lips. I was, indeed, unprepared for such a mark of honour, and immediately took the cup in my hand. "*Mitog, mitog*; do not care for this trifle - go on with your work," said his holiness. At three in the afternoon we asked his leave to go to Lupa Gyantsan's house. He permitted us to go to Shiga-tse with some reluctance, and in fact did not like our going to the house of so insignificant a man as Lupa. I understood the Minister's object in hesitating to give us permission, but Ugyen Gyatsho, on account of his promise to Lupa, could not be prevailed upon to let me remain at home. I, however, delayed starting, and Ugyen went alone to Shiga-tse. Lupa not seeing me, sent two of his servants with a pressing invitation. At last at half-past 4 P.M. I started by the road leading to Shiga-tse town and running by the east of Kesar Lhakhang. The eastern part of the town was filled with groves and handsome lawns. I rode on the pony which had been kept for trial, and which I now made up my mind to buy for Rs. 56. Lupa Gyantsan gave me a warm reception, his wife and himself coming to help me in dismounting from my pony. Both husband and wife conducted me to the first-floor, which was lately completed, and which contained his chapel. I was asked to occupy the highest seat just below the chapel. Ugyen Gyatsho occupied a seat further below and to the left of mine. First *chhang* was served. I did not touch it. Then tea (*cha*) was brought by his young daughter, a girl of ten, while his wife placed a wooden bowl of barley-flour and some pieces of boiled mutton on a little table. Lupa Gyantsan then, taking off his turban, respectfully begged that I should take *sol cha* (prepared tea), and consider that I was dining at my own home. Shortly after, Ugyen, according to the Tibetan custom, made a short speech, in which he exhorted the Lupa always to inquire after my health during his absence from Tashi-lhunpo, and to furnish me with any articles of food, &c., which I might think of buying during his absence. He thanked them both for their kindness, adding that he (Lupa) and I being old acquaintances, should ever continue to be friends, and that he would with my permission take the liberty to say that men who, like us, have been friends, must behave to each other as brothers born of the same parents. So saying, he presented them each with a rupee and a piece of scarf, putting the coins in their hands and the scarves round their necks. They received these with much pleasure, and rising from their seats said that they considered it their duty to serve me as my devoted servants. Ugyen then put a scarf on our servant Lhagpa's head, observing that it was given him ever to serve me faithfully and obediently. Lhagpa, joining his palms, saluted me, and said that he would never prove false. We then took leave of our hosts, wishing them a happy new year. I had inquired if it was a purely Tibetan custom, and from their reply I guessed, and very rightly, that this was the new-year's day according to the national Tibetan custom of the pre-Buddhist period. This is the only remnant of ancient Tibetan usage which has not been entirely displaced by Buddhism. The Buddhist new year commences in February, which the Lamas observe very carefully. At the time of taking leave of the hosts, Ugyen told them that I would very much like to know of passing events and occurrences in Tibet from time to time. Before we got up from our seats, Lupa's daughter, having dressed herself in her gala-dress, danced and sang a Tibetan song. Ugyen asked Lupa if she knew to dance like the Chinese, whereupon she danced very prettily in the Chinese fashion, and also sang a Chinese song, Lupa himself playing an accompaniment on the pipe (*ling-bu*). When the girl sat down, an old woman sang a Tibetan song, wishing us a happy new year. At 7 P.M. we returned to Tashi-lhunpo.

21*st January*.—This day was also observed as a holiday by the Tibetan laity. Very few men assembled at the *thom*, so that Ugyen could not make purchases of provisions for us. After breakfast we went to the presence of the Minister, who graciously insisted upon my putting up with him at his own residence Phuntsho Khangsar. He offered to accommodate me in the library-room, adjoining to which there was one waiting-room and a bath-room. I gladly agreed to the proposal, and heartily thanked him for his very kind offer. Ugyen Gyatsho and myself then begged him to keep the gold and the proceeds of the sale of pearls in his chest for safe-custody. In the evening Nima Dorje, the eldest son of Chhyan-dso Kusho of Dong-tse, arrived and was kindly received by the Minister. After conversing with his holiness for a few minutes, Nima Dorje came to me, and showed me his eyes. I saw that a cataract had formed in his right eye. He told me that, hearing his uncle

Kusho Jambala's eyes were improving under my treatment, he was emboldened to try my medicines, and that, with the permission of his father and the Minister, he was come to consult me. I told him I was exceedingly sorry I had no medicines with me to suit his case; that we, however, proposed to send Ugyen Gyatsho to Calcutta to bring certain articles, along with which some medicines would also be brought. As soon as the *lam-yig* was obtained, Ugyen Gyatsho would start for India. Nima Dorje then smilingly said that the *lam-yig* was being prepared by the Dahpon, and it was to ask the Minister about a certain point to be inserted in the *lam-yig* that he had come here. He hoped the *lam-yig* would be ready within a day or two. He confidentially told me that if I could cure him of the defect in his eye, he would present me several thousand silver coins. I replied that I would care more for his recovery than for his money.

22nd January.—We resumed reading English and working sums in arithmetic with the Minister. After reading a few lines of the First Royal Reader, his holiness turned over the pages of Ganot's Physics and desired me to explain to him the diagrams on telegraphy and the camera obscura. There was nothing in that book which he did not like to be explained, but unfortunately for me I was not myself acquainted with most of the subjects which excited his curiosity. Not prepared to expose my own ignorance, I often dwelt longer on questions and points which I could best explain and with which I was familiar. In spite of all my careful attempts to evade his inquisitiveness, the shrewd Minister had gauged me well, and often expressed his earnestness to meet with such men as Dr. Sircar and my brother Navin Chandra. "Amchi-chhenpo" (Dr. Sircar, of whose disinterested zeal and earnestness for the cultivation of science in Aryavarta I had often told him in course of conversation), he said, "cannot be expected to visit this country. He is a great man. He will not probably take the trouble of crossing the snows. But could not you arrange to invite your brother, who, as you say, has carefully studied this interesting book?" While we were thus engaged in conversation, several visitors were announced as waiting for an interview with his holiness, so that I had to withdraw to the library-room. In the afternoon Nima Dorje brought the *lam-yig* and presented it to the Minister. We were called to his presence and shewn it. Ugyen Gyatsho disapproving of it, as nothing was mentioned in it of his return journey, it was returned.

23rd January.—Crowds of visitors came to receive the *chhyag-wang* (benediction) from the Minister's hand. Among them were many Kulmuck pilgrims from Khalkha and other remote provinces of Mongolia. The leader of the Khalkha Mongols was Lobssang Arya, now a respectable man, having been promoted to the *Gyer-gyan* (eldership) of Khalkha Kham-tshan. It may be remembered that he had served me as a cook for more than a month during my residence at Tashi-lhunpo in 1879. The Minister talked with him in Mongolian, after receiving the pilgrims with much kindness. The Mongols are greatly devoted to his holiness for his affability and acquaintance with their language, customs and manners. Some of the Mongols peeped from the window of the waiting-room at me, wishing evidently to talk with me. Some asked me to explain to them the map of Asia, which was hung on the wall of the waiting-room. Besides this map there was a beautiful bird's-eye view of Rivo-tsena, the superb residence of Arya Manjusri, or the god of learning and wisdom in China, in the neighbourhood of Pekin. I explained to them the latter, and shewed them the cities of Lhasa, Gaya, Urga (the capital of Khalkha), Calcutta, &c., on the English map. The mention of these names startled them very much. They gazed at me with wonder, and evidently took me for a pilgrim who had been all over the world. "Have you been to those places?" inquired they, opening wide their oblique eyes. "No," said I, "I have not been to those places, still I know them." "How can that be unless you be a miracle-worker?" I then added that I could at once tell them by looking to the *satha* (map) the distance of one place from another in Mongolia. After silently wondering at what I said, and saluting me by touching their head to my forehead, they bid me good-bye.

24th January.—Early in the morning I was called to the Minister's presence, when a young monk of Nagpa Ta-tshang (Tantrik school) came and sat by me. The Minister asked him to show me his eyes, which were both a little swollen. His holiness reminded me that the young monk had served him devotedly during his residence at the Nag-khang, and was deserving of my attention. I opened Moore's Manual of Family Medicines in his presence and read the symptoms mentioned under the heading Muscæ volitantes. "That is precisely the disease this young Gelong is suffering from," said his holiness. The monk also said that he saw spots and a kind of web-like haze before his eyes. I gave him a few doses of alum lotion to wash his eyes with, and made him promise to walk round the monastery during fair weather several times a day.

In the afternoon I took tiffin with Kusho Tungchhen, and conversed with him on the topics of the weather and the high winds which now every day blew invariably in the afternoon. He talked of Phagri pass and told me that the *Serpon* (customs collector of Phagri) was his friend. If Ugyen Gyatsho returned to Darjeeling by the Phagri pass, he could give him a letter of introduction to that officer. I thanked him for his kindness, and added that Ugyen would prefer the Lachen pass, as he had obtained a *lam-yig* from the commander of Shiga-tse, whose jurisdiction did not, as he knew, extend to Phagri-jong He then requested me to indent for a few good Malacca rattans and a few yards of merino cloth for his own use.

25th January.—In the morning as usual I went to the Minister's presence and had my breakfast with him. He told me that in certain star maps he had seen figures of the different constellations and had understood they represented *real* figures to be seen in the sky. To satisfy his curiosity in this respect he had bought a large telescope at much cost. Not knowing how to use it and what to see by it, he had not been able to put that fine and valuable instrument to any practical use. He therefore desired me to write to my master in India to select for him a well illustrated work on astronomy. He also remembered my saying that the regions of the moon, saturn, and even of the sun were said to be visible through the medium of the telescope: now he was very curious to know what those luminaries contained and what was the natural aspect of their surfaces, lying under the effusion of streaming light from them. I told him that I could satisfy his curiosity to some extent by showing him the use of the telescope, although I could not possibly tell him all that scientific men had learnt about them by means of their researches. He smilingly observed that hitherto he had been under the impression that the sun and moon and the numerous other planets and constellations were angelic luminaries, who for the excellence of their moral merits were promoted to the celestial mansions at different heights, to shed forth their radiant lustre and thereby guide all living beings of this earth to the path of *dharma*; but if the enlightened *Philings* had discovered hitherto unknown secrets regarding those luminaries, which it was nothing impossible for them to do, he would like to know their true character before he could accept them as correct and real. While we were thus engaged in conversation, Nima Dorje arrived and presented the *lam-yig* to his holiness. After perusal the Minister handed it over to me, and I in turn passed it to Ugyen Gyatsho. The Dahpons, we found, out of anxiety for the prevention of small-pox, had instructed the Jongpon of Khamba to examine the contents of the boxes to see that nothing defiled or contagious was brought with them. This would put the Jongpon in a position to extract from Ugyen Gyatsho any amount of money they might choose. I inquired, reading the passage in question, how it would be possible for the Jongpons to ascertain if there was any contagious matter in the boxes Ugyen Gyatsho was now going to fetch. As it would be inconvenient to wait a few days more for a corrected *lam-yig*, the Minister advised Ugyen to be satisfied with the one in hand and to make the best use of it according to his own intelligence and judgment. Nima Dorje again reminded me of his eye-disease, and begged me to indent for the best medicines obtainable from Calcutta. Kahchan Gopa likewise asked me to procure him a very good stereoscope from Calcutta, of which he would bear the cost.

26th January.—The Minister proposed that I should put up with him at Phuntsho Khangsar, assuring us repeatedly of his kind protection. Ugyen Gyatsho undertook to go to India, on the understanding that Phurchung's services were to be lent to him for a period of six months at the most: without Phurchung he would not proceed a single step towards Khamba-jong. After breakfast, before we again met, the Minister consulted with Tungchhen and Gopa about keeping me with him. They readily agreed to it, but objected to my keeping Lhagpa as my servant, and the Minister told us that Lhagpa being a Shiga-tse man could not be trusted, as Shiga-tse men were very deceitful and cunning, and at the same time faithless. Although I spoke favourably of Lhagpa, the Minister could not be persuaded to believe in his honesty, and observed that as he had undertaken to look to my wants and comforts, there was not the least necessity of entertaining a servant to wait upon me at my expense. Fearing if I still persisted in my wish to keep a servant, that the Minister might suspect me of entertaining some ulterior objects, I at once agreed to abide by his decision. Of course it was my intention to keep myself informed of the daily occurrences in the town and the monastery, and I thought Lhagpa, not having much to do at Phuntsho Khangsar, could easily rove about the town and monastery in search of information, as I myself would be practically confined within the walls of Phun-tsho Khangsar, being required, according to custom, to wait upon his holiness. Everything being settled about my residence, we were now to equip Ugyen Gyatsho and Phurchung for a journey to India *viâ* Khamba-jong and Lachen pass. They were very reluctant to journey at this season of the year, as it was midwinter and snow must undoubtedly have fallen in the lofty regions of the south. The Minister expressed his anxiety at Ugyen's delay to start, and I was equally anxious to start them, that I might hear from home and friends at Calcutta. After supper I prepared my letters for home, indulging hopes of receiving letters through Rinzing.

27th January.—After returning from the *thom*, Ugyen and Phurchung busied themselves in preparing for the journey. I allowed the former to take with him a pair of Gyan-tse blankets and a suit of lambskin clothes to protect himself from the severity of the cold. He purchased a large quantity of sheep's fat to distribute among the Sikkimese on the way. Dried mutton, barley-flour and sheep's fat are special dainties to the Sikkimese, which they value above all other articles of food. I gave Phurchung a pair of my own blankets for his use during the journey. With my permission they hired four ponies for the conveyance of themselves and their indispensables. In the evening we were invited to take tea with the Minister, when Ugyen, after three profound salutations to his holiness, prayed that his blessings may always be on him, and that by the mercy of the sacred Buddhas he might reach his destination safely. When the Minister withdrew to his prayer-room, we went down to the second-floor and conversed for a short time with Kusho Tungchhen.

28th January.—To-day, the 10th of the 12th Tibetan lunar month, was considered very auspicious to start for India. At six in the morning, Uygen, Phurchung and I went to the Minister's presence. His holiness, after a short prayer, wished Ugyen a safe and pleasant journey, and placed a long scarf on his neck. Phurchung also received one, shorter and inferior to Ugyen's. At the latter's special request I desired Phurchung in a short speech to serve Ugyen as he would serve me. Phurchung answered my exhortation with

La lasso, lasso (yes sir, yes sir). Then we returned to Thorgod Chyikhang, our lodging, where after breakfast, I presented parting scarves to my faithful companions. The scene was extremely touching, and they shed tears to leave me alone. I, too, could not suppress my feelings when I exhorted them to take care of themselves in the snows and to be prepared for any heavy snowfall. Ugyen Gyatsho assured me he would exert himself to the utmost of his power to establish friendly relations with the Jongpon of Khamba and the Lacheu Peepon. I gave him leave to spend a reasonable sum in making presents to them, and secretly told him that if he succeeded in making friends with either of them or both, it would be of great service to our cause, and that I would gladly pay him the expenses of *tog-chhang* (or friendship wine). He smiled at my suggestion, and said he would do everything in his power to please me and return to Tibet in April next. I thanked him heartily for his kindness, and also Phurchung, who having obtained a pony for himself to ride up to Khamba-jong, was wholly taken up with that pleasurable prospect. Both now in excellent spirits rode off towards Delel. I sent Wang Chhyug Gya*l*-po and Shabdung to fetch my clothes, utensils, &c., from Thorgod Chyikhang. They brought some, and told me that our servant Lhagpa was clandestinely removing some of my kettles, enamelled plates, &c. I immediately went to Thorgod Chyikhang and asked him to produce the missing articles. He denied any knowledge of them, and said the *de* (devils) must have removed them. Surprised with his replies, I at once sent for Nerpala and Kusho Tungchhen. Nerpala arrived first; and though we could plainly see Lhagpa's great pocket enormously stuffed out, yet as it was impossible to search his pocket, we confined ourselves to drawing out a list of things that were missing. Kusho Tungchhen, who presently arrived, smiled at the roguery of our trusted servant Lhagpa, and made me understand that our knowledge of the Tibetans was very small, and that we should not have trusted in Shiga-tse people. He then drew out a list of things we had with us, and at the conclusion locked the doors of Thorgod Chyikhang, and told Lhagpa to return quietly to his home. My bedding and books were removed to the library-room, which henceforth became the place of my residence.

29th January.—Early in the morning, after performing the morning service, his holiness suddenly came to my room, accompanied by Kusho Tungchhen. I rose and respectfully begged him to take his seat on a raised cushion near my table, to which his holiness said, *mitog-mitog* (be not anxious for that). He observed to Kusho Tungchhen, "This library-room will hardly in its present state be comfortable to Pandibla. Will you fetch me the hammer, a few nails and a piece of screen cloth?" Tungchhen ran to bring them, and soon returned with the things, when the Minister proceeded to fasten the curtain with his own hands. I begged to be allowed to fix the curtain myself. He replied that he felt much pleasure to make me comfortable. "This room," he said, "is filled with books, most of which are of arsenical papers. You will fall ill if you constantly inhale the air of this place." The curtain divided the room into two parts, the books lying in the northern part and my seat and bedstead in the southern half of it. Underneath the floor was the *sol-thab* (or cook-room), the heat of which kept the library very dry and warm. There was only one window in the room, about four feet square, through which a view of the Narthang group of hills could be obtained. At 9 A.M. breakfast was announced, when Nerpala conducted me to the Minister's presence. Tea was poured in a pretty China cup. Kahchan Gopa fetched me a bowl of barley-flour and a few slices of boiled mutton, and marking my difficulty in making a paste of the barley-flour with tea in the cup after the Tibetan manner, made the thick paste for me by twirling the cup on his palm while mixing the flour with his fore-finger. In the dining-room there was a parrot, lately presented to the Minister by the Chhyan-dso-shar of Tashi-lhunpo, and a small saffron plant with very pretty flowers, resembling the marigold. Nerpala took much care of this plant, keeping it inside the house during the night, and exposing it to the sun during the day. The Minister told me that a Kashmir merchant had brought a few saffron seeds from Kashmir and presented them to him. The plant throve well, but yielded no saffron. After breakfast I returned to my room to my studies, and with the permission of the Minister commenced a search for Sanskrit books in the library. At noon Machen, the cook, placed near me a teapot of steaming tea, kept on an earthenware stove. I was told that it was injurious to drink cold water in Tibet, and was recommended to use hot tea. The Tibetans very seldom drink water, but the lay people quench their thirst with draughts of cold fermented barley liquor, and the Lamas with warm tea. In the evening the cook replenished the teapot. As the Minister, on account of his vows of monkhood, was debarred from taking any meat in the afternoon, evening, or night, he desired me to take supper with Kusho Tungchhen; accordingly after the lamp was lighted I went downstairs and sat to gossip with Kusho Tungchhen in the *sol-thab*.

30th January.—To-day I discovered three Sanskrit works written in the Tibetan character, (viz. "Kavyadarsha," by Acharya Sri Dandi; "Chandra Vyakarana," by Chandra Gomi; and "Svarasvat Vyakarana" by Acharya Anu,) and was transported with joy when I saw that they contained explanations in Tibetan. Now that my companions had left and I was alone, having none to speak with, except the Tibetans, who were perfect strangers to my native tongue, the author Sri Dandi, himself a traveller, was my only agreeable companion. In the afternoon I showed this author to the Minister, who to my surprise was able to give me more information than I had expected. He had committed the entire volume to memory. "Dandi," he said, "must have lived some thousand years ago." I asked how he came to that conjecture. "Well," said his holiness, "this work was translated into Tibetan by one of the Sakya hierarchs who lived about 600 years ago, and it was probable that the work was not very new when it came to be known in this country." In the evening I took my supper with Kusho Tungchhen, and talked on various subjects. As my candles were all consumed, I begged some oil from Kahchan Gopa to feed my lamp, and remained engaged with my books till midnight.

31st January.—The preparation for the new year's ceremonies now occupied the attention of all classes of men. Large numbers of men came to receive the first vows of monkhood from his holiness, and Kahchan Shabdung brought a number of his monk-pupils for ordainment into the great order of Bhikshu. The Minister was largely taken up with these religious duties, and could hardly see me for more than ten or twelve minutes. When I withdrew to my room, the astrologer, Lobssang, came to see me. He was busy with his new year's almanac, and frequently turned its pages to see if there were no mistakes. The Minister was to examine it before submission to the Grand Lama. The astrologer was curious to know what the stones and wheeled apparatus lying near my table meant. I told him what they were. He begged me to explain the process of printing, but I politely evaded his request, as I had been told not to talk of the press to outsiders. In the evening Deba-shikha arrived with a large supply of yak butter and barley-flour, evidently for the approaching new year's ceremonies.

Henceforth I applied myself deeply to the study of the sacred books and histories of Tibet. When I felt tired of Tibetan, I refreshed my mind with the melodious *slokas* of Kavyādarsha, both in the text and in a translation. During my leisure hours I conversed with Kusho Tungchhen, Nerpala, Kahchan Gopa, Kahchan Shabdung, Kusho Dichhang-pa, and a host of other well-informed men. I ceased to write my diary regularly, but only noted such information respecting the customs and manners of the country as appeared interesting.

15th February.—The winter was very severe, or I felt it to be so, during the first part of this month. Daily the north winds blew, raising storms of dust in the plains situated to the west and south of Tashi-lhunpo. The grand monastery being on the south and lee-side of Dolmairi, the north winds, made to shift by the obstacle, blew upon it from the west. The falling of sand and small bits of stone raised by the fitful gusts, on the papered shutters of my room disturbed me very often. There were two holes in the shutter, through which, as the air rushed in, a kind of shrill whistle was produced. I saw people busily engaged in out-door work, such as collecting fuel and tending cattle. In fact, this was in a manner the busiest part of the year, when the Tibetans remain on the move for the purpose of buying and selling. At a time when the extremely dry cold winds blowing from the Arctic regions wither up the vegetation, freeze the streams and fountains, harden the soil as if it was baked with cold, and blast the skin of travellers, the period of universal merriment begins. Greater agility and briskness never mark the habits of the people in summer or autumn than at this time. The monks, like the lay-people, are remarkable for their habit of early rising, and I did not know any monk within the walls of the monastery who rose later than 5 in the morning. The usual time for getting up from bed was 4 A.M., and those who slept later than that without any special cause were sent to the discipliner of the Tshogs-chhen for correction. At 3 in the morning the *dung-chhen* (great trumpet) is blown to summon all the monks to the congregation hall to attend the daily religious service. Whoever fails to attend is punished next morning. No register is called, no attendance recorded, yet the church discipliner could tell what monk out of two thousand absented himself on a particular day. I was the only man who slept up to six in the morning, and sometimes I lingered in bed till seven. The monks of Phuntsho Khangsar used often to remark that, were I a regular monk of the monastery, the Gyekoi's birch would have stript my body of its flesh. I smiled at the remarks, and told them that in fact I slept less than they were used to do. The Minister himself sometimes in the morning used to walk quietly into my room and awaken me, and excused me on the ground that he often found me up with my books till midnight. Sometimes he used to peep in by raising the screen of my room to see if I was not awake, for being himself a great lover of study, he appreciated the habit of study in others. Fortunately for me I was the only man within the large premises of Phuntsho Khangsar who kept up at night like himself; but the Minister used to rise early, while I used to get up late in the morning. The room in which I slept was warm and well-ventilated, my woollens fresh and soft, and my stuffed bed, though about nine inches high, thick enough to keep off the cold of the floor, which was glossy, and reflected some of the furniture of the house. Whenever the winds subsided I used to go out for a stroll round the monastery. At all other times I used to confine myself and my acquaintance to books alone. The repairs of the lofty *chhorten* which stood to the west of the monastery opposite our house were commenced this morning. About twenty monks, assisted by about forty laymen labourers, were engaged in dismantling the gilt spiral ornamentations fixed just above the cupola, or in Tibetan the *pumpa*, of the *chhorten*. This *chhorten* is called Damdul (*Da* enemy, and *dul* vanquished), on account of its having been erected at the time of the last Nepal war, by which meritorious act the enemy were believed to have been defeated by the imperial forces. The late grand Lama Tanpai-nima had consecrated many charms and mystic incantations inscribed in silk scarves, which were preserved within the cupola of the *chhorten* to keep off enemies. The repairs lasted three days, during which the noise of the workmen, their songs and their shouts in dragging heavy rocks, &c., much interrupted me. I was told that the labourers were employed by force, and that they received neither wages nor food, which latter they had to bring from their homes. On the ground-floor of our house, opposite the big ladder leading to the first floor, half a dozen monks were engaged in making cakes, bread and biscuits, and large caldrons full of butter were kept boiling to fry the twisted biscuits, &c.

16*th February*.—In the morning Deba-shikha, dressed in a brown broadcloth robe, arrived, accompanied by his son Damdul, a boy of eight, bringing for the Minister a few pots of *ti* (a kind of cream made from the first milk of a newly-calved *jo*). I was sitting in Tungchhen's room on the first-floor, and Tungchhen-la asked me if I would taste the *ti*, recommending it to me as very nutritious and cooling; and accordingly Deba-shikha sent two pots of *ti* to my room. At noon several Mongolian pilgrims came to receive the minister's *chhyag-wang* (benediction). I spoke to some of the respectable-looking Mongols who were waiting in the lobby for an interview with his holiness, asking them in Mongolian "*amar si-eng ba ya-no*" (are you in good health?), when all smilingly replied "*si-eng, si-eng*" (very well, very well), and in turn asked "*bi-si-eng baya-no*" (are you well?), and seemed amused at my attempt to talk with them in their mother-tongue. I had picked up only a smattering of the Kalmuck language, and my curious pronunciation of their aspirates, especially the *kh* and *h*, caused some merriment. I observed that they invariably pronounced our *h* as *kh* and the aspirate *k* as *h*. As I did the reverse in my pronunciation, and that repeatedly, they thought my pronunciation very bad, no doubt. When we were thus engaged, the Minister came out of his room, and the Mongols at once prostrated themselves before his holiness, and he touched their heads with the palms of his hands. One of them, probably the devoutest of the number, in a kneeling posture addressed his holiness to this effect:—"Oh, thou who hast been for unnumbered ages the deliverer of souls and hast taught men and gods, vouchsafe thy blessings to me, that I may be born in the happy land of Shambhala." He spoke half in Mongolian and half in Tibetan, mixing both the languages in a curious way. His holiness made a suitable reply in Mongolian in a low voice.

The Mongols had brought him presents of horsehoof-shaped silver ingots called *tamig-ma*, each of the value of Rs. 125. They also presented him with different kinds of carpets, brocades, scarves, rubies, jades, cats-eyes, &c. In the evening Deba-shikha came to my room and asked me if I would go to see the *chham*, the grand annual Lama dance. I told him that I was afraid if I joined the vulgar spectators, I could hardly expect gentle treatment from the *Dsim-gag-pas* (the stage guards), for I had seen whips freely used on the heads of the crowded spectators. He said that he would arrange for a reserved seat for me; but the messenger whom he sent returned with the information that, not to speak of seats, even the balconies and roofs of the buildings round the grand courtyard had been engaged by the officials of Labrang and the Mongol pilgrims. However, Tungchhen assured me that he would accompany me himself to the *chham*.

17*th February*.—Early in the morning there was a procession of the Newars (Nepalese Buddhists), which went round the monastery singing Sanskrit hymns to the noisy music of cymbals and bells. There were above forty to fifty Nepalese and twenty to thirty Tibetans in the procession. At 8 A.M. men and women of all classes, dressed in their best commenced to stream into the monastery. At 10 A.M. Kusho Tungchhen, Deba-shikha, a respectable Lama who had come to see Tungchhen, and myself, started to visit the Nag-khang chapels. The streets were filled with spectators, and there was a great concourse of monks round the great *chhorten* and the *gya-phig* (tombs of the grand Lamas). I was dressed in Tungchhen's best church dress, his clothes fitting me very well. We walked slowly and looking straight before us, as only high class Lamas do. Before entering the Nag-khang we paid a visit to another old chapel situated on the east of it, which contained several inscriptions consecrated by Gedundub, the founder of Tashi-lhunpo. Here I was shown the mark of a horse's hoof miraculously impressed on a rock. People in passing by this place touch this sacred hoof-print with their heads. The priest of the temple touched my head with the mask of Ge-nen Dharma Tala, the greatest promoter of Buddhism in China. We then entered the Nag-khang, a place which was very familiar to me, for during our first residence in Tibet we used to come here very often to visit the Minister, and most of the monks were known to me. Kusho Tungchhen being the *ex-chhyan-dso* of this school was received by the monks and the present *chhyan-dso* with much cordiality. We visited all the chapels of the Nag-khang and the several *chhortens* where the remains of the illustrious predecessor of the Minister were embalmed, and at about 11 A.M. we took our seat on the balcony of the second floor of Nag-khang building facing south to see the *chham* (grand dance) which was to take place in the courtyard of the Tsug-la-khang. First of all were unfurled one by one the twenty-four sacred flags made of best embroidered China satin, with figures of the terrific dragon and other monsters worked in threads of gold on them. Each flag, in my opinion, must have cost more than five hundred rupees. Ordinary square parti-coloured flags were hung all round the Tsug-la-khang. The flagstaffs were tall, and made of slender poplar logs, with two stout men to each of them About a dozen coats of mail were worn by the monks, who were in masks mostly representing eagles.

Before the arrival of the principal *chham* was announced, the assembly dissolved for a while, when Kusho Tungchhen conducted me to the presence of Kusho Billûng, an incarnate Lama, who was studying in the Nag-pa Ta-tshang college. I received his *chhyag wang* and returned to my seat, and I was introduced to several of Tungchhen's friends The dancers, each performing his part, entered the stage one after another, and were followed by Kusho Yong-dsin Lhopa, the abbot of Nag-pa Ta-tshang, holding a *Dorge* in his right hand and a bell in his left. He wore a mitre-shaped yellow cap, the corners of which, covering his ears, hung down to his breast. His stature was tall, his looks intelligent, and his complexion fair, and though young his manners were very grave. He acted his part very cleverly, and as soon as he had finished the first portion as the stage master, the flag-bearers, the masked troops, the guards, &c., proceeded towards the courtyard of the grand Tsug-la-khang of Tashi-lhunpo, and the spectators dispersed in haste to reach the place where the dance was to take place. Deba-shikha, Nerpala and a monk of Nagpa Ta-tshang conducted me to the western balcony of the grand Tsug-la-khang. From the Tashi Lama's palace gate to the Tsug-la-khang, a distance of 600 yards, a piece of red cloth was spread for the grand Lama's reception. Kusho Tungchhen conversed for a while with an officer of the Labrang, and obtained from him a high table that I might see the dance standing upon it. The grand Tsug-la-khang was about 300 yards long and 150 feet broad. Round this rose the storeys of the building, four in number, each being ten to twelve feet high. These spacious, handsome, pillared balconies all faced the court where the dance was to take place. From my seat I could see the performance, as well as the principal personages who were present at the *chham.* The grand Lama's seat was just overhead in the second balcony of the first-floor. The long balconies on the east and south were occupied by the families of the chiefs and nobles of Tsang. In the fourth line of balconies were accommodated the Mongol pilgrims and some respectable merchants of Shiga-tse. The four abbots of the four Ta-tshang were assigned the first seats just above the gallery of the Nag-pas. About 50 senior Nag-pas, assisted by their Om-dse and the Dorje Lopon, conducted a short service, Kusho Yong-dsin Lhopa being the president and stage master on the occasion. The Nag-pas sat on very handsome square Khamba rugs. Two high stuffed seats were given to the Om-dse and Dorje Lopon, who held in their hands a pair of cymbals and a tambourine. The stage master only made peculiar figure with his hands while holding the *Dorje* and the bell. At the termination of the service came that august personage the Hwashang, the well-known Dharma Tala who had invited the sixteen Buddhist sages called *sthaviras* to hold a convocation in China for the diffusion of Buddhism in that vast country. His mask was painted dark and represented one completely overpowered by devotion, the yawning mouth, though meant to indicate ecstacy, being very ludicrous. He gazed generally upwards and received presents of scarves which were flung towards him by the spectators. His two wives, with rather well-painted yellow complexions, acted their parts well, and collected the numerous scarves which were thrown towards Dharma Tala. When Dharma Tala and his wives left the scene, there came the four kings of the four quarters of the world dressed in the gaudiest apparel and ornaments, fantastically arranged to illustrate the barbaric splendour of the dress of the High Asian kingdoms. When these masqueraders withdrew, there came the sons of the gods, about sixty in number, dressed in beautiful silk robes and glittering ornaments of cloth of gold, precious stones and pearls. These were followed by Indian acharas, whose black and bearded faces and rude Indian dress excited loud laughter in the crowds of spectators. These clowns in their turn were followed by the four warders of cemeteries, whose skeleton-like appearance was meant to remind the spectators of the terrors of the grave. At about three the dead body of the devil in effigy was burnt, a pile of dry sedge being set on fire upon it. The dance being over, we returned to our house. Incense was burnt on the *Lhakha* of Dolmairi and other mountain-tops in the neighbourhood. I requested Kusho Tungchhen to give me an account of the history of the dance, and he promised to obtain for me the information through one of his Nagpa friends. I heard that there are several works on the art of the religious dance and also on religious music. The accounts that I obtained about the numerous festivities and dances will be included in the chapter on the Tibetan year.

18th February.—Early in the morning the Om-dse of Nag-khang came to our house with a thick razor, the blade of which was about three inches broad (the very sight of it frightened me), with which he intended first of all to shave the Minister's head. Formerly he used to wash his holiness' head with water and *sug-pa* powder, but now he was doing the same with a cake of Pear's transparent soap. I quietly placed my old English razor on the Minister's table, and begged him to try it. The Om-dse took it up, admired it, and with a few strokes of it finished his business. At about 8 A.M. arrangements were made for a religious service to be held in the Minister's reception hall to ordain some monks into the superior order of *gelongs* and some young men into priesthood. Our old acquaintance Kah-chan Machanla was also waiting to take part in the service. At 10 o'clock about a dozen young men in yellow church dresses were admitted into the service room, being the candidates for monkhood. The service lasted till three in the afternoon. The servants of Phuntsho Khangsar were engaged in cleaning the furniture and utensils, and rubbing the floors, when Kusho Tungchhen and I went out for a *kor* (walk) round the monastery. A chill piercing wind was blowing from the north-west, the sky was clear, but the sun's rays were ineffectual against the wind. We dressed ourselves in our lambskin coats, and each with a *thengwa* (string of beads) in his hand, went out by the private entrance to the south of our house, intending to include Damdul *chhorten* in our walk. This *chhorten* was about sixty paces from the entrance. Proceeding in a north-easterly direction for about three hundred paces, we came to a flight of stone steps below the western gateway. This gate was provided with massive doors, which are closed after sunset and opened at sunrise, and is the principal entrance to the monastery. I guessed it to be twelve feet high and eight feet wide. Proceeding about fifty paces further north, we came to a point in a line with the row of glittering *gya-phig* (gilt temples containing the tombs of the grand Lama). Here another flight of about 60 long steps, some made, some cut out of rock, brought us to the north-western corner of the monastery.

Being now on the slope of Dolmairi, we obtained a good view of the whole monastery and the surrounding villages and mountains. Proceeding in a north-easterly direction by a narrow rocky path for about two hundred paces, we came behind the Nag-khang. Here there were several *chyangma* (a species of willow), all in flower. I wondered how in the depth of winter and in a rocky place these trees could thrive and bear flowers! Here we met several hoof-marks which some pilgrims and monks who preceded us touched with their foreheads. Kusho Tungchhen-la told me that the hoof-marks were *ran-jûng, i.e.*, real and not artificial, being the foot-marks of the miraculous chargers of Bodhisattvas. There were several starved pariah mastiffs lying about and looking at us with half-open eyes. Kusho Tungchhen remarked that these dogs were undergoing the miseries of metempsychosis: who knows that they were not sinful *gelongs* in their former lives? He regretted that we had not brought with us a few morsels of parched barley for them.

Proceeding further north-east for upwards of two hundred paces, we arrived at the court of the huge lofty stone building called Kiku Tamsa. I counted nine storeys in it, and guessed its height at about 90 feet: its length was sixty paces and breadth about thirty. People say that its height is equal to its length; but I did not think it to be so. Though it is upwards of two centuries old, yet in spite of all kind of wear and tear from weather, rain and wind it appeared to be in excellent condition, the rubble work being of the very best kind. A sketch of it was obtained by George Bogle, who mistook it for a religious building. Now-a-days this lofty house is used as a godown for dried carcasses of sheep, yak and goats. In the latter part of November a religious service is held here, when all the sacred pictures and paintings of Labrang (the church Government) are hung here for the benefit of the public. People receive benediction from the gods and Buddhas by touching these pictures with their heads. The court of this gigantic building was paved with large slabs of stones neatly cut. We enjoyed from here a very fine view of the grand monastery and town of Shiga-tse and the neighbouring villages. After a while we descended towards the eastern gateway of Tashi-lhunpo. Here we met two Ladaki Tibetans in woollen clothes lined with goat-skin, standing enraptured apparently with the magnificent view of the monastery. Kusho Tungchhen asked who they were and whence they came. They replied that they came from the Chyang-thang, or the desert in the north-western part of Tibet. From here I was shown the Dong-tse Kham-tshan, where all the tribes of Dong-tse and its neighbourhood find accommodation. My friend pointed out to me the bush of juniper which was planted by Gedundub, the founder of the monastery, in which that saintly Lama's hair is still said to exist. I was also shown the spacious buildings of Thaisamling college, the Kyil Khang Ta-tshang and the Shar-tse college. The descent was very steep, and in one place I was about to slide down the smooth surface of a rock. There is an easier but roundabout passage down. Here there were several prayer cylinders fixed in rows of three, four and six, which we twirled one by one as we passed.

Proceeding in a little south-easterly direction by some irregularly cut stone steps, we traversed a distance of nearly five hundred paces, and had to twirl about two dozens of prayer cylinders attached to a *mandang* situated at some distance from the eastern gateway. To the south-east of this *mandang* lies the grove attached to the monastery, and at the north-eastern corner is a stout tall flagstaff. At this spot several beggars were supplicating for alms: some blind, some maimed. These were the outlaws exiled from their native place in lower Tibet by Government for high crimes. From here a well-beaten road goes towards Shiga-tse *viâ* Mani Lhakhang. Proceeding nearly seventy paces along this road in a south-westerly direction we passed the Mani Lhakhang, which is about 25 feet long, and a *mandang* nearly seventy paces long. Nearly twenty paces from the western corner of the latter is the eastern gateway of the grand monastery. On the front of the gate are inscribed in stereotyped letters the sin as well as the penalty of smoking; tobacco smoking being strictly prohibited within the walls of the monastery. Both the red and yellow hat schools of Buddhism strongly denounce tobacco smoking, particularly by monks. In the same direction, at a distance of nearly a hundred paces, is the eastern end of the *mandang*, where a road leading to the southern gate runs in a south-westerly direction. Here is a road dividing the monastery from the grove of Kiki-naga. A second road runs in a westerly direction past the Lhopa-kham-tshan, which it leaves to the right-hand side, and leads on to the Labrang Gyal-tshan-thonpo, or the court of the Tashi Lama.

From the flagstaff we went southward, and proceeding about two hundred paces along the monastery wall, which was on our right-hand side, and above which rise lofty poplars, now entirely leafless, we found ourselves opposite the grove of Kiki-naga, where the grand Lama's mother resides. Then walking south-west for nearly three hundred paces, we came to the gateway of Kiki-naga. There was a turret-like room above the gate, which reminded me of the garden gates I had seen in the suburban gardens and groves of Benares and Gya. Proceeding for a distance of nearly two hundred and forty paces, we came in front of another gateway of the monastery, the doors of which were locked up. Looking northward we saw a beautiful cone-shaped mountain with a *lhakha* on its top, situated to the east of Ssampa-shar bridge. The latter bore due east, the Panjor-sher hill being to the south-east and the Digparaja mountain near Tashi Gyan-tsa, on which there is a solitary temple, to the south. From this gateway, proceeding for about a hundred paces, we came to the southern gate, opposite which is the Chhyag-chha-khang, in front of which people are required to dismount from their ponies and conveyances before they enter the monastery. Here is a flagstaff and several *chhortens* and *mani lhakhang* outside the monastery wall, into which two roads run, one towards the west and the other in a south-westerly direction. Then walking a distance of nearly one hundred and twenty paces we came to the south-western corner of the monastery, whence about one hundred and eighty paces brought us to the plinth of Damdul *chhorten*. It was dusk when we entered the monastery, and with this *kor* round the monastery we finished the year. In some of the houses lamps and oil-burners fed with butter and oil were lighted to bid farewell to the parting year with cheerfulness.

19*th February*.—The Minister got up from bed in the third watch of night and drank *thon-ja* or the night tea, and commenced a thanksgiving prayer service. I did not get up, but listened attentively to what was going on in the adjoining rooms. All the houses and rooms were swept, and the oblation cups rubbed bright. At dawn Wang Chhyug Gya*l*-po came to sweep my room, when Kusho Tungchhen also came in and said, "Pandibla. get up; to-day is the new-year's day." Grand preparations were made to celebrate the new-year's day by Tungchhen and his subordinates. Several persons were employed in making different kinds of dishes and dainties, and there was no end of provisions in the kitchen, where the blowing of the fire was continuous. A large party of Tsang notables were invited to dinner by his holiness. At 10 A.M. the young incarnate Lamas Kusho-Dechan Tul-ku, Tu-Tulku, Kusho Billung, and the Khanpos of Shar-tse, and Thoisamling, Kusho Dechhang, besides a host of learned Lamas and monks, came to Phuntsho-khangsar. The young incarnate Lamas came to my room before sitting to dinner. They rummaged among my things and picked out my metallic pocket-books, spectacles, pencils, and some other stationeries as articles of curiosity, playfully saying they would steal them. One of them called me Achara.

On the new-year's day the Minister visited the grand Lama, who presented him with a flower vase as ja*l*-rten, or token of interview. On his return the Minister told me that the grand Lama had graciously inquired if I was come to Tashi-lhunpo. Kahchan Gopa told me that his holiness the grand Lama had graciously inquired after me several times before, and on one occasion had observed that Pandib must have been prevented from coming on account of the closing up of the passes. I asked the Minister if what Kahchan said was true. He replied "The grand Lama remembers you very well, and whenever any Sanskrit translation is needed his holiness asks me, "Why is it that Pandib has not returned to Tibet as he promised to do? His holiness has given me one hundred and twenty pages of headings which he wishes you to translate. Will you do it? The grand Lama has written a volume on sacred literature, which contains one hundred and twenty chapters. At the commencement of these chapters he will put Sanskrit headings to indicate their subject-matter." I begged that he would be pleased to take me to the grand Lama that I might have the honour of an interview with his holiness. The Minister said that as soon as I had finished the translations he would take me to the grand Lama's presence. In the evening a messenger arrived from Dong-tse, who handed over a letter to the Minister. This was from Chhyan-dso Kusho, who on behalf of Dahpon Phala entreated him to be pleased to start for Dong-tse to exert his sacred influence in propitiating the gods for his wife Lhacham's recovery.

20*th February*.—Early in the morning the Minister saw the grand Lama, and obtained his leave to go to Dong-tse. Arrangements were made for conducting the new-year's service in his absence, and Kahchan Gopa and Shubdung were ordered to accompany him, while Kusho Tungchhen and myself were to remain at Tashi-chunpo. In the afternoon the Minister went to Gya-tsho Shar to spend the night there and to be at Dong-tse on the following evening. I spent the last week of this month very pleasantly in the excellent company of Kusho Tungchhen, who spared no pains to make me comfortable Every evening we used to discuss the severity of the weather outside with a continuous supply of steaming tea to our lips. Our conversation often turned on the customs, manners and habits of the Tibetans, as well as contemporary events at Lhasa. The venerable Om-dse of Nag-khang, Kahchan Sabdungla, the well-known professor of Tibetan literature, and other friends of Tungchhen, used occasionally to join us in our evening table-talk.

28*th February*.—The grand Lama sent a messenger to our house with a letter to request the return of the Minister to Tashi-lhunpo. Considering the nature of the message, we conjectured that some urgent matters were required to be discussed, so we sent Lhagparida to Dong-tse with the grand Lama's letter. Kusho Tungchhen also addressed a letter to his holiness at Dong-tse. The Minister returned to the capital on the 2nd March, and had an interview with the grand Lama on the following morning, but did not tell us what the conference was about Kusho Tungchhen conjectered that it related to the misunderstanding between his and the Dalai Lama's Government caused by some of the courtiers of Gya*l* tshan thonpo in connection with some disputes respecting the U-yug district. The real secret was that the Dalai Lama's Government had protested against the conduct of the Tashi Lama in some religious matters. It was an open secret that the Tashi Lama had taken the vow of monkhood from Sakya Panchhen, the hierarch of the Sakya school and a Lama of the red-hat school, for which he was charged with encouraging heresy, if he was not altogether a heretic himself. It was for this reason that the authorities at Lhasa did not invite his holiness to ordain the supreme ruler of Tibet to the great order of monkhood; for the Dalai, as the head of the Gelug-pa, or the yellow-hat school, could not have any connection with the heretical school of which the Sakya Panchhen was the hierarch.

In the afternoon the man from Targyepara of Shiga-tse came to beg me to see his wife, who was seriously ill. At Kusho Tungchhen's suggestion, he presented a scarf and a *tanka* to the Minister to grant me permission to accompany him to his house at Shiga-tse The Minister declined the prayer, and said that I was too important a person to go out to see patients. I gave the man a few doses of sal-ammoniac, and asked him to report to me the effect of it on the patient the following morning.

4th March.—To-day a religious service was held in which a few Nag-pa monks took part, preparatory to the service for the ordination of some forty monks into the higher vows of Bhikshu. The Minister was engaged in this important ceremony during the whole day. Formerly the grand Lama used to ordain ordinary monks into the higher grades of Gelong or Bhikshu. Now-a-days he has delegated a large portion of his religious duties to the Minister, which includes this most important business, which has afforded to the Minister an opportunity of becoming the spiritual father of hundreds of influential people.

6th March.—Norpu Tondub, the assistant of Chhyan-dso Kusho, arrived at Phuntsho Khangsar with letters from Dahpon Phala and Chhyan-dso Kusho to invite the Minister to Dong-tse. We offered him tea, and after a short conversation with him respecting the health of Lhacham, I retired to my room, and he was conducted by Nerpala to the Minister's presence Next morning the Minister asked me if I would accompany him to Dong-tse to be of any service to Lhacham. He also asked my opinion on the question of his going back to Dong-tse, as requested by Dahpon Phala. "Lhacham Kusho," he added, "is still laid up, and the Dahpon has been summoned to Lhasa to proceed there forthwith. By this time he must have started from Dong-tse. Both Dahpon and Chhyan-dso have entreated me to stay a few days at Dong-tse to look after Lhacham and the family." I replied that if the grand Lama himself wished to oblige the Dahpon and his uncle, it would be desirable for the Minister to proceed to Dong-tse, as the Phala family had been much devoted to him. To do this the Minister ought personally to show the Dahpon's letter to the grand Lama. As for me, I would be right glad to accompany him to be useful to him, as, besides, I could make arrangements for going to Lhasa during the summer season. At night the Minister saw the grand Lama, who gladly gave his assent to the proposal, seeming willing to oblige the Phala family and give a favourable turn to the strained relations existing between his holiness and the Dalai Lama's Government. This time Kusho Tungchhen and I were ordered to accompany the Minister in addition to Kahchan Gopa and Shubdung. In the afternoon the man from Targyepara reported to Kusho Tungchhen that his wife was allright. In the evening we conversed with Norpu Tondub to ascertain the real nature of Lhacham's illness, but I could gather nothing from him with the exception that Lhacham frequently complained of giddiness and want of appetite. Kusho Tungchhen said that he was pretty sure that my medicines would cure Lhacham.

7th to 8th March.—On the morning of Wednesday, at 7 A.M., we started for Panam Tashigang. We had a stiff and tedious ride, during which we took rest at the Mani-lhakhang opposite Patsha*l*, which is situated on the Panam river. On the way we met flocks of wild ducks, geese, cranes, and here and there solitary rabbits ran, startled at our approach, on either side as we passed along. The streamlets were dry or with thin crusts of ice on them. The husbandmen—those mindful of commencing work early—were busying themselves in ploughing, while others were collecting manure. The trees were all still bare, but showed traces of reviving life in fresh shoots. In the afternoon there was a strong gale. We were respectfully received by the hostess, an elderly woman, but I was so fatigued that I fell prostrate on alighting, my knees being very much pained on account of the shortness of the stirrups. Tea was poured in my cup. I had no desire for tea or anything.

9th to 22nd March.—We left Tashigang a little after sunrise and arrived at Dekiling at about 2 P.M. From the road the Minister was escorted to a beautiful garden-house situated at the centre of a spacious *chang-sreb* (grove) belonging to Sawang Phala by Phuntsho Yugya*l*, the third son of Dong-tse Chhyan-dso, and a respectable looking gentleman named Deba Reshi. Arrived at the house, the Minister was conducted to a raised seat which resembled an altar. Tea was served, and was followed by *bre-se* (buttered rice with sugar). I was very much fatigued, but was quite refreshed by this arrangement, which enabled me to rest for a while under the grateful shades of the garden-house on its east front. At about 3 o'clock we resumed our journey, and arrived at Dong-tse *Phodang* at about 4 P.M. Lhacham, a lady of about thirty, and Je-tsun Kusho, Phala's sister, an elderly lady, were seated on two stuffed seats in the central room of the fifth floor of the building. A cushion was placed on an altar confronting the seat of Lhacham. When the Minister had taken his seat, Kusho Tungchhen, Kahchan Gopa, and I seated ourselves on low *bodan* (stuffed) rugs spread on the right of Chhyan-dso Kusho's seat, just below the altar. Lhacham was dressed in a Mongolian princess' dress; her head was covered with a crown-like head-dress studded with precious stones and numberless pearls of all sizes; pearl necklaces, amber and coral strings, hung down to her breast; and the richest Chinese brocades and Tibet serge were used in her vestments. Je-tsun Kusho, being a nun, was dressed very plainly; but though other nuns usually crop their hair, Je-tsun allowed hers to grow. She belonged to the Ningma school, which allows its nuns some extraordinary privileges. On the following day I prescribed some medicines for Je-tsun Kusho, who was suffering from bronchitis. A physician from Tse-chan monastery was treating Lhacham, who complained of giddiness and debility, but on the fifth day of our residence at Dong-tse I prescribed some medicines for her, which, however. did her no good. The Minister seemed much concerned at the failure of my medicines. I tried a second dose, which also had no effect. Lhacham, finding herself worse than before grew fretful and said that malignant stars were now ascendent in her *kham* (the place in the zodiac), and were bent on her ruin. Although people said that she was being troubled by some wicked spirits who had followed her from Tengri, she did not believe them or the stories about her, but observed that the heavens alone were against her recovery. The Minister looked towards me and asked me how it was that my medicines were fruitless in Lhacham's case. In the midst of a dead silence, I told him slowly that different medicines administered by different physicians to Lhacham were not harmonious in their action on her system. I was not sorry that my medicines did her no good, for if these had done her any good, I would surely have prescribed stronger medicines, which would have acted differently, if not altogether adversely: that I had heard Lhacham say she had first tried the medicines of a Chinese quack, then those of a Nepalese physician, and lastly the medicines of several learned Tibetan physicians, all of which had had no effect: that, under these circumstances, I should not have prescribed any medicines at all, but as every one expectantly wanted me to give her medicines, I had done so; but now, from the nature of her ladyship's illness, I could tell that the best remedy that could cure her was *no medicine* at all.

They seemed to think my reply reasonable, and Lhacham herself admitted its truth, and resolved not to take any medicine for a fortnight. In the course of the next ten days she felt a marked improvement in her health. I daily used to hold conversation with her, just after breakfast, on the manners and customs of the Indian people, and on the condition of women in India, which interested her very much. The existence of *Suttee* formerly, of poligamy and life-long widowhood now in India, roused the liveliest surprise in her. She often wondered how human selfishness could reach such extreme limits as to behave in such a cruel and inhuman way towards the female sex. On the contrary, she was glad to hear that the English people who ruled over India adored their females. The rulers and the ruled in India, she said, seemed to entertain the extremes of opposite feelings, which would some day or other cause a happy combination of the two, so as to elevate the condition of women in India.

Lhacham seemed to entertain a kind regard for me, as being a pandit from India, and also for my knowledge of Tibetan history, and to set a high value on my daily conversation with her. One day the Minister suggested that it would be a very good thing if I could be sent to Lhasa to see Lord Buddha and the incarnate Chanrassig. Lhacham approved of the suggestion, and promised to help me with accommodation in her residence there, and also to favour me with her kind protection if I happened to go to Lhasa.

23rd March.—I left Dong-tse to-day at 10 A. M. accompanied by Kusho Tungchhen, having taken leave of the lady by presenting her with a scarf. Her expressions to me were very kind and assuring, and Chhyan-dso Kusho promised to arrange about my journey to Lhasa. I gave some rewards to the menials of Lhacham and Chhyan-dso Kusho. We met Gopa at the end of the first mile from Dong-tse. The skies were cloudy, and at noon a strong gale blew. We saw flocks of wild ducks and cranes here and there in the Nyang-chhu, and lambs picking the fresh shoots of grass. There was no ice in the irrigation passages and upland streamlets. We met several pony-dealers proceeding towards Gyan-tse *thom*, but did not talk with them. Beyond Norpu Khyung-dsin we saw and read from a distance many inscriptions in gigantic Tibetan characters, consisting of the sacred phrases "Om vajra Pani hum," "Om Wagishvari hum," "Om Ah-hum," &c. These were engraved on the rocky flank of a projection of the Norpu Khyung-dsin hill. At some distance from Dekiling, while observing the cultivators at work, and looking at the travellers coming from an opposite direction in hopes of seeing Phurchung among them, I had slackened the reins of my pony, so that while crossing a ditch its forefeet slipped and it tumbled in, and I fell to the ground, which was soft, slightly hurting my knees. The cultivators were busy, some driving their teams, some calling their yaks and *jomo* to put them to the *ña-shing* (yoke). The yaks were adorned with red, yellow, blue, and green tufts of hair and with garlands of coloured fleece and cowries. The soil was just being released from the grasp of winter, and the frozen and incrusted surface of the ground under the genial rays of the sun was just soft enough for the ploughshare.

We halted for the night at Tashigang in the house of Ang-putti, who was suffering from toothache. Toothache is a general complaint of the people in Tibet, who I was told in the remote province of Chyang-thang, owing to the extreme rigour of the climate and the coldness of the water, lose their teeth before reaching the age of 30. Ang-putti entreated me for some medicine, but I was sorry I had none to relieve her.

24th March.—We left Tashigang after breakfast. A little above Shalu Gonpa we met a gang of sinister-looking beggars, who supplicated for alms, but Kusho Tungchhen did not reply to their supplications, and his perfect gravity repulsed them and relieved me of my apprehensions, for I thought they were highwaymen, and I had about 60 *tolas* of gold in my pocket. At 3 P.M. we reached Gya-tsho Shar, where we were warmly received by Deba Shikha. As soon as we entered the Deba's house, a heavy shower of snow fell, which whitened the upper parts of the hills.

25th March to 4th April.—I witnessed the ceremony of commencing the work of husbandry. The prayers offered by the ploughmen when fixing the yoke to the necks of the *jo* teams, and their attempts to run ploughing races, were very amusing. We left Gya-tsho Shar in the afternoon and arrived at Tashi-lhunpo at 4 P.M.

At Tashi-lhunpo I applied myself to studying Jamling Gyashe and other important works under Kusho Tungchhen, and ceased to keep my journal for a long time.

PART II.

NARRATIVE OF A JOURNEY FROM TASHI-LHUNPO TO LHASA.

I.—JOURNEY FROM TASHI-LHUNPO TO YAMDO SAMDING.

25*th April* (7*th of the* 3*rd Tibetan lunar month*).—The *Tshembu-pa* (tailor) whom I had engaged to prepare the outfit for my journey to Lhasa made his appearance to-day. Kusho Tungchhen, who had kindly furnished me with two pieces of *chying-dse*, or country-made broad-cloth, for my upper robes and jacket, made a list of things he had supplied me with through the tailor, and I cleared up all my accounts with him. I paid at the rate of one *tanka* per day to the tailor for the number of days he worked for me, and at two annas a day to his boy assistant. The *Tshembu-pa* being one of the best and quick-handed tailors of Tsang, was entitled to an allowance of a *tanka* daily. He generally worked from 7 A.M. to 6 P.M., with but little interruption. We used to supply him with food twice a day and tea during the whole day. I told him that if he accompanied me to Lhasa I would present him with a sewing-machine from Calcutta, by means of which he could alone do ten tailors' work. I tried to give him some faint idea of the working of a sewing machine, but he seemed to be quite unable to understand how the sewing was done by *philings*, *i.e.*, clock-like self-working machines, but begged earnestly to be supplied with one. He had prepared me a serge *chhuba* (outer loose robe), a *khen-dsa* (jacket), a pair of *torma-pishu* (trousers), a silk *cho-sha* (church hat), and a pair of leggings after the Chinese fashion. I dismissed him a little before sunset with suit-able rewards for his labour. After dusk, I arranged for one of Tungchhen's ponies to convey my traps, for my own being by this time fit for work, I did not trouble Tungchhen for a second pony.

26*th April* (8*th of the* 3*rd Tibetan lunar month*).—On Wednesday, the 8th of the third lunar month of the Tibetan year, called *Chhuta*, or *water-horse*, dressed in my newly-made monkish raiments, I left Tashi-lhunpo to make arrangements at Dong-tse for my proposed journey to Lhasa. Dao-sring, our cook, who was ordered to proceed to Dong-tse, now for the first time, after nearly a decade, washed his face and hands: the former, lately jet black with a little gloss on it, now becoming fairly white, and the wrinkles and other prominent features of his face made their appearance. The Nubian black was no more, and those who had nicknamed him "Uncle Daw" (*Aku-chyarog*) now smiled to see him no longer justify that epithet. He now, putting on his newly-bought *Kham* shoes and a *tamuksi* hat, walked to the court to hold my pony. Handing over my letters for India to Nerpala, and thanking him for his kindness towards me, I left Phuntsho Khang-sar at 2 P.M. Several of my acquaintances came to bid me farewell, and after the Tibetan fashion all of them offered prayers to the Three Holies that I might return in their midst safe and sound. With a copious exchange of *La la-so* and *La thug-ge-chhe*, I walked off to the gate to mount my pony near Damdu*l chhorten*, Wang Chhyug Gya*l*-po accompanying us some distance out of respect to Tungchhen, his master. Tshering Tashi, who was appointed to accompany me to Lhasa, was fully equipped with all the necessaries of a long journey. Butter, meat, spices and rice he had bought in reasonable quantities, besides a copper cook-ing-vessel, an iron pan, flint-stones, tinder, and bellows. He now also purchased a bag of pounded dried mutton. Kusho Tungchhen had kindly given us about 20tbs.of best barley-flour for my use, nearly 40tbs. of second quality flour, and enough of *chhura* (vermicelli of dried boiled milk), peas and pea-flour for the use of our servants and ponies. Of all the indis-pensables bought, he valued most the bamboo tea-churner as the prettiest and most portable thing in our possession. I tied my English medicine-box to a bag attached to my saddle on one side, and hung the bundle of my wearing apparel on the other side. Our party consisted of five persons, all on horseback. Kusho Tungchhen rode first, I followed, Tshering Tashi riding third, Dao-sring and Lhagpa-rida, the groom, following us in a train. After an hour's swift ambling, and crossing many irrigation channels filled with water drawn from the Nyang-chhu, we arrived at Chyang-chhu Shikha at 3 P.M. Our host Deba-shikha not being at home, his wife, Cheh-lá, received us very kindly, and the maid-servant, Dao Do*l*ma, served us with tea and barley-flour. After tea Tungchhen and myself went to pay our respects to the old lady Ang-la, who was now in the 81st year of her age. She blest us repeatedly, saying "May the Three Holies make you happy and grant you long life." Her daughter, Cheh-la, who is 38 years old, looked rather younger, probably because the winter had passed away. She spared no pains to prepare a good dinner for us. There was a slight gale accompanied by sleet before sunset. I was somewhat unwell that evening, at which both Tungchhen and his sister expressed themselves much concerned; but having a good appetite, I took a hearty meal of *gya-thug* (Chinese gruel), and showed much dexterity in the use of the chop-sticks. After a few minutes' chat with the Deba, who had just returned from inspecting his cultivation, I went to bed rather early. Deba himself wrapped me with thick blankets of his own, thinking that my clothes were not sufficient.

27th April.—I got up from bed at 7 A.M., and felt little better. There was a slight snow-fall, about two inches, during the night, and a cool breeze blew, with the skies slightly foggy, the atmosphere surcharged with moisture, and the hill-tops all round pretty white with snow. After breakfast, which consisted of *pag-thug* (barley gruel), the national food of the Tibetans, I went for a walk accompanied by Kusho Tungchhen round the Lobding and the *Changra* grove of the Minister. We entered the Lobding, where poplars and willows and several kinds of tamarisks and *deodar* grew in rows, as well as different kinds of saffron (*kurkum metog*). Deba, who had accompanied me, asked me if I could oblige him with some Indian flower-seeds. I promised to supply him with various Indian and European seeds, provided he undertook to make a large collection of Tibetan flower-seeds for me. At 10 A.M. a messenger arrived from Dong-tse, and delivered to Tungchhen a letter from the Minister with enclosures of a key and scarf. Kusho Tungchhen was requested to open the Minister's box to fetch him some cash and also to take with him his revolver. In front of our residence, at a distance of about 100 yards, some cultivators, men and women, were engaged in digging the ground for the purpose of collecting a kind of under-ground grass called *rampa*. These in some places acquired a length of five to six feet, and grew in abundance. In the beginning of spring, when all other vegetables die out, this grass becomes fit for provender, and is then dug out. I went to see this operation in one place, and found a good network of it under the ground. The spring being also the ploughing season with the Tibetans, the digging of the *rampa* facilitates the work of ploughing. The cultivators know this grass by the offshoots above ground, which are dry and stunted in growth, and which absorb sunlight. I was told by the cultivators that where these offshoots are found green and luxuriant, the sub-soil *rampa* is neither good nor well-grown, external heat favouring the external growth and hindering the sub-soil growth during the season. This year's *rampa* were not good on account of the low temperature during the season. The wind ceased to blow at noon, when there was a brilliant sun, which soon melted the snow lying on the roofs and the courts of the hamlet. Tshering Tashi, who was appointed to accompany me, now arrived from Tashi Gyan-tse, where he had been detained to make some purchases. Both Chehla and Deba busied themselves in completing our outfits. In the evening tea was served by Po-kah-chan-la, a grey-haired monk, who generally works on the estates of the Minister at Tanag. He related to me the particulars of a journey which he had made to Dinajpur Rungpur and Purneah some 30 years ago. His account of how the jackals filled the forests with their nocturnal cries, how Bengalis roasted crabs and other fresh-water fish on frypans, &c., was most ludicrous. He also gave a comic description of the half-naked, savage-looking appearance of the low-class Bengalis. I was indeed forced to admit that the dress of the Bengalis was not so good and decent as that of the Tibetans. Po-kah-chan also said that the Bengalis never approached the places where his party used to encamp: not to speak of any molestation, they even avoided the sight of the Tibetans as much as possible. Po-kah-chan had also travelled up to Kongpo, Naga, and among the Mishmis and Tsari in Eastern Tibet, and related to me how the savage tribes of the Lho-khabra harassed the Tibetan pilgrims, and also how the river Tsang-po entered the country of defiles in Eastern Bhutan to rush out in a tremendous waterfall from the top of a gigantic, solid precipice called *Singdong* (or lion's face). In the evening I had a conversation with Ang-la about the road to Lhasa and the price of provisions in it, but the old lady observed that it was many years since she had gone on pilgrimage to Lhasa, so that she had forgotten much about the country and its people.

28th April.—In the morning we breakfasted at 8, and talked at table with Kusho Tungchhen and Po-kah-chan about the snowfall. I said that while in Sikkim we had observed snow fall in January and February: here in Tibet it was strange to remark that I never saw any snow fall in winter. "Is it," added I, "that snow never falls in Tibet proper during the middle of winter?" Tungchhen replied "It is only this year that no snow has fallen during the middle of winter. The falling of snow in April is not auspicious, as the seeds that have just been sown would be frozen. Times are altered. The power of sin is growing more and more paramount, and the snow has come in April instead of falling in February or earlier." The present snowfall, though dangerous to young seedlings, yet, according to him, would be of great benefit to the herdsmen, since it would grow grass on the hill-tops. In fact the continued drought in winter had almost baked the soil. Two of Deba-shikha's largest ewes had died the previous evening from starvation. At the time of parting, Tungchhen's sister presented me with a *tashi-khatag* (or auspicious scarf), at the same time wishing me a prosperous journey, while herhusband, Deba-shikha, helped me in mounting my pony, and Ang-la uttered her *monlam*, or prayers, for our safe return after a successful journey to the sanctuaries of Central Tibet. Tungchhen rode ahead, and we followed him at a gentle amble.

The villagers—men, women and children—had assembled to bid us farewell and to express their good wishes for our happy return. We met many flocks of *tontong*, or large cranes, and several flocks of wild ducks in pools that were now filled with water from irrigation canals. I admired the industrious habits of the people, which had covered the fields with a network of irrigation channels. It is no doubt very easy and convenient for the people to cut channels to draw water from the Nyang-chhu, but it is at the same time creditable to them that they avail themselves of the advantages of cultivation so afforded by nature. On the banks of Nyang-chhu, opposite to and eight miles below Shalu Gonpa, we were overtaken by wind and sleet. Herds of goat and sheep were here feeding on the fresh shoots of grass, and brown, red-necked ducks were swimming in the river. The ride was a pleasant one. Advancing forward, I conversed with Tungchhen La on the subject of my proposed journey to Lhasa. Here and there the cultivators were engaged in driving their hairy teams, with their heads decorated with tufts of coloured yak-hair and garlands made of coloured rags. The distant mountains were clad in freshly-fallen snow, above all of which towered the Chomo Lhari, so famed in Tsang as the great haunt of *Mamo* hobgoblins. Near Pishi Lhakhang we witnessed the practice of ploughing and sowing together. After the land is made ready for receiving the seed, the ploughman drives his plough, behind which the sower scatters the seeds. This process is resorted to to protect the seeds from being picked up by birds, large flocks of which commit great havoc over the fields. At Pishi Mani Lhakhang we refreshed ourselves with tea, biscuits, chinese cakes and *chhura* (vermicelli of dried boiled milk). The *Namo* showed much kindness towards us in paying attention to the tea-making and supplying forage to our ponies. Resuming our journey at 2 P.M., we reached Tashi-gang. Ang-putti, who was alone in the house, received us with her usual kindness. A young girl, the daughter of one of her near relations, about eight years old, poured tea into our cups after we had taken seats in the first room. Ang-putti's favourite cat, slowly approaching me, at once leaped into my lap. Tungchhen got out some biscuits and *chhura* from his saddle-bag, and pressed me to eat some. While we were engaged in conversation about the fatigues of the journey, Ang-putti drew near Tungchhen, and in a whisper told him that her landlord was trying to harass her by demanding from her more money than was actually due. She showed him one of the documents, but was sorry to have lost an important paper. I regretted that I had no medicines with me to relieve a toothache of which she complained, but said, if she did not get well within two months, I would treat her with fresh medicine after my return from Lhasa. Rice was now cooked, and some *phing-sha* (curry made of mutton and *phing*) was prepared for our dinner. In the evening Ang-putti milked one of her *jomos* and kindly gave me some to drink. There was a strong gale in the evening, which made the weather very severe. Tshering Tashi, well known as a skilful cook, could not, however, cook rice. The Tibetans steam their rice, but the Bhuteas of Sikkim, Nepal and Bhutan, who do not use steam, turn out an equally good dish by boiling it in water. Rinzing, the servant of Ang-putti, took care of our ponies. There was sleet and snow accompanied by wind, and our ponies being exposed to the inclemency of the weather, we felt somewhat uneasy for them Our servants, however, had taken the precaution of bringing them at midnight under the roof of the *hokhang*, or the godown-like hall of the house.

29th April.—In the morning, at 6 A.M., we breakfasted on *pag-thug* (Tibet gruel), boiled mutton and a few cups of tea. At the time of parting Ang-putti presented me with a couple of *tankas*, two pairs of garters, and a piece of blanket, all of her own manufacture, and some coins, with a request to burn incense in the great temple of Buddha and other sanctuaries of Lhasa for her benefit. With the exception of the *kerag* (garter), I declined to accept the rest, and, thanking her warmly for her kind wishes and presents, at 8 A.M. resumed our journey. The country all round was covered with snow, and the mountains, the table-lands and the river Nyang-chhu, all presented a uniform white appearance. Contrary to our expectation, the weather was pretty temperate, so that we held the reins without any freezing of our fingers. We never used gloves, and in fact the Tibetans never resort to such a protection for the fingers. The sun shone with unusual brightness, and I was again reminded of the journey I had made in the snows of the Kangla-chhen. The glare of the sun was not so great as to make the wearing of blue glasses necessary. Before arriving at the *Rissur*, where the Nyang-chhu washes the edge of the mountain, we saw the Dahpon (commander) of Shiga-tse, with his party and an escort of a dozen *sowars*, marching at a gentle trot by the road on the other side of the Nyang-chhu, a distance of nearly three to four miles from us. As I was very anxious to make the acquaintance of the Dahpon, I regretted his early departure from Dong-tse. Kusho Tungchhen told me that Lhacham, the Dahpon's wife, was the greater personage of the two, and that as I was assured of protection from her, I need cherish no uneasy thought about a journey to Lhasa. A little above the village of Thaimen, on the bank of the Nyang-chhu, we dismounted from our ponies to rest for a while and refresh ourselves with curds and twisted sugar-biscuits prepared under Tungchhen's supervision at Tashi-lhunpo. I did not like the greasy Chinese cakes of which Tungchhen had an abundant supply. At 4 P.M. we arrived at Dong-tse, and found the snow that had fallen there had almost disappeared, only the distant mountain-tops being still clad in white. The wind was moist and cold. Both Tungchhen and I took up our accommodation in the Chhoide, and did not proceed to Dong-tse Phodang, where the Minister was staying as a guest of Lhacham. In the evening Deba Chola came to invite us to avail ourselves of the company of the Minister at Dong-tse Phodang, to which we readily consented.

30th April.—The Minister asked if I had any news respecting Tashi-lhunpo and Shiga-tse. I told him of the arrival of several Mongolian high-priests and incarnate Lamas at Tashi-lhunpo, as well as of some Kulmuk merchants who had brought a large caravan of double-humped camels and Tartar ponies. We were told that the Tartar merchants had brought a large quantity of *Tamig-ma* silver for presentation to the Grand Lama and the Minister. As the latter was away from Tashi-lhunpo, and as Dong-tse was rather an out-of-the-way place, it was not probable that they would take the trouble of coming up to pay him their respects there. The Tashi Lama was, at the time we left Tashi-lhunpo, preparing to proceed to Bur-tsho, the famous mineral spring of Tanag, whither Kusho Dichhang-pa, our good neighbour of Phuntsho Khangsar, was ordered to accompany him, and at the time of my leaving Tashi-lhunpo he was negociating to buy a well-known, swift pony from a certain incarnate Lama. The weather at Tashi-lhunpo had been pleasant, although a strong gale blew every evening, so that the husbandmen were putting their shoulders to the field work in right earnest. I also informed his holiness of my earnest desire to proceed to Lhasa; but as the Tah Lama of Dapung and Mirkan Pandita of Mongolia, who had kindly promised to take me with them to Lhasa, would stay a few months at Tashi-lhunpo, there would be considerable delay in carrying out that desire. I therefore prayed that I might be allowed to avail myself of the earliest chance that offered, for although it was arranged that the Tashi Lama would proceed to Lhasa to ordain the young Dalai into the monkhood, yet rumours were rife about the differences which had lately arisen between the Governments of Tsang and Lhasa, in consequence of which the Gya*l*-tshab would, though contrary to the usage of the country and the church, impose upon himself the duties of officiating as the spiritual guide of the grand hierarch. Such being the case, it was doubtful whether the Panchhen would at all go to Lhasa. I also represented that even if the Grand Lama were to go, it would not be comfortable for me to accompany his followers, who would march in a ceremonial procession. The Minister told me that he had lately received a letter from Mirkan Pandita, in which he begged to be allowed to meet him at Dong-tse. It would therefore be possible for him to arrange with the Pandita for my safe journey to Lhasa. In the evening I paid my respects to Lhacham and Chhyan-dso Kusho, who were glad to see me back. Lhacham was somewhat better for not having taken any medicines at all during the last three weeks.

1st May.—Kusho Tungchhen informed the Minister that the clergy of Tashi-lhunpo were anxiously waiting for his return. Hundreds of monks were to be ordained into the order of *Bhikshu* or *Gelong*, and there was not a single sacred learned Lama who could conduct that ceremony, with the exception of the Minister. In fact, Kusho Billung-pa, one of the chief incarnate Lamas, was very young, and himself a novice in *mantra* ritual, and Kusho Yong-dsin Lhopa, who was at the head of the Nagpa Ta-tshang, was too heavily pressed by his own duties to be able to attend to other work, while the incarnations of Dechhen Tanga and Tu-Tu*l*ku were mere boys, not yet initiated into the vows of monkhood. For these reasons the Minister's absence was keenly felt at the capital. Tungchhen also added that Mirkan Pandita intended to come up to Dong-tse to take lessons in sacred literature from the Minister, and had begged him (Tungchhen) to arrange for his accommodation in a corner of the Minister's residence. Mirkan was no ordinary personage, being a very important *Khutukto* of Horchan, whom the Khans of Mongolia revered, and who had come from the remotest corner of Mongolia with the sole object of studying the sacred Buddhist scriptures. The Minister carefully listening to what Tungchhen related, said that he was aware of the importance of his returning to the capital, but that Lhacham would not let him go before the religious observances lately commenced by her to propitiate Dorje Jig-je were finished. Lhacham, her husband the Dahpon, and the Shape, were his devoted friends: he could by no means displease them. At the same time it would be undesirable to disregard the sacred duties of a divine Lama, which consisted in expounding *dharma* to lay devotees. After a pause, his holiness ordered Tungchhen to write to Mirkan Pandita not to start for Dong-tse before hearing from him of the exact date when the Minister could make it convenient to converse with him on religious matters. The Minister then, turning towards me, asked if it would not be convenient to receive Mirkan in the Dong-tse Chhoide instead of in the Dong-tse Phodang. I replied that that proposal was the best, as an incarnate Lama of Mirkan's position and rank could by no means be entertained in a house, however grand and large it may be, where there were women. It was accordingly decided to receive Mirkan Pandita at the monastery, and that I should wait upon him with a view to cultivate his acquaintance.

2nd May.—To-day the monks of Dong-tse, headed by Punlo Kusho, a learned old Lama of seventy years, arrived at our place, Dong-tse Phodang, to commence reading the "Kahgyur" scriptures. Arrangements for the worship of Dorje Jig-je were made in the *Ñihok*, in the middle of which was a small glazed house. *Torma*, or offerings to terrific evil spirits, were placed in the Nihok,* and in the glazed house were spread two rows of rugs, four feet by twelve, on which the *Gedun-pa*, or clergymen, were to take their seat. A little chapel was placed in one corner of the house, in front of which was the raised seat or dais for the Minister. A complete set of church furniture was arranged in front and about the chapel, of which the *tshegi-pumpa* (or "the bowl of life") was the most important article. It was to propitiate the Buddha Ayusmata that the service was undertaken, and Dorje Jig-je is the terrific spirit who keeps the Lord of Death under his power. The worship began to-day and was continued on the following two days.

5th May.—Tshing-ta (Tshering Tashi) in the morning went to the *sho* (town) to arrange with Pador, whom Chhyan-dso Kusho had appointed to accompany me, to hold himself in readiness to start. He was told to arrange with somebody to plough his *phashi* or paternal acres and to execute the *oolag-pa*, or personal service to Chhyan-dso Kusho. Pador's possessions consisted chiefly of a pair of donkeys, two cows, three *jo*, and a few implements of husbandry, for which he showed much anxiety. He, however, agreed to serve us, and begged that he might be formally granted leave by his lord Chhyan-dso Kusho. I was required to advance him a few *tankas* to enable him to make some purchases for his old father. Pador was a stalwart young man, taller than Phurchung, and swifter in walking. He had

* Ñihok is the open space upon the roof of a building, on at least three sides of which there are walls.

been several times to Lhasa, and knew many people there and on the way. Chhyan-dso Kusho generally employed him in heding the caravans he had several times sent to the metropolis last year.

6th May.—At noon, after the first part of the religious service, I and Tungchhen were invited to join the Minister, Lhacham and Chhyan-dso Kusho at dinner. We quietly took our seats showing our good manners and knowledge of state etiquette in our way of sitting, looking and replying to those who were above us. The young Ane-tung, who sat close to his mother, ran every now and then to the Minister's side to whisper a word or two of his childish jokes. When other topics were exhausted, Kusho Tungchhen introduced the subject of my journey to Lhasa: how I apprehended danger at the hands of robbers and highwaymen, how I daily brooded over the thought of seeing Lhasa, and how I needed particular help from persons of Lhacham's position and influence. She was graciously pleased to say that life and death were matters over which no human being had command, but that she would readily undertake to help me in all other matters during my journey to Lhasa. Pandibla, she added, need not be anxious: she would take him with her and lodge him in a corner room of her own house. The Minister heard this assurance of help with interest, and thanked her warmly for it. Pandibla, he said, was a good man, and deserved to be treated as such. I was delighted to hear these august personages talk so kindly of me, and especially to know that I should be allowed to accompany Lhacham to Lhasa, and was impatient to ascertain the exact date of their leaving Dong-tse. In the evening the Minister, accompanied by me, Kah-chan Gopa and Shabdung, went to take a walk round the monastery. The country was covered with snow and enveloped in fogs; the mountains towards Gyan-tse and in our neighbourhood were all white, and indicated by the cloudiness of the horizon towards the east that the snowfall was still going on towards Gyan-tse. The Minister drew my attention to the white appearance of the mountains, and asked if I could take a good photograph of the scene. I said that with his holiness' leave I could immediately photograph the landscape, but that it was late in the evening, and some time would be needed to set the camera and mix the chemicals. He thereupon patted me on the back and observed that Dong-tse being his birthplace, he would first of all like to take a landscape view of the "uplands" or *phug*, with his native place dotted on, and then photographs of Gopa, the convents, and the town, and looking towards the monastery he said, "Could we not wait till Pandibla returned from Lhasa?" 'Yes, venerable sir," said Gopa, "we must not allow Pandibla to stay long at Lhasa. His presence here is essential for your holiness' progress in Sanskrit, and we must say we like to have him in our midst." Looking towards the Minister, I asked "Sir, do you think I will ever be able to go to Lhasa, and if there, I will be back to see your holiness' feet again here?" "What fear is there, Pandibla?" replied his holiness.

7th May.—Deba Rheshi, one of the *shi-ñer* under Chhyan-dso Kusho, arrived in the afternoon, and after exchanging compliments with me for a few minutes, entered the store-room to see what was falling short in the stock. I then walked up to the roof in front of the *Tsan-khang*, or the particular chapel where wrathful spirits are worshipped. Here, in the presence of Je-tsun Kusho, Lhasre, the eldest son of Lhacham, was having his head shaved with a very bad substitute for a razor, namely, a piece of brass obtained from a broken waterpot. Seeing me, Lhasre was reminded of my razor, and at once asked me to fetch it for him; but it was locked up in the Minister's box. Gergyan-tung now sharpened his knife (a two-blade Rodgers' penknife), and tried it with some success upon Lhasre's head, which was to be shaven in the Chinese fashion. It took nearly two hours to shave his head, although a central patch of hair round the pig-tail was left untouched.

8th May.—Je-tsun Kusho took her breakfast before eight and prepared to start for her convent, Rinchhen-ling, situated in the Dong-tse *phug* (uplands). She had two maid-servants, the younger of which had been suffering for the last eight years from dysmenorrhœa, and when I went to pay my respects to Je-tsun, she pressed me to breakfast with her, and begged me to see if I could do anything for her poor maid-servant As a token of respect, I accepted a cup of *pag-thug* (Tibet gruel) from her hands. She smiled when she remembered the ludicrous name (*rilpo*) I had given to *pag-thug*. In her presence I made my earnest *monlam* or prayer that I might again see her saintly smile, and that she might not forget to extend her kindness to me. To all my grateful expressions she replied, "*La laso thug-je-chhe*," with a gentle nod each time, and when I finished what I had to say, she begged me to pay a visit to her convent after my return. Lhasa, she said, was not a very distant place, and I was promised patronage by Lhacham, so that there would be no difficulty in my safely returning from there; she had herself lately returned from Lhasa, when it took her only five days to reach Dong-tse. After presenting my *khatag* (scarf) and a rupee as parting gift, I walked up towards my room, which was opposite to hers, but before I came to the skylight which intervened between her room and ours, Gergyan-tung put into my hand five *tankas* with a scarf of auspicious parting (*tashi-khatag*). I returned the money, but kept the scarf. The two Lhasre Kushos and Gergyan-tung joined me in conversation about my journey to Lhasa. The former promised to render me every possible help, but feared lest orders had been issued against foreigners coming to Lhasa, for the protection of the young Dalai Lama against small-pox. In that case it would be difficult for me to visit Lhasa. After breakfast, I requested Kah-chan Gopa to draft the promised letter introducing me to Sawang Rampa. The Minister himself drafted it, and calling me to his presence, read it for my information. He also secretly wished me not to speak to Lhacham about this letter, for then she would be displeased, as, having already undertaken to help me at Lhasa in every matter, she would hardly like another person being also requested to aid me. A letter to Sawang Rampa, his holiness said, was unnecessary as long as I remained under Lhacham's protection; "but as you are anxious that you should have in your *amba* (breast-pocket) additional resources and means of protection, I give you this letter, but you must never show it to Lhacham." He then ordered Gopa to enclose in the letter one *sho, i.e.* a guinea-weight of gold dust, wrapped up in a white silk scarf. News arrived to-day to the effect that small-pox was raging at Lhasa and other places of U (Central Tibet). Several persons had died at Gyan-tse, and three or four stations between Gyan-tse and Lhasa were also affected by it. The dread of small-pox greatly preyed upon the mind of Lhacham, as she and her three sons were all unprotected against it. She confined herself to her private sitting-room, refusing admission to outsiders. Several of her agents and rent-collectors had arrived to pay their respects to her with presents, to all of whom she refused an interview. Dinner was announced by Chhyan-dso Kusho at 2 P.M., when Deba Chola, dressed in his official robes, entered Lhacham's chamber with the first course of dishes. A few minutes after, I was called to dine with the Minister, in our rooms, where Chhyan-dso Kusho, Ané-tung, the Minister, myself, and Kusho Tungchhen were served with two courses of dishes—the first of Chinese and the second of national Tibetan dishes. Tungchhen and I were provided with four kinds of Chinese dainties in four China cups The tender shoots of peas, a kind of green Chinese grass called "swallow's nest," mushrooms, a kind of black hill fungus called *magrum*, were the vegetables cooked with mutton.

9th May.—At 2 P M, Lhacham left Dong-tse Phodang. Kusho Ané, her third son, who being selected for the church, was required to remain with the Minister, appeared in very low spirits, even to tears. The mother too shed tears, and was unable to take a hearty meal. The Minister tried to console them, but to no purpose. I went to the balcony to see to the equipment of the ponies and the servants and the escort. Chhyan-dso Kusho, his son Deba Chola, and Deba Norpu Dondub now appeared dressed in their best apparel, the former carrying in his hand a bundle of incense-sticks. His *serchan bogto*, or yellow turban-like head-dress, was very handsome, and his satin robe most gaudy. Lhacham, after taking leave of the Minister, prepared to make obeisance at the different chapels of the palace. Her sons, Lhasre Kusho and Kundi Kusho, dressed in their Chinese costumes, followed her, Chhyan-dso Kusho heading the party, while I stood at the corner of the top of the ladder leading to the fourth floor. On my bidding her farewell by lowering my hat, she smiled and asked me to meet her at Gyang-khar castle, her principal residence at Gyan-tse. It took them nearly an hour to visit all the chapels, after which the party returned to the fifth floor, where the Minister was sitting. She begged him to look to the health and education of her darling Ané, whom she was leaving with him. Then receiving his *chhyag-wang* (benediction), the whole party descended by the ladder to the courtyard, where a white pony with handsome housings of embroidered cloth and beautiful Tartar saddle was in waiting, held by one of her richly-dressed grooms. She was helped by Chhyan-dso Kusho to the saddle, on which she sat astride. With her pearl-studded head-dress, her amulets of gold and ruby, her string of coral and finest amber, and her dress made of best satin and kinkob, she looked more like a heroine or a goddess. While they rode along the road past the Phuntsho Linka park, the Minister, myself, and Kusho Ané looked towards them from the balcony. Ané, who was a child of ten, and who had never known separation from his dear mother, sobbed bitterly. The occasion was most touching, and the Minister himself seemed moved. When the party vanished from our sight, the Minister went for a walk in the park accompanied by Ané. I remained in my room, being somewhat unwell.

10th May.—To-day the Minister, accompanied by me and Kusho Ané-tung, left Dong-tse Phodang to take up his residence in the monastery of Dong-tse Chhoide. Chhyan-dso Kusho went to reach him there. The Om-dse (high priest) of the monastery, with the help of his two assistants, had constructed a splendid mansion to the Kalachakra Tantrik god. On a smooth floor, about 20 feet in diameter, in the northern room of the third floor of the Tsug-lakhang, was described a large circle with coloured barley-flour. Within this were described the entrance, spires, doors and domes of the Kalachakra mansion. The presiding deity is a many-armed, tall deity, with several heads. The attendant deities were all of the Tantrik school. The whole was a grand painting made with solid pulverized paints and coloured flour. The grand worship at this Kalachakra *mandala* was to commence to-day, and Chhyan-dso Kusho being the first patron, was invited to see the performance, Punlo Kusho, the Minister and Kusho Tungchhen accompanying him to explain the *mandala.* He praised the Om-dse for this grand work, and gratified the monks, eighty in number, with a present of half a *tanka* each and an entertainment of tea and barley broth. The Minister performed the inaugural ceremonies of erecting a gilt *Gyal-tshan*, or the Dvaja of the Buddha religion, and a pair of sacred domes (*Ganjera*). Artizans from Shiga-tse had arrived, and were arranging to commence their work. The Minister, after presenting them with his sacred *chhyag-wang* (benediction), gave them a *solra,* or reward, to make them set zealously about their work. Chhyan-dso Kusho Tungchhen and others took an active part in the opening ceremony, every one attesting his zeal in the Minister's service, but owing to my illness I could not join them, and had to retire to my room after a few minutes' stay at the Dukhor Lhakhang.

11th May.—Though feeling somewhat worse. I got up early and waited in Kah-chan Gopa's room to take an early opportunity of begging the Minister to write a few lines for me to the Regent. As soon as his morning service was over, I entered his room and, seated on a rug below his raised seat, made my request. The Minister replied that the letter of introduction he had given me the other day to Sawang Rampa was sufficient. As my object was to make pilgrimages to the different sanctuaries, any introduction to the Regent would not only be unnecessary, but might be productive of *tog-pa*, or suspicion, for no pilgrim needs any introduction to see the Gyal-tshab, who, being a sacred personage, is accessible to all. If he thought that such a letter was indispensably necessary, he would surely have given it me unasked, but Sawang Rampa, who headed the most powerful of the *Shapes*, being his greatest friend, would protect me from any troubles that might befall me. Besides, he said the Regent was not personally known to him. As for securing me a permanent *lam-yig*, or road bill, that no obstacles might be put in my future residence or admission to Tibet, he advised me not to talk of that at present, for if the matter got wind, the Regent and the Ampa would surely attach a political significance to it. A messenger arrived in the evening to inform us that Lhacham would be off from Gyan-tse next morning, and that we would do well to meet her at Gyankhar castle before she left it. Norpu Tondub, the chief assistant of Chhyan-dso Kusho, was ordered to proceed to Gyan-tse in order to escort Lhacham up to Lhasa. As this man was a devoted friend and admirer of the Minister, I was glad when I heard he would come presently to see him. The Minister was also pleased to hear that Norpu Tondub was to go at the head of Lhacham's escort, and promised to speak to him to help me on the way if necessary. My ponies were brought inside the monastery from Dong-tse stables, and Pador announced that all was ready for a start. Although my illness had increased greatly, yet, thinking the present opportunity a capital one, I made up my mind to start for Lhasa. At 5 P.M., accompanied by Kusho Tungchhen, I went down to Dong-tse Phodang to pay my respects to Chhyan-dso Kusho. Tungchhen very kindly spoke to him for me, saying that my past conduct fully entitled me to his kind patronage. While walking up the Chhoide hill, I felt much oppression at the breast, and entertained serious forebodings of sufferings from an increase of my illness. In ascending three hundred feet I took breath twenty times, and pondered how it would be possible for me to journey in such a state of health to Lhasa, a distance of more than one hundred and fifty miles. I did not come to any conclusion save that such a grand opportunity would never again occur of going to Lhasa.

12th May.—A little before dawn a messenger arrived from Gyan-khar to inform the Minister that Lhacham wished to start for Lhasa positively to-day, provided he declared it to be auspicious and predicted that the journey would not be unfortunate. Chhyan-dso Kusho personally came up to the monastery for the Minister's reply. Hearing much whispering and stir in the Minister's waiting-room, I got up from bed, guessing that some change must have taken place in the programme of Lhacham's journey. What I feared most was that the message might be for my detention at Dong-tse. When I was so pondering, Tungchhen arrived and told me to be ready for setting out. I at once ran to my servant's place to see if my traps were packed up, and found Tshing-ta and Pador sewing the mouth of a yak-hair bag in which our provisions were packed. At 6 A.M., Tshing-ta and myself saw the Minister, and with profound salutations, before taking his final leave to start, implored his sacred protection (*kyab-ju*), and begged to be favoured with his *sûng-ta* (precepts and prediction). As is usual on such occasions, each of us presented him with a scarf, in the corner of which was tied a few silver coins wrapped in a piece of paper containing a petition for his *kyab-ju*. Then leaving his room quietly, we inquired if Norpu Tondub, who was to accompany us, was come. Being told that he was gone up to the *Lha-sol* to offer prayers to the spirits and demi-gods, we did not wait for him. After a hurried breakfast, while my servants were engaged in saddling and packing up my things, I went, accompanied by Tungchhen, Tshing-ta and the Om-dse of the monastery, to make obeisance to Buddha in the *Tsug-la-khang*, and present scarves to the sacred images of Buddha, Maitreya, Tsong-khapa, and Tashi Paldan Yeshe. Om-dse prayed that the sacred Buddhas and Bodhisattvas might bring us back to Dong-tse after a successful and safe pilgrimage to the sanctuaries of U, while I distributed alms to the monks who were assembled in the court to offer prayers for me. Returning to my room, I took out the longest and the best scarf from my bag to present to the Minister. His holiness very graciously touched my head with the palms of his hands, and in solemn tones said "Sarat Chandra, Lhasa is not a good place. The people there are not like those whom you meet here. The Lhasa people are suspicious and insincere. You do not know, and in fact you cannot read, their character. I advise you not to stay long in one place there. Lhacham Kusho is a powerful and influential personage in Lhasa. She will protect you, but you should so behave as rarely to require her protection. Neither should you stay long in the vicinity of Dapûng or Sera monastery. If you intend to stay long at Lhasa, you should choose your residence in a garden or village in the suburbs of Lhasa. You have selected a very bad time for your pilgrimage, as small-pox is raging all over U. But you will return safely, though the journey will be trying and fraught with immense difficulties." Having listened attentively to all the advice of his holiness, I made a profound salutation and received his benediction. His treatment of me at this time of parting was extremely kind. In fact, he treated me as his spiritual son, and I looked towards him with the veneration and high regard due to a saintly personage. Tshing-ta, who was appointed by Tung-chhen to accompany me, was now called to the Minister's presence, when Kahchan Gopa wrapped a piece of *tashi khatag* (auspicious scarf) round his neck. The Minister then turning towards him, said "Tshing-ta, I believe you know whom you are accompanying. You should serve him as you would serve me; your relations with him must be *Phama dan pu* (like parent and son)." "Venerable sire (*La kah pheb-rang-nang*), be it as you command," he meekly replied, and making three low bows withdrew. I then presented scarves to Tungchhen, Gopa and Ané Tung, all of whom evinced deep concern in my welfare, and prayed that I might return safely in their midst after a successful termination of my pilgrimage. The Minister gave some silver coins and *khatag* as *solra*, or consideration, to Tshing-ta and Pador, with a request that they should serve me well, and then came down to the top of the staircase, while Tungchhen and Kusho Ané-tung hung round my neck the auspicious *khatags*. The former followed me up to the last step of the stone staircase leading to the Minister's residence. The skies towards Gyan-tse were covered with nimbus clouds, and a few drops of rain were falling at Dong-tse. Tungchhen therefore sent his Chinese umbrella, lately indented from Terchindo, for my use. I walked down to Dong-tse Phodang by the southern road past the *chhortens*, where Chhyan-dso Kusho received us very kindly. His son, Phuntsho, poured tea in a China cup for me, Tshing-ta was provided with a seat by my side, and Pador was asked by a gesture to sit down on a long rug at a distance of about ten feet from us. Chhyan-dso Kusho then ordered Deba Reshi to fetch me some presents of Gyan-tse rugs, blankets and provisions. Thanking him cordially for his kindness, I begged him to let my men choose such things out of the presents as they could conveniently carry with them for use during the journey. Chhyan-dso Kusho ordered Tshing-ta and Pador to be presented with scarves and silver coins as *solra* or binding pledges that they would serve me faithfully and honestly. To the former he also gave three *tankas* and to the latter two, and ordered them to pay particular attention in preparing my food, as, being a man of Ayravarta, I was used to clean living and board. He also jocosely observed—"Pandib is a child; he does not know to put on his clothes!" In fact, I never succeeded in tying my *kamurbund* round my waist in the way that distinguishes a Pa*l*po from a Tibetan: whenever I tied my *kamurbund* myself, I looked like a Pa*l*po Nepali merchant. After making *chhyambul*, by taking off our hats, we presented him our parting scarves. He did not accept them, but hung round our necks longer scarves. After repeated exchange of thanks, and after he had desired me to see his colleague the Chhyan-dso Kusho of Gyan-khar, we took our leave.

It was 8 A.M. when I mounted my pony to start for Gyan-tse. The entire expedition consisted of two ponies, Tshing-ta, Pador and myself. Thus did I embark on a journey to a hostile, inhospitable, and unknown country with only two men, strangers to me, as my companions. Proceeding a few hundred yards along the road, on both sides of which were ploughed fields, in some of which men were still ploughing, I arrived at the foot of a huge willow stump, where I waited for a few minutes for Tshing-ta. Two *jo* were fighting close by. Pador, leading the pack-pony, proceeded ahead of us to fetch his lance, as he said, from his friend's house in the neighbourhood. When Tshing-ta arrived, he was quite delighted to see irrigation water running forward from a full pool along the side drain in the direction we were going. "Mark that auspicious sign," said he, "the water runs forward with us." I looked towards it with a smile and said that it was very good. If my companion had seen an unlucky omen, I do not know what turn his thoughts would have taken. Proceeding a mile, we arrived at a *chhorten*, on one side of which there was a pool of water. Alighting from my pony, I sat down on the plinth of the *chhorten*. Within half an hour Pador made his appearance with a lance full six feet long in his hand.

At 12 A.M. we arrived at Gyan-tse and passed by the *thom*, which was now full. There were dealers of ponies, blankets and grain assembled together below the *chhorten* of the *thom*. I did not look much towards the people there, lest some known faces should meet me in this strange place in a strange dress. Shortly after, we arrived at Gyan-khar castle. I waited a minute in the outer court, while Tshing-ta ran to intimate my arrival to Chhyan-dso Kusho, who sent his daughter to receive me. I alighted from my pony with the help of Pador, and was conducted by the young lady to the second-floor, mounting the ladder leading to it with difficulty. My illness was now much increased, oppression at the chest, difficulty of breathing, and dry coughing at intervals being my worst complaints. Hearing of my arrival, the Lhasre Kusho came running towards me, exclaiming *Pandibla phebsong*, *Pandibla phebsong* (Pandib is come, Pandib is come). I smilingly replied *la-yin, la-yin* (yes, sir; yes, sir). How sincerely kind and loving they were to me! and their honest smiles of welcome yet remain impressed on my mind. A religious service was being conducted in the chapel of the castle, which was enlivened by the sonorous music of *gyaling* (Tibet trumpet) and tambourines. I guessed that this service was conducted in honour of Lhacham's departure from Gyan-khar. Chhyan-dso having to accompany Lhacham in *chhoijal* (visit to chapels), I engaged in conversation with his wife and daughter. They described the nature of his illness and the different treatments he had undergone, and begged, presenting me their scarves, to prescribe good and effective medicines for his quick recovery. The *chhoijal* being over, Lhacham returned to her room, and Chhyan-dso Kusho came to be introduced to me. I paid him my *chhyambul* (respects) by taking off my hat and presented him a long scarf with three *tankas*, and made a similar present to his wife; but he forced Tshing-ta to receive back the coins and the scarves. Then, exchanging compliments with me for a few seconds, he hastened to Lhacham's presence, where he was seated on a raised seat, and the retinue, escorts and the menials of Lhacham, all one by one received presents of scarves from his hands as they walked away after paying their *chhyambul* to him. I observed the ceremony with interest, and was pleased with the show. At 1 P.M., Lhacham, accompanied by her sons, started for Lhasa. As she passed by me, she asked me in a low, gentle voice to give Chhyan-dso Kusho excellent medicines and to meet her at Gobshi in the evening. Lhasre Kusho and Gyergyan-tung also begged me, as they passed, to give the best medicines to their master. I was now surrounded by the ladies and maid-servants of Chhyan-dso Kusho's family, who had learnt that I was the Indian Amchi of whom they had heard so much of late. Chhyan-dso Kusho, now free from business, presently arrived, and expressed his delight in having been able to see me. "In former times," said he, "communication existed between India and Tibet, but unfortunately it has now ceased. It was owing to our *monlam* (prayer) that you have come in our midst, and your coming has made me hopeful of my recovery." I asked him the particulars of his illness, and found that it was chronic bronchitis, which eventually might end in consumption. I gave him a few grains of quinine and some doses of paregoric elixir, with instructions to regulate his diet. I told him that when I returned from Lhasa I could pay proper attention to his case, and assured him that his illness would not grow worse if he was careful in diet for the next six months. Every one grew cheerful when, in a grave and thoughtful tone, I declared that Chhyan-dso Kusho's illness was curable. I begged him to let me go, for if I delayed I could hardly overtake Lhacham's party on the way. While I was getting up the old gentleman and his wife seized my hands and pressed me to resume my seat. *Gya-thug* (Chinese gruel), rice and boiled mutton were brought in tinned copper dishes for my entertainment. I tasted a little of all the preparations, and then laid aside the chop-sticks to indicate that I had finished. Cham Kusho now placed before me several rolls of blankets and rugs, balls of butter and a few silver coins for my acceptance. I begged them respectfully to excuse me from accepting the presents, for as I was going on pilgrimage I could hardly put the articles to any use. As for money, I added, I would refer him to Lhacham and the Minister; it was known to them that I made it a rule not to receive any fees for medical aid, and that I did not come to Tibet to earn money or a livelihood by selling medicines. They, however, pressed my companions to accept presents that were made to them. I then got up from my seat, and Chhyan-dso Kusho, his *cham* (wife) and daughter came to reach me to the gate, where, mounting my pony, I bid them farewell.

We now journeyed on the high road between Lhasa and Gyan-tse. It was in some places more than twenty feet broad, but in others, specially in gravelly and rocky places, the road appeared hardly wider than a track, and in the neighbourhood of arable fields it served the purpose of a drain as well. In fact it resembled an unmetalled Indian road in summer. The Government pays very little attention to road-making, though the arid climate of the country affords excellent means for the construction and preservation of roads. Thus far I had not seen any wheeled conveyances, and I was told that such things are unknown in this part of the world. To the right-hand side of the road we saw the extensive *linga* (grove) of Chyanglo Chan, with a lofty palace-like building on the riverside. Proceeding two furlongs towards the east, we saw on the left the Gelug-pa monastery of Gahdan Chhoiphe*l*-ling. To our right-hand side we left several hamlets, included in the village of Da-khu. Both the monastery and the village, we were told, belongs to the Tsang Government. A chill breeze now blew and rain-clouds covered the skies, and as soon as we arrived in the vicinity of some ruins, probably of an ancient castle and a fort, we were overtaken by a snow-storm. Tshing-ta pointed out to me with his finger the road to Phagri and the monastery of Na-ñing, which formerly was, as Gyan-tse now is, a place of great trade. We next followed the course of the river Nyang-chhu, now a muddy torrent. Passing the ruins of the town of Gyang-ro, which anciently was a place of considerable trade, we entered the *rong* or defiles. Formerly this part of the country was occupied by three tribes of pastoral herdsmen called Gyang-ro, Ñing-ro, and Gang-ro, who carried on a thriving trade in yak-tail, felt turbans, soft felt and blankets. From an easterly direction we now turned towards the north-east, the road running along the steep banks of the Nyang-chhu. The nature of the soil and the rocks now changed, red slate and mica abounding on the roadside. Our road now became a mere track, and I wondered how the Tibetans using the road from time immemorial could have allowed it to remain in so primitive a state. A nation so superstitious as to view all improvement and progress as against custom and usage cannot indeed be prosperous and civilized; but that those who look to the improvement of the soul with such extraordinary interest and zeal should care very little for the material prosperity of the country seemed strange. At 4 in the afternoon, after passing several hamlets and small religious buildings on the way side, we entered a narrow valley where the Nyang-chhu suddenly changed itself into a rushing hill torrent. We crossed it at Ku-dung *ssampa* (bridge), where we met two of the female attendants of Lhacham. Some of the mountain-tops were covered with snow, and here and there on the roadside fresh snow had fallen. At dusk, overtaken by rain and sleet, we arrived at the village of Gobshi, where Lhacham with her retinue and escort had arrived a little before us. Norpu Tondub asked to help me, and conducted me to her presence. Her face was overcast with melancholy, for she had learnt that small-pox was raging all over this part of the country, and that the very *mi-tshang* (family residence) where she was now accommodated contained five patients. But my arrival cheered her, and she accorded me a very warm reception. She asked me to sit in her presence on the same seat with her eldest son, and told me that she apprehended great danger in having to stay in a village filled with small-pox patients. She inquired after the Minister's health, and if he was taking care of her darling Ané-tung. I gave a very interesting account of Ané-tung: how Ané wept when she left Dong-tse; how the Minister consoled him; on what friendly terms I was with him; how, in short, her lovely child was an idol with us all; listening to all which Lhacham forgot for a while that she was in an infectious place. She then ordered her attendants to fetch me *sol-shib* and *sol-tsi*—flour and meat—for my dinner. Gergyan-tung, in the presence of the whole audience, asked me to vaccinate every one of Lhacham's party, as they were all unprotected. Both he and Lhacham had heard from the Minister that I knew the best remedy for small-pox, and that I had brought with me some virus which, when inserted in the arms of an individual, brought him immunity from small-pox. What a grand opportunity this was for me to have introduced vaccination! But alas! the vaccine matter had not now even entered Tibet. My companion Ugyen Gyatsho, by mistake, had put the virus tubes in my chest of chemicals, which was detained at Lachan pass. I expressed my regret in not having the vaccine matter at hand, as Tung-yig La (Ugyen Gyatsho), whom we had sent to Lachan Pass with the *lam-yig* or passport issued by her husband Mije-chhenpo, had not arrived with my things. The disappointment was equally felt by Lhacham and the whole party. My attendants came and asked if I would like to sleep in a room where there were small-pox patients. On my saying no, Lhacham wished me to go and personally find out sleeping accommodation for myself. It was raining now, with a slight gale, and the court of the house was muddy. My companions were also much afraid of the contagion of small-pox, and begged me to pass the night in the yak-shed adjoining the stables where Lhacham's servants and escort had accommodated themselves. The ponies and *jo* were all tied in the open court, where they kept frequently fighting with each other. The latter did not much annoy us, but the fighting and kicking of the ponies, and their violent neighing, was a great nuisance. At midnight there was a snow-storm, when I found my woollens insufficient to keep off the cold. My fever increased; I felt oppression at the chest; the difficulty of coughing increased, and with much exertion I expectorated small quantities of stiff phlegm.

The places of any importance which we passed in our journey from Gyang-khar castle of Phala were the following:—Phala, containing about two hundred houses, belonging entirely to Lhacham's husband; Charong-shikha, Chhe-ningpa, Ta-chong-thanka, Gahdan, Chhoiphe*l*-ling monastery and its *sho* or lay village; Doisa, Jewa Cha wang, Tha-ring, Kudûng, Chyama and its monastery in the uplands; Gyaridom and Gobshi. The Chyama monastery belongs to the Dorje-Thag monastery, and is now under the abbotship of an incarnate Lama of the red-hat school.

13*th May*.—At sun-rise, when I got up from bed, Lhacham's men were busy starting the *Thél-pa*, or laden mules. Tshing-ta soon prepared tea and wished me to sit at breakfast. Norpo Tondub now made his appearance, and inquiring how I had spent the night, rode off in haste to reach Ralung in time to make arrangements for Lhacham's accommodation and dinner there. After breakfast we resumed our journey; but before we had proceeded a few yards, we were met by two gaudily dressed Tibetans, whom we took for military men. Near the village *mandang* two mendicants implored alms, chanting some hymns. I heard them address me as Mankyi Gya*l*-po (or the Prince of Physicians); so, ordering Tshing-ta to give them a silver two-anna bit, I rode down to the river-side to cross the bridge. Gobshi is a large village containing about fifty houses, of which three were large and respectable looking. There were a few poplars and pollard willow trees planted in front of the village, while the barley fields, in terrace steps, were behind the village on the river side. Two *chhortens*—one large and the other small—marked the entrance to the village from the east. This place was noted formerly under the Sakya hierarchy for its large monastic establishments. To the left-hand side of the confluence of the two streams—one of which comes from the south-east and the other from the east—there was a flour-mill turned by water, with a few willow stumps in the neighbourhood of the mill-house. On the top of the hill, over-ranging the mill-house, was a temple-like old building, a portion of which was in ruins. Two rivers meet below the hill on which the *jong* is situated: the one coming from the north, or felt-hand side, being the Nyang-chhu, and the other from the south, the Niro-chhu. The name Gobshi means four gates, and in former times, when the Sakya and Phag-modu dynasties were in power, this place was celebrated as a place of pilgrimage, being situated in a gorge surrounded by wild rocky mountains imparting much religious mystery and sanctity. Its four entrances are poetically described by the Tibetans as Chhoikyi-go, the eastern gate, facing the Ralung monastery; Ning roi-go, the spirit-entrance, facing the south; Do-chag-gi-go, the adamantine gate, which leads to a cave-temple consecrated to Yama or the lord of death; and Gya-tag-na-go, the western entrance, or the pilgrim's gate. To the south side of the village there are eight mountain peaks standing in a row, and venerated by devout people as the eight self-sprung images of *Gur-lha*, the lords of the Buddhist tabernacle. A little to the east, in the uplands above the junction of the two streams, is situated a Pon monastery, named *Khyung-nag* (consecrated to the black eagle), of very ancient date. During the Dikhung hierarchy in the 15th century, this monastery became very famous, and pilgrims from different parts of Tibet proper and Kham visited it. Tshing-ta told me that the old house on the top of the hill was a *jong* (fort); but Pador, whose knowledge of this place seemed intimate, for he had often come here to collect rent, corrected his colleague and said that half of the village belonged to Lhacham's father-in-law Sa-Wang Phala, and to her husband. From Gobshi our next stage was Kha-vo monastery, which formerly, under the name of Khyung, belonged to the Pon religion. It is now a Ningma religious establishment. The monks of Khavo generally follow agricultural pursuits for a livelihood, and the barley fields that we passed belonged to them. I was struck with the industrious habits of the people, and the immense labour with which they reclaimed the bleak and barren nooks of mountains wherever the water percolated. The religious buildings and the cells of monks were externally decorated with blue and red stripes, and Tshing-ta told me that now-a-days such stripes are painted on the outside of the walls of houses to show that they are the residence of the Ningma Buddhists. Our next stage was Go-chye village, situated on a narrow table-land about 300 feet above the river, but a snow-storm overtook us when we had proceeded a short distance from Kha-vo. Here we overtook Norpu Tondub in a narrow rocky path where two ponies could hardly pass together, and I stayed behind for a few minutes to let Norpu Tondub and his companion pass first. From Go-chye I came to Salagang, riding very slowly in consequence of my illness. Here we descended to the margin of Nyang-chhu, along which our way now began to thread. Proceeding for about a couple of miles eastward, we came to Shetoi, where we crossed the river on horseback. Reaching the opposite side of the river, I alighted from the pony to take a short rest, and then joined Lhacham's party a little below the village of Shetoi, the Lhasre Kushos preceding Lhacham, while I followed. Lhacham kindly ordered her head groom, Tshering-tenpa, to help me in steep places. From Shetoi there are two roads leading to Ralung *ssampa*. The road which runs by the right bank is generally frequented by travellers, but the one we followed was a short cut. At Longma we crossed the *Shing ssampa*, or wooden bridge, about 30 feet long, and, following the course of the river, we arrived at the village of Pesar. The barley-fields here, cut in the shape of terrace steps, appeared to be fertile and well manured. At about half-past 3 in the afternoon we arrived at the town of Ralûng-chhong-doi. I was completely exhausted by the fatigues of the journey, and my illness much increased by exposure to the foul weather. The Gyanpo of Ralûng had already made arrangements for Lhacham's reception. In a snug little house carpets were spread on the floor and curtains hung to conceal the unevenness of the walls. I was accommodated in a side room adjoining Lhacham's, and two stuffed rugs and a pair of pillows supplied me by the Gyanpo, to whom I promised some consideration at the time of leaving the place. He also supplied us with fuel and water. When all were seated, Lhacham asked me to sit at dinner with her sons, and ordered *phing-sha*, or meat cooked with *phing*, to be served for me. Although very ill, my fever having increased, I took two cups of *phing-sha* with barley-flour. A chill, moist wind blew, accompanied by sleet, for an hour before sun-set. The country was all white with snow. After dinner I felt a shivering cold, my blankets being insufficient to protect me, and I begged Tshing-ta to borrow a pair of blankets from the Gyanpo, which he at once did and wrapped me up in them. Ralûng is one of the most important sacred places of Tibet. It was here that the great *Dukpa* school of the red-hat monks first originated, which is still very powerful in Tibet, having numerous adherents in southern, northern, and eastern Tibet. Besides, the whole country of Bhutan is designated by the name *Dukpa* owing to the prevalence of that school there. A little into the interior, south-eastward, is situated the famous monastery of Ralûng or Ralûng-thil, the head-quarter of the Dukpa school: the hills surrounding the great monastery being compared to the petals of a lotus, the monastery itself being the corolla. Indeed, the devout Buddhists see many sacred objects all over the Ralûng hills. A little before sun-set two Chinese officials arrived with an order for *Ta-oo* (relay of horses), and our host the Gyanpo hastened to attend to their requirements.

14*th May*.—Without even a cup of tea or gruel we set out on our journey. Lhacham told us that she intended to reach Nangar-tse-jong that day, which was a long distance to travel. Hearing that the hilly country between Ralûng and Nangar-tse was a dreadful solitude where robberies are not of unfrequent occurrence, I was anxious to keep up with the party. My health was pulled down and my complaint of shortness of breath and difficulty in expectoration increased to an alarming extent, yet the fear of being waylaid and robbed forced me to follow the fast-trotting *sowars* of Lhacham. At about 7 A.M. we rode along an extensive flat above the Nyang-chhu, overhung by a lofty mountain running behind us to our right. Here I kept myself in the middle of the train, Lhacham riding before me, and frequently asking me if I was not fatigued or hungry or thirsty. Sometimes her two sons came to my side and stirred up my pony with their whips. Our way till now lay to the south of the Nyang-chhu. To our right and left we left many *Dok-pa* tents made of yak-hair and sheltering herdsmen's families. Leaving the vicinity of the river-side, we now ascended a lofty and extensive plateau, to the north-east of which the snowy ranges of Noijin Kang-ssang reared up their white heads. The two highest of the snowy mountains between Om-thang and Tagla are Kang-ssang and Noijin Norpu-ssang-po. The legends say that at the command of the Buddhas to guard Buddhism, the Saint Kuntu-ssang-po was born as the son of Kang-ssang, the king of goblins, and was called Norpu-ssang-po. The devout Buddhists go further than this. They say that the mountain peak Norpu-ssang, holding as it were in its hand the Dorje in which is consecrated the power of all Buddhas, is a manifestation of Chyagna Dorje, or the lord of mysticism. Legends connected with the snowy mountain Noijin Kang-ssang have been graphically narrated by Pama-karpo, a well-known scholar of the Dukpa school of Buddhists. He says—"The uppermost part of Nyang district includes the group of lofty, snow-clad mountains called Ha-hu Kang-ssang, with which is connected the legend of the three Noijin goblins—Kang-ssang-po, Chhovo-ssang-po, and Norpu-ssang-po. The chief of these, Noijin Kang-ssang-po, sits exalted surrounded by his sons Norpu, Chhovo and Kharo, the last of whom has five hundred fierce demon retainers. The Chief Kang-ssang being possessed of various auspicious symbols and beauties, is supremely magnificent in appearance. His whiteness, variegated with many shades of colour, is most magnificent to the view. The Tibetan poet Kunleg describes him thus :—

"In yonder bounds of earth, the quarter of the setting sun,
Beneath the white clouds, that float in glorious array,
Like a truncated marble block, shooting to the skies,
The divine Kang-ssang, the powerful goblin lies."

A certain Ningma Lama having performed a very difficult ascetic ceremony according to the Kalachakra *tantras*, is said to have transformed his body into a condensed heap of glorious lustre, and was then called upon to be the spiritual adviser of this mountain king. Keeping the peak, with its divinely glorious hues right ahead, and proceeding to a half day's journey, one will arrive at a sanctuary called Kamoling, where exists a sacred cavern consecrated to saint Padma Sambhava. There are several springs and rills, the water of which is held in high sanctity : the milky water, impregnated with a sweet scent, being reputed to have the property of restoring life to the dead. The plateau reminded me of the description of steppes I had read in books, being covered with pastures, with numerous herds of yaks grazing by the side of some rills or fountains. These rills seemed to be lateral feeders of the Nyang-chhu, which has its source in the glaciers of Noijin. The part of the plateau we traversed could not be less than five miles; but to what length it extended towards the north and east I could not guess. Shortly after we arrived at the topmost part of the plateau, our way turned towards Kharula. This high plateau is called Omathang (or the milky plain). The Dok-pa village, overhung by a snowy peak, and consisting of three or four houses, which stands at the entrance of Kharula Pass, is also called Omathang, but Tshing-ta told me that he had heard it called Pamthang. Two rivers here flow in two different directions: the one running towards the south, after a short westerly direction, is said to be the head water of Nyang-chhu, and the other, which flows towards the east, is called Kharnang-phu-chhu. Leaving Omathang village to our left, we ascended the steep slopes of Kharula. Here grew a species of thorny shrubs about four feet high, the like of which I had never noticed in other parts of Tibet. The thorns were long, and the stems and leaves of the shrubs of a grey ash colour. Proceeding further on for two miles, we came to the foot of the famous Noijin Kang-ssang mountain, where the river Kharnang-phu-chhu turns northward through a glen. Over the two channels of this stream there are two stone bridges. Then proceeding eastward for a short distance, we came to the Lab-tse, where there is a high mound of stone, probably a sacred cairn, with a *chhorten* close by. Here Lhacham with her retinue halted for tiffin, and she invited me to sit by her eldest son. I had very little appetite, having a fever in addition to my other complaints, but as she pressed me to take some biscuits covered with treacle, fearing she might take offence, I at last tried a few. The sun was strong, and the umbrellas being with the attendants, I offered a Chinese wicker-work hat to Lhacham to protect her head from the sun, which she declined with thanks. After half-an-hour's rest we resumed our journey. Lhacham appeared to be in a very sprightly mood, and wished me to make my pony amble; so she, myself, and her two sons rode together for a short distance, when my pony alone was found to amble with something like regularity in lifting its legs on each side alternately. When the race was finished, she patted my pony on the back, saying *Aih-hai* (bravo). Her two sons being ashamed of this defeat, challenged me to a second trial, and, though feeling very unwell, yet fearing the Lhasre Kushos might take offence at my not complying with their request, I whipped my pony and made it amble for a short distance, when the amble changed into a slow trot, whereupon the Lhasres laughed exultingly at my failure. When I alighted from my pony for rest, I gasped, breathing hard and quick. If I had won, which they did not like me to do, and which I purposely did not, the Lhasre Kushos would surely not look towards me with their usual kindness. When we had advanced far in the solitude, the Lhasre Kushos did not like to go alone further, so they rested themselves on the ground beside me, and noticing my illness expressed their regret at it. When Lhacham and party arrived, we mounted our ponies and resumed our journey. The mountain slopes were steep here ; the soil of a reddish colour interposed with brown, slaty rocks. The glens, where only brown boulders were visible, were deep on either side. Our way now lay through a bleak and verdureless ravine which terminated at Dsawa. The descent to this place was very steep, and the road for a length of two to three hundred yards was along a loose, sandy and gravelly bank. Here we dismounted and walked down on foot. Norpu Tondub, who had arrived here before us as *Ngondo*, now came to receive Lhacham. He conducted us to a herdsman's house situated on the top of a hillock overhanging the Gya-Khang, or the Ampa's circuit-house, which is situated on the flat of Dsara. This house was built of loose stones piled one upon another, the roof being low and constructed of slate and stone slabs. Here, in a cell-like room, her head touching the roof, Lhacham seated herself for refreshment, while her sons sat by her side. Not finding me near her, I having gone to wash, she sent Tshing-ta to call me. When I was conducted to her presence, she at once ordered her attendants to cook my food in a clean pot and to fetch me the best mutton available. Tea was served as usual. I asked her if she was not tired with riding such a distance : as for me, I was completely tired, and my illness *woo-sag-pa* (shortness of breath) had increased. She replied that she was tired, but being used to this kind of journey, the ride to this distance was no hard work to her. I observed "*Kusho khayn* (your ladyship), riding is indeed pleasant to one in health, but when one falls ill, and especially a female, it cannot be a pleasant affair. What kind of conveyance do you use to take the sick from one place to another? I know conveyance by *shing chyam* (sedan chair) is not allowed to anybody except to two or three great personages." She replied: "It is true that only the two Grand Lamas, the Ampas, and the Regent occasionally are allowed the privilege of using the *shing chyam*. No other persons, however great they may be, can use it." I said that in India any man can use a wooden conveyance at a trifling cost of from two to four annas, and asked how it was that the Tibetans attach so great an importance to *shing chyam* conveyances. She answered: "Pandib La, to use human beings as beasts of conveyance, and thereby to degrade them to a lower level, is a cruel thing. It would be disgraceful to our *misser* to yield to such an indignity." "How is it," said I, "that the Tibetans do not feel ashamed to carry the Ampa, who is no holy personage at all." "Yes," replied she, "the Imperial Resident is the representative of the Emperor of China, who is a Bodhisattva incarnate. Both the Grand Lamas and the Regent are divine beings." The cook now brought a fat piece of boiled mutton and placed it on a dish before her. She sliced it and placed some of the best parts on my plate, saying that Pandibla must have the best of things, being from India, a very remote country. At this the herdsman and outsiders, who were waiting outside, looked hard at me, and I winked towards her not to mention that I was from India. But she did not choose to notice it. At this Gergyantung, who was sitting at some distance from our seat, said with great presence of mind "Kusho Pandibla looks like a Palpo, and his pronunciation resembles that of the Nepalese merchants of Lhasa." Lhacham then jokingly said: "Pandib, if some one now comes here and takes you down to Lhasa for being a native of India, what will you do?" I replied "I shall see Lhasa before I could otherwise expect to see it." "If they give you trouble, and beat you, then what would you think of your coming here?" I replied "I am now under the protection of one of the greatest ladies of Tibet, for your ladyship occupies the highest place in society, there being no queen in Tibet, and the King of Tibet being himself an incarnate Lama. You are the wife of a Shape and daughter of the Dahpon (commander) of Lhasa." "No," she replied, "we are not the only *Ponpo* (chiefs) of Lhasa: there are many like us there. Yes, when you are at Lhasa, do not say that you are from India." I told her that there was no law prohibiting the admission of the natives of India into Tibet: all the saints and sages who appeared here in Tibet in ancient time, and do appear now, were, and are, from India: in fact, the Grand Lamas were all from India. But to change the topic I said "Does not your ladyship think that pony conveyance is not suited to women, for if a lady falls ill in the middle of a steppe while crossing it, how would she be conveyed to her home? As, unlike the natives of Sikkim and Nepal, the Tibetans do not carry either loads or human beings, the want of proper conveyance is most keenly felt, and if your ladyship introduces the wooden conveyance into Tibet, and would make your own *misser* carry the sedan chair, you would confer a benefit on future generations." "Yes," replied she, "if we forced our *misser* to carry the *shing chyam* (sedan chair), they would feel greatly disgraced in the eyes of their countrymen, and would in consequence leave our estates." Our refreshments being now finished, we prepared to resume our journey. I walked down to the gate of the Gya-khang (Ampa's circuit-house), in the court of which our ponies were tied, but my pony was let loose to graze on the grassy flat of the Dsara rivulet, there being no forage for him, although Lhacham's men had brought a few morsels of forage for her ponies. I and the Lhasre Kushos rode together, Lhacham and her escort following us at an amble. The valley of Dsara-chhu rivulet now gradually opened towards the east. At a distance of about two miles from Dsara we saw the ruins of two or three *ritoi* (recluses' cells) on the steep edge of a rocky precipice. There is a long wall, probably the revetment, which protected the cells and the passage leading to them. Here two streamlets coming from the right and the left join the Dsara-chhu and form a valley of several spacious flats, where yaks and sheep were grazing. The combined streams flowed towards the east under the name of Kharnang-phu-chhu, on the left bank of which lay our way. We followed its downward course for about six miles up to Rhingla village, where the river turned towards the north to empty itself in the Yamdo-yum-tsho lake. From Rhingla, where the extensive table-land of Nangar-tse begins, the monastery of Samding is faintly visible. As soon as Lhacham and her party arrived at this place the ponies quickened their pace; and now that the *rong* (defiles and ravines) were passed, and the way lay along the middle of an extensive plain, the animals seemed to be in their proper element. I was not prepared for a hard ride on account of my illness, but as our companions could not, at this late hour of the day, travel slowly, I was obliged to follow them to be able to reach Nangar-tse before 5 P.M. Lhacham here asked me how much gold I had with me and how much I possessed at home. I told her that I was a poor man in India, though the income of my family was about five *dochhe* a month, but that while starting for Tibet my master had given me some gold that I might journey in Tibet. That gold was deposited with the Minister, and her ladyship had probably seen it. At the time of starting for Lhasa the Minister had only advanced me two *dochhes* (Rs. 250) to meet my expenses during the trip, and assured me that if money fell short, I could apply to her ladyship for a loan. "Yes," she replied, with a smile, "the Minister has asked me to help you on your journey to Lhasa." She then asked me, her eyes filling with tears, how her darling Ané-tung was doing with the Minister, and how Tungchhen and Gopa liked him. I talked flatteringly of her son's good conduct, and what a favourite he was with the Minister. She listened with much attention to what I said, and I think it was to hear more frequently of her son that she wished me to ride close by her. Beguiling the way in such pleasant conversation, we arrived in the neighbourhood of Nangar-tse jong. The houses of the fishermen and of the *misser* were perched on the hill-side overhanging the *jong*. The blue expanse of the famous Yamdo-tsho (Lake Palti) bounded our sight towards the north-east, while sheep dotted the *thang* (plain) we were passing through. Here Lhacham dismounted, when the whole escort also alighted from their ponies. She changed her upper garments for new and more decent-looking ones, and put on her costly *patug* (crown-like head-dress), which was a mass of the choicest pearls, rubies and lapis-lazuli. Then remounting her white palfrey she trotted swiftly on, and we followed her without delay. When we arrived at the gate of Nabo Chhokhen, we saw a raised platform erected, covered with soft blankets, upon which Lhacham alighted, while her sons and other followers alighted from their ponies outside the gate. As all were busy, I remained outside the gate for a few minutes, waiting for somebody to come to help me in dismounting, as the saddle and the short stirrups were so bad that I feared to get down alone, and my knees were almost paralyzed with keeping them bent and strained for such a length of time. At last Tshing-ta came and brought me down from my high-peaked saddle. For a few minutes I could not walk without limping, but slowly ascending the ladder, arrived at where Gergyan Tung and others were sitting. The Lhasre Kushos seeing me, at once ran to their mother to ask where she would wish me to sit. A room next to hers was selected for me, where I laid myself down, quite prostrated with fatigue. The house in which we were accommodated was a spacious one. The rooms were large, the roof high, the door-frames neatly made and the floor well beaten, being constructed of pebbles laid in layers, as is usual in most Tibetan houses. Lhacham was accommodated in the chapel-room, of which the ceiling was of China silk and the curtains of Nepal chintz with Buddhist images painted all over. The walls mostly contained frescoes descriptive of scenes in religious tragedies. The host appeared a well-to-do man, his dress being respectable and his earrings valuable. The head-dress of his wife, though not well studded with corals and pearls, was yet a tolerably good and handsome one. The brother and nephew of our host were laid up with small-pox, and in one corner of the house some Lamas were reading texts from Buddhist scripture for their speedy recovery. As soon as Lhacham was informed of my arrival, she at once sent her sons to conduct me to her presence. "Amchila," she said, "my heart is palpitating with fear; we are now in the heart of *mi-tsang-ma* (defilement) owing to the prevalence of small-pox. Every one in this house has suffered from small-pox, and two or three are laid up in the adjoining room. What do you think will befall us? If I or my children fall ill on the way, it will indeed be a very unfortunate affair." To allay her fears, I said "Your ladyship should not apprehend much danger from small-pox. Many people, we are told, are attacked with *lhan-dum* (small-pox), but we do not hear that there has been much mortality from it. If we remain aloof from the patients, there will be little chance of our catching the contagion." "How could we be clear of infection?" replied Lhacham; "the very rugs and carpets on which we sit must have been used by the patients." As this kind of topic did not appear pleasant, I diverted her attention by telling her a few stories respecting Dolma (goddess Tara) and other female deities, for Lhacham seemed to think that she had in her the spirit of the divine mother Tara, and in fact she was well versed in the literature and *shastras* of Tibet, used to read letters and dictate correspondence to Gergyan Tung, and directed the management of a large portion of her husband's estates. The Minister had also told me that she was more influential than her husband. In the course of conversation, I told her that Tara was the goddess of transcendental wisdom or *Prajna* (in Tibetan *sherab*), and that those who possessed learning and wisdom had the spirit of Tara in them. She was quite edified with this compliment. In conclusion, I observed that she ought to have made arrangements for tents, which would have saved her from her present apprehensions of danger and uneasiness of mind. Opposite to the portico of the ground-floor, in the court, a man lately arrived from Lhasa was lying down, while two *Gelongs* (priests) were chanting some religious *mantra* to the disagreeable music of a bell and *damaru* (a small hand drum made of a human skull and fish skin). Lhacham pointed out to me this patient, and smilingly said that small-pox was now a general complaint throughout Lhasa. After dinner I returned to my room. The hard journey of the day had quite exhausted me, and the moment I covered myself up a shivering cold overtook me, and I required more woollens to wrap myself with. Lhacham's men could not let me have their blankets, nor could I ask the host to lend me some, as they were all used by small-pox patients. The chill developed into fever, and I began to cough. There was no expectoration, but the cough was violent, half lifting me from the bed. I took a dose of cough-mixture, but the fever increased during the night. For a few hours I slept restlessly, and in the third watch of night I felt much oppression at the chest. I called Tshing-ta and Pador to my help, and to watch the progress of my illness. I was afraid of being left behind by my companions. The worst part of the journey, I was told, lay between Nangar-tse-jong and Khamba Par-tshi, where robbery is frequently committed on lonely travellers. I thought my illness would be my ruin. Tshing-ta and Pador sat down near my bed, felt my pulse, examined my chest and eyes, and said the disease was serious and that I could by no means journey with Lhacham. I then, with the help of Tshing-ta, prepared four doses of cough-mixture with paregoric elixir and ipecacuanha wine, of which I drank one. The medicines which I had taken at bed-time last night had rather aggravated the disease, and I entertained little hope of obtaining relief from the present mixture.

15th May.—There was a brisk movement among Lhacham's servants a little before daybreak, some engaged in packing up, some in saddling the ponies, and others in preparing tea. My illness assumed serious proportions, the paroxysms of coughing increased, when with painful efforts I could throw up a yellowish mucus from the lungs. Tshing-ta informed Norpu Tondub and Gergyan Tung of my state, who anxiously came to see me, and expressed much sorrow at my helpless condition. "In this *changthan* (desert-like place) how will Amchila remain alone," said Norpu Tondub, "where there is no physician to give him medicines?" It was broad daylight when the latter half of the party, headed by Norpu Tondub, left Nangar-tse. The Lhasre Kushos also came to see me, and sat for a few minutes near my bed, embracing my hands, and were indeed very sorry to hear that I would be left alone at Nangar-tse. Our host, Chhokhen, next came in, examined my pulse, tongue and eyes, and turning to Tshing-ta and Gergyan Tung, whispered that the disease was a very serious one and required skilful medical treatment. He said there were no *Amchis* at Nangar-tse, but there were two very learned physicians at Samding monastery, by whom, a few days ago, a similar case had been cured. He also mentioned the name of the medicine which they would at the first instance administer to me. The two chief maid-servants of Lhacham, named Apenla and Patononla, also came to see me. "*Akkha-kha*," they said, "the illness is *tshub-chhen* (very serious). How will we leave him alone, having accompanied him thus far?" The former, an elderly woman, drew near me and whispered in my ears "Amchila, ask Lhacham to give you a letter of introduction to Dorje Phagmo, the incarnate lady superior of Samding. Lhacham and Dorje Phagmo are fast friends; they are sisters." She then left me, being required to wait upon Lhacham. I then asked our host how far Samding was from Nangar-tse. "Oh, Sir, it is nearly a pag-tshad and half" (equal to seven miles). "Could I ride to it?" said I. "Yes, the road is easy; but the question is whether Dorje Phagmo will (*jalkha naug-ong*) grant you an interview at this time;" for it was rumoured that owing to the prevalence of small-pox she had stopped admission to pilgrims into her monastery. Tshing-ta said "Sir, if you could go to Samding, it would be possible to consult some sacred Lamas to examine your fortune, propitiate the gods by some religious observance, and arrange about your medical treatment. We hear that there are two good physicians, one of whom is old and the other young. Our *Nabo* (host) says that there is no knowing if Dorje Phagmo will see you." Gergyan Tung assured me not to be uneasy, as presently Lhacham would arrange for my accommodation. Shortly after Lhacham came to see me, accompanied by her two sons, and after examining my eyes and tongue observed that the case appeared hopeful: there would be much suffering, but she feared no fatal end to the disease. She and her sons, however, seemed very much moved. The *Nabo* presently came, and said that we should go to Samding where, even if we failed to see Dorje Phagmo, we would still be better off than here; for there I could get medical help, accommodation, and also means to propitiate the gods for my recovery. I then begged Gergyan Tung to ask Lhacham to favour me with a letter of introduction to Dorje Phagmo, that I might go there for medical treatment. Saying "*laso, laso,*" he at once went to Lhacham to plead for me. A few minutes after he returned to my room, and asked if I had a good scarf to enclose the letter of introduction in. Tshing-ta immediately opened the bundle of scarves which I had bought from Kusho Tungchhen, and selected a very good one as *shuten*. The letter being immediately written and sealed, Gergyan Tung handed it over to Tshing-ta, and told me that Lhacham, moved by compassion for me, had written to Dorje Phagmo to take care of me and to look to my wants. Shortly after, Lhacham came to take leave of me, and could hardly forbear from tears when she saw mine flowing at the fear of death in an unknown and friendless country. "Don't cry, *ogo* (will you)?" she said, "I have asked Dorje Phagmo to help you to the best of her power; you will get all sorts of necessaries as long as you remain there. When you get well, will you come over to our house at Lhasa, *ogo*?" I replied in a faltering tone, "Your ladyship will not forget this humble stranger; he has none in this distant and strange land to show mercy to him, save your ladyship and that fountain of mercy, the Minister." "Fear not, Pandibla, Dorje Phagmo will be as kind to you as myself. We have no hand in the inevitable consequence of *las* (karma). You must submit to it, but I am glad that you have fallen ill here instead of at another place, for here we can send you to Dorje Phagmo. Come directly to our house when you recover." She charged Tshing-ta and Pador to serve me to the best of their power and ability, and warned them not to desert me. The Lhasre Kushos also exhorted Pador to be a faithful and devoted servant to Pandibla, and serve him to the last. Lhacham, I was told, had, as the last thing before her departure, desired the *Nabo* and *Namo* to accommodate me in their house as long as I liked to remain at Nangar-tse.

II.—ARRIVAL AT YAMDO SAMDING, AND RESIDENCE THERE.

When the *Nabo* and *Namo* returned to the house after reaching Lhacham to a short distance from the gateway, Tshing-ta, with my permission, presented the former with a couple of *tankas* for my accommodation. He seemed to be very obliging and willing to serve me. Tea being prepared, I raised myself to sit reclining on my blankets, and drank a cup. After breakfast, feeling a little better, I asked Tshing-ta if he and Pador, travelling on foot, could reach Samding before noon. The Nabo immediately said it could be reached in a couple of hours. I was much encouraged to learn that the distance was so very small, and almost made up my mind to leave Nangar-tse, for if the physicians from Samding were called to attend on me here, they would charge me heavily. Besides, there was a scarcity of fodder at Nangar-tse; so about half an hour after breakfast I prepared to start for Samding. Pador and Tshing-ta wrapped me with the woollens and blankets, carefully tied the head-tie round my head, and protected my neck with my comforter. The weight of the clothes pressed heavily on my neck. It was about 9 A.M. when I set off towards Samding. At a distance of about two miles from Nangar-tse, we met a sluggish stream which flowed towards the Yamdo-tsho. The rivulet was teeming with a kind of small fish and overgrown with a kind of sedge, over which green moss was scattered. The plain over which we travelled was extensive towards the north and south, and terminated at the Samding mountains on the north and west. Crossing three or four limpid but sluggish streams, all on their way to join the great lake, we arrived at the eastern side of Samding monastery, which, perched on the top of a barren hill, looked most picturesque. The appearance of its lofty *tsug-la-khang* (grand hall of worship), of the residence of the abbot, and of the surrounding houses, induced me to think that Samding monastery must have once been a very impregnable fortress. The flight of stone steps from the foot of the hill to the top of it, along which a zig-zag pathway wound up, lined by a stone wall about six feet high and three feet broad, filled me with the greatest dismay: how could I ascend to that height when my heart throbbed even while I was seated on the pony! Arrived at the foot of the large *chhorten* where pilgrims generally halt and encamp, Tshing-ta asked two men, who were coming down from the monastery, if Kyab-gon (protectress) Dorje Phagmo was accessible to pilgrims, and if the two Amchi Kushos (physician gentlemen) were at the monastery. Being answered in the affirmative, I dismounted from the pony, and sat down gasping on a stone step. The stone wall was in a dilapidated state, and the steps, though constructed of stone slabs, were ugly-looking and evidently in a ruinous state. After a few minutes' rest, we commenced our wearisome ascent. Taking rest at every bend of the stair, we reached its top, which I guessed to be about 300 feet in height. The top of the steps, however, was not the end, for a narrow pathway thence led us further up to the foot of the monastery. From the eastern edge of the hill we now came to the north-western face of it, whence we enjoyed a grand view of the inner lake of Yamdo. I could not long keep my eyes fixed on the surrounding scenery, troubled as I was with the glare of the sun, a headache, and above all the hard breathing. Towards the north-west I noticed a group of sombre hills topped with grey snow. The lake seemed to have been fed by the streams caused by the melting of the glaciers in those hoary mountains. But this was now no time for conjectures, for at intervals of a few minutes—sometimes of seconds—difficult expectoration bent me down to the ground with the effort of coughing. On the left-hand side of the road leading to the entrance of the monastery, two huge *dokhyi* (watch-mastiffs), fastened with stout chains, howled and attempted to jump towards us, but a wooden railing in front of their kennels prevented them. While at Tashi-lhunpo I heard that the mastiffs of Yamdo were very large and fierce, and these dogs convinced me of the truth of what I had heard. Ascending a few steps, we arrived at the northern gate of the monastery, which faces the inner lake called Dumo-tsho. I seated myself on a stone slab lying on the plinth of the monastery. My sickly appearance, the frequent hard coughing, and my covering of thick woollens, made the circumambulators of the monastery look with pity towards me. I saw with surprise several gentlemen walking round the monastery and continually twirling *manikhorlo* (prayer-wheels), for I thought men, excepting pilgrims, had no access to the great monastery of which the presiding head was an abbess; but the number of monks seemed to be more than that of the nuns among the circumambulators. Two or three monks enquired whence I came, and what my illness was. I told them it was *lo-chham*, or cold in the lungs. Pador stood at a distance from me, holding the pony and watching our traps, while Tshing-ta, with a scarf in his hand, entered the monastery in search of the two physicians. After an hour's absence he returned, and to my enquiries if the *Amchis* had been found, he replied *La, Amchi gyanpa dug, shonpa mindug* (Yes, sir, the old physician is present, the junior not; the former is just coming). I was then led towards a lane to the north-east of the outer wall of the monastic building. The lane was narrow and scarcely more than six feet broad, lying between the monastic building and the monastery wall. After a few minutes the Amchi Chhenpo arrived, and with an appearance of kindness and sympathy, while feeling my pulse, said "Don't you shed tears, *ogo* (will you)? You are come from a great distance. I will give very good medicines; don't you weep, *ogo*." I said "*Kusho* (sir), I see my death is near; I have fever, my breath is short and difficult, and I do not think a man in such a state of illness can last long." "*Mitog, mitog*, do not fear do not fear so much; we will presently give you medicine." He then examined my eyes, tongue and expectoration. He appeared to be about 70 years age, quite grey, but with a frame still strong and sturdy, of middle stature, with agreeable features, broad forehead and dignified looks. Helped by Tshing-ta, I followed him, and after ascending two ladders we arrived at the portico of the Amchi's house. The old man, while twirling his prayer-wheel with the right hand, and frequently taking snuff with his left, observed the working of my lungs with attention as I walked and climbed up. He gave me a medicinal powder to be taken with a spoon of warm water, and ordered his cook to supply me with *cha-thang* (light plain tea), and then accompanied by Tshing-ta went to the residence of her holiness Dorje Phagmo, carrying Lhacham's letter in his hand. Tshing-ta represented my case to her through Amchi Chhenpo, and paid five *tankas* and a scarf for her *Sung-ta*, or benediction and protection. In the evening, at about 5 P.M., I was conducted to the house of one Geleg Namgya*l*, a monk, situated at the western end of the monastery. Although Amchila had offered us accommodation at his, yet the bath-room being on the ground-floor I preferred Geleg Namgya*l*'s house to his. But when I arrived at Geleg Namgya*l*'s I found there was no accommodation for us inside the house, so our rugs were spread in the portico. Tshing-ta returned at dusk, and told me that her holiness having carefully examined my fortune, had found that the illness being very serious, though not apparently fatal, the speedy observance of some efficacious religious ceremonies would be urgently required. As I had come from Tashi-lhunpo, and with a letter of introduction from Lhacham, she would be glad to see me presently, and also conveyed to me her leave to freely ask for anything we might require for subsistence during our stay at Samding. This assurance was most cheering, and enlivened my drooping spirits. Tshing-ta having arranged for our cooking, went again to *tshog-chhen*, or the evening assembly of the congregated monks, leaving Amchila to wait upon me. He presented the assembly with enough of tea and butter, and also a few *tankas*, together with a scarf, requesting them to pray for my recovery, at the same time presenting two *tankas* to the deities in the grand hall. The monks with one voice prayed that the gods might extend their mercy to me—a pilgrim from a distant land. At bed-time I took another dose of the powder, and being wrapped up with all my woollens, laid myself down in the portico, half exposed to the wind and cold. The fear that my servants would forsake me when my illness became protracted, leaving me in some *dur-toi* (cemetery) where, while still alive, my limbs would be torn by hungry vultures, wolves and dogs, ever distressed me. In this miserable plight, while passing a restless night, at times startled by the howling of the wind blowing below the eaves of the house, I thought of the world where I would be hurried soon, and absolutely resigned myself to the mercy of Him who had brought me into this existence.

16th May.—Owing to the fatigues of the previous day and the exposure to the weather, my illness in spite of Amchila's drugs, increased The night passed away, and when I saw day-light I wondered I was still alive. Tshing-ta and Pador thought that Amchila's medicines had done me some good; so, as soon as they awoke from sleep they asked me hopefully how I felt. "A little worse," replied I. But the former, who was certain I was better on account of the reception Dorje Phagmo had given me and her prayers for my recovery, was full of spirits. He asked me if he had my permission to entertain the congregated monks, numbering about eighty, with *mang chya*, *i.e.* tea, and also to distribute alms to them at the rate of a *karma* (two annas) a head. My voice was now sunk; however, with much exertion I told him that all my money and properties were in his hands: I would not object to his spending something for pleasing the monks, Dorje Phagmo, and the gods; but in doing so he should exercise his discretion. Tshing-ta having obtained my leave, and also being encouraged at Dorje Phagmo's kind assurance to supply us with necessaries, went to the *tshog-chhen* (grand congregation) and arranged to entertain them in a respectable way. He also made offerings to the several deities that were pointed out to him, that they might drive away the goblins that were believed to surround me now, having followed me from Dong-tse. After the entertainment of the monks, which cost about 80 *tankas*, Tshing-ta made offerings and suitable presents to Dorje Phagmo, and received a sacred pill containing a particle of Kashyapa Buddha's relics, who is supposed to have lived nearly 10,000 years ago. Having obtained this pill, Tshing-ta came running to me and said that he had got a very efficacious medicine which would cure me at once. Although I guessed what that *rinsel* (sacred pill) was worth, yet under present circumstances I could not avoid taking it with much apparent veneration for Buddha Kashyapa. I asked Amchila, who was sitting by my side, if the pill would not interfere with the working of his drugs. "No," said he "that is a *jinlab* (blessing)." He then advised me not to drink cold water, specially unboiled water. "The water of Yamdo," said he, "is very *chibu* (heavy); it does not agree with many persons even in health. How can it suit you who are so very ill and come from a distant country?" He advised Tshing-ta to keep a supply of boiled water in an earthen jug and to give me only a spoonful at a time when I felt very thirsty.[1] He also superintended the preparation of tea, taking particular care that it was light and free from butter. He

---

[1] I obtained the following note on water from a learned physician of Tibet:—

Water free from impurities removes illness, and on account of its wholesome action on the constitution also prolongs life. Foul water being fraught with poisonous substances, produces different disorders which shorten life.

There are eight kinds of water, of which three are good and the rest bad—

(1) The best is rain-water (*namchhu*) and water from melting snow (*gang-chhû*).
(2) Fountain-water, which comes from a distance after percolating through a great number of sandy, rocky and boulder beds.
(3) Spring water, which rising from a great depth, is cool in summer and warm in winter. These three kinds really resemble divine elixir in their wholesome action on the human constitution.

The following five kinds are foul:—

(1) Well water, never touched by the wind or the rays of the sun, moon, and stars.
(2) Water which comes down from the top of high mountains carrying mineral poisons such as verdigris and sulphates of lead and magnesia.
(3) Jungle water, which contains much lithic and vegetable poisons.
(4) Marsh water, which has been poisoned by putrid leaves and contains mud and insects.
(5) Stagnant water of pools and the water of salt lakes.

Good water, when kept long in pots, either in its natural state or after boiling, turns bad. If bad water, immediately after it is drawn, be filtered and warmed without being allowed to eject bubbles, it may become serviceable.

When it is difficult to find out which water is good and which bad, the easiest mode of distinguishing them is by weighing equal quantities in a sensitive balance (*rgya-ma*). The light one is to be preferred to that which weighs heavier. Autumn water is generally light and good; summer and winter waters are tolerably so. In Tibet, spring water, if heavy should be used with caution. Water should not be kept in leathern sacks more than six hours, in copper and bronze vessels more than a day, in wooden vessels more than two days, in iron pots more than three days, in earthen pots and black bell-metal vessels more than five days, in porcelain more than six days, and in tin more than a week. When kept longer than these limits, water turns foul from external substances being mixed with it. Water in tinned vessels does not soon become bad. When it is necessary to keep water for a good length of time, a little of "*chûgang*" (a medicinal drug) should be thrown into the pot. When *chûgang* is not available, the precious stone called *kêtaka*, or amber, may supply its place.

*

offered to supply me with *sol-shib* (fine barley-flour) from his house; but as our barley was the very best, having been brought from Tashi-lhunpo, we declined his kind offer with thanks. In the afternoon he again came to see me, when Tshing-ta too returned and asked him to induce Geleg Namgya*l* to remove his bed to his store-room and to let to us his bed-room on a rent of 4 annas per diem. This offer he considered too much for such a miserable hovel like his. However I thought I would do well by renting the house at once. There were two rooms and a small portico in front of the principal room, which was 6 feet by 8 feet. The roof was about 6 feet high with a slit in one corner of it. There was a kitchen attached to the house at the western extremity of the court. This latter was about 10 feet by 12, and was protected by a stone wall towards the north. Geleg Namgya*l* having agreed to our proposal, my bed was removed to his room, which contained a few small dining-tables and about half a dozen manuscripts kept on two large boxes and on the walls. In one corner there was a small wooden chapel with the images of Guru Pema Chaurassig and Dorje Phagmo hung by its sides. During the night my illness reached an alarming stage, for at midnight I found my gullet choked with dry mucus, and I thought I would die very soon. I called Tshing-ta and Pador to sit by my side, and though much fatigued they attended to my call. With their help, though prostrate in bed, I prepared a dose of cough-mixture according to Dr. Moore's prescription. This medicine did me no good, and in fact, made my condition worse, as the expectoration, instead of becoming free, became more obstructive and dry. Tshing-ta did not like my taking English medicines. He said I made my condition worse by taking different medicines in a day without waiting to see the action of a particular medicine. I asked him to sleep by my side, but after half-an-hour's stay they returned to their bed in the portico. It seemed they feared to sleep by me, as they believed I was attended by the *Tsan* (or evil genius) of Dong-tse. I dreamt many hideous visions, and once got delirious, which alarmed them more, and convinced my attendants of the evil genius being about me. Geleg Namgya*l*, who slept in the next room, did not fear so much as my friends did.

17th May—To-day being the new moon. the monks of Samding got up early to assemble at the grand hall of congregation to perform solemn religious service, as the fourth month of the year, called *saga-dao*, the holiest in the Buddhist calendar, was to commence to-morrow. Our host and neighbour, Geleg Namgya*l* dressed himself in his church dress, and Tshing-ta, who was very anxious for my recovery, got up early from bed to attend the service, and to present them with *mang-ja* (tea for many) and offerings of money. At the conclusion of the service he saw Dorje Phagmo, to inform her of my condition. By presenting her with a couple of *tankas* and a scarf he obtained another sacred pill. The old Amchila with his assistant Jerung, who is said to be a better physician than himself, came to see me. The junior happened to be an acquaintance of Tshing-ta, and promised to pay special attention to the selection and preparation of medicines for me. Tshing-ta presented him with five *tankas* and a scarf, and Amchila with two *tankas*. The latter begged me not to try Indian drugs any more, for Yamdo was a very high place, and its water and climate very different from those of other places, so that I should not think of other medicines than those of Yamdo, which alone could do me good. Both of them advised me to avoid falling asleep during the day-time, telling Tshing-ta that if the patient did not sleep during the day-time he would get well. My diet now consisted of plain tea and about an ounce of barley-flour a day. I was reduced to a skeleton and could hardly stand erect. With what faithfulness these men served me, and how deeply indebted I should be to them for their invaluable services! I occasionally got a glimpse of the lake and its surrounding hills and mountains, standing leaning on my friend's arm. The bleak and desolate appearance of the surrounding mountainous countries, the dark blue expanse of the lake, and the windy weather of Samding, always heightened to my mind the fearfulness of this strange land. As the evening advanced my illness increased. It being the new moon, I thought, now overpowered by a superstitious idea, that I would breathe my last during the night. It was the day of the eclipse of the sun, and as I was born on the new moon, I thought I would be taken away on that day. At midnight I called Tshing-ta and Pador, and asked them to fetch me my note-book that I might leave a record about myself and a note for the disposal of my properties as well as for the guidance of my assistant. They brought it: with a shaking hand I wrote a will. Then looking towards them, I said "You have served me well. I leave directions to my friends, and particularly to my protector the Minister, to reward you sufficiently for your excellent conduct towards me." After sitting about an hour besides me, they returned to their beds. They thought that the *Tsan* was now bent upon my ruin, and after my death would seize them. This was evidently the secret of their unwillingness to sit near my bedside. I dreamt a series of dreadful dreams, sometimes even in my waking hours. At about 3 A.M., with the help of Pador, I tried a new medicine given by Jerung, which brought me some relief from the obstructiveness of the yellow mucus in my throat. At day-break both Tshing-ta and Pador came to my beside, and were delighted to see that I was alive. The dreadful night was over; hopes of recovery gleamed in my drooping heart; I prayed to Heaven, and absolutely submitted myself to His all-seeing and merciful providence.

18th May.—Early in the morning Tshing-ta went to the *Tshog-chhen* to make them the usual presentation of *mang-ja* and silver coins that they might propitiate the gods for my recovery. He also saw Dorje Phagmo, from whom, after again presenting two *tankas* and a scarf, he received another sacred pill. On his way back to our lodgings he met the ex-incarnate Lama of Tshe-chhog-ling of Lhasa, who had been expelled from his high office on account of a secret connection with a woman. Although he has lost his holy character, yet, according to Tshing-ta, he was not entirely devoid of holiness. He therefore presented him with three *tankas* and a scarf to obtain his so-called sacred protection. Seeing no decrease in the disease, he visited Dorje Phagmo in the afternoon and paid her ten *tankas*, with a scarf, to propitiate the *lokapala* deities for my recovery, doing all these things out of his own sincere eagerness for my welfare. Not satisfied with the above means for my speedy cure, he went so far as to induce Dorje Phagmo to undertake the tedious service of propitiating the Ausmata Buddha and the god Mahākala to extend my life beyond the term originally granted to me. This is called *Tshe-dub*[1] or life-propitiation. She also gave a long list of religious observances, which, according to her, were urgently necessary for my recovery, and which she desired might be immediately conducted by engaging some learned priests.

19*th May.*—The list of religious observances that were drawn up by Dorje Phagmo as being most necessary for my speedy recovery was as follows:—

1. The reading of the sacred Buddhist scriptures called Gya*d* *s*tong-pa or Ashta-sahasrika Prajna Pāramita, together with their supplements. This would require about twelve monks to go through in two days.

2. Chha-*g*sum (or the three-share offerings), consisting of painted wafers of barley paste and butter. These are divided into three parts. The first part is offered to the ten Dik-pālas, viz.—

(1) Gya-byin (Indra or Jove).
(2) Me-lha (Agni or God of Fire).
(3) Shin-je (Yama or Pluto).
(4) Srin-po (Rakshas, goblins).
(5) Chhu-lha (Varuna or Neptune).
(6) Lung-lha (Pavana or God of Urāds).
(7) No*d*-byin (Kuvera or God of Wealth).
(8) Vyan-phyag (Iswara).
(9) Tshangs-pa (Brahma or the God of the Heavens).
(10) Sa-dag (the chief of the Nagas Ananta, the gods of the earth or nether regions).

The second part is offered to the *h*Vyang-po (Bhuta or spirits), viz. Lha (gods); *g*Lu (Nagas or serpents); Lha-min (Asuras or demons); Dri-sa (divine musicians or Gandharvas); Yidvags (Pretas or the damned spirits of Tartarus).

The third part is offered to the host of demi-gods called or gana vinayaka, of whom Ganesa is the chief. When these three-share offerings are made, a quick cure from all sorts of diseases is said to be surely obtainable.

3. Gya*l*-*g*sol;—In this the several genii, such as Pehar, the five *v*Gya*l*po-sku *l*nâ, are worshipped with a view to remove uneasiness of mind, to free one from oppressive and hideous dreams, and divers disorders of the body. There are different rites for conducting their propitiation.

The following hymns are recited when offerings are made:—

D Vang-po *r*Dorje-*h* Chhang-vahi Lha; Lha-yi *r* gyal-po *g* don-gyi *b*dag Shar-phyogs *g* don-gyi tshogs *b* chas la Chhod ching *bs* tod de phyag *h* tshal.	Oh god Indra, the holder of the thunder, The king of gods and lord of spirits divine, Thee, together with the eastern legion of spirits, We adore, praise, and revere.

The following *dharani* is uttered by the prists, all in one voice, at the end of each service:—Om a hya hi loka kā raya; Deva, Nāga, Yaksha, Gandharva, Asura, Karut Kinnara, Mahoraga, Manusha, Amanusha, Sapōriwara Samaye Svā hā.

The following hymns are sung by the assembled priests, to the music of the bell, the tambourine, cymbals, and *damaru*:—

Kai phyogs phyogs deni pha gina Ñima shar-phyogs pha gi na Dung-gi pho brang nang she*d* na. Denā *r* Gyal-po Chenpo *b* shugs.	Say in what quarter you live! To the east where the sun gleams, You dwell in a place of conch shells, There as a great king you reside.

[1] Tshe-dub, or the propitiating of the gods of life:—For the prevention of fatal occurrences to one's self the three deities of life, called Tshe-lha, viz. Tshe-*d* pag-me*d*, *g* Tsug-tor *r* Gyal-ma, and *s* Grol-*d* kar are worshipped. The propitiator must be a sacred person of pure morals. He must have taken the vows of abstinence from wine, women, and meat, and also of not killing or causing lives to be taken away. On the day of propitiation such a priest is required to bathe and then to meditate on the moral merits of the gods of life, and recite one hundred thousand hymns in honour of them. The following are the beginnings of their respective hymns:—

(1) Om Amarani Jivantiye Svā hā. (Tshe-*d* pag-me*d* or Ausmat Buddha's hymns.)
(2) Om Bhrum svāhā, Om Amrita āyurdate Svāhā.
(3) Om Tāre tuttāre ture mama āyur jnana pushtinkuru ye Svāhā. At the end, from the pot called the 'jug of life,' water is sprinkled on the pills (made of barley-flour scented with sandal, &c.), which are called life-pills.

The following *mantras* are also recited by the priests in one voice :—

Om maharaja sapariwara i dam ballingta khakhā hi khāhi khāhi.

4. *g*Ser-*s*kyem*s* or libations to gods. This is considered as one of the most efficacious means of propitiating the gods. People in Tibet generally resort to this when they fail to obtain relief from diseases or dangers by all other means. Libations may be made to the saints, *yidam* or guardian angels, Buddhas and Bodhisattvas, the Dakinis called Khadomas or fairies, Dharmapalas, and the solemnly sworn guardian of the country, demi-gods and the Shibdag (Nagas). By making libations one's desires are fulfilled, and escape from fatal accidents is ensured. There are different sorts of rites prescribed in the liturgy of Tibet about libations. When I first heard the name *Ser-kem*, I did not fully understand what it meant, and most Tibetans misinterpret its meaning. The word *g*ser means gold and *s*kyem is the honorific synonym for *thung* or drink. It is for this combination of the word *g*ser with *s*kyem that the Tibetans put a piece of gold in the wine bowl at the time of making libations, in order to make the sacred drink partake of the nature of the golden drink.[1]

The following hymns are sung by the priest or person offering the libation :—

"Tsa *r*gyu*d* *b*lama yidam *d*kon *m*chhog *g*sum,
Pah-vo *m*khah *h*gro chhos *s*kyong *b*srung-mahi tshog*s*;
Sol-lo *m*chhod-do *b*chol-vahi *h*phrin la*s* *m*dsod :
The patriarch Lamas, spiritual guides, tutelary deities, and the three ratnas,
The deified heroes, the angels, dharmapalas, and the assembly of the defenders of faith,
We pray and adore you; lend us your aid."

The following *mantras* are chanted at the end by the assembled priests together, or, if none is present, by him who makes the libation :—

"Om vajra amrita kundali hana hana hum phat."

5. *h*Chhi-*b*slu (ransoming one's own life). When all means, either medical, religious, or mystical, fail to obtain cure from a fatal or serious disease, ultimately the ceremony of *h*chhi-*b*slu is resorted to. In this an image resembling or representing the patient is constructed, before which a full suit of his dress and enough of his usual food and drink are placed. Two learned priests in church dress bless it with their mystic *mantras*, ringing a bell and holding a *dorje* with a peculiar configuration of the hands, called *mahamudra*. At the end of the service, of which exhortations and threats are the principal parts, the officiating priests or the patient himself supplicate Yama, the lord of death, to accept the image in the place of the patient. There are different rites and ceremonies in connection with *h*chhi-*b*slu. My companions and the Amchila did not let me know what they were going to do about me. In fact, they despaired of my life, and therefore were driven to offer this last service to the lord of death. Had they told me the particulars of this service, I should have been most amused to see my friends satisfy the great lord of death by presenting him an effigy of mine.

The following invocation is made by the priests :—

"Ho *h*chhi *b*dag *g*shin-*n*je *r*gyal-po la.	Oh! Thou, King Shin-je, the lord of death,
Lu*d* dang *g*torma *h*di *h*bul gyi.	I make these offerings and ransom to thee;
Sha*s* la tshe yi par chha*d* sol.	Accept them, and remove the dangers of life;
Du*s* min *h*chi-va *b*slog-tu *g*sol.	Vouchsafe me freedom from an untimely death.

The following Sanskrit charms were also cited at the conclusion of the service :—

"Om thagu nagu da gu sváhá."

This mantra is said to have been introduced by Atisha, a learned pandit of Bengal, in the first part of the 11th century.[2]

6. Srog-*b*slu (ransoming another's life). To release animals which are being slaughtered or are taken to be slaughtered, from the butcher's hands, is the principal object of srog-*b*slu. This is also called mi-*h*jigh*s*-pa*h*i *s*byin-pa, or life-saving charity. It brings much moral merit to the ransomer, and gives him longevity and worldly prosperity. Those who can afford the expense should save hundreds and thousands of lives from death by ransoming. The saving of men, beasts, &c., and particularly of fish in this way, is calculated to bring immediate immunity from death. When Tshing-ta proposed to me this observance, I at once agreed to it, and asked to arrange to save five hundred fish; but as we had no trustworthy men to send on the errand we doubted whether this pleasing affair could be successfully conducted. Pador's presence near me was necessary, and Tshing-ta was our life and soul in all matters. While we were engaged in thinking over the solution of this difficulty, Amchila arrived and sat by my

[1] Lama Londol Rimpo-chhe, one of the greatest scholars of Tibet, has observed that the Tibetans erroneously put gold and grain in wine at the time of making libations. The word *g*ser also means face, something like *g*ser-shal, or 'golden face.' When a king is addressed or talked of, his face cannot be called face, but golden face. In the same manner the honorific of 'drink' is 'golden drink.'

[2] In one of the *h*chhi-*b*slu ceremonies performed for the late Emperor of China, about Rs. 2,500 were spent for the image (effigy) and its equipments, &c., to make it acceptable to the lord of death.

side. He offered a pinch of snuff to Tshing-ta, who gladly received it, and asked him how we could best ransom fish life. Amchila replied this work could not be entrusted to another's hands; but as it was a very effective mode of prolonging life and curing disease, he would himself undertake to go to the fishermen's village, a distance of three miles from Samding, if we only lent him our pony, his ponies being sent to the pasture lands. We gladly agreed to his proposal, and he returned to his house to put on his usual dress and to start forthwith towards the fishermen's quarters. At about 4 P.M. he returned, delighted with the successful execution of his mission. He told me that he had saved five hundred fishes, and that much moral merit would accrue to me thereby. While restoring the fish to their element, one has to make the following *monlam* or prayer :—

"By the virtue and moral merit of my having ransomed the lives of these animals, let there be prosperity, longevity and health and perpetual happiness to me.

"Dag-gi*s* sem*s*-chan *h*di dag-gi,
Srog *bs*lus *d*ge-va*h*i phan yon gyi*s*
Tshe-ring na*d* ma*d* phun sum tshog*s*,
Tantu *b*de va thob-par shog !"

20th May.—The old Amchila's medicines having exhibited no perceptible effect, and my condition not being better than on the previous night, Tshing-ta requested Jerung-la to try one of his lately-prepared medicines. Amchila told us that his medicines, though very good and costly, were somewhat less effective owing to their being old. But Jerung's medicines also failed to shew any improvement on his master's pills and powders. They both examined my pulse, and by their manner shewed that they were very skilful in that operation. I was told that all diseases are indicated by the motion of the pulse.[1] So long Pador had obtained forage from the *sho* or village of Samding, but now no hay could be obtained. To go to Nangar-tse for provender would be a waste of much time, but, however, as the pony could not be left to starve, we sent Pador to Nangar-tse for a load of hay. On his return Pador said that it would be impossible for him to serve me well if he were required to go daily to Nangar-tse; so I asked Tshing-ta to appoint an assistant to Pador. Geleg Namgya*l* recommended one of his acquaintances named Omje Tondub, a tailor by profession, for the work.

---

[1] *The Pulse.*—The best time for feeling the pulse is when the morning sun shoots forth his beams on the mountain-tops, and when the patient has not yet risen from his bed, nor his body and mind been agitated, and when he has not taken any food or drink. The physician should also satisfy himself that the patient has not been fluttered by any irregularity in behaviour and food. His hand must be pliable, neither warm nor cold. The physician should feel the left hand of a male patient with his right hand, and the right hand of a female patient with his left.

Position of the pulse.—Measure one thumb-breath from the wrinkle of the wrist, and on the artery in the first furrow of the bone of the forearm, apply *evenly* the three fingers, viz. the fore, middle and the ring finger, so that they may not come in contact with each other. The forefinger should only press the skin, the middle finger the flesh, and the ring finger the bone. By this it is meant that the pressures transmitted by the second and third fingers should be twice and three times that of the first. The tip of each finger can, by its upper and lower parts, feel two kinds of pulsation. The upper tip of the forefinger of the physician's right hand feels the working of the heart and the lower part that of the bowels. In the same way the middle finger by its upper and lower tips feels the workings of the spleen and the stomach, and those of the ring finger of the left kidney and the vessels of the semen virile, respectively. Again the upper and lower (that is the right and left) tips of the forefinger of the physician's left hand feel the workings of the lungs and the mesenteric gut, those of the middle finger perceive the state of the liver and the bile, and those of the ring finger the action of the right kidney and the urinary bladder.

In women, instead of the action of the heart, that of the lungs will be perceived, and *vice versâ ;* while other indications will remain the same.

The indications regarding each region are conveyed by veins connected with it. They are divided into two classes called—

1st, Don *r*tsa, the system of veins connected with the heart, lungs, liver, spleen and bowels.
2nd, *S*no*d*-kyi-*r*tsa, the system of veins connected with the remaining organs, such as the bladder, kidneys, bile, mesentric gut.

The first system is clearly indicated when the patient exhales, and the second system when he inhales.

When during every act of respiration of the physician (who must be a healthy man and free from disorders) there are five pulsations of the patient, he must be considered to be in health. If the pulsations exceed five, there is heat in his constitution. If their number falls below five, cold is indicated. The heat is gentle when the pulsations are six, temperate when seven, and great when eight. When they are nine and upwards, the pulse is said to have "passed the mountain," and the case is rarely curable. On the other hand, if the pulsations fall down to four, the cold is slight; if to three, it is middling; if to two, it is great. When they fall below (this is, when the pulse sinks) it is difficult to save the patient. These are the general indications of the pulse. To come to details.

The attenuated but strong pulse is indicative of fever and increased irritation The empty and weak pulse indicates spasm and cold. If the pulse is much accelerated and appears empty, it must be understood that fever based on weakness and spasm is indicated. Again, if the pulse shows strength, but a slight acceleration, cold spasmodic condition based on fever is indicated. The largeness and emptiness of the pulse indicate the action of air within the system and a plethoric state of the body. The pulse then also becomes intermittent and irregular in its beats. The abundance of blood and bile is indicated by a strong and quick pulse, phlegm and acidity by a soft, weak and sluggish pulse. When the pulse beats with difficulty and is tremulous, the working of the *chhin-sen* humour is indicated. If the trembling resemble that of the cross threads of a loom, putrid matter or *pus* is present internally or externally. If the pulse appear rough, but strung and short in its motion, it forebodes danger. If it cannot be clearly felt by the lower part of the middle finger tip, some sort of sore or ulcer, internal, or external, is indicated. If it is attenuated feeble and sticks, a dropsical condition is indicated. If its motion is flat, the patient is attacked with what is called strin-*nad* (worms or canker). If when the pulse is pressed to the bone it does not stop beating, the dangerous disease called *skran* is indicated. If strange indications present themself to the experienced hand, the working of poison is to be apprehended in the patient's constitution. If there be many variations in the motion of the pulse, the patient is possessed by the devil. If the accelerated pulse move like a torrent, and at times become changeable, the patient's affection is chronic and of a nervous kind. If the heart vein beat more forcibly than usual, and the liver artery beat less, there is cold and spasm of the liver and irritation or inflammation of the heart. If the pulse moves like a banner, or like drops falling through a leak, or like the quivering of a falcon's tail, and the indications of the arteries of the heart, liver, lungs and kidneys be incomplete the patient's death may happen after the 1st, 2nd, 3rd, 5th or 8th day, respectively.

External symptoms of approaching death.—When the patient's tongue turns back, the pupils of the eyes turn upwards and dilate, the nostrils collapse, the lower lip hangs down, and there is deafness, his death is certain. If the patient be found to indulge in habits and thoughts diametrically opposed to those to which he was known to be used his death must be guessed to be near at hand.

In the evening Tshing-ta brought, with Dorje Phagmo's leave, a piece of felt from the *Labrang Dso* (the church store) and gave it to Omje to make a *khan-tsa* (waistcoat) for me. I now felt keenly the effects of solitude. During the day-time not a soul used to remain in the house, and I had not a friend or a stranger to talk to. On all sides I saw dreariness—both nature and men in this part of the world alike seemed cheerless ; the sun, the wind and the solitude were objects of terror to me. In this dismal state I resigned myself to the mercy of Him who had thus far spared my life.

21st May.—The Tshe-chhog-ling Tu*l*paiku, now an expelled abbot, was my next-door neighbour, and now and then sent his servant to enquire after my health. Having lost his holy character, he is never consulted by anybody either in religious matters or on occasions of illness. But our companion had made him a present of about nine or ten *tankas*, in consequence of which he seemed to be much interested in my recovery, for if I got well, probably he would to some extent recover his lost reputation. To-day he sent me some *snags*-chhu (or charmed water) ; but with all its charms his consecrated water did me no good. The grand annual lama-dance of the monastery commenced to-day. Geleg Namgya*l* dressed himself in a dragon-silk costume, and carrying a hideous mask in his hand, evidently to be put on by and bye, went to the congregation hall. I was indeed sorry that I could not witness such a grand and curious show, which I was told would last three days.

22nd May.—My companions were tired of constantly attending me. Pador, who had to work hard in fetching water from the well at the foot of the hill, and purchasing hay for the ponies from a great distance in the interior of Yamdo district, besides doing other, work was unable to keep up at nights for my sake ; yet he worked with great readiness and alacrity. Tshing-ta, though he served me with unflagging energy, yet did not at night regularly attend to my frequent calls. Through illness I had become very fretful. Our funds were growing less, and the *chhumthung* (pea flour for the ponies) Tshing-ta had brought from Dong-tse was nearly consumed. Forage was very scarce in the country. In the afternoon Tshing-ta saw Dorje Phagmo, and making her a present of a scarf and five *tankas*, asked her holiness if by her divine knowledge she perceived that our present physician was the right man to attend me. She came out to the portico of her house and consulted her gods and cast dice, when the fates declared that the two physicians could be depended upon. Returning to me, he communicated to me this result of his interview. Accordingly we sent for the physicians, and on their arrival I paid them five *tankas* each, with a scarf, and entreated them to prepare a new and more effective medicine for me. In the evening Jerung brought me some pills, which smelt of musk, and some powders, probably those called *kurkum-chusum*. I took a dose of each alternately. At midnight I felt somewhat better. the expectoration being a little looser than before.

23rd May.—In the morning I felt better and almost able to sit reclining on my blankets. The two physicians came early to enquire after my health, and were delighted to see me somewhat better. The news of this favourable change was reported to Dorje Phagmo, who advised Tshing-ta to observe the propitiatory rites of Tomdin, Dorje Phagmo, and the divine eagle *Khyung*. Of these three, the first, she said, must at all events be conducted. He at once agreed to commence the propitiation of Tamdin and Dorje Phagmo. After presenting seven *tankas*, with a scarf, he begged her to graciously undertake the service of the propitiation of those two powerful deities. In the afternoon he had an interview with the ex-abbot of Tshe-chhog ling, who secretly told him that the genius who had followed me from the west was bent on doing me mischief. When in the evening Amchila came to see me, I begged him to favour me with a picture of Dorje Phagmo and an account of the sactuary of Samding.

24th May.—Amchila came early this morning. Looking with much cheerfulness at my face, he said : "The danger to life is now over ; the fatal stage is past. You can now by degrees take barley and a little fresh boiled meat and soup." Cheered with this hopeful assurance of Amchila, I ordered Tshing-ta to make him a present of a few bundles of *phing* (caseine from peas) which I had brought from Shiga-tse. Amchila was exceedingly pleased with the present. A man was sent to Nangar-tse to buy some mutton for me. In the village of Samding there were several flocks of sheep, but the season to cure mutton being past, nobody sold *shya-mar* (fresh or red meat). I now felt much better, and took some exercise by walking in the court-yard, and the fresh air seemed to possess a miraculous power of healing. As our friend, the old physician, was much addicted to snuff-taking, I asked him if he derived any benefit from it. I also asked his views on diet.[1] In the evening Amchila brought me a history of the Samding monastery.

---

[1] *Diet.*—One-third of the quantity of food that the stomach can hold should be taken at a meal, one-third should be filled with water, and the remaining third left empty for the free play of the digestive functions. This rule, when attended to, ensures good health. Hunger and surfeit are the chief causes of innumerable diseases and disorders.

Fermented liquors, taken in excess, work as poison, but in moderate quantities act as nectar. Spirituous drinks, such as *arrack*, produce inflammation and irritation of the liver. Smoking tobacco in excess affects the lungs. Snuff affects the chest and the eyes. Tobacco, if chewed or smoked from a *hookah*, affects the bile and lungs. The use of opium was unknown in Tibet, but the few Chinese who live there are now initiating the Tibetans in its use. Opium-smoking is considered the worst kind of slow poison The fear of being attacked with heart-disease, or at least of being debarred from the use of wine, is the chief motive which has arrested the progress of opium-smoking in Tibet.

25th May.—I felt much better than yesterday, got up from bed without any assistance, and walked to a short distance in front of our lodgings. The vast expanse of the lake which spread itself in a tortuous manner at some distance, the snow-topped mountains which bounded the horizon on the north and west, the bleak and desolate appearance of the surrounding hills, impressed me with feelings of awe and dread. If I had died, I would, according to the custom of the country, surely have been thrown into the lake, for I was told that in the district of Yamdo dead bodies are neither burnt nor buried, but are cut into pieces to feast hungry vultures and dogs. A gentle, cool breeze blew, which now seemed to me very bracing and pleasant. At about 9 P.M. Amchila arrived, bringing a bag from which he produced several walnuts (*targa*) and apricots (*ashu*). Pador and Tshing-ta ate some and put the remainder in our saddle-bag. The latter carefully prepared my breakfast of rice, *phing* and mutton cooked together. The superior tea, called *dhuthang*, was also prepared, churned with fresh yak butter. Accompanied by Pador and Tshing-ta, carrying a large bowl of clarified butter, a bundle of incense sticks, and about 50 scarves, I started on *Chhoi-jal*, or visit to the shrines and deities of Samding, in spite of my suffering from difficulty of breathing—so strong was my curiosity to see Dorje Phagmo and the famed monastery of Samding. This the monk of Samding and Amchila and our friends took for an instance of my zeal for *dharma* or Buddhism. We first went to the house of Amchila, a two-storied building. I was conducted to the first floor by Pador, where Amchila came and received me at the entrance. I was struck with the neat and clean appearance of the flooring, which was constructed of fine pebbles, beautifully laid and beaten. The surface was smooth and glossy, and the articles of the house were dimly reflected on it. The drawing-room, in which Amchila also receives his guests at dinner or on ordinary visits, had its walls painted in different colours, Buddhist symbols, trees, and the hideous figures of Lokapalas being the most prominent frescoes. The furniture consisted of four painted chests-of-drawers and half a dozen miniature dining-tables, painted bowls of wood to hold barley-flour, two wooden chapels containing a number of deities, and about half a dozen carpet rugs spread on stuffed mattress-like cushions. Screens and curtains of silk were also hung, the latter to cover pictures and to keep off dust, and in one corner of the wall there was a buckler and a knife. Both the physicians lived together. As soon as we took our seat the old man prepared tea, and Jerung-la poured it in China cups. When we left Amchila's house, at the court I met Geleg Namgya*l*, our landlord, who asked for the keys of the house. I gave him one, but not the one he required. At about noon, accompanied by Amchila and Tshing-ta, I entered the grand court-yard of Samding. It was more than one hundred and fifty feet long and nearly a hundred feet broad. On three sides of it the monastic buildings of Samding reared up their tops, and only on the west a row of wooden posts supported a balcony. There were three broad ladders, the steps of which were erect, lined with brass and iron plates. The central ladder is used by her holiness only. The left broad ladder, resembling a staircase, landed us on the first floor of the grand monastery. In the passage to the third storey two women were engaged in husking barley and peas. I and Pador waited in the hall, while Tshing-ta called at the Donner's room. He was told that her holiness was engaged in the service of Tamdin, and would presently see me at its termination. We therefore withdrew to the roof, and feasted our eyes with the grand scenery of the great lake district of Yamdo. I cannot describe the wild and fantastic appearance of the mountains on all sides, and the interior of the lake, that now presented themselves before us. After above half-an-hour Amchila arrived and conducted us to the different chapels and shrines. The most dreaded of all is the *gonkhang*, or the house where the images of the most fearful demons and genii are collected, their heads, lest men become terror-stricken at the first sight of them, being generally kept veiled with scarves. Almost all the images were dressed in coats of mails, iron helmets, and held in queer attitudes different weapons, bucklers, &c. The images of Chandika and Pehar occupied a conspicuous place in the house. Tshing-ta presented every one of the deities with a scarf and an incense-stick, while Pador poured clarified butter in the brass and silver oil-burners, which are never extinguished. The *ku-ner*, or keeper of the idols, begged for some *bukshish*, and we satisfied him with a two-anna piece. In the largset room of the first floor are the tombs of the former incarnations of Dorje Phagmo. The largest and richest of these, constructed of silver, was erected in honour of the founder of the monastery, Je-tsun Thinlas Tshomo, and contained his remains. It is gilt all over, and studded with large turquoises, corals, rubies, emeralds and pearls. It resembled in shape a *chhorten*, 6 to 7 feet square at the foot, and contained the foot-mark of its illustrious founder printed on a slab of stone. I was not able to ascertain whose tomb the second silver *chhorten* was. It was of the same size and make as the first. The third, round which some English porcelain and glass toys were placed as rare curios, was in memory of Nag Wang Kunssang, the predecessor last but one of the present Dorje Phagmo. It appeared also to be a very neatly and handsomely executed piece of silver work. The top of the tomb was tastefully decorated with work in gold and precious stones. The taste with which various precious stones and pearls were laid and studded over the different faces of the tombs deserved particular attention. I was variously told that they were the work of the Nepalese Buddhists and of Tibetan workmen. In another room, to which the public are not admitted, are collected the remains of the different incarnations of Dorje Phagmo. It is said that every Dorje Phagmo once in her life pays a visit to the hall of her ancestors' remains to make obeisance to them, and that the inner lake of Yamdo, called *Dumo-tsho* (or demons' lake) ever exerts itself to heave up and thereby to flood the whole of Tibet, but that the Samding monastery presided over by Dorje Phagmo keeps it down.

After visiting all the shrines and chapels, we returned to the hall, where I was given a stuffed cushion to sit on. The Donner and the Ssimpon of her holiness received me very kindly, having had to deal so long with Tshing-ta for my recovery. A number of respectable looking men and women had also assembled there to receive the *Chhyag-wang* (benediction) from Dorje Phagmo's hands on the occasion of her propitiating Tamdin and the divine Dorje Phagmo. There also was present the ex-abbot of Tshe-chhog-ling. When all the men and women were seated on rows of Tibet rugs before the altar on which Dorje Phagmo sits, I was conducted by the Donner to a seat immediately on her left. The ex-abbot of Tshe-chhog-ling occupied a seat higher than mine, but a little to the back of the altar. This consideration was shewn to me, I came to know, on account of my being a pupil of the Minister of the Tashi Lama and a protegé of Lhacham Kusho, Dorje Phagmo's half-sister. Besides, the service was conducted for me and at my cost. Dorje Phagmo was assisted by the head Lamas of her monastery, about a dozen in number, all dressed in lama church costumes. The service lasted upwards of two hours, and appeared most tedious to me. At intervals Dorje Phagmo sprinkled sacred water from the "jug of life." The sprinkling stick was tufted with a few peacock's plumes and *kusha* or sacred grass, and the water was stained yellow with saffron. I failed to catch the *mantras*, which she uttered rapidly to finish the service soon. On account of my illness I did not like to be much sprinkled with water, but the largest quantity fell on my head. It was a demonstration of kindness and special favour for which others wished much but got little of it. Tshing-ta was allowed to sit close to me, but Pador occupied a seat some twenty feet behind mine. At the termination of the service sugared balls of barley, of the size of large bullets, were distributed among the audience. Some of the balls were painted red with a kind of dye-root, and a large quantity of these fell to my share. Our friend Amchila was present at the service. The spectators, before receiving the ball, thrice prostrated themselves before her holiness, and quietly walked out with much demonstration of awe and reverence. As soon as the ex-abbot of Tshe-chhog-ling left the room, Dorje Phagmo asked me to draw near her. She said that she was exceedingly interested in my recovery, and that Lhacham was her great friend and relation. Tshing-ta now thrice prostrating himself before her, and presenting a silver coin with a scarf, said "Your holiness, now that our Pandib has to some extent recovered his health by the grace of Konchhog (God) and yourself, we beg to be permitted to set out on our journey to Lhasa. We left Tashi-lhunpo for that purpose, and it was to make a pilgrimage to the great shrine of Buddha at Lhasa that our friend has come thus far after encountering immense difficulties." Dorje Phagmo did not allow the prayer to be continued further, but, looking towards me, said "It does not appear that you have recovered from your illness : you are very weak ; how will you travel up to Lhasa in such a state of health?" I replied in a faltering voice, "*Kusho*, the holiest of the sanctified days of the year is the 15th of the present month. If I can see the sacred image of Buddha that day, I shall deem myself fortunate. This is my only reason for wishing to leave this place so soon." She heard my prayer with attention ; but asked again how she could advise me to undertake a tedious journey in this condition of health. Thereupon Tshing-ta rose a second time to urge his request, to which she replied that she must satisfy herself, before giving me leave, that my illness was decreasing. The result being satisfactory, she granted her leave and asked me to remember her to Lhacham, adding that she had heard of the Minister's fame, and very much wished to see him. She assured me that there was no more danger to my life, and that I could proceed to Lhasa as soon as the symptoms of recovery became more evident. At the time of parting, she gave me three sacred pills, and ordered her Ssimpon to shew me the different rooms of her palace. The furniture consisted mostly of chapels made of beautifully carved timber in which, the dragon and the eagle were ever present ; of dining-tables, painted wooden chests, painted shelves and drawers, cushions stuffed with musk-ox hair, silk hangings, swords, shields ; of bell-metal, brass and silver cups ; and of images of gold, silver and copper, neatly arranged along the sides of the chapels. In fact her taste in furniture resembled those of the Minister. I was conducted into half a dozen rooms. Dorje Phagmo never sleeps as others do, being required to sit in a meditative mood during the hours of night, but in the day-time she may sit reclining or on a chair, but cannot rest at full length. She allows her hair to grow long, although it is against the custom of nuns, and enjoys this privilege for being a Tantrik nun and an incarnate on

---

[1] The consecration service and also sanctifying of the sacred pills called *tsheril*, or life-pills.

The pupil or person wishing to be consecrated either for admission into the holy order or doing any grand religious work first of all makes ablution, and presents the presiding Lama or priest with a complete series of offerings called *mandal*. The Lama then addresses him, exhorting him to obey his prohibitive commands, delivers a sermon, and recites some anecdotes from the sacred books. He then touches the pot of life (Tshe-*h*bum) to his head and utters sacred *mantras* to the music of the bell and cymbals. Thereafter sacred pills made of different kinds of fragrant substance and barley are given him. Then he presents the pupil or devotee with *Tshe-chhang*, or the elixir of life (consecrated wine). At the conclusion he touches the devotee's head with the sacred flag called m*dah dar*, and offers prayers to the gods, saints and Buddhas. It is believed that if the officiating Lama be pure in his morals, the devotee by such a consecration gets immunity from death for one year. Dorje Phagmo kindly consecrated me.

earth of the divine terrific Dorje Phagmo. The name of this intelligent and learned lady is Nag Wang Rinchen Kunssang Wangmo. She is about 26 years of age, of middle stature, with a well preserved body and countenance; her looks agreeable, and her manners grave, but without the dignified demeanour and polite manners of her half-sister, to whom in personal accomplishments she was far inferior. The Ssimpon also showed me the library, which contained about a thousand volumes of block-prints and manuscripts, of which one hundred and eighteen volumes were said to be composed by Podong-chhog leg Namgya*l*, the illustrious founder of the sect to which Dorje Phagmo belongs.

On our return to our lodgings we found the tailor Tondub had fled, after having stolen a few articles belonging to Tshing-ta and Pador. The fellow had also carried away the money we had given him to purchase good mutton for us. On asking Geleg Namgya*l*, he said he knew the man but had never associated with him, but we suspected that the object of Geleg Namgya*l* in asking for the keys was to get entrance into our house to steal some of our properties. After a short rest, I turned over the pages of the book Amchila had kindly lent me. In the evening the old physician arrived and brought me a picture, in which there were above two dozen images of Dorje Phagmo, all seated in a tranquil and meditative mood, with this peculiarity, that they had each a sow's head on their crowns. I made a present to Amchila of a large quantity of *chhyugra* (vermicelli) made of dried boiled milk and dried cream. He said he did not see that I would derive any good by prolonging my stay at Samding, where good meat was not available and forage for ponies scarce, besides the climate of Yamdo being too severe for me, and its water too heavy. According to him, the climate of Lhasa being warmer and the water lighter, if I went there I might be spontaneously restored to health. The old man's advice was sincere and good, and I at once made up my mind to start for Lhasa as soon as I obtained Dorje Phagmo's leave.

26th May.—My companions were busy early preparing tea and arranging to start for Lhasa. They obtained barley-flour from Amchila's house and pea-flour and gram for the ponies from Samding *Sho* (village); but as meat could not be had in the neighbourhood, they went to a branch monastery of Samding, situated at a distance of one mile, in search of mutton or sheep. They got the latter only, and after the animal was slaughtered, the monks of the monastery asked for a half share. Her holiness accordingly ordered Tshing-ta to take all the provisions, &c., for our journey up to Lhasa from her store, and expressed a wish that I should visit Samding on my way back from Lhasa. Tshing-ta replied that in case we returned by Nangar-tse I would surely come to pay my respects to her holiness, who had been so very kind to us. She said we could proceed slowly towards Lhadan (the honorific name of Lhasa). My long stay at Samding, the gracious treatment I had received from Dorje Phagmo, and particularly curiosity to know what made the people call such an august personage the "diamond or venerable sow," naturally impelled me to inquire into her origin and history. Amchila referred me to the Ningma works, Pemakathang and Serteng, from the former of which I obtained a very strange and interesting account of Dorje Phagmo and her husband Tamdin.

THE MYTHOLOGICAL ACCOUNT OF THE SUPPRESSION OF RUDRA (MATRANKARU) BY TAMDIN AND DORJE PHAGMO.

Previous to the advent of Buddha śakya śinha, in the latter part of the religious epoch of Buddha Dipankara, there lived in the country of Du-dsom-tsham a householder named Kankala. He had a son named Kankunti, and a servant Pramadeva. At that time there also lived the ascetic monk Sramana Kumara. The son of the householder and his servant having both imbibed faith in Buddhism, once approached the Sramana, and reverentially exclaimed, "Venerable Sir, the migratory world is full of misery: all things are transitory, and all matters are in their very nature void." The Sramana, struck with these utterances, admitted them into the sacred order of monkhood, giving them the religious names Tharpa-nagpo and Danphag, and began to instruct them in the sacred metaphysics of the wheel of law. Tharpa-nagpo one day addressed his teacher thus, "Venerable sir, pray tell us what is the true way for deliverance from all miseries of the migratory existence?" The teacher, pleased with the question, said, "To the immaculate spirit which has in itself the nature of the sky, both virtue and sin are alike like clouds: through the enjoyments of the five organs of sense, it becomes externally tarnished, but in its essence continues immaculate and stainless. If you can so think and conceive, you will attain the way of sainthood; there is no other way for salvation." Tharpa-nagpo and his servant being greatly edified with the explanation, praised and reverenced the teacher, and cheerfully returned to their homes. But not being able to understand the real meaning, but catching only the word, Tharpa-nagpo failed to cast off sin, and engaged deeper and deeper in the practice of vice. Failing to accomplish his religious aims, though professing to be in the service of the church, he perpetrated physically all sorts of sinful actions, and thereby prepared the way to damnation. On the other hand, Danphag, reflecting on the real meaning of his teacher's words, by his intelligence avoided sin, shaped his character according to righteousness, and meditated on the acquirement of moral merit. By subjecting his mind and body to peacefulness and tranquillity, he disciplined his soul.

Though both master and servant received the same instruction from the same teacher, yet each having understood the same subject in diametrically opposite ways according to their own bent to virtue or vice, they disagreed. Tharpa said to his page, "We two have heard religious instruction from the same teacher; yet how is it that we behave differently?" Danphag replied, "I have not strayed from the real meaning of our teacher's instruction." "I too am confident of the correctness of the meaning I have attached to our teacher's sermon, and am acting accordingly. The mystic Tantras are what I follow literally," said Tharpa. "Yes," objected Danphag, "you are acting contrary to the theory and practice of the Tantras." To this Tharpa replied, "Moral sins and divine wisdom spring from the same cause. Perfection or Buddha-hood cannot be attained by doing good actions, such as worshipping, giving alms, performing religious rites and ceremonies, for when the mind is kept in a state of supreme inaction, sins cannot harm it. What are called sins cannot or should not affect it, inasmuch as good or virtuous actions do not or cannot alter its condition." Danphag replied, "When the conscious existence (soul) is liberated from the hold of moral corruption, it gets into a state of divine wisdom; so long as it is not cut off from the grasp of sin, it remains tied to the transmigratory world of misery. Wherefore one's principles should be high, his moral conduct pure, and his body and mind peaceful and disciplined to avoid sin. But you are observing both in theory and ritual a perfectly contrary method." Tharpa, enraged at this exclaimed, "Which of us is correct will be known if we refer the question to our master." So they went to their teacher, who, to the disappointment of Tharpa, said that Danphag was right. At this Tharpa being exceedingly enraged, said, "It is strange that there should be two different interpretations of the same theory taught by the same teacher, and these two at variance with each other." He dismissed Danphag from his service, left the place himself, and turned his mind to do mischief to others, and, finally, to the conquest of entire states and kingdoms.

The teacher, Sramana Kumara, died of a broken heart. But, determined to do mischief, Tharpa devised all sorts of plans to destroy Dharma. He never thought of the Buddhas and gods, never meditated for the welfare of all living beings, but betook himself to the pleasures of this world. In fact, he became a perfect heretic, faithless to Lamas and to his benefactors. He drove away men from his presence. Not satisfied with ordinary articles of food (being a perverse Tantrik), he feasted upon human flesh and blood in the dreadful solitude of cemeteries: he wore human skins, and trained up numerous ferocious animals and birds of prey to kill innocent creatures: he became the chief perpetrator of sinful deeds and unholy actions: and after an impious and vicious life of twelve years, he died. Thereafter he was born as a wolf, a dog, a fly, a worm, and other creatures which feed upon dirt and defilement. He was next consigned to Tartarus, and lastly to hell, there to suffer endless miseries with other damned creatures. At the termination of these stages of damnation, he was born in the land of cannibals as the son of Kuntugyu. The child was born nine months after conception with three heads, six hands, four legs and wings, and three goggle eyes in each head. As soon as he was born, many portentous signs were observed: evil omens, diseases, plagues, disputes, war and famine inflicted the world, and his mother died nine months after his birth. His countrymen, terrified at the ominous birth of the child, wished to destroy it, and removed it to the cemetery where its mother's corpse was lying. In that cemetery, where tigers, venomous serpents and vultures all together feasted themselves on dead bodies, the Srinpos (cannibal goblins) had erected a corpse shed where all dead bodies were heaped. Now, the dead body of the Srinmo was also thrown there, together with the living body of the child, which, after sucking dry its mother's teats, next sucked her yellowish juice and cold blood. By and bye it began to subsist on the brains and the fat of the knees, wrists and other joints of its mother's body. On the forty-second day of this existence the child moved round, whereby the *rokhang* (corpse-house) was thrown down. From among the ruins he looked upwards, and saw several aërial monsters and Sha-ssa Khadoma (cannibal hobgoblins) feasting on dead human bodies. Following their example, he too began to feed upon human bodies, to wear human skins, and to drink from bowls made of human skulls, wherever he came. Many venomous serpents did he twist round his limbs, hands, legs and neck, by way of bangles, chains, bracelets and other ornaments. When he came across dead bodies of elephants, he ate the flesh and carried away the skins on his back, in order to use them as wrappers, just as he converted horse skins into trousers. In consequence of eating the dead bodies of all kinds of animals, he emitted a most offensive smell from his mouth and body, and on his teeth different curious figures appeared. He rubbed the ashes and dust of the funeral place all over his body. Of his three heads, the right-side one was white, the left red, and the central blue; the colour of his body was ash-grey; the flesh of his calves and muscles very rough-looking and ugly; so that with his gigantic body he made a terrible figure. He wore a string of human skulls, some dry and others fresh and wet, and painted his body, cheek-bones and temples with spots of blood. The hairs of his body resembled the bristles of pigs, and were in colour the darkest yellowish-black. He let half the hair of his head flow down loosely, and bound up the remainder on the crown of his head with a snake coiled round it. His hands and feet were furnished with claws resembling those of the eagle, and always armed with different kinds of weapons. From the vapour of his mouth, from his breath, eyes, ears and the lower orifices of the body, there issued forth obnoxious diseases, contagious and infectious maladies, plagues, obstruction of the passages of the body, and needle-like pricking pains to afflict others. He showed various mischievous and miraculous omens, and people called him by the name of Matrankaru. At that time in Bullira, Malaya, Jalendhra, Godavary, &c.—twenty-four countries of Jambadvipa—there ruled Devas, Gandharbas, Yakshas, Rakshas, Nagas and demons, oppressing the people and reducing everything to chaos. The hurtling of destructive weapons, such as axes, javelins, swords and arrows over the country, and other inauspicious and diabolical sights of the most terrific kind, were of the commonest occurrence. The evil spirits, dressing themselves in the relics of cemeteries, such as skulls, bones, skins, &c., infested the whole of Jambadvipa. All the Devas, Nagas, &c., had become supremely arrogant through unrestrained exercise of power, there being no supreme rule to check them, so that every one said that there was none over him nor any equal to him. At last, after a number of years of anarchy and confusion, the Devas, Asuras, Yakshas and Nagas agreed among themselves that if they had a chief to rule over them, there would then be an end to internal dissensions and disputes, and their lives and properties would be safe. "Now that in this world," they said, "Matrankaru has become most powerful, having vanquished all the gods and demons of the three worlds, let us elect him to rule over us." Wherefore the living beings of this world unanimously selected Matrankaru as their sovereign ruler, and all with one voice solemnly agreed and bound themselves by oath to obey his commands. In fact, they declared him to be the lord of their body, soul and spirit. Henceforth, Matrankaru's power became unlimited, and numberless warriors enlisted themselves under his banners. Filled with pride at having reached this position, he arrogantly exclaimed again and again: "If there be any one who is greater than myself, let him come and I shall subdue him:" so that his vaunts were heard in all the ten quarters of this world, and all living beings became confounded and paralysed thereat. Just at this time the goddess Du-tshan-ma was heard saying: "On the summit of mount Malaya, called Nam-Chag Bar-ma, stands the great city of Lankapuri, where reigns the king of Srinpos (cannibal giants), who had once been a disciple of Dipankara Buddha. He is greater than you, oh Matrankaru!" Burning with rage, the demon instantly flew towards heaven and landed on the summit of mount Malaya, and boastfully uttered the challenge, "Who is greater than Matrankaru, let him come forward to fight with me." Through fear of this terrible demon, the city of Lankapuri, quaked, and the country groaned aloud. The king of Lanka now thought this fearful enemy no ordinary demon, and remembered the prophecy mentioned in the aphorisme of Yontondsin: "One who disturbed the mind of his Lama and broke his solemn vows, whose lips were thrice damned by sin, must vanquish the king of Lanka. He in his turn will be subdued by the horse and the sow." Believing that prophecy was now about to be realized, he thought it was time for him to submit to this demoniac conqueror and become his vassal. From that time the country of Lanka, the king and his subjects, passed under Matrankaru's rule. Having conquered Lanka, the land of the Srinpos, Matrankaru's arrogance knew no bounds. Again and again he vaunted aloud: "Is there any one who is greater than me?" To this the goddess Du-tshan-ma again replied: "Greater than thou, oh Matrankaru! is Mahakaru, the lord of the Asuras. He alone excels thee in power and miraculous feats." Burning with wrath, the demon Matrankaru became converted into a huge flame of fire, and descended to the land of Asuras (goblins). There he showered weapons and destroyed their armies. Seizing him by his right leg he whirled Mahakaru round so violently that the latter's brains became muddled, and hurled him down on Jambuling (Jambudvipa), and flung his remains to the eight sacred places of the earth. Thereafter, Matrankaru subdued the eight planets, the twenty-eight constellations, the eight *Nagas*, the gods and all the demons. He next built the great city of Bam-ri-thoi-khar, where he fixed the flag of victory over the demons. That place, formerly pleasant to behold, now looked fearful with sharp and pointed weapons fixed all over the battle-field. By his miraculous power he could now lift the Rirab (Sumeru) mountains on the tip of his thumb; and so again, bursting with arrogance, he vaunted aloud: Is there a greater person than me?" And again the goddess Du-tshan-ma replied to his vaunts: "Greater than thou is the saint Dampa-tog-kar of Gahdan, who is possessed of boundless power of working miracles and great strength. He preaches *dharma* to all the gods and receives their homage, and is the object of their worship and mystical prayers." Matrankaru, full of fury, assumed a most hideous form, and flew towards the abodes of the gods uttering a terrific yell, at which the earth quaked, and the teacher of gods, Dampa-tog-kar fell down from his exalted celestial throne, and at once entered his mother's womb to be born as Gautama in Jambudvipa. Conquering all the celestial regions without resistance, Matrankaru proclaimed himself the king of gods and men, and proved himself a demon of demons, the like of whom the world never saw before. Human flesh was the greatest dainty to him, and the sight of human misery was his greatest entertainment.

Thus, when this world was groaning under the weight of the wicked actions of this arch-demon, a council was held in the superb mansion of Hogmin by Dorje-chhang, Chhyagna Dorje, Kantu-ssang-po, the five Dhyani Buddhas, Jamyang, Chyan-ras-ssig, the twelve divine Rudras, and the whole host of Bodhisattvas, to devise means for his suppression. Unless the dreaded Matrankaru were subdued by the united strength of all the Buddhas, Buddhism could not be diffused, and all living beings would be inevitably damned by sin. After a long conference, the Buddhas and gods saw, through the medium of divine fore-knowledge, that Chyanras-ssig must miraculously change himself to Tamdin ("the horse's neck"), and his wife Dolma assume the shape of Dorje Phagmo ("the diamond sow") in order to vanquish him. Accordingly Tamdin and Dorje Phagmo repaired to the summit of Malaya mountains, where, assuming the most frightful forms and making the most hideous gestures, Tamdin neighed three times to stun the arch-enemy with terror, and made the mountains of Lankapuri re-echo with his terrific voice. After him his redoubted colleague, Dorje Phagmo, grunted five times to freeze Matrankaru's wife with fear. To this the great demon replied. "What do you, horse and pig, mean by these frightful yells; know you not that all the gods, demons and other fearful beings of this world have been subdued by me? They all obey my commands with abject submission, they look for favour and mercy towards me, and in their minds hopes and fears alternate when they observe the changes in my looks. Know also that I conquered Dampa Togkar. I did not disturb you. What makes you disturb my peace with such unusual cries?" So saying, he stretched his arms, and pressed both horse and pig down by the necks. At this opportunity Tamdin slipped from his hands. Tamdin laid the arch-enemy down with his limbs outstretched. Wherefore, on the head of Matrankaru appeared the head of a horse—green, owing to the colour of the enemy's brains. In the same manner Dorge Phagmo manifested herself on the head of Matrankaru's wife, but black, having similarly contracted that colour. Both husband and wife lay prostrate on the ground, but were not dead, for the Bodhisattvas, being merciful, did not kill them. Thus the enemies being vanquished, Tamdin again neighed thrice to inform the world of his triumph, and his wife followed his example by grunting five times. The prostrate enemy, unable to bear their sufferings, supplicated for mercy and help, and loudly bewailed their lot, crying *Phama-Hoo-yu*. Thus Tamdin and Dorje Phagmo conquered the enemy and made Buddhas and Dharma triumph over sin and unrighteousness. The orthodox Buddhists regained their place on earth, and the heretics were displaced. The gods conquered the demon, the fire burnt the woods, the water put out the fire, the winds dispersed the clouds to clear the sky, the adamant rocks were turned into mines of precious stones, the root of the wishing-tree (*kalpadruma*) penetrated to the land of Nagas, its leaves reached the abodes of demons, and its fruits ripened to be plucked by the gods from their celestial mansions. Matrankaru was converted to Buddhism and henceforth proved a devout follower of Buddha. With his followers and retinue he was sworn as defender of the faith and given the name of Mahākāla. Having converted the arch-enemy to the religion of the sacred Tathagata, Tamdin and Dorje Phagmo returned to the mansion of Buddhas and the gods, whence they sent forth their divine rays for the good of the world.

Amchila and Jerung-la told me that at the particular request of the first Dalai Lama, Dorje Phagmo introduced the *Tshan-nid* (meditative service) in her monastery. Early in the morning the monks dressed in yellow, exactly like the monks of Tashi-lhunpo, congregate in the worship-hall to read the sacred scriptures called the Dulva Vinaya (or the disciplinary precepts of Buddha). At other times and services they follow the Ningma liturgy. Dorje Phagmo belongs to the school founded by Podong Chhyog-leg-Nam-gya*l*, which differs slightly in liturgy from the Nyingma school, and accordingly takes her lessons in the sacred literature from a Karmapa Lama of Lhobrag. The monks have some reputation for their morals. I found most of them wearing the *chhab-lug* as a sign of having taken the vows of monkhood. Dorje Phagmo enforces a strict discipline among the monks, who are not allowed long vacations or leave to absent themselves from the monastery for long periods, and neither the monks nor the nuns are allowed to lend money and other things on interest. There is a convent at some distance from Samding, where Dorje Phagmo spends a portion of the year. In the congregation-hall, called *h*Dus-khang, we were told that there exists inscriptions on the walls recording how Dorje Phagmo miraculously saved the monastery of Samding from the hands of the conqueror Jung-gar (the ruthless persecutor of the Nyingma school) in the year 1716.

When the Jungar Chief with his army arrived at Nangar-tse, hearing that Dorje Phagmo had a pig's head in the shape of an excrescence behind her head, he spoke in ridicule of her in public, and sent a messenger to Samding to summon Dorje Phagmo to his presence, that he might examine her holy character and see if she really possessed a pig's head. Dorje Phagmo did not return an angry reply to this insulting message of the Mongol Chief, but desired him to give up his evil designs upon her monastery. Burning with anger, the conqueror invaded the monastery and destroyed its walls; but on entering it he found it was entirely deserted: not a single soul, man or woman, of whom he could make enquiries! He only found eighty pigs and eighty sows grunting in the grand congregation hall under the lead of a big sow. He was struck with this singular frustration of his projects; for he could not now plunder the monastery, it being disgraceful to take away properties guarded by, or belonging to, pigs. When they found that he was not bent upon plunder, the pigs and sows disappeared, and their place was occupied by venerable-looking monks and nuns headed by the most venerable Dorje Phagmo! Out of faith and veneration for the sacred character of the miraculous lady, the Chief made immense presents to Samding. Such is the history of Dorje Phagmo, whose recognised incarnation so graciously treated me during my few days' residence at Yamdo Samding monastery. I inquired from well-informed and learned sources why it is that Tamdin did not become incarnate to enlighten the people in the sacred religion, and was told that the Dalai Lama being the real embodiment of Chanras-ssig (the peaceful mood of Tamdin), no other incarnation of his could be recognized, and that, besides Dorje Phagmo, there is no other incarnation of Tara in Tibet. I also made inquiries respecting the extent of the great Yamdo lake, and was told that one could go round it in eight days, although it is commonly believed that its external area cannot be traversed in less than eighteen days. In the afternoon we cleared our accounts with the landlord and made arrangements for our journey to Lhasa. Yamdo is a poor country in which very little barley grows. There was at this time, in fact, a scarcity of forage throughout the lake district. The extreme severity of the climate, its bleak and barren appearance, its desolate aspect, made me particularly anxious to bid it farewell as soon as possible. My companions were also tired of the place.

III.—JOURNEY FROM YAMDO SAMDING TO LASHA ARRIVAL AT LHASA.

27th May (*the 10th of the 4th lunar month of the Tibetan calendar*).—We left Samding to-day. Pador, who had prepared three small flags, with some red cloth and yellow calico borrowed from Amchila, now tied these to his long spear-head. Old Amchila brought us a basketful of dried apricots and a dish of rice as presents, and begged us to call at his brother's house in the upland of Ka*l*ssang Ssampa. Geleg Namgya*l*, our host, brought us some eggs of the wild goose, but I did not accept them on religious grounds. Tshing-ta and Pador were in excellent spirits now that their toils were apparently at an end, I having recovered from my illness. My two ponies during our fortnight's stay here had picked up flesh and were fit for a long journey, and at 7 A.M., after breakfast, we bid farewell to the thrice holy monastery of Samding. Standing on an eminence behind our lodgings, I enjoyed for a while the grand and awful scenery of the lake country, bounded by endless ranges of sombre hills backed by snow-tipped peaks. Though Dorje Phagmo had desired me to visit her monastery on our return journey towards Tashi-lhunpo, I entertained very little hopes of being able to see her again. I cast a glance towards the lake (Dumo-tsho) into which lately five hundred fish had been ransomed for my recovery by Amchila, and also the particular place where the dead bodies of the inhabitants of Samding are thrown into the water to be devoured by fish and sea fowls. Dead bodies in other parts of Tibet are disposed of by being cut into pieces for distribution among vultures and dogs, but at Samding a different usage holds, and the following story which Kusho Tung-chhen had told me about lake Yamdo came to my recollection :—It is believed all over Tibet that at a depth of about 500 feet there dwell in the interior of the great lake a number of *Nagas* (serpent demi-gods), who keep the key of heaven in their custody, and in a palace of crystal in the deep recesses of the lake resides their chief. The Samding monks, and generally the Yamdo people, throw their dead bodies into the lake there with a hope that they might reach heaven by serving the king of the *Nagas* during the period of *pardo* (interval between death and regeneration). We descended from Samding hill by the western road, when a mastiff belonging to the monastery followed us; we threw stones at him, but to no purpose. My companions considered the dog's following us as something very inauspicious, and, in fact, thought it to be some evil spirit. Arriving at the foot of Samding hill, I cast a long look towards the flight of stone steps leading to the monastery, the *chhorten*, the monastery wall, about 300 yards in length, and all that I had passed by when I was in immediate fear of death. At the foot of the Samding hill is the little hamlet of Gag-tsa (grass-place), exclusively inhabited by the grass-keepers of Dorje Phagmo. Close to it is a *mandang* about 300 yards long. A few minutes' slow ride brought us to the side of a deep irrigation canal about 12 feet broad. There was no water in it, but the sides were steep, and I had to dismount to cross it. We now passsed through cultivated fields, where the ponies sank up to their knees in mud, and found ourselves in a spacious steppe where herds of wild goat, sheep and a few musk-deer were grazing. These looked so tame and heedless of our approach that at first sight I took them for domesticated animals belonging to Dorje Phagmo. But when we arrived at a distance of about a hundred yards from them, they quietly withdrew towards the hill-sides. Dorje Phagmo is a particular protectress of these wild animals. Within the lake district of Yamdo hunters are not allowed admission, and the natives do not kill the *ridvag* (wild animals, such as musk-deer, stag, rabbits, goats, sheep, &c.).

After half an hour's ride we arrived at the extensive plateau of Nangar-tse, where we met several yak-herds and shepherds, tending their flocks. Pador talked with two or three of these men who were standing in front of their black yak-hair tents. At about 10 A.M., we reached Nangar-tse Jong, when I sent Pador to Chhoikhang, our late kind *Nabo*. A little above and beyond Nangar-tse Jong there is a hamlet belonging to one Tshering Jordan, the Government grass superintendent. Above this is situated Nangah-chhoi-de monastery belonging to Samding. I saw another monastery called Jam-joi about four miles from the town of Nangar-tse, and towards the Thonang district. Proceeding a short distance towards the north, we came to the margin of the far-famed Yamdo (Palti) lake, where several *kodu* (hide boats) were being dried, by being placed

*

in an erect position, each on two supports. I was told that these were fishing-boats from Naugar-tse. At a distance of about a mile-and-a-half is the village of Hang, situated on the margin of the lake. Flocks of wild geese were swimming in the lake, and the yaks that were grazing near it appeared to be of a superior breed to those I had hitherto seen on the way. In the rocky slopes of barren mountains which overhung the lake on our left-hand side there were grazing several herds of sheep and goat. The vast expanse of the lake extending towards the north and the north-west was a novel sight to me, and the small glacial lakes I had hitherto come across in the northern slopes of the Himalayas compared with this fell into insignificance. In Tibetan books it is called Yum-tsho or the turquoise lake, for which name there is ample justification in the green blue appearance of the lake. On the way between the villages of Hang and Nyen, the latter of which has a long *Mandang*, we met several caravans of donkeys and ponies carrying *argol* (dried dung) and barley. Travelling along the lake side for nearly six miles we passed by the villages of Hailo, Dab-lung, and Dephu. At Hailo there were above a dozen houses inhabited by cultivators and fishermen. On the sides and in front of three or four houses we again saw a few hide boats kept in an erect position. Two or three boats were also floating in the lake in front of the village. The village of Dab-lung, consisting of several scattered hamlets, is situated on the eastern slope of Noijin Kang-*ssang* mountain, and is divided into two parts, Dab-lung Dah and Dab-lung Phu. We had a glimpse of the latter. Dephu is an inconsiderable village, situated at a distance of 500 yards from the margin of the lake. A small stream of water flows by the village to the lake, past the barley fields, from which the villagers raise a scanty crop. The soil there presented an extremely barren appearance from a distance. Proceeding thence about three miles, we obtained a distant view of Pa*l*di-jong, which seemed perched, as it were over the lake. The road which wound along a steep narrow bank was now within 20 to 30 feet from the water, and turned directly westward along with the lake. We saw the village of Samding on the receding bank of the lake and Phugpa a little above in the uplands. The furthest extremity of the lake on the west is called Yar-see or Yar-ssig. Several flocks of *tung-tung* (a long-billed, white-breasted crane) were picking up their food in the water. At about 1 A.M. we arrived in the vicinity of Ka*l*-*ssang* *Ssampa* (bridge), where we met two Tibetan officers, in military uniforms, riding on two spirited ponies towards Nangar-tse. We had not the courage to ask who and what they were, but one of them asked Tshing-ta who we were and whence coming.

Being now much fatigued after a continuous ride for nearly five hours, I halted in a gap, a little above Kal-*ssang* *ssampa*, through which a stream of water flowed to empty itself in the lake. The men collected dried dung for fuel. Pador hastened to fetch water and Tshing-ta busied himself with the skin bellows to blow the fire, while I sat on a rug. Presently came two elderly-looking men leading two ponies and three donkeys. They asked Tshing-ta whence we were coming, and one of them told him that the place where we were halting was not safe, and that we had better finish our refreshments soon. Hearing this, Tshing-ta asked me to load my revolver, and Pador, presently arriving with a bowl of water, got hold of his lance, and flourishing it, said that he did not fear any *chag-pa* (robber). I tried my revolver, but the first and second cartridges missed fire. I then dried some of the cartridges, and succeeded in firing one. After tea we resumed our journey. The Ka*l*-*ssang* *ssampa* is no bridge at all, but a long embankment dividing a long neck of the lake into two parts, with three or four passages cut in it for the water of the upper part to flow down to the lower or main lake. About 100 feet of the middle portion of the embankment is constructed of rubble, and the whole is about three to four hundred paces long and twenty feet broad, and extends from north to south. Then, proceeding eastward along the northern shore of the great lake by a foot-path along the ledge of the precipitous sides of the rocky mountains overhanging the lake on the north, we arrived at a narrow saddle-like pass. At a place where a string of coloured and inscribed rags was stretched between two needle-shaped rocky points, Tshing-ta made me dismount. He then ascended a large block of rock, where he scattered a few pinches of barley-flour, and striking the flint-stone, he lighted an incense-stick which he fixed in the cleft of the rock. At a distance of about thirty feet from the place where we stood, two dead bodies were floating in the water of the lake. This place is called Sharui-theng on account of its being the haunt of some fearful genii. Travellers, when they pass by this extremely

---

Ovis Ammon—(The Tibetan *nyan*).

This is a native of the lofty north and north-western desert regions of high Asia. In its love of cold and high elevations it even surpasses the musk-deer. In size the *nyan* is little bigger than the Tibetan bull. In shape and appearance it resembles the sheep, of which it is believed to be the prototype. Very large, massive, and long horns grow on its head, which instead of rising upwards like the antlers of the stag grow downwards in screw-like coils. In eight or nine years these horns grow so long that they touch the ground, and thereby prevent their owners from picking grass. Most of these animals are said to die in this posture, in which they are discovered by the nomad shepherds. Such of them as are not strong, when by accident or being chased by hunters, they have once fallen forwards or on their backs, cannot get up, their horns being driven into the ground, in which state they die. The *nyan* horn is of use in rims na*d* (infectious fever).

*

narrow passage, are expected, according to my companion's account, to pay them homage, and those who neglect to do so incur their serious displeasure. At about 4-30 P.M., after traversing a circuitous path by the lake margin, we reached Pa*l*di-jong, which appeared to me about six miles from Ka*l-ssang* Ssampa. A slight shower of rain, accompanied by sleet, had fallen the previous evening, which had set the dust of the road. Pador conducted us to a house Dekhang, belonging to an acquaintance of Lhacham Kusho. Lhacham herself had passed one night at Dekhang on her way to Lhasa, and had mentioned me to the host, and desired him to help me. Our ponies and things were accordingly readily admitted into his hospitable house, and one large room was given to us for our accommodation. There was a spacious court in front of our host's house, the two sides of which were provided with stalls for ponies and cows. The *namo* provided us with water, firewood, and two earthen cooking-vessels, and then went to milk her cows. We bought from her some milk and a few eggs, and some malt beer for my companions. The one-anna measure of beer here is comparatively smaller than at Gyantse or Shiga-tse. Our *namo* told us that some fish were brought for sale by a fisherman: would I buy some? But, having ransomed the lives of 500 fish, and also fearing that it would be inconsistent with my character of a pious pilgrim to eat fish when it was religiously forbidden by the Dalai Lama's Government, I refrained from giving her an answer. The Grand Lama, I must mention, having lately taken the vows of monkhood, had issued edicts to prohibit his subjects from killing or eating fish for the space of one year. Pador also brought us a rumour that Lhachan would shortly return to Tsang, the gods having declared that her health would not improve if she stayed at Lhasa during the summer. A good shower of rain fell at dusk. There was no door to our room, but there was a large one at the entrance of the court. Pador assured me of the honesty of our host, and that I could sleep without the least anxiety about being robbed by anybody. I was still very weak, my headache had not yet left me, and my difficulty in breathing was still very painful. There was a delightful moonlight: the town of Pa*l*di-jong appearing bleached, as it were, in the moon-beams, and the *jong* (castle) looming magnificently on the margin of the great lake.

28th May.—We got up from bed at 3 A.M., and re-packing our baggage, resumed our journey a little before four in the morning. We were not the only early-risers that day, for two parties of travellers, leading packs of laden ponies and donkeys, had already preceded us. The Tibetans are a very early-rising people, and early as it was, I saw some husbandmen of Pa*l*di going to their work in the upland fields of the town. Our way was along the north-western shore of the great lake, whose calm surface was slightly ruffled by a gentle wind, the waves running towards the east along with us and the wind. We passed Tong-chhen-chobgye, so called on account of its rock caverns, eighteen in number. I obtained some legendary accounts of Pa*l*di-jong from a well-informed man, a native of a village situated in the neighbourhood of Pa*l*di-jong. Anciently the town of Pa*l*di was famous as the seat of *Ningma* (the oldest Buddhist sect) learning, and the lake used to be called after it by the vulgar people. (The English name, lake Palti, seems to have been evidently derived from the name of this town. The Tibetan *d* is generally pronounced like *t*. The Jesuits who visited Tibet in the 15th and 16th centuries must have heard the lake called after the name of the town of Pa*l*di). The Jongar (a nomad Mongol tribe) invaders, after demolishing many of the *Ningma* monasteries of Lhasa and other places in U and its neighbourhood, crossed Nabso-la with the object of suppressing all *Ningma* schools and monasteries in Tsang. Just at this time there lived a very learned and sacred personage called Pa*l*di Shabdung, who was believed to be an incarnation of the famous saint Thangthong Gya*l*pa. He was versed in the sacred books, and particularly in the *Ningma* rituals, such as Tertanlingpa's introductions, and also in the Kahgyur and Tangyur scriptures. He was famous as the only person of his time to whose will the tutelary deities were subservient, and people used to say that the gods were enslaved by him. He composed several religious works, which are known as the Khye*d*-Chho*s*, the "particular works" of Pa*l*di Shabdung, and owing to his special proficiency in the *Ningma* rites, the votaries of the oldest Buddhist school of Tibet increased in number. Just then the Jongar invasion took place, and the dreadful news that the invader was a sworn enemy of the *Ningma* sect created a panic in the mind of all the adherents of Padma Jung-ne. Pa*l*di Shabdung, while sitting in contemplation, saw two divine beings, exquisitely beautiful, whom he understood to be the guardians of the great lake, issue forth from the middle of the lake, who approached and addressed him thus:—"Oh, venerable Lama, a great and inveterate enemy to the cause of the *Ningma* church has just come to Tibet to demolish all temples and religious institutions of our creed in U and Tsang. He will shortly arrive here. Before he reaches this place it is meet for you to adopt means for his destruction." They then instructed him how to perform certain Do[1] rites and religious ceremonies for the propitiation of the lake gods. Accordingly Pa*l*di Shabdung performed the rituals at Sharui-theng, and thereby propitiated the deities of the lake, who now solemnly promised to do him services considered impossible hitherto, and particularly to destroy the sworn enemies of his creed. The Jongar armies, crossing the Nabsola Pass, encamped at Yar-ssee, whence they saw what they thought a plain of fine verdure extending between Yar-ssee and Sharui-theng. Tempted with its

[1] The Do (*m* Do*s*) rites of sorcery are very curious. The priests generally construct certain miniature figures resembling ship-masts, in which the place of ropes is supplied by coloured strings. I was told that the magical rites originated from the Pon religion, and are still practised by the Tantrik Buddhists who practise incantations.

beauty, on the following morning they marched to cross it to sack Pa*l*di-jong, but the whole detachment was drowned in the lake, not one out of several thousands of men being saved. Another detachment, which came *viâ* Khambala, retraced their steps on finding that the first detachment did not arrive to co-operate with them. So Pa*l*di-jong was saved by the magical intercession of the gods of the lake who were propitiated by Pa*l*di Shabdung. From this fabulous account some glimpse of an actual occurrence may be obtained. Either there must have been a sudden increase in the volume of the lake by the excessive supply of water from the glacial streams of the Noijin, or the soldiers might have been deluded by a mirage. The portion of the lake above Ka*l*-*s*sang Ssampa was overgrown with a long grass called *dam-tsa*, and it is not impossible that the shores of the lake below the Ssampa at some part of the year are covered with vegetation, for even so late as that time the water of the lake is said to have stood very high. The large village of Yar-ssee, situated a few miles above Ka*l*-ssang Ssampa, was believed to be situated at its tail and Talung at its head: for people believe that the great lake is of the shape of a scorpion laid flat on its back on the ground.

On the way we met two solitary monks from Dapung, armed with a matchlock and a long lance with a red banner flying at the top of it. I was told that those monks were highwaymen; and their stalwart appearance, ruffian looks, and their arms seemed to confirm it; for if they were *bonâ fide* travellers they should have at least got their woollens to carry with them. Why, again, did they carry such weapons if they had no property to defend? At 10 A.M. we arrived at the foot of Khambala, the mountain which divides the lake from the river Tsang-po. Ascending about three hundred feet, we saw a tiny spring, whence water trickled down in drops. At about 11, after breakfast, we resumed our ascent of the *La*, and after two bends of the road, came to the side of the mountain, which overhangs the village of Tamalung. There was a tolerably good foot-track, repaired in some places, winding up over the mountain, by which we reached the top of its southern flank after a gradual ascent of an hour-and-a-half. On the surfaces of the perpendicular or sloping rocks numerous images of Buddhas and Bodhisattvas were painted. The mountain on the other side of the lake, and the continuation of the Khambala towards the east, at the foot of which numerous villages nestled, presented a novel and picturesque sight to my enraptured eyes; for I had never witnessed such sights in the Himalayas. The snowy mountains of Lhobra, the lofty peaks of Noijin Kang-*s*sang and numerous other mountains, broke the dull uniformity of the prevailing blue of Tibetan scenery; from Tamalung a road meandered along the craggy shore of the lake towards the east and south-east; and the serpentine bends of the lake, with its spacious nooks and gaps on both shores, could be surveyed as far as the eye could follow the horizon. The height we had reached was about a thousand feet above the level of the lake. Passing this summit, which faced the lake, we proceeded toward the *Lab-tse*, the culminating point of the pass. Here two large cairns stood on either side of the road, where my companions, taking off their hats, uttered *mantras* to invoke the mountain deities. According to religious custom every-one who passes by this place adds a stone to these votive cairns. I saw some travellers going towards the east by the road which traverses the summits of the continuous range of Khambala above Tamalung. Tshing-ta told me that many robberies are committed on solitary travellers at this place, and that I would do well to see if my revolver was in good order. I asked him if the mountain gods would not take offence at my disturbing the atmosphere by a loud report. He said they would not, if I only fired to warn off brigands. So I loaded the revolver and handed it over to Tshing-ta. Both he and Pador expected to hear a loud report from the tiny thing, but were much disappointed. Tshing-ta attributed this to the course of the wind, but thought it might also be owing to the sound being dispersed in the open space, there being no obstruction to echo back the sound. Advancing a few paces behind the sacred cairns, I came to a point whence I saw one of the grandest views of Tibet. It was that of the valley of the far-famed Tsang-po, whose sublime and majestic scenery, the like of which I never beheld before, quite ravished my heart. The impression of the scenery in my enchanted mind was full, and I liked to enjoy it to satiety. In the snowy Himalayas there are torrents and rapids rushing down with impetuosity, and when I looked from a lofty summit toward the deep valleys, the streams there dwindled down to silver threads, meandering in deep gorges. But the scene here was otherwise: the great Tsang-po flowed at the base of a gigantic, yawning chasm, which extended for miles between two ranges of lofty, dark mountains, whose flanks overhanging the river from the north were covered with dark forests of fir-like trees. At the foot of those lofty mountains, but still in the upland, there were pretty-looking villages with castle-like whitewashed houses, most of the larger houses being surrounded with tall trees. A village on the other side of Tsang-po was particularly conspicuous for amazing depth in the valley at which it was seen from the *Lab-tse* of Khambala, surrounded by rugged and sombre mountains. My companions fixed a flag to the *Lab-tse*, and as required by religion and usage, burnt incense, strewed flour, and sprinkled dust instead of wine for the acceptance of the mountain god. While making the offerings they made the following invocation:—

Kyai! Lama yi-dam khah-gro dang.
Chho*s*-srung nor-lha *g* ter-*b* dag dang.
Yul-lha shi-dag khor cha*s* kyi*s*.
Sang*s* dang phye-mar *g* ser-*s* kyem*s* sog*s*.
Chho*d*-pa gya-chhen di she*s* la.

Oh, Lamas, tutelars and soarers in the skies,
Ye guardians of *dharma* and the gods of wealth,
Ye demi-gods and local deities,
Together with your trains pray accept
This offering of incense, flour, and copious drink!

After this invocation they made the following prayer :—

To us, together with our retinue,
Vouchsafe the chief blessings of health and life;
Make us happy without risk to life.
We beg you to grant us prosperity and wealth,
Sweet food, cattle wealth, and fine dress.
Protect us from evils and befriend us wherever we go.

At the conclusion they shouted—

Lha sol-lo Lha sol-lo.
Offerings and libations are made to gods!
Offerings and libations are made to gods!
Lha gya*l*-lo Lha gya*l*-lo!
Victory be to the gods, Victory be to the gods!
Kei—Kei—Ho, Ho—!

Surveying for a while the grand scenery of the valley of the Tsang-po, and the tortuous windings of the great lake from this commanding point, we descended towards the province of U. I was told that there was a passage westward along the continuous summits of the Khambala range towards Paldi-jong. Proceeding for seven miles, one comes to Nabsola, whence Pa*l*di is five miles. I walked down for a short distance though the zig-zag road was somewhat steep for a few hundred feet. On the road-side two clownish-looking men were lying fast asleep, one of whom on our near approach awoke, and Tshing-ta asked him whence they were and where going to. The man replied that he was a courier of Sawang-Rampa, the senior *Shapé*. Thereupon Tshing-ta inquired after that great man's health and if he was residing at Lhasa, for Rampa being a devoted friend of our patron the Minister, the news of his being at Lhasa would be welcome to us. These men were going back to Tsang. Descending a short distance, we met two men who, leading several ponies, were proceeding to Khambala, riding fast, so as to reach Tamalung before sunset. At about 3 P.M. we arrived at the foot of the La, traversing a tedious zig-zag about five miles, where there is a fine wooden bridge with stone approaches. Different sorts of brambles and wild roses grew on the sides of the road, and a few conifers and rhododendrons broke the dull uniformity of the barren soil. Here we saw two flocks of sheep, each numbering more than three hundred heads, picking fresh shoots of grass, and tended by two shepherds, whose stone hovels (*Na-tshang*) were perched on a flat slope near the way. We now followed the course of a sluggish stream carrying down muddy water, and proceeding further down saw a second stream joining the former. The way was now gravelly and full of debris of splintered rocks. By its side there was an irrigation channel cut to carry water to the barley fields we had passed through before reaching the village of Khamba Partshi. The houses of this straggling village, numbering upwards of 40, were all wretched huts, and though built of stone and surrounded with walls, evinced on all sides the miserable condition of the people. Our way after we left the village lay across a barley field, along both sides of which there were a few pollard willows, now partially green with fresh leaves. At the north-western corner of the village and about 300 yards above the river Tsang-po, and about half a mile from the upper part of Partshi village, is situated the *Gya-khang*, or circuit house of the Ampa. The banks of the Tsang-po are sandy, heaps of sands being also seen in the upland-nooks of the lofty mountain, undoubtedly accumulated by the sweeping of the incessant gales which blow over the Tibetan plateau during eight months of the year. There were also extensive alluvial deposits on both banks of the great river. In some places cultivators were reclaiming land. It was about 3 P.M. when we reached the river-side and climbed up a precipitous, narrow passage over rocks overlooking the great river, in the stagnant pools and nooks of which we saw fine fish. The way for a short distance was dangerous, being extremely narrow and situated on the edge of steep and bluff rocks. Proceeding further on, we arrived at Tongbu, about a mile from Partshi, in a tolerably level valley called Khamba Chyang-thang. This place, both in the uplands and the lowlands, was sparsely occupied with villages. The fields were green, the seedlings here being now four to six inches high. In some places cultivators, both men and women, were picking out weeds, &c., from amidst the seedlings. Here we were overtaken by a chill gale followed by rain. Two women who were engaged in picking up weeds approached us with bundles of barley seedlings in their hands, and presented them to me. Tshing-ta explained to me their object in so doing: they wanted money to aid the work of cultivation. I did not reply to their entreaties, but passed on listlessly. They followed us to some distance and then stopped. This custom, called *Lubul*, I was told, is universal all over Tibet, and well-to-do men generally give something when so supplicated; but we had only a few two-anna pieces with us, and had we given anything to one or two parties, several others would surely have troubled us for alms also. Our way now lay on the sandy banks of the Tsang-po. On our right-hand side we passed the village of Thoi-tsi with about a dozen houses. In one place two women were engaged in making bricks, which I guessed measured a foot by a foot-and-a-half and between six and nine inches thick. Several donkeys and yaks were employed in carrying the dried bricks, led by an old woman and two boys. They told Tshing-ta that the bricks were being taken to build a house at the foot of the Palchhen Chhuvori. On our right-hand side we left the insignificant hamlet of Chyan-bu with four or five dilapidated houses. Then proceeding nearly two miles along this side of the Tsang-po, we came to the foot of an old *chhorten*, which probably marks the entrance of the famous Palchhen Chhuvori monastery. On the sacred hill there are said to exist 108 temples, 108 *chhortens*, 108 cemeteries, and 108 springs. The principal cemetery is said to be the counterpart of the celebrated Himashila cemetery of Magadha. We passed a second *chhorten* of like construction and size, when the way ascended over a steep rock rising abruptly from the river. Proceeding for above four furlongs we arrived at the monastery of Palchhen Chhuvori, which stands on the eastern approach of the iron chain-bridge *Chag-ssam*. This chain-bridge was constructed by the illustrious sage Thang-Tong Gya*l*-po, who, in the first quarter of the 15th century after Christ, having discovered extensive iron mines, caused its contents to be utilized as materials for a bridge. According to the Ningma Lamas, the sage Thang-Tong Gya*l*-po constructed 108 hanging bridges over the Tsang-po; but the information supplied to me by the Gelug-pa Lamas, which I accepted as accurate, credits him with the construction of only eight bridges. I was told by a certain Lama that the library of Palchhen Chhuvori contains two large volumes of the life of Thang-Tong Gya*l*-po, which are not shown to the public. I obtained certain legendary accounts about him from a learned Gelug-pa Lama on my return from Lhasa, which I embody here :—

The sage Thang-Tong Gya*l*-po was born in the year 1385 A.D. He is said to have possessed a part of Chyan-ras-ssig's spirit. Fearing the miseries of this world very much, he managed to remain sixty years in his mother's womb, where he sat in profound meditation with perfect concentration of mind on the well-being of all living beings. At the termination of a full cycle of sixty years his meditation broke, when, seeing how unkind he was to his mother (for while meditating for the good of others, he neglected her sufferings), he forthwith quitted the womb, and was born in this world with grey hairs, having attained already to a good old age. Just after seeing light, he made profound salutations to his mother, whom he addressed thus: "Mother, pardon me. I have put you to endless troubles, but I was exceedingly comfortable during my long residence in your womb." He then, observing that nowhere in this world there exists so soft and comfortable a place for residence as a mother's womb, sat for a while cross-legged, absorbed in meditation. Those who were about him at this auspicious time were struck with the beauty of his person, which resembled that of a child of three years in its whitish-red colour, and its remarkable softness. It sent out a lotus-like fragrance, so that those who saw him from a distance took him for a reflected image. Remaining in the same position for seven days, during which time he did not move his limbs, he acquired the size and stature of youth, and when he had reached that of an adult man he got up to walk. It is said that while he was in his mother's womb, the latter did not suffer as ordinary mothers do during pregnancy. She rather felt easy, light, and cheerful, and during sleep used to have pleasing dreams. Thang-Tong Gya*l*-po was not nursed like other children, and he learnt to eat within about a fortnight after his birth. As soon as he put on clothes, he began to lecture on the sacred scriptures of the Buddhists. The manner of his conception was thus :—Once his mother, when only sixteen years old, while crossing a desert plain, being fatigued with journeying, fell asleep. She saw a white, angelic person, diffusing lustre as it passed. Shortly after she conceived this child. On account of this vision in Thang-Tong (bare and desert plain), the child was called Thang-Tong Gya*l*-po (or the Prince of the desert plain). By virtue of the moral merits and acquirements of his former life he soon learnt to read and write with facility, with very little teaching, and his former wisdom and foreknowledge returned of their own accord to his saintly mind. He soon acquired the power of working miracles, and being celebrated for his vast learning contributed much to the diffusion of the sacred *dharma*. Among his chief works for public welfare were the construction of eight famous hanging chain-bridges over the Tsang-po and the erection of one hundred and eight temples, one hundred and eight *chhortens*, &c., on the hills of Chung-Rivochhe in Tsang and Palchhen Chhuvori in Ü. He also discovered many self-sprung images of Buddha and Bodhisattvas. According to popular belief, he achieved all these great deeds with the aid of gods and *Nagas*; for where else could he get wealth and power to accomplish such great works as do not fall to the lot of kings and princes to achieve, if he were not assisted by supernatural agencies! Many strange stories are related about the building of the temple on Rivochhe. One man is said to have commenced dragging huge loads of timber posts, &c., fastened together with ropes to a consecrated stick, with the warning that he should not look back on any account. But the man having proceeded to a considerable distance, and hearing a rattling sound behind him, out of curiosity, forgetting the sage's warning, looked back, when the wood ceased to move: up to that place the gods and demi-gods had helped him in the carriage of the timber load. But they now departed in anger and the sage was compelled to erect, unaided, the monastery of Rivochhe. The people of the country are said to have witnessed loads of iron being carried by four giant-like men during the hours of night. Those who obtained consecration and benediction from his hand are said to have lived unusually long. His likenesses and images are worshipped by many people

Whatever might have been the story of his extraordinary stay in his mother's womb, it is certain that he attained an unusually long life, having lived to see one hundred and twenty summers. The devout Ning-ma Lamas believe that he was conducted to the mansion of rest by an escort of fairies. Thang-Tong Gya*l*-po is said to have appeared in Tibet as Je-tsun Milarapa in one of his transmigrations, and one of his later incarnations is said to have been Lama Shab-karpa of Amdo.

The monastery of Palchhen-Chhuvori is in excellent condition. The entire income of the ferry toll is set apart as an endowment for the monastery, which supports upwards of one hundred monks. On the side of the eastern approach of the bridge, and to the west of the monastery, the entire plot is occupied by the *sho* or lay village, by one of whose narrow lanes we passed. In an enclosed court two or three calves were confined, and some *jomos* were chewing the cud, lying in the court. The huts of the *sho* were in good condition. There were a few pollard willows along the river-side, and also some poplars (*shovo*) to the west of the *sho*. Several hide boats were kept in an erect position for drying in the sun, and about half a dozen wooden boats were tied with hair ropes to huge boulders on the *ghât*. Two long, heavy chains, a little thicker than the anchor chains of British ships, were suspended over the narrowest breadth of the river to support the bridge, which was about 400 feet broad here. The eastern ends of the chains were fastened to a huge log fixed in the middle of a *chhorten* situated at the western entrance of the monastery, which being situated at the foot of the Chhuvori hill on the rocky slope, its position is secure; but the western approach of the bridge is very insecure, being at the extremity of an extensive sand-bank formation; the remaining two ends of the chains are likewise fastened to a well-built stone *chhorten*. I did not get an opportunity to enter it to see how the chains were fastened. This *chhorten* was larger than the other, and stood on a base of about 20 feet square, round which there were several poplars and willows grown to a good height. The river at this time of the year was about 700 feet wide. I and Pador proceeded towards the northern end of the *ghât*, where two oblong boats were tied by ropes to two huge boulders. The boatmen were gone to their houses, thinking that there would be no passenger during such a stormy evening. It was past five, and we had waited for nearly an hour standing on a slab of rock, the lower part of which was being washed by the waves of the river. When the boatmen arrived, there was a regular storm, which fearfully ruffled the river and made the boatmen afraid to attempt crossing; but Tshing-ta entreated the head boatman to call all his men to ply the boat, as we could hardly get *na-tshang* (lodgings) for the night if we delayed longer on this side of the river; for neither himself nor Pador knew anybody in Chag-ssam village in whose house we could obtain accommodation for the night. Besides there was no provender to be had in the village for our ponies. The head boatman seemed to be a gentlemanly person, polite in manners and obliging, and I promised him *chhang-rin* (wine-money) if he would immediately start his boat to take us to the opposite bank. He accordingly called his men and proceeded to the boat. Just then about two dozen donkeys laden with grain bags came up attended by several men and women, who engaged two hide boats to cross over. The waves were furious, yet the hide boats steered across with wonderful agility. The two wooden boats were heavily laden with passengers, for we were altogether a dozen in one of them, which looked like a shallow box without the lid, above 20 feet long and 8 feet broad, the planks joined by nails. Indeed, the Tibetans seemed to be perfectly ignorant of the art of boat-making. I asked the boatmen if the Ampa and the great Ministers ever crossed the river by such boats. "Yes, Sir," said the boatmen, "these are the only conveyances we have for this Chagssam ferry. All men, great or humble, cross by these boats." One of the crew baled out the water accumulated from the numerous leaks, by means of a large hide scoop. We paid the captain at the rate of a *tanka* for the ponies and 2 annas per head for men. Our ponies stood quietly, though the donkeys were frightened by the rolling of the boat. We landed near the *chhorten* on the opposite bank; but the river having overflooded its banks, we had to wade for about fifteen minutes in the shallow water alongside of a stone embankment. Having passed this, we had a tedious march along a sand bank, a distance of about half a mile from the *chhorten* connected with the chain bridge. Pador knew the way, and guided us, and a little before sunset we arrived at the village of Dsim-Khar, which looked from a distance like a castle. There is a fine *chhorten* in front of the village with spacious open lawns on its east and south. Our host's house was high and commodious, and of a stately appearance. Two men and a woman were engaged in circumambulating and uttering frequently, but indistinctly *Om mani pame hum*, while two men were engaged in threshing corn in a corner of the court of a neighbouring house. I waited at the gate of the house of Dsimkhar *Gyanpo* (headman) for above a quarter of an hour, while Pador knocked at his door several times. Two fierce-looking mastiffs, chained on the roof of the doorway, made savage attempts to break loose, when a servant of the Gyan-po came out and asked what we wanted. Pador entered the inner court, saying that the Gyan-po was an acquaintance of his, and asked for a night's *na-tshang*, which was granted on our agreeing to pay one *tanka* as *na-la* or house-rent for the night. His servant conducted us to a sheep-fold, filled with hay and a number of kids. These latter were driven out and the hay removed to make room for our accommodation. All the members of the Gyan-po's family were laid up with small-pox, the Gyan-po himself having lately recovered from that disease. He regretted that he had no other place to accommodate us. The kids were very pretty-looking, hardly more than a month old, and frisked and cried as they were driven out of the house. The floor having been swept, Pador spread a rug, on which I seated myself. The Gyan-po guessed that I must have been ill. Close to our lodgings, a number of travellers arrived after we had taken shelter under the roof of our host. It rained at dusk, and the roof leaked in several places. Our host kindly lent us the use of two earthen bowls to cook tea and rice. Pador slept outside the house to look to the ponies that they might not be stolen away. In the stables of our host there were nine ponies tied in a row, whose kicking and neighing disturbed our sleep. Besides this nuisance, the leaks, which under heavy showers at night became numerous, made us very uncomfortable.

29th May.—Just before dawn we resumed our journey. The village of Dsim-khar belongs to the estate of Namgya*l* Ta-tshang, the great monastic establishment of Potala. South-east of Dsim-khar is the village of Sagong with about ten houses. Proceeding for nearly a mile towards the north and west from this village we arrived at the village of Dsim, whence the road running along the steep rocky bank of the Tsang-po, took us to the village of Chhushu*l*-jong. On the rocky edge of the great river there were several old stumps, probably of willows, and some old pollard willows grew overhanging the river, which would most probably during the rains be swept away. It was now morning, and we got sight of the ruins of Chhushu*l*-jong, which stood in their fallen greatness on the craggy ridge of a low hill overhanging the Tsang-po. Some two hundred years ago Chhushu*l*-jong was a place of some importance. The Jongpon was a rich and powerful noble, who married a handsome maiden, sprung from the family of the illustrious minister Thonmi-Sambhota, the father of Tibetan literature. The brother of the maiden was the Dahpon (commander) of Lhasa, who, on account of some family dispute created by his brother-in-law insulting his sister, invaded Chhushu*l*-jong and destroyed it. From Chhushu*l* we enjoyed a fine view of the junction of the Kyi-chhu with the great Tsang-po. The latter, turning a little to the north and then to the south-east, flows towards the east, being joined by the Kyi-chhu. A shower of rain had just fallen to swell the feeders of the river. The heat of the summer had melted the glaciers of the snowy mountains which feed the Tsang-po, causing it to rise to some extent. The head feeders of the Kyi-chhu, I was told, did not originate from any glaciers of Central Tibet; owing to this and to there being comparatively less rains in the interior of Tibet, the Kyi-chhu had not at this time risen much in its level. But I entertained much doubt about this assertion. The village of Chhushu*l*, which I guessed contained about 60 houses, stood in the midst of extensive fields, growing rich crops of barley, rape, buck-wheat, and wheat. At a distance of one mile from Chhushu*l*-jong, towards the south-east, is the junction of the river Kyi-chhu with the Tsang-po. The monastery of Chhoikhor-ling, with a few willows and poplars in front of it, was perched in the uplands to our left, to the south-west of Chhushu*l*. and seemed from a distance to be in good condition. A streamlet coming from the west passes towards the east at the entrance of the village of Chhushu*l* to discharge its contents into the Tsang-po. There is a stone bridge, about 20 feet long, across the streamlet, which we crossed. Several hamlets surrounded by clusters of poplars and other trees dotted the table-land which we now entered. Proceeding about half a mile along a sandy plain, we reached the banks of a shallow streamlet coming from the west, with a marshy basin, in some parts of which there were deep pools. Crossing this rivulet on foot, we proceeded westwards for about half a mile, when we came across a *mandang* about 30 feet long and 8 feet broad. The images in relief on its four sides were freshly painted, though the *mandang* was an old stone pile. Two ragged monks, probably fatigued, were lying below its plinth on the east side, but we did not disturb their slumbers to make inquiries as to their destination. Travelling on a sandy plain for nearly four furlongs from this *mandang*, we arrived at the *dah* or foot of the monastery of Chhyang-chhub ling situated in the uplands to the north, and about half a mile to the left. The monastery appeared to be a respectable institution, for I was told that it contained upwards of a hundred monks. It was now past 7 A.M., and the husbandmen were out weeding their fields and collecting pot-herbs. There was slight rain, or rather a heavy dew-fall, and we met two parties of timber dealers proceeding towards Lhasa, leading laden yaks and donkeys. Then travelling forwards on a flat sandy slope for above three miles in a northerly direction, we arrived at a place called Tsha-khang. Here our way for a distance of nearly three hundred paces lay on marshy soil, where the ponies in some places sank up to their knees. These sands I guessed to be the deposits of the Kyi-chhu. Passing this with some difficulty, we arrived at the Semu hamlet, which contained four huts. I now felt very hungry, and Pador gave me a piece of boiled mutton from my saddle-bag, which I ate leisurely as we journeyed on. There was a dense fog enveloping everything around us, so that I could not see the river Kyi-chhu, while a range of rugged, forky, and bare cliffs obstructed our view towards the north and east. Proceeding nearly a mile towards the north-west, we arrived at the ruins of a fort called Tsha*l*-pa-naug, which evidently had been destroyed by the Kyi-chhu. Here we met our friends Norpu Tondub, Gergyan Tung, and others who had gone to escort Lhacham to Lhasa. The moment they saw me they dismounted from their ponies and, seizing my hands, every one of the party greeted me with the utmost cordiality at seeing me recovered from my illness. I told them how kind Dorje Phagmo had been to me, and how much my servants had helped me during my worst hours. We all sat down on the walls of the ruins to converse, but as two Kashmiri merchants and a Nepalese trader accompanied them, I talked in good Tibetan to escape detection. They looked hard at me, but I always avoided looking towards them. My friends did not care for the Kashmiris, and in course of conversation frequently addressed me as Pandibla, which I did not like. But fortunately the word was so much Tibetanized in pronunciation that the Kashmiris and the Nepalese could not make out what it signified. Our happy meeting lasted about an hour, when my companions hastened to resume the journey, as they intended to reach Nethang that day before sunset. Norpu Tondub advised us not to delay any longer at Tsha*l*-pa-nang, as then Nethang could not be reached before dusk, and Gergyan Tung told us that we could get very good accommodation for the night at the Gya-khang (Ampa's circuit-house). Norpu also secretly gave a *tanka* to Tshing-ta, with a request that he should serve me as faithfully as he had done at Samding. After expressing my thankfulness to both for the kind help they had lent me in times of need, I took leave of the party and we resumed our journey. The village of Tsha*l*-pa-nang contained several hamlets scattered over the valley of the Kyi-chhu, surrounded by groves of willows and poplars. In some ruins two or three poor families of herdsmen resided, and in the western corner of the ruined fort many cakes of cowdung were stuck on the ground to dry. The gateway under which we passed had still remains of grandeur. Passing this half-ruinous village we entered another gravelly and sandy plain, one part of which is washed by the Kyi-chhu. The plateau is nearly four miles long and about three or four broad. We met several rabbits on the way, which at our approach ran for life to the neighbouring mountains. Proceeding eastward along this plain for about four miles, we arrived at the village of Jang-hôg, or Lower Jang, in a fine flat country. The whole of Jang-hôg was green with vegetation, the young barley being eight to twelve inches high, and in almost every field one or two boys or women were picking a kind of edible herb which grew wild. Two women and a girl approached me with bunches of barley plants in their hands, and begged alms to help them in their work of cultivation. I did not reply to their supplication, and Pador told them that we were poor pilgrims who required money ourselves, so after following us for a short distance they fell back. This large village contained about a dozen hamlets and as many groves. Travelling upwards of a mile north-eastward, we arrived at the village of Jang-toi, or Upper Jang, which appeared to me still richer in vegetation, and indeed charmed me with its beauty. The pea, a kind of bean, and the white mustard now in blossom, brightened the places we passed before halting at 12 o'clock in a willow and poplar grove in the neighbourhood of a hamlet of this village. A limpid stream flowed by the middle of this grove to join the Kyi-chhu. Tshing-ta helped me in dismounting, and Pador spread my rug under the shadow of a willow. The scenery of the place was really refreshing, and though still an invalid, I stood for a while leaning on the bent stump of a willow to feast my eyes with the grateful scene of this fine village. Pador, who had gone to it in search of *chhang argol* (dung fuel) and eggs, returned after half an hour's absence with plenty of *chhang* and a little butter, besides some milk. Tea was prepared and poured in my China cup, when a *Chhangma*, or wine-seller, with a large bowl of wine in her hand, and two Dokpas with a few balls of butter, came to our little camp. I bought about five pounds of good butter from the latter for 12 annas, and gave a two-anna piece to Tshing-ta that he and Pador might refresh themselves with some wine. They got about a quarter gallon of barley-beer for that sum. Two other travellers cooked their food near us, and left the place before we had finished our breakfast. It was half-past one in the afternoon when we resumed our journey along the side of barley-fields. A gentle breeze blew, and a brilliant sunshine lighted up the scenery. This village contained about half a dozen hamlets with a few groves (*linka*). From Jang-toi, proceeding nearly three miles by a narrow, precipitous passage along the side of the river, we arrived at the village of Nam, which contained four hamlets. The lands here did not look fertile and the cultivation was scanty. Our way lay by the house of a villager who had several *jomos*, two of which he had yoked together to plough his fields. His cultivation was evidently rather late. From the uplands of this village due west comes down the streamlet Nam-chhu, which flows down to the Kyi-chhu. Immediately beyond the village of Nam, the road becomes a mere track along steep rocks and boulders overhanging the Kyi-chhu. It is called the *Gag-lam*, or " the contracted passage." This was the worst part of our journey. The river rushed at the foot of the *Gag-lam* with impetuous speed, and in some places there were large sand-banks which tempted us to leave the steep track and try to walk over the sands, but our fellow-travellers warned us not to do so, and to be careful in walking along the *Gag-lam:* a single false step here would plunge one in the eddies beneath. The whole of this dangerous passage extended nearly a mile and a half, and I was told that it was with great difficulty that the two elephants presented by the Sikkim Rajah to the grand Lama had passed this place. We saw many herds of yaks grazing in the pasture-lands along the banks of the Kyi-chhu. Passing this dreadful place we came to Lachhen-Lachhung, where our way lay sometimes on the rocky banks of the river, and at others on the sandy plain formed by its alluvial deposits. Here we were left behind by our fellow-travellers of Jang-toi. After a tedious journey of about three miles along the sands and rocks of the Kyi-chhu, we got sight of the famous village of Nethang, watered by a streamlet coming from a north-westerly direction and flowing into the Kyi-chhu. The plain of Nethang is very fertile, and is dotted with groves of willows, poplars, &c. Though still unwell, my spirits were enlivened by its refreshing scenery and its touching historical associations, for it was here that Atisha died. From a distance we saw a large barrack-like stone building, and proceeding for about half a mile we arrived at its gateway, where two mastiffs came howling towards us. The house, which was two-storied, about 50 feet long and 30 feet broad, did not appear to contain many inmates: only two women engaged in weaving blankets in the eastern portico and several *jomos* tied within the enclosed court. The windows and shutters were painted dark red, and contained carved ornamental work. I guessed it to be the property of some great man. There was not a single tree around or near it, probably because the lands here had been encroached on by the Kyi-chhu. Then travelling onward we entered a country covered with trees and verdure, and watered by numerous irrigation channels flowing with a gurgling noise through grassy plains overgrown with different kinds of shrubs now in blossom. Here we met an old man of whom Tshing-ta asked if we could get *na-tshang* (lodgings) for the night in any house in the village. The old man conducted us to the village, and arranged to put us up in a dilapidated but walled hut. I asked him if there were *da-shig* (demon-bug) in the house, when he replied, "Oh, sir, none can escape here from the bite of the *da-shig* at this season." So I declined to dismount from my pony, as I disapproved of the accommodation. An old woman then conducted us to the Gya-khang, or the Ampa's circuit-house, it being the nearest stage to Lhasa. At the gate of the circuit-house there was a signboard containing inscriptions in Chinese and Tibetan characters, and two flag-poles on two sides of the gateway. The Gya-khang resembled in its outward appearance a Calcutta native gentleman's house, and there were flower-vases kept in the verandah of the house in earthen vessels. The *Nabo* and *Namo* of the Gya-khang appeared very obliging and hospitable; and though they had other travellers in the house, on our promising to pay a *tanka* as *nala*, or house-rent, for the night, they accommodated us in one of the well-ventilated outer rooms, the inner rooms being reserved for the Government officials and particularly the Chinese resident and his staff. Although travellers are not ordinarily admitted into the Gya-khang, yet the keepers privately shelter them in the out-offices and the outer rooms. The flooring of the house was not good, the stones being very irregularly laid. As I preferred to sleep in the varandah, my companions hung two curtains in front and on the exposed side to shelter me from the rain and wind. After we were seated to refresh ourselves with tea, Pador told me that the back of one of the ponies was so swollen that it would hardly be able to carry its burden the next morning. But not minding him, I reflected on the past, and could not forbear shedding tears of joy that the All-merciful Father in his endless mercy had brought us safe thus far, that I could feast my eyes with the sight of that antique and sacred spot where one of my illustrious countrymen had preached the sacred tenets of pure Buddhism to the great Tibetan nation. With what pleasure I reflected on the life of Dipankara-sri-jnana, that saintly native of Bengal to whom the revival of Buddhism in Tibet was chiefly due! I was proud to think that I was the second native of Bengal who, after a lapse of nearly a thousand years, had visited this sacred country of the Boddhisattvas, a land which is little known to the civilized world. The name *Atisha*, by which Dipankara-sri is universally known in Tibet, is deeply venerated by all sects and denominations of Buddhists of high Asia. Tsonkhapa merely revived the school which Atisha had founded in Tibet, his Lamrim-chhenpo being nothing more than an elaborate commentary on the Sal-don-me, or Pradipa of Atisha. Dipankara-sri is therefore the greatest of saints that ever visited Tibet after Padma Sambhava. The history of the latter is shrouded in myths, but the life of Atisha is free from extravagance and is a historical fact of undisputed authenticity. In fact, the real history and chronology of Tibet based on genuine facts commences from the days of Atisha.

A SHORT LIFE OF ATISHA.

In the country of Bangala, which lies to the east of Vajrsana (Buddha Gaya), there was a great and populous city (Sahor), the metropolis of Bangala, called Vikramanipur. Including its suburbs, it contained two millions and seven hundred thousand souls, 720 groves, 1,025 tanks for bathing, innumerable palm-trees, 363 bridges and culverts, besides 1,025 golden *dvajas* (domes). The central palace was thirteen stories high, each of which was adorned and marked by a golden dome constructed in the shape of the sacred car. Round the palace compound there were seven concentric courses of railings. The chief of this city was named Bhu Indra Chandra, who by his wife, Prabhavati, had three sons, viz. Padma Garbha, Chandra Garbha, and Sri Garbha. The first succeeded to his father's dignities, and married five wives, by whom he had nine sons; and the last betook himself to monkhood, became an ascetic, and was known by his religious name of Virya Chandra. The second son was the illustrious Atisha. He was born in 1815 of the Buddhist era (corresponding with the year 982 A.D.) according to the chronology of Bromtan. Atisha, from his early boyhood, was a devoted votary of the goddess Arya Tara, whose blessings he enjoyed. Up to the 21st year of his age he devoted his time to the study of grammar, rhetoric, logic, arithmetic and medicine according to both Buddhistic and heretic (Brahmanical) systems, in all of which he acquired great proficiency. In the twenty-second year of his age he commenced taking instructions in religion from Rahula Gupta Vajra, who gave him the secret name of Jnana Guhya Vajra. During his study of the *Tantras* he is said to have been miraculously visited by his tutelary deity, who helped him to become an adept in the Sunyata philosophy. He held controversies with the Brahmanical pandits, most of whom he converted to Buddhism by his powerful logic and reasoning. At the age of 29, under divine inspiration, and being exhorted by some saintly sages, he received the vows of monkhood from Acharya Shila Rakshita, who on that occasion gave him the name of Dipankara Sri Jnana. Subsequently he assiduously applied himself to the investigation of the sacred books of the Brahmanas and the Sramanas, in which task he received hints on sacred literature from about 50 learned professors, and became a profoundly read scholar. At last, without a rival in the knowledge of the *Tantras*, he fancied within himself that there were few books which he had not read; but this conceit was subdued by his being miraculously shewn by the gods numberless other books on religion and literature. Hearing now the fame of a learned pandit of Serling (Svarnadvipa, probably the modern Burmah or Siam), named Dharma Kirti, he visited that famous country in company with some merchants. The party crossed the great sea in a large ship moved by sails, passing on the voyage a colossal statue of Buddha under whose outstretched legs the ship had to pass, and on which flocks of birds had perched. Atisha also stated in his diary that he had seen sea-monsters, such as gigantic alligators, sharks, &c., in the seas and rivers between Jambudvipa (India) and Svarnadvipa. Arrived at Svarnadvipa, he introduced himself to the sage Dharma Kirti, and stayed with him for twelve years. During this long period he learnt the language of the country, and held exhaustive discussions with the sage on metaphysics and religion, and as a learned pandit of India, visiting Svarnadvipa, Atisha obtained great celebrity all over that country. After twelve years, joining a company of merchants, he returned to Jambudvipa (India). On his return to Bangala he was invited by king Mahapala to fill the Abbotship of Vajrasana (Gaya), and was subsequently appointed to the Abbotship of Vikrama Shila. At the invitation of king Chyang Chub-hod of Tibet he visited Tibet in the 72nd year of his age. After visiting different sanctuaries in U and Tsang, such as Lhasa, Samye, &c., he returned to this place (Nethang). Here, in the temple situated at the upland, he meditated for the welfare of all living beings for a period of seven years, and we were shewn the yellow temple situated in the middle of a *linka* (Atisha's hermitage), where his remains were entombed.

The village of Nethang contains about 40 to 50 houses, all clustered together. The people obtain their water from the streams and also from wells. The houses by the way-side were closely constructed, rising sometimes from two to three stories high; but some were of a very mean and filthy appearance. At dusk a party of travellers arrived, consisting of about a dozen men and several ponies and donkeys, and spent the night in the court of the Gya-khang. These men, I was told, were servants of Sawang Rampa, the Chief Shape (Minister) of Lhasa. One of the party, a groom, was an acquaintance of Pador, and kindly promised to apply medicines to our pony's back next morning. Pador also begged the *Nabo* to engage a pony or donkey to carry our baggage to Lhasa, as our pack-pony was ailing, and he accordingly sent the *Namo*, his wife, to the village for the purpose, but she returned at about 9 P.M. unsuccessful. A gale blew at midnight. Early in the morning Pador went to the village in search of a pack-pony for hire. The villagers had many donkeys and pack-ponies, but they would not let only one or two on hire: if I agreed to take at least half a dozen animals, they would readily agree to enter our service; so the negociation for a pack-pony failed, and Pador returned to the Gya-khang disappointed.

30th May.—We hastened to take breakfast and resume our journey as early as possible. Two boiled eggs and a few slices of mutton with a handful of barley-flour were given to me, with which I fortified myself to stand the fatigues of the day's journey. Proceeding eastward, we waded along a narrow road now filled with water. We passed by several respectable houses, gardens, and orchards. The hamlets of Norpu-gang and Chhumig-gang contained handsome, respectable-looking buildings, which, I was told, belonged to some of the distinguished Dung-kors (civil officers) of Lhasa. Then travelling along the table-land, the upper part of which was filled with gravel and splintered rocks, we came to a gap between two rocky cliffs which from a distance appeared like a gigantic gateway. Here a ragged woman, engaged in removing sharp and pointed stones from the middle of the road, begged for *bakshish*, and I gave her a two-anna piece. The river Kyi-chhu flowed at a distance of half a mile to the south-east to our left, and turned behind this gap towards the north to wash the hill-side along which our way lay. For a distance of nearly four miles both on the right and left of our way there were sand-banks and stagnant pools of water caused by the changes in the wild and meandering course of this stream. Then we arrived at a place where a magnificent view of Potala and Chogpoiri, with their lofty buildings surmounted by glittering gilt domes, presented itself, most imposing from this distance. I was transported with the fulfilment of my hope of one day being able to see Lhasa—a long-cherished dream of my life. There were no clouds in the sky, and the gilt domes through a serene and clear atmosphere glowed with the reflected rays of the sun. Here we took a short rest under the shade of a rock. My knees, on account of the shortness of the stirrups of the Tibetan saddle, pained much, and I could hardly stretch my legs. I wished much to walk, but my health did not permit me to do so. Here was painted a gigantic fresco image of Buddha on a stone slab, about 16 feet high. On the shoulders of the image was a rainbow-coloured nimbus. On the top of the rock slab was a flat wooden roof supported by six beams and two walls on the right and left of the image evidently to support the roof. The whole structure had the appearance of a chapel. The image, I was told, was seated so as to look towards the great image of Buddha at Lhasa. Numerous pigeons roosted in the lower side of the roof. Proceeding for a little more than four miles along a tolerably good road in the lower part of the great village of Toilung, we reached the Thi-chhu *ssampa*, a very large and handsome stone bridge, and I was struck with the excellent stonework of the piers and the approaches of the bridge. Underneath it flowed a rivulet which came meandering from the north-west uplands, where, I was told, the famcus monastery of Tshorpu is situated. That monastery was founded by Karma Bag-shi, one of the two celebrated Lamas who were invited to the imperial court of China by the Emperor Khublai in the 13th century. The bridge is supported by large wooden beams, and is about 120 paces long and six to eight paces broad. The plain of Toilung, being watered by numerous streamlets cut from the Toilung river, and being situated immediately above the Kyi-chhu of which it is the valley, is extremely fertile, with numerous hamlets dotted over it. Tall poplars and branching willows planted in little groves by the villagers added much to the beauty of the place. The country was now green on all sides, and the barley, buck-wheat, and wheat in some places were a foot high. We crossed several streamlets which irrigated this rich table-land. Parties of grain-dealers and *argol* carriers with trains of donkeys, mules, ponies, and yaks followed and preceded us. The tinkling of the bells attached to the necks of the donkeys served to announce the movements of parties of traders to each other from a distance. Proceeding about half a mile we passed by the hamlet of Ker-tsa with half a dozen houses lying on the road-side. About half a mile further off were the villages of Shing-Donkar and Tahje, the latter lying on the road-side, and the former with half a dozen houses about a hundred yards distant from the road-side. It was surrounded with tall poplars planted in rows and small willow trees planted irregularly. We halted for breakfast in a small grove in front of the village of Shing-Donkar. Two spirited ponies were tied to a willow stump close to where we had sat down to cook our food by a stream of clear water. Pador first attended to the ponies, and carefully examining the back of the pack-pony, told me that it was fit for work. Tshing-ta cooked *phing-sha* and tea for us, with which we made a hearty breakfast. In the village a religious ceremony was being conducted by about eighteen monks from Dapung monastery. A large mastiff was tied at the entrance of the village. A few beggars who had come to supplicate for alms from the villagers stopped on their way at our halting-place, and begged some barley-flour from Tshing-ta. Pador obtained about four pints of malt beer from the village for one *kha* (anna). An elderly-looking woman who came to pour the liquor from her wine bowl into our companions' cups told us that all the villages near Shing-Dongkar on this side of Toilung belonged to Sa-wang Ragasha, one of the senior *Shapes* of Lhasa, and that the monks were assembled to perform religious ceremonies for the recovery of the *shiner*, or farm headman, from an attack of small-pox. The houses in the village were respectable-looking and seemed to be the residence of well-to-do people. A paper-seller came to sell nice *daphne* paper, but as we expected to reach Lhasa within a few hours, Tshing-ta did not allow me to buy more than eight sheets, which I got for one *kha* (anna). Some radish-sellers also came and importuned us to buy some radish from them. At about 2 P.M. we resumed our journey. Proceeding a little more than a mile, we arrived at the village of Donkar, situated on an eminence, and consisting of upwards of twenty families. This place is said to be the first stage up to which people travel at the public expense when availing themselves of their road bills. It is commonly called Sa-tsi, or the "first stage" for conveyances from and to Lhasa. Several coolies were engaged in road-making, whom we had to pay about half a *tanka* as encouragement in their work. They told us they were not paid by Government, but were working under forced labour rules. Proceeding in an easterly direction along a tolerably good road, we arrived at the village of Cheri, which contained twelve houses; and close to this village was a large grove, surrounded by a stone wall, about 400 paces long, which we passed on our right. Inside the grove several monks were sitting on the grass under the cooling shades of willow and walnut trees, and behind it at a short distance was the slaughter-place where daily hundreds of sheep, goats, and yaks are killed. Adjoining was a small tank in which the carcasses are washed. Quite a small mound was formed by heaping the excrements from the stomach of the animals killed. The scavengers had not yet removed these, and they emitted an offensive smell. The Tibetans do not spare even the intestines of animals, but eat them, together with the gristle of the joints after pounding them. The Kashmiri Mussalmans come here to buy meat. Although the Mussalmans are known to be very strict in observing the orthodox manner of slaughtering animals, yet these Kashmiris of Lhasa evince great laxity in that respect, and readily eat yaks slaughtered by the Tibetans with arrows or knives driven in their stomachs. Proceeding northward we came near the *sho* or lay village of Daru, at the foot of the hill on the upper flank of which the famous monastery of Dapung is situated. Here Pador asked my leave to go into the village to engage one of his most intimate friends to serve me, and pointing out to me his friend's house with his finger, ran off towards it. Several Tibetan gentlemen rode by casting an occasional look towards me. Some admired my pony; others inquired where that sick man, meaning me, was going. Some replied to such inquiries by saying "he seems going to Lhasa;" others, "he is probably going out of Lhasa." But none asked me any questions whatever. Here on the road-side there were heaps of sheep and goat-horns which were evidently thrown away by the butchers as useless. Extending to the front of the monastery of Dapung to our left hand side was the great park belonging to Dapung.

After half an hour's absence Pador returned without bringing anybody with him: his friend was not at home, having gone to the market of Lhasa. So we slowly proceeded onwards. A table-land now opened extending to Lhasa to the east and to the Kyi-chhu to the south-east. I saw large stumps of old trees resembling *shovo* (poplar), but could not ascertain the names of the several kinds of trees, which were large and old enough to attract anybody's attention. Proceeding a few hundred paces eastward we came in front of the far-famed temple of Nachhung Chhoikyong, the oracle by which the Government of Tibet is guided in all important matters. The temple is a fine edifice of a dark red colour, surmounted by a gilt dome, constructed after the Chinese fashion. The several tall trees which surround the monastery being all within the walls of the premises, considerably added to the beauty of the place. Our way now receded towards the direction of the river Kyi-chhu, whence I obtained a magnificent view of the renowned city, as it now appeared to our north-east-by-east, with the slanting rays of the sun falling on its gilded domes. It was indeed a superb sight, the like of which I never beheld in India. The monastery of Dapung, perched on a distant hill-side, was partly seen and partly hid under a ledge of the Dapung hill, but this we soon left behind, and Potala and Lhasa now engrossed my entire attention. Passing by the grove sacred to Nachhung, we entered a marshy flat intersected by numerous water-passages. Several of these I crossed riding. Crowds of people were proceeding towards Lhasa, some on horseback, some on donkeys, and many on foot. Several monks, probably from Dapung, were also proceeding towards the same destination. We now found ourselves in a marsh overgrown with rank grass. This marsh is called Dam-tsho, and the grass, *dam-tsa*. Channels cut to drain the water of the marsh flowed towards the Kyi-chhu across our way. To the north-north-east of this marsh at the foot of some barren hills stood the monastery of Sera. Passing by the Dam-tsho we arrived at the great *maidan* of Lhasa called *Nehu-sing*, which was covered with verdure. The grass was in blossom, which gave the *maidan* the appearance of a carpet variegated with beautiful flowers. Numerous gardens and groves were dotted over it. On our right hand side we saw an extensive embankment like an accumulation of sand, on the further side of which is situated the great park called Norpu-linga, containing a beautiful palace, while immediately on our left hand was the pasture-land Kyang-thang Naga, to the north-east of which extended the beautiful grove of Kemaitshal with a palatial building in the middle, the property of Lhalu, the father of the late Dalai Lama. We then passed by the meadow Chyaray, where we saw several monks lying down idly as if they had no anxieties whatever. It was about 4 P.M. when we arrived in the vicinity of Kunduling, the residence of the regent, the *de facto* King of Tibet. Tshing-ta now begged me to dress myself properly like a Tibetan, that I might not appear like a *Palpo* (Nepalese merchant). I covered my head with a piece of coarse red silk, and put on my spectacles that I might see everything. My companions objected to this, but I told them that the use of spectacles in Tibet was general, and that if my appearance did not betray my foreign nationality, the spectacles would do very little to prejudice the people and authorities of Lhasa against me. Tshing-ta pointed out to me the hills Chogpoiri and Pamoiri. On the top of the latter I was shown a temple named Gya-lha Khang, which is the place of worship of the Chinese exclusively. Just as I was entering the city gate called Pargo Kaling Chhorten, I saw the elephant which was lately presented to the Dalai Lama by the Rajah of Sikkim. This was the survivor of the two elephants presented by the British Government to Sikkim a few months ago.

IV.—RESIDENCE AT LHASA.

30*th May* (*continued*).—It was past 4 o'clock in the afternoon when we entered the renowned city of Lhasa by the western gateway, called the Pargo Kaling chhorten, having the grand palace of Potala, the residence of the Dalai Lama, on our left. The lofty buildings of Potala, with their towers and numerous gilt roofs, and the *Sho* (lay town), with its lofty white-washed houses, engrossed all my attention. People, monks and laymen, looked out of their windows as we were passing by. The architectural peculiarity of the houses of Potala, especially the prismoidal shape of the windows, fringed below the lintels, and their curiously painted cornice, arrested our attention at the very entrance. The broad road along which we travelled was lined with aged trees. The Chinese-fashioned houses, roofed with bluish glazed tiles, having turrets in the middle, the numerous festoons of inscribed and painted rags which stretched from one turret of a house to another, the green appearance of the meadows, all combined to give a majestic and imposing appearance to this renowned metropolis of Tibet. Pador walked ahead of us, shouldering his long lance, on the point of which a red banner fluttered to the wind. Tshing-ta followed him, whip in hand, leading the pack-pony. I came last. People and the *korchagpas* (Lhasa policemen) marked us as new-comers, but none cared to ask who we were and whence we came. My head drooped with fatigue, the goggle spectacles covered my eyes, and the red cloth *pagri* gave me the appearance of a Ladaki coming from the farthest west of Tibet. People evidently took me for a *Nepa* (a sick man) attacked with small-pox and eye-disease, for some Tibetans, standing in front of a Chinaman's pastry shop, said to one another—"Look there, another *Nepa* is coming. His eyes appear to be affected by *lhandum* (small-pox). The city is filled with *Nepa*: what an unlucky time it is for Tibet this year!" Such an observation from the Tibetans was most welcome to me, and I smiled within myself, thinking how safe it was for me to pass for a *Nepa*, whom all pity but loathe to converse with! A few minutes after we came to Yuthog *ssampa*, a small stone bridge with a turret and a large gateway, where the *korchagpas*, headed by a monk-sergeant, keep watch. Fortunately I was not interrogated by anybody, and we crossed the *ssampa* quietly. Both Pador and Tshing-ta, whose anxiety on my account was very great, now smiled with joy, for at the gate even Tibetans are examined and required to state the object of their coming to Lhasa. On our right we had left the Doring, on the monolith of which there are inscriptions in Tibetan and Chinese. As I had read an account of those inscriptions in Dr. Bushell's contribution to the Royal Asiatic Society, I carefully looked at the inscriptions to see if they were not much worn out and obliterated; but though nearly a thousand years old, yet little affected by the weather or by time's unsparing hand, they could be easily read by a careful epigraphist. The monolith from a distance appeared to be about 8 to 10 feet high. Its pedestal was very low. I saw several Chinese houses, roofed with glazed tiles, before entering the city of Lhasa, which, properly speaking, commences at the Yuthog *ssampa*.

Both sides of the street were lined with shops kept by Tibetan and Chinese merchants. In front of every shop and house there was a chimney-shaped pyramidal clay structure in which incense is burnt as offerings to gods. The dried leaves of the juniper and different kinds of arborescent firs, obtained from Tsari and other places, were being burnt as we passed, and smoked profusely, emitting a peculiar fragrant smell. We then came to the street on the south of Ki*l*-khording, on both sides of which stood the shops of the Nepalese merchants, two to three stories high. The Chinese shops were adorned with beautifully arranged China articles, such as porcelain, silk fabrics, different kinds of brick-tea, &c. From the street we were led into a lane, proceeding along which for about three hundred yards I was shown the residence of Sawang Phala, called Bangye-shag, a castle-like building three stories high. We did not go to the front of it, but Pador took us to the postern, where, asking me and Tshing-ta to wait, he entered the servants' quarters to inquire if Lhacham was at home and if we could pay our respects to her. Pador being an old servant of Sawang Phala, had a good many acquaintances among the menials there, and had free access to the lower story, where Phala's *amlahs* sit to do office work. After a few minutes' absence, he returned with the news that Lhacham was engaged in conversation with a lady of rank, who had come to see her. Tshing-ta then left me alone at the gateway, and entered the house in company with Pador, to present Lhacham my scarf of respect, and to ask if we were to wait upon her ladyship at Bangye-shag. When both were gone, a beggar came with three ewes to where I stood holding the two ponies by the bridle, and relieved me of this task unasked. I had a chat with him, from which I came to know that he occupied a small cell in one of the out-offices of Bangye-shag. Presently Pador and Tshing-ta came back with downcast looks of disappointment. Tshing-ta said that Lhacham declined to give us *Na-tshang* (accommodation) at Bangye-shag, but had asked him to take me to Pa*l*-jor Rabtan, belonging to the Tashi Lama, where all officers and monks from Tashi-lhunpo generally get quarters. If there were no rooms at Pa*l*-jor Rabtan, she would make arrangements for my accommodation elsewhere. She did not tell him the reason for her declining to accommodate us at Bangye-shag, but had offered to do all in her power to protect me, and to see that I might not be put to inconvenience for anything during my stay at Lhasa, and concluded by asking Tshing-ta to take me to her presence on the following day. So, after this somewhat unexpected and indifferent reception from Lhacham, we slowly moved towards Pa*l*-jor Rabtan, situated between Ki*l*-khording and the great monastery of Tangye-ling. I waited in a lane at a distance of about a hundred yards from the gate, while Pador and Tshing-ta went to ask the *Khang-ner* (the officer in charge of the premises belonging to the Tashi Lama at Lhasa) leave to occupy two rooms in the Pa*l*-jor Rabtan. An old woman who occupied one of the out-offices asked if I was not from Tashi-lhunpo, and if I did not like to take rooms at Pa*l*-jor Rabtan: if so, she would fetch water for us and serve us obediently. I did not reply to her inquiries, but turned my pony aside to let her pass. After she had passed, a monk and a respectable-looking layman asked me where I intended to put up, to which I replied at Pa*l*-jor Rabtan. My companions returned shortly after with smiling looks, and Tshing-ta said that he had obtained the *Khang-ner's* permission to occupy a room in Pa*l*-jor Rabtan. "What kind of accommodation? Are there any *dashig* (demon-fly)?" said I. "*Gahmo dug*, the accommodation is good, but there are *dashig*. There are very few houses in this city which are free from that pest," said Tshing-ta. I hesitated to go; but as my companions remonstrated against my staying in the street any longer, as that would excite the curiosity of the neighbouring householders respecting ourselves, I reluctantly proceeded towards the gateway, which was about 8 to 9 feet high and 5 feet broad, and from the lintels of which fringes about a foot and a half broad fluttered to the wind. Two stout flag-poles, about 20 to 25 feet high, carrying inscribed banners, stood on two sides. Ascending a steep staircase resembling a ladder, we came to an open verandah, opposite to which was a pretty glazed house, the residence of the *Khang-ner*. We waited here for a while to allow our room to be dusted by Pador. After we had entered, an elderly woman, an acquaintance of my companion, who lived in an out-office, came in and after serving me with tea from a *chambim*, and Tshing-ta with *chhang* in his *phorpa* (wooden cup), conversed with him about her other acquaintances and friends.

At 6 a heavy shower of rain fell and a high wind blew, but it soon cleared up, when from the window of our room I could see the *damra*, the grove of poplars and willows on a marshy belt of land round the monastery of Tangye-ling, which adjoined the premises of Pa*l*-jor Rabtan, while to the far west shone the lofty gilt domes of Potala. The skies were again covered with rain clouds, and chill blasts rushed into my room, when I resumed my seat. I asked Tshing-ta how I could save myself during sleep from the attacks of the *dashig*. Tshing-ta ominously replied that the *dashig* would come out from the holes in the walls at midnight to suck our blood, but that they could not be seen now. I was very much frightened at this account of the demon-bug, and asked Tshing-ta to find out a spot within the spacious premises where I could sleep without disturbance from those blood-thirsty pests. It was raining heavily at this time. Pador had prepared some tea, with which I managed to eat a few balls of barley paste. I was much fatigued on account of the journey and my ill-health. At 7 P.M. my rugs were spread on a heap of fleece lying in the inner open verandah of the house, as it was thought to be free from *dashig*. After wrapping me with my woollens, my companions retired to their sleeping places—Tshing-ta to the room where our things were lying, and Pador to the stables downstairs. After an hour's rain, the skies cleared up, there was brilliant moonlight, and the whole vault was illumined with stars.

31*st May*.—The morning was fine, and the scenery all round was delightful. The magnificent view of the lofty buildings of Potala, Tangye-ling, Ki*l*-khording and Rading, the gilt domes of which glittered in the slanting rays of the morning sun, enraptured my heart. I was impatient to visit them, and anxiously waited for the arrival of Tshing-ta, who was gone to see Lhacham Kusho. Pador was busy with the ponies, the back of one of which was still swollen. Both from the roof, and from the western window of our room I viewed the distant mountain sceneries of this lovely country. Though not well recovered from my late illness, and still suffering from dry coughing and shortness of breath, my spirits were high, now that the goal of my journey was reached. This dreamland of my life was now a waking reality with numberless objects for patient and life-long study. At 7 A.M. Pador cleaned the room, arranged our things, and then brought a kettle of tea prepared in the house of our water-carrier. I did not like it on account of the lard mixed with it instead of butter, as the water-carrier's wife had stolen our butter and replaced it by sheep's lard; so I ordered my servant to cleanse our own hearth and to prepare fresh tea for me. Shortly after Tshing-ta returned with a pair of stuffed seats, a pair of tiny dining-tables, and a pair of pillows which he had borrowed from Lhacham Kusho. He was delighted with the reception he had met from Lhacham, and conveyed to me her sincere congratulation for my recovery, and her desire to see me in the afternoon if that would be convenient for me. After breakfast, my companions went to the Lhasa *thom* to make purchases. A list was drawn up by Tshing-ta of articles for religious service, which I considerably curtailed on the ground that as our object was not to make a name, but to make obeisance to the all-knowing Buddha, we should only limit ourselves to the purchase of articles indispensable for conducting an economical service. I felt somewhat chill and unwell as I lay alone covered with my woollens. In the rooms adjoining ours were some monks from Tashi-lhunpo and Upper Tibet, who had lately been attacked with small-pox. One of them, named Tomola, now convalescent, came to my room, and, seeing me laid up, warned me not to sleep, as that would make me worse. Two other monks living in the same house, and the wife of our water-carrier, also came to see me. They too warned me not to sleep in the day-time. A little after noon Tshing-ta and Pador returned from the market, and hastened to equip me for a visit to Bangye-shag. I shaved myself, and dressed in my Lama costume, with my goggles on, slowly proceeded towards Lhacham's residence by a short lane running straight from our house through Pa*l*-jor Rabtan to the front of Ki*l*-khording. Then taking the grand road, we arrived at the northern gate of Bangye-shag. The two sides of the road were lined with shops kept by Kashmiris, Nepalese, and Chinese merchants. The Tibetan shops were few and very poor, while the Chinese shops were well adorned with articles for show. The Nepalese being largely employed in trading in piece-goods, Chinese satin, and precious things, were less showy than the Chinamen. I feared coming across known faces, from whom alone I feared any injury, consciously or unconsciously. The distance from our lodging to Bangye-shag was about a mile. Arrived there, I waited in the lobby of the ground-floor and sent in Pador, who, being an old servant of Phala, was well-known to all the domestics and members of Phala's family. Bangye-shag is a lofty flat-roofed castle, three stories high, with two large gateways on the north and south. The ground-floor is used as a store-room and quarters for the *amlahs* of the estates of the Phala family in the province of U. The building was constructed of finely-dressed stones, and little mortar was used. The beams, the external cornice, and the window frames were painted red. Some of the windows were glazed, but most were papered. Presently Pador arrived and conducted us to the second floor, where Lhacham waited to see me. I carried the *jahdar* (visiting scarf) in my hand and a gold *sho* (about a tolah weight) to present to her ladyship. As soon as I came to the second floor, the *Shetama* (maid-servants) Apela and Patonla greeted me, joining their palms and saying "*Kusho Pandibla, Chhyag phenag chig.*" They were delighted to see me again, but remarked that I was extremely reduced in health. They hastened to bring tea and pressed me to take one or two cups of the steaming draught. Presently I was conducted to Lhacham's presence by Apela, where, taking off my hat, I presented the scarf to her ladyship, together with the *sho* of gold. Silently ordering Apela to present me a scarf in return, "*Chyag-phe nang chig, Pandibla*" (welcome, Pandit sir), she said in a gentle voice, and graciously inquired after my health. "Is all right now with you?" inquired her ladyship. "No, *Kusho-khyen* (your gracious ladyship); I am far from being so. I feel great difficulty in breathing, especially in making ascents. In ascending the staircases of your ladyship's residence I had to take rest twice or thrice. I am very feeble yet." "*Akka-kha* (what sorrow), I hope you will now gradually recover; your eyes look better; of course it will be some time before you get restored to health," said she. I thanked her warmly, and rising from my seat saluted her a second time, taking off my hat. She seemed much gratified by this appreciation of her kindness and pointing with her hand said, "*Pandibla, Shu-dan Shag, Shu-dan Shag*" (Pandit, sir, take your seat, take your seat). She then inquired after the health of Dorje Phagmo, and the treatment I had received from that incarnate Abbess of Yamdo. "Kusho-khyen, through your kindness, we were accorded a very cordial reception in the Yamdo Samding monastery. As soon as Dorje Phagmo received your ladyship's letter, she ordered her Dsim-gag-pa to conduct me to her presence; but as I was unable to ascend the several staircases which lead to her lofty residence I failed to see her the day I went to Samding. She promised every help, and indeed lent me all the assistance I asked of her. I must now, as in duty bound, say with a grateful recollection of my residence at Samding, that I owe my recovery, nay, my life, to the kindness of that merciful and blessed Lady of the Lake. I would also now take the opportunity to say that my feelings of gratitude to your ladyship know no bounds, and that even if I knew the language of Tibet thoroughly, I could hardly have found words adequately to express them." After a little more talk I took my leave.

1st June.—To-day being the holiest day of the year—the anniversary of Buddha's *nirvana*—the burning of incense in every shrine, chapel, monastery, and house had almost darkened the atmosphere with smoke. Even on the lofty *lhakha* (mountain-top) shouting invocations of the gods and dark fumigations were noticed as early as day-break, and the entire city of Lhasa was thrown into a state of religious insanity. Men, women, and children were hastening to the sacred shrine of Ki*l*-khording to do homage to the *Chovo* (Lord Buddha) and to obtain his blessing. They carried in their hands bundles of incense-sticks, bowls filled with melted butter, and scarves of different sizes and qualities. Our neighbours also hastened to the Cho-khang (the temple of the Lord Buddha), calling at my room as they passed. Pador prepared tea and barley paste, off which I breakfasted in haste, fearing if we delayed the Cho-khang would be thronged by pilgrims. I proposed to leave Pador to guard our little possessions, but Tshing-ta represented that Pador would be disappointed if we left him behind at this auspicious time of *sagadawa* (anniversary of *nirvana*), and besides he would like very much to be in our company to hear the explanation of the historical and sacred images in the Cho-khang, so I agreed to my companion's proposal, when a flush of cheerfulness glowed in Pador's face. He locked the room and gently led me downstairs by the hand. The lane which divided Panjor Rabtan and Chyan-Sreb, our lodging, was extremely filthy. Crossing this infernal lane, stopping my nose with a handkerchief, we entered the premises of Pa*l*-jor Rabtan, generally called Panjor Rabtan. Tshing-ta talked with an acquaintance of his while passing below the balcony of a two-storied house, and though pressed to take tea with him, he did not delay here, but hastened to conduct me out of the alley, which was too narrow to allow two men to pass together. Arriving at the broad street, we waited for a few minutes in front of a shop, until Pador made his appearance, when we all proceeded to the Cho-khang. A broad street runs from north to south in front of it, while the western grand road, which comes from Pargo Kaling gate, terminates at the western entrance of the Cho-khang. At its junction, but a little to the west, bordering the Panjor Rabtan, is a tall branching poplar, which is said to spring from the consecrated hair of Buddha. Here also stands the most ancient *doring* (monolith) erected by the Tibetans to commemorate their victory over the Chinese in the 9th century. I was told that it also contained inscriptions of a treaty between the Emperor of China and King Ra*l*pachan. The grand and magnificent temple of Buddha, more a palace than a temple, now engrossed our attention. In front of its entrance stood a lofty flag-pole, the shaft of which was forty feet high. At its foot and sides two tufts of yak hair, some inscriptions, and several yak and sheep horns, were tied. A gentle breeze blew, which set in motion the leaves of the poplar. At the entrance of the Cho-khang was a fine frontispiece containing inscriptions in Chinese and Tibetan, probably setting forth the year, name, and titles of the princess who had erected this far-famed temple. The entrance, or more properly the portico, was a thick colonnade of wooden pillars, each of which was three to four feet in girth and about twelve feet high. Here upwards of a hundred monks were engaged in making profound salutations to the shrine. We next entered the Tsang-khang (principal shrine), where the holiest of holies was seated, looking towards the west on an exalted throne. This image of Buddha, called Chovo-Rinpo-chhe, is said to have been constructed in Magadha during the life-time of the great teacher, who had personally consecrated it after it was recognized to be his youthful likeness. Tradition ascribes its origin to Visva-karma, the divine architect who, under instructions from Indra, constructed it of an alloy of the "ten celestial and terrestrial precious things," such as gold, silver, zinc, iron, lead, copper, and the five "precious articles" of the gods. Whatever may be the legendary accounts of the origin of this famous image, it is certain it was constructed with an alloy of equal parts of the five metals that were known to the ancients. The "five precious articles" must have been diamond, ruby, lapis-lazuli, emerald, and *Indra nila*. We saw plenty of these precious stones in the decorations of the person of Chovo. From Magadha the image was sent to the metropolis of China at the special request of the Emperor, and in return for his helping the King of Magadha against the invasions of Yavanas from the west. The princess Konjo, daughter of Emperor Thaijung, as a condition of her going to Tibet and for her consolation during the exile, obtained the image as a part of her marriage dowry. This took place in the second quarter of the seventh century A.D. The image, which was life-size, was exquisitely modelled and glittered with gold gilding. The crown on its head is said to be the gift of Tsong-khapa, the great reformer. We were told by the Kuner that the image was a likeness of Buddha when only twelve years of age, so that being then a prince and dressed in a princely costume, he could not be represented in his appearance of Buddha-hood: hence it was that the image was unlike the common images of Buddha seen in the temples of Magadha, Singhala, and Serling. The image was truly lovely, and represented, not the great Sramana, but a prince of handsome person and countenance. On four sides were four dragon pillars of silver gilt with gold which supported the royal umbrella like a canopy. On its right and left were the bronze images of Maitreya and Manjusri. Behind Buddha, we were pointed out the most sacred image of Buddha Dvipankara, behind which was seated the image of Tathagata called Gang-chan-hogya*l*, constructed by Ssankhar Lo-tsava of Kashmir. On the right and left of the latter image stood in votive mood twelve Bodhisattras, the disciples of Buddha. Behind these we were shown the image of Maitreya and Manjusri, constructed by the well-known chief of Ling-chhyag. We were then shown the image of the great reformer Tsongkhapa, near which was the fossil rock, called Amolonkha, discovered by Tsongkhapa himself in a rock cavern in Tibet. On the rock was placed the historical bell with a gem as its handle, said to have been used by Moungalputtra. Next to the image of Buddha the most conspicuous figure was that of Chanrassig chu-chig shal (the eleven faced Avolokitesvara). The origin of this is ascribed to King Srong-tsan gampo. Once the king heard a voice from heaven, saying that if he constructed an image of Chanrassig of the size of his own person, his wishes would be fulfilled. Accordingly King Srong-tsan constructed an image of the eleven-faced Chanrassig. The materials used in it were the branch of the sacred Bodhi tree of the Vajrasana brought by a miracle-working *Gelong*, the soil of an oceanic island, the sand of the river Nairanjana, the pith of sandal-wood, a piece of Gourshish, the soil of the eight sacred places of ancient India, and very many other rare and valuable articles pounded together and made into paste with the milk of a red cow and a she-goat. This clay paste the king touched with his head, and prayed to the all-knowing Buddhas and the host of Bodhisattvas that by the moral merit of making that image there might be god-speed to the great work he had undertaken, namely, the introduction and diffusion of Buddhism in Tibet. The gods, Buddhas, saints, &c., filled the aërial space to listen to the prayer of the mighty and pious king, and blessed him and retired when the ceremony of consecration was over. The king then ordered the Nepalese artist to quicken the completion of the image, and to heighten its sanctity he ordered that the sandal-wood image of Avalokitesvara obtained from Singhala by the miraculous *Gelong*, might be put inside this image, together with the relics of the seven past Tathagatas. When the work was finished, the artist said, "Sire, I cannot say that I have made this image, but it has passed into self-grown existence." Instantly the lowermost face of the image was miraculously drawn up a little above its left knee, and from the insteps of its feet flashed forth a current of lightning. Afterwards the souls of the king and his queens are said to have been absorbed in it, in consequence of which this image is called the Na-dan rang-chyung, or "the five absorbed self-sprung" It occupies the northern chapel, and the space to the right of it was occupied by the images of Jig-ten Van-phyng, Khro ñer-chanma, Vyang chanma (Svarasvati) and Amrita Kundali, while on the left were seated in graceful attitudes the glittering images of *Hod*-sser chan (Prabhavati), Gro*l* ma (Tara) and Tamdin (Haya-griba). In the outer court-yard of the Tsang-khang were placed in a row the statues of Thang-tong gya*l*-po, Dam-pa Sang*s* *rgyas*, Bilwa-bas the Saint, and Shakya sri Pandita of Kashmir. In the porch were the images of the Buddhas of the past, present and future times.

We were next shown the very old images of Byampa Gon-po (Maitreyanath) constructed by Ssankar-lo-tsava with the earth obtained from the site of King Srong-tsan's bathing-stand. This image holds in its lap a very pretty sandal-wood image of Manjusri. By its side was a bronze image of Ayusmat, also called Amitáyu Buddha, constructed by the pious King of Ser-ling (Burma) in the tenth century of Christ. There were also the bronzes of Jam-yang, the four-handed Chanrassig, Tsong-khapa, the image containing the relics of the sage Leg-pa*h*i She-rab, the bronze of Arya Tara, the Bum scriptures written in gold for the absolution of sins committed by a butcher of Meru-tse, a miniature tomb containing the relies of Tson-du ñingpo of Nari, and a hundred and eight oil-burners cut out of rock under Tsong-khapa's supervision.

In the outer impluvium we were shown the stone slab, called the Padma-pûng-pa, sitting on which King Srong-tsan and his wives used to bathe, the red image of the god of physicians called Man-pa Gya*l*-po constructed by Lama Ne-chhûng ripa, the bronze of the great Indian Pandit Shanta Rakshita constructed by the famous Ningma Lama Padma-lupa, and the images of Padma-sambhava and Kamala-shila, the philosopher who vanquished the heretical Hwashang Mahayana. Inside a room enclosed by iron-wire lattice (where numerous rats were running about), we were shown a life-size statue of Tsong-khapa, said to have been consecrated by the reformer himself. On its left were the bronzes of Kungah Tashi and Sonam Gya*l*-tshan, two famous Sakyapa hierarchs of Buton Rinpo-chhe, the great historiographer, constructed by Lotsa-va Chyang-chhûb-tse, Gya*l*-sre Thogme, Dorje Gya*l*-tshan of Musri, of the famous Karma Rang-jung Dorje, and of the wrathful deity Chhyagna-dorje (Vajra Pani), consecrated by King Srong-tsan himself. This last image was first seized by the apostate King Langdarma when he commenced his persecution of Buddhism by destroying Buddhist images. The valet who tied a rope to the neck of this image in order to drag it out became insane and died of vomiting blood, in consequence of which people approach it with feelings of awe and dread. The remaining divinities of the Tsang-khang were the following :—Buddha Amitabha (immeasurable light) surrounded by Chanrassig, Bhumigarbha, Dile-nomsil, Shunya garbha, Kuntu ssang-po (Samanta bhadra) Manjusri, Vajra Pani, and Maitreya, all of which date as early as the age of King Srong-tsan.

Inside the Tsang-khang and in the galleries, numerous mice were scared at our approach and ran in every direction, presenting a very amusing sight. Coming out from the Tsang-khang in the *khyamra* (outer court) we saw the fearful deity Thovo-me-tsig pa, by the side of which were lying the heirlooms of the Minister Gar's cunning and dexterous exploits in the court of the Emperor Thaijûng. When, immediately after the death of King Srong-tsan, Tibet was invaded by a million of Chinese troops, and the Tibetan soldiers could no longer defend the country against their overwhelming foes, this fearful image is said to have been propitiated as a last resort. By his miraculous intervention the Tibetan troops, animated with fresh spirit, completely routed the Chinese armies and saved the country. Owing to this, people attach much importance to the *Chhyag-wang* (benediction) of this fearful deity. Near it the statues of Srong-tsan and his wives, constructed by Tshal-pa Thipon, the images of Buddha Thong-wadon yo, the terrible images of the four guardian kings of the world, called Gya*l*-chhenshi, a pair of pillars said to be consecrated by one of the Chhoigya*l*s, and a number of huge yak horns, were the most notable objects in the porch pointed out to us as worthy of the notice of all pilgrims. An anecdote is connected with these antique yak horns, which the Kuners relate to respectable and inquisitive pilgrims :—Ra-chhûng-pa, the chief disciple of Milarapa, visited Arya-varta, where he studied general science, and particularly the esoteric branch of the sacred literature of the Buddhist, under many learned Pundits and Buddhist sages, and returned to Tibet filled with conceit about his acquirements. Milarapa, reading by his prescience his disciple's mind, in order to subdue his pride went to receive him on his return. While tutor and pupil were travelling conversing together, it occurred to the latter that he, having come from such a distant land as Arya-varta, after performing an arduous task and suffering immense privations, might naturally expect a grand reception in the house of his own tutor ; but his tutor's circumstances being rather unenviable, as was evident from his dress and the state of his person, such an expectation on his part was merely a delusion. Milarapa perceiving what was passing in Ra-chhûng-pa's mind, on arriving in the middle of Pa*l*moi pa*l* thang (desert), wished the latter to fetch him a pair of huge wild yak's horns which were lying there. Ra-chhûng said to himself "Ah ! there is nothing that my Lama does not require for his use : sometimes he becomes as fretful as an old cur, at others he evinces the childish fancies of old men for novelties. What on earth does he require these yak-horns for? They cannot be eaten or drunk, or worn as clothes ?" So he asked Milarapa what use these dry horns might be put to. The sage smilingly replied, "Although it is not possible to say in what contingencies these may be useful, the time will come when their usefulness will be seen. But Ra-chhûng thought it useless to listen to his Lama's words and passed on, while Milarapa picked them up himself. When they arrived at the middle of the desert, where there was not even a hole for a rat to conceal itself, they were overtaken by hail-storms and rain. Clouds covered the skies, and a high wind blew. Ra-chhûng, bewildered, could not tell either where he was or where his Lama was gone. He covered his head and body with his cotton raiment, and sat on the ground to protect himself against the inclement weather. When the storm subsided, Ra-chhûng-pa searched for his Lama, but in vain. Disappointed, he sat for a while, when from an elevation in the neighbourhood a voice was heard. He ran up to it and saw his tutor sitting at ease within one of the yak horns. Milarapa had not contracted himself, nor was the horn enlarged, yet the saintly ascetic sat in it and looked like a reflection in a mirror. Milarapa, seeing his pupil, said "if the son has attained a position of equality with his father, let him accommodate himself in the hollow of the remaining horn." Ra-chhûng-pa, thinking he could do so, approached the horn, but lo ! it was too small even to serve him for a hat ! He was struck with the miracle, and was convinced that he had not arrived even at half the stage of his Lama's perfection. Milarapa came out of his shelter when the rains cleared up and the storm subsided. He carried the horns to Lhasa, and presented them to Chovo Rinpo-chhe."

In the outer gallery of the Tsong-khang we saw the image of Munindra, Atisha, Bromton and Arya Tara—the last reputed to possess a special sanctity. Once on a time Phagapa Rinpo-chhe, the spiritual guide of the Emperor Khublai, after he had finished presenting scarves to all the deities of the temple, had one left. So he addressed all the gods in a body. "Say unto what deity shall I offer this remaining scarf." "Let me have it" said a voice from the image of Tara, and the scarf was placed upon it.

After visiting the chapels on the ground-floor, we slowly ascended the second and third floors, where several Nepalese Buddhists were chanting Sanskrit *Mantras*. This sound was most welcome to me, and I listened to it attentively for a few minutes, when my companions hurried me to the different chapels. The number of visitors was not so great here as in the ground-floor, where one is not allowed to stay more than a minute. The rush was indeed very great in the chapel of the Chovo. Paying a flying visit to the Goddess Pa*l*don Lhamo and a few other divinities in the third storey, we descended to the Tsang-khang by two different ladders, and again presented ourselves before the grand Chovo. This time the Kuner asked Tshing-ta who I was and whence I came. My companion replied by saying that I was from Tashi-lhunpo and was very ill. He sympathized with me and asked him to perform some religious service for my speedy recovery. By this time Pador had emptied the butter-bowl, as he had poured butter into every oil-burner lighted that day in the chapels.

About five thousand of these were lighted in the court-yard alone to illuminate the Tsang-khang. Those before the image of the Chovo were all of gold, and each must have contained ten to twelve pounds of melted butter. The uttering of *Om mani Padme hum, om A-hum,* &c, was unending. Owing to my ill-health and the long time I had been on my legs, I felt completely exhausted, and pressed my good companions to hasten to return home. "Are you satisfied with visiting the shrine and seeing the venerable face of Buddha?" asked Tshing-ta. "Yes, thank you, the temple is the grandest that I ever beheld, and I am really fortunate to have seen it. I must attribute this to the mercy of Kon-chhog (god), for otherwise, I could never have come here to see these wonders." Pador was also delighted with the visit, and remarked that my *kal-pa* (fortune) was very good. We then slowly walked to our lodging. Two of our neighbours, who also had come from Tashi-lhunpo, asked if I was pleased with the *chhoi-jyal*. A *Donner* of Tashi-lhunpo, to whom Tshing-ta had introduced me, graciously inquired after my health and about the *chhoi-jyal*. I then sat reclining on my blankets, while Pador busied himself in preparing tea and Tshing-ta cut slices from a piece of boiled mutton for dinner.

Namola, who fetched water for us, supplied us with a bag of dried cow-dung, which we used here for fuel. In the evening a number of Ragyaba beggars clamoured in the court of the Donner Chhenpo of Tashi-lhunpo, whom the Grand Lama had deputed with presents to his holiness' representative on the occasion of the young Dalai's ordainment into monkhood. At intervals, when they ceased their howling, as if to take breath, the Ragyabas said—"Kusho, months have elapsed since you arrived here, yet you have not satisfied us hungry beggars: we won't leave this place without receiving *solra* (gratification) from you." I heard this distinctly, as the court was about twenty yards off from our window, and observed to Tshing-ta that these Ragyabas were a dangerous set of people, the pests of Lhasa: "Why does not Government take steps to suppress this nuisance?" My companion replied: "Sir they are the sons of earth and work with the sons of earth." After dinner, a little before sunset, I went to the roof of our house to enjoy the panorama of the city. The sunset on the western group of sable hills was glorious. The gilt domes of Potala and the spires of Tangye-ling glittered with the slanting rays, and the spire of Rading palace was a mass of blazing gold. The moon was rearing her bright orb to bleach the religious city, when for fear of cold I returned to my homely room. I begged Tshing-ta to pour sufficient water round my bed-stead to keep off the *dashig* which infested our house. The nearness of Tangye-ling to our house was not an advantage, as the disagreeable music of the cymbals and conch shells continued for hours after sunset to resound in the atmosphere.

I went to bed early and asked Tshing-ta to sit near me. He rendered me an account of the day's expenses, and said that, although his anxiety for me was diminishing, his thoughtfulness for his own and Pador's health was increasing, for the *Khang-ner*, with his wife and children, were laid up with small-pox; every one in the house and the neighbour-hood was laid up: some recovering, some falling ill, was the order of the day: if he and Pador fell, who would look after them, and who would attend upon me? He then poured water a second time on the ground round my bedstead, and muttering some sacred *mantras*, covered himself with his woollens opposite the fire-place. He did not care for the attacks of the *dashig*, for, said he, these pests do not attack people whose blood contain a kind of poison. I jokingly asked if *his* blood had poison in it to repulse the *dashig*. He smiled and went off to sleep. I now thought of jotting down my experiences of the day, but felt too fatigued even for the exertion of writing. Having seen the grand image of Buddha, of whose sanctity and celebrity I had heard and read in numerous books, my thoughts were now bent towards seeing the famous shrine of Ramo-chhe, and I was determined to see it on the following morning at all events.

2nd June.—After an early breakfast, accompanied by Tashing-ta and Pador, I went to visit the famous shrine of Ramo-chhe. Our equipment was as usual a bundle of incense-sticks, clarified butter, and a few scarves. I was dressed in my church costume, and wore my goggle spectacles to conceal my eyes, and pulled the *cho-sha*, or monk's hat, over my forehead. We proceeded by the narrow lane, running eastward. Owing to the rains of the previous night, the lane was disgustingly muddy and full of offensive smells from the heaps of filth lying on it. Stopping my nose, I passed this lane and landed on a cleaner road which ran northward crossing the Potala road at a short distance from the north-western corner of the Kyi*l* khording square, or, as it is called, Thom-se-gang. We left the lofty Wangdu *chhorten* on our right. This *chhorten* was erected in ancient times in order to bring all the neighbouring nations under the power of the Tibetans. (*Wang* in Tibetan means "power," and *du*, to "bring under.") But in the days of Wang and Gung of Tibet, when the Ming dynasty ruled the destinies of China, Lhasa is said to have been over-run by numerous Chinese troops, of whom about one hundred thousand occupied the plain to the north of this *chhorten*, for which reason this place is called Gya-bum gang, or the landing-place of a hundred thousand Chinese.* To the east of Gya-bum gang is the pottery

* The above is the Chinese account of Gya-bum gang. But the Tibetan account is quite different. After the death of King Srong-tsan Gampo, two hundred thousand Chinese soldiers invaded Tibet. The veteran general Gar defeated the Chinese troops in a pitched battle near Gya-bum gang, and buried one hundred thousand Chinese troops on the site of Gya-bum.

*

market. Our road turned westward by the side of a long Mandang. I carefully left it to my right-hand side, since, *to have kept it on my left would have been heretical.* A few hundred paces brought us to the gate of the famous temple of Ramo-chhe, erected by the illustrious Princess Konjo, daughter of the Emperor Thai-jung, and wife of King Srong-tsan Gampo. It is a lofty edifice, flat-roofed and three stories high, surrounded by a stone wall, with a high and wide porch. The frontispiece of the building contains a very old inscription in Chinese, which probably gives the name, year, and the history of the shrine erected by the first Chinese Princess who introduced Buddhism into Tibet. The courts on the east and west were spacious, and were lined with a few old *shovo* (poplars). About thirty monks were solemnly seated to perform a religious service on two sides of a row of pillars which supported the roof The passage to the image of Mikya Dorje (Vajra Akshoba), which was brought by the Nepalese Princess, lay midway between the pillars. The image was grand looking; and though its face was gilt with gold, yet its antiquity was manifest in its ornamentation and in the rest of the body. I was impressed with feelings of awe and reverence for those Chinese and Indian sages who had toiled in this remote country for the diffusion of the religion of Tathagata. The sight of the remains of antiquity, and particularly when they are connected with history, cannot fail to excite such feelings. Lay monks, called *Serkem-pa*, generally perform religious services in Ramo-chhe, and only one Kuner, with half a dozen monks, occupy the upper floors of the temple. With the exception of a small gilt dome constructed after the Chinese model, I did not see any remarkable Chinese architecture in Ramo-chhe, which fell far short of the ideas I had formed when reading the accounts of the building of Ramo-chhe by Chinese architects sent by Emperor Thaijung at the earnest solicitation of Princess Konjo. Probably the ancient edifice was demolished by the apostate Langdarma in the beginning of the tenth century. The rebuilt shrine is also very old. In the northern lobby of the temple there were heaps of ancient relics. such as shields, spears, drums, arrows, scimitars, sabres, long knives, trumpets, &c. In a room to the left side of the entrance, enclosed by iron lattice work, a few images, consid red very sacred, were kept. We were shown a brass mirror, called *melong*, which is said to be possessed of wonderful charms. My companion gave a two-anna piece to the *kuner* of Ramo-chhe, and we then came out of the shrine, keeping the line of smaller chhortens situated in the court-yard to our right, and returned to our house by another road. A party of mendicants, street-singers by profession, followed us. Tshing-ta wished to dismiss them with a *tanka*, but I advised him not to give them anything. They waited and waited, clamouring all along for *solra* for about one hour, when we dismissed them with a *karma* (two-anna piece). Had we been more liberal, they would have recommended other parties to visit us for *solra*. In the afternoon, after dinner, we went to Phala's residence for an interview with Lhacham. The Shetamas (female attendants) told us that the lady was gone to see her father, Dahpon Ssaur-khang, who was laid up with small-pox. They pressed us to take tea, but we thanked them and returned home. In the evening two of our neighbours came to our room and chatted for about an hour with Tshing-ta about the scarcity of mutton and butter and the dearth of barley in the market. This they attributed to the fear of small-pox, which deterred the people of the interior from coming to Lhasa for selling provisions. The *Khang-ner* with his family was still laid up. in consequence of which Tshing-ta could not arrange for a better house for my residence. I requested our friendly neighbours to engage a house for me even at double the usual rent, that I might live more comfortably. The *phing* that we had brought from Tashi-lhunpo was all consumed, and good meat was not available. The mutton of gram-fed sheep was plenty in the market, but my companion thought that fat meat would be injurious to my health, and lean meat was what I very much disliked. Having to pass for a monk, it was impossible for me to take fowls, which were very cheap, and my companions would not let me take eggs, as they were believed to be injurious in my convalescent state.

3rd June.—Owing to the fatigues of the previous days, and the fall of temperature due to the late rains, I felt very unwell to-day; the difficulty in breathing increased, and I did not get up from bed. Two of Tshing-ta's acquaintances came to see him in the morning, whom he introduced to me. They expressed much sympathy at my helpless condition so far away from my home. At about 10 A.M. Gelong Pomda, a native of Pomda in Kham, to whom I had been introduced by Kusho Tungchhen at Tashi-lhunpo, hearing that I was come to Lhasa and was putting up in the Chyan-sreb-gang of Panjor Rabtan, came to see me. Seeing me laid up, he observed that small-pox was not a dangerous illness this present year, but was rather welcomed by many. But when he came near my bed to feel my pulse, he found out his mistake. I told him that my illness was a dangerous one and had nearly put an end to my life at Yamdo. Pomda sympathized with me, and talked about the happy days he had spent in the company of Kusho Tungchhen at Tashi-lhunpo, adding that as I was that good man's friend, he would by all means help me at Lhasa. He told us that he was waiting for the arrival of nine mule-loads of silver which were coming from Tashi-lhunpo: as soon as the money arrived, he would leave Lhasa for Western China, stay a few months at his home, travel further into China, and then return to Lhasa in the month of March or April. I had heard at Tashi-lhunpo that Gelong Pomda was the head of a caravan consisting of 700 mules, and carried on trade between Tar-chindo and Lhasa *viâ* Kham. The brigands know him, and never molest him. His person is gigantic, being a little higher than 6 feet, corpulent and muscular. Having obtained his assurance, I revived in my mind the idea of visiting Kham-Amdo and ultimately Pekin. It also occurred to me that the Kham people, though naturally wild, are entirely devoted to their friends. Kusho Tungchhen had often told me that if once I became intimate with a Khamba, I might be sure that he would serve me to the last. This emboldened me in my desire to trust in the good faith of Gelong Pomda, and I said in a whisper that if he could wait for about a month at Lhasa, I would accompany him to his native place. He shook his head and said *Aih yo*, meaning he doubted if he could wait about a month. Some of our neighbours arrived and seated themselves near my bed. They often warned me not to fall asleep, and conversed on several matters, such as the death of the Meru tah Lama, the Chyi-khyab Khanpo, from small-pox, some of them observing that the Lama did not listen to the advice of his friends, and drank curd while attacked with small-pox. This aggravated the malady, and carried him off. Meru tah Lama was one of the most profound scholars of the day in Tibet, and his death was greatly deplored by the people During my idle hours I collected information on the customs and habits of the people. The following story about the Regent Tshomoling and the practice of the women of Tibet will not be uninteresting :—

In the north-western border of Kham, within the province of Amdo, lies the district of Tshoni, whence a mendicant came on pilgrimage to Lhasa. Arrived at the outer court of Sera monastery, he fell asleep from the fatigues of the journey. That night the Mo*d*pa Khanpo of Sera dreamt that within the sacred precincts of the monastery there lay a lion, and next morning he sent one of his attendants to conduct to his presence any man who might be found near the monastery gate. Accordingly the mendicant of Tshoni was brought to his presence, and on being asked his business there replied that his simple prayer was to be admitted as a monk into the monastery. The Khanpo was pleased with the reply of the mendicant, who he thought would have prayed for money. The mendicant was promised admission into the monastery, and the Khanpo appointed a learned Mongolian Lama to be his tutor. Although according to the customs of Tibet a man of one nationality is not appointed as tutor of one of different nationality, yet the Khanpo, believing that the mendicant was no ordinary person, entrusted his education to the charge of the warlike Mongol. The mendicant soon mastered the different branches of the sacred literature, and obtained the approbation of his superiors. A few years after the Mongol tutor, who possessed some wealth, began to sell off his effects with a view to return to his home. The pupil, who had entertained hopes of receiving a share, was somewhat disappointed, but reached his tutor to a short distance. At parting the Mongol told him that he had left for him a pair of earthen pots, a scarf and bag of barley, as a legacy, which he said were the best things he possessed. The pupil, not satisfied with the gifts, but rather indignant at their meagreness, went to the market and sold the pots for half a *tanka*. With this silver-piece he bought butter and offered the same to the great image of Buddha, praying that if he ever attained to the rank of Regent of Tibet, he would introduce reforms into those old customs of Tibet which were liable to abuse, and make fresh laws to displace the rude usages of ancient times. On his return to his cell, while opening the bag of barley, he found that it was filled with gold and silver. He now realized the meaning of his tutor's hint, and, reflecting on the sage's parting instructions, applied himself to study. In course of time he succeeded to the dignity and position of his tutor, and ultimately to that of his patron the Khanpo. A few years after he was appointed Regent, and the first act of his administration was directed against loose women. He expelled all prostitutes from Lhasa, and subjected their accomplices to cruel tortures. He also compelled all the women of Tibet to disfigure their faces (particularly the cheek) with a thin pigment of catechu, and thereby to prevent their ruddiness from being exposed to the public view. The women of Tibet wear an entire conch-shell in the place of bangles in their right hand. This is believed to be a preventive against their being subjected to handcuffing for any kind of guilt or crime. From that time also the women of Tibet began to wear a thick breast-covering, called *Pang-den*, above their petticoats. Tshomoling also compelled them to make modifications in their head adornments. The *Patug*, or the head-dress of the women of Tibet, is a modification of the ancient *Patug*, which now is alone used by the Lhachams (wives of Shapes). The line of Tshomoling incarnations originated from him, and continues up to the present day. I was shown the great monastery of Tshomoling, which is situated in the middle of an extensive grove behind the famous shrine of Ramo-chhe.

4th June.—After breakfast we visited the Chokhang. After paying reverence to the Chovo and circumambulating his sacred throne, we were going to visit other deities of the Tsang-khang, when the Kuner of the Chovo offered us the *Thui*, or consecrated ablution water of Buddha, pouring the same from a golden jar. Having received the consecrated water with both my hands, I proceeded towards the southern chapels of the Tsang-khang. Here in one of the minature *chhortens* is placed the most ancient bronze that exists in Tibet. Legends say that this bronze, which is made of *Limar*, or red bell-metal, was constructed by King Kriki at the epoch when human life extended to 20,000 years by virtue of his faith in Maitreya, and was consecrated by Kashyapa Buddha. It remained in the chapel of the early Kings of Nepal for many centuries. The Nepalese Princess who was married to King Srong-tsan brought it to Tibet, and placed it in a conspicuous position in her famous shrine. Tradition has it that the image, while being carried in Tibet, travelled miraculously in the steepest parts of the way. Being very handsome, and of well proportioned features, it is considered transcendentally holy and possessed of miraculous powers in blessing its devotees. In one of the door-sides we were shown the images of Tshangma (Brahma) and Gya-Jin (Indra), which were constructed by King Ra*l*pachan the warlike, who is believed to have been an incarnation of the fearful Chhyagna-Dorje. In the niches of the outer gallery were prominently placed the following divinities, deified saints, and personages :—

Divinities.

Tshe-*d*pag-me*d*	Aparimita yusha Buddha.
*S*pyan-ra*s g*ssig*s*	Avalokiteshvara Bodhi sattva, with four arms.
Pa*d*ma *h*byung *g*na*s*	Padma sambhava, placed in a niche constructed in the shape of a *swastika* figure.
*H*jam-*d*vyang*s*	Manjusri, who was the tutelary dety of King Ho*d*-sser Gochha (jyoti varma), father-in-law of King Srong-tsan.
Jambhala	Kuvera, god of wealth, constructed by Pandita Tshul Khrim*s* nor, through the moral merit of which he obtained great quantities of silver.
Byam-pa*s*	Maitreya, constructed of solid silver by a Kashmerian Pandit named Utpala, who lived in Tibet.
Khasar-pani	Khasharpana Bodhisattva, by Lume, a well-known learned Pandit of Tibet.
*B*chu-chig shal	Ekadsha mukha Bodhiattva, which is said to have been consecrated by Buddha Kashyapa.
*R*Dorje sem*s*-*d*pah	Vajra Sattva.
*S*tong-chhen Rab-*h*byam*s*.	
So sor *h*brang-ma.	
*G*Shin-*r*je *m*thar-bye*d*	Yama-antaka. Lord of death.
Pa*d*ma-*m*thar-bye*d*	Padmantaka.
Bgeg-*m*thar-bye*d*	Vinayakantaka.

Sainted Lamas.

Grub-chhen Bilwava.
Sa-chhen Kun *d*gah *s*ñing-po.
*R*je-*b*tsun-*b*so*d* nams tse-mo.
*R*je-*b*tsun Grag*s*-po *r*gya*l m*tshan.
Sa-*s*kya Pan chhen.
H gro *m*gon *h*phag*s*-pa.
Don-yo*d r*gya*l*-*m*tshan.
*B*so*d* nams *r*gya*l*-*m*tshan.

} These are Sakya Hierarchs.

Deified personages.

King Khri-srong *l*de *b*tsan.
Two of his wives, constructed by Tsha*l*-pa khri-*d*pon.
Mon-*b*ssah khri *l*cham, the third wife of King of Srong-*b*tsan.
Prince Gung-gung *b*tsan. (Sron-*b*tsan's son).
Minister Thonmi.
General *M*gar.
And several other ministers.

Inside the northern wing of the temple, called *K*Lu-khang, or the house of the serpent demi-gods, are the following :—

Sang*s* rgya*s k*lu *d*vang rgya*l*-po (Buddha Nagendra Raja).
Mahakala.
Dasha Skandha, the King of cannibal Lanka.
S Sur-phu*d*-*l*ñapa, the chief of the divine musicians.
Nanda, the King of Nagas.
Upa Nanda.
Yaksha Chief Kuvera.

To the south and north of the Seng-dong (lion-face) gate of the Lukhang are the bronze images of Trag-sha*d* and Chhyog-don. In the second story, called Bar-khang, are the goddesses Lhamo Magjorma and Tamdin. In the centre of the Tsang-khang of the western wing of the Bar-khang were the images of the past seven Buddhas, consecrated by King Srong-tsan, and of the members of the royal family of Srong-tsan, constructed by Lama Dung-karpa of Tsongkhapa, and his two spiritual sons. In the upper porch-room were the beautiful bronzes of Do*l*-kar, Tamdin, &c. We were also shown the paintings of Pa*l*-dan Lhamo, executed in the days of King Srong-tsan, the cells of the ascetic Lamas Thang and Loponchhenpo. Just above the golden canopy over the image of Thug-jechhenpo, were the bronzes of the eight Sugata Buddhas, the lords of medicine, with their retinues. Above the grand image of the Chovo on the four sides were arranged in order the five

Pancha jati Buddhas, the eight Sattvas called sem*sd*pah-*b*rgya*d*, the oracular goddess Sung-chyon-ma, and the terrific spirits Tamdin and Chhyagdor. The image of Pa*l*dan Lhamo, on the upper story, is the most important of all the deities in the shrine, except the Chovo. The face of this goddess being most terrific, is always kept veiled, but the Kuñer kindly took up the veil at our request and favoured us with some *T'hu*, or ablution water, to sanctify ourselves with.* Tshing-ta told me that by the *jin-lab* (charm) of the *T'hu* my illness would be much diminished. The whole chapel of Pa*l*dan Lhamo was infested by numerous tiny mice, which even crept on to the person of the Kuñer. People say that the mice are all metamorphosed *Gelongs* (monks). Two or three Nepalese Buddhists were uttering Sanskrit hymns in honour of the dreaded goddess, and a number of Nevers were making *chhoi-kor* (circumambulation). There were some paintings on the walls, said to have been painted with blood that oozed out of the nose of king Srong-tsan. In the Na-chu Lhakhang chapel, erected by one of the Sakya Lamas named Wang Chhyug Tsondu, were the most remarkable statue-like images of the sixteen Sthaviras called Natan Chudug, arranged to represent the scene of their reception by Upashaka Dharma Tala, one of the most celebrated and devout Buddhists of ancient China. Besides these there were the Dikapalas, most gaudily dressed, and bearing their respective weapons. We returned to our house at about twelve, and meeting in front of the western gate of the Chokhong several itinerant book-sellers, I asked my companion to tell them that we required several books, and would give them orders for some copies of manuscript histories, such as Kachhem-kakholma, Gya*l*-rab-Jonshing Gya*l*rab-Salvai-Melong. Arriving home very much exhausted, I fell asleep. The brick tea No. 2 (Duthang ñipa) which Tung-chhen had given me for my use during the journey, being now all consumed, I had to drink the worst kind of tea, called Gya-pa. Although Tshing-ta bought some tea from the market for me, which was sold as Duthang ñipa, I did not like it at all, and I asked Gergan Pomda to procure me a brick of No. 2, as I preferred it to No. 1 (Duthang), which, though flavoury, is very strong. Different kinds of brick tea are known in Tibet. In ancient times, not earlier than the tenth century, when tea is said to have been first introduced here from Western China, few kinds of tea were known, but during the times of the Sakya hierarchy, and also during the reigns of the Phagmo-du kings, the use of tea in Tibet became general. During the first century of the Dalai Lama's hierarchy the tea trade was a monopoly of the Government, which ceased in the first part of the present century. But the officials who privately carried on trade in tea took advantage of the former monopoly of the Government and replaced it by an unauthorized monopoly of their own. At Kirong and other distant districts of the country tea is compulsorily sold to the people in the name of the Government. The different kinds of brick tea which were formerly in demand are not much valued by the people now-a-days.

---

* Pa*l*dan Lhama (pronounced as Pandan Lhamo, or Srimati Devi).

This terrific goddess is propitiated by the northern Buddhists and particularly by the Tibetans, who regard her as the greatest guardian deity of the Dalai and Tashi Lamas. By some she is identified with the goddess Kali of the Hindus, whom she greatly resembles in appearance and in her fabulous exploits. Many extravagant stories are related about the unrestrained character she is said to have borne during her different metempsychoses in the worlds of demons and men. In short, in all her numerous existences, whether in the region of the Nagas, or of demons, gods or men, she was notorious for the free life she led everywhere with impunity. Some legendary accounts identify her with the *Sakti*, or the female energy of nature, a condition which naturally joined her with the male energy. But the well-informed Buddhists generally deny her such a high position on account of her being originally a Tirthika goddess, the renowned wife of Maheshvara, whom Buddha conditionally permitted to become a guardian of Buddhism on his becoming an Upasaka, but who never reached the position of a Bodhisattva. She is only a female Upasaka. It is said that she is an emanation from the Goddess Yang-chhen-ma (Svarasvati, the goddess of learning). In the days of Budha Kashyapa, while she appeared in the abodes of gods and men as Ganga Devi, Pa*l*dan Lhamo fervently prayed that she might become the staunchest guardian of Buddha Shakya Simha's doctrine.

For one of her earliest chivalrous demonstrations in the abodes of demons, Buddha Vajra Dhara gave her the name of Mag-jar Gya*l*mo, or the "War-making Queen." On the occasions of her triumphs over the demons she got various other names. Chhyagna dorje (Vajra Pani) gave her the name of Remati—the black gown hobgoblin; Tamdin (Hayagriba) called her Vidun-megha Sena; and Mahesvara gave her the name of Guhya Ghana Narana, &c. In India she is once said to have become notorious as a *Mamo* (nymph) under the name of Vasankuruni. In China she became famous as the wife of one of the Emperors, and bore the name Gya*l*-mo Din-ssang. In Hor (Mongolia) she was the wife of nine Tartar heroes, all brothers. In Tibet she had appeared once, when she was called by the name Pandan Achhyima. What names she bore in her numerous transmigrations is not easy to mention; suffice it to say that in the ether she is adored by the Genii under the name of Pa*l*mo-tsan. In the celestial regions she is the renowned Uma, the daughter of Indra. In the nether regions—the abodes of Nagas—she was the daughter of the serpent king and bore the name of Tsugna-mani dsung (she that holds a gem in her head). In the land of *Srinpo* (cannibal demons), while born as the daughter of Srinpo King, she was unequalled by any in feats of strength. So violent was her conduct among the *Srinpos* that she spread havoc over them, and would have extinguished their race had not she taken a fancy to wear a chain on her legs, when, according to a certain legend, she was laid in chains by her *Srinpo* husband in order that she might not lead a notoriously unrestrained life. The King of Death being enamoured of her most dreaded charms, took her to his abode, still unreleased from the iron fetters on her legs.

When she was converted into Buddhism and given the name of genius Remati by Buddha himself, she solemnly undertook to defend the religion of Tathagata. Having spread the terror of her power over all the worlds below (*i e.* "Shin-thul wang-ji"), she obtained numerous followers from among the gods, nagas, yakshas, divine musicians, demons, hosts of death, cannibal-goblins, &c. For her triumph over the enemies of Buddhism she was loaded with numerous presents from different quarters. The goddess of the sea who guards the pearls and conch shells presented her with a chestnut-coloured mule colt, the offspring of a red ass and a winged mare. This mule possessed the power of flying like birds. A saddle made of the skin and bones of cannibal-goblin Yaksha-gora was also presented to her. Using venomous snakes as bridle and cruppers for this wonderful mule, she could fly round the Jambudipa thrice within a day. The genius Kyadorje presented her with black and white dice, to stake the lives of all living beings. Tshang-pa (Brahma) presented her with an umbrella of peacock's feathers. Khyab-jug (Vishnu) presented her with the two great luminaries, the sun and moon, of which she put the latter on the crown of her head and the former on her navel. The great king Nam-thoi-sre presented her with a lion, which she placed in her right ear. Nanda, the king of the Nagas, presented her with a giant serpent, which she hid in her left ear. Chhyagnadorje presented her with a huge club which she carried in her right hand. The numberless legions of the Srinpo presented her with a string of numerous skulls filled with blood, which she held in her left hand. She tied to her girdle the cross-like weapon of the demons called Thamka. The hobgoblins who haunt cemeteries presented her with numberless corpses, which she feasted upon with ghastly smiles, singing songs of revelry.

Dressed in all the paraphernalia of terror, such as tiger gowns tied with venomous snakes, ornaments of skulls, &c., she began waging war with the enemies of Buddhism. The image of this goddess in the third storey of Kyi*l*-khording is said to be very wonderful, as oracles are delivered at it. She is feared all over Mongolia, Tibet, and China. The monks and authorities of the monasteries of Sera, Dapung, Gahdan, and the great hierarchs of Lhasa and Tashi-lhunpo, believe her to be the greatest of all guardians of Buddha Dharma.

The discovery of the present Dalai Lama.

Formerly the selection of the incarnate Lamas depended on the concurrent opinion of the College of Cardinals, but subsequently that system being found unsatisfactory, tests were introduced for identification, in which laymen also had a voice. Together with this the hints (if any) left by the defunct incarnation respecting his re-appearance as to the particular locality and time were taken into consideration to confirm or refuse the claims of pretenders.

In the middle ages the system of selection by the throw of dice and trial of chances was greatly in vogue. Since the middle of the seventeenth century, the practice of propitiating the *ser-bum* (golden jar) was generally resorted to for finding out the real person from among many pretenders to the office of a defunct divine Lama.[1] After the death of a recognized incarnate Lama, his soul is said ordinarily to remain in the spiritual world for a space of at least forty-nine days. This period or stage of existence is called *Par-do*. There is no fixed limit to *Par-do*, but forty-nine days is the minimum time assigned to the Bodhisattvas who have chosen to appear in this world for the good of all living beings. By the force of impersonal prayer, or what is called *monlam* in Tibetan, it is within the power of every being to extend or shorten the limit of *Par-do*, although the efficacy of such prayers is varied by the consequence of *karma* (or acts) of former existences. For instance if a man intensely wishes that he should in his future existence become a successful pretender to the Grand Lama's throne, there would be every probability of his attaining it as long as intenser prayers from other quarters did not counteract the fulfilment of his desire. On this principle the usurper Dayan khanpo is said to have prayed not long ago that he should one day sit at the head of the Government of Lhasa to be able to injure the Dalai Lama's supremacy. In order to prevent his evil spirit from being successful in its designs, the Government of Tibet has made some radical changes in the system hitherto in force for discovering the real person from among the many pretenders to the office and possessions of a particular defunct incarnate Lama.

In 1875, one year after the demise of the late Dalai Lama, Thin*le* Gya-tsho, the Regency and the College of Cardinals at Lhasa consulted the celebrated oracle of Nachung chhoikyong about the re-appearance of the Dalai. The oracle declared that the Grand Lama would be discovered only by a monk of the purest morals. In order to find out who that monk was, the Government sent emissaries to different quarters of Tibet, who all returned without being able to trace him. The oracle was again consulted for finding out that particular monk of pure morals, and declared the Khanpo (prefect) of Shar-tse of Gah-dan to be that monk, and that he would have to go to Chhoikhor Gya, as the gods divined that the Grand Lama would appear somewhere in the direction of Kong-po. Accordingly the Shar-tse Khanpo of Gah-dan monastery, who was well known for his purity of morals and his profound knowledge of the sacred books, proceeded to Chhoikhor Gya, where he sat in profound meditation for full seven days. On the night of the last day he saw a vision, in which a voice from heaven directed him to go and see a miraculous sight in the Yu-tsho lake of Chhoikhor Gya. Awaking from his sleep, the Khanpo went to the lake, where in the unruffled crystal-like water he saw the incarnate Grand Lama sitting in the lap of his mother and caressed by his father. The house with its furniture were also visible. All on a sudden this mirage-like appearance disappeared, and he heard the neighing of a horse. So much of his dream being fulfilled, he proceeded towards the province of Kong-po, when, on the way, he happened to call at the house of a rich and respectable family of the district of Tag-po. Here he recognized the house, the family, and the child he had seen in the lake, and at once declared that the real end of his journey was obtained. On his report the Government officials and the College of Cardinals, headed by the Regent, visited Tag-po and escorted the infant with its parents in great pomp to the palace of Rigya*l* near Lhasa. The princely child was only one year old when he was discovered. He is now ten, and bears the name of Nag-wang Lo-ssang Thub-dan Gya-tsho. (Sumati bag-indra Dhimansagara, the lord of speech, the powerful ocean of wisdom).

5th June.—Early in the morning, when I was yet in bed, feeling unwell, one of Lhacham's servants came to invite us (Tshing-ta and myself) to dine at Phala's residence. I was too feeble to walk even to a short distance; but to decline the honour of dining with her would be perhaps to offend Lhacham. I consulted Tshing-ta as to the course I should follow, and he advised me to proceed slowly to Bangye-shag in order to show the state of my health to

---

[1] The propitiation of the *serbum* (golden jar) was resorted to for ascertaining the real incarnation both in Tibet and China till 1860. In the third year after the death of an incarnate Lama, reports are obtained from different quarters about his re-appearance. The names of several pretenders are sent to the Regency (in the case of the Dalai Lama) for examination and final identification, and are received with much veneration. The President of the conclave, in the presence of the Regent and the ministers, inclose in barley balls the different pretenders' names with slips of paper, some blank, others with "yes" or "no" written on them; all of which are then mixed together with barley-flour and placed in a golden jar. This last is then placed on the altar of the grand chapel of Lhasa, and the gods are invoked for a week to help in finding out the real incarnation. On the eighth day the golden jar is twirled round in order that the barley balls may come out to the surface, when the number of turns are recorded. That name which turns out thrice with slips containing "yes" is considered as the real one. The others are rejected. Then the child singled out is brought in state (in the event of its being the Dalai or Tashi Lama). Men who go to escort the infant ask certain questions, answers to which are obtained in signs made by the infant elect. Sometimes the rings, strings of beads, cups, and mitres of the deceased Lama, mixed with some ordinary ones, are presented to the pretenders for him to single out the ones belonging to the late Lama. About the year 1860, Dayan Khanpo became very powerful, and wanted to do away with the Dalai Lama's hierarchy. At the time of his death he is said to have prayed to be revenged upon the Government by any means, fair or foul, so that it is feared his evil spirit might tamper with the names in the *ser-bum* (golden jar) and then set up a false pretender to the throne of Potala.

The lake of Chhoikhor-gya is called Muli-ding-ki chho. It is very deep and several miles in area. In the ritualistic works of Sikkim it is called yutsho-muli-thing-ki-tsho.

Lhacham. Accordingly, dressing in my church suit, with the assistance of Pador, I slowly climbed down the ladders of our house and proceeded towards the Thom-segang square, which was lined with shops kept up by Nepalese and Kashmiri merchants. I had put on an eye-veil made of horse-hair, generally worn by men suffering from eye-diseases. Now-a-days people use coloured glass spectacles, but the horse-hair veil has not yet gone out of use. Arrived at Bangye-shag, we found the ground-floor filled with men engaged in weighing and measuring grain and corn-flour. The principal ladder, which more resembled a staircase, was also filled with menials. We therefore went to the southern central stair-like ladder and commenced ascending the steps, but my difficulty of breathing was so great that after climbing two or three steps I stood for a while to draw breath, and when I had managed to crawl up the steep ladder to the third story, I fell on the floor completely exhausted. Pador helped me, and the *Shetama* Apela, who came running and crying "*Akha-kha!* Pandibla has not been restored to health," conducted me to a seat in the reception hall, where a large paper lantern was hung. I surveyed the room, and smiled at the homeliness of the furniture of Bangye-shag, Phala's famous residence. There was not a single shade or glass light, or any kind of chandelier in it. About ten or twelve Gelug-ug monks came out from a room to the north of the reception hall, probably having finished a religious service. A slight shower of rain fell at this time. Tea was about to be poured in our cups, when Apela came to say that Lhacham had returned from the house of Dahpon Ssur-khang, her father. She received me very graciously, and conducted me to her drawing-room, which fronted the south. The room was about 16 feet long east to west and 12 feet broad north to south. Against the eastern wall stood two chests of drawers made after the Chinese fashion, on the tops of which China cups were tastefully arranged. The western wall, as also the northern partition wall, were covered with Chinese pictures, mostly picnic and dancing scenes. Excellent Yarkand and Tibet carpets were laid down; the ceiling was of the finest China satin. Nicely polished dining-tables, wooden bowls to hold barley-flour, small fancy tables, stuffed rugs covered with satin, made up the furniture of the room.

Lhacham sat cross-legged on a rug spread opposite the western wall just to my left. Tshing-ta was offered a seat to my left, but did not avail himself of the honour, being a man of obscure origin and position, and withdrew to the outer room, where guests are received. The finest tea, called Duthang, was served, and one of the *Shetamas* placed a trayful of sugar-biscuits on my table. Shortly after Lhasre Kusho, Lhacham's eldest son, came and sat by her side. He had covered himself with a wrapper, and said that he felt unwell; his joints were aching, and there was pain all over his body. She remarked that small-pox was raging, and that the other day her father was attacked with that disease when we called on her, and expressed her regret at having failed to see me then owing to that event. After a short conversation she left the room while I was engaged in conversation with her eldest son. Shortly after the *Shetama* conducted me to the different rooms of Bangye-shag castle.

The furniture of the rooms were of the same description as those of Lhacham's, except that they were of inferior quality. I did not enter the Shapé's room, as I had not been introduced to him. The bedsteads were low, and the bedding resembled those of the Chinese. In one room there was a net-cloth curtain, evidently intended for show, as mosquitoes and flies were little troublesome; with the exception of the demon-bug (*dashig*), I did not notice other fleas. I was told that *khyi-shig*, or the dog-flea, infested old and delapidated houses and those where dogs were kept. The articles of luxury, such as imitations of chairs and couches, lanterns and chandeliers, which adorned the drawing-rooms both of the Shapé and Lhacham, were ludicrously rude. The walls were painted green and blue, the uniformity of which was relieved in some places with pictures of processions, demons and tutelary gods. The doors were roughly made: nowhere did I notice pannels of the description we meet with in Indian or European houses. The shutters, though neatly and beautifully executed, were of one or two patterns only. They were all papered, with the exception of a central patch in each, where there is a pane of glass fitted in a frame. Not a single room was furnished with chimneys of any description. The *jala*, or earthenware stoves, took the place of heating stoves. Opposite the windows of some of the rooms there were flower-pots. The rooms, which were not provided with ceilings, did not look ugly, as the close, small beams which supported the roof were painted and carved in some places.

After half an hour's absence Lhacham returned and resumed her seat. She twirled a golden prayer-wheel with her right hand, while with the left she caressed her son. She asked me if her son could eat meat, as without animal food he could hardly make a full meal. I told her that from what I had heard of small-pox patients in Tibet, it would be better to avoid fat meat and milk, cooling medicines and diet being advised by doctors in such a state. She pressed me again to take tea and biscuits, and some bread made of buck-wheat with malt was placed on my table. At about 12 noon she ordered dinner to be brought, saying that Tshing-ta had not till then returned, and she could not wait for him any longer. Both he and Pador had probably returned to Panjor Rabtan. Several china cups and maple-knot cups mounted with silver and gold were then brought out from a chest of drawers, and a cleanly-dressed boy brought a tray filled with cups containing different dainties. Before beginning, I inquired of Lhacham if there was yak-beef in the dish. "Madam," said I, "I have a great repugnance to beef, never having tasted it in my life." "No, no, all that you see in the plate and cups are mutton of the first quality. Although we prefer *chhyug-sha* (yak-beef) to mutton, yet knowing that you Indians have a repugnance for that delicacy of Tibet, I ordered our cook to take care not to mix beef with mutton," said Lhacham. However, seeing me still hesitate to eat the meat dishes, she assured me that she did not mean to play practical jokes on me by inviting me to dinner at her house. I then busied myself with the chop-sticks and the pins, which latter served for forks. I relished the dishes very well, either not having tasted such food since leaving Dong-tse, or on account of the excellency of cooking. She occasionally took a sip or two of tea and conversed with me, showing great interest in my narration of the customs of Indian marriages and the seclusion of the native females there, and much horror at the revolting custom of *Sutti* in force in India till very recently, when it was abolished by the enlightened Philing. But when I related to her that in India one husband had several wives, and that among the Philings and the enlightened natives of India monogamy is alone practised, she stared at me with wonder, and expressed much curiosity to hear an account of such strange customs. "One wife with one husband only!" she exclaimed in comic surprise. "Do not you, Pandibla, think that we Tibetan women are happier than the Indian or Philing women, of whom the former must be the most miserable!" "Indeed, they are so," replied I. "It is fair that one woman should have one husband, but how monstrous it is that one man should marry several wives!" exclaimed Lhacham. "Pray tell me, is it not inconvenient for one wife to serve many husbands?" said I. "I do not see," observed Lhacham, "how the Indian women are happier than the Tibetan women while the former have to divide among many the affection and property of their single husband, whereas in Tibet the housewife is the real lady of all the joint earnings and inheritance of several brothers who are sprung from the same mother, and are undoubtedly the same blood, flesh, and bones. Their persons are one, though their souls might be different. Does not in India one man marry several women who are strangers to each other?" "I understand then that your ladyship would like to marry several sisters to one husband," asked I. "That, too, does not alter my point: that is, that Tibetan women are happier than Indian women," replied Lhacham. To shorten the discussion, I said that I did not object to Tibetan ladies making themselves happy with their several husbands; I would like to see them happy; and if they were indeed happy, I should be satisfied.

She then changed the topic, and inquired why I had not brought my wife with me to Tibet. She had heard from the Minister that I was a married man; if so, how many children had I? curiously inquired Lhacham. On my telling, she said that she would very much like to see my wife. "Why did you not bring her here, how cruel of you not to bring her." "Madam, it was with extreme difficulty that I succeeded, although alone, in entering Tibet. How was it possible to bring one's family to a place where he has no friends?" said I. "Is not the Minister your best friend? He would have helped you and your wife," replied Lhacham. She seemed to think that the condition of Indian women was like that of the Tibetans, and had no idea of the *zenana* system which makes our country-women the most miserable of the female race. I did not, however, now remind her of the accounts I had given her while at Dong-tse respecting the position of women in India, but said, "Madam, if you can procure me a *lam-yig* (passport) from the Ampa and the Regent to enable me to come to Tibet freely, it will be possible for me to bring my wife to Tibet. Could you do so?" "Yes," said she, "I will undertake to procure you a *lam-yig* if you will promise to bring your wife with you next time that you come here." "I must consult her wishes as to visiting Tibet before I promise to bring her. If she does not like to come, how can I force her to accompany me. If your ladyship does not like to go to Shiga-tse, can Mijechhenpo (the Dahpon, her husband) force you to go there?" asked I. She said, "If you wish to bring her with you she will surely like it." I then said that if I failed to bring my wife I would send a likeness of her as a present to her ladyship, and promised to send suitable presents to the Lhasre Kushos (her sons) as soon as I reached my home. She then inquired if I had not paid a visit to the Dalai Lama (Kyapgon). I replied in a pathetic tone that I was come to Lhasa at a most inopportune time, when small-pox was raging all over the country. At a time when interviews were denied to the chiefs and nobles of Tibet, it would be most silly for *me* to hope to see the incarnate Chanrassig. She then pressed me to take the *gyathug* and *momo* sweetmeat, which I only tasted, and begged to be excused for having failed to do justice to the dishes on the ground of my being an invalid. Apela said that, judging from my appearance, she thought I had no positive illness; but that I was only not restored to health, so that I would do well to take nutritious food. After dinner Lhacham asked me if I would like to be presented to the Shape, to whom she had already mentioned me. I thanked her for her gracious kindness, and said I would avail myself of the honour of the presentation some other day. At three o'clock Tshing-ta and Pador returned, and were served by the *machan* with dinner in the *solthab* (kitchen). The *shetama* whispered in my ear that Kusho Sangyela, a distinguished monk of Tangaing, versed in fortune-telling, was there, and if I would consult him. At 4 P.M. I took leave of Lhacham and returned to our lodging.

Gelong Pomda came at 5 P.M. with a trayful of Chinese cakes and bread. I received him with much respect, and thanked him for his kind presents. I distributed some of the cakes among my companions. Gelong Pomda also gave me half a brick of No. 2 Duthang tea, which was most welcome at this time. In the evening I sent a rupee with a scarf to the *shetama* to consult Kusho Sangyala, the Shape's nephew, about my fortune.

6th June.—My companions told me that yesterday they had consulted Gahdan Thipa, now residing at Lhasa, if in his opinion it would be safe for them to proceed to Samye *viâ* Gahdan. The great Lama found that both Tshing-ta and Pador would eventually be attacked with small-pox: they would therefore do well to return to Tsang or stay a few days at Lhasa, or return to Tsethang before making a pilgrimage to Samye As I was still an invalid, I could hardly be expected to help them in the event of their falling ill. They therefore begged me to give up the idea of proceeding to Samye or Gahdan. I told them if I failed to avail myself of the present opportunity to visit Gahdan and Samye, it would hardly be in my lot to see Samye, and asked them to go to Champa Rinpo-chhe, who was now staying at Potala as guardian of the young Dalai, and gave them a couple of *tankas* and a scarf as consultation-fee for the Champa Lama. Being alone in the house, while I was lying in bed, two of my neighbours came and warned me not to sleep, and when I *did* fall asleep, they awoke me saying that such slumbers would make me worse. They also in course of conversation said that the Doñer Chhenpo had been unnecessarily detained at Lhasa by the Gya*l*-tshab's Durbar; that the Regent having delayed to acknowledge the Tashi Lama's letter and presents, the two governments were not on good terms; and that the Regent was not satisfied with the presents which the Tashi had sent for the young Dalai. They did not tell me the cause of the misunderstanding which worked at the bottom, and which, in fact, was creating a gulf between the divine and spiritual brothers. They also related a cold-blooded murder committed only a few days ago by two monks of Dapūng, who had given shelter in their house to a rich trader. The case was under investigation. They also informed me of another case in which a pupil was charged with the murder of his tutor. I felt much concern to know what punishment the murderer would get.

7th June.—I felt very unwell in the morning, and did not get up from bed till 8 A.M. Apela, the chief *Shetama*, came to see me. She brought for me a few cakes and some *bag-leb* (unleavened bread), and said that apparently I had no illness of a serious nature, but was only in a convalescent state. She recommended yak-beef and soup made of yak-marrow. "Alas," said I to her, "I have a great repugnance for beef; how can I restore my health with beef?" She said that good mutton could not be had in the *thom*, and gram-fed mutton being too fatty might increase phlegm, but promised to fetch me some good mutton from her mistress' store. She related to me how her son, Nima-tshering, disgusted with a layman's life, was constantly pressing her to let him become a monk, and knowing I had influence over Kusho Sing-chhen Rinpo-chhe, she begged me to introduce Nima-tshering to his holiness, and to help him as a friend. After talking for a short time with Tshing-ta, she again came and sat by my bed, and expressed her sympathy for my helpless state. "Oh, your wife and mother do not know that you are so ill in this foreign land, nor how and where you are, or who nurses you!" she exclaimed. The very mention of my dearest ones at home brought tears to my eyes. At noon I sent Tshing-ta to buy some bread cakes and *phing* from the *thom*. At about three I dressed two trays with the painted biscuits and sent them to Gelong Pomda as return presents. Tshing-ta then prepared tea, which I took with moistened barley. Shortly after arrived the Parpon of Potala *sho* with about 60 volumes of printed books, according to the list I had drawn out a few days ago; but he did not bring the life of the Regent Desi Sangye Gya-tsho, which I required most. He told me that historical works, such as Khachem, Kakholma, Ga*l* rab Jonshing, &c., were very rare, but he would be on the look out for them. We pressed him to take tea, which he did with reluctance. He expressed great regret at my illness, and shutting his eyes for a few seconds, made prayer for my recovery. He told me that he lived in the house of Shapé Yuthogpa, which was not far from Panjor Rabtan, and that he would supply me with printed books at the rate of 30 pages per *tanka*. I spoke to him about my messenger Phurchung who would soon be at Lhasa to fetch the books. I did not take charge of the books, but referred him to Apela. He agreed to my proposal, and went away after the usual *chhambul* (salutation).

After sunset, water was sprinkled all round my bed to prevent *dashig* from swarming into my blankets. There was a slight rain and gale. Tshing-ta asked if I still desired to proceed towards Lhokha (Samye, Chethang, &c.). I told him that, having come thus far from the remote country of Aryavarta, I would not limit my journey to Lhasa, but would proceed further towards Gahdan and Samye. At this both he and Pador looked with surprise towards me, and said, "Sir, do you like that we should die?" "Far from wishing it, I would myself rather perish than retrace my steps towards Tsang from Lhasa," said I. "Very well, if you say so, we shall go with you. *A-oosee A-oosee* (we don't care, we don't care). Yes, sir, according to you, it does not make much difference if we die," said Tshing-ta with dissimulated anger. "The Minister, Chhyan-dso Kusho, and Lhacham, have all requested you to help me in my journey; our lot should be the same. I am already ill; you are afraid that you may fall ill. How is it, Tshing-ta, that you now reply to me in such a manner?" asked I. He and Pador then said that they would serve me according to the Minister's command, and that they would not care for their lives. I asked them to consult the Abbot of Gahdan and to fetch me a written *sûng-ta*, or divination, which would enable me to arrange about the course of my journey. "Sir, he lives at a distance of about fifteen miles from here, and it is doubtful whether he will interview us at all, the time being very unfavourable," replied Tshing-ta.

8th June.—This morning I felt somewhat better, and expressed my desire to visit the Chokhang. Pador reported to me that the sore on the back of our brown pony was gone, and that both the ponies were perfectly fit for use, and begged me to ride on one of them as I was going out. I preferred walking to riding, and entered the Chokhang in company with Tshing-ta at about 8 A.M. The most remarkable parts of the Chokhang at the entrance and on the ground-floor are the numerous wooden pillars which support the upper floor. The chief of these are called *Ka-wa shinghlochan*, having capitals decorated with sculptured foliage. At their base beneath the ground, treasures of gold and silver are believed to have been concealed. Those who offer prayers to these in the name of Buddha for wealth and enjoyment are believed to have their wishes generally fulfilled. At the foot of the pillars called Dul-go-chan (dragon-headed capital), there are concealed many charmed inscriptions, possessed of wonderful efficacies in subduing devils, curing diseases, and particularly in repelling invasions and evil designs of enemies on Buddhism and the Government of the sacred Lamas. Beneath the base of the pillar called *Sengo-chan* (the capital of lion's head) there are hidden under ground many bundles of inscribed benedictions called *Yang-yig*, through the enchanted efficacy of which Tibet traditionally derives excellent harvests of nutritious corn. Many *Yang-yig* with precious things packed in the skins of the snow-fox and snakes are said to have been buried underneath the floor of the Lukhang shrine, in consequence of which it is believed that the cattle-wealth of Tibet remains undiminished. Under the ground below the image of Dsambhala is concealed a box made of onyx filled with consecrated *Tag-sha* (a kind of medicinal plant growing in Tibet), in virtue of which precious stones, wool, grain, and cattle abound in the snow-girt country of Tibet. The famous mendicant's platter made of lapis-lazuli is said to be preserved for the maintenance of the peace and prosperity of the Tibetans in ages to come. Besides these there are underneath the Kyil-khor (sacred circle with geometrical figures and ornamentations) a giant image of Naga Kuvera, in the right loin of which are concealed many precious stones of immense value to serve as endowments for the repairs and maintenance of this great religious establishment in the remote future.

Both inside and out of the Par-kor, or central passage for circumambulation, are the Dolma-lhakhang (temple consecrated to Arya Tara) erected by Rinchhen Tag-pa, and Ary-lhakhang (temple of the venerable), containing a bronze of Chanrassig with a thousand arms and eyes, and with eleven heads. Besides these there are the images of Chyamba (Maitreya) called the seer of the market, constructed by Lodoi Gyal-tshan, a devout Buddhist king. On the outside of the outer passage for circumambulation is a cavity in the rock, which on account of its not being covered or overgrown with moss or grass is believed to be able to retard the progress of the Kyi-chhu towards the Chokhang. To the north of this passage formerly existed a fountain, the water of which possessed healing virtues, and was as delicious as nectar. To the west of the Chhyi-kor stood the stone monolith containing an inscription of the treaty concluded between China and Tibet, which is a monument of the chivalry and power of King Thi Ralpachan. It is also said that there is a stone pillar buried underground which contains many inscriptions of the ancient kings. King Nahdag Nang and Tarton Chhoi-wang made presents of a great number of gold and silver oil-burners to the Chovo. King Gewa-bum gave thorough repairs to the great shrine, rebuilt its outer walls, and provided it with a gilt dome constructed after the Chinese style. The beautiful tapestry and wall-curtains of the Chokhang were repaired and new paintings added to them by Dao-*hod* shonnu. The tapestry of the grand chapel of the Chovo was supplied by Shakya-Ssangpo, the first chief of the Sakyapa hierarchy. The chief Tshal-pa Thipon erected the chapel, which contains sixteen pillars, and is generally kept covered by a network of iron wires.

9th June.—After tea I proceeded towards Ramochhe, accompanied by Tshing-ta and Pador, by the north *Linkor* road, keeping the Gya-bum Chhorten to our right. Here we met many Ragyabas (scavengers) in companies of eight and more, strolling in the roads and on the look-out for new-comer, stranger, or pilgrim. I was much perplexed when I saw them, lest they might fix their attention on me. But my sickly appearance and homely dress helped me to pass unnoticed. I was told that these pests, when they see any new-comer, first surround him and clamorously supplicate for alms; but if their solicitations are not listened to, they thrust their filthy and offensively smelling hats in the faces of the strangers, at the same time pouring on them the most vulgar and insulting language. If any one takes offence at this conduct, and asks the cause of their insolence, they at once say, "No, my lords, we are simply saluting your lordships." It is said that the Ragyabas of Lhasa are not all born of Ragyaba parents. The convicts, such as thieves, bad characters, &c., after punishment are sent to their village headmen, who are required to keep an eye on them and their behaviour. When the authorities fail to ascertain the homes and the name of the headmen of the villages to which the criminals belong, they generally make them over to the charge of the chief scavenger, who admits them into the class of the Ragyabas. At present the head of the Ragyabas of Lhasa, named Abula, about 50 years old, takes charge of all such vagabonds and unclaimed convicts, and employs them as scavengers. The children of all Ragyabas, whether born or employed as Ragyabas, are destined to be scavengers by profession. Abula is a well-known individual. He wears a Purug kho (long loose coat made of scarlet serge) and yellow turban, and is a prominent figure among the scavenger race. The law does not allow Ragyabas to live as gentlemen, or to make any show of wealth. They are precluded from erecting houses like other Tibetans. A Ragyaba, however rich he may be, must live in a house made of horn walls, and must not dress like a gentleman or live in a stone or brick-walled house. As regards the life of Ragyabas, the common saying has:—

"Chhyi Rwa cho rong rong
"Nang Do-tha*d* rong rong."

"The outside of a Ragyaba's house must bristle with points of horn, though the inside of it may be studded with coins."

From a distance the Ragyabas' houses look handsome, but when one comes near them their appearance is simply loathsome. In some of the walls the horns, mostly of sheep, goat, and yak, are bound together with their convex sides upwards, in a curious way. I was told that the interior of these walls are filled with such rubbish as bones of animals, hair, and refuse fleece of sheep and goat. There are two celebrated cemeteries in Lhasa, where the bodies of dead Ragyabas are disposed of, being cut into pieces to satisfy the hunger of vultures and dogs, over which also Abula's jurisdiction extends. Cursed is the lot of the Ragyaba race, and cursed is Abula if on any day no corpse is brought to these cemeteries, observed one of our informants. People believe that it is ominous for Lhasa if one man does not die every day.

We at last entered the court of the antique shrine of Ramochhe, built by the illustrious Kong-jo, the daughter of the Emperor Thaijung, who was married to Srong-tsan Gampo. The Princess being thoroughly versed in astrology, astronomy, and particularly in the mystical sciences of divination called *Porthang*, which was derived from the symbolical figures discovered on the back of a tortoise, found that there was a spot in the new-built city of Lhasa which was connected with hell, and underneath which there was a crystal palace inhabited by the Nagas. On that plot of ground she erected the shrine of Ramochhe, which she consecrated to Buddha, and placed his famous statue brought from China on the chief and central altar of it. Thus, in the language of the Gya*l*-rab, she designed to intercept the progress of misery in this world by obstructing the way of the damned towards hell. Whoever at the time of death was brought to this great sanctuary was delivered from hell and destined to be born again in this world of men and gods. It is true that both the great sanctuaries of Lhasa, viz. Rasa T'hulnang-ki Tsuglakhang and Ramochhe, were finished in the same year, and also consecrated by King Srong-tsan Gampo at the same time. On a former visit I only noticed a few monks who were engaged in conducting religious service in this shrine; but this time there were many monks reading the sacred books and chanting hymns very gravely. It is said that about three hundred learned monks from Dapûng and Sera every month come here to study and perform ritual services.

After the death of King Srong-tsan Gampo during the reign of Mang-srong Mang-tsan, when Tibet was overrun by the Chinese, the Tibetans, fearing that the holiest of the holies might be taken away to China, concealed him within the southern door called *Melong-chan*, which was covered by plaster on both the sides. During full three generations did the image remain hidden from public view. At last Kyim-Shing Kung-Jo, the mother of King Thi-srong-de-tsan, unearthed it and transferred it to the great shrine of Rasa-thulnang, where it still remains. The image of Chovo Mikyo-dorje (Lord Vajra Akshobha), which was seated on the principal altar of Rasa-thulnang after it was brought from Nepal, was at the same time transferred to the shrine of Ramochhe. Legends say that this image was constructed by Indra, the Lord of the dwellers of heaven, and consecrated by Buddha himself. Many extravagant stories are related about its miraculous powers. When it was being brought to Tibet from the principal shrine of Nepal by the Nepalese princess, on account of the steep and rocky nature of the passage it was left on the way. But Thi-tsun, the princess, by force of her prayers induced the image to walk where men had failed to carry it on their backs! Among the principal divinities and objects which we noticed in this shrine were the following:—

- An image of Do*l*-ma (Arya Tara), made of sandal-wood.
- An image of Thug-je chhenpo (Chanrassig), of sandal-wood.
- Two *chhorten*-like tombs containing the relics of King Srong-tsan and Princess Konjo.
- The images of the eight principal disciples of Buddha, constructed during the time of King Srong-tsan.

On the right and left of the principal entrance were the two terrific images of Chhyagna-dorje and T'ho-vo Vyug-ñon-chan, consecrated by Tsong-khapa himself. On the walls were painted the images of one thousand Buddhas and the ten exploits of Buddha Shakya Simha. It is well known that the sanctuary was much patronized by King Lha-je Ge-vabûm, and Ñimahosser, who largely endowed it with funds and presents. The celebrated sage Sakya Ssangpo rebuilt the altar, together with the hinder wall of the central chapel. Tshal wa T'hipon gave thorough repairs to the whole shrine. Among the most remarkable curiosities of Ramochhe are the following:—

- An image of Thug-Je Chhenpo, made of conch shell.
- An image of Ton-yo-dub, made of jade.
- An image of Do*l*-ma, made of turquoise, which is believed to be able to deliver oracles.
- An image of Tshe-pag-me (the god of unlimited life), made of coral.
- An image of Chhyagna Dorje, made of *mumen*, a kind of bluestone.

Besides these there are several images of enchanted women and fairies, miraculously obtained by Thantong Gya*l*-po, the principal of which are the following:—

- An image of Dorje Khadoma, made of conch shell.
- An image of Padma Khadoma, made of coral.
- An image of Rinchhen Khadoma, made of amber.
- An image of Laki Khadoma, made of turquoise.
- An image of Sangyas Khadoma, made of *mumen*.

There were also several jars and bowls of gold and jade of very ancient date. While returning to our lodging a householder who had heard of me saluted me as Amchila, and entreated me to see his old father who was dying. I saw the old man, felt his pulse, and said to his disappointment that, as I had no medicines with me, I could not treat him. In the afternoon two respectable men, hearing that I was a physician of Ladak, came to our house, and begged me to attend a case of erysipelas. I declined to take up the case on the plea of my own illness. I was, indeed, surprised to see that even at Lhasa I was gradually being known as an Amchi (physician). I suspected that Tshing-ta and Pador must have given out that I was versed in the healing art.

At about 3 P.M. we went to see Lhacham, who received me with her usual affability. She was not cheerful to-day, and said she felt feverish. Her second son was laid up with small-pox. Her father, Dahpon Ssurkhang, who had lately been attacked with small-pox, was recovering from it. She said that by constantly having to go out to see her father and sisters, she was falling ill. While talking to me she was twirling a prayer-wheel. I expressed much sorrow at her illness, and sat for a while with downcast eyes. "How is it, Pandibla, that you too seem to be so very sad," said she with a sigh. I replied "Kusho Khyen, blessed madam, your ladyship, depending on whom I have come to this strange land, has to my utter misfortune fallen ill. I myself am also a helpless invalid. My great object of coming to Tibet, and particularly to Lhasa, was to see the blessed face of the incarnate Chanrassig, the lord of Tibet, and to see the far-famed image of Chovo Rinpochhe. I have seen the latter, and had I been fortunate enough to obtain at least a glimpse of the *Kyab-gon*, the lord protector of Tibet, I could have returned to my country with satisfaction. But, alas! I did not acquire enough moral merit in my former life to be able to see Chanrassig in flesh and blood." "Do not you be sorry, Pandibla, I will arrange for your interviewing the *Kyab-gon*. The chiefs and nobles of Tibet, nay even the Shapes, cannot easily get admission into the presence of the most holy Chanrassig. It is a bad time for you, but yet I shall try for your seeing the Dalai Lama," added Lhacham, and looked at me in a very gracious manner to notice if cheerfulness was returning to my face. I gravely replied, "Madam, it is very kind of your ladyship to assure me that your ladyship will arrange for my visiting Potala and the grand Lama, but Madam, I am diffident of my ability to scale the hill and the lofty palace of Potala: for I feel difficulty even in ascending the ladders of your ladyship's residence; besides, if that living divinity be not easily approachable to Shapes, how will it be possible for me to see him at such a time?" She did not say anything in reply, but kept on twirling her prayer-wheel and smiled. Tea was served to us by her servants, and a tray of cakes and bread placed on my table by Apela. She showed me the beautiful bangles made of the purest jade and brought from Kham, which her father had presented to her the other day.

10th June.—Early in the morning, when after getting up from bed I was sitting at tea, Pador informed me of the arrival of a *ku-dag* (gentleman), who was waiting to see me. I went out to the verandah to receive him. He said that Kusho Lhacham of Phala had arranged with the Donñer Chhenpo of Potala for my interview with the Dalai Lama to-day, and that he had come to ask me to make myself ready for the same as soon as possible. On my begging him to tell me who he was, he said that he was a Dungkhor of Potala, and belonged to Bangye-shag. He then politely bid me good morning, and walked towards the east lane, promising me to return shortly after. I never dreamed that Lhacham would take so much interest in my seeing the Dalai Lama. Although transported at the prospect of seeing the Vice-Regent of Buddha in the flesh, yet I feared I would hardly be able to ascend to the top of the grand palace after climbing up many a steep ladder and flight of steps. If I failed to reach the top of Potala, my companions and acquaintances would laugh at me and call me *sonam manpa* (one of low moral merits). This thought prevailed in my mind when Tshing-ta and Pador were hastening to equip themselves for going to Potala. I wavered for a while, but at last resolved not to lose this grand opportunity of paying my respects to the holiest of the living holies. Finishing breakfast as quickly as possible, I busied myself in dressing. My companion assisted me in putting on the church dress and in tying the *kerag* (garter) that I might not appear like a *Palpo*. Chola Kusho, accompanied by a servant, now arrived, and wished me to start at once. Forthwith with three bundles of *puo* (incense-sticks) in our hands and a roll of scarves in our breast-pockets, and chanting the several hymns and particularly the mystic *Om mani padme hum*, we sallied out, and on coming to the street saw a calf sucking milk and several women fetching water in our direction. My companions smiled at seeing these auspicious omens, and Chola Kusho observed that I was a lucky fellow. I rode on my pony and Chola Kusho on his white charger. Arrived at the eastern gateway of Potala, we dismounted and walked up a long hall, on two sides of which were two rows of prayer-wheels, which pilgrims twirl at the time of going in and coming out from Potala. We then commenced ascending a flight of stone steps eight to ten feet long and about three feet broad. This passed, we arrived at a landing-place, in the middle of which stood a *doring* (stone monolith) the sides of which were smooth. I did not see any inscription on it, with the exception of some sacred symbols. Two long flights of steps ascend towards Potala from this place. We rested here for a few minutes, our ponies being made over to a bystander, who was known to Chola Kusho. No one is allowed to ride further up. We took out the scarves to be in readiness for presentation. A young monk now came down to conduct us to Potala, and we proceeded towards the palace with slow paces, looking only towards the ground before us. The difficulty of breathing compelled me to take rest frequently to draw breath. However, I mustered all my strength and walked up holding Tshing-ta's hand. Chola walked first, the young monk second, Tshing-ta and I, followed by Pador, walked last.

At the termination of the stone steps my difficulty increased. The several ladders which conducted us from one story to another were steep and placed in dark halls. I counted five long ladders which took us to the ground-floor of Phodang Marpo, or the red palace built by the first Dalai Lama with the assistance of his illustrious Regent Desi Sangye Gya-tsho. Fortunately for me my difficulty of breathing diminished as I ascended upwards, and my companions wondered at this miraculous change in my constitution. I found an explanation of it in the help which Tshing-ta lent by pulling me upwards by his hand, and the exertion I myself made to avoid shame. But this was not evident to them, and they frequently remarked "Yam-tshen" (how strange) it is that he succeeds in ascending these difficult ladders! Half a dozen ladders still remained to be scaled. I took rest for a few minutes, but the young monk, who thought we might be late, pressed me to make haste. At about eight we reached the top of Potala, where a number of monks were waiting with anxious expectation for an interview with his holiness. I was pointed to a seat by Kusho Chola, who was being greeted by several monk officials. Tshing-ta sat near me, and smilingly observed that I was a saint born on account of the sins of my former life in India, where there is no Buddha. From the top of Phodang Marpo (red palace) we enjoyed the grandest panorama of Lhasa and its suburbs, together with the extensive flat valley of the Kyi-chhu, in the centre of which the great city stood, with numerous groves all round it, and the great monasteries at the foot of two long ranges of bleak and lofty hills, the green tanks and reservoirs for water situated in the midst of the several Linga (groves), the gilt domes of the Chokhang and the gilt spires of several palatial buildings and monasteries of Lhasa. I could distinctly make out the groves of Norpu Linga, Tse-dûng Linga, Chhyag-dso Linga, Shar chang sreb, and Kushu Changsreb, all now green with fresh foliage. Shortly after some high rank Lamas dressed in loose yellow mantles arrived, with all of whom Chola Kusho exchanged greetings. They entered the hall of reception one after another in solemn array. We were in anxious expectation of being summoned to his holiness' presence, and had our eyes fixed on the door of the entrance. At last three respectable Lamas arrived, and said that the Dalai Lama would presently conduct a divine service in honour of, and for blessing the departed soul of, the late Meru Tah Lama, and that we would be allowed to attend it. They then asked us to come in a row one after another. Walking very gently, we arrived in the middle of the hall, where one of the Donners (scarf collectors) received the presentation scarves from our hands. Chola Kusho here in a whisper advised me not to put any silver or gold, if I had any to present to the Grand Lama, in the hands of the Donners, but to place it on a casket in the presence of the Grand Lama. Accordingly, when in my turn I was presented to his holiness, I unexpectedly placed a piece of gold weighing a *tola* on his lap. This surprised all the officers, who looked toward me, surprised at my boldness. Chola Kusho drew near the chief Donner and whispered something in his ear, probably introducing me to him. We were seated on rugs spread in about eight rows, my seat being in the third row, at a distance of about ten feet from the Grand Lama's throne and a little to his left. When we were all seated, there was perfect silence in the grand hall. The State officials walked from left to right with serene gravity, as becoming their exalted rank in the presence of the Supreme Vice-Regent of Buddha on earth, headed by the Kuchar Khanpo, who carried in his hand the bowl of benediction containing the sacred *thu* (oblation water painted yellow with saffron) intended to be sprinkled over the audience. The carrier of the incense pot suspended by three golden chains, the Solpon chhenpo, who carried the royal golden teapot, and other domestic officials, now came up, and, arrived in his holiness' presence, stood motionless as pictures without looking on this side or that, but fixing their eyes and their attention, as it were, on the tips of their respective noses. Two large lamp-burners made of gold resembling flower-vases flickered on two sides of the throne. The great altar resembling an oriental throne and borne by lions carved in wood, on which his holiness, a child of eight, sat, was covered with silk scarves of great value. It was about four feet high, six long, and four broad. A yellow *kinkob* (mitre-hat) covered the Grand Lama's head, the pendant hoods of which veiled his ears, a yellow mantle covered his person, and he sat cross-legged with the palms of his hands joined together to bless us. In my turn I received his holiness' benediction and surveyed his divine face. Other Lamas approached his holiness with downward looks, and resumed their respective seats, never having the audacity to look up to the Grand Lama's face. I wanted to linger a few seconds in his holiness' presence, but was not allowed to do so, other candidates for benediction displacing me by pushing me gently. The princely child possessed a really bright and fair complexion with rosy cheeks. His eyes were large and penetrating. The cut of his face was remarkably Aryan, though somewhat marred by the obliquity of his eyes. The thinness of his person was probably owing to the fatigues of the ceremonies of the court, of his religious duties, and of ascetic observances to which he was subjected since taking the vows of monkhood. Remembering the accounts of the freaks of fortune which had lately brought him to this proud position. and which compelled his predecessors to undergo untimely transmigrations, I pitied his exalted position; for who knows that he will not be forced to undergo another transmigration before reaching his twentieth year? The reception hall was spacious, measuring, according to my guess, about 40 feet by 30 feet and 15 feet high. At the centre of it there was a skylight opening below the eastern end of the roof, through which the gilt domes of the tomb of the first Dalai Lama were partially seen. The roof was supported by three rows of wooden pillars, each row containing four pillars. The furniture of the room was of a description generally seen in great Buddhist monasteries, with this difference, that all the hangings were of the richest brocades and embroidered cloth of gold, the church utensils of gold and silver and the wooden articles, such as the back of the throne, tables, capitals of pillars, most exquisitely painted after the Chinese style. The walls, which were beautifully plastered, contained beautiful paintings descriptive of the exploits of Buddha, of Chanrassig, and other great saints, besides the images of the successive incarnations of the Dalai Lama, and the scenes of Tsong-kha-pa's religious achievements. The part of the hall behind the palace was decorated with beautiful tapestries and satin hangings in the shape of the sacred Gyal-tshan, or cylindrical flag of the Buddhists. The floor was remarkably smooth and glossy, but the doors and windows, which were painted in dark red, did not impress me with favourable ideas as to the skill of the Tibetan carpenters. The outside of the walls of the whole gigantic fabric and of the uppermost buildings of Potala were painted dark red; the central building, which is nine-storied, is called Phodang marpo, or "red palace."

When all were seated after receiving benediction, the So*l*-pon Chhenpo poured tea in his Holiness' golden cup from a teapot made of gold. Four assistant So*l*-pon poured tea in the cups of the audience, consisting of the head Lamas of Meru monastery and ourselves. Before the Grand Lama lifted his cup to his lips a grace was solemnly said, beginning with "Om āh hoom," thrice chanted, and followed by this prayer, "Never even for a moment losing sight of the three Holies, always make reverence to the Triratnas (Trinity). Let the blessings of the three Konchhog (the Trinity) be upon us," and so on. Without even stirring the air by the movements of our limbs or our clothes, we slowly lifted our cups to our lips and drank the tea, which was delicious and flavoury, taking care that no sound or noise was made by the lips or tongue in drinking. Three times did the assistants of the So*l*pon serve tea, and three times we had to empty our cups, after which we put them back in our respective breast-pockets. Thereafter the So*l*pon Chhenpo placed a golden dish full of rice in front of his holiness, which he only touched. The *Shalag* (remainder) was distributed among all the gentlemen present. I obtained a handful of this consecrated rice, which I carefully tied in one corner of my handkerchief. The following grace was then uttered by the assembled monks with much gravity:—

> The most precious *Buddha* is the most perfect and matchless teacher.
> The most unerring guide is the *Sanga* (Church).
> The most infallible protection is in the sacred *Dharma*.
> We offer these offerings to these three objects of refuge. Reverence be made to them.

Then his holiness in a low indistinct voice chanted a hymn, which I understood to be a blessing for the translation of the soul of the late Chyikhyab Khanpo to the mansion of Devachan at the expiration of the *pardo* (the space between death and transmigration or translation into another world). Then the assembled monks in grave tones repeated what his holiness had uttered. The late Chyikhyab Khanpo, well known as Meru Tah Lama, had lately died of small-pox. He was one of the most distinguished scholars of Tibet, and held the highest position in the Court of Potala. The interval of forty-nine days after his death was not yet expired. To-day, I believe, was the twenty-seventh day of his *pardo*. Then a venerable gentleman rose from the middle of the first row of seats, and addressing the Grand Lama as the incarnate Lord Chanrassig, made a short address reciting the many deeds of mercy that that patron saint of Tibet had vouchsafed towards its benighted people. At the conclusion of his address, he made offerings of many precious things to his holiness for the benefit of the soul of the late Meru Tah Lama. I heard the last words of the address distinctly, which were to this effect:—

"Om vajra Bhumi āh hoom. On this mighty earth, Om vajra rishi āh hoom, surrounded by the outer wall, lies the great world, at the centre of which stands the Mount Rirab, the King of Mountains. To the east of Rirab lies the continent of Luphags-pa; to the south Dsambuling; to the west Balang Choi; and to the north of it lies Daminan. Besides these there are great islands, such as Lui, Luiphag, Nayab, Nayabshan, Yodan, Lamchhogdo, and Daminan Dao, &c. The mountain of precious stones, the enchanted tree which yields everything, the wonderful milch-cow, the uncultivated harvest, the precious wheel, the precious commander of forces, the precious princess, the gem, the prime minister, the prince of elephants, the king of horses, the bowl of treasure, the dancing girl, the garland maker, the songstress, the dancer, the flower supplier, the perfumer, the incense burner, the illuminator, the sun, the moon, the umbrella of precious things, the cylindrical flag of victory, these, together with this work, at the centre of which exist all sorts of precious articles, accumulated by the joint good luck of gods and men, I reverentially present to the most perfect Lamas and spiritual guides, and particularly to Arya Chanrassig and the whole body of gods who form his staff and retinue. I reverentially pray that you most graciously accept these presents for the good of all living beings." At the conclusion of the address he thrice prostrated himself before his holiness' throne, when a solemn pause in the ceremony followed, after which the audience rose and the Grand Lama retired. The Donñer Chhenpo accompanied by two of his assistants called me to his presence, and pointing to me asked one or two questions to Chola Kusho. One of his assistants gave me two packets of pills, and the other tied a scrap of red silk round my neck. The pills I was told were *chinlab* (blessings consecrated by Buddha Kashyapa and other saints), and the silk scrap, called *sungdü* (knot of blessing), was the Grand Lama's usual consecrated return for presents made to him by pilgrims and devotees. We received these with profound veneration, and gently walked out of the hall of ceremonies.

At the entrance we were met by Chola Kusho's younger brother, who is a monk of Namgya*l* Tatshang, and lives within the eastern cells of the Grand Lama's own monastery, which is attached to the palace. Both Chola Kusho and his brother kindly conducted us to the different rooms of the palace, and explained the history and tradition connected with them to us.

First of all we visited the chapel containing the image of Arya Lokeshvara (Chanrassig) with eleven heads and a thousand arms, in the palm of each of which there was an eye. Near it was another image with four arms; the chapel contained many golden miniature *chhorten*, bronzes, and silk hangings. We were next conducted to a hall, with an old throne-like altar in it; opposite this there was a group of images of the family of King Srong-tsan-Gampo. The illustrious king was seated in the middle; on his right and left sat his two celebrated wives, the Nepalese and Chinese princesses. In his front, but a little to his side, stood the veteran General Gar, Prince Gungri Gung-tsan, and the Minister Thonmi Sambhota. In front of one of the principal pillars of the hall stood the fearful image of Jampa*l* Shinji with six faces, said to be possessed of great sanctity on account of its having been consecrated by Buddha Kashyapa. Tradition has it that when the shrine of Ho*d*-chhong-do was set on fire, this image, miraculously flying up into the sky landed here. Chola Kusho then conducted us to the grand hall, where the first Dalai Lama Nagwang Lo*b*-ssang used to hold his court. The throned altar, the sandal-wood image of Gonpo, a terrific deity, the eleven-headed Chanrassig, and Tamdin (Hayagriba), were the principal objects of sanctity in it. There were hung from the capitals of the pillars the ancient tapestries containing pictures of King Srong-tsan's family, Chanrassig, and the first Dalai himself, all of which were belived to be indestructible by fire and possessed of great sanctity. We were then led to the hall, where the illustrious Desi Sangye Gya-tsho used to hold his council. The most important and conspicuous thing here is the gilt tomb called Dsamling Gyan of the 5th Dalai (first Gya*l*-wa-Rinpochhe), Nag-wang Lo*b*-ssang, which is double-storied. The dome is covered with thin plates of gold, which have stood the wear and tear of nearly three centuries, and still retain much of their original freshness. We were told that there is contained inside the golden chapel the Dalai's remains surrounded by numerous precious stones. The tomb also contained many articles of the richest design brought from China, Mongolia, and other remote parts of High Asia, the people of which pay homage to Buddha's Vice-Regent in the flesh.

From the time of the erection of this celebrated tomb the custom of erecting a gold-gilt tomb to cover the remains of the successive Dalai Lamas originated. Those that we saw to the right and left of Dsamling Gyan were small compared with it. One of these contained an image of the eleven-headed Chanrassig, about which a curious story is related Once the mother of Dalai Ka*l*-ssang Gya-tsho ransomed the life of a sheep, which as soon as it was released from the butcher's stake, went to graze in the field, where with its hoofs it dug out a miraculous image of Chanrassig, the eleven-headed deity. In one chapel there were about a hundred golden oil-burners presented by the celebrated Lama Longdo Rinpochhe. Whoever pours butter in these burners and lights a lamp in honour of Buddhas and the saints, obtains perfection within a very short time. Thus visiting the chapels and the historical halls of former Dalai Lamas and kings, beginning from the top, we descended by ladders which led us to the Namgya*l* Tatshang. So puzzling is the plan of this palace that I could not discover the design on which such a huge fabric had been raised. In fact an entire hill was covered with lofty buildings; the walls built of stones were massive, varying from two to four feet in thickness. In some parts the stones were beautifully banded, no mortar being used. In the thinner walls mortar was visible through cracks. A part of this gigantic building lately underwent repairs. Very little care is taken for sanitation, and as we passed by a narrow passage between two walls the stench from the watering places was intolerable. Presently, we were led into a small room about ten feet by six feet. This was the cell of Chola Kusho's brother, who is a monk of Namgya*l* Ta-tshang. We were seated on a *khamba* rug, and three little tables placed before us. A companion of our monk host poured tea into our cups, and begged us to moisten barley. A very fair-complexioned, tall monk entered the room just as we had lifted the tea-cups to our lips. As we wanted to rise from our seats in honour of his arrival, he prevented us from doing so by saying *La ma shang, ma shang* (Sir, don't you get up). He, it seemed to me, was the *gyergan* (tutor) of Chola Kusho's brother. After enquiring after our health, he asked if we were pleased with the visit. After exchanging compliments, he ordered some mutton steaks (*momo*) to be brought for our entertainment. After refreshments we rose up from our seats and approached Chola Kusho with scarves and a few coins in our hands. Perceiving our intention, he said that it was not the custom (*lug sol*) to receive remuneration for such trifling services: he had come to help us at Lhacham's request and to enquire if we were satisfied with the interview and with visiting the different chapels of Potala. We then offered five *tankas* as presents to his brother, who too declined with thanks. It was nearly noon when we took leave of Chola Kusho to return to our lodging. I gave some reward to the man who had held my pony near *doring nangma*, or the inner monolith.

From Potala we returned by the Ling-kor road. I have already mentioned that an extensive marsh lies to the north-west of the road leading to Lhasa from Dapung, intervening between Sera and Dapung, drained by numerous tiny outlets in summer. At the entrance of the city there was a stone bridge over an outlet of the marsh, about

40 paces long and 12 broad, with parapet walls three feet high on both sides. The two piers of the bridge, roughly and irregularly constructed, were about ten feet high and six thick. The stream at this time was teeming with fish. From this bridge the road goes towards the north-east by east for a distance of 200 paces to its junction with the *Ling kor*, or circular road round Lhasa. From the bridge Potala is due east, Chogpoiri south-east, while Kunduling lies in a south-south-easterly direction, and Kesar Lhakhang, which stands midway between *Chhorten* Kaling and Kunduling, bears slightly to the south-east. To the south, beyond the river Kyi-chhu, were two *Lhakha* (flags placed on the tops of lofty isolated peaks in honour of the sylvan gods) visible a great way off. To the farthest north of Lhasa were seen three lofty peaks of barren mountains without any votive flags. From the junction of the *Ling-kor* road with the roads coming from the bridge, at a distance of 200 paces, was a rivulet stocked with fish, crossing the *Ling-kor* road and bridged by a culvert about 20 feet long and nine feet broad. Long stone slabs and beams were laid on the piers instead of planks and wooden beams. The grand road extends in a due easterly direction from this culvert up to Chhorten Kaling, the entrance of the city, where it slightly bends northwards to join the Potala *Sho* road. At a distance of nearly half a mile from this culvert, in a north-easterly direction, we met a small culvert under which a tiny stream flowed listlessly. The road running in a north-easterly direction for a furlong and then turning due east, passed by a park on the left side, where there was a shed for an elephant. The elephant itself was standing in a barley-field A hundred paces further on was the gate of the temple called Lukhang Thamo (the house of party-coloured Nagas), situated exactly behind the hill of Potala. This shrine, which had a small gilt Gya-phig (dome) on it was about 60 feet long and 25 feet broad. At the further termination of 200 paces of the road was the junction of a lane leading into Lhasa with this road. To the right hand side were numerous groves and gardens, and to the left suburban villages with numerous barley-fields, now green with barley and pea plants. The *Ling-kor* road runs eastwards for 300 paces, and slightly bends southwards, whence the monastery of Rigya*l*, where the Dalai Lama resides during his infancy, is clearly seen. From this point Sera, which is about three miles off, bears to the north, and Potala south-west by west. A road from the suburbs coming from the north joins it here. Proceeding further for half a mile the road passes the gateway of the celebrated shrine of Ramochhe, whence at a distance of 200 paces on the *Ling-kor* road are the junctions with it of a road leading to Sera and of another leading to the Chokhang. The latter is above half a mile off from this point. The circular road here bends towards the south-east, and passes for a distance of nearly 300 paces by the filthy village of the Ragyabas (scavengers), which is distinguished from others by its huts made of horns. The road continues running in the same direction for about a furlong more, and then bends towards the south and joins a street coming south-south-west from Lhasa. Then running for about half a mile in the same direction, it passes by the walls of Lhasa, here about 10 feet high and 4 feet broad, and by the antique *chhorten* which commemorates the site of the spot where the first Chinese princess, on reaching Lhasa, made profound salutations towards the palace of Potala and to her saintly husband King Srong-tsan Gampo. Now-a-days the place round the *chhorten* is used as a cemetery where the dead bodies of the town people are disposed of. The pigs, which feast on the dead bodies here, are said to yield most delicious pork. Every day at least one dead body is considered necessary for the preservation of the honour of the cemetery, otherwise it is ominous for the city. The road then turns towards the west, and running for about five hundred paces makes another bend at a second *chhorten* containing another cemetery. The entire land to the left of the road and the Dur-toi (cemetery) is filled with the horn huts of Ragyabas. From this Dur-toi *chhorten*, at a distance of about half a mile, is the junction with it of the ferry ghât road which comes from Tshe-chhogling monastery, and also of a broad street coming from the interior of Lhasa. The Kyi-chhu makes its appearance here. On the left side of the *Ling-kor* road up the bank of Kyi-chhu the entire land is filled with numerous gardens and groves, tastefully planted with different kinds of trees, and containing tanks and nicely lined avenues. The Kyi-chhu, nearly a mile wide at this place, running due west for a distance of three hundred paces, passes by the residence of the Lhading family of Lhasa, the chief of whom is one of the leading Dung-khors under the Government. From Lhading the southern gate of Lhasa, called Lhogo, is only one hundred paces, whence the city wall runs westward. At the gateway several helpless beggars were supplicating for alms, and many *pariah* mastiffs where lying down listlessly on the road. The road leading to the interior of the city from this gate is about thirty feet broad, and is irregularly lined with many old willows and other trees with large stumps. Some of these are said to be upwards of a hundred years old. A little off from this gate, towards the west, there is a small *chhorten* which is not used as a cemetery, but which on account of its charms is believed to arrest the progress of the Kyi-chhu towards Lhasa. It was erected by some saintly Lamas, and consecrated for the purpose of saving Lhasa from the encroachment of the river. At a short distance from the *chhorten*, the river bends southward, where an extensive park comes to view. This is the famous Norpa Linga, where there is a palace for the retirement of the Dalai Lama from the bustle of the court. From this place Potala bears north and Chogpoiri north-north-west. At a distance of nearly a furlong from the *chhorten*, a road from the interior of the city joins the *Ling-kor* road, and the city wall turns northward in the direction of the Doring. Here is a huge cairn which receives a stone from every passing pilgrim or traveller as a tribute of reverence to the sacred city, and particularly to the great sanctuary of Potala.

At a distance of 250 paces from this cairn there lies another still larger cairn. From this latter to the Chhyag-Chhegang (the place of offering profound salutation), which contains about a dozen small cairns, the distance is 100 paces. To the right hand side of Chhyag-Chhegang lies a garden, the walls of which are low and adjoining the road. At a distance of 200 paces from Chhyag-Chhegang there is an approach of a deep channel of the river Kyi-chhu, which, for a distance of another 200 paces, runs touching the *Ling-kor* road. Here the Tibetans, fearing further encroachments of the river towards the city, have erected a revetment wall from the very edge of Kyi-chhu. Had it not been for this wall the river would have ere long washed away a part of Lhasa. Further off the river recedes leaving a sand-bank between it and the *Ling-kor* road. People come here to bathe during the summer and autumn. From the side of the sand-bank the road bends northward, and running for a distance of 500 paces stops at a culvert constructed on a deep canal teeming with fish. The culvert rests on a single pier and a bluff rocky ledge of Chogpoiri, which runs over the stream. A steep passage over the southern flank of Chogpoiri now takes the place of the *Ling-kor* road, and in one place it runs for a distance of 200 paces over a precipice overhanging a stagnant pool of the Kyi-chhu. It is very dangerous for travellers on account of its extreme narrowness, as well as for its being overhung by rough forky rocks. Here many niches are cut out, inside of which are carved many relievo images of Buddhas and saints. Many of the images were painted blue, red, and yellow. Several monks, almost continually engaged in painting and repainting the faded frescoes of old niches, supplicate for alms from passers-by. This is a kind of profession to them. At a distance of 400 paces from the culvert was the sentry-house, where the Government had stationed guards to watch the movements of strangers and travellers. The passage here gradually becomes broader, and, running past a pair of *chhorten* for a distance of 100 paces from the guard's house, joins a well-beaten road which comes from the Norpu Linga. The *Ling-kor* road now runs direct north for a distance of 350 paces, leaving the gateway of Kunduling to the right-hand side and that of Norpu Linga to the left. Then leaving the gateway of Norpu Linga the road runs slightly north-eastward for a distance of three hundred paces and meets the Dapung road, by which we had entered Lhasa. The grand street of Lhasa runs in a north-easterly direction for a distance of seven hundred paces between Chhorten Kaling and Doring, the part of the city lying on both sides of this road being called Bana sho*l*. But the well-known Bana sho*l*, with which the following anecdote is connected, is situated to the north of Kyi*l*khording:—Once on a time a monk of Potala clandestinely came to make himself merry with a woman of Bana sho*l*. He was somehow or other detected and publicly punished to serve as a warning to his fellow monks. Hence whenever a monk goes to a town or village or to a layman's house he is commonly ridiculed as having gone to Bana sho*l*.

When Tsongkhapa first visited Lhasa, he went to the houses of many laymen to buy curds; failing to obtain that delicacy of monks, he knocked at the door of a woman's house, and was received as a mendicant inside the house. The housewife asked Tsongkhapa what brought him there, to which he replied that he came from Tsongkha, a remote place of Ando, to make pilgrimage at the shrine of Buddha, and that he was very thirsty, and would thank her for a little curd with which to quench his thirst. The housewife asked him if he could pay for it, but as Tsongkhapa had no money in his pocket, he said that if she would do an act of piety by helping him he would prove to her that he was a Lama. After drinking the curd he tried to wipe out what curd stuck inside the pot with his fingers. At this the housewife observed that if he was a Lama he could as well by his saintly power turn the pot inside out, and thus easily lick up the contents: when lo! the pot was immediately turned inside out to the housewife's surprise. Tsongkhapa blessed the woman for her kindness and hospitality, while she, charmed with this miracle, fell on the ground prostrating herself to make obeisance. Tsongkhapa then made some predictions respecting her descendants. These are now the most prosperous residents of Lhasa at the present day.

In the evening a caravan of donkeys with barley-flour and butter arrived from Gyan-tse and halted in a house near Panjor Rabtan. Tshing-ta met the headman of the party, who communicated to him the sad news of the Minister's being attacked with small-pox. He told him that his holiness very much wished to see us back at Dong-tse as soon as possible. As our whereabouts were not known, no letters could be addressed to us, but he had instructions to tell us his holiness' wish if he happened to meet us at Lhasa. This news made us very uneasy. But as small-pox was not now generally considered fatal, we had some consolation in the hope that he would soon recover. My companions, who only wanted an excuse to return to Tsang on account of their aversion to accompany me to Samye, now began to press me to prepare for returning to Dong-tse. Pador went to arrange with the *Pon-gu-pa* (conductors of the donkey caravan) to carry our things, but returned disappointed, as none would leave Lhasa shortly. Although I had fixed tomorrow for going to see Shape Rampa, yet Tshing-ta began to throw obstacles in the way by saying that that nobleman would not much help us in any way, that Tibetan high officials are procrastinating and ceremonious, that if he at all granted me an interview, he would do so only after we had waited upon him several days, and that as the object of my coming to Lhasa was simple pilgrimage, it was not good for me to see this man or that man. I did not give much heed to his gratuitous advice, but I found that they were bent on returning to Tsang, and no amount of persuasion could prevail upon them to alter their intention. I obtained a very interesting legendary account of the origin of the Dalai Lama's line, which I afterwards verified by comparing it with the accounts mentioned in the Gyal rab.

Once on a time, when Buddha was sitting in Venu Vana, surrounded by his disciples and followers, from the hair of the crown of his head, which was the repository of perfection and contemplation, there issued forth a flash of light, combining all the colours of the rainbow, which propagated itself towards the kingdom of Himavat. Looking at this phenomenon, Bhagavan smiled. At this one of the Bodhisattva begged him to enlighten him as to the cause of his so doing. Bhagavan said "Noble sir, in time to come in that country of Himavat, to discipline which all the former Buddhas failed, and which is the abode of evil spirits and hobgoblins, there will be diffused the religion of Tathagata as glorious and bright as the rays of the sun. All living beings will then be conducted to the path of emancipation from earthly miseries. The patron and discipliner of that border country is Arya Chanrassig. When in a former existence that saint was engaged in practising the different Bodhisattva rites in the presence of the thousand Sugata Buddhas, he prayed that he might conduct the living beings of Himavat, the border country never touched by any Buddha, to the path of sainthood; that that border land might be the sphere of his vicarage, and the natives of that country, including the *devils* and *srinpo*, who dwell there, his children, whom he might conduct to the path of Nirvana, like a lamp to destroy the gloom; and that he might establish on a permanent basis the church of the Tathagata, and diffuse the teaching of all the Sugata Buddhas in Himavat, so that the natives there, on hearing the names of the three holies, might seek refuge in them, and reaching the prosperity and enjoyments of the celestial regions, might gradually with his help attain Bodhisattva perfection. Owing to the intensity of this prayer the Land of Snow became the province of Chanrassig's apostolic vicarage, and from his inner being a ray of white light issued forth, which, illuminating in its way this earth, proceeded towards the mansion of Devachan, where it melted away, being mixed with the radiant lustre of Amitabha, the Buddha of immeasurable light. Again, from the heart of Buddha Amitabha issued forth a ray of light, which, falling on the lake Pemachan, melted away. This was an omen of the appearance of a divine incarnation who was destined to convert the country of snow into Buddhism. The mansion of Devachan is unlike this material world, but is a spiritual world where the spirits of the blessed enjoy beatitude. In the mansion of Devachan the basis of matter is a combination of precious things, which, though variegated like the squares on a chessboard, yet do not resemble nor are named after the elements which form this earth. The fire of bright knowledge gives light, though it is very different from the terrestrial element of fire. The stream of divine drink flows perpetually, though there the earthly element of water is unknown. No trees or woods find place there except the wishing-tree of the Bodhisattva knowledge, which alone flourishes there. There people eat the food of contemplation, but there is no such thing as bodily hunger or thirst in Devachan. People dress in the clothes of morality and modesty, as there is nothing like the covering of the nakedness of the body. In that blessed land there is no sun or moon, for people there are lighted by the glorious lustre that emanates from their own spiritual person. No strife nor quarrel disturbs the serenity of the moral atmosphere, as all are possessed of the power of forgiveness and charity. All is beatitude, and there is nothing like misery or suffering. There is found perfect deliverance from misery without any preliminary migratory existences; sacred images of Buddhas and Bodhisattvas, but no mundane living being; immortal spiritual life, but nothing like old age and death and sickness. There they are born in a miraculous way in lotus stems, for which reason the four kinds of birth are there unknown. At this time, when lake Pemachan was miraculously illuminated, King Ssangpo Chhog, who reigned at Devachan, in order to make offerings to Buddha, sent his followers to collect flowers on its shore. They there saw a stem of lotus, of which the leaves were like shields, and which bore a shining fruit as big as a jug, resting in the middle of a flower having a thousand petals. They at once informed the king of their discovery, who, accompanied by his ministers, went to the spot in a boat. "What might be this wondrous fruit; does it contain a gem or jewel divinity?" said the king to his ministers. By the intensity of his prayer the fruit burst, and there came forth a wonderful figure of that miraculous saint who was destined to be the lord patron of the land of snow, with one head and four hands, and sitting cross-legged in a contemplative mood. With the first pair of his hands joined he paid homage to the Triratnas. With the outer right hand he held a string of beads of white rock crystal, and with the left a white lotus opposite his left ear. Decorated in brilliant colours adorned with most exquisite ornaments and precious stones, and dressed in various scarves, he sat motionless like a picture. The colour of his person surpassed the whiteness of snow under the sun. A fine antelope skin covered his body from the left shoulder to the nipple. His locks were tied in five kinds of knots, and a crown studded with precious stones adorned his head. He sat smiling. A halo of light, a perfect nimbus, illuminating the ten quarters, shone round his person. The very sight of this miraculous celestial manifestation threw the king and his ministers into ecstacy, and they immediately carried the saintly child to the palace in a triumphant procession, enlivened by divine music. Then the king, approaching the most perfect Buddha Amitabha (immeasurable light), thus addressed him—"Most reverend sire, say if this wonderful child, whose beauty is unspeakably ravishing, is a saint miraculously manifested here to be the heir of my crown, or to be the teacher of all living beings of the mortal world?" To this Buddha Amitabha replied—"This lotus-born miraculous child is no other than the self-caused manifestation of the most merciful Chanrassig, who careth not to succeed to your celestial throne. He will be born on earth to extend Nirvana to the living beings of the mortal universe, and particularly to convert the savage beings of Himavat, the land of snow." Then placing his hands on the child's head, he addressed him—"Oh, thou, the jewel in the lotus, noble child, be blessed and victorious! By the force of thy prayer to subdue the living beings of Himavat, that country which baffled the efforts of all Buddhas to convert it, will be converted to Buddhism. Oh, Arya, when the natives of Himavat will see thy image, or hear the invocation *Om mani padme hum,* (Oh, thou! the jewel in the lotus) they will immediately obtain deliverance from the three kinds of damnation, and joyfully proceed to paradise. As soon as the dwellers of Himavat, demon cannibals, hobgoblins, evil spirits, devils, genii, and other mischievous and blood-sucking animals, who do injury to person and life, will see your blessed image, or hear the sacred mantra *Om mani padme hum* they will be freed from evil thoughts and intentions, and be inspired with generous feelings. By their saintly proclivities they will show compassion and charity to all living beings. The animals of Himavat, such as tigers, leopards, bears, hyenas and other hurtful and carnivorous animals, as soon as they hear thy noble voice, will be subdued, and will lose their mischievous and brutal propensities when they see thy image or hear the invocation *Om mani padme hum.* The natives of Himavat will behave to each other with kindness and generosity. They who suffer from want of food or drink will, when they see thy image or hear the sacred invocation, drink nectar and eat ambrosia. The sick, the blind, the mischievous, the maimed, and the helpless, will find refuge in thee, and when they see thy image or hear thy invocation, will have their wants supplied. In the land of snow, Oh Arya! the honour of being patron and tutelary deity will fall to thy share. Depending on thee as a patron and tutelary god in time to come, numerous Buddhas and Bodhisattvas will become incarnate in the country of Himavat for the propagation of the sacred Buddha Dharma. Based on the sacred invocation *Om mani padme hum,* the precepts of Buddha will be diffused over the land of snow. Let the sacred Dharma be blest. Let it prosper in thy name and in the invocation *Om mani padme hum.*" Such were the benedictory expressions of Buddha Amitabha towards the miraculous image of Chanrassig when it first became manifest in the mansion of Devachan. Then the venerable Chanrassig, intensely thoughtful of the good and prosperity of the living beings of Himavat, and moved with Bodhisattva feelings, falling on his knees, approached Buddha Amitabha, and prayed thus—"Let me place all the six kinds of mortal beings of the three worlds in happiness, and particularly devote my attention to the interest of all the living beings of Himavat, to lead them to the path of happiness. Let me undergo every trouble and fatigue in conducting all living beings to a state of happiness. Until I succeed in that great work let me deny myself all sorts of comforts and repose. If ever a desire for happiness or rest steal into my mind, let my head, bursting into pieces, be scattered to the ten quarters of this world, and my body split into a thousand pieces like the petals of the cotton flower." Then Chanrassig miraculously visited purgatory, where, explaining the meaning of his *vija mantra* (*Om mani padme hum*), he led the sufferers of hell to a state of happiness, alleviating the miseries of the damned, who were being scorched in the extremes of inconceivable heat and cold. Then visiting Tartarus, where the Pretas (manes of the dead) were being tantalized with food and drink, he preached the sacred Dharma and led them to a happy state of life, removing their thirst and hunger. Then proceeding to the animal kingdom, he preached the Dharma to deliver them from the misery of slavery to mankind. Then visiting human beings, he preached unto them the sacred law of Buddha, and delivered them from the mundane miseries consequent on birth, death, sickness, and old age. Next visiting the abodes of the Asuras (demons), he brought them to a stage of happiness by means of the Buddhist law, and saved them from the miseries of eternal fighting and strife. Going next to the celestial region, he preached Buddhism there and delivered its inhabitants from the fear and miseries of migratory existence. At last returning to the kingdom of Himavat, he found that Upper Tibet, including Nari, was submerged in a lake, its shores infested with wild animals; Amdo, Kham, and Gang formed extensive fields flocking with birds; and U and Tsang, a gloomy marsh, was choked with weeds. Then arriving at the top of Marpoiri of Lhasa, he saw that the lake of Hothang was the abode of many wretched beings, whose intolerable sufferings, specially from hunger and thirst, and burning diseases and wailings, moved him to compassion, and tears gushed from his eyes. In consequence of the tears of his right eye, the goddess Do*l*-ma Thonerchan miraculously presented herself before him and said, "Venerable sire, let not thy mind be ruffled; I shall in time come to help thee in the great work of converting the people of Himavat to Buddhism." She then disappeared and fulfilled her promise long after by making the Nepalese princess Thi-tsun marry King Srong-tsan Gampo. In consequence of the tears from his left eye there appeared the goddess Arya Tara (Dolma), who in like manner promised to assist him in the work of introducing Buddhism into Tibet, and similarly kept her promise by bringing about the marriage of the Chinese princess with King Srong-tsan. Then Arya Chanrassig going to the shores of the lake uttered the sacred *mantras* and, moved with unlimited compassion, expounded the fundamental truths of the sacred Dharma and

Thus, for the first time, the invocation *Om mani padme hum* (Oh thou! the jewel in the lotus), being the address of Buddha Amitabha to Chanrassig, was heard by the gods, who instantly showered forth flowers.

made the following prayer: "May these sufferers, who for their sins accumulated from time immemorial, and immeasurably deep-rooted and intolerable, are sunk in misery, obtain deliverance! May these who swim in this boiling lake of poison, tormented by hell fire, plaintively crying under tormenting pains, be refreshed by the cool breeze of prosperity. May the millions of wretched beings who suffer from the agonies of extreme hunger and thirst, all quitting their mortal frames, be born in my celestial abode as pious and venerable beings!" Accordingly, by this prayer, many a living being of that earthly Tartarus were delivered from misery. Thus having visited the three worlds, and particularly the country of Himavat, and accomplished much for the deliverance of migratory beings, the venerable Chanrassig sat in a contemplative mood to refresh himself after the fatigues of his spiritual rambles.

But now looking from the top of mount Potala towards hell, to his infinite grief he found that not one-hundredth part of the wretched sufferers of Himavat were delivered from the torments of hell; and because he had availed himself of ease before the completion of his vow, by the power and efficacy of his former prayer, his head, bursting into ten parts, was flung into the ten quarters, and his body torn into a thousand fragments. At the time of this sad event Buddha Amitabha came to his deliverance, and collecting the scattered parts with his own hands, uttered the following charm: "All things are effects based upon desire. Whoever makes a prayer obtains what he prays for. Yes, Oh noble child! let not sorrow overpower thee. Let, by the force of my benediction, your head, which was split into ten parts and scattered, be turned into ten full heads; let your body, which was torn into a thousand parts, now turn into a thousand arms to represent the thousand Emperors of the world, and let each of these hands be possessed of an eye in the centre of its palm to represent the thousand Buddhas. Thus, for the conversion and disciplining of the living beings of Himavat, the venerable Chanrassig assumed many a miraculous form, and performed many a deed of grace for the deliverance of mundane sufferers.

The following parable from Do Samatog illustrates the real aim of Buddha Dharma, and its ideas of virtue, sin, and happiness:—Once on a time several merchants of southern India, of very little moral merit, embarked on a voyage in the outer ocean in order to purchase gems. On the seventh day of the voyage an adverse gale arose; at midday the clouds whirling in the skies screened the sun and shrouded the world in darkness, and a fearful tempest followed, shaking the earth and felling the trees of the forests. The billows of the sea leaped like enraged lions, and the waves dashing against each other burst towards the skies. At last the ship was wrecked on a rock, smashed into pieces, and the merchants were cast on the shores of Singhala Dipa. The Srinmos (hobgoblins) of Singhala, transforming themselves into handsome damsels, approached them with presents of delicious drinks, and beguiled them with pleasant conversation into love and revelry. They warned them not to go to the uplands, but each with a merchant went to her respective home, and they lived for some time as husbands and wives, and begat children. Thus when they were passing their days in thoughtlessness, forgetful of their past sufferings, there was heard a voice from heaven, which said, "Oh, luckless merchants, damned on account of your sinful actions, and thrown on this island by adverse winds like animals astray in the wilderness, ye have been seized by the lord of death. There is no means of escape from here as long as ye are infatuated by thoughts of merriment. Ye have forgotten your former sufferings which you remember like midnight dreams, being now lured by the nymph-like damsels of the Srinmos and their delicious food and drink." This brought the Depon, the leader of the merchants, to his senses, who now, alarmed at his being in the land of Srinmos, was overwhelmed with grief and with fears of death. Suspecting now that there must have been some reason for the damsels forbidding them to go to the uplands, Depon, at night, when his mistress was asleep, secretly sallied out thither. Arrived there, he heard some plaintive cries issuing out from a doorless iron house, and he climbed up a tree which stood overhanging it. From the tree-top he enquired who was inside, and a voice replied that they were unfortunate merchants who, having been beguiled by the Srinmos, had been thrown into this fearful place; that their former mistresses, whom they never suspected to be Srinmos, and by whom they had begotten many children, had confined them in that doorless iron house, from which they daily picked out one and ate him. "Beware of these cannibal Srinmos, and fly hence ye hapless merchants, for it is high time to run away. If you are once thrown into this iron prison, it will be impossible for you to escape." The Depon asked, if running away was the safest way of escape, how it could be effected. The sufferers replied there was a way to escape from the horrid snares of the Srinmos if they could only overcome their attachment to them and resist their fascinating charms, their weepings, and their persuasions. "There is a pass on yonder hill, which crossed, you will arrive at a golden sand-bank, in the midst of which there is a fountain of delicious turquoise-colored water. Around that fountain the land is covered with emerald and lapis-lazuli instead of verdure. On the day of the full-moon there will alight from heaven on moonbeam the king of horses, Balaha, majestic in appearance, and able to carry a hundred persons at a time on his back. After drinking water from the turquoise lake and refreshing himself with the emerald verdure, and rolling his body thrice on the golden sand, Balaha will stand up, and shaking off the dust, will call aloud with a human voice 'Ye merchants, and ye who are here in the land of Srinmos, having lost your way from Jambudipa, all come and mount upon my back; I will take you to your native land.' Attend his call, and mount him without delay, and he will fly away with you from this fearful place. Listen not to the hollow and luring calls of the Srinmos, nor let your mind be attached to pleasures and enjoyments with them." The Depon, resolved to act according to his advice, returned to his house. Next morning he secretly informed his companions of their dangerous position, and proposed to follow the advice of the sufferers in the iron prison. They agreed, and on the night of the full-moon, when the Srinmos were fast asleep, the Depon and his companions went to the pass beyond which lay the golden sand-bank, and saw the king of horses descending on moon-beams and landing on the sand. After drinking water from the turquoise lake and grazing on the emerald verdure, and thrice rolling himself on the sand, he called aloud to the misguided and shipwrecked merchants to mount his back. The Depon addressed him thus: "Oh thou! the miraculous prince of horses, who hast come to conduct us from misery and danger, we, the unlucky shipwrecked merchants of Jambudipa, who, by freaks of fortune, have fallen into the fearful snares of the Srinmos, take refuge under thee. Rescue us from this fearful state." So saying, he and his companions mounted on his back, forsaking their mistresses and children. Balaha, warning them not to listen to the cries of the children and Srinmo women, who would implore them to return to their houses, flew towards the skies. His flight awoke the Srinmos, who with their children called to them in pathetic voices to come back. "Oh merchants," they cried, "where do ye go forsaking your children, the flesh of your flesh; where do ye go unmindful of delicious food and drink, unmindful of your sweet home and loving wives;" and some of them lifted up their children towards their flying fathers. Hearing their pathetic cries, all the silly merchants, with the exception of the Depon, thinking that they were wronging their innocent wives and children, and unable to bear their weeping, which pierced their hearts as arrows, dropped down from Balaha's back one by one to the ground, whence they were picked up by the Srinmos and at once confined in the iron prison. The Depon, who alone remained on Balaha's back weeping, asked his fleet companion where he had thrown his followers. Balaha, also wiping with his paw the tears which gushed from his eyes, said: "Oh Depon, your merchant companions, unmindful of their real homes, through attachment to the Srinmos and their children, and the false bliss of sensuality, have dropped down to suffer the miseries consequent on their sins." Then the divine Balaha, who was no other than the all-merciful Chanrassig, preached to him the sacred *Dharma* of the four-fold truth, and reached him home, where he passed the rest of his days in prosperity and ease. He had won the jewels of the sacred doctrine of virtue and piety, but his companions, plunged in the sea of misery, now awaited their turns for death and damnation.

11th June.—Early in the morning, after tea, we went to Bangye-shag, and waited for about half an hour in the waiting-room. Lhacham then received us, and said she was very glad to learn from Chola Kusho that I obtained a very successful "Ja*l*kha" (interview) with the Kyab-gon. I thanked her warmly for her kindness, and said that it was solely through her gracious exertion that I was able to see the Dalai Lama and his renowned palace. She observed that it does not fall in the lot of even the great Shapes to obtain such unusually long interviews with the holiest of holies. I told her how my difficulty of breathing diminished as I ascended higher and higher towards the top of Potala, on which she observed, "When we go near the image of Chovo in the sanctuary of Kyi*l* Khording, the mind becomes as it were unburdened from fears and anxieties. Exactly the same has happened to you, Pandibla." She was unable to speak much, and frequently complained of feeling feverish. Her two sons were still laid up with small-pox, and she was exceedingly anxious for the health of Ane-tung, her youngest son, whom she had left with the Minister at Dong-tse. She too, it seemed to me, was being attacked with small-pox. I now thought I would do well to return to Tsang, as every one at Lhasa was suffering from fears of small-pox, and strangers were not allowed to approach the Gya*l*-tshab or the great sanctities, such as Gahdan Thipa, Chyamba Rimpo-chhe. I asked her advice as to returning to Tsang, as my companions were very anxious to do so at the earliest opportunity, and were unwilling to accompany me up to Samye. She said that their fears about small-pox were natural, and that this was a very bad time for me to stay at Lhasa: if I wished to come back, I could do so at any time now that I had become acquainted with several people at Lhasa: she would therefore advise me to return to Tsang as soon as I found it convenient to do so. Thanking her warmly for her extreme kindness towards me, I saluted her, and taking off my hat, and presenting a scarf, said that I had made up my mind to be off at once. One of her servants taking a long scarf, placed it on my hand, and wished me god-speed in my return journey to Tsang. Returning to our lodging, I sent Tshing-ta back with a scarf to pray for a loan of 200 *tankas* from Lhacham, but he did not succeed in obtaining an interview with her. In the evening, however, Apela came with the money. Now also came the Parpon (head printer), whom I dismissed by paying him his dues. The old Shetama entreated me to take care of her son Nima Tshering, who would shortly take his admission in the monastery of Tashi-lhunpo. She was followed by two of Lhacham's servants, who brought a load of gram and pea-flour for the use of our ponies on the way and a second load of provisions, such as meat, barley-flour, &c., for our own use during the journey. These were very welcome presents to us.

12th June.— Apela came again in the morning to bid us good-bye and to return the razor which she had taken to sharpen. Then came two respectable gentlemen, very decently dressed. These were the two principal disciples of Amchi Rivola, and I received them with much politeness. They told me that their master Amchi Rivola, the State physician, was suffering from cataract in his eyes: if I would only go over to their place on Chogpoiri, they would really feel very thankful to me. So saying, the elder of them presented a long scarf to me. I explained to them the state of my health and my hurry to start for Tsang.

But they replied that there was no auspicious day for starting till the day after tomorrow, and, rising again from their seats and presenting a scarf, begged me to see their master by any means. One of them felt my pulse, examined my eyes and tongue, and gave me several powders to take, two at a time at night. At the time of leaving me, I presented them with five *tankas* as the price of the medicine they had given me, but they walked off hurriedly to avoid taking the money. In the afternoon Pador told me that the ponies were in excellent condition and could carry our things with ease. Tshing-ta went to the *thom* and bought for me a pice of mutton and two *tankas* worth of *phing*. In the evening he saw the Khangner and paid the house-rent, which amounted to about 20 *tankas*, or Rs. 7½ for a fortnight. He was much pleased with that sum, and asked Tshing-ta to bring me to his house next time I happened to visit Lhasa.

The following is a list of the important places of Lhasa, such as public buildings, religious institutions, residences of chiefs and nobles, parks and groves, &c. :—

Potala (the Dalai Lama's residence and court), together with the Nam gya*l*-Ta-tshang monastery.

Kyi*l*-khording (pronounced Kinkhording), also commonly called Chokhang, *i.e.* the house of the Lord, is the principal shrine of Buddha. Ramochhe is one of the oldest shrines of Tibet.

Tangye-ling (*B*stan *r*gya*s*-*g*ling), the wealthiest and the most richly endowed of the four Lings (monastery).

Tshomoling (*M*tsho-mohi-*g*ling), one of the four Lings.

Kunduling (Kun-*h*du*s*-*g*ling), one of the four Lings, the abbot of which is now Regent of Lhasa.

The Residency of the Chinese Ambassador or Ampan.

Gah-dan Khangsar.
Lukhang.
Khar-nga-dvng (the castle of the kettle-drum).
Doipa*l*.
Nubtong.
Doring Nangma lhakhang.
Lhogo (southern gate).
Doring Chhima.
Rigsum Gonpo *chhorten*.
Tag-Go kaling. The Kaling gate. Entrance to Lhasa from the west.
*G*yu-thog Tsampa (bridge).
*G*shi-de-ta-tshang.
Chhoira.
Manithang.
Tshoiling Chho*s*-ra.
Changsreb shar.
Gya tsho Damra.
Lukhang Dungkhorpa.
Doling Chhung.
Yuthog.
Wang-Chhen-linga.
Nungna*s* lhakhang.
Manithang Gyami dungra.
Tshe-pag-Lhakhang.
Hor tshong doi.
Damra.
Mesa ssampa. Chinese temple.
Gya-*l*hakhang.
Tse-dung linga.
Chhyag-dso linga.
Gyu*d*-ma*d*.
Meru monastery.
Kones and Tanning.
Pottery market.
Thomsi-gang, the great market.
Nos-dub ding na.
Nam de-leg.
Doi cho ssampa.
Gya bum gang.
Gya-khang.
Pa*l*-jor rabtan.
Doring.
Darpoling.
Nepalese shops and market.
Rag-ga shag.
Jovo Wu-ta.
Chhamra.
Mondo*l* *r*dse khang.
Ludûng.
Nag-toi.
Tsha*l*-yang-tse.
Shingra.
Labrang ñingpa.
Ssur-khang.
Gah-ru shar.
Shar gyari.
Meat market.
Pony market.
Hong tong shingkha.
Chinese shop line.
Hakong ssakhang.
Shing-gi gyaphig (timber houses built after the Chinese style).
Dong-tse ssur.
Rang chyon.
Pa*l*-jor ling.
Rabsa*l*.
Kun-ssang-tse.
Kah shag lho (Southern Magistrate's Court).
Gya*l* ton-jong.
Karma Shar-Chog.
Bangye-shag (Phala).
Chang chan ta phug khang.
Gya gyog og sha thom (second meat market).
Ani ssakhang (Nuns' Hotel.)
Hong doi shikha.
Mon khang (Hospital).
Gya*l*-morong gyu*d*.
Cha ko-chhe.
Khachhe lhakhong (Mahomedan mosque).
Tha*l* pung gang
Chhyag tshal gong.
Rama gang ferry.
Norpu linga.
Chogpoiri.
Shalu.
Numri.
Ka*l*-ssang-ling.
Rig tong.
Chogpoiri (Medical College).
Barla lu-gug.
Lu gug naga.

V.—RETURN FROM LHASA TO DONGTSE.

13th June.—Early in the morning, as soon as the bells of the Chokhang tolled, and the great church trumpets of Tangye-ling summoned the monks to the morning service, we busied ourselves in the work of packing our things for an early start. Cheerfulness glowed in the countenances of my companions, though I was heavy at heart, having through mere ordinary circumstances to quit Lhasa so soon. Had I been well, I could certainly have remained at Lhasa by engaging new servants to replace Tshing-ta and Pador, who now obstinately refused to follow me a step further in an onward journey. When the sun was peeping from the eastern horizon I went to the roof to enjoy a view of the sacred city. The gilt domes of Potala, the eastern elevation of the red palace, the gilt spires of Rading Tangye-ling, and the glittering domes of Kyi*l*-khording, the tapering Ganjira, all lay before me, and I lingered for feasting my eyes with scenes that I thought I would never see again. What joy these magnificent sights produced in my mind, what sudden emotions overtook the heart, it is hard to describe; but the happiness was transient, for the next moment took me to a world of anxieties and troubles. After breakfast we went to the Chokhang to pay our parting homage to Buddha, whence we returned to our house at half-past six. At about seven, when all our co-lodgers and neighbours had bid us farewell, we left our lodging. Several Nepalese merchants passed us at the gate of the house we were new quitting, most of whom looked closely at me, probably taking me for a Nepalese. Several women were drawing water with raw skin buckets from a shallow well on the roadside. The wells of Lhasa, which yield excellent water, are all very shallow, the best and deepest wells having four to five feet of water with the surface below four feet. It is for this reason people say that Lhasa is situated on a lake. A servant of our landlord, and the old woman who supplied us with water, conducted us to the courtyard of Tangye-ling, there being a short cut from it to the Potala road. As soon as we reached there, the gardener of Tangye-ling required me to dismount from my pony, and told Pador to take off the *lingsha* (string of small bells) which Tshing-ta had tied round the pony's neck. The rooms of Tangye-ling, seen from a distance, appeared very spacious, and the cells of the monks more comfortable than those of Tashi-lhunpo or Dâpung. As I did not enter the monastery, I could not know other particulars about Tangye-ling. In front and to the north of Tangye-ling runs the Potala road from east to west. It is about thirty feet broad. To its north there are many groves and gardens with large buildings in them. For a short distance to the south of it we saw native residences. While passing by this road we encountered a party of *Ragyabas*, who began to clamour for alms as soon as they saw us. I rode off leaving Tshing-ta and Pador behind to dismiss them. The long lance which Pador carried signified that we were leaving Lhasa, and some of the *Ragyabas* regretted that they had not traced us out before. After a hard struggle Tshing-ta cleared them off with a *ñanpa* (reward) of a *tanka*. Amchi Rivola's man did not wait for us at Doring or the Kaling gate, as it had been arranged on the previous day. We saw several *Korchag-pas* at the gate. From Kaling we went southwards along a road leading to the top of Chogpoiri along the side of a *Linga*. Several villagers were engaged in washing clothes in a small tank of this *Linga*. In Tibet there is no system of washing, nor washermen, as people seldom wash their clothes, and the natives wash their own clothes only when they find that they cannot any longer keep them unwashed. This they do more from fear of damage to the clothes than from any idea of cleanliness, which is altogether foreign to them. Arriving at the foot of Chogpoiri, I alighted from my pony and took rest for a while sitting on my saddle rug. Pador unloaded the other pony, and took them both to a grassy nook of the *Linga*. Then, accompanied by Tshing-ta, I slowly climbed up the hillside by a rather steep zig-zag. Here I met one of Amchi Rivola's pupils, who was coming to receive me. He presented, me a scarf, and stretched one of his hands to help me in the ascent. I was conducted inside of a nice snug room, which contained a few neatly finished tables and chapels, and in the walls of which were hung beautiful tapestries containing the images of Man-lha, the god of medicine, and his retinue. Silk ceilings and satin hangings of various kinds decorated the room. The floor was glossy, and reflected some of the furniture of the house, specially the finely painted chapel with its divinities. I was seated on a high, stuffed seat, Tshing-ta to my left on a lower rug. A very handsome China cup was placed on a little table, into which a rose-coloured tea of excellent flavour was poured. At first sight I thought the tea was coloured with some dye, but it was not so. The tea, I was told, was of the finest description, and the finest yak butter had been mixed with it in the preparation. A few minutes after, Amchi Rivola was announced. He was a gentleman of a strong-built constitution and a majestic demeanour. We all rose up from our seats, and he introduced himself to me, saying that fortune had favoured him till lately, when she was pleased to afflict him with two cataracts in his eyes. He was (he continued) the principal of the Vaidurya Ta-tshang of Chogpoiri (which is the College of Physicians of Tibet) and consulting physician to the Regent, whom he frequently attended. But all his happiness and prosperity were marred by the loss of his eye-sight. If I, whom Lhacham had recommended to him as being a skilful Indian physician, succeeded in curing him of his eye-disease, he would ever remain indebted to me. If I liked to remain at Lhasa, he would accommodate me in his own house, introduce me to the Regent, and procure me a decent means of living. He begged me to stay with him and to postpone my journey towards Shigatse for the present. Tshing-ta here in an unmannerly way interrupted him with "*La tenda Kah manang* (Sir, pray do not make such commands). Kusho Pandib must return to Tsang on some urgent business." The venerable gentleman did not like the interruption, but took no notice of it. This was indeed a very good opportunity to make myself famous at Lhasa, but unfortunately I had no medicines whatever for eye-diseases in my medicine-chest; besides Amchi Rivola's case was a difficult one, which would baffle the skill of professional experts. I told him plainly that all my medicines were exhausted, and that what I had was left at Tashi-lhunpo with Kusho Tungchhen Rinpo-chhe; but now that I was going to Tsang I would take the opportunity of sending him some medicines for washing his eyes. His chief pupil now placed a bowl of barley and a dish of boiled mutton before me, to which Rivola politely invited me by a movement of his hands. I thanked him for his kind assurance to help me if I happened to come back to Lhasa, adding that as the present was an inopportune time to stay at Lhasa, I was returning to Tsang, but would probably be back after a couple of months. In the meantime a servant of mine would come to Lhasa to fetch some of my books, with whom I would surely send some medicines for Kusho Rivola's eyes. The venerable old physician, placing his left hand on his forehead, pathetically observed that he had tried every medicine which the skill of Tibetan physicians could prescribe, but all with little effect. But hearing of my fame from Kusho Lhacham, he entertained some hopes of a favourable turn of the disease, which in his opinion was curable. It was a *Linto* or *chhyi-deb* (external cataract) only, which could easily be removed by a skilful operation, but he knew no such operator in Tibet, and no physician ventured to undertake the operation. If I cured him, he would do everything in his power to make me known at Lhasa and other important places of Tibet, by introducing me to the Ampas, Regent, and the powerful chiefs of the country. He would place his entire fortune—the earning of his whole life—at my disposal, as, being a monk, he had no family to support or heir to provide for. I told him that I clearly understood his position, and was aware of the divers advantages his recovery under my treatment would bring upon me. Had I any medicines with me I should certainly have prolonged my stay at Lhasa, but now that I had nothing in my possession by which I could make myself useful to him, he had better grant me leave to proceed to Tsang. So saying I rose up from my seat, and his pupils came to reach me up to the road at the foot of the hill. The old man continued sitting in a pensive mood, his mind overcast with sorrow and despair.

We now proceeded by our fórmer route, the Dapûng road, leaving the Na-chhung on our right, where in the grove of Kyang-dang gang an old stag with ten antlers was grazing. The shrine of Na-chhung, with a gold gilt dome in the middle of its roof, is a remarkable edifice; not less remarkable is the oracle it contains. Hence we proceeded towards Nethang, which we reached at 4 P.M.

14th June.—Starting early from Nethang, we breakfasted on the banks of the Jangtoi, sitting under the grateful shade of a group of poplars. The Jang river was full now, and a further rise of it might have caused flooding on both sides of its way to the Kyi-chhu. Several parts of the road were submerged in water, in consequence of which we experienced some difficulty in riding and in wading across them. At Chhushu*l* a shower of rain fell, which wet our clothes. We saw a caravan of yaks and donkeys halting at the court of a farmer's house. Among the people sitting round a fire in the portico of a house, I saw somebody who looked like Phurchung, but as the rains increased we hurried on our journey without making inquiries if our friend, who was expected there, was come. At 5 P.M. we reached Dsimkhar, where we took shelter under the hospitable roof of our old host. During the night heavy showers fell.

15th June.—In the morning, at about 6 A.M., the rain, which was accompanied by a gale, slightly abated, and we resumed our journey. Near the iron suspension bridge the Tsang-po had overflown its banks, and the embankment leading to the bridge, together with the sand-banks surrounding it, were now under water. I rode the pony as it waded along led by Pador, who walked along the edge of the boulder and ballast embankment, which was carried away in several places. Arrived at the *chhorten* of the suspension bridge, we met several people with laden donkeys and barley bags waiting to cross the river. Several *ko-wa*, or hide boats, were launched from the other bank, and the boatmen were straining every nerve to reach this side of the river first and obtain the largest share of passengers. The *ko-wa* were remarkably swift, and tossed over the rough and rapid river with wonderful agility. We did not risk ourselves in these hide boats, but signalled to the *tu-pon* (head man of the ferry) to send for us a large junk from the opposite bank. In our boat there were taken half a dozen donkeys with their loads, our two ponies, and ourselves. The crew consisted of six men, who begged for *chhang-rin*, or wine money. On reaching the opposite bank we satisfied them and walked off towards the Chhuvori monastery. At about 10 in the morning we came to the rock-cut road which leads to the village of Khamba Par-tse. Here we met several yakmen leading about thirty or forty yaks laden with salt and soda. At Par-tse we breakfasted in the court of the house of an acquaintance of Pador, and at about 11 o'clock resumed our up-hill journey along the steep zig-zags of this side of Khamba-la, which was most fatiguing. The ascent from the bed of the Tsang-po to the Lab-tse of Khamba-la is five times greater than the same from the margin of Yamdo lake, along the serpentine bends of which threads the road to Pa*l*-de jong. We reached the Yamdo side of Khamba-la at about 3 in the afternoon, whence we walked down to the margin of the lake. Here we met several *ta-oo* pony suppliers returning to U, after reaching some big people to Nangar-tse. As our ponies were extremely fatigued, we felt it necessary to relieve them by a fresh relay, and offered three rupees for a couple of ponies to convey our packages to Pal-de jong. The *Ta-oo* men agreed to it, and immediately changed saddles. We now fixed our eyes on the castle of Pal-de jong, which we were anxious to reach to-night. A gentle breeze blew, and the western skies glowed with clouds of various hues, the reflected images of which streamed with the running waves of the great lake. In the deep dark-blue water of Yamdo there floated no boats, no vegetation, and no birds, save the red-breast ducks and the tall-necked Ang-pa (goose). The water of the lake had risen high since we had left these shores not three weeks ago; the way was solitary, the scenery impressively serene, and inspired our minds with feelings of awe as we passed silently, observing on all sides numberless ranges of stupendous mountains, which in the distance resembled the billows of a solid and unmoving sea. No fear occupied my mind, no dread of brigands uneased it, no mundane thoughts agitated it; but I was absorbed, while passing along these dreaded solitudes, in feelings of gratitude to that Infinite Being who had called me to enjoy these wonderful sights where His unspeakable majesty alone turned the wheel of nature. We were overtaken by night about five miles above Pal-de jong, which we reached at 8 P.M. Our hostess was not at home, and her daughter and servants did not reply when we knocked at the door. At last an old woman kindly inquired who and whence we were. Tshing-ta replied that we were Tashi-lhunpo men returning from Lhasa. "Come in if you are from Tashi-lhunpo; I am always hospitable to the monks of that excellent monastery. I serve them with pleasure." When we had seated ourselves round her fireplace, Tshing-ta asked the old lady how it was that she liked Tashi-lhunpo people better than others. She said in a whisper that she abhorred the monks of Sera, Dapûng, &c., the very mention of whose name frightened her. "They are all scoundrels," she added in a still softer whisper. We were really glad to hear that the name of Tashi-lhunpo was honoured everywhere in U, and its monks looked upon as gentlemen. The old lady supplied us with fuel, cooking vessels, and water. Pador took the ponies to the margin of the lake to drink water. Though Yamdo is a fresh-water lake, yet people always, when possible, avoid using its water for cooking or drinking purposes, as it was supposed to contain certain deleterious substances injurious to the human constitution, but not to cattle. It is for this reason that Yamdo lake is not considered very sacred, whatever sanctity it possesses being due to its having numerous monasteries round and inside of its vast area. There was rain and a storm during the night, and the sound of the rushing waves was distinctly heard from inside our house.

16th June.—We left Pal-de jong at sunrise. The morning was lovely, the sky clear, and the waves of the great lake, which had so lately dashed furiously against the rocks under the way and the walls of Pal-de jong, now lay in an unruffled calm. Before we had advanced a league we met a train of thirty or forty men and women coming towards Pal-de jong. On inquiry we learnt that six men among the party, who were handcuffed and tied with ropes, were the brigands who had, two days before our first passing by Pal-de jong, waylaid two natives of Nangar-tse, one of whom they threw headlong into the lake from the cliff of Sharu-theng, but the other escaped from their hands by running away. These six men with their families were now being taken to Lhasa for trial. The Jongpons of Nangar-tse and Pal-de jong had jointly exerted themselves to detect the felons, and succeeded in tracing them to their hiding-places in a village near the Rong Chyamchhen district. The policemen were armed with matchlocks and long spears, and some of them had slings. At 8 A.M. we reached Yar-ssig, where we cooked our breakfast sitting in the court of a gentleman's house. Yar-ssig is a large village containing about 200 families. We obtained enough of yak milk, eggs, butter, and flour, and all at a comparatively low price. Some *khamba* beggars came supplicating for alms. These mendicant people, I was told, in their annual depredations over different parts of Tibet, rob the weak and fight the rich. They are very sinister-looking. After a short conversation with the householder respecting the rains and the pasturage of Yamdo, and also of the revenue which people pay to the Government, we bid them farewell. The rains had been uniform in Tsang, and an excellent crop was expected this year. The pasturage of Yamdo was most luxuriant. The upper part of Yamdo, which received the glacial melting of Noijin Kang-ssang, extends in front of and beyond Yar-ssig. It was overgrown with long rank grass, upon which hundreds of yak and *jomos* were feeding. Their very sight reminded me of the common story that yaks and buffaloes were brothers formerly. The younger brother chose to live in Tibet, the land of snow, and so his body became covered with hair; the elder brother retired to India, where he sought the coolness of the water by grazing in marshes and wallowing in mud, and consequently lost his hair. As to the revenue, the old gentleman told me, with a sigh, that the Government officials were unrelenting and exacting. They never cared to acquaint themselves with the condition of the people, their happiness or misery; that money was exacted from them on various pretences; and that a fixed revenue was altogether unknown, as they had to pay hundreds of contributions to the Church and to the State. Proceeding for about a furlong towards the east along the head waters of the Yamdo lake, and passing here and there by solitary hamlets, we reached a prominence, which probably forms the water-parting of the north-western slopes of the Noijin Kang-ssang range. To the east of this ridge lay the feeders of Yamdo, and to the west of it was a marshy flat, to cross which we had to wade through mud in several places. Numerous yaks were grazing on the pasture lands, and we saw several *dok-pa* tents smoking in the distance. In the depression of this flat, shallow pools were formed, connected with one another by narrow channels. This flat is called Tsa-thang, or "the plain of pasture," and is in fact the source of the Rong-nag-chhu, or the "black river" of the Rong district. Several mendicants from

Kham Gya-rong were passing along the *dok-pa* tents in search of alms on their way to Shiga-tse. Proceeding about two furlongs westward down the stream, we met a torrent, which coming from the Noijin Kang-ssang range flows into the Rong-nag-chhu. Then walking about a mile down the stream we came near a lofty *chhorten*, about sixty feet high. Then crossing the Rong-nag-chhu by a bridge, we reached the left bank of the river, whence, proceeding about a furlong up, we arrived at a large village the houses of which were built altogether in a different style. The walls were of bonded stone, strong though slender in appearance, and evidently capable of resisting the strongest gales. From inspecting some of the ruins we inferred that no wooden beams to support the roof or lintels were used—only long slabs of stone, which supplied the place of both. In this village, called Tsesum, there were about forty houses. Then proceeding about two miles down the "black stream," which now meandered in the defiles, we came across another stream, a feeder of the Rong-nag-chhu. This passed, we travelled for more than a couple of miles along the margin of the stream through rocky passages along the edge of cliffs before we reached the valley of Rampa.

We now entered the district of Rong proper, or the country of defiles. Here the physical aspect of the country entirely changed, the sluggish, limpid streams of the Tibetan plateau now giving place to mountain torrents, its extensive corn-fields to cultivations on narrow terrace flats, and its easy roads to steep zig-zags. Passing many ruins of ancient Tibetan villages situated on both sides of the Rong-nag-chhu, we reached the village of Rampa at 6 P.M., where we took shelter in the *mani-lhakhang* of Deba Rampa. Rampa is a pretty village, containing many huts, scattered over the rough slopes and flats of Rampa hill and the Rong-nag-chhu. The valley seemed to be fertile, judging from the nature of the vegetation and the luxuriant growth of the autumn crops. There were several *changs reb*, containing tall groves, poplars, and willows, on the river-side flat. The *mani-lhakhang*, which properly speaking is a small shrine, was under the charge of *Kuner*, a nun of twenty-five. She kindly accommodated us in a nice little room situated to the north-east, and supplied us with fresh butter and mutton, and several bottles of barley-beer, at a trifling charge. She seemed to be a pious and good-natured nun, and continually kept herself engaged in counting the beads and chanting *mantras*. When we were sitting to take tea, several villagers arrived to perform *chhoikor* (circumambulation) round the *mani-lhakhang*, to-day being the day of the new moon. As they passed round they occasionally peeped at us. Before leaving they paid their respects to the *Kuner*, who touched their heads with her prayer-wheel and talked to them of certain ceremonies in connection with the funeral of an old woman who died two days ago, and a man whose body still lay in a neighbouring house undisposed. Both Tshing-ta and Pador made two or three *chhoikor*. Some of the visitors and the *Kuner*, observing my pale looks, expressed their sympathy for me, and the latter begged my companions to look after my health and to serve me well. She, it seemed to me, feared that I would not live long, and that my companions might desert me when they would find me incapable of journeying further, and repeatedly appealed to their tender mercies to serve me to the last. Before going to bed, we paid her the *nala* (house-rent) and the price of the different article we had bought of her.

17th June.—We left Rampa at 4 A.M. at cock-crow, when it was still dark, and the starry vault still retained its glory. A chill breeze blew from the south-west against us. The castle of Rampa, with its aged willows surrounding it, presented a very imposing spectacle. Bidding good-bye to it and the village, we began our day's journey, and suddenly entered a deep gorge where the stream assumed the form of a torrent. At sunrise we arrived at the village of Srang-yul, belonging to Sawang Rampa, whence proceeding for about four miles we entered the district of Rong-chhu-tshen. The valley from here seemed to broaden westward, and the banks on either side, over which our way alternately lay, gradually rose higher and higher above the river. There were several hamlets on either bank. This district is said to belong to the Rong-chyam-chhen monastery, Deba Rang-hok, and Dahpon Yu-la. There is a hot spring near the roadside, about thirty feet round, the water of which was steaming hot when we passed by it. People resort to this spring from the different parts of Tibet for the benefit of their health. There are other minor hot-springs in this district, but less easily accessible than the one near the road. Then passing many villages on either side of the river, both in the uplands and lowlands, and crossing a bridge of stone, we reached the large village of Gyamo-kho-tshog, where we halted for breakfast, having travelled this morning sixteen miles and upwards. There were upwards of one hundred walled huts in the village, which occupied an uneven flat on the Rong-nag-chhu, the black rushing stream of which flowed at a depth of about a hundred feet from the place where we sat. The hut in which we sat for refreshment was wretched, the court being filled with sheep-dung. The wife of our host threw two yak-hair sacks towards Pador, who spread them to serve us for rugs. This part of the country seemed to be rich in cattle wealth. Herds of yaks grazed on the river-sides and the slopes of the hills. The people are also very industrious, as was evident from their reclaiming the rocky nooks of the mountain for cultivation, and from the irrigation passages cut through rocks along the steep side of a cliff, and extending to a distance of about a mile. Finishing our breakfast, we resumed our journey. Proceeding about a mile, after passing by the village of Thom-pa, we entered an extensive flat filled with splintered rocks and boulders. It was two or three miles long and a mile and a half broad. This is called Rong-do-thang. In the uplands, at a distance of about half a mile, is the celebrated shrine of Dur-mig Do*l*-ma Sûng Çhon-ma. The image is believed to be possessed of miraculous powers, and the shrine having been erected in ancient times, is considered only second in sanctity to the great temple of Thandub-Do*l*ma Shakhang of Yarlûng. The following is the legendary account of the origin of the goddess Do*l*-ma or Tara, who is the presiding deity of this antique shrine:—

In ancient times, when there was no measure of time, and when this world was called the "light of various colours," the doctrine of *Tathagata* (drum-sound) was followed by gods and men. In those days reigned a celebrated king who was reverenced by all, and was called the "Lord of reverence." He had a daughter, the princess Yeshe-dao (the moon-beam of knowledge), who for a hundred thousand years made innumerable offerings to Buddhas and Bodhisattvas. Every day she used to cover extensive fields with offerings of sacrifices, gold, silver, precious things of various kinds, and luxurious edibles. At last she prayed that by her accumulated moral merits she might be born in the state of a *chyang-chhub* or enchanted saint. As many among the male sex had attained sainthood, she desired that she might, after attaining sainthood, devote herself to the furtherance of the happiness of the female sex, among whom, till then, few had gone up to the path of Buddhisattva stage. Thereafter she contemplated on the moral virtues of the Buddhas for another hundred thousand years, when, becoming possessed of saintly merits, deep meditation, and purity of morals, she became absorbed in the contemplative state called "the *yoga* of deliverance of all living beings." She henceforth became a devoted propagator of the sacred *Dharma*; so much so that she never used to take any food in the morning before converting a hundred men and women to the religion of *Tathagata*. Having worked with the utmost perseverance and zeal during a great period in bringing all living beings into the path of deliverance (or do*l*-ma), she became universally known by the name Do*l*-ma or Tara, the goddess of deliverance. The Buddha Drum-sound now observing the immense accumulation of her moral merits, graciously ordained "Princess, may thou henceforth bear the name of Do*l*-ma for the deliverance of all living beings till you attain the most immaculate state of *Nirvana*." In the age called *kalpa nampar gyapa*, when Buddha Tonyodub turned the wheel of law, she protected numberless beings from the grasp of misery, and took vows to deliver them from damnation. Sitting in the deep contemplation called "the *yoga* of vanquishing the devils," she released hundreds of thousands of demons every night from mundane suffering. For the attainment of her pious ends she had to manifest herself in this world under the names of Pah-mo, Demo, Gemo, Shimo, Dung-mo, and Do*l*-ma. Again, in the age called *kalpa thogme*, when that celebrated and patriotic saint Chanrassig, who in his former existence was the monk Vimala prabha, being ordained and sanctified by the combined glories of the Buddhas of the ten quarters, became the pith of foreknowledge and divine wisdom of all the five Dhyani Buddhas and Boddhisattvas, there emanated from that assemblege of divine lights ten rays, the first five of which concentrated themselves to form a male in the soul of Chanrassig, and the other five to form a female angel in the soul of Do*l*-ma. This was the origin of Chanrassig and Do*l*-ma. Living now as male and female, they jointly worked for the deliverance of all living beings from mundane misery. Then the saintly Do*l*-ma having served the cause of all the living beings during several succeeding ages, at last attained *Nirvana*, and became the female energy of all the Buddhas. In the present age a ray emanating from her divine soul shot forth towards Ri-Potala (Potala hill), which enlightening the heart of many a poor soul of undefiled birth propagated the sacred *Dharma*. Among the numerous branched emanations of that light, the following are well known in this world:—Princess Konjo, Thi-tsun, and Dorje Phagmo, Lhamo (Magjor Gya*l*-mo), Yang-chanma (goddess of learning), Kurukulli and Sang-wa yeshe of Aryavarta, Machigdubpai gya*l*mo, &c. In Tibet the female saints Machig-Labdon, Khado-Yeshe-tsho gya*l*, and Dorje Phagmo of Yamdo lake, are very famous.

Leaving the Do*l*ma Lhakhang on our left, we entered a deep gorge lying between two lateral ranges extending from Yungla mountains in a north-westerly direction. The gorge then gradually expanded its valley into a table-land about a mile long and half a mile broad, filled with an immense collection of splintered rocks and boulders. This was evidently an extensive moraine in ancient times. Here and there we noticed large horns, skulls, and bones of yaks, much worn out by age. The place was lovely and most solitary, there being scarcely any living being on the hill-side or in the valley. Then crossing it we saw a foot-track, following which for a short distance we arrived at the head of a stream which flows towards Yung-na-chhu. Crossing a second ledge of hills, we descended to the valley of Yung-na-chhu, which rises from the Yungla mountain. Then sometimes following the course of this gurgling stream, at others ascending to the upland slopes above it, we entered into an inhabited valley dotted with villages—an oasis in this barren country. It was past 2 P.M. when we arrived at the village of Umi. Pador bought one anna worth of *chang* (barley-beer), which he shared with Tshing-ta. The rain clouds had gathered in the sky and a cool breeze blew. Then hurrying on our journey we reached Yungna, the largest village in the valley. There were many willows and poplars round the village. A number of men and women had collected near the gateway of a rich man's house. We did not loiter in this village as we did at Umi, but hurried on to reach our night's stage, the village of Yakpe. A slight shower of rain fell while we were passing by the village of Lucho, after which we reached the village of Dargye Shikha. Beyond the latter, in the upland, we saw two villages overhanging a grove of willows. We saw many yaks tethered in front of a house. A severe gale blew, dispersing the rain. I felt the keenness of the cold wind very much, as it penetrated through the torn patches of my garment. Then a short but steep ascent brought us to the foot of the village of Yakpe. Two ponies were halted in the court of a house along which the passage to the Gambo's house lay. Two women were fetching water, whom we asked to conduct us to the Gambo (headman of the village). We waited outside the walls of the court for a few minutes, when the water-carriers returned shaking their heads, meaning that there was no *na-tshang* (accommodation) for us. But Tshing-ta ascertained that small-pox had not spread here as yet, and that the villagers declined to receive guests in their houses for fear of small-pox. He went to two or three houses to beg for a night's shelter, but returned without success. At last Pador induced one of his acquaintances, an old widow, whose sons were away from home, to receive us. We assured her that we had no small-pox with us. We bought some excellent yak butter and milk from her, and she presented us with some parched barley and an edible shrub, more resembling the lily, which grows on the hill-tops, in return for which we made her partake of our barley meal and tea, which pleased her very much. The interior of the hut which sheltered us from the inclement weather was filled with barley sacks, donkey pack-saddles, yak-hair ropes, dry dung of cattle, and some old and broken earthenware vessels. There was a slit in the roof to let out smoke, with the neck of a broken wine mug by way of chimney. The stone walls, though constructed of loose slabs without any mortar, were thick, and prevented the wind from penetrating through the crevices. Through our hostess we engaged two ponies to carry us up to Gyan-tse.

18*th June*.—We left Yak-pe a little before sunrise. The ascent towards the Yungla pass was for about half a mile, somewhat steep. We met several *dok-pas*, who had halted during the night this side of Yak-pe. I walked on the steeper slopes that the pony I was riding upon might not get knocked up. We heard the howlings of mastiffs in the distant valleys, from which we inferred that *dok-pas* were encamped there. At nine we reached the La*b*-tse, about 17,000 feet high, where my companions uttered the usual *Lha-sol* invocation to the mountain deities. Descending a few hundred paces from the La*b*-tse, we came to a spacious flat from which we obtained a grand view of the Tibetan plateau extending to the north-east of Gyan-tse and the entire mountainous region lying to the south-east of it. From this flat we gradually descended to a saddle-shaped part of the La, where there were a few sheep-folds. Here I dismounted from the pony at the suggestion of my companions, as the descent for a considerable distance was very steep, and along the side of a sandy and rocky precipice. Fortunately there was no snow, for had there been any our difficulties in crossing the Yungla would have been great. There was no water on the Yungla to enable us to cook our breakfast. At about 11 we came to the village of Jilung, containing half a dozen families, situated at the foot of Yungla. Pador spread my rug in the shade of a bluff ledge overhanging a sluggish stream flowing towards the Nyang-chhu. Jilung belongs to Sa-wang Phala, and Pador had many acquaintances there. My companions bought for me a few eggs, some curds and fuel from a villager. We cooked our food sitting in the shade on the river-bed.

We left Jilung at noon, and for a short distance following the course of the Jilung river, entered the great plateau which terminates at Gyan-tse valley. Two ranges of mountains extended on our left and right, which diverged further and further as we proceeded towards Gyan-tse. Though this part of the country was barren and bleak, yet the number of villages in the uplands was not inconsiderable. There were *dok-pa* villages in the recesses of the mountain, the inhabitants of which tend numberless cattle. In the valley of the Jilung rivulet we noticed the villages of Tsho-chan-Tagang, Nortondab, Tara, Jaye, Chabe, and Gyan-khar. At Jaye there is a large monastery, the monks of which are under the jurisdiction of the Sakya Panchhen. Pador told us that the Jaye monks were notorious for the immoral life they now-a-days led, and that the monastery possessed many valuable images and manuscripts. Standing on a flat rock of the valley near Jaye, we enjoyed a very fine view of Gyan-tse jong. At about 3 P.M. we passed by the village of Chabe, whence I obtained a view of the Gyan-tse valley, now green with cultivation. When we arrived at Gyan-tse we were overtaken by a slight shower of rain. Here we dismissed the Yak-pe ponies, and reloading our own ponies, resumed our journey. My companions advised me to halt here during the night; but as there was enough time to reach Dong-tse, I determined upon doing so to-day. The Nyang-chhu was overflown and the bridges carried away; but being pointed out the *Rab*, or the ford, we attempted to cross it riding. First our things were taken to the opposite side of the river by Pador on the pony, which swam with exertion. Then I crossed the stream, being helped by Pador. We reached Dong-tse *sho* at 10 P.M. As I did not like to go to the monastery at such a time, we halted at Pador's house, where we passed the night.

VI.—RETURN TO TASHI-LHUNPO, AND SUBSEQUENT MOVEMENTS.

19*th June*.—Early in the morning, accompanied by Pador's brother, I rode to the monastery gate and met Kusho Tungchhen at the entrance of the Tsug-lakhang. He received me with great cordiality, and conducted me to the Minister's presence. Kusho Ane-tung, though also laid up with small-pox, getting up from his bed, sat near me and inquired of his dear mother's health. The Minister's face was swollen, and the small-pox eruptions covered his tongue, throat and lips, so that he was hardly able to speak, yet, in a faltering voice, he asked me if I thought he would recover. I told him that I thought the dangerous stage was over and the illness about to take a favourable turn. He took me by the hand and said that the gods had miraculously brought me back from Lhasa. When the Minister fell asleep, I left the room and sat to tea with Kusho Tungchhen. He asked me if I had not met Phurchung, whom he had sent to Lhasa only a week ago with my letters and a fowling-piece. Ugyen Gyatsho, he said, had come back with the packages that were left at Lachen, and very much wished to go to Lhasa in order to be useful to me. Tungchhen requested me to put up in the same room with him, which was filled with all sorts of provisions, such as barley-flour, wheat, rice, butter, meat, &c , he being now busily engaged in making preparations for the ceremonies of consecrating the newly constructed *Ganjira* and *Gyal-tshan* on the roof of the Tsugla-khang. On account of my illness, and also there being nothing remarkable to observe at Dong-tse Chhoide, I discontinued writing my diary, contenting myself with now and then taking notes of passing events.

At Tashi-lhunpo Ugyen Gyatsho was actively engaged in collecting plants. According to the instructions I had left with Nerpala for his guidance, he kept a diary to record information respecting the customs, legends, &c., of the people. From this diary I am able to give the following particulars :—

In the evening of the 19th June one of Ugyen's monk friends, named Tomrampa Gyal called at his lodging and jokingly asked if he liked to be greeted like a Golog gentleman of Amdo. Ugyen said he would like to know what kind of greeting it was before he submitted to it. Tomrampa laughed and went on to describe it. In the country of Amdo there is a nation of brigands called Golog. The Golog people, who are Buddhists, have a few monasteries in their country, the head Lamas of which are appointed from among the monks of the great monasteries of U and Tsang. Their principal Lama, whom the Golog chief recognizes as his priest, is appointed by the Panchhen Rinpo-chhe from the graduates of Ñag-pa Ta-tshang of Tashi-lhunpo, and after five years' stay at the chief Golog monastery generally returns to Tashi-lhunpo. Not long ago one of those Lamas returned to Tashi-lhunpo after five years' residence in the Golog country, during which he had enjoyed the confidence of the people as well as the reverence of the chief and his family. He had amassed considerable wealth, out of which he spent several thousand rupees in entertaining the entire body of Tashi-lhunpo monks, and in giving alms to them at the rate of an ounce of silver each. Two years ago the wife of the Golog chief came to Tashi-lhunpo on pilgrimage. After visiting the Ñag-khag she expressed a desire to see the Lama lately returned from her country. But the Lama did not make his appearance, although he was then residing within the Ñag-khag premises. In Golog people greet one another, even their female acquaintances, with a kiss, and whoever omits the kiss at the time of meeting or parting with a respectable acquaintance is considered rude and unmannerly. The Lama, who had kissed this lady hundreds of times by way of greeting, now felt a delicacy to appear before her, for how could he kiss her in the presence of the assembled monks? And particularly as the Panchhen Rinpo-chhe was present at Tashi-lhunpo, how could he hope to escape with impunity after committing what was considered in Tsang an act of gross immodesty? The lady, however, before leaving Tashi-lhunpo, invited him to a dinner. He went, and when she entered the room, he suddenly shut the door and greeted her with a kiss on the lips, and explained to her the reason of his failing to see her as early as he was expected to do, and the embarrassment he had felt in approaching her in public.

In Golog, which, partly owing to bad communications, cannot be traversed in one or two months, there are no cultivations nor good pasture-lands like those of Tibet Proper. No barley is grown, nor do the people care to live like peaceful *misser*. But they breed numerous ponies, which they use in making raids and over-running the settled border countries. The entire Golog population follow brigandage as their sole profession for earning a livelihood, and the chiefs and heads of village are all hereditary brigands from ancient times. The chiefs exact a kind of black mail called *Chagthal*, or "way-laying tax," from the people, and indiscriminately rob all people who happen to fall in their way, except those who produce *Lam-yig* from their own chiefs. It is for this reason that the Tibetan Lamas, who return from lower Mongolia and Golog, do not start before providing themselves with the necessary *Lam-yig* from the Golog chiefs through whose country they have to pass in reaching Tibet.

Again, in the Bardom district of Kham, there is a curious custom of greeting. There, when two acquaintances meet, they touch each other's foreheads together by way of salutation. It is well known that a Mongol salutes his friend by touching his own ears.

20th June.—Ugyen visited Shiga-tse *thom* at noon, and found the price of mutton unusually high—two *tankas* for a leg. In the afternoon he dined with his friend Tshul-thim, a monk of the Ñag-pa Ta-tshang, who, in course of conversation, related the following account of a conspiracy at Lhasa to kill King Mi-wang :—"In the days of Panchhen Chhoi-gyan there took place a dispute between U and Tsang. Of the four Kahlons of Lhasa, one or two are generally selected from among the nobles of Tsang. At that time Mi-wang was the only man who represented the interests of Tsang at the Court of Lhasa. Two of Mi-wang's colleagues, named Kong-bu-na-ba and Kunpang, formed a conspiracy to kill him. The fourth Kahlon, named Jáhrah, who was a friend of Mi-wang, felt great anxiety to save him. He could not secretly write to his friend about the matter, nor send any verbal intimation, for fear lest he might be betrayed. After long deliberation he wrote a letter on thin paper, which he twisted into a string for beads. He then sent this string to Mi-wang through a servant of his, requesting him verbally to count the beads as often as possible. On receiving the beads, Mi-wang, reflecting there might be some object in his friend sending the present, counted it as desired. Shortly after the string broke, and he found it was made of a slip of paper twisted. He read the letter, and understood the hints about the conspiracy, though garbed in an enigma. So he forthwith left Lhasa and rode to Tsang. Arrived at

Tashi-lhunpo, he consulted the Grand Lama as to the course he should take for the success of the Tsang army. The Grand Lama told him that as the great image of the Chovo (Lord Buddha) sat facing towards Tsang, it would not be possible for him to fight the U armies by a manœuvre from the west alone, but the Tsang forces were to attack the Lhasan army from two directions, east and west. Those from the west were to act on the defensive, but those from the east were to take the offensive. Accordingly Mi-wang went to Nahri and Chyang-thang, whence he recruited a large army from the Dokpas, with whom, traversing the Chyang-thang, he surprised the Lhasan army by a move from the west.

21st June.—When Ugyen was reading a Tibetan manuscript, his friend Tshul-thim came and sat by him for a chat. He asked Ugyen if he knew the origin of the name Yu-thog-pa, borne by one of the Shapes of Lhasa. On our friend's replying that he did not, he went on as follows:—"In ancient time there lived at Lhasa a very wise and learned physician. One day, packing his medicines in the saddle-bags, he rode off to see one of his patients who lived in a distant place. While passing through a wood, he met a wild man who stopped him, and tying his pony by its bridle to a rock, took him and his medicine-chest on his back and climbed up a cliff. Beyond the cliff was a rocky gorge filled with human skulls and bones. Here the physician was landed in a fearful dark cave, where the wild man's wife was sitting in a gloomy mood, and he thought that within a few minutes his limbs would be torn off to satisfy the hunger of the cannibal pair. Trembling with fear, he implored Buddha for help, and, as if in reply to his prayer, shortly after, the female cannibal began to cry pitifully. The wild man brought her near the physician, who, opening her mouth, found her suffering from an obstructed gullet. The wild man now produced the medicine-chest, and the physician extracted a human bone which was stuck in her gullet, and applied some ointment to the sore. The wild man then brought back the physician to the place where his pony was left, and returned to his den. The physician lost no time in mounting and riding off, but had not gone far when he heard the wild man following at a swift pace to overtake him, and, this time, thought he, to devour him, so in desperation he whipped his pony, and, luckily arriving at a village, took shelter in a house. The wild man, who had followed all the way, finding his pony at the gate, put the saddle-bags, which the physician had left behind in his haste, in their proper place and returned to the mountain recesses. The physician came out of the house accompanied by his host, opened the saddle-bags, and found them filled with turquoises, jades, corals, and a pearl head-dress. From this circumstance he was called Yu-thog-pa (*Yu*, a turquoise, and *thoh-pa* or *thob-pa*, a gainer).

22nd June.—Tshul-thim again made his appearance to-day and told another tale to Ugyen Gyatsho as follows:—"In times of yore, when beasts could talk with one another, a leopard met an ass. Although the leopard very much wished to kill the ass, yet, taking him for a powerful animal, on account of his loud braying, he did not attempt it, but proposed friendship to the ass on condition that he watched his den with its booty when he went out in search of game. The ass agreed to the proposal, so the leopard sallied out, after a tremendous roar by way of prelude, to the day's work. Shortly after there came rolling, from the top of the cliff overhanging the leopard's den, a wild yak's body killed through fright at the roaring of the leopard. When the leopard returned and saw the dead *dong*, the ass told him that he had killed it himself, and stretching out his tongue shewed it all bloody in proof of his prowess. The leopard believed him, and promised to help him in times of need, and still taking the ass for a powerful companion, sent him to graze alone in the meadow on the other side of the hill. The ass one day, after filling his stomach with grass, brayed continually twenty-five or thirty times through sheer wantonness. The leopard, thinking that his friend was really in trouble, came to his rescue, but the ass told him that he was braying merely for pleasure. Another time a pack of wolves attacked the ass, when he brayed several times, imploring help from his friend; but this time the leopard thought that the braying was merely for the sake of amusement, and did not come to his rescue, so he was torn to pieces by the wolves."

23rd June.—To-day being the 7th of the 5th Tibetan month, there was a grand review of the Tibetan soldiers. Annually two *mag-chyang* (reviews) take place, one in summer and the other in winter. An occasional *mag-chyang* also takes place when the Ampa comes here on inspection tour. To-day more than a thousand soldiers were collected and a sham fight took place before the Dahpon. The *thom* was unusually crowded on account of the review.

24th to 26th June.—Ugyen was laid up during these dates on account of acidity and headache. The 25th June is considered to be the longest day in the year by the Tibetans, who follow the Kalachakra system of astronomy. It is called *Yar-ñi-dok*, or the midsummer day.

27th June.—To-day was a holiday with the Chinese. At Pangja and other quarters in the town of Shiga-tse, where the Chinese reside, there were much festive demonstrations. The beating of kettle-drums, cymbals, *gongs*, and the blowing of trumpets, &c., were deafening at Kesar Lhakhang. In every Chinese house there was dancing and music going on, and much preparation for entertainment, and brisk movements of men coming and going. A few Chinamen, who had painted their faces in five different colours, performed a comic dance. The guitar seemed to be the musical instrument which attracted the largest audience. Some Chinamen performed theatricals, in which the exploits of king Kesar were represented. Ugyen Gyatsho, not understanding the Chinese language, could not fully enjoy the amusements.

28th June.—The Chinese festivities did not end yesterday. At Pangja the Chinese dance still went on. The acting of the religious part being over, the monk spectators retired to their respective cells in the monastery, a few Tibetans only remaining. The majority of the Chinese were engaged in eating and drinking. Daloye, the captain of the Chinese militia, was present on the occasion. The actors, before commencing their respective parts, made some highly humorous discourses. Most of them wore long, flowing beards, and all had their faces painted in different colours. One was most gorgeously dressed in a yellow silk vestment and brocades, and probably represented the warlike king Kesar, in whose presence his generals fought their enemies with swords and shields. Among the masqueraders were many wearing heads of tigers, lions, eagles, monkeys, and demons, armed with various weapons and clad in coats of mail. Some with heads of frightful demons had the bodies of beasts. In the middle of the masqueraders the image of that terrific deity—Magjor Gya*l*-mo (queen of war)—was most conspicuous, kept in a standing position with outstretched tongue. On her right was placed the image of Norpo Ssangpo, the prince of merchants. At every available creek and corner of the premises of Pangja were Chinese wine and pastry shops crowded with spectators. There was not a single Chinese woman, their place being supplied by the Tibetan women, whom the Chinamen keep during their stay in Tibet. One could make a very full meal from a Chinese *Ssakhang* (hotel) by paying only three annas. A bottle of best *arrack* sold at five annas. The Chinese admitted all classes of spectators into the Pangja premises free of charge, it being a gala-day with them. The Daloye asked Ugyen if he had any watches to sell. Not liking to say that he had one, he replied that he had seen one in the *thom*. This did not satisfy the Daloye, who repeated his question. Ugyen replied that he *had* a watch, but begged to be excused for not wishing to sell it. Before returning to the monastery, he circumambulated round it.

29th June.—Great preparations were made to-day to celebrate the summer prayer ceremony called *mon*l*am*. At Chhyag-tsha*l*-gang all the monks of Tashi-lhunpo, numbering upwards of three thousand, had assembled. A gigantic state canopy was stretched, underneath which the throne of Panchhen Rinpo-chhe was placed. The Grand Lama being unable to attend the ceremony through indisposition, his church mantle and mitre were placed on the throne, round which thronged the monks in order of precedence and rank, those of higher rank and grade having their seats near it, and the inferior monks standing at proportionate distances. The plain of Chhyag-tsha*l*-gang was enclosed by a satin wall called *gyab-yol*, which was about a thousand feet round. The people of Shiga-tse also assembled there, some under tents, some under sheds extemporized with cypress and willow twigs, and all amusing themselves with songs and repartees. A tall mast, about 120 feet long, was lifted from the ground by the monks with much uproar, from the top of which ropes were stretched to the foot of the great Kiku building, with other ropes tied to the top of the Kiku, against which it leaned. The base of the Kiku was 60 paces long as measured by Ugyen, and its height was a little more than its base. On it were hung numerous pictures containing the paintings of the entire Buddhist pantheon. At Shiga-tse the people were engaged in racing and military exercises, the cavalry exhibiting their skill in shooting from horseback. Those who failed in this feat, or lost their hats in racing, were marked for being degraded in rank. A heavy shower of rain fell in the afternoon.

30th June.—To-day being a holiday in honour of Dipankara, Buddha of the past age, the pictures that were exhibited on the western face of the Kiku building yesterday were taken off and replaced by others in which Buddha Dipankara was prominent. This image, which was skilfully worked on many-coloured satin, was about 100 feet high. On two sides of it two other gigantic images of Buddha were also exhibited. Under the great canopy of Chhyag-tsha*l*-gang almost all the monks of Tashi-lhunpo had assembled, as well as the nobility of Shiga-tse, with their wives and children, dressed in their gala dresses. All were engaged in making themselves merry in a hundred different ways. Sumptuous dinners, cooked by skilful Chinese and Tibetan cooks, were served to the great personages of the monastery and of the Government. Private gentlemen had their own tents pitched in the neighbourhood of the grand canopy. With the exception of the Panchhen, all the chiefs and nobles of Tsang were assembled there. It was rumoured that the Grand Lama, being laid up with small-pox, was residing at Thobgya*l*, whither he had repaired after visiting the hot spring of Tanag. The *Ling-kor* road round the grand monastery was thronged by a moving crowd of foreign and local pilgrims. From morning to evening there was the continuous and deafening music of kettle-drums, drums, cymbals, and trumpets. On two sides of the huge nine-storeyed building of Kiku, two gigantic lion-like monsters were kept, and now and then moved this way and that by men who had concealed themselves inside. This was indeed a great holiday for the Tsang people.

1st July.—To-day being the full moon of the fifth lunar month, was sacred to Buddha Shakya Simha. The picture of Dipankara Buddha was accordingly removed and its place supplied by a very splendid picture of gigantic size, in the centre of which Buddha Shakya Simha was seated surrounded by a number of past and future Buddhas. This was brought out from the monastery with great *eclat*. The church music was simply deafening. The procession was imposingly grave. Ten *Nag-pa* priests, who were well versed in *Tantrik* ritual, conducted a solemn religious service, assisted by 300 monks of Thosamling in chanting the sacred hymns and prayers. In the plain of Chhyag-tsha*l*-gang, the assembled monks and spectators cooked their food, entertained their friends, and during the whole day remained engaged in decent festive merriment and enjoyment of pleasures.

2nd July.—To-day the pictures of Buddha Shakya Simha and his retinue were displaced by those of Maitreya, the coming Buddha. The service conducted was similar to that of yesterday. The monastery was declared open to the female population of Shiga-tse for to-day only, for women are not publicly allowed to visit the monastery at all times in the year. In consequence of this, crowds of women, dressed in their richest holiday attire, entered Tashi-lhunpo to visit the different shrines and sacred objects contained in it. In the evening all classes of people received the *chhyag-wang* (benediction) of the coming Buddha by touching with their heads the pictures of the Kiku. The head-dress of some of the ladies were of immense value. One was estimated by Ugyen at Rs. 40,000.

In the afternoon Phurchung returned from Lhasa, carrying with him the books that I had left with the Parpon. When Phurchung reached Lhasa, Lhacham was seriously indisposed with small-pox. The Shetamas had shown him much kindness. He put up at Yuthog castle, with the Parpon. who received him with great hospitality. Phurchung stayed only five days at Lhasa, after which he returned to Tsang, being unsuccessful in finding me out. With the exception of Tungchhen and Phurchung, everyone in the house was laid up with small-pox. The Minister and Kusho Ane-tung had recovered. The climate of Dong-tse not being agreeable to my health, the Minister permitted me to spend a few days in his *Lobding linga* of Gya-tsho shar. At sunset a monk from Tashi-lhunpo arrived to take me to see a friend of the Minister (at the latter's special request), who was lying on his death-bed.

3rd July.—Accompanied by Phurchung and Pador, I left Dong-tse after breakfast. We were overtaken by a shower of rain a little beyond Dekiling, and passed the night under the hospitable roof of Angputti.

4th July.—At 3 P.M. we reached Gya-tsho shar, where Ugyen Gyatsho was waiting for me. He delivered to me the letters he had brought from India.

5th July.—Accompanied by Phurchung, I visited Tashi-lhunpo. The streamlets and irrigation cuts were swollen, and we found much difficulty in crossing them. The sick man, an ex-Gyekoi, was abandoned by all the physicians of Tsang as incurable. I shook my head when asked if he would live.

I returned to Dong-tse, on the 26th of July, and put up with the Minister in the Tsug-lakhang of Dong-tse Chhoide. Ugyen Gyatsho at the same time started for Sakya to collect plants. On the 31st I visited Gyan-tse at the invitation of the Chhyan-dso kusho of Gyangkhar, and stayed there a fortnight. I returned to Dong-tse on the 1st of the seventh lunar month, corresponding with the 14th of August. On the 29th of August his holiness the Panchhen Rinpo-chhe breathed his last, and the sad tidings reached the Minister on the evening of the 30th. Nobody ventured to say in public that the Grand Lama was dead. The Minister was overwhelmed with sorrow when he heard the sad news, and the whole of Tsang fell into deep mourning, which, according to the prevailing usage, was to be continued for a period of seven weeks. Kusho Tungchhen told me that the Grand Lama had died of pneumonia, but rumour had it that his holiness had fallen a victim to small-pox. The devout and the faithful, however, never believed this. According to them, the Grand Lama left this world because disgusted with the conduct of the government authorities at Lhasa, who disregarded the spiritual relation ever existing between himself and the Dalai Lama. According to time-honoured custom, said they, the Panchhen, and not the Gya*l*-tshal, should have ordained the young Dalai Lama into the grand order of monkhood. The Minister received another private announcement of the Grand Lama's death on the 31st. At 4 P.M., on the 1st of September, the official announcement of the sad event reached the Minister, when he stopped the religious service that was then being performed at Dong-tse in connection with the erection of some sacred symbols. On the evening of the 4th September the Minister received a letter from Shapé Mereh, pressing him to return to Tashi-lhunpo in order to discharge the spiritual duties in honour of "the retirement of the august personage from this mundane existence," and to arrange for his funeral. The coffin was to be brought in state to Tashi-lhunpo on the 10th instant. Dahpon Phala being laid up with small-pox, Dahpon Yula was in attendance on the coffin at Thob-gya*l*.

Ugyen Gyatsho with his companion Chhoitashi returned from his botanical tour to Sakya on the afternoon of the 6th. Chhoitashi went to Lhasa on the following date. Both the Minister and Ugyen left Dong-tse on the 9th and reached Shiga-tse on the morning of the 10th. Ugyen started on a second journey to Western Tsang to collect some information respecting the Pon religion. I left Dong-tse in the afternoon and arrived at the Gyan-tse castle at 5 P.M., where I was warmly received by the Chhyan-dso Kusho. I stayed in the castle enjoying the hospitality of the Chhyan-dso till the 4th October, when, accompanied by Ugyen, I returned to Dong-tse, whence on the 7th October we returned to Tashi-lhunpo. On the morning of the 17th, Ugyen started for India, carrying with him all my Tibetan manuscripts and things. On the afternoon of the same day, accompanied by Phurchung and Gopon, a servant of Gyangkhar Chhyan-dso, I started on a journey to Sam-ye.

On the 18th we reached Tashigang and arrived at the Gyangkhar castle in the evening of the 19th. Equipping ourselves with all the necessaries of a long journey, we left Gyan-tse at 6 A.M. on the 21st and reached the village of Gyaridong at half-past four. We halted at the following places:—

22nd October—At the foot of Bomdong la in a Dakpu shed. This is the entrance to the Kharu la pass.

23rd „ —Yamdo Taglung, a large village containing two monasteries and several recluse cells.

24th „ —Shari village, situated on the lake, containing two large buildings and several small huts.

25th „ —Kha-mado *viâ* Lonagla is an extensive plateau of arable lands and pastures.

26th „ —Village of Thib, below Thib la Pass, in an upland valley containing many huts and two large houses : the people were harvesting.

27th „ —Kidisho or Chidesho, a town of some importance, on the Tsang-po, containing a large fort, now in ruins, two monasteries, and a school. There is a beautiful park attached to the Sakyapa monastery.

28th „ —Village of Tag below Tag-yong-dsog monastery, surrounded by several groves of willow, poplar, and *ombo* tree.

29th „ —Sam-ye, the most ancient monastery, of Tibet, founded by Padma Sambhava under the auspices of King Thisrong.

2nd November—Taga sho, in the uplands of which is situated the monastery of Owen. Taga sho is a large village with extensive orchards and groves. The villagers appeared to be well-to-do men.

3rd „ —Thensa thee*l*, once the seat of Je-Phagno du, one of the leaders of the Kah-gyu schools.

4th „ —Jang, a small village with two large two-storied houses and half a dozen huts.

6th „ —Che-thang (Tse-thang). The fourth town of Tibet, and the emporium of the trade of Eastern Tibet.

7th „ —Tag-chhen Pûmpa, situated at the head of an upland : half a mile south of it there are one hundred and eight *chhortens*.

8th „ —Rechhung-sho is a large village containing about 100 houses.

9th „ —Tse-thang.

*

10*th* *November*—Chinchholing village on the Tsangpo, containing half a dozen houses. The autumn crop had failed here. The people are rich in cattle wealth.
11*th* „ —Mindolling monastery, the most celebrated of Ningma monasteries, has a market frequented by Kashmir and Nepal merchants.
12*th* „ —Kidisho.
13*th* „ —Gongkar jong, a very old town, now in ruins, commanded by a fort, very strong. The monastery of Dorgidas overhangs the lay town.
14*th* „ —Tamolûng, a picturesque village at the foot of the Khambala towards Yamdo side.
15*th* „ —Dablûng, a large village containing half a dozen hamlets. The yaks and sheep of Dablûng are very fat.
16*th* „ —Omothong below Bongdong La.
17*th* „ —Gobshi.
18*th* „ —Gyang-khar.
21*st* „ —Dong-tse.
23*rd* „ —Tashigong.
24*th* „ —Tashi-lhunpo.

We left Tashi-lhunpo on Thursday, the 30th of November, with a view to visit Sakya, Phun-tsholing, and Lhar-tse. On the 1st of December we halted at the village of Ge-chhûng.

2*nd* *December*—Lhûng-po-tse (Ssamdong).
3*rd* „ —Jig-kyou.
4*th* „ —Sakya.
5*th* „ —Village of Chhu-sho.
8*th* „ —Chiblûng valley at Dongang village.
9*th* „ —Dobtha Chikhang.
10*th* „ —Khamba Jong.
12*th* „ —Kongra Lamo pass, above Geu-gang.
13*th* „ —Thangu.
14*th* „ —Zemu Ssamdong.
15*th* „ —Lamoteng.
17*th* „ —Ssampa Kongma.
18*th* „ —Tumbong.
19*th* „ —Chakoong bridge.
20*th* „ —Nangama.
21*st* „ —Sontam.
22*nd* „ —Ting-chem.
23*rd* „ —On the river bank below Silling thang.
24*th* „ —Lingmo.
25*th* „ —Temi.
26*th* „ —Nam-tse.
27*th* „ —Darjeeling.

THE GOVERNMENT OF TIBET.

THE DALAI LAMA OR SOVEREIGN.

The Dalai Lama's supremacy, both spiritual and temporal, is acknowledged all over Tibet. His position as a sovereign resembles that of the Pope in Europe. He is believed by the Northern Buddhists to be Buddha's vice-regent incarnate on earth, to uphold Buddhism and particularly to protect Tibet. He never dies, though at times, being displeased with the sins of all living beings, he retires to Gah-dan,[1] the paradise of the Buddhists, leaving his mortal frame on earth. His death or temporary absence from the world is generally attributed to the want of moral merit in the inhabitants of this world rather than to any want of mercy in him. He is called Thug-je-Chhenpo,[2] Chanra-ssig, or the most merciful Avalokitesvara. The ancient records of Tibet show that he appeared on earth only fourteen times within the long period of eighteen centuries intervening between Buddha's death and the year 1400 of the Christian era. In the year 1474 was born Gedun[3] Gya-*m*tsho, the embodiment of the spirit of Gedundub,[4] the last recognized incarnation of Chanra-ssig, who founded the famous monastery of Tashi-lhunpo,[5] in Tsang,[6] in the year 1446. Gedun Gya-*m*tsho was elected Supreme Lama of Tashi-lhunpo in the year 1512, which office he resigned on being invited to fill the chair of the Supreme Lama of Dapûng,[7] the chief monastery of Lhasa. He erected the palace of Gah-dan Phodang[8] at Dapûng, which henceforth became famed as the principal seat of learning and the head-quarters of Buddhism. He, in fact, was the founder of the hierarchy of which the Dalai Lama is the head. His successor, Sonam Gya-*m*tsho,[9] who was famed far and wide for his holy character and vast learning, was invited to visit Mongolia by Althan Khan,[10] the celebrated Mongol conqueror after Chhingis Khan. On the Lama's arrival at Mongolia, Althan presented him with an umbrella of peacocks' plumes, besides numberless presents in gold and other precious things. Shortly after, in 1576, the Supreme Lama founded the monastery of Chhyi-Khor Theg Chhe-ling[11] in Mongolia. Althan Khan, while making offerings and presents to this Supreme Lama, addressed him in Mongolian as Talai Lama, the word Gya-*m*tsho in Mongolian meaning *Talai* (ocean). The Supreme Lama's predecessor also having borne the name of Gya-*m*tsho, Althan thought that it must have been his family name; but it was in fact a religious title given to him by his spiritual guide at the time of his ordination to the sacred order of monkhood. It was therefore by accident that he and his predecessor had become invested with the name of Gya-*m*tsho. It is commonly known in Tibet that Althan had invested the Supreme Lama with the title of Talai when making presents to him. For this reason Sonam Gya-*m*tsho's successors have up to this day continued to affix the name of Gya-*m*tsho as a surname to their spiritual names. The name Dalai is evidently an European corruption of the Mongolian word "Talai," meaning ocean. The title of "Ocean of Learning," of "Wisdom," or of "Virtue," are of Indian origin, corresponding to Vidyá Ságara, Jnána Ságara, or Punya Ságara. Sonam Gya-*m*tsho literally means "Ocean of Virtue" (*sonam*, virtue, and *gya-mtsho*, ocean).

The following are the names in Tibetan of the first four Supreme Lamas who presided over the Gelugpa[12] Church, by filling the chair of the Supreme Lama of Dapûng. The names rendered into Sanskrit, Mongolian, and English stand thus:—

1.	Gedun Dub	... Sángha Siddhi	... Hobrag-butekhu	... The accomplished church.
2.	Gedun Gya-*m*tsho	... Sánga Ságara	... Hobrag-Talaí	... The ocean of the congregation.
3.	Sonam Gya-*m*tsho	... Punya Ságara	... Pu-yn-Talaí	... The ocean of moral merit.
4.	Yonton Gya-*m*tsho	... Guna Ságara	... Eertini-Talaí	... The ocean of talents.

In the year 1642, Kushi Khan, the powerful chief of Khokonwar,[13] in Mongolia, conquered Tibet by defeating the armies of Deba Tsang-pa, shortly after which he presented the fifth

---

[1] *D*Gah-*l*dan means joyful—the mansion of joy. In Sanskrit it is called Tushita. At present Maitreya is believed to be the King of Tushita.

[2] Thug*s* *r*je-Chhenpo, the most merciful *s*Pyan-ras-*g*ssig*s*, the All-seer. His other names are Lokesvara or *H*jig-*r*ten *d*Vang Phyug, Padma Pani or Phyag-na-Pa*d*ma, Tho*d*-Chan, or one wearing a crown, &c.

[3] *Dge-h*dun *r*Gya-*m*tsho, the ocean of priesthood or congregation of monks.

[4] *Dge-h*dun grub, the accomplished or perfect priesthood. Grub is pronounced as dub.

[5] *B*kra-shi*s* lhun-po, the heap of glory, from *b*kra-shi*s*, glory, and lhun-po, mass, the capital of Tsang and residence of the Tashi Lama. *B*kra is pronounced as ta.

[6] *G*tsang*s*, the western province of Tibet proper, which lies to the north of Nepal and Sikkim. The word *g*tsang*s* literally means pure.

[7] *H*bra*s*-*s*pung*s*, the name of the most important and largest monastery of Tibet which is situated a couple of miles to the west of Potala. *H*bra*s*-*s*pung*s* literally means a heap of rice, from *h*bra*s*, rice, and *s*pung*s*, heap. In ancient India there existed a famous monastery called Sri Dhanya kataka, or the glorious heap of rice. The Tibetan monastery is said to have been named after that monastery. *H*bra*s* is pronounced as da.

[8] Pho-brang, a palace. Brang is pronounced as dang, except in the word *b*la-brang, which means the church.

[9] *B*so*d*-nam*s* *r*Gya*m*tsho.

[10] Althan-Khan is a purely Mongolian word meaning the golden prince—althan, gold, and khan, a prince. He was a very devout Buddhist.

[11] Phyi-*h*khor theg chhe-*g*ling. Phyi is pronounced as chhyi.

[12] *D*ge-lugs-pa, the celebrated yellow hat school of the Buddhists. The Dalai Lama is the grand hierarch of this sect. It was founded by the famous reformer Tsong-khapa. *D*ge means auspicious or propitious, and lug*s*, a sect or order.

[13] Khokonwar or Kokonor is the great lake of southern Mongolia. The lake country is also called Khokonwar. Khoko, sometimes pronounced as khokho, means blue, and *nwar* or *nor* means lake. The Tibetans call it *M*tsho-ñon-po, or the blue lake.

Dalai Lama, Nag-Wang[1] Lo-ssang Gya-*m*tsho with the sovereignty of Tibet. Kushi Khan, however, continued to rule as *de facto* King of Tibet, and appointed the Chief of Lhasa, Sonam[2] Chhoiphel, as Desi[3] or Governor to administer the temporal affairs of Tibet. By this arrangement he left the spiritual rule of the country in the hands of the Dalai Lama. Although he professed to have made a gift of the sovereignty of Tibet to the Dalai Lama, yet, finding the latter not capable of defending himself, he continued to reign as the Sovereign ruler of the country. The Dalai Lama, in his capacity of Grand Hierarch, conferred on him the proud title of Tan-dsin[4] Chhoikyi Gya*l*-po (the upholder and king of the Buddhist religion).

During Kushi Khan's reign the Dalai enjoyed only spiritual supremacy over the country, though secretly he wished much to be invested with the secular concerns of the State. But the time was not come when Kushi could safely entrust him with the sovereignty of Tibet. It may be mentioned here that Kushi had also presented the Grand Lama of Tashi-lhunpo with the province of Tsang and had appointed a Desi to govern it for him. His relations with the Dalai and the Tashi Lama were therefore the same.

In the year 1645 the Dalai Lama erected the famous palace of Potala, previous to which he and his predecessors used to reside in the palace of Gah-dan Phodang at Dapûng. During this time Kushi Khan resided in the palace Gah-dan Khangsar at Lhasa. Kushi, who had assumed the name and dignity of Gya*l*-po, gradually became more and more devoted to his spiritual guide the Dalai, so much so that he agreed to apply the revenues of the State solely to religious purposes, and undertook the permanent protectorate of Tibet in order to defend it by the aid of his Tartar soldiers against the attacks of internal or foreign enemies. But engrossed with the consolidation of his own kingdom of Khokonwar, he remained sometimes in Tibet and sometimes in Mongolia. Though the dual Government still remained, Kushi gradually transferred much of his kingly powers to the Dalai Lama, at the same time increasing the responsibilities of the Desi.

Having proved himself eminently the upholder of faith, Kushi died in the year 1654. The faithful Desi, who, for his devotion to the cause of the reformed Gelugpa school and for his zealous administration of the government of the country, was universally believed in Tibet to be an incarnate Chhoi-srung or guardian of Buddhism, followed his master two years later. By this time the Dalai Lama had assumed such a large share of the kingly duties that during an interregnum of five years no anarchy or confusion had occurred; and during the years 1658 and 1659, when there was neither king nor Desi to look to state affairs, the Dalai Lama had so ably conducted the government that throughout the country peace and prosperity reigned.

In the year 1660 Dayan Khan, the eldest son of Kushi Khan, arrived at Lhasa to succeed his father as the Gya*l*-po of Tibet. He appointed Jaisang Teba, a Mongolian Chief, as the Desi of Tibet. After a peaceful reign of eight years, Dayan Khan died. His Mongal Governor followed him in the same year. No important events mark Dayan Khan's reign. All that can be said from the records is that he and his Desi were mere puppets in the hands of the now powerful Dalai Lama.

In 1669 the Grand Lama himself appointed his Spiritual Minister Chhoi-pon-Deba[5] as Desi. In the following year Ratna Talai Khan, the eldest son of Dayan Khan, became Gya*l*-po (King). No events mark his reign, and in fact the power of the Gya*l*-po waned as the power of the Grand Lama increased. The management of state affairs had now entirely passed into the hands of the Grand Lama, his own Desi being now at the head of the administration. But the Chhoi-pon-Deba did not long sit at the head of the Government. In the year 1675 Desi Chhoi-pon-Deba retired, leaving his exalted office to Lo-ssang Jinpa,[6] another Tibetan of noble extraction. The Grand Lama had delegated to these dignitaries such high authority in state affairs that Talai Khan found himself to be a nobody in Tibet, for which reason probably he retired to his native country. In 1680 the Dalai Lama, struck with the remarkable intelligence, ability, learning, and wisdom of young Sangye Gya-*m*tsho, appointed him Desi, and conferred on him much authority in secular matters, placing implicit confidence in his ability and honesty, so much so that henceforth Sangye Gya-*m*tsho[7] united in himself the offices of King and of Desi, under the designation of Sakyong-wai-Chhyan-dso, or the Governor-Treasurer. The Dalai Lama, who had discovered rare talents in this newly-appointed Desi, and, in particular, extraordinary administrative abilities, instructed him to remodel the Government and to introduce reforms in every branch of the service by defining the duties of the various public officers.

In the kingdom of Tibet, according to the common saying, there are seven great personages, viz.—

The Grand Lama, the Desi, the four Kah-lons,[8] and the Chyikhyab[9] Khanpo.

The Government of Tibet is conducted by the following officers, viz.—

1. Desi or Sakyong-wai Chhyan-dso[10] the Governor assisted by a Secretary, called Chasag.

---

[1] Nag *d*vang *b*lossang *r*Gya-*m*tsho.
[2] *Bsod* nam*s* chho*s* *h*phel.
[3] *S*de sri*d*.
[4] *B*stan-*h*dsin chho*s* kyi *r*Gya*l*-po.
[5] *M*chho*d*-*d*pon *s*de-ba.
[6] *B*lossag *s*byin-po. *By* is pronounced as chy.
[7] San-*r*gya*s* *r*Gya-*m*tsho.
[8] *B*kah-*b*lon.
[9] *S*pyi-khyab *m*khan-po. *Py* is pronounced as chy.
[10] Sa-*s*kyong va*h*i phyag *m*dso*d*. *Phy* is pronounced as chhyi.

2. The Council of five Kah-lons, of whom four are laymen and one a monk, assisted by one Secretary, called Kahdung,[1] and an Accountant-General called Tsi-pon.[2]
3. The Jong-pons or district officers.

The following constitute the Court establishment of the Dalai Lama :—

Chyi-Khyab Khanpo, Prime Minister.

Staff	Sol-pon Chhenpo[3]	The Chief Steward, who superintends the cooking establishment.
	Ssimpon Chhenpo[4]	The Chief Chamberlain.
	Chhoipon Chhenpo[5]	The Chief Priest.
	Kuchar Khanpo[6]	The Private Secretary.
	Chhyag Tshang Chhenpo ...	The Bearer of the emblem of benediction.
	Doñ-ner Chhenpo[7]	The Chief Receiver of guests and petitions.

THE SAKYONG OR DESI (THE GOVERNOR OR REGENT).

In order that the Grand Lama might be better able to attend to spiritual matters, and specially to mental abstraction, and to meditation on the welfare of all living beings, he delegated a large portion of his sovereign duties to the Desi, who, consequently, was called by the people Gya*l*-tshab (Regent) and sometimes Gya*l*-po (King). Thus the Grand Lama having practically withdrawn his attention from the affairs of the state, the Desi became the permanent Regent.

From the commencement of the present century, unfortunately for Tibet, the Dalai Lamas have all died before coming to age, which circumstance, as a matter of course, necessitated the continuance of the Regency. When the Dalai attains majority at the age of eighteen the Regent, in the presence of the assembled ministers, chiefs, and nobles of the country, presents to him the seals of both the spiritual and the temporal Governments.

The office Gya*l*-po or Regent being the most important and powerful in the kingdom, after the expulsion of Pon-Wang[8] (who had succeeded his father, King Mi-Wang[9]) was, with the sanction of the Emperor of China and the consent of the lords, spiritual and temporal, made elective. In order that the Regent might not declare himself independent of the Grand Lama, and do away with the hierarchical form of government, it was ruled that no layman could hold it ; and at the same time the incarnate Grand Lamas of the four monasteries of Tangyeling,[10] Kunduling,[11] Tshe-chhogling,[12] and Tshamoling,[13] were made by preference eligible to it. The spirits of the four most celebrated and loyal ministers of the first monarchy were propitiated and besought to unite with the spirits of these four Grand Lamas. For instance, the spirit of Lonpo Gar, the famous Minister of King Srong-tsan Gampo,[14] was said to have united itself with the spirit of the Grand Lama of Tangyeling. To these four monasteries princely endowments were made that the Regent selected from them might not be a burden on the state ; but, however wise and well-conceived this policy may be, it has not fully answered its object. The Dalai Lamas have not been allowed to reach the age of majority and to assume the reins of the Government, and on several occasions the Grand Incarnate Lamas of the four *Lings* have had to give way to abler men like Desi Shata,[15] Rading,[16] and others.

Now-a-days the Regent is generally selected from among the Incarnate Lamas of the four *Lings*—first by the council of Kah-lons and the Chyikhyab Khanpo, whose selection is next confirmed by the oracles of Nachhûng Chhoi[17] kyong and Lhamo Sung-Chonma ;[18] and lastly, the sanction of the Emperor of China is obtained to the appointment. The establishment of the Regent consists of a Chasag (Secretary) and two De-Chhang-pas[19] (Treasurers).

The appointment of the Chasag is also subject to the confirmation of the Emperor. The Chasag is a powerful officer, who sometimes exercises the functions of his master, and no petitions, proposals or official business can reach the Regent without passing through his hands. The Regent, who generally confides much to the honesty and ability of the Chasag, scarcely passes any order on important matters without consulting him. He is entrusted

[1] *B*ka*h*-drung. Dru is pronounced as du.
[2] *R*tsis-*d*pon. *R*tsis means account, *d*pon, chief.
[3] *G*sol-*d*pon chhenpo. *G*sol means food.
[4] *G*ssim-*d*pon chhenpo. *G*ssim means slumber.
[5] *M*chhod-*d*pon chhenpo.
[6] *S*ku-*b*char-*m*khanpo, also Chhyag-tshang chhenpo.
[7] *M*gron-*g*ñer chhenpo. *M*gron, pronounced as don, means entertainment; hence donpo, a guest, *g*ñer is a keeper.
[8] *D*pon-*d*vang.
[9] Mi-*d*vang.
[10] *B*stan-rgyas *g*ling.
[11] Kun-*h*dus *g*ling.
[12] Tshe-*m*chhog *g*ling.
[13] Tsha-mo *g*ling.
[14] Srong-*b*tsan *s*Gam-po.
[15] *h*shad-*s*gra Gra is pronounced as ta.
[16] Rva-*s*gring pronounced as ra-ding.
[17] *G*nas-chhung chhos *s*kyong.
[18] Lhamo *g*sung by on-ma.
[19] *L*de-*h*chhang ; *l*de, key, *h*chhang, a hand.

with the state seal, and when any state paper or letter is prepared by the Kah-dung or the Chief Clerk, the Regent, after approval, sends it to the Chasag to be sealed, who sometimes represents the necessity of its reconsideration. The word *Chasag* literally means a sieve for tea, this dignitary being so designated as he is considered to be the test and model of refined merits.

The De-Chhang-pas are Treasurers. The word is derived from *De*, a key, and *chhang-pa*, one holding in his hand.

The following is a translation of an extract from "Dvang shel melong," being a code of regulations drawn up by the Regent Sangs *r*gyas *r*gya-*m*tsho under the directions of the first Dalai Lama for the guidance of all the Government servants in Tibet. It is the standard code which even now guides the Government. In the translation I have omitted such portions as appeared to me unnecessary and uninteresting :—

The duties of the Sakyong.

The first and the greatest bounden duty of the Sakyong is implicit obedience to the commands of his Sovereign. He should never finally decide matters of importance without soliciting the Sovereign's opinion (*gong-len*) thereon.

In matters where black acts and sins are involved, requiring the infliction of severe punishment, as well as in unimportant matters, the Sakyong should himself cut "the string" (*thag choi*), *i.e.*, pass final sentence without reference to the Sovereign, as such cases are calculated to disturb his serenity and contemplations.

With regard to strength and moral courage, which are chiefly essential in the discharge of public duties, the ethical work called Shes-rab *s*Dong-po has the following :—

"On him who has the six virtues of firmness,
Assiduity, diligence, and strength,
Prudence, and bravery in vanquishing foes,
Even the gods look with fear."

The Sakyong should always, with a perfectly pure heart, adore and venerate the *Konchhog*[1] (Rare Trinity). He should, particularly, have unshaken faith in the Gelugpa doctrine (the reformed school of Buddhism). The work Phar Phyin *bs*dus has the following :—

"If the moral merit of faith had a shape,
This world would be but a small vessel for it :
The great ocean is the repository of water ;
Who can measure its extent with a spoon ?"

The work called *bs*Kal-*b* saang also says—

"Who can seize with his mind the bounds of the skies,
Or by drops measure the volume of the sea ?
So to comprehend the extent of merit is hard,
Even by one's faith in the most perfect saints.
So, before reaching the beatific state of *Nirvána*,
Such a person will not suffer the miseries of hell.
When he has attained that stage of saintly merit,
He is praised and worshipped by the pious."

Again Grub-chhen Las kyi *r*Dorje observes—

"Lossang Tag-pa[2] being unrivalled by any,
Founded his faith in the Prince of Shakyas ;
In this world he spread *tantra* and *mantras* ;
Passing hence he has gone to Gah-dan,
As Jampa*l* Ningpo, Maitreya's chief son,
Where he will soon become a Sugata.

Thus according to these sayings this marvellous country of Tibet is the seat of the Gelugpa doctrine and of the great body of Buddhist ministers, among whom the chief hierarch is the Dalai Lama, the Sovereign Ruler : he being presented with the kingdom of Tibet with all its subjects by Tan-dsin Chhoikyi Gya*l*-po as a memorial of his sincere faith in his Holiness.

The Sakyong bearing this in mind should not make the country of Tibet the scene of enjoyment, nor make large presents for the sake of fame and self-aggrandizement. He should administer its Government so that there may be no waste or spoliation of its resources and revenues. He should, always maintaining a close supervision over the public and the Sovereign's domestic treasuries and over the officers of State, exert himself to increase the public revenue and the well-being of his subjects. He should consolidate the kingdom by serving his Sovereign with ability and wisdom, by paying attention to the service of the church for increasing the welfare of all living beings, by establishing friendly relations with the tribes of the frontier countries, particularly by carefully watching the affairs

---

[1] *D*kon-*m*chhog. *D*kon, rarity ; *m*chhog, chief : chief of rarity means god.

[2] *B*lossang-*g*rags-pa, the name of the great reformer Tsong-khapa. *B*lossang, excellent heart, Sans., sumati. *G*rags-pa, pronounced as tag-pa, means famous, or Sans. kirti.

of the border states and establishing harmony in the political relations of his own Government with them, and by satisfying the devout believers and useful allies of the sacred church. He should so enrich the state treasury that it may be compared with that of the God of wealth. In expenditure he should be strictly economic, but in supplying the royal and church treasuries with funds from the state treasury he should not act like the *yidvag*[1] — the spirits of the misers, consigned to Tartarus, who naturally look on everything with discomfort and envy, not even sparing the treasuries of the God of wealth. He should follow the example of the former Buddhist Kings of Tibet in the administration of the laws of the ten moral virtues—in extending charity to the subjects and in divers other means of increasing the happiness of the people. With regard to giving help to the subjects of his Holiness, articles which if kept for a long time would not be of much use to the Government, or when distributed to the people might be turned to good account, should largely be spent in charity.

In the work called "*g*Ser-ho*d* Dampa" is stated the following :—

"For the sake of usefulness to one's self and others, the country should be entirely governed by religion. If deceitful practices are discovered, they should be cut short by punishment sanctioned by law and religion."

Again, in the ethical work of Chanaka Gya*l*-po it is stated—

"The King being skilled in all matters, carefully examines and discriminates his servants, and by comprehending truth and faith, always governs the people and the realm righteously."

Again, we find in another place—

"To compare the wealth of a country with honey,
It is not meet to kill the bees living therein ;
As the owner milks his own cow,
So the king should govern the state ;
Thus the land governed by his efforts
Grows happy, as his fame and longevity increase."

In the laws of dGe-*b*chuhi Khrims,[2] promulgated in Tibet by King Sron-tsan Gampo in the seventh century, the killing of fish, deer and other animals of the chase, being prohibited, the Sakyong should issue notices and edicts for the conservation of harmless wild animals in the hills and valleys of Tibet. Such edicts should be placarded on all the thoroughfares and public places for general information. In this way the virtue called *Mijigpai Jinpa* (life-saving charity) should be extended. He should also protect the *misser* (subjects) by lightening as much as possible the burden of personal labour upon them, except when in the interests of the church he is under the necessity of imposing on them forced service, for instance in times of war. But in times of peace, unless it be for a particular sacred service, the Sakyong should not issue *lamyig* (road bill) to anybody at the instance of another, since forced service entails much trouble and suffering on the *misser*.

He should administer even-handed justice in accordance with the law of the country, without the least partiality to suitors or petitioners, whatever their respectability—Lamas, chiefs, landlords, clergy, laity, great or humble. He should administer justice according to the ancient laws, and particularly the code of revised laws called the Sha*l*-chhe-*b*chu drug-pa with its appendix.

The state being extensive, and the number of civil servants (*Drung-khors*) rather large, it can hardly be expected that they are all excellent officers. For the administration of large and important *jongs* (districts) such officers should be selected who by their ability and power of organization are capable of ruling over different sections of the people. They being duly qualified by their faith in the pure doctrine, and also by purity of morals, should be men in whom Government can have confidence. Men who are corrupt in the administration of justice, wicked in nature, greedy of gain, and given to partiality, should never be appointed to the important and responsible post of Jongpon.

The Sakyong should not be too ready to initial the petitions and applications of landlords and other people, nor be lavish in promises. He should inquire into the ins and outs of all important cases, regardless of the position of the parties concerned, whether great or humble, and should always personally examine doubtful points, as all *facts* are of importance to him. He should carefully weigh the comparative importance of different questions, and give early attention to matters of public interest. The taking of security in disputes, and the final disposal of important petitions, claim his early attention. Many civil cases in which the interest of landlords is involved, applications for confirmation and sanction which, when disposed of, numerous other cases will follow, one after another, like the waves of the sea, should be disposed of according to their importance and value.

Civil and criminal suits, when it is necessary to be strict to the oppressor, should be dealt with accordingly. Although it is necessary to investigate the accusations preferred, chiefly against Jongpons, Nerpas, accountants, revenue collectors, and other Government officers who have shown partiality to the subjects, or have served their own interest at the expense of the state, or acted contrary to the rules laid down for their guidance,

---

[1] Yi-dvag, pronounced as yi-dag, means *preta*, the manes of the dead.
[2] *D*ge-*b*chu*h*i khrim*s*, the laws of ten virtues (moral virtues according to the Buddhist law).
[3] *G*shi-*g*ñer, the manager of farms

or neglected to receive information of importance, yet it must also be borne in mind that as such charges are generally preferred by malicious and disaffected men, unless their truth seems probable from the evidences of independent parties, no investigation should be made on the receipt of such complaints. In some important cases he should try to learn the truth regarding such charges from the accused himself.

With the exception of all registered documents, of which the titles are important and which are entitled to particular exemption from rent, all other later grants which have obtained the Dalai Lama's sanction should be carefully examined as to their wording. The particular sanctions issued under joint orders of the grand Lama and the Emperor of China, and other old original documents which require confirmation, should receive his careful attention. When free grants are made to monasteries and individuals for any religious or charitable purpose, they should only be made for a term of five years, so that when the conditions and objects are not fulfilled they may be resumed by Government. Grants to religious institutions should be made on definite conditions, which not being fulfilled the lands should be resumed. As full justice in all important civil and criminal matters cannot always be expected from the Jong-pons who generally delay in settling questions, the Sakyong should order that such cases may be committed to him or to higher courts for settlement as soon as they are instituted. When ordinary petty cases are decided by the lower courts of Jong-pons and revenue collectors by taking evidence from witnesses, and the decision is not considered satisfactory to the minor parties concerned, the case should be transferred to the Sakyong or to some other higher court. Matters of significance should be left by him to be decided by the respective Jong-pons of the districts. In fact, the Sakyong will be the court of final appeal against the decisions of other high courts.

Commercial intercourse should not be stopped or interrupted. As traders travel at their convenience and pleasure, at all times and with no certainty, they should be allowed to pass freely after payment of the established *sho thal* (customs duty) on loads of goods and heads of travellers. There should be no restriction on the Khampa in passing through Tibet, which they generally do up to mid-winter; but Kashmiris and Nepalese, when their Governments cease to be friendly, should not be allowed admission into Tibet.

Seekers of alms and subscriptions, with the exception of those who come from "our quarter," *i.e.*, outsiders coming from other countries, should not be permitted to collect subscription and alms in Tibet. Men from remote quarters of this country, the object of whose journey, whose conduct, and due payment of customs duty are satisfactory, and men who come into the country to make offerings or presents to sanctuaries and Lamas, should not be stopped on their way.

The Sakyong should also enforce the observance of funeral obsequies and mourning in accordance with the prevailing customs, and particularly in the event of the death of people who have no friends, relations, or heirs, be they rich or poor. For such persons religious observances should be conducted on the forty-ninth day or hundredth day, or at the end of the sixth month from the day of death, according to the national custom.

Lists of remittances of money or things to students from Mongolia and other places, reading in Tibet, and of their properties, of offerings for the obsequies of the dead, and of presents to the Government, should at every important station on the way be examined by the Jong-pons or custom officers, to make sure that no loss has occurred on the way before reaching Lhasa. No customs duty should be levied on such articles, but the list accompanying them should receive the custom officer's seal. With the exception of these no articles should be passed free.

A knowledge of accounts and of writing being most essential for conducting Government business, the Sakyong should encourage the study of figures and letters by establishing schools. Much attention should be paid to the practical training of boys to proficiency in arithmetic. On calculating income and expenditure, if surpluses or deficits are shown in the figures while they do not exist in reality, the account is a mere waste of time, labour, ink, and paper. Of course, when there is any deficit shown, the cause should be at once traced out, and the amount falling short realized. There cannot be any excess unless it be due to excessive collection from the *misser* (tenants) or to a difference in the weights and measures used in receiving the revenue in kind. In such cases the revenue collectors should be punished with fines, it being unbecoming on the part of the Government to receive more than is actually due from the subjects. In cases of deficit, when it is owing to ignorance or to personal obligation or to compassion for those who plead inability to pay what is due from them, the revenue collector, if new to his work, should be excused; but if he did such things knowing them to be wrong, he should be suitably punished. When the collectors receive revenue from one party and pay it to another party, or what is called in Tibetan idiom— "taking with the right hand and paying with the left"—the excess or deficit can easily be accounted for.

In collecting from the herdsmen and shepherds a revenue which is always variable, consisting as it does of cattle, butter, milk (dried), wool, yak-hair, &c., the collector cannot adhere to any rule. He must sometimes collect less, at others more, for cattle are not a constant and unvarying form of wealth to the people. In respect of revenue receipts in gold, silver, iron, and copper, great care should be taken in the weighing, for the difference caused by weights and to the peculiar handling of steel-yards, is much to the advantage of the artizans or workers in metal. When metals are entrusted to the hands of artizans, care should be taken that they do not replace or steal them, or give bad workmanship or inferior metal. The Jong-pons and Nerpas of Shikhas,[1] on whom devolves the work of buying or constructing articles for the Government (such as religious symbols, chapels, and *chhortens* of gold or silver), should carefully watch the artizans, after handing over to them the metals in the presence of respectable witnesses. But no witness is necessary at the collection of the revenue, for a large share of confidence must be placed on such responsible officers as the collectors.

ADMINISTRATION OF JUSTICE.

The due dispensation of justice results in much usefulness and moral merit. Public officers sitting as judges, when receiving complaints, should carefully examine into their correctness and ascertain the nature of the charges through the evidence of witnesses. According to the importance of the interests concerned, they may challenge the contending parties to undergo some ordeals, or allow the parties to challenge each other to do the same.

The court does not always take down the depositions of the parties, but in the generality of cases the parties are required to make statements either in their own writing or in that of their paid advocates, which, when the case comes on for hearing, should be read publicly in court. The portions of the statements which treat of indecent or unbecoming matters, and are unfit to be read, should be suppressed or omitted. Murderers and perpetrators of black acts, when imprisoned or under arrest, may be kept in government custody, or may be made over to the charge of some parties connected or unconnected with the Government under judicial decree. But the culprits from Sera, Dapûng and Gah-dan, when committed in chains and handcuffs to the court of the Regent for trial (the monastic authorities being incompetent to try for serious offences), should always be kept in the government lock-up. They should be tried regularly, the evidence from witnesses being invariably considered as the best means of testing their guilt, but they should not be given the option of trial by ordeal. The monastic authorities are required to submit to the Regent a judicial decree against the criminals in every case of committal. In all important and serious cases, elaborate judgment based on the evidence from witnesses should be passed, including the contentions of all the parties concerned and the arguments for and against. In unimportant cases short notes or memoranda are sufficient, and judicial decrees need not be delivered. Although in ancient time Judges used to deliver verbal decrees, now-a-days that practice does not suit the people, grown suspicious of the veracity of both Judges and rulers. Therefore the Judge, to quiet the fears and distrust of both parties concerned, should always write down the evidence, depositions, and decision, in which all the principal points should be noted to the exclusion of irrelevant and minor ones. At the conclusion the Judge should order the payment of the *thim-teg* or law-fee in proportion to the importance and value of the case. The charge should be proportionately borne by both parties according to the interests at stake. Besides the *thim-teg*, the parties are also required to pay the *myug-rin* or writing-fee, which is the emolument of the court clerk.

When the Judge has settled the principal points at issue, he should definitely state what one party will have to lose and the other to gain. The legal form of judicial decree should be always adhered to, and the subject-matter only be commenced at the conclusion of the formal heading, in which the gods are called to bear witness to the justice of the decree. The decree should be written accurately, much brevity or diffuseness being alike avoided in its wording. The different points in simple cases should be divided into three heads. At the conclusion of the decree, the terms of agreement or of payment of fines, as consented to by the parties, should be written down. Disobeying the order of the court, or not acting according to the judicial decree, should be treated as a high crime, like murder, exposing the offender to a fine of three gold *srangs*[2] (Rs. 180): should he, however, be above the lowest class (*thamai thama*), the fines must be higher and according to his social rank.

True copies of the judicial decree, duly numbered and dated, should be given to the parties concerned.

When in complaints, statements, or petitions the defendant is charged with defying or slandering the Government or court, due investigations should be made, and if the charge is proved, he should be flogged. But if after inquiry it be found that the charge was false, and that the party accused did not slander the Judge or defy the law, the complainant or the informant should be fined, but not corporally punished.

Although it is enjoined on the Sakyong that he should always assiduously adhere to the *white acts, i.e.*, those conducive to the good of the people, yet the perpetrators of black acts or sinners, not being deserving of his kindness and sympathy, should be punished with imprisonment, corporal punishment, or, in extreme cases, death, according to law, and thereby the way to sin be closed.

With regard to assistants, helpmates, and servants employed on business requiring despatch, no report should be made on petty faults; for dissensions between master and servants in such cases is to the injury of the former. The work called Shon-nuvi-gul-gyan has the following lines bearing on this subject :—

> " Even if servants act a little amiss,
> Express it not in speech, but hide it in the heart ;

---

[1] *G*ner-pa, a keeper, steward : *S*hikha is a farm or estate.

[2] *Srang*, the same as the Chinese *tael*, equivalent to a crown or Rs. 2½. In Tsang *srang* is pronounced as hrang. In U it is pronounced *sang*. Six *tanka* and a *sho* make one *srang*.

'Good or bad,' say, 'all is known to me.'
He who rules by love is a chief indeed.
To blame or punish for a little fault,
Or shower reproof in angry words,
Is not good; it only brings mischief:
Such is a bad master—his servant's foe."

When, however, subordinates persist in neglect and mischief, they should, though respectable, be removed from service or degraded; and their properties, both moveable and immoveable, confiscated by Government, to make them severely feel the consequence of their misconduct. No leniency should be shown to them for their position or as a personal consideration.

The work Dang-thig Thong-wa Dsum-shor has the following bearing on this point:—

"Let not the head of the high grow stiff;
Despise not nor cast away the humble for his birth:
Observing every good and evil work of men,
He that trusts is the best of chiefs."

The Northmen (Mongolians), being the principal objects of the hospitality and patronage of the state, should always be treated with consideration and respect according to custom. In showing attention to them, the Sakyong should not forget differences in rank and order; but those who deserve less respect should not get precedence over their superiors, for this may give rise to discontent and indignation among the devotees. He should in dealing with the Mongolians consult the guide book called Sog-deb Muthilai Thi-sing, and should not act under the influence of friendship or patronage. Men who have been mischievous and hostile to the state and to the cause of religion should, according to the directions in the Registers, be suppressed and treated with harshness. Those who during war have served with zeal and devotion, and during peace practised themselves well in military exercise, and are firmly attached to the state, should be promoted in the order of precedence registered in the book of Records.

If Mongolian servants of the Gya*l*-po (King), his door-keepers, and soldiers, who have fought for the defence of the state and religion, come to ask for remuneration, they should be presented with tea, butter, &c. Similarly, other men of respectable position and rank in Tibet who have served the state in time of war and in the executive administration, and also the indigent and the sick, should be refreshed with tea and butter, and not sent away empty-handed. But there should be a limit to charity, although there is no limit to the seekers of charity: idle beggars, who do not come under the category of the poor, the helpless, and the sick, and who have done no service either to the state or to religion, should not be given anything. Thus it has been observed—

"With kindness and consideration treat the humble and the poor; give not lavishly; keep yourself within proper bounds, &c."

Dung-khors and other executive officers deputed for special work should be immediately admitted when they ask for an interview with the Sakyong, and dismissed with the usual *thon-chha*[1] (starting or parting gift). The Sakyong should personally instruct the senior Dung-khors in the nature of the work entrusted to them, and also command them to discharge their duties honourably. To officers inferior to the above, the Sakyong should only read the government instructions; and to the ordinary Dung-khors he should communicate instructions through other officials. Dung-khors and other public servants required to start on special duty, both civil and military, should arrange for their own equipment and ponies. But when they are sent suddenly on urgent business, they should be provided with government ponies and equipments, which they must return at the termination of their special work. Monks and others, when required to start on special government service, should also be provided with *tsi-ta*[2] or government ponies, to be afterwards returned. When such *tsi-ta* die by accident, the officers are not to be held responsible for the loss.

When such senior Dung-khors as are well known for their zeal and usefulness in the public service set out on government service, the Sakyong should present them with a complete suit of wearing apparel, boots, the finest tea, butter, &c., as a particular mark of kindness to them. For meritorious junior officers on such occasions a brick of black tea is sufficient; for ordinary senior officers a brick of *ya-ju* tea with a scarf each, and for the last class of officers half a brick of common tea. In conferring *sol-re* or presents at the time of starting for special work, the Government should follow the *Tsi-shi* or code of regulation. The Sakyong should not be too liberal or too tight-handed on such occasions, but should encourage the officers with a show of gracious attention for special service. He should not accede to any requests on the part of the officers for special consideration in the distribution of *thon-chha* (starting present). The Dung-khors, when they wash and dress their locks once every month, should be allowed *ta-cha*[3] (hair tea), consisting of half a brick of tea.

---

[1] Thon-cha, tea presented to officers at the time of starting for executing any important work or mission.
[2] *Rtsis-r*ta, a Government pony, the use of which is allowed to privileged officers for a stated period.
[3] Kra-cha kra, is pronounced as ta, and means hair—the allowance of tea granted to Dung-khors at the time of washing their hair, which they do once in a month.

When any superior officer of state falls ill, the Government should on the tenth day of his illness and subsequently inquire about his health, the medical treatment he is receiving, his accommodation and diet, and send him medical aid and advice gratis, together with a present of tea, butter, &c. The Government should not forget to show marks of kindness to officers sick in remote places, and to respectable landlords and chiefs, by such "health presents;" and should also according to the Code of Service contribute to the funeral service and obsequies of meritorious and faithful Dung-khors who have served for a long time. Of the confiscated properties of officers banished for misconduct or imprisoned, durable articles (such as accoutrements, sacred images, and books) should be appropriated to Government use, but perishable articles like grain, tea, butter, meat, should be exchanged or sold. Such properties should not be disposed of, unless for special reasons, before the death of the officer banished or imprisoned. The Government may give to trustworthy Dung-khors suits of official apparel for occasional use. At the termination of service, these, unless quite worn out, should be returned to the government storekeeper (Dvang shel melong).

THE KAHLONS OR MINISTERS AND COUNCILLORS.

In the classical works of Tibet the Minister of State is called Chhying-Sang[1] or Dun-na-dun;[2] but the popular and general designation of a Minister in Tibet is Kahlon. The vulgar people generally call him by the title of Shab-pé, or the "lotus feet." As the Kahlons are generally selected from among the wealthy and powerful nobles of the country, the title of Sa-wang[3] (the power of the land) is ordinarily affixed to their names.

Formerly, the wife of a Gya*l*-po, and latterly the wife of a Desi, enjoyed the privilege of being addressed by the proud title of Lhacham. Now-a-days, as both the Sovereign and the Governor are selected from ordained and anointed monks, the wives of Kahlons alone are addressed as Lhacham,[4] or lady of the King. Similarly, the sons of Kahlons are called Lha-sre[5] or Princes.

The affairs of the Government are ordinarily conducted by the Council of five Kahlons, four of whom are as a rule appointed from the laity and one from the clergy. Formerly there were only four Kahlons, but latterly the predominance of the clergy forced the Dalai Lama to appoint a Lama-Kahlon to represent the church in the Council. This dignitary being a high-rank Lama, is given the top seat in the Council Hall, the Senior Minister, called Kahlon[6] Thi-pa, or the President of the Council, occupying the next highest seat. The Council, which sits daily between the hours of 9 A. M. and 2 P. M., conducts the judicial, political, and executive administration of the Government. But it is not a legislative body, for there is no fresh legislation in the country, ancient laws, customs, and usage being the chief guide of the Government.

The Council is called Kah-shag[7] Lhengye. The Councillors sit cross-legged on thick stuffed mattress-like cushions placed on raised seats, and drink tea in the open court. The clerks and secretaries who sit in separate rooms and halls also have seats of different heights assigned to them. All sit cross-legged on stuffed cushions, each having a small dining table before him. A cup of tea always remains on the table of every officer; and when it is emptied, the court So*l*pon replenishes it immediately. Sometimes visitors, if they place their cups on the small tables before them, get a supply of prepared tea to drink. All the officers dine daily at the state expense while sitting at their work in office.

The Court or the Council Hall, called Kah-shag, is also the principal Court of Justice, the Kahlons being the Judges. It hears appeals from the decision of the Jong-pons or from the Court of the Thimpon[8] of Lhasa, called Nagtsa-shar or the Black Court. The Council of Kahlons is a permanent organized body, which cannot be dissolved at the will of the Sovereign, and whose members are appointed for life. Estates called *Lonshi*[9] are set apart for the maintenance of each of the Kahlons. But it generally so happens that some of them being very rich do not avail themselves of the income of the *Lonshi*. The Kahlons are not allowed the privilege of being conveyed in the sedan chair or Pheb-Chyam,[10] the Ampa,[11] the Dalai, and the Panchhen Lamas, and occasionally the Regent, being alone privileged to use the sedan. The Kahlons dress in the yellow flowing tunic-like robe, and wear the *Sog-sha* (Mongol hat) with a coral button on top.

When the office of a Kahlon falls vacant, the Regent, in consultation with the other Kahlons, selects two or three names from among the Dah-pons (Generals), and sends them to the oracles of Nachûng-chhoikyong[12] and Lhamo Sung-chonma of Potala for their opinion. He

1 *H*phying-sang. Phying is pronounced as chhying.

2 *M*dun-na *h*dun.

3 Sa-*d*vang pronounced as sa-wang. *Sa*, land, and *dvang*, lord or power. It is a contraction of the word sa-*h*i *d*vang-po, the lord of the land or country.

4 Lha-*l*cham, literally a queen.

5 Lha-sre*s*, a prince, son of a god or king.

6 *B*ka*h*-*b*lon Khri-pa, the presiding minister. Khri, pronounced as thi, means a chair, khripa a chairman.

7 *B*ka*h*-*b*lon shag lhen-*r*gya*s*, the council of the ministers. Shag means a court and lhen-*r*gyas, together; hence means the court and council of the Ka*h*lons.

8 Khrim-*d*pon, the chief justice, ordinarily a magistrate or a judge.

9 *B*lon-*g*shi, the Government land or estate set apart for the support of a minister while in office.

10 Pheb*s* byam or shing byam. Byam is pronounced as chyam. Is a wooden conveyance like the Indian tang-jam or the Chinese *sedan* chair.

11 Am-pan.

12 *G*nas-chhung, the little place. The presiding deity of this oracle first asked for a small plot of land to erect a temple near Lhasa.

is appointed as Kahlon in whose favour the oracles decide unanimously. When all the names are disapproved, fresh names are submitted for approval. In this way much heart-burning and discontent are prevented, for all men are alike bound to abide by the decision of the gods.

In the Kahshag, or Court of the Kahlons, there are three Kahdung (Secretaries) appointed from among the Dung-khors, and one Kab-shopa or Chief Clerk. The Kahdungs are the chief officers, under whom 175 Dung-khors or civil officers work. As the Kahdungs sit in the Kahshag, where the Dung-khors have no place, the Tsi-pon, the Chief of Accounts, presides over them.

The Dung-khors are appointed from among the successful students of Yu-thog *Lob-ta*[1] (school) at Lhasa, where the sons of nobles and respectable men get their training in letters and figures. The Dung-khors learn accounts by serving as apprentices in the Tsi-khang, or account office, for a period of five years. The allowance of a Dung-khor is inconsiderable, hardly exceeding what is necessary for his maintenance at Lhasa. But as they are selected from among the well-to-do men and landlords, the question of the smallness of the allowance is never raised. The Dung-khors are deputed to do various acting duties in connection with the executive or revenue. When they acquire experience by long service, they are appointed to the posts of Jong-pons. All Dung-khors are laymen. They have a peculiar way of dressing their hair, by which they are distinguished from other officers.

In like manner sons of respectable men of Lhasa, who choose to betake themselves to a monkish life, are trained in the Tse-lobta[2] or the palace school of Potala. Here one of the four Tung-yig-Chhenpo (Secretary-in-Chief) of the Namgya*l*-ta-tshang in rotation teaches the boys, with one pupil-teacher as his assistant. The successful candidates from here are admitted as Tse-rung,[3] or monk-officers. The total number of Tse-rung cannot exceed 175. In all posts of trust and responsibility two officers are jointly appointed, one of whom at least is a Tse-rung. For instance, to conduct the office of Chhyan-dso (Treasurer) of Potala, there are now three officers—two Tse-rungs and one Dung-khor. The office of Labrang-chhyan-dso[4] similarly is held by two Tse-rungs and one Dung-khor. These and other offices of responsibility are tenable for three years.

The duties of Kahlons as defined in the Dvang-Shel-Melong.

In the work Lug*s* kyi-*bs*tan *b*chho*s* of Chanaka Gya*l*po appear the following lines :—

"Learned and efficient in all kinds of works,
Well versed in philosophy and the sacred books,
He who ever performs the duties of the King,
Is indeed a Lonpo or Minister of State."

The Kahlons or the members of the Kah-shag (Court of Ministers) are the highest dignitaries of state. Accordingly, being the pillars of the sacred Government of his Holiness the Gya*l*wa Rinpo-chhe,[5] they should consider his Holiness' properties, personal and public, as sacred, and discharge their high functions with moderation and economy, in accordance with the directions of the *Tsa-tshig*, or code of regulations.

In the work *s*Kye*s* buhi *r*nam *h*bye*d g*shon-nui *m*gul *r*gyan the following is mentioned with reference to a Minister's duty :—

"That Lonpo (Minister), though learned and wise,
Who quarrels and annoys, is a devil to his King."

The Ministers should as minutely as possible examine into state affairs of every kind, and particularly into the accounts branch. He should not be remiss with the idea that everything will go evenly on in its course, nor should he do any disloyal action. In reference to this a Tibetan author writes—

"Quick in perception, dexterous in means,[6]
Loyal to the king, firm of purpose;
His nature artless, straight as an arrow,—
That person is fit to be a Minister."

When the Sakyong does anything through mistake or inadvertence, which is likely to be against the interests of the state, the Kahlon should represent it to him. The Minister, not allowing himself to be led away by personal influence or delicacy, should with strict impartiality conduct the administration of the Government. He should examine with due attention all letters from and to his Government, edicts, and judicial decrees on state-

---

[1] *G*yu-thog *bs*lab gra. Gra is pronounced as ta, the school for boys first established by minister Yu-thog.
[2] *R*tse-*bs*lab gra, the school attached to the Dalai Lama's palace.
[3] *R*tse-drung, a clerk of Potala, also a head clerk.
[4] *B*la brang-phyag-*m*dso*d*, the chief treasurer of the church establishment.
[5] *R*gya*l*-va, the victorious.
[6] Quotation from the ethical work called she*s*-rab *s*dong-bu :—
"Ji-*l*tar *r*gya*l* sri*d bs*kyongva dang
"*Bs* Do-vahi *d* gra *r* nam*s h*dul va dag,
"*H* bang*s* la reva ma *h* jog par.
"Shal *b* shug*s* tshe na myur du *m*dso*d* also
"Byahi thab*s* kyi gra*s* bye*d* na.
"*B*Lo *l*dan dag la dri var bya."

ments of accounts. Shrewdly inquiring into all information from all kinds of men respecting the internal or external relations of the state or of the frontiers, and examining the faults and merits of the officers, he should bring all important matters to the notice of the Sakyongs Thus it has been said—

> "He is a friend who is capable of secrets :
> If he reveals them, he is hollow right through."

Accordingly, the Kahlon preserves perfect secrecy in important state matters, whether internal or external, never communicating them even to his best and most intimate friends or relations.

The work on politics called Gyal *b*lon gyi *m*dsan*s* yig leg*s* *b*sha*d* *h*phreng has the following lines about the qualifications of a Minister :—

> "Noble in birth, great in wealth,
> Large-hearted and with few desires,
> Prudent, polite, intelligible to all,
> Such a man in this world is chief.

"He who returns kindnesses, knows not waste, is good to friends, never lets slip any opportunity to look to his own interests, is skilful in conversation, wise, intelligent, and considerate in his dealings with all men, is indeed in this world a prudent man.

"He who sets himself to work after examining all works, is agreeable to all, does no evil, puts none in confusion, and pleases all by his truthfulness and amiableness, is in this world a really good man."

The Minister should be free from corruption. If in homage to his exalted position people make him presents, he should accept such presents publicly. In appointing Dung-khors and Jong-pons, the Kahlon should carefully consider the qualifications of the candidates, their eligibility, and the doctrines and faith they profess. He should not under the influence of partiality forget former usage and custom in such matters. He should always see that such matters as receiving or making over charge of offices, payments, collection of revenue, distribution of lands, are done according to rule and custom, without deviation from them, except when constrained by unavoidable circumstances. He should report without concealment to the Sakyong the merits of all public servants, so that those who have done excellent work with purity of purpose may be rewarded according to their desert, and the incompetent and idle punished. He should direct and control the works of all government servants. He should conduct all religious ceremonies and services of the state according to former practice and custom, always making the expenditure commensurate with the income and resources of the state. He should always be careful that in church services none of the necessary articles prescribed in the sacred books be wanting, for then the service will be incomplete.

When reports reach him about oppression over subjects, he should engage truthful agents to bring him the real facts of the case. Thus, referring to this, an author says—

"The chief duties of a Lonpo are of four kinds : the worship of the sacred images, the internal consolidation of the state, the external administration of the Government, and the establishment of a benign control over the subjects."

The Kahlon should be chivalrous, wise, good, upright, resolute, penetrating, generous, and straightforward ; accomplished in letters and figures ; skilful in exactly hitting off the means of making the subjects prosperous and happy, and always bent on doing good to others : possessed of these virtues, he should govern the state, and be the object of admiration of all over whom he rules.

THE JONG-PONS.

The Jong-pons are the district officers, who, in addition to their revenue and executive duties, are entrusted with powers to try civil and criminal cases within the limits of their *jongs* or districts. The chief duty of the Jong-pon is the collection of the Government revenues, and of occasional taxes levied by the issue of *kargya* or *purwanas* from the Court of Kahlons. His power, therefore, is very great in revenue and executive matters. To every *jong* two Jong-pons, with equal powers, are appointed from among the most distinguished Dung-khors.* The Jong-pons of Tibet closely resemble in their duties and powers the district officers under the British Government, with this difference that the Jong-pons have also to do military duty in times of war. In military matters the Jong-pon is subordinate to the Dahpon (General) and the Ampa (Senior Imperial Resident). Annually he has to render an account of the military stores, &c., to the Resident, and also to display his dexterity in shooting, racing, and other athletic sports in the presence of the Dahpon and the Ampa. For military service he receives distinction from the Ampa's hands, which consists of *momay* (blue stone) and crystal buttons of the third and fourth class, to be worn on the top of his official hat. The establishment of the Jong-pon consists of one or two Dung-khors and two store-keepers called Jong-ner, and several menials. The heads of circles of villages, called Tsho-pon, the village head-man, called Mipon, and

* Dung-khor is pronounced as Doong-khor, or ordinarily as Toong-khor.

the elders, called Gyanpo, who are annually elected, are all subordinate to the Jong-pon and are bound to obey his orders. The appointments of Jong-pons are transferable. Successful and efficient Jong-pons are promoted to the rank of Dahpon, while weak and corrupt Jong-pons are degraded to the rank of Jong-ner, or to that of ordinary Dung-khor.

The following is a literal translation of a note written in the third quarter of the 17th century by the Regent Sangyasrgya-*m*tsho on the duties of a Jong-pon :—

"At the time of appointing a Jong-pon the most trustworthy and loyal person should be selected for the office. The candidate appointed should exert himself devotedly in the cause of religion. If by chance he is involved in any serious affray, looking to the present and future interest of all—of himself and of his Government—he should fight even to death, never surrendering the *jong* to the enemy."

The ethical work Sherab-dong-bu has the following :—

> "How to govern a kingdom,
> To subdue dangerous foes,
> Without depending on his subjects,
> *   *   *   *   *
> How to do a work if asked,—
> He should consult those who are wise ;
> Not to speak of a successful issue,
> Even failures so brilliant appear pleasant."

In business requiring despatch, unless unavoidably prevented, the senior of the two Jong-pons should always consult the junior Jong-pon, no matter whether he is more or less learned and intelligent than himself. No Jong-pon should alone by himself decide finally any matter "according to his wish" as it is called. He should not allow his subordinates and servants to find fault with one another, or to behave wilfully and improperly, nor should he himself do so. The Jong-pon should always remain present in the head quarters of the *jong*.

The common saying is :—

> "In the custodian of a large district,
> There should be shrewdness, skill, and exercise."

Accordingly, both within and without his *jong* and jurisdiction, the Jong-pon should exercise diligent supervision. He should not neglect to look after the *jong* buildings, the supply of grass and firewood in it, the conservation of forests and pasture lands, the planting of trees, the dismantling and repairing of houses, to be done by employing the *misser* in forced labour during their leisure time, without subjecting them to difficulties or inconveniences. He should constantly be watchful lest the *jong* house be set on fire by some carelessness.

In doctrine and principles the Gelugpa school being the purest, he should chiefly follow it. But although the Ning-ma school, unlike the Gelugpa school, has some alloy in it, yet as it is useful in religious services for removing certain diseases and injuries, while the Sakyapa school being of the same extraction as the Gelugpa school, its followers should not be treated with harshness. People should be freely allowed to observe their funeral obsequies and religious services for the welfare of the living according to its former custom. But although it is unfair to treat with partiality the followers of the different religious schools and persuasions in general, yet, since the Karmapa and Dukpa schools had opposed the Gelugpa church with violence, and their doctrines were heretical like those of Hwashang Maháyána, and they had converted many to them, it will be the duty of the Jong-pons to put them down as much as lies in their power.

If prisoners and exiles are treated with leniency by the Jong-pon, the strictness of the law is violated, and at the end harm befalls himself.

Whenever petitions or applications are made, either personally or through some officer, the matter should be carefully inquired into. In uprightness and justice to all classes of men, great or small, monk or laymen, no partiality should be shown. Uninfluenced by gratifications or the fear of unpleasant criticism, the Jong-pon should administer even-handed justice. Questions of jurisdiction, of revenue due from the *misser* (tenants), and of forced labour, should be adjusted according to the directions laid down in the *Tsa-tshig* of the *jong*. The number of villages, houses, and inhabitants should annually be counted and examined, and compared with former records. Those who have deserted the country should, after thorough investigation, be brought back if possible ; and particularly *misser* who have left the district not more than five years ago should by all means be induced to return to their homesteads. The servants and working men of the *jong*, respectable or menial, should not be made to work privately for the Jong-pons, who should not keep more servants than is allowed by the *Tsa-tshig* (code for guidance). It being his duty to show kindness to the *misser*, the Jong-pon should not without a cause enter into disputes with his neighbour Jong-pon, the interests of the Government being the same in both cases. He should not allow the government lands to be encroached upon, and tenants to be taken away, by the Gerpas (landholders). The arrears of revenue and property given in loan should be realized without delay.

Women should not be accommodated or allowed to remain in public in the *jong*, and the Jong-pon particularly should not even flirt with another's wife. The work of the sentries of the gateways should be closely watched and supervised. Looking to the distances the message-runners have to traverse, and the difficulties they have to surmount, arrangement should be made for running them by stages. No partiality on this point should be shown. To merchants on Government business and to messengers no journey-provisions should be given if they fail to produce a *lam-yig* or road bill. On the other hand, the messengers of the frontier states conveying foreign or political messages should receive suitable provisions. If anybody without a letter of authority from Government obliges the *misser* to supply him with forage or firewood, his name should be forwarded to the Government. Frontier or foreign merchants who can produce no *lam-yig* should not be allowed to leave the country. Men residing on the frontier should always be watched that they may not be taken across. Any secret information regarding the affairs of other quarters, if obtained, should be communicated to Government. Men who come to Tibet as spies, and Tibetans who give out state secrets to others, should be carefully examined. They should be called back, and either arrested or sent out of the country. Loyal and considerate officers should be kept on the frontier, which should also be guarded by brave soldiers.

THE JUDGE.

The Sha*l*-chhe-pa (Judge) is the chief dispenser of justice. He is also called Shu-lenpa or the receiver of complaints and petitions. Sometimes the Shulenpa does the work of an advocate; for instance when the Delai Lama, the Sakyong and the Kahlons sit as Judges or Sha*l*-chhe-pa, the Shulenpa acts as a separate officer, undertaking the part of an advocate. The latter also sits as judge in the absence of the former, and hence the distinction between a Sha*l*-chhe-pa and a Shulenpa is not exactly like that between a Judge and an advocate in this country. In Tibet the executive officers sit as Judges and decide both civil and criminal cases. In the monasteries of Sera and Dapûng the abbots try all sorts of cases, mostly criminal, of offences committed within the monastery limits. As has been mentioned elsewhere, they commit all serious cases to the court of the Regent and the Kahlon Shag. The other monasteries are not allowed such privileges: in their case offences which come under the monastic regulations are alone tried by the abbots; but all offences which have no relation to religion are tried by the Jong-pons and other executive officers. Although bribery is strictly prohibited by edicts and rulings, yet there are few Judges in Tibet who do not consent to receive secret gratifications: all parties when they first come to the court are required by usage to make presents to the Judge as fees for receiving their petitions. Generally the defendants have to pay more than the plaintiffs.

When the case is decided, the Judge fixes the amount of *Thim-teg* (law fee), which both the plaintiff and defendant are required to bear equally: the custom of settling disputes by a committee of village elders (*r*Gyan-po) also holds in Tibet, in consequence of which the Jong-pons have very few petty cases to decide. It is optional with the parties either to move the Jong-pons or the Kahlon Shag to settle their dispute. But all cases of theft, robbery, and murder are tried by the Jongpons and the Kahlon Shag. The Tibetans are very little disposed to litigation, being simple, peaceful, and of an admirably even temper, easily reconcilable and amenable to reason. Custom is a sacred thing with them, which they uphold with great pertinacity; but when reason upholds any reformation or innovation, they demolish custom with equal vehemence. This is well exemplified in the progress of the Gelugpa school of Buddhists in Tibet. Unfortunately for the people there has been no revolution in the laws and legal usage of the country since the days of Desi Sangye.

The following are a few hints by that learned administrator Desi Sangye on the duties of a Judge.

The work *r*Gyal *b*lon *m*Dsang*s* yig leg*s* *b*sha*d* *g*ser *h*phreng has the following :—

"That man in this world is a Judge who, without wavering and impartiality, does the work of the state; uses agreeable language; is disinterested by nature; is cautious and does not deceive others."

Nagarjuna also observed :—

"That Judge who takes bribes,
Does in fact fling justice to the winds;
That youth who steals and robs,
Does ruin both himself and others."

The Judge having heard attentively and patiently the petitions of both plaintiff and defendant, should proceed to enter into details. He should accordingly take their evidence, and in their presence discard any unsupportable allegations. When one party has finished addressing the court, the other party should be allowed his turn. There should be no partiality in this respect at all. When he has taken the evidences, he should see in what points the parties differ, and also where they waver. All unsupportable points should be re-examined and the witnesses subjected to cross-examination for extracting the truth from them. When by questions and answers the real facts have been well established, the Judge should pronounce his decision. When a Judge, knowing what is true and what is false in a case, bends himself towards injustice through partiality or for the sake of secret gratifications, he fits himself for a place in hell.

Referring to this, the work *n*Do *m*Dsangs *b*lun has the following :—

"The Judge who wilfully commits injustice is destined to suffer different kinds of miseries, being compelled by *Karma* to be born in the infernal regions. Even after deliverance from hell, he must for five hundred births be born as a round lump of flesh without any of the five organs of sense. In this state he will resemble 'Man ji byi la' of *m*Do *m*Dsangs *b*lun (a Buddhist work on the wise man and the fool)."

The main points of the complainant's statement (which is generally coloured by passion), together with collateral facts, should all, dressed in clear and plain language, be laid before the Sakyong by the Shulenpa. If the judicial decree passed by the Sakyong on the question be not satisfactory to him, the Shulenpa should represent the case for further consideration. When delivering his final decree to the parties, he should clearly state the penalty to which they should be subjected in case they fail to abide by it ; and should also receive the *Thim-teg* and other fees equally from both parties. In realizing fines, he must not accept articles and other things in kind when cash payment in gold or silver can be obtained from the party. If gold-dust containing foreign substances and alloys in it is offered in payment, he should only accept the *silma* or melted gold at the current price, weighing the same by the *Thim-sho* standard weight in a correct steel yard. When he cannot help receiving articles, no gold or silver being forthcoming, he should consult the Sakyong about it ; but he should not receive the following articles—cymbals, saddles, matchlocks, ponies, helmets, coats-of-mail, shields, church furniture, images, books, lean cattle. But whenever he receives articles in default of money or silver and gold, he must estimate the local price of such things and reduce it by one-fourth as discount for acceptance by Government.

Being a public servant, and supported at the expense of the state, he should always be free from corruption, and remain satisfied with the *r*kang-*g*la or travelling fees and *m*na*h n*ten or oath fee. If outsiders make him presents in his official capacity, he may accept them publicly. He should never alter his convictions under the influence of recommendations or entreaties for mercy, and thereby frustrate the ends of justice, but he should always be amenable to reason, and only inclined to reconsider a case when he is satisfied with reasons adduced for so doing. For the preservation of the state and for the good of great and small alike, the impartial administration of justice is essential.

Sakya Pandita has said—

"The ingenuous Lonpo who is upright,
Serves both his lord and subjects alike ;
When an expert shoots a straight arrow,
Wherever it is aimed it hits aright."

Also in another place—

"They who by nature resolute and wise,
Without partiality govern the people ;
Always good and kind-hearted to others :—
Those are really great among men."

Half the justice of a case depends upon the complainant. The Judge should administer even-handed justice without looking to gain or gratification, or to feelings of his friends or acquaintances, or of the rich or noble, but should follow the example of King Melong Dong.

REVENUE.

Land and moveable property tax.—In Tibet taxes are paid in kind and in money. Apart from the lands held by chiefs and nobles, there are altogether 53 *jongs* or districts under Jong-pons and 123 sub-districts under Jong-ners. These constitute what is called the Shung-shi or Shung-sa (state lands). Each *jong* on an average contains 500 families* of *misser*. Each family on an average possesses two to three *kangs* of arable soil. The ordinary *kang* is a measure of land in which about 400℔ of seed-grain can be conveniently sown. The seed sown in spring grows in summer, and yields a crop in autumn. If one *khal* (50℔) yields nine to ten *khals* of autumn crop it is considered a good harvest; six to eight *khals* is a tolerable outturn, four to six *khals* a bad one. The Government revenues for each *kang* is on an average 50 *srangs*, or Rs. 125, and about one hundred and fifty *khals* of grains. The Crown revenue, if entirely taken in kind, would therefore amount to 26,25,000 *khals*, which (keeping nine-tenths for the maintenance of the people) would be equivalent in money to Rs. 20,00,000. If the price of a *khal* of barley be estimated at one rupee, the total revenue would amount to Rs. 20,00,000 from *Shung-sa* or Government lands, which is partially expended by Government in the service of the church and in distributing alms to the whole body of Lamas belonging to the monasteries of Potála, Sera, Dapûng, Gahdan, &c. According to a custom handed down from ancient times, the Tibetan *missers* are required to furnish means of conveyance to all sorts of travellers, private or public, who travel under a pass (*lam-yig*) from Government. There is no fixed rule to determine what particular class of

* One wife with all her husbands and children, widows and unmarried women and servants, form the family of a Tibetan *misser*. A *misser* in Tibet is something like an English farmer. The men working on a farm are called *oo-lagpa*.

subjects should be made to bear *oolag** (conveyance duty). All *missers* generally, and those who hold above one *kang* of land, must supply *oolag* and *ta-oo*, which consist in supplying either one coolie or pony free of charge when the traveller can produce his Government *lam-yig* for *oolag* and *ta-oo*. The system of levying *oolag* is a kind of indirect taxation, accounts of which are kept by the Tsho-pon (village headman). Some families supply 100 *oolags* in one year, others only ten or five. If a *misser* fail to supply *oolag* once in a year, he will be required to pay the arrears in the following year. The duty of *oolag* is levied on all kinds of Government lands and subjects. Freeholds and private properties granted to sacred personages entitle them to immunity from this hateful tax. Lands purchased from Government or received as gifts are also liable to taxation of this kind. Under the Lhasa Government there are about one hundred and twenty landlords, out of whom about twenty are very powerful and rich. The Gya*l*-tshab Rinpo-chhe (Regent), who virtually exercises the sovereign power in Tibet, holds one of the largest estates in U. The present Regent Lama Ta-tshag Rinpo-chhe of Kunduling has upwards of 3,000 *missers* on his estates in Kham and Tibet Proper. Lama Demo Rinpo-chhe, the ex-Regent of Tan-gya*s*-ling, whose estates lie in Kongpo, possesses about 5,000 *missers*. Lama Yong-dsin Rinpo-chhe of Tshe-chhog-ling, and Lama Tsha-tur Noman Khan of Tsha-mo-ling, from among whom the Regent is also elected, possess 1,000 *misser* each. The greatest noble of Tibet is Phag*s*-pa-Lha of Chhab-*m*do, who is lord over 10,000 *missers*. Among the four Ministers of the Lhasa Government, Minister Phala, whose guest I was during my residence at Gyan-tse, and who was senior in rank to many of his colleagues, is the master of upwards of 1,000 *misser*. The Lord Treasurer (Chhyag-dso-chhenpo) of the Lhasa Government, Kab-shipa of Gyan-tse, owns an estate of upwards of 1,000 *missers*. People say that his *missers* equal in number those of the Tashi Lama. The three Kahlons, Raga-sha, Rampa, and Yu-thog-pa, also representatives of very ancient families, are no way inferior to Phala. There being no system of remuneration by salaries in Tibet, all high officials are elected from such hereditary chiefs and nobles of the country as have entered the service as Dung-khors. The great monasteries of Lhasa and its neighbourhood, such as Sera, Dapûng, Gahdan, Samye, &c., hold numerous rent-free estates. Besides the above-mentioned, there are more than 300 landholders or zemindars called *Gerpas*, who pay a nominal revenue to Government. I divide them on the *average rule* into three classes, the first class contributing an annual revenue of 30 *dochhes* (Rs. 3,750) to Government, the second class 20 *dochhes* (Rs. 2,500), and the last class 10 *dochhes*, (Rs. 1,250) each. The landholders, called *Gerpas*, are also liable to furnish *oolag*, *ta-oo*, and other indirect taxes. Government cows, *jomos*† and she-yaks, kept in charge of *Dokpas*, are calculated to yield at the rate of 5lb of butter per head a year. In the province of Kongpo and its neighbourhood numerous pigs are reared, and rich families count their pig-wealth by thousands. The Lhasa Government levies a tax of one *tanka* for every pig. Lama Sherab Gya*m*-tsho, who spent 12 years in the district of Pemakyo*d* on the farthest east of Kongpo, informed me that the pig tax forms no despicable part of the Dalai Lama's revenues obtained from Kong-po and Pema-kyo*d*. The chief district officers (Jong-pons) appropriate to themselves the revenue of their respective *Jongshi* or grants of land set apart for the maintenance of Jong-pons. The independent tenants under a *jong* contribute ten days' manual labour per head for the ploughing or sowing or harvesting of Government land. This is called the *Las-thal*, or the labour tax.

Taxes levied from traders.—There is no fixed rule or rate for levying duties on traders. Goods are neither weighed nor valued for fixing the duty. There is no such thing as a regular custom duty in Tibet. Rich merchants who come from distant countries are required to pay a customs duty of 50 *srangs* to Government annually: second class merchants are charged 25 *srangs*, and the lowest class 3 *srangs*. The yearly trade duty on foreign merchants therefore varies from 50 *srangs* to 3 *srangs*. Petty shopkeepers and pedlers pay 5 *shos* (Re. 1¼) annually. Khamba itinerant hawkers, who carry their own loads, are charged half a *tanka* per quarter year both in U and Tsang.

Minor taxes.—For crossing large bridges the charge is from one *kha* (anna) to one *tanka* per head per man, and a *karma* (two annas) to a *sho* (four annas) for ponies. The cattle toll for pasturing ranges from 5 *shos* (Re. 1¼) to three *shos* yearly. Besides these there is a capitation tax of two to three *srangs* (Rs. 7½) on people owning no lands, but only homesteads. The revenue collectors and their servants get conveyance, ponies, and yaks at every stage free of charge. The villagers also furnish them with attendants, fuel, water, and shelter. The revenue collectors can appropriate to their own use all the *khatags*, scarves, butter, tea, and silver coin which the *misser* may offer them as presents. They are also authorized by Government to kill one out of every 100 sheep belonging to the *missers* for consumption while on tour. In all other matters they are guided by the usage and laws of the country. No Government official, revenue officer or Jong-pon, may oppress the poorest *misser*. When a *misser* fails to pay the revenue in money, he may pay it in blankets, tea or butter, which are accepted as equivalents of money; but live goods, except when it is unavoidable, are not so accepted. The cattle property of the Lhasa Government, consisting of ponies, cows, yaks, *jos*, sheep, goats, and donkeys exceeds 1,000,000 in

---

* *Oolag* consists in supplying beasts of burden, ponies, mules, yaks, and donkeys. If the *missers* have no ponies, they can furnish yaks or donkeys. Where no ponies nor yaks can pass, the *misser* must supply a porter for conveying the traveller's goods. In default of these they are required to pay compensation for carriage or conveyance.

† Female *jo*, a cross between yak and cow.

number. There is a superintendent of these cattle properties, who at the end of every year submits an account of the live and dead animals. In order to satisfy the authorities, he is required to produce the entire dried carcasses of the dead animals, with their tails and horns. These superintendents are annually selected, and as a consequence they take every advantage of making their fortune at the expense of the state before the expiration of their service.

In every *jong* (district) there are two stores, one the *kar-gya* or reserve store, and the other *jong-dso* or the repository of the *jong*. The keys of the former always remain with the Kah-lons, so that it is opened only once or twice in a year. The Government annually sends a revenue commissioner to check the accounts of the Jong-pons and revenue collectors, and to take over the revenue receipts from them. He, in fact, does the part of a controlling treasurer. The following translation from the Revenue Code of Tibet will show the nature of the duties a *Kargya-pa* has to discharge :—

The officer in charge of *kargya* should always bear in mind the following lines from the She-*s*rab-*s*dong-bu :—

"Follow the ants in hoarding wealth,
Spend as you spend medicine for the eyes ;
He is really a wise financier,
Who makes the loss less than the gain.
The ant-hill or the honey of the bee,
The crescent which grow fuller and fuller,—
These with the King's wealth compare,
Spend and hoard by little his store to fill."

On arriving at a *jong* for the purpose of inspecting the *kargya*, the officer should first of all examine the weights and measures, and see if they agree with the Government standard ones. The false weights should be kept apart from the correct ones in order to guard against deception. The good grain and miscellaneous articles should always be kept separate from that which has been spoilt. In receiving revenue in kind (other than grain) from the revenue collector, he should clearly put down in the account book how much is bad and how much good. The same should also apply to cattle revenue, whether dead or alive. In every collection the greatest care and attention should be bestowed on the weights and measures. As regards the supplies of fuel, dried dung of cows and ponies, and other less valuable property, he need not go to the trouble of measuring or weighing them, nor interfere with the accounts submitted by the Jong-pon, but may, if he chooses, transfer them to the *Tsi-thi* accounts of the Jong-pon or Jong-ner. As to hay and firewood, he should see if they are supplied in proper quantities as mentioned in the *Tsa-tshig* or register of the *jong*. Grain of bad quality (damaged by hail or snow) should be kept separate from the good. The former must be taken out of the reserve store and replaced by good grain. Very old grain should also be taken out from the *kargya*. Old, dried flesh, butter, hair, and wool should always be disposed of by sale or otherwise, and their place supplied by fresh articles. If the supply of fresh articles is insufficient, the old articles, if unspoilt, should be allowed to remain in the store.

The measures, such as *hbobre* and steel yards, should be compared with those used in the *jong*. When any variance is noticed, the officer should enquire whether the difference is due to the order of the Jong-pon or to the custom of the place, or other circumstances. When allowances are required to be paid to monasteries, pensioners, &c., the officer should satisfy himself that the parties are in existence. When endowments and allowances are made to a body or a general establishment, he should see that the full number of individuals mentioned in the grant letter is still maintained. Carcasses of cattle, hides, and all other articles which are liable to damage by worms, should not be received in the reserve treasury. These, except in unavoidable cases, should always be transferred to the *tsi-thi* of the Jong-pons. Helmets, armour, shields, metals such as bell-metal, copper, brass, &c., may be received in the *kargya*. The receipts of butter from Government cattle should be distributed to the *jong* for use. The greater portion of the butter, &c., obtained from the subjects as revenue should be remitted to Lhasa. Revenue receipts in gold and silver should be remitted to the chief treasury at Lhasa. The Kargya-pa should himself perform the duty of making payments, and not delegate it to others. He should keep an eye on the Government properties and lands, that there may be no encroachment or spoliation. The causes of decrease and increase in lands and subjects should be carfully noted by him. As regards the furniture of the *jong* and *kargya*, he should, when possible, replace the unserviceable by new articles.

*The duties of the Revenue Collector or Khra*l-*s*du*d-pa*.

This officer is sometimes deputed directly by the Court of Kahlons to collect revenue from the Government lands. But as the Jong-pon is the chief head of a district, the collection of revenue is his principal duty. In order to help him at this work, the court of Kahlons generally send Dung-khors with the designation of *Khra*l-*sdud-pa*, or revenue collectors. The chief revenue of the country is obtained from two sources, viz. the family tax and the land tax. The former is generally realized in silver coin and gold, and the latter in kind. On the Jong-pon, who can seldom leave the *jong*, but remains at head-quarters throughout the year, the collection of the family tax devolves. The *misser* are allowed to pay this tax at any time within the year, but the greatest rush for payments takes place in the months of December and January, when the Jong-pons, Jongner, and Shiñers remit their respective collections to the state treasuries at Lhasa and Tashi-lhunpo. In every *jong* are registers, in which are entered the receipts of the revenue of past years, and the quality of the lands under cultivation. The collector, after careful examination of these state documents, goes to the fields to inspect the harvest and to guess the probable outturn of the season. This he compares with the outturn of the preceding five years, and then fixes the share of the yield the *misser* will have to pay to Government. Generally when after examination the outturn is found very good, two-fifths of the produce (being the maximum allowed) is appropriated to Government use. When the yield is below five years' average, the collector satisfies himself with accepting only one-third of the produce. The collector's first duty is, therefore, to know the *thon-skor* (the outturn of the field).

When questions arise about newly-reclaimed lands, there being no records to guide him in fixing the revenue, the collector personally watches the harvesting and measures the field, and accordingly settles the share to be received by Government, two-fifths being the maximum rate fixed in the *tsi-shi* (revenue register) for the best lands. In fact, the rule of equal division of the produce between the Government and the tenant holds throughout Tibet. The average yield of a given plot of cultivated land is generally estimated at five-fold of the grain sown, so that one part being reserved for the seed-grain, the remaining four parts are divided equally between the Government and the tenant.

The revenue collectors are prohibited from assessing revenue on lands through agents or by guesses based on information supplied by outsiders. They are authorized to receive revenue in three instalments, during the months of November, December, and January only. Forced recovery of revenue is also prohibited, and the revenue collectors are generally warned not to extort more revenue than is due from the tenants. Regarding the collection of revenue, the following hints by Desi Sangye will be interesting :—

"The author, Chanaka Gya*l*po, has wisely observed :—

"As by milking the cow you get milk to drink,
It is not proper to kill the cow,
So the king preserves his men
In time by degrees to increase his wealth ;
If you break the thigh of the cow
No milk will the milch cow yield."

"So by extortion people become poor. It is indeed very bad for the state if its people are impoverished or compelled to run away through rough and relentless treatment on the part of the collector for the realization of revenue. Therefore the collectors should in hard cases always strike a mean between extremes in realizing arrears of revenue. Of course, they should not be lenient to those who, although able to pay, wish to deceive the Government by evasion and by pleading poverty. Although as a general rule the collectors should not receive other articles in place of money or grain, yet, where it is unavoidable, they should make accurate price-lists of such articles. The collectors are prohibited from appropriating to their own use articles received as revenue and replacing the same by others. They are strictly forbidden to oppress or put the *misser* to unnecessary expense on any account ; those who are really so indigent that nothing can be squeezed out of them should be excused for the time being from the payment of revenue ; but they should be made to agree to pay the arrears from their subsequent earnings, or from the year's produce. In making price-lists of articles in default of payment in money or grain, the collectors should draw up an average from the local prices of the preceding five years, which should first be exactly determined.

"When from hail-storms, frost, damage by water, or other natural causes, there is failure of the crops, the collectors may, when they think there are sufficient reasons, remit portions of the revenue, in proportion to the estimated loss. In doing so they must give due consideration to the interest both of the state and of the *missers*. When making payments on account of endowments, they should be satisfied that they pay to the real persons and not to fictitious claimants who may produce receipts. If the receivers of pensions and allowances are dead, payments should be stopped.

In reference to the treatment of *missers*, Sakya Pandita observes :—

"The king's treasure is for the sake of increasing the *misser* :
Collect not much. fill the treasury by little and little.
The ants raise hills, and bees gather honey,
The waxing crescent gradually to full-moon grows ;
The king who avoids injuring his subjects,
With wisdom and sense collects his dues ;
In obtaining resin from the juice of the *sâl*,
When much is drawn out, the tree withers."

"The collectors are prohibited from worrying the *misser* for revenue during the months of spring and summer, for then their pockets and stores are both empty. In all such matters they should be guided by the code on revenue collection. In collecting revenue in kind, the collectors should always take the best grain from the landlords and other well-to-do people, but in the case of poor peasants, they may sometimes rest satisfied with inferior grain full of chaff. In fact, the collectors must so behave in discharging their duties that the *misser* may not feel the payment: as eggs are quietly taken out from underneath fowls when they are hatching, without destroying their nests, so the collectors must collect revenue without oppressing the *misser*."

AMBASSADORS AND ENVOYS.

Phoña and Gser-yig-pa.—These dignitaries in Tibet occupy a position which is next only to that of the Kah-lons. They are generally selected from among the Dah-pons; but in matters of great political importance, from among the Kah-lons. In the early history of Tibet, mention is made of a Prime Minister being sent as ambassador to the Court of the Emperor Thai-jung of China. This was the celebrated Prime Minister Lonpo-Gar, who visited China and Nepal to negociate the marriage of King Srong-tsan Gampo with the princess Kon-jo and Thi-tsun. In later times, Kah-lons Ssur-khang and Sha-ta were deputed as plenipotentiaries to Kashmir and Nepal to sign treaties on behalf of the Government of Lhasa with Maharjah Golab Singh and Sir Jung Bahadur.

Now-a-days occasional embassies are sent from Lhasa to Pekin and the Khanates of Upper and Lower Mongolia. But the political relations between Tibet and China are now so intimate that within the last half century no envoy extraordinary, except Kong-thong (known in English accounts of China by the name "Kishen") and Chanky Rolpai Dorje, has been sent either from China to Tibet or from Tibet to China. The Imperial Residency established at Lhasa in the first quarter of the eighteenth century has in fact converted Tibet from a protected state into a dependency of China.

The Grand Lama of Lhasa being a sacred personage, the Buddhist spiritual guide of the Emperor of China has the privilege of visiting Lhasa at the state expense in order to confer on church affairs, accompanied by the envoy of the Emperor, called *g* Ser-yig-pa, or the bearer of the golden letter of his celestial Majesty. These two high officials sometimes spend twelve months on the journey either way. The spritual guide can, if he likes, take a supply of merchandise to sell at Lhasa or on the way there; and the envoy, though by law forbidden to carry on trade, does sometimes carry merchandise at state expense to sell at Lhasa. All arrangements for their conveyance and the transit of their goods are made by the Tibetan Government when they cross the Chinese frontier, at Dar-Chin-do, generally 300 to 500 persons being engaged in the *oo-lag* to forward them and their luggage. Their conveyance, consisting of a greenish-yellow sedan chair carried by four bearers and a train of sixteen relay bearers, together with their daily board, are arranged for by the Jong-pons through whose districts they happen to pass. When such arrangements are not needed by these august travellers, they generally receive their travelling bill, amounting to three *Dochhe* (Rs. 375) per diem. The Imperial envoy, the Spiritual Guide, the Residents, and such persons as are invited by the Emperor to visit Pekin, and, in case of death, their corpses, are also entitled to these privileges. The *misser* inhabiting the country between Dar Chindo and Lhasa, within a distance of 20 miles on either side of the grand road, are required by Government to supply *oo-lag* and make arrangements for conveyance of those officials, and in return enjoy immunity from all other kinds of taxation or payment of revenue.

The envoys of the Grand Lamas of Lhasa and Tashi-lhunpo have the privilege of occupying a seat eighteen inches high in the Imperial Court. Being ushered into the Court, he first presents the Dalai and Panchhen Lamas' letters and the presents accompanying them. Then follow ceremonial prayers and the recitation of the high titles of the Emperor, after which the envoy, making his own presents to the Emperor, stands ready to answer the gracious inquiries of his celestial Majesty. The Emperor's inquiries are few, such as the following :—*Emperor.*—Are their Holinesses the Dalai Lama and the Panchhen in the enjoyment of sound health and mental prosperity? *Envoy.*—Yes, your immaculate Majesty; their Holinesses are so. *Emperor.*—Were you not much fatigued in the journey? *Envoy.*—By the mercy of your gracious Majesty, this humble servant arrived in this celestial country in perfect safety and happiness.—Thereafter he is conducted to his seat, and entertained with tea and refreshments according to the Tibetan custom. The envoy is granted a second interview when leaving Pekin for Tibet.

The following is a translation of the codified directions respecting the duties of an envoy or state messenger :—

The *g*Ser-yig-pa should consider it his first duty to make the least delay on the journey. He should chiefly look to the interest of his own Government, and always avoid minding his personal interest and his merchandise. After presenting the state letters and presents, together with his credentials, to the Emperor or to the Kings and Princes to whose court he might be sent, he should make his own present, and wait most ceremoniously for replies and inquiries.

Chanaka Gyalpo, in his ethical work, has the following :—

"That man deserves to be a Phoña (Envoy)
Who knows how to answer the questions of a Prince;
Who possessed of shrewdness and wisdom,
Can understand the workings of another's heart."

Such a person deals with the concerns of the state as if they were his own. Speaking considerately, he uses few words, comprehensive in meaning and replete with sense. Envoys deputed to the courts of Mongolian Princes and chieftains should bear in mind that the Grand Lama has assumed the spiritual sovereignty of Tibet for the peaceful government of the country and to put an end to all disputes and political commotion, and they should always remember the following proverb of Sakya Paudita :—

> " By softness the soft is subdued,
> To softness the rough also yield ;
> Wherefore by softness all can be done ;
> Softness by nature is sharp, the sages say."

The envoy should not oppress the *misser* on the way for supplying him with food, conveyance, porters, beasts of burden, &c., but should take only such help from the people as he is authorized to demand by letters-patent from his Government. In demeanour, behaviour, and manner of walking and sitting he should manifest suitable dignity, modesty, and intelligence, regulating them by a studied regard to his own position.

Regarding the envoy's treatment of people of humble position, the Code has the following quotations from the religious work called La*s* *r*nampar *h*bye*d*pai-*m*do.

" To take what has not been given is to fill up the measure of one's own impious actions. Such actions are visited with the destruction of the harvest by frost and hail-storms, by birds, oxen, rats, worms, and insects. Those who commit such sins do really ruin their own good fortune and prosperity. The work called *r*Nampar-*h*gyur-vahi-*m*do points out how from the commission of such corrupt acts people grow poor and miserable. This arises from the following ten moral demerits, viz :—

1. Taking what is not given.
2. Praising for taking what is not given.
3. Coveting or wishing to take what has not been given.
4. Stopping or reducing the maintenance allowance of one's parents.
5. Doing injury to religious service, colleges, monasteries, and the place of residence of those who are already in the way of emancipation.
6. Envy at another's gains.
7. Putting hindrance in the way of another's gains.
8. Rejoicing at another's not gaining.
9. Rejoicing at the occurrence of famines.
10. Misappropriating or reducing endowments to Lamas or monasteries.

The envoy should always bear these demerits in mind, and behave with strict disinterestedness in the performance of his duties, and by no means, because in an exalted office, oppress the people on his way.

When the Imperial Ambassador announces his arrival, the Governments of Lhasa and Tashi-lhunpo send two high officials to wait on him at Nag-chhu, the north-eastern military outpost of Tibet. On his reaching the capital, the Regent, the Ampas (Imperial Residents), the Kah-lons, Cha-sag, and the Dung-khors, marshalled according to official precedence, receive him. He is then carried on a small yellow sedan chair, borne by sixteen bearers, to the palace, where both the Dalai and the Panchhen meet him in the lobby. Arrived in their Holinesses' presence, he takes his seat in a kneeling posture on a high cushion to the left of the throne, when tea and rice are served. Then presenting the Imperial letters and presents to the Grand Lamas, he resumes his seat with his palms joined together. The secretary-in-chief or the chief interpreter opens the covers and places the letters and tablets on the table of their Holinesses. The great respect shown to the Imperial Ambassador seems to account for the high position of that official in China. Such ceremonies were observed when Kishen was sent to Lhasa to dethrone Regent Tshomoling.

POSTAL ARRANGEMENTS.

Nothing like the postal arrangements of India exists in Tibet. Letters are carried by messengers and special couriers, called *Chhib-ssampa* or *Ta-ssampa*, literally "horse-bridge." The message is called *Te-si* in ordinary official language, but in literature it is always called *shu-yig*, or, when applied to the letter of a great personage, *gser-yig* (golden letter). The couriers generally discharge their duties with admirable efficiency, and people help them with great promptness. The Government messengers are invariably provided with the best and swiftest ponies, and during a halt are furnished with lodging, water, and firewood. The heads of villages also supply them with a *thab-yog* (cook). The couriers on foot generally travel 20 to 25 miles per day, while those who ride generally do 30 to 35 miles. The latter is the express rate, for which the Government generally gives an extra remuneration to the couriers. The Government couriers alone get *ta-oo*, or ponies for travelling. The private letters of officials are generally carried by the Government couriers, if their destination lies on the way, while common people make their own arrangements for the conveyance of their letters. There is little correspondence between one person and another in the country. Couriers who carry their own provisions for a journey are called *pang-chhenpas*. Government couriers do not bring separate letters to show to the *misser* for *ta-oo*, but on the covers of their letters a slip is generally labelled, on which the following words are written for the guidance of the Gyanpos or Gopas (head-men) of villages: "Gormed she-kyel, Goi gyur tshan-chas, tshathing, &c." "This letter is despatched from Lhasa at such an hour. It is required to be sent off without delay to reach such-and-such place at such an hour."

There is a special class of trained men employed on postal service between Lhasa and China. The distance between Lhasa and Pekin is divided into 120 *gya-tshug* or postal stages. The average distance between a *gya-tshug* and one next it is about 80 to 90 *lebor*, a *lebor* being equal to 720 yards. This distance of nearly a thousand *lebor* is required to be travelled by the *te-tsi* (the state couriers between Lhasa and China) in seventy-two days. They are generally allowed a delay of five days, but when they exceed that they are punished. On occasions of great importance and urgency the express rate of running is 36 days. During the last affray between the junior Ampa and the people at Shiga-tse the express took a month and a half to reach Pekin.

A well-informed Lama supplied me with the following account of the express between Lhasa and China:—"The express courier is dressed in a tight, blue-coloured dress, the tape fastenings of which are tied on his head, and the knot sealed. He is required to subsist daily on five hen's eggs, five cups of plain tea, a pound of corn-flour, half a pound of rice, and a quarter pound of lean meat. He is forbidden to take much salt, and strictly forbidden to take onions, garlic, red-pepper, butter, or milk. At midnight he is allowed to sleep in a sitting posture for three hours, after which he is awakened by the keeper of the postal stage-house. It is said that the couriers generally take certain medicines to give them the power of endurance against fatigue. The letters are enclosed in a yellow bag, which the courier carries on his back, generally putting some soft vulture plumes below the bags where it comes in contact with their backs. They get relays of ponies at the end of every five *lebor*. Arriving at a stage, they fire a gun as a notice to the keeper of the nearest postal stage to make ready a post pony. At every such stage a relay of five ponies is usually kept. The courier is allowed to change his dress once a week."

THE ARMY.

Military Resources.

In Tibet there is a regular army of about six thousand trained men. Besides this there are *yul-mag*, or "country soldiers," who form no regular army, but are recruited from the *jongs* during war or emergency. Every family or house throughout the country is bound to furnish one ready armed *yul-mag* at the call of the Government. The Kah-lons, Jong-pons, and particularly the Gerpas (landholders) furnish quotas of one regular soldier with weapons, and a servant to carry his provisions, for every *kang* of land they hold. An ordinary *kang* is a measure of land in which 10 yak-loads of barley can be sown, or which annually pays a revenue of 50 to 55 *srang* (Rs. 120-8 to Rs. 132-8) to the Government. During the invasion of Tibet by a horde of nomad Mongols in the beginning of the 17th century, the Tibetan chiefs mustered 100,000 men, and defeated the enemy in battle at Kyan-thang-gang. In the ancient historical accounts of Tibet, it is mentioned that upwards of one hundred thousand Tibetan soldiers mustered under the command of King Ra*l*pa-chan and his successors to fight against the Chinese invaders.

The number of houses (families) in Tibet Proper, *i.e.*, Tsang and U, estimated in the beginning of the 11th century by Bromtan Gya*l*wai Jungne, was 50,000. But now the population is said to have increased about ten-fold. Accepting this conjecture only approximately, the number of families may now be estimated at *not less than* 350,000. The average number of souls in a family being taken as *ten*, the population of Tibet Proper would stand at three and a half millions. The population of Amdo and Kham, which constitute Pyo-chhen, or Great Tibet, is said to be one and a half times greater than that of Tibet Proper. The population of the two—Tibet Proper and Great Tibet,—therefore, according to hearsay, would exceed eight and a half millions. But the great province of Kham is ruled by 18 chiefs, who owe a nominal allegiance to the Dalai Lama, and Amdo is virtually a Chinese province, being under the direct administration of the Governor of Silling.

The Dalai Lama's Government therefore extends over a population of about four millions of people, including the monks of the great monasteries and also the few districts of Kham, including Nyagrong, &c., within the political boundaries of Tibet Proper. If on a call to arms one man were to answer from each family, the Commander-in-Chief of Tibet could muster a force of 300,000, making allowance for absentees. But as the country extends over an immense distance, there would be extreme difficulty in mobilizing this force. Only a fifth part of this (60,000), recruited from U and Tsang, could conveniently be mobilized.

The Government having to support an immensely large body of monks, generally collects the revenue in kind, in consequence of which a large supply of grain always remains in the Government store godowns at Lhasa, Tashi-lhunpo, Gyan-tse, and Tse-thang. As the country abounds in ponies, mules, donkeys, and yaks, these could easily be utilized for commissariat purposes. Besides, in every part of the country there are flocks of sheep and goats, which would also help the army in making a protracted defence against foreign invasion. As the Tibetans mainly subsist on flour made of parched barley, moistened with tea or whey, and dry mutton, they have an advantage over their enemies from Nepal, Sikkim or Bhutan, who subsist on cooked rice and meat or vegetables.

The Chiefs, Kahlons, Jong-pons and Dah-pons furnish quotas of *ta-mag*, or cavalry. Those who merely bring ponies are included in the cavalry, but all others are ranked as infantry and armed with bows and arrows in quivers, sabres, slings, long knives, and matchlocks. In ancient times the Tibetan *Ta-mag* used to dress themselves in coats of mail and helmets (*r*mog), and carried shields. Now-a-days, I am told, these are gone out of fashion owing to the introduction of the Chinese method of warfare and military equipment. An army is called *Mag-pung* and the Commander-in-Chief *Mag-pon*. Immediately under the Mag-pon are the *Dah-pons*, or commanders, who exercise great influence and authority over the divisions under their respective commands. The battalions are commanded by the *Rupons*, who, when they head a thousand soldiers, are called *Tong-pons* (chief of a thousand). An officer at the head of a hundred soldiers is called *Gya-pon* (chief of a hundred), while a *Chupon* is the chief of ten soldiers. An encampment is called *gar* or *mag-gar*. The tents of the soldiers are very strong and durable, being generally made of yak-hair. The tents used by the officers are made of Chinese canvas brought from Dar-chindo or Centifu. They are of a picturesque appearance on account of the different ornamental figures sewn over their sides.

Military Establishment.

The Ampa, or the Imperial Resident of China, is ordinarily the head of the Military Department. His staff consists of an assistant Ampa and two captains, called Daloye, and a *phog-pon* or paymaster. He ordinarily resides at Lhasa, and annually goes out on an inspection tour towards the Nepal frontier *viâ* Shiga-tse up to Tengri-jong. Sometimes he sends the Assistant Ampa on inspection tour, when he inspects the military stores of the different *jongs*, examines the Jong-pons, Dah-pons, and the forces under them in field exercise and the manipulation of arms. The Ampa is the medium of all communications between the Tibetan Government and China. Through him the Emperor communicates his edicts and wishes to the Tibetan Government, and also receives their replies. He settles, or is expected to settle, all political differences between the various states and the Government. He confers honours and titles on the military officers. On the other hand, he has no jurisdiction over the internal administration of the country. Immediately under him in official rank are the Dah-pons, who are the generals of the Tibetan forces.

The following is the distribution :—

Ampa	*Residency Staff.*
Assistant Ampa	
Two Daloye	
One Phog-pon	
One Mag-pon	*Military establishment.*
Six Dah-pons	
Six Rupons	
Nyagrong Chyikhyab or Commissioner of Nyagrong in Kham	
Garpon of Rudok	
53 Jong-pons	

The Mag-pon or Commander-in-Chief is selected in times of war from among the distinguished Dah-pons. He takes instructions from the Council of Kahlons in matters connected with war. Constitutionally he is not bound to take any instructions from the Ampa. Out of six Dah-pons who command 1,000 soldiers each, two are posted in the city of Lhasa, two at Shiga-tse, one at Gyan-tse, and one at Tengri-jong. Out of six Rupons, three belong to the north or central Province, and three to Tsang. The Rupons are purely military officers.

The Chyikhyab of Nyagrong is virtually a Jong-pon, but his position and responsibilities being of a higher order than those of the ordinary Jong-pons, he has precedence over the 53 Jong-pons. The Garpon of Rudok and Gartog hold a position which is second only to that of the Chyikhyab.

The Jong-pons, as I have mentioned elsewhere, are civil officers, who also hold military responsibilities in addition to their civil duties. In times of war the Jong-pons raise soldiers by conscription.

The regular army consists of 6,000 men, out of whom 3,000 are kept ready for service and the remaining 3,000 engage themselves in agricultural pursuits like other *misser*, when they receive only half-pay. The pay of a Tibetan soldier is two *srangs* or five rupees a month, and that of a Chinese soldier six *srangs* (15 rupees) a month. The latter return to China after three years' service in Tibet. The Tibetan soldiers remain three years on active duty, after which they return for a period to their respective homes, and are called the regular *yul-mag*. After this period the regular *yul-mag* may return to active duty. Although the expenditure in maintaining five thousand soldiers, including the Chinese contingent of 500 men, is inconsiderable, considering the extent and resources of the country, yet it must be borne in mind, while estimating the military requirements of Tibet, that the Government revenue is drained off by the heavy expenditure necessary to support 30,000 idle monks who may be considered as so many undisciplined soldiers. If the great body of monks were trained in the art of war, which Buddhism does not permit, Tibet would have been a power stronger even than Nepal.

The commander of the soldiers of a *jong* is called *Ding-pon*. The soldiers do not ordinarily wear uniforms. They have, however, a kind of black uniform, partly resembling the Chinese uniform and partly their national dress, so that whoever dresses in black is taken for a soldier. They are armed with long Chinese matchlocks (*mendah*) with a bore resembling that of a rifle, with bows and arrows in quivers (*shu-dah*), long spears (*dung*), and slings (*ordo*). The Tibetans prepare a coarse kind of powder from saltpetre and sulphur which occur in several mines in Chyang and Tsang provinces. A superior breed of mules called *silling* is bred in Lower Tibet, and an inferior breed called *dode*, much valued by Tibeto-Chinese merchants, is reared in Kham. These are excellent animals for military conveyances, and hardier than those we meet with in the plains of India.

A fort is called a *khar;* its chief, *Khar-pon*. The forts are generally temporary constructions. The *jongs*, the standing forts of the country, are of great strength and generally difficult of access.

The duties of the d*Mag*-d*pon (General)*.

The work *m*Non-par *h*byung-vahi *m*do has the following lines with regard to the qualifications of a Mag-pon :—

"Able to lead, halt, or to call at will ;
He is a gallant and great General,
Who with a valiant and determined force
Subdues the foe, one and all."

The work called *b*De-*m*Chhog *m*Chho*d* Phreng, written by Tsong-khapa, has the following :—

"He is a General valuable and brave,
Who perceives, without being told, the will of his liege ;
Knows all duties, and discharges them well :
To lead, to stop, or to call back his men."

The work Shes-rab *s*dong-bu has the following lines on the same subject :—

"Who by stratagem subdues the opposing foe,
Least by might, but more by skill
(A lion, though valiant, once on a time
Lost his life by a rabbit's stratagem),
Who owns skill, courage, and sense,
Does indeed possess power and strength.
What can valour do without skill and means ?"

Accordingly, although the most important function of a King is the prosecution of war, yet in this country there being, properly speaking, no King, but merely sacred personages engaged in the service of the church, the General should avoid involving himself or his country in warfare. The Kings of other countries, who, to satisfy their vanity or greed for fame and territorial possessions, invade one another's possession or wage war, cannot be compared with the ruler of Tibet, for here the consideration of the present and the future are paramount in the governing class. Heroism, quick perception, and wisdom being united in a General, he does not succumb to the fear of death, but is able fearlessly to combat the enemy. He never yields through fear, but only when forced by very strong reasons for the safety of his men. Although it is necessary for him not to be over-sensitive in the work of the destruction and capture of the enemy's people and possessions, yet he should always refrain from destroying or burning or plundering religious institutions, temples, and monasteries or things consecrated to the service of divinities and divine persons. He should direct the manœuvres or the bivouacking of his army, examining carefully the circumstances under which he and his enemies may be acting. He should not fail minutely to observe the behaviour of his soldiers, and notice their good or bad conduct, that he might bring the deserving and meritorious to the notice of the Sakyong, recommending them for remuneration, and demand punishment for the cowardly and the disloyal.

It is not meet to harass the people on the pretence of war. In exigencies the General should not wait for instructions from his superiors, but should himself decide such points as cannot conveniently be referred to the Government during active military operations. But where discretion is allowed it should not be abused. The General also should not in the time of war, or under pretence of military requirements, or at other times, make the *misser* work in his private concerns; and if there be anybody in the encampment who is guilty of such unfair practices, he should be brought to trial. Property of value obtained on a large scale from subdued or retiring enemies should be divided among the soldiers and officers, things inconsiderable in value and quantity being left to be enjoyed by whoever may pick them up. Weapons and gold should be taken to the Government store. The innocent, peaceful *misser* of the enemy should not be molested, plundered or subjected to rough treatment for the sake of plunder. The General should always give full consideration and due weight to the opinions of his colleagues, and should never fail to confer with them in maturing his plans for carrying out military operations. He should explain to his subordinates the exact nature of their duties, and also point out to the army the vital interests which will be endangered by their irregularity, want of discipline, or desertion. The General, in leading his men to attack the enemy, to halt, or to move, should always be guided by mature considerations as to the comparative strength and resources of both himself and the enemy. Upon this question his utmost skill as a General should be brought to bear.

The duties of the Dah-pon (Commander).

The work *m*Dsang-*s*yig legs-*b*shad *g*ser *h*phring has the following lines about the qualifications of a Dah-pon :—

> " Possessed of valour, skill, and lion's might,
> Strategy, quick perception of right and wrong ;
> Strong armour, sharp weapon, swift steed, and brave men—
> That man alone is fit to be a Tong-pon."

The Dah-pon always keeps his soldiers well drilled in field exercises to make them adroit in military operations. He looks after their discipline and morals. He exhorts them to behave well according to the requirements of the military code. He sets himself with assiduity to acquire proficiency in physical and military exercises. At the time of war he behaves so as to keep up the spirits of the courageous and to inspire terror in the minds of the wavering, according as he thinks the one course or the other advisable. At the termination of the war he remunerates and confers marks of recognition of merit and services on those who have fought gallantly and bravely. He also receives back from them government uniforms, armour, and accoutrements, according to the rules of *Tsi-thi.* He carefully superintends the military stores, such as weapons, coats-of-mail, shields, tents, gunpowder, and such other articles which are liable to be damaged by rust or moth or damp, and sees that they are carefully kept and ready for service.

As regards soldiers, such men should be chosen as are capable of fatigue, courageous, skilful in athletic exercises, and without physical disabilities or diseases. None should be admitted as a soldier who is below the age of 18 or above 60. Unknown or unfit men or vagabonds should not be enlisted as soldiers. Men belonging to an opposite party should also be cautiously employed. Leave should not be granted ordinarily to soldiers unless satisfactory and grave reasons, such as disease, or the death of a relation, justify their absence from the army.

LAWS OF TIBET,

WITH OCCASIONAL NOTICES ON CUSTOMS, &c., OF MONGOLIA AND WESTERN CHINA.

DIVISIONS OF THE PEOPLE IN TIBET FOR LEGAL PURPOSES.

In Tibet there are three distinct classes among the people, lay or clerical, which are determined by birth, office, rank, and social position. Each of these has three sub-divisions. They are as follows :—

First or highest classes "*Rab.*"	*1st.*—" Rab-kyi-rab." The best of the highest class, or the highest in the realm, includes the King, members of the royal family, and incarnate Lamas who have appeared several times on earth. *2nd.*—" Rab-kyi-ding." The middle of the highest class, including the Desi or Governors, ordinary incarnate Lamas, and the Ministers and Councillors of State, the learned Lamas or Abbots, and Professors of important monasteries. *3rd.*—" Rab kyi-thama." The lowest of the highest class includes Secretaries to the Government, Dah-pons, Jong-pons (or district officers), and inferior Lamas or Abbots.
Middle classes "*Ding.*"	*1st.*—" Ding-kyi-rab." The best of the middle class, including families which for generations have possessed great wealth, the landlords who do not claim heritage from illustrious ministers or warriors, the Dung-khors, the oldest families, and such men who, though newly risen, have contributed much to the welfare of the country, and lastly the Jong-ners. *2nd.*—Ding-kyi-ding." The middle of the middle class includes the Dung-yigs or clerks, stewards, chamberlains, head-grooms, head-cook, and other petty officers. *3rd.*—" Ding-kyi-thama." The lowest of the middle class includes soldiers and subjects (*misser*).
Low class "*Thama.*"	*1st.*—" Thamai-rab." The best of the low class are the grooms, menials engaged in domestic service, and other hired servants. *2nd.*—" Thamai-ding." The middle of the low class are those who do not live as householders, men who lead a life of libertinism without taking a wife, or women without husbands that lead an unrestrained life, professional beggars, vagabonds, and destitute people, when they are free from guilt. *3rd.*—" Thamai thama," *i.e.*, the lowest of the low class, are the butchers, scavengers, disposers of dead-bodies, blacksmiths, and goldsmiths.

(*s*Tong *d*pon means a chief over a thousand soldiers).

MURDER.

Punishment for murder consists of the following fines:—(1) "Tong Jal," life-compensation; (2) "Ge-tong," fines for the performance of funeral obsequies and religious ceremonies of the murdered; (3) fines paid to Government; (4) consolation fine.

Life-compensation is called "Tong Jal" in Tibetan. If a man kills a member of the first sub-division of the first class, he must in the first instance be required to pay a quantity of gold equal to the weight of the corpse. In the event of his killing a member of the second sub-division, he will be required to pay a quantity of gold equal to the weight of the upper half of the dead body, and of silver equal to the weight of the lower half. In case of a murder of one of third sub-division, the life-compensation consists of a weight of silver equal to the weight of the corpse.

In murder of one belonging to the fourth sub-division (first of the second class), the payment of 1,000 silver *srangs*, equal to Rs. 2,500, is necessary; of one to the fifth, 500 silver *srangs* (Rs. 1,250); of one to the sixth, 250 silver *srangs* (Rs. 625).

In the case of the murder of one belonging to the seventh sub-division, 125 *srangs* (Rs. 312-8); of one to the eighth, between 60 to 70 *srangs* (Rs. 150 to Rs. 175); and for the last sub-division, the life-compensation ranges from 10 to 30 *srangs* (Rs. 25 to Rs. 75).

All cases of murder (including homicide) are tried by chief courts of justice. The above-mentioned life-compensations fixed by law cannot be exceeded. Besides the *tong-jal*, the offender is required to pay a fine to the court; secondly, a certain amount of money to meet the funeral obsequies of the dead; and thirdly, the "consolation fine."

The least amount of fine which a criminal is required to pay to Government for killing the vilest of the vile in the ninth sub-division is 5 silver *srangs*, and any grade higher up, according to the proportion of the *tong-jal*, the fine will increase by multiples of 5 *srangs*. Although the law enjoins the strict observance of the above limits of *tong-jal*, yet, as it is impossible to produce as much gold as will weigh equal to the dead body, the dispenser of justice is allowed the discretion of imposing payment of the *tong-jal* upon the heirs and claimants of the murderer. Instead of being required to produce gold equal in weight to the corpse of a man of the higher rank, the amount fixed by the court is divided into three equal parts. The first part must consist of gold, the second of silver, and the third of other articles and cattle, each being estimated to be one-third the value of the whole.

The life-compensation fixed for the murder of one of the middle class is paid in two equal parts—one consisting of silver and gold and the other of cattle and other articles. In cases of murder of the lower class, the property of the murderer, when not sufficient to meet the several fines, is entirely confiscated by Government to meet the compensation fee and expenses for performing the obsequies of the murdered (*ge-tong*). For the offence of killing a man of the higher class, he will be required to pay 60 silver *srangs* (Rs. 150), 60 yak-loads of barley, 30 *chamkas** (30℔.) of butter. For killing a man of the middle class he will be required to pay half of the above, and for killing one of the third class he will get his release by the payment of one-fourth of the above, the least amount chargeable being one silver *srang*, one yak-load of barley, and 2℔ of butter for the least culpable murder.

The consolation fine to be paid to the friends and parents of one of the higher class amounts to one very good *khatag* (scarf), and five gold *srangs* cash (Rs. 300); for the middle class it consists of five silver *srangs* and a *khatag* of good quality; and for the lower class an ordinary *khatag* and a *tanka* or two, in cash. In default of payment of any portion of the fines, the criminals are thrown into prison and laid under heavy chains for life.

When a man is killed by a lunatic, or by a boy below eight years throwing a stone or a piece of timber, accidentally or intentionally, the offence is not considered as amounting to murder, and consequently the parties guilty are not to be punished as murderers. Their friends, if there be any, are required to pay only the usual *ge-tong* for the obsequies prescribed for the murdered. If a man be killed by a beast, such as a cow, yak, or horse, the owner of the beast is required to pay one-fourth the usual *ge-tong* for the funeral service.

When a husband kills his wife or a master his servant, he is required to pay the usual fines to Government to the exclusion of the *tong-jal* or life-compensation and the consolation fine, there being none to claim them.

When a man kills another's wife with whom he has had illicit connection, he should be laid under heavy chains for life, besides paying certain fines.

The above are the general laws observed in the country, but now-a-days offences against *individuals* of the higher class are very rare, though general risings and political disturbances are frequent. Cases of murder in the second class are occasional, and in the third class are very rare. When the murderer's case is espoused by some powerful noble or officer, the ends of justice are generally frustrated by corruption and partiality.

In Western China all offences of murder, whether of a father, mother, son, daughter, brother, friend or relative, servant or slave, are punished by sentencing the criminal to death by beheading.

In Mongolia the murderer, after rigorous imprisonment for three years, is banished from the country. Although the custom of punishing by compensation, as in Tibet, to some extent prevails there also, yet people on account of their poverty abide very little by it. When they can afford to pay the fines, the murderers are released. The proportion of fines is smaller in Mongolia than in Tibet, the *tong-jal* for the first class being 3,000 silver *srangs*

---

* Chamka is equal to half a seer.

(Rs. 7,500), for the middle class 2,000 *srangs* (Rs. 5,000), and for the lower class 1,000 *srangs* (Rs. 2,500). The fine to be paid to Government is 300, 200, and 100 *srangs*, respectively. The proportion of the other two fines is comparatively lower than these two. In Mongolia, when a man is found by the evidences of trustworthy eye-witnesses to be guilty of causing death by poisoning or by malevolent incantations, he is thrown into the river, packed in a leather bag; but now-a-days payment of fines, as in cases of murder, is generally accepted and the culprit released.

One is required to supply three horses of equal value as damages for killing one; for killing a cow the damages are two cows; for killing two goats, sheep, or pigs, three of the same animal. Killing dogs is severely punished. In Tibet, as in Europe, the dog is prized by all classes of men as a most useful animal. If a dog is killed by blows on its hinder parts, it is to be taken for granted that it was to some extent blameless, as it must have been running away for its life on being chastised or pursued. In such instances the compensation for a good house-dog is 15 *srangs* (Rs. 37-8); for a *dokpyi* or mastiff, 10 *srangs* (Rs. 25); and for common dogs, 5 *srangs* (Rs. 12-8). If a dog is killed by blows on its head, the offence is considered very light. In such cases the dog is considered to have been the offender and to have been killed in self-defence, so that there is no punishment; only the offender will be required to offer a *khatag* to the owner of the dog.

ROBBERY, DACOITY, AND THEFT.

When a man commits theft in the houses of the king, chiefs, landlords or the heads of towns and villages, he should be required to pay according to the ancient laws. Ten thousand times the value of the property or *thi-jal* was fixed as a fine for stealing the king's property, but generally a fine of one hundred times the value of the property stolen was inflicted, and granted as compensation to the owner. When a man steals property belonging to the church or any particular priest or Lama, or what is consecrated to deities, he should be required to pay 80 measures of the stolen property, namely, for stealing one *tanka* he must return 80 *tankas*. If he steals the property of his fellow-villagers, he is required to return the purloined article, together with seven times the value of the property. When he robs his neighbour, the compensation must amount to nine times, together with the property stolen.

In all these several cases of theft, if the fines are not fully paid up, the thief must be punished corporally, but in a slight measure, according to the proportion of the fines levied on him. Law does not fix any definite corporal punishment, which is left to the discrétion of the Judge; but the spirit of the law requires that he should not inflict severe punishment when the fines are paid.

If the thief be an idiot or dumb, or one from the border-land, or a foreigner ignorant of the language of the country in which he commits theft, or if he lives a vagabond life, or is being forced by hunger or driven by adverse circumstances to commit theft, the stolen property only should be recovered from him, if possible, and he should be fined in proportion to his means, if any. If he fails to pay the fine, service should be exacted from him by the owner for a definite period.

When the theft is of a heavy and serious nature, and the thief a notorious offender, he should be severely dealt with. After the fifth repetition of the same crime, his hands should be cut off. After the seventh instance the sinews of his legs under the knees should be cut to disable him from walking. After the ninth instance his eyes should be put out of their sockets. The infliction of punishment is generally left to the discretion of the Judge, who can modify the severity of the law by diminishing the magnitude of the punishment, but cannot exceed it. Instead of cutting off both the arms, he can order one to be cut off, or neither. For petty thefts, such as stealing eatables and drinkables, the punishment is very light. For stealing saddle-horses or ponies, cattle used in ploughing, milch-cows, *jomos*, pack-horses, war-horses, cooking utensils, implements of war and husbandry, for breaking into store-houses and house-breaking, which constitute the first class of offences, heavy fines are prescribed by law. For thefts of gold, silver, jewelry used by males and females on their persons, very heavy punishments in fines are inflicted. Petty thefts, such as of clothes and apparel, are not considered as serious crimes.

The most serious and daring cases of *dacoity* (called *Chagpa* in Tibetan) are very severely dealt with, the offenders being packed in leather bags and thrown into a river. Offences of a less heinous nature are dealt with by banishing the offender out of the country to remote wildernesses in the border territories. Sometimes the criminals are loaded with chains and thrown into prison. Offences of a light nature are dealt with by subjecting the convict to 500 stripes, inflicted at intervals. In all cases of *dacoity*, be they serious or light, the criminals are thrown into prison till they confess the real facts of their guilt. In order to bring out the truth, they are daily interrogated, teased or tortured lightly till everything is revealed. After subjecting them for three days to this treatment on the mere suspicion of guilt, if no admission is obtained, they are partially released. If after 100 days' crucial examination no clue is obtained to their guilt, they are unconditionally released, no matter how grave the offences they were charged with.

In Western China, when a man is found guilty of a theft of Rs. 2,500 or upwards, he is at once beheaded. For a theft of Rs. 1,250 and upwards he is banished from the country. For all sums below that and above Rs. 125 he is sentenced to three years' rigorous imprisonment.

In Western China, when a *chag-pa* (robber) is detected in the act, or in using violence, he is confined in a wooden cage, where he can neither stand upright nor sit, but is obliged to stoop, bending his knees and lowering the head. He is not allowed a grain of food or a drop of water, and is starved to death. For the gravest offences he is crucified. His hands and legs are stretched on a large public gate and nailed down; or the criminal pays the last penalty of the law by decapitation. The head is suspended with a short account of his crime labelled on it, or placarded in a public assembly or market-place.

The Mongolians punish the gravest cases of robbery and plunder by tying several ropes to the limbs of the criminals and the other ends to the saddles of fleet chargers, which are then whipped and tear the convict's body into pieces. In cases of robbery of a less offensive character, the criminals, put in heavy chains, and seated on donkeys, are led in infamous procession round the cities and villages for several days. Others are banished from the country. In cases of light offences, the guilty are obliged to pay two or three times the value of the property robbed, and are also lightly punished before being released.

In Tibet, when a man is falsely or maliciously charged by a third person with theft, and the real thief be not detected, nor the property recovered, the accuser should be required to pay the value of the lost article to each of the parties—the owner and the accused. In the event of the owner himself falsely or maliciously charging an innocent man with theft, on the charges being dismissed, he should be obliged to pay the value of the article pretended to have been lost to the accused as damage, and a benedictory scarf (*khatag*) by way of apology.

When a man, on finding lost or left property, conceals it, or neglects to restore it to the rightful owner, or denies knowledge of it, his offence should be treated as theft, there being no great difference between direct and indirect stealing. He should be required to pay the prescribed fines to the owner, and be corporally punished according to the discretion of the Judge. But if he restores it to the owner without showing any desire of misappropriating it, the owner should reward him with half the lost article or half its value. But if he misappropriates it he should be dragged to the court. When the thief desires to come to an amicable settlement with the owner, the prescribed fines should be exacted from him through mediators, and the owner abstain from further proceedings. But if he fails to pay the fines, he must liquidate his liabilities by personal service. In the first instance of theft amicable settlement is permitted; in case the offence is repeated, it is not permissible. If the owner, seizing the thief, thrashes him so as to inflict wounds on his body, the thief will not be liable to a second punishment by any court of justice, nor will he be required to pay any fines or compensation. If the owner fails to seize the thief, but succeeds in killing him while running away by an arrow or a sling from a distance, he should be obliged to pay compensation for his life to his family, but will not be required to furnish funds for his funeral service and religious observances. But when the thief, being caught by the owner, is killed by a sword or spear, the slayer must be required to pay the compensation value for the deceased's life and also the necessary expenses of his funeral and other religious services as prescribed by law. If the thief, being seized and confined by the owner, die in confinement without any maltreatment or violence on the part of the owner, the latter will be required to pay a sum of 5 silver *srangs*, or Rs. 12-8, as compensation for the deceased's life. In instances when thefts are committed by men of high rank or official position, such as chiefs, Lamas, and nobles, all complaints must be made before the Government or to the court of justice. They must be required to pay only twice the value of the stolen property to the owner; and if they are confined in prison, they are not to be treated with rigor like ordinary convicts, but are to be consigned to civil prisons. No corporal punishment can be inflicted on them. Before the expiration of the term of confinement, they are not to be permitted to leave the prison, nor allowed to mix or talk with outsiders or their relatives and friends. In the event of the criminals being public servants, they are to be degraded from their rank in service, according to the gravity of their offence. But whenever an officer's offence, whether light or grave, is proved, he is to be punished. Even if he is not degraded his promotion must be stopped for a period of ten years.

When thefts like the stealing of crops are proved, the guilty are required to pay fines amounting to three times the value of the crop robbed. For stealing garden fruit, trees, and water from another's house, the fine is also thrice the value.

When ponies, donkeys, and oxen are found straying in corn-fields, plantations, or gardens, no matter whether any damage is done or not, for each animal the owner is required to pay in damages four *tankas* (Re. 1-8), being one *tanka* for each leg. For goats and sheep the damages are half those for the larger animals. But if the animal be found to have eaten anything, five tankas should be charged, four for four legs and one for the mouth. If the animal causes damage to a crop during the day-time, the owner will be required to pay damages to the extent of six *bres* (6 lb); if during the night, he should be required to pay 12 *bres*. If the owner of the crop or garden beat the cattle and injure it, he should be required to pay half the price of the cattle to the owner. For a simple beating he forfeits the fines, but if through his beating the cattle dies, he should be required to pay its full value or give the owner one of equal value, in which case he should be allowed to take away the skin and flesh of the cattle he killed. When a pig damages a crop or garden, for which it is killed, its owner must be content to get its flesh only; the killer will not be required to pay its price.

Boys below 13 years of age are exempted from all sorts of punishment for theft; only the parents are remonstrated with for their children's conduct.

If a dog eat or steal meat or butter from one's house, its owner should be required to pay half the price of the article stolen or damaged. When lost ponies or donkeys, goats and sheep are found and restored to their owners without having been saddled or sheared, the owners should be required to pay one-fourth their price as reward to the restorer. But if the finder saddle them for use, or shear their fleece, or milk them, he forfeits the usual reward. Finders of other lost articles are paid the rewards and entertained with food and wine according to the value of the thing recovered and the wealth of the owner. In all cases rewards should be adjusted according to the value of the recovered article. In cases of this nature recourse should not be had to the courts of justice or to Government. When a lost pony or other lost article is found, the obtainer must restore the article to the rightful owner within three days. If within that period the owner is not found out, the matter should be reported to the head-man of the village or town. If he fails to do that, he should be found guilty of misappropriation.

If a woman commits theft, the payment of prescribed fines and corporal punishment should be borne equally by herself and her husband or friend in whose keeping she is. No corporal punishment can be inflicted upon women in a state of pregnancy or after childbirth, till the time of suckling expires. Diseased persons, male or female, those who have been bereaved of their parents or children within one month, or those who have passed the 70th year of their age, are exempted from corporal punishment. Slight corporal punishment only can be inflicted on those who are aged from 13 to 19 or 61 to 69. Bodily punishment of any degree or kind can be inflicted on persons who are between 19 and 60 years of age.

When stolen property is discovered in the possession of a trader or merchant, it should be brought out to the market and exposed. If the owner can identify it, the trader will be held guiltless only when he can produce the seller or the thief from whom he obtained it. If he cannot produce the thief, he will be required to produce witnesses who saw him buying the article. If he cannot bring forth witnesses, and if the owner can produce witnesses who will testify that they saw the article in his possession, the owner will be allowed to take away the article from the trader. When there are witnesses to support the statement of both parties, the owner will have to pay half the price of the article to the merchant.

The giver of shelter to a thief is a greater offender than the thief himself. The abettor of theft, or one who invites another to steal, or to cause a third party to steal, is also a graver offender than the thief who committed the theft.

According to the custom of Western China, when a traveller's or merchant-traveller's riding-horse or luggage or goods are robbed on the road, he must complain to the chief of the country, who will take masures to detect the robbers and recover the stolen properties. If the property be not recovered, nor the robbers detected within a week's time, the Government makes good the losses sustained by the traveller, and dismisses him without further detention. The traveller himself cannot search the villagers to find the robbers; but the villagers are held responsible for making good the traveller's losses. In Tibet and Mongolia, if after close search and investigation the property be not recovered nor the robbers detected, the Government does not reimburse the traveller.

When a thief steals a lock or key or a watch-dog from a house, his offence will be tantamount to stealing the contents of the house or store to which these belonged. The stealing of a lock or key or a dog is the same as robbing the treasury which they guarded. When a man sees a thief in the act, and does not raise a hue and cry, he is equally guilty with the thief himself. When a thief, stealing a cow, kills it and eats its flesh, and another man, aware of the theft, partakes of the meat with the thief, his offence should be considered as serious as that of the thief. But when he is ignorant of the theft, he will not be guilty even if he were to eat up the entire cow. If a theft of property belonging to a party included in the family circle is committed by any member of a family, either by the father, mother or the children, by the tutor or his pupil, layman or priest, in the house itself or outside of it, the matter should not be reported to the court of justice nor received by it when applied to; but the guilty party should be punished by the head of the family.

RAPE AND ADULTERY.

When a man is found guilty of rape upon the lady of a king, prince, noble or chief, he should be punished by having his testicles extracted and with a payment of gold to the party or parties injured equal to the weight of the testes; but when the crime is considered very grave, the above punishment will not suffice: after having paid the aforesaid penalty, he should be required to pay nine articles, consisting of ponies, yaks, *jo*, &c., one *khatág*, nine articles consisting of skins, nine articles consisting of carpets, and blankets, &c., to the parties injured, besides a law fee of Rs. 900 (15 gold *srangs*). In default, he should be banished from the country.

If a man has immodest intercourse with the wife of a man of his own rank and position in society, he should be required to pay the husband a compensation fee of 5 *srangs* or Rs. 12-8, and a series of seven articles as mentioned above. To the woman abused, he should be required to give a complete suit of dress. He should find a security, and bind himself to pay a fine of 15 gold *srangs*, or Rs. 900, to ensure non-repetition of a similar offence with the same party, and pay a law fee of 15 silver *srangs*, *i.e.* Rs. 47-8.

When a man commits adultery at the request of the woman, he should be required to present a *khatag*, wine, and 3 silver *srangs* (Rs. 7-8) only to her husband as compensation. He must also be required to bind himself by oath, or by a letter duly signed and sealed by himself before witnesses, not to repeat the offence with her. When a simple letter signed by the guilty party is not accepted, he is required to find securities. When one of high rank commits adultery with a woman of inferior class, he is required to present the woman and her husband with a robe each and a sufficient quantity of meat, wine, flour, and butter, to gratify them.

In instances where the husband is impotent, and the woman unwilling to live with him, the adulterer, when he is much attached to her, must supply the injured husband with a suitable substitute, *i.e.*, one to his satisfaction, and in addition pay the marriage expenses which the husband had incurred on the first occasion.

In China, when a man commits adultery with another's wife, when the guilt is proved, both the parties are beheaded. If the adulterer be a man of high rank, he is degraded, or has to pay a compensation fee of 10 *dochhe* (Rs. 1,200) to the husband of the adulteress.

INTERCOURSE WITH UNMARRIED GIRLS.

When a man of inferior rank has immodest intercourse with a maiden of high rank, such as the daughter of a Lama,* king, prince, noble, or chief, he should be compelled to serve the parent of the maiden gratuitously for a number of years. If the guilty person be very rich, he will be required to present a *khatag* to each of the parents, together with his riding-pony, saddle, carpet, and bridle, besides a petition fee† of 50 silver *srangs* (Rs. 125) in cash. When both the parties are of equal rank, the man is required to marry the maiden and live with her in her father's house. If he fail to do so, he should be required to present a *khatag* to each of her parents and a sufficient quantity of wine, and a married woman's gown to the maiden. When one of high rank is found guilty of this offence with a maiden of inferior rank, there is no punishment for him except that he will be slightly put to shame by those who may hear of the affair. But if he bears much attachment to the maiden, he can take her for his wife.

When a man, be he great or humble, without wedding a maiden, makes her pregnant, so that she falls ill, he should be required to furnish her with proper medicine and medical treatment, necessary religious ceremonies for her speedy cure, and sick-bed attendance. He should also be required to furnish her with food and wine, clothes and bed-covering till she is free from the effects of childbirth. To the parents of the maiden he should present *khatags* and wine. He must be compelled to entertain all his fellow-villagers or townsmen with meat and wine, according to his means. This is called *yusang* or "the ceremony of cleansing of defilement."

In China, if a man be found guilty of committing illicit intercourse with the daughter of the King, or of a minister, governor or any high official, the offender pays the penalty with the loss of his head. If a man is found to have committed unlawful intercourse with a girl of inferior rank, he must, after having asked pardon from her parents, either keep it secret or take her as his wife. If the matter is brought to the notice of the Government, the parents are required to serve him for a period of three years as a punishment for lax morality. In this respect the Chinese laws being very strict, in spite of the vastness of the population, cases of this kind I am told are very rare. In the generality of cases the parents jealously guard their girls from coming in contact with men. Those who come in contact either marry, or have the good sense to preserve their virginity till they are married.

According to the custom of the Mongolians, if a man of inferior rank is found to have committed adultery with the King's wife, a princess, or the wife of a chief or minister, he is remonstrated with for his conduct, and receives very slight punishment. In fact, law and custom prescribe no penalty for adultery among the Mongol people. Chastity or modesty is a virtue unknown to them; girls and young men are at liberty to practise unrestrained intimacy with each other, sometimes even in the very face of their parents. Custom allows promiscuous intercourse everywhere. Where the parties consent, there is no offence. When one finds that his wife indulges in immodest intercourse with another, he cannot say a word to him nor to her, nor can she tell him a word when she finds him with another's wife. Marriage is a contract by which both parties can have access to each other's person, and live for the fulfilment of conjugal duties; but by marriage the Mongols do not lose their right, as they consider it, of having sexual intercourse with those whom they love. In consequence of such gross laxity of morals, jealousy is unknown among the Mongols. When a Mongol host is very much pleased with the amiability and gaity of his guest, he presses him to make merry with his beautiful wife. So also in order to please his guest and to add to his comforts he presses him to sleep with his wife. Such offers are frequent when they find that their wives are handsome and will be acceptable to the guests. It is not the custom of the Mongols at all to watch the modesty of their girls. When a girl gives birth to a child, the father is required to present the nomad villagers with one sheep at least. When a Mongol princess in this way gives birth to a child, she blushes for her conduct, and that is considered a sufficient punishment.

* All Lamas, with the exception of those of the Gelugpa sect, generally keep female company.
† This fee is paid to the party applied to, and not to the Government.

CAUSING GRIEVOUS HURT, WOUNDS, AND BLOODSHED.

Fines for these offences are included under the general term of *Son-jal* or "life compensation." The entravagant punishments enjoined in the ancient droconic codes of Tibet are now to some extent repealed by the Government, being considered impracticable. In them the value of each drop of blood of the higher class is fixed at one gold *srang*, and of each drop of blood of the middle class at one gold *sho* (Rs. 9-8), and of each drop of blood of the lower class at one silver *sho* (4 annas). Now-a-days in the transactions of ordinary business the subjects and servants exchange words very often, and it is not unusual for them to assault and inflict severe wounds on their masters and superiors. In such cases, according to the gravity and character of the hurts and wounds, corporal punishment is inflicted on the offender. For offenders possessing some property the fines range from a *khatag* and one gold *sho* to three gold *srangs*. If the master be a chief or a man of position, and causes grievous hurt of any kind to his servant, he should be required to furnish medicine and medical treatment and attendance, and also to pay a suitable amount of reward in money or other articles to the party to console him for his disgrace, but he shall pay no life compensation in consequence of the relation in question being one of master and servant. If a man assault or cause hurt to or wound one of his own position or class after mutual exchange of abusive language, false accusations, or fighting, he should only be required to take measures to heal the wound. In such instances the law would not make him pay a life-compensation to the injured when wounds are inflicted on the bodies of both the parties. The provoker, after being examined, if found guilty, should be required to give the necessary compensation. If one party on account of superior strength receive no wound or hurt, and the other party be grievously hurt and bleed much, the former should be required to give the latter a blanket of superior quality as compensation for the wound (called *mag-gos*. or the *wound-dresser*) and a wrapper and white woollen rug as compensation for the blood shed (called *t'hag-den* or *blood-rester*), besides the supply of medicines, religious ceremonies, medical treatment, diet, and other necessaries of life, till the wound gets healed. After these he should be required to pay compensation for shedding of blood in the proportion mentioned above. Again, there are instances in which the wounds are measured as to their extent and depth. If the depth be more than a finger's breadth, the party accused should be required to furnish the injured with a gold *srang* for each finger's breadth of the wound. In cases of less depth the compensation is one gold *srang*. When any fracture happens, compensation is made in gold to the weight of a similar bone. Where the party hurt or wounded is found guilty, he should be required to make his antagonist the present of "three kinds" or "five kinds,"* who should, as usual, pay him the necessary life-compensation. If a man be found guilty of knocking out the tooth of another, or of tearing out his hair, for each tooth he should be required to make compensation with a pony and for each hair a sheep. But now-a-days the penalty fixed for pulling out hair is altered. For pulling out hair (any quantity) for each offence the compensation is only a "gold *sho*" (Rs. 9½). For causing grievous hurt to the organs of sense or the limbs, such as the eyes, nose, ears, and hands or legs, so as to make them unserviceable, the compensation is equal to half the sum fixed for murder, for the loss of an eye or hand is considered equal to the loss of half one's life. In cases of light hurt the compensation is paid in the proportion of one-fourth, one-fifth, &c., of that of murder.

In cases of battery, when no wound or bleeding is caused, but only swelling and pain, the assaulter should be required to present a *khatag* and three *srangs* to the injured. In light offences one or two *srangs* are accepted as compensation. When both the parties are found guilty the provoker is punished by the court with a fine, the amount of which varies with the nature of the offence, but never exceeds the *Son-jal*. Flourishing a sword in a threatening manner, or drawing a knife as if to stab, is considered a grave offence. The fine or compensation for such an offence is one gold *srang* (Rs. 60).

In China the abettors of a fight and the parties fighting and those who cause hurts or wounds, are put in chains as soon as they are arrested. For offences of this nature, rigorous imprisonment for a number of years, according to the gravity of the crime, is inflicted. Payment of a simple fine or compensation, as it holds in Tibet, is not to be met with in China.

In Mongolia the using of disrespectful or abusive language or assaulting those who claim descent from Jengis Khan is severely punished; for using foul language one must lose his horse together with saddle and bridle. For blows and causing hurt he must be banished from the country. For causing grievous hurt, or bleeding or wounding, he must be committed to a Chinese court to be tried with a view to his being beheaded, for the Mongols do not take life for life nor, do they throw convicts into river, their only capital punishment being to tear the limbs of the criminal by tying them to horses. With the exception of the descendants of Jengis Khan, for causing grievous hurt or wound to any nobles or great men, the compensation is one camel; to middle class men, one horse; to one of the lower class, one sheep. The amount of fines exacted by Government is not fixed by law. In the case of rich folk 1,000 silver *srangs* is sometimes not considered much, and in the case of the poor the presentation of a *khatag* is thought enough. In Tibet, if a man

---

* These consist of different sorts, three at a time or five at a time.

causes a large wound to a pony, cow, or yak, he is required to feed the animal thus hurt with grass and gram, or supply the means of cure as long as the wound does not heal up; when perfectly cured, he returns it to the owner. If he hurts it in the eye or limbs, so as to make it almost useless, he is required to pay half its price to the owner.

OATHS AND ORDEALS.

In doubtful cases, where the judge or the arbitrators fail to decide, oaths and ordeals are ultimately resorted to, such being considered as conclusive tests for the court of final appeal. When the dispensers of justice and the, mediators fail to ascertain the guilt or innocence of the contending parties, or even, knowing the circumstances connected with the offences, cannot for want of evidence convict the offender, they are required, in extreme cases, to permit the plaintiff to challenge the defendant to undergo an ordeal or make a deposition on oath. Of all penalties these two are considered the most horrid as well as the most repulsive. Very few cases happen in which ordeals or oaths are taken. In Kham and Amdo thése practices are now being gradully abolished, but in Tibet proper they are still in vogue. On account of the diabolical nature of oaths and ordeals the Tibetan law exempts a certain class of men from them as being morally incapable of undergoing them. Lamas, teachers, *Ge-ñen* (*quasi*-priestly householders), monks, and adepts are not allowed to take oaths and pass through ordeals. Tantriks (religious sorcerers) and other practitioners of mystic incantations, who are supposed to be able to counteract the fearful consequences of an oath by means of their powerful spells, are also exempted. Destitute and famished people to whom food and clothes are all-in-all, and men who will do anything they like, unmindful of the consequences of sin in a future existence, are not allowed to make a deposition on oath. Wives and mothers, who can easily be persuaded to swear in the interest of their husbands and children, are also not admitted by the court as capable of taking the oath. Besides these, young boys, lunatics, and the dumb, who do not understand the difference between good and bad, or happiness and misery, are also exempted. All others not included in the above, who are honest, know the difference between good and evil, believe in the inevitable consequences of one's actions (*Karma*), or have foresight and sense to see the present and future, are considered proper persons to come under the operation of oaths and ordeals. The party (generally the plaintiff) who challenges his opponent to take the oath is required to pay the defendant the "oath compensation." This varies from a trifling amount to a very large sum, according to the nature of the case. But for one of considerable importance the usual compensation is 50 *srangs* (Rs. 125) and a yak, which is claimed for what is called the "oath flesh" (*Nah-sha*) and "oath blood" (*Nahtha*).

Description of a Tibetan oath.—First the swearer offers prayers to the all-knowing gods (Buddhas and Bodhi-sattva), to earthly gods and godesses called *Srungmas*, the demi-gods of the land, and the fierce goblins and nymphs who live in the land, invoking them to bear witness to his solemn deposition. Then he begins by saying, "What I depose is the truth and nothing but the truth." He then sits on the reeking skin of a cow or ox newly slain, with his face and body all naked, smears his body with the reeking blood of the ox, and places the image of Buddha, with some volumes of religious books, on his head. Next, after eating the raw heart of the ox and drinking three mouthfuls of its steaming blood, he declares to the spectators, "There is certainly no guilt in me, but if there be any, may the guardians of the world, the gods, before the end of the current month or year, make me cease to exist." He then receives the oath compensation and the slain ox. It is the universal belief among the Tibetans that when the swearer perjures himself, before the expiration of one hundred and seven days he either turns insane or dies, vomiting blood. When these do not happen, some sort of calamities must happen to him, such as the loss of wife or children, entanglement in quarrels, enmity, and loss or destruction of property. Death is believed to be the most frequent consequence of perjury.

The undergoing of such an oath liberates the swearer from the penalty of death and compensation in all cases of robbery and murder, as well as from all civil liabilities, such as debts, even of thousands of *srangs*, and disputes about lands. On the other hand it is believed that if the challenger be really guilty of false and malicious accusation, all sorts of evils that were reserved for the perjured swearer shall fall upon him.

In certain cases by the throw of dice the guilt or innocence of contending parties is ascertained, that party being exculpated who gets the greatest number of points.

Ordeal of white and black pebbles.—All important cases of murder, robbery, and theft are decided by ordeals. The first kind of ordeals consists in picking out white and black pebbles from a bowl of boiling oil or marsh water; the second in handling a red-hot stone ball. In the presence of the prosecutor, the witnesses, the judge or his representative, and many other spectators, the swearer invokes the gods and the demi-gods to bear witness to his statement. He then declares that he tells the perfect truth. A copper or iron bowl filled with boiling oil or marsh-water is then brought before him, in which two pebbles of the size of an egg, one white and the other black, each tied and wrapped up in a bag, are thrown. The swearer now washing his hand first with water and then with milk, hears the reading of the section of the law written on a tablet with the blood of the cow slain for the occasion. Then, again affirming that his statement is true, he thrusts his hand in the boiling oil or water, and takes out one of the pebbles. If he can take out the white one without scalding his hand, he is believed to be perfectly innocent, but if in getting it out his hand gets scalded, he is considered partially or half innocent, but if he misses the white stone altogether and also gets his hand scalded, he is pronounced guilty. The second ordeal consists in making a stone ball of the size of an ostrich-egg, red-hot in a coal fire and then placing it in an iron vessel, freed from the burning embers and ashes. The swearer then washing his hand in milk and water, with perfect composure of mind, and without shrinking, seizes the ball with his hand and walks with it to a distance of 7, 5 or 3 paces, according as the party aggrieved is of the 1st, 2nd or 3rd class. Then his hand is immediately put in a bag made of white cotton cloth, and in the presence of those assembled to witness the scene, it is tied and sealed. At the end of the 3rd, 5th or 7th day the bag is opened and the palm examined. If it is found unscorched but with only a pale yellowish line or stain on it, he is declared innocent. If there appear a blister of the size of a pea, he is thought a little guilty. If three blisters of that size appear he is considered half guilty. If his hand be scorched all over, he is looked upon as the guilty culprit, and the full punishment for his offence is inflicted upon him.

It is believed that if the swearer be really innocent and honest the white and black pebble or the red-hot stone ball will cause very slight injury to his hand. When he is declared innocent he gains the challenger's wager together with the case. But when he is found guilty he must undergo the full punishment required by law.

In China this systems of oaths and ordeals does not prevail. In Mongolia the oath system only is in vogue, there being no system of ordeal. The system of casting dice is also practised all over Kham and Amdo, but chiefly in the former province, where its efficacy is believed to be productive of much good. The oaths and ordeals above described are between enemies. But there are some which are resorted to for establishing friendships. When a man contracts friendship with another, he first arranges for a festive dinner He then, in the presence of the emblems of the "three holies,"—the images of Buddha, Dharma, and Sanga, – invokes the gods and demi-gods to bear witness to his contracting the friendship. Then the two friends clasping each other's hand solemnly swear that they will never think of doing mischief to each other either by cheating or practising fraud ; that they will through life, to the best of their power, try to contribute to each other's welfare, service, and good. This is called the "oath of concord." When such friends prove faithless they are universally hated as bad characters, but no complaints in the absence of regular offences can be preferred against one by the other People believe that men who do not agree with each other after such solemn vows of friendship are born as devils in another life ; and that false swearing after the manner above described, unscrupulously practised by evil characters, generally entails disease, plague, and famine on the country in which the vows were taken. The authorities of Government generally select desert and uninhabited places, where tents are pitched, for the taking of oaths and ordeals.

USURY, CONTRACTS, AND TRADE CUSTOMS.

According to the laws of the Tibetan Government, the interest on articles of exchange—money, grain, or any other substance—is 20 per cent., or one measure for five measures yearly. For instance if one borrows five *srangs* or five *bre* of grain, he shall have to pay six (5 + 1) *srangs* or *bre* at the end of the year. All calculations are made in this proportion. The courts in a few cases admit contracts on a higher interest than 20 per cent. as valid. Those who claim more according to their contract deeds, are sometimes punished as covetous, but sometimes have their claims allowed. All contracts of usury are required to be made on written documents, executed before witnesses, and duly signed and sealed. The interest is required to be paid at the end of the year. If the debtor absconds, the witnesses are required to make good the loss thereby sustained by the lender. If the debtor having died or become insolvent, the money be not realized, the witnesses are not held responsible. If the money belongs to Government, to certain monasteries or Lamas, or to the *phog-pon* (paymaster) of the army, the amount is realized from the relations, witnesses, and neighbours of the debtor. In Tibet, at every military station, a certain amount of money is generally laid out by Government, from the interest of which the militia is paid by the Phog-pon. This officer is one of the chief Government money-lenders. In urgent cases 33 per cent. interest is also sometimes agreed upon. There are instances in which 25, 20, 15, and 10 per cent. interest is charged by mutual agreement of the contracting parties. When the parties soliciting a loan are not known, and when doubts about their honesty are entertained, taking security or pawning is resorted to. When pledge-bonds are exceeded, claims on the pledged deposits are forfeited by the debtors. The creditors are then free to dispose of the article.

In Mongolia the usual rate of interest fixed by law is 30 per cent. per annum. Higher or lower rates are very rare : when the interest equals the principal, the latter ceases to bear interest. The accumulated interest produces interest, but when the compound interest equals the simple interest, it also ceases ; so that the entire interest on any loan cannot exceed twice the principal within three years of contracting the debt. The creditor exercises much power over the debtor. After three years the power of his claims decreases. Not so in Tibet, where the lender is known to use his power over the debtors for three generations. The more the debtor exceeds the fixed term, the more urgent is the creditor in his demands on the debtor. The court, when it sees that the creditor has extracted much compound interest for many years from the debtor, can put a stop to the accumulation of further compound interest ; but there is no fixed period mentioned in the law after which compound interest must cease to accumulate.

In Mongolia the debtor, on the creditor's preferring a complaint against him after six years, can free himself of all liabilities by payment of half the sum, after nine years by one-third, and after ten years no claim is admitted at all. In Tibet, Mongolia or China, when a man comes to ask for a loan, the creditor generally entertains him with good food and drink. If he has a mind to refuse the prayer, he will behave with great politeness, not to make the solicitor feel the bitterness of disappointment; and instead of dismissing him with an abrupt refusal, he will entertain him with the best food, and at the end communicate his inability to comply with the request. Both in Tibet and Mongolia the loan of such articles as utensils, implements of husbandry and war, drinking cups, borrowed articles, articles kept on trust, landed estates of which the revenue is paid to Government, and images of gods, are never given in loan or mortgaged.

When a man has a single pony, one milch cow or *jo*, one pair of ploughs, a team of bullocks or yaks, or one suit of a monk's dress for his own use, nobody can ask for a loan of any of these articles without committing the offence of 'impudence,' for which he may be severely rebuked. The creditors, whether Government or private parties, cannot also dispossess the *misser* of any one or more of these properties. This is the grand charter of the Tibetans. No creditor can by force seize the property of his debtor. If without the debtor's permission he removes one *srang*, he forfeits his entirec laim on a loan of 100 *srangs*; if two, on 200; and so on. Nobody, be he a public officer, landlord, master, or creditor, can for any kind of pecuniary claims exercise violence on the *misser*. If being in possession of means the *misser* refuses to pay off his liabilities or debts, the creditors should call mediators, or institute a law-suit in a court of justice, to settle the differences; but if, without resorting to those means, he beats or practises any kind of violence on the debtor, he foregoes all his claims on him.

The rate of hire for a pony or mule between Lhasa and Shiga-tse, a distance of eight marches only, is five *srangs*; for a donkey or yak, two *srangs*. This is of course for known parties, neighbours, and official travellers. For urgent cases where despatch is needed the rate is one *srang* for every pa*g*-tsha*d*, or Tibetan mile, which is equal to nearly five English miles. For a complete set of implements of husbandry, the daily hire is 20 *bre* of barley. If a horse, yak, bullock, *jo*, or donkey die in the charge of the hirer, he should be required to pay the price of it, or give one of equal value in exchange. If the animal die within six hours after being returned, the hirer is held responsible for it, but if it die after six hours, the owner cannot lodge any claim against the hirer. If the animal be overworked and returned lame or useless on account of sores on the back, the owner can realize half, one-third, or one-fourth of its price from the hirer. On the Chinese frontier pony or mule hire is charged at the rate of three *sho* (12 annas) per diem. In Mongolia no hire is charged from known parties for draught or pack-animals, and from strangers, traders, or revenue collectors very trifling sums are charged. For long distances the rate of hire increases in proportion. If the animals taken on hire be returned without apparent illness, and yet die soon after, the owner cannot charge the hirer for damages after he has gone out of sight.

During the grand religious prayer assembly of Lhasa, called Monlam-chhenpo, which takes place on New Year's Day (Tibetan year), when pilgrims come from different countries of High Asia and China, a great demand arises for Lama costumes on hire. The richest apparel, consisting of the upper garments (like petticoats) of the Lamas (*stod agag*), the gown (*sham thab*), the girdle (*skérag*), boots, hat, the emblems of ordination (*chhab-blug*), and the rosary is charged at the rate of 10 *srangs* per diem (Rs. 25). The outfitter can charge heavily for damage done to the clothes by carelessness, such as oil or tea stains. At Tashi-lhunpo for such a suit of dress three *srangs* are charged. For ordinary clothes, both at Lhasa and Tashi-lhunpo, the rate of hire does not exceed one *tanka*, accompanied by a *khatag* per day. In Pekin, I am told, when on certain occasions the grand nobles, ministers, vassal-kings, and chiefs assemble to pay their respects to the Emperor, a great demand exists for State costumes. There are nobles who hire clothes at the rate of Rs. 7,500, or 60 *dochhes* per diem! In Mongolia there is no such system of letting clothes on hire.

If after buying an article the customer wishes to return it, he will have to return the article together with one-tenth of its price. If he returns it on the second day, he will have to pay one-fifth of the price of the article, together with the article itself. If he delays two days, he must return it with half its price as a fine. After the third day no goods can be returned. If a house-keeper himself cheats a merchant-lodger, for every *srang* worth of article he should be required to pay 5 *srangs* as compensation. If a trader deceive his customers, by using false measures and weights, or by selling spurious or imitation goods, gems, or jewels as genuine, or by managing to give currency to false coin, he must immediately be handed over to the police, and committed for trial. If the merchant convicted be a subject of the Tibetan Government, all his goods are confiscated by Government, and he is sentenced to penal servitude for a certain number of years. If the merchant be a subject of some foreign Government, such as China, Mongolia, Kashmir, or Nepal, a certain amount of fine, as prescribed by law, is exacted from him, and a list of his goods is made. The Government seizes and examines all his goods, and after securely packing them, sends them and the merchant himself in charge of the police to his own Government, together with a letter of representation from the Tibetan Government, complaining of the conduct of the merchant, and stating the amount of the fines exacted from him as punishment. The Tibetan and Mongolian merchants sell goods in a way that suits them well. They are not so calculating as the Chinese of Shensi and Yúnnan, who generally return to their country after earning 300 per cent. profit clear of all expenses. The Pekin merchants who come to Lhasa sell their goods at six times the cost price. They generally raise 400 per cent. on original stock. Brokerage and commission are only paid on Chinese goods when the bargain is great. In Mongolia no such custom prevails. In China no custom exists of paying hire for borrowed articles. Both in Tibet and China, when one fails to return the borrowed articles in good order, he is required to replace the loan by a similar article if possible. In Tibet if a borrower wickedly denies that he borrowed anything, and refuses to return the article he had borrowed, he is treated as a thief. In Mongolia such a criminal is set free on the payment of half the price of the property demanded.

In Western China the penalty for practising extensive fraud by using false weights and measures is death. For cheating and using counterfeit coin the penalty is banishment. The Mongolians being a straightforward people, are not known to commit such crimes. Among them for slight offences of this nature the criminals are whipped. In China, when a purchaser wishes to return the goods after having paid its price, he can only do so by paying five *sho* (Re. 1-4) for all articles of the value of one *srang* and upwards. If he has walked seven paces after the bargain, the article cannot be returned. In Mongolia the purchaser can only return the article as long as he has not walked to a distance whence his hat cannot be seen. If he has walked to such a distance, he must pay one-tenth of the value of the article bought, to have its price refunded to him. In Tibet, there is a great demand for several Chinese commodities of merchandise. Supplies from China consist chiefly of Chinese silver, silk, raw and manufactured, satins of various kinds, *khatags*, tea, China-ware, porcelain saucers and cups, embroidered Chinese mandarin hats (*sertheb*), Chinese chintz, coarse Assam silk-cloth (*sburés*), kincobs (*hor-goo*), different sorts of Chinese hats white jade (*yang-the*), Chinese velvet boots, bridles, brass and bronze cups (*sil-nyen*), musical instrument made of brass plates, cymbals, gongs, incense-burners, flower-vases, yellow silk, wood, &c.

HOUSE-RENT.

In Lhasa, Tashi-lhunpo, and Shiga-tse, houses ordinarily used by monks and traders are let on an annual rental of 10 to 50 *srangs*. For good and commodious accommodation, higher rates are charged. In Mongolia, where people live in felt tents, there is no custom of renting house, strangers being either accommodated gratis or entertained as guests. In China, I am told, the huts of poor people, which are occupied by dealers and traders generally, fetch from 5 *tong-tse* (Chinese copper coins) to 20 *tong-tse* a month. At the time of the Emperor's visit to the principal monasteries, chiefly at Revo-tse-lña,* the ministers and other high officers crowd in the houses of the monks. For good houses they are known to pay from 25 to 50 *srangs* for a night's lodging. The general rate of rent for ordinary houses which merchants occupy ranges from Rs. 125 to Rs. 375 per annum. In Tibet house-keepers exercise great influence in matters of trade. They serve in most cases as brokers. Merchants from distant countries as a rule go to the houses of their old acquaintances who furnish them with lodgings. The new merchants secure introductions or make acquaintances through these friends. According to the custom of the country it is a most important duty of a house-keeper, in whose house a merchant may be admitted, to arrange for the proper sale of the merchant-lodger's goods and to guard against others deceiving him and using false measures and weights; at the same time he himself is required not to deal unfairly with his lodger, or to defraud him. By arranging the sale or purchase of 50 *srangs*, the house-keeper can legally demand a commission of one *srang* from either party, which is equivalent to two per cent. from each, or four per cent. on the whole. If the house-keeper defrauds the trader who is his lodger, or exact more than the usual commission from him, he is guilty of breach of trust.

---

* The five-peaked mountain.

H. P.—Reg. No. 13339J—100—27-3-84.

Sheet No. 6 of NORTH EASTERN FRONTIER

TRIGONOMETRICAL BRANCH, SURVEY OF INDIA.

Parts of TIBET, SIKHIM and BHUTAN

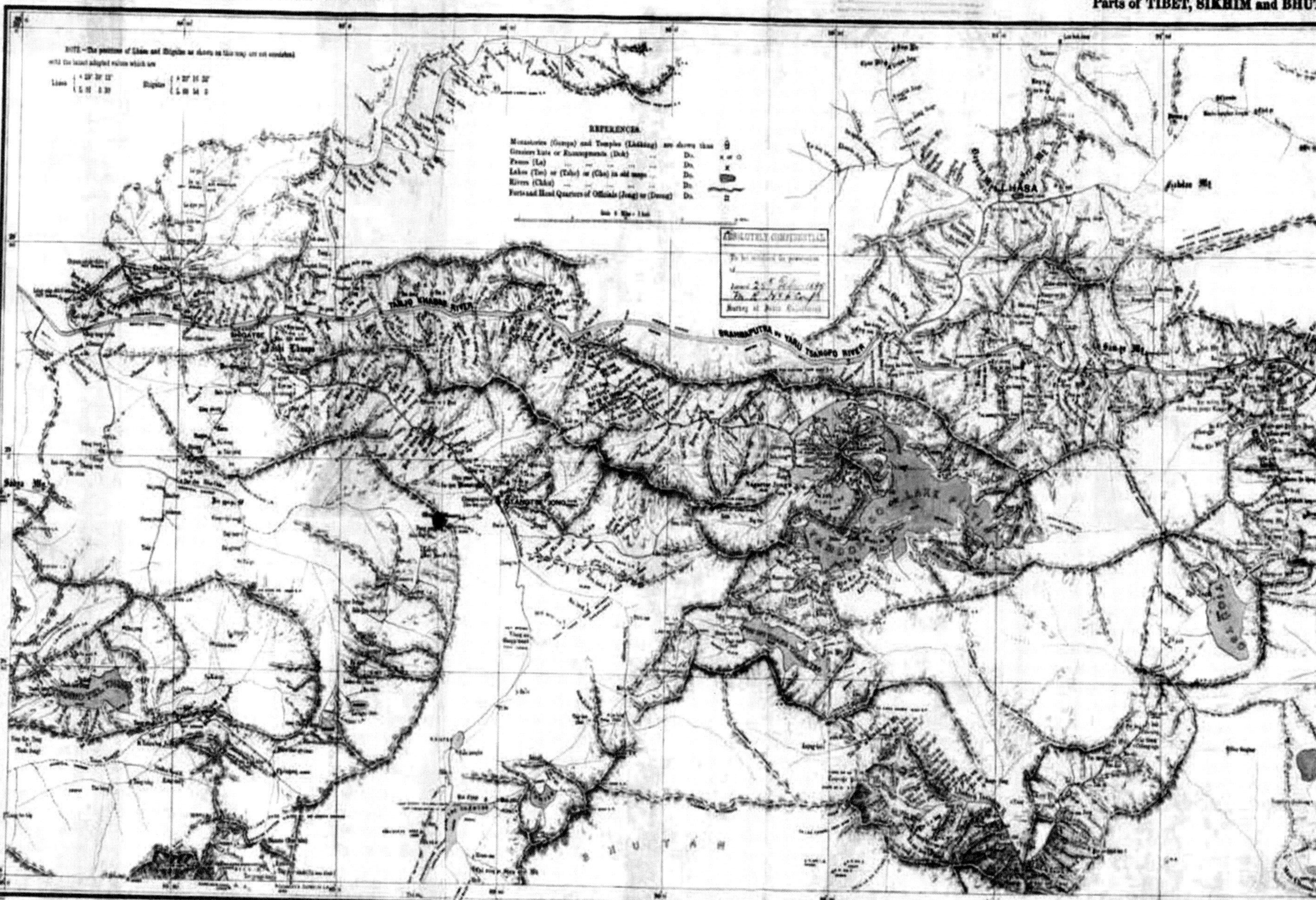

Published under the direction of Colonel G. C. DePrée, S.C., Surveyor General of India.

Compiled under the direction of Colonel G. C. DePrée, S.C., Surveyor General of India and under the Superintendence of J. B. N. Hennessey, Esq., M.A., F.R.S., Deputy Surveyor General in charge Trigonometrical Branch, by Colonel H. C. B. Tanner, Bo. S.C., Deputy Superintendent.

Hill shading by Mr. J. Peyton.